Pleasure in Profit

PLEASURE IN PROFIT

Popular Prose in Seventeenth-Century Japan

Laura Moretti

Columbia University Press *New York*

Columbia University Press
Publishers Since 1893
New York   Chichester, West Sussex
cup.columbia.edu

Copyright © 2020 Columbia University Press
All rights reserved

Library of Congress Cataloging-in-Publication Data
Names: Moretti, Laura, (Senior Lecturer in Pre-modern Japanese Studies) author.
Title: Pleasure in profit : popular prose in seventeenth-century Japan / Laura Moretti.
Description: New York : Columbia University Press, 2021. | Includes bibliographical references and index.
Identifiers: LCCN 2020012016 (print) | LCCN 2020012017 (ebook) | ISBN 9780231197229 (hardback) | ISBN 9780231197236 (trade paperback) | ISBN 9780231552059 (ebook)
Subjects: LCSH: Japanese prose literature—Edo period, 1600–1868—History and criticism. | Popular literature—Japan—History and criticism.
Classification: LCC PL747.4 .M67 2020 (print) | LCC PL747.4 (ebook) | DDC 895.63/3—dc23
LC record available at https://lccn.loc.gov/2020012016
LC ebook record available at https://lccn.loc.gov/2020012017

Cover image: Detail from Sumiyoshi Gukei, *Tohi zukan* (or *Tohi emaki*), ca. late seventeenth century. Bookshop and *terakoya* school. Courtesy of Konbuin, Nara. Licenced image provided by the Nara National Museum.

Cover design: Milenda Nan Ok Lee

To my parents and Trevor
for their unconditional love and support,
without which this book would not have been possible.

Ai miei genitori e a Trevor
il cui amore e supporto hanno reso
questo libro possibile.

Reading is a craft that enriches the text conceived by the author, deepening it and rendering it more complex, concentrating it to reflect the reader's personal experience and expanding it to reach the farthest confines of the reader's universe and beyond. Writing, instead, is the art of resignation. The writer must accept the fact that the final text will be but a blurred reflection of the work conceived in the mind, less enlightening, less subtle, less poignant, less precise.

—Alberto Manguel, *Curiosity*

Contents

Acknowledgments xi
Note to Readers xv

Introduction: Reclaiming the Great Unread 1

1. The Culture of the Written Word 25
2. The Publishing Business 67
3. Negotiating the Way 97
4. Civility Matters 133
5. Say It in a Skillful Letter 178
6. A Commitment to the Present 221
7. The Triumph of Plurality 255

   Epilogue: Wayfinding 294

Notes 299
Bibliography 369
Index 397

Acknowledgments

Writing can be an extremely humbling experience. It certainly is for me. This book is the result of a project that has developed over many years, possibly too many, as some of my closest friends might observe. As the project grew, I came to appreciate what Patricia Nelson Limerick suggested in her compelling article "Dancing with Professors: The Trouble with Academic Prose" (*New York Times*, October 31, 1993): carpenters and other artisans can act effectively as our emotional model. As I overcame the fear of scrapping ideas and the frustration of losing big chunks of writing, the manuscript, too, evolved through numerous drafts. In the process, I was constantly inspired by the research of scholars in early modern literature across the globe, and I have been supported by a number of wonderful people. It is now time to let the project go. I can offer only an imperfect list of all to whom I owe my heartfelt gratitude.

I would never have embarked on exploring seventeenth-century popular prose had I not had the privilege to learn from and work with scholars who have profoundly molded the way in which I do research. During my formative years Fukasawa Akio, Nagashima Hiroaki, Nobuhiro Shinji, and Oka Masahiko taught me how to work with early modern Japanese primary sources. I am too well aware that the scholarship I have produced in this volume is still far from the standards that these phenomenal scholars expect. But without their insightful teaching and patient guidance, I could not even have begun to conceive this project. Peter Burke had been for years my unseen intellectual hero before

I was given the opportunity to join Emmanuel College and meet him in person in 2012. Since then, he has been a terrific mentor and a sharp reader of my work.

I have benefited greatly from a number of colleagues and friends who read the manuscript as it was taking shape. Richard Bowring was an exceptionally lucid reader, whose honesty made it possible for me to completely rethink the trajectory of the project before 2017. His wise advice saved me from regret. Linda Chance gave crucial feedback on chapters 4 and 5. She has also been an unparalleled source of intellectual inspiration and warm friendship. Mary Elizabeth Berry provided excellent comments on chapter 4 and offered significant insights that helped me flesh out the arguments running through the book. Peter Burke has been a real treasure, not only reading the manuscript twice—including the much longer version I originally submitted—but also providing me with precious information about publications on popular literatures around the world. Ellis Tinios generously shared with me his exceptional bibliographic knowledge of early modern books. He also offered especially helpful comments on chapters 3 and 5. As if this were not enough, he has been a marvelous friend, always ready to encourage me whenever the project seemed too daunting. Alessandro Bianchi did a wonderful job of double-checking the information on my primary sources. The anonymous reviewers of the manuscript gave me superb feedback. Their knowledgeable, acute, and detailed comments guided me in bringing the book to its present form. Many thanks to you all!

Along the way, I was blessed with the intellectual generosity of a number of scholars. Oka Masahiko was incredibly kind in granting me access to the unpublished data that he has gathered over the years from surveying seventeenth-century colophons. These data cover the period from 1658 to 1703 and complement his coedited *Edo jidai shoki shuppan nenpyō* (Tokyo: Bensei Shuppan, 2011). Without these, chapter 2 would have looked very different. Nagatomo Chiyoji was most helpful in his advice on primary sources, which I have incorporated into chapters 1 and 2. Ishigami Aki, Rosina Buckland, Nagashima Hiroaki, Satō Katsura, Michael Kinski, Yamabe Susumu, David Atherton, Thomas Gaubatz, David Howell, Julie Nelson Davis, Joshua Scott Mostow, Amy Beth Stanley, and Barbara Wall answered a number of questions and suggested useful readings. Barak Kushner, Haruo Shirane, and Satoko Shimazaki very kindly gave support when I was putting together the book proposal.

In collecting images and acquiring rights to reproduce them, I was assisted by several people and institutions. Muraki Keiko of the Gotoh Museum offered invaluable assistance in liaising with Konbuin (Nara) and the Nara National Museum to access the image featured on the cover of this book. My thanks extend to the abbot of Konbuin, who granted permission to use the image, and to Taniguchi Kōsei, Sasaki Kyōsuke, and Sakamoto Naoko of the Nara National Museum. I am grateful to the team at the Tokyo National Museum for their assistance, in particular Imaichi Kaoru and Oyamada Shūya. Tim Clark of the British Museum alerted me to the existence of the Hishikawa Moronobu image included in chapter 2. It is hard to forget the excitement of viewing this fabulous scroll with Tim in the Asia study room. My thanks also go to Elizabeth Bray for help with securing new photography and the rights to use it. Mary Redfern and Jenny Greiner of the Chester Beatty Library (Dublin) were very kind in granting access to the scroll featured extensively in chapter 1. Koizumi Yoshinaga was uncommonly generous in permitting me to use a book from his stunning collection. Nishiguchi Tōru of Kawade Shobō Shinsha was marvelous in granting permission to use images from works issued by this publisher. Special thanks also to the National Diet Library and the National Institute of Japanese Literature. Their recent policy to make a substantial number of early modern archival materials available digitally and to allow reproduction without the need for permission is commendable and exemplary. My gratitude goes also to other institutions that made their materials accessible, digitally or otherwise: Art Research Center (Ritsumeikan University), Ebi Bunko, Ehime University Library, Hirosaki City Public Library, Osaka University Library, Tenri University Library, Tohoku University Library, Tokyo Gakugei University Library, Tokyo Kasei Gakuin University Library, Tokyo Municipal Central Library, Tokyo University Library, Tōyō Bunko, and Waseda University Library. Kristin Williams, head of the Japanese section at Cambridge University Library, and her predecessor, Noboru Koyama, were immensely helpful to me in acquiring necessary materials over the years. In purchasing primary sources that have proven essential for my research, I was assisted by several antiquarian booksellers: Nagumo Shoten, Ōya Shobō, Rinrokaku Shoten, Seishindō Shoten, Shibunkaku, Tōjō Shoten, and Yagi Shoten.

The core of the project developed after I moved to Cambridge. Special gratitude to Mikael Adolphson, Keidanren Professor of Japanese Studies at Cambridge. He has been absolutely amazing in his support, care, and advice over the years. We are very lucky to have him as our "coach." Many thanks also to Barak Kushner for being such an encouraging colleague. The generous research funds I received from the Faculty of Asian and Middle Eastern Studies and Emmanuel College helped offset the production costs of this book. For this, special thanks go to the Japanese Studies Group at Cambridge and Mike Gross. My students have been a constant source of energy and inspiration. Working with my graduate students always offers valuable food for thought. In particular, Elena Follador shared with me her interest in cognitive studies and Helen Magowan is exploring *nyohitsu* texts similar to those that I cover in part of chapter 5. Teaching and supervising my undergraduate students bring a much-needed break from what are often solitary ruminations and infuse vitality into my research.

I am honored that Columbia University Press is the publisher of this book. Christine Dunbar has believed in this project since the very beginning, for which I am deeply grateful. Her dedication, passion, and understanding have been inspirational. Christian P. Winting was extremely helpful throughout the whole process. Milenda Nan Ok Lee created a wonderfully eye-catching cover and book design. Zachary Friedman helped hone the language of the marketing copy. Leslie Kriesel ensured that the production of the manuscript proceeded according to plan, despite the fact that we were going through the COVID-19 crisis. She also meticulously combed through the text at the proof stage. Anne Holmes and Rob Rudnick produced a thorough index for the book. I am also grateful to Amy Reigle Newland for her initial copyediting of the manuscript.

None of this would have been possible without my family and Trevor. Dina and Elia have always been understanding when it came to my studies and work, which often forced me away from home. The love and friendship that unite us bridge any geographical distances. Thank you for always being there. Trevor has steadfastly believed in me, my work, and this project. His love, patience, support, encouragement, understanding, and tremendous help have made all the difference. Thank you for being the sun of my life.

Note to Readers

Japanese personal names are rendered as family name followed by given name, except in citations of English-language materials. I also adopt the common practice of referring to early modern Japanese authors by their given name or pseudonym. Asai Ryōi, for instance, is referred to as Ryōi. I consciously opted for *ee* and not *ei* or *ē* in names such as Chōbee.

A few choices have been made to ensure accessibility for a wide readership. I have kept the amount of Japanese characters to a minimum. Names of early modern people—including authors, illustrators, and publishers—are accompanied by their Japanese characters on first occurrence in the body of the text. Reading early modern Japanese names can be extremely challenging, in particular for publishers' names. I have cross-checked several sources, including Web NDL Authorities, the Waseda University Library's Kotenseki Sogo Database, and the Union Catalogue of Early Japanese Books.

Titles of early modern works in Japanese are given in transliteration, with characters appearing only in the bibliography. At their first appearance, such titles are accompanied by a literal translation into English. These translations are for reference only and should not be considered definitive or authoritative. The choice to use Japanese titles throughout the book is informed by the insightful remarks in Suzuki Jun and Ellis Tinios, *Understanding Japanese Woodblock-Printed Illustrated Books: A Short Introduction to Their History, Bibliography and Format* (Leiden: Brill, 2013), 54, 132.

Depending on the primary source under scrutiny, I have made use of originals from the archive, diplomatic transcriptions, or modern critical editions. In the notes and bibliography I give clear indications of the format I accessed. For archival materials, I include the name of the library or collection holding the original printed text and its shelf mark number. All page citations consist of the number of the leaf and an abbreviated indication of recto or verso—for example, 14r. For diplomatic transcriptions, I cite both the folio in the original printed text and the page number in the transcription. For critical editions, I refer only to the page number in the modern edition.

Beginning with chapter 3, where I undertake close readings of chosen seventeenth-century texts, the title of a primary source is accompanied on first appearance by an endnote containing the following information: (1) the format I have used, (2) a synopsis of the early modern publishing history of the text in question, (3) an indication of what kind of data are recorded in book-trade catalogues about it, and (4) any additional remarks, including English translations that I am aware of.

Introduction

Reclaiming the Great Unread

> ... a different conception of the history of literature: a history that takes for its potential subject the entire field of word-made objects; that refuses to assume a fixed, a priori distinction between one kind of writing and another; that concerns itself with the practical uses of such distinctions as emerge in any epoch; that looks skeptically upon the celebration of autonomous individuality; that understands that all literary creativity involves a complex global circulation of social energies.
>
> —Stephen Greenblatt, "What Is the History of Literature?"

The bookshop is a space that breathes dazzling plurality. Once you have stepped into this space—be it physical or digital—you cannot but be mesmerized by the cornucopia of materials that spark curiosity, awaken imagination, and activate the senses. Shaped as a condensed version of the world, the bookshop offers much more than a few fictional stories canonized as "literature" by centuries of Eurocentric critical pronouncements and curricular decisions.[1] Each of us goes to the bookshop motivated by different interests. Some relish the aesthetic process of reading, savoring the visual and auditory nature of words. Others delight in the emotional and cognitive excitement generated by fiction and nonfiction. Still others revel in reading texts that quench their thirst for knowledge, humans' innate *libido sciendi*. After all, as Latin American writer Gabriel Zaid notes, "What matters is how we feel, how we see, what we do after reading … whether reading makes us, physically, more alive."[2] Transformative literature—this is what some crave. An etiquette manual can be a source of great enjoyment for those who want to master a more genteel deportment. Philosophical ruminations delivered in essay format can provide gratification to those trying to make sense of the world they inhabit. Travel writing can offer more than practical information or fantasies of distant places: as British writer Robert Macfarlane puts it, travel writing can be felt in one's feet, it speaks to one's soles, and invites us to march out into adventure.[3] The pleasures of reading are as manifold as the books on the shelves of a bookshop. Publishers and booksellers are invested in a commercial enterprise that shapes what Umberto Eco viewed as the network of texts produced for "humanity's own enjoyment—and which are read for pleasure, spiritual edification, broadening of knowledge, or maybe just to pass the time."[4] Eco held that it is precisely this network of texts that embodies our "literary tradition."[5] As such, literature expands beyond the rigid constraints of the canon in the eclectic space of the bookshop.

Now step back in time, to seventeenth-century Japan. Imagine yourself on Teramachi Street, in the heart of Kyoto (fig. 0.1).[6] This area was home to a number of publishers, which also operated as bookstores. The space they created was no different from the one limned in the preceding. The business established by Akitaya Heizaemon 秋田屋平左衛門 (dates unknown), probably in 1644, was located in front of the temple known as Enpukuji (fig. 0.1, no. 1). In addition to

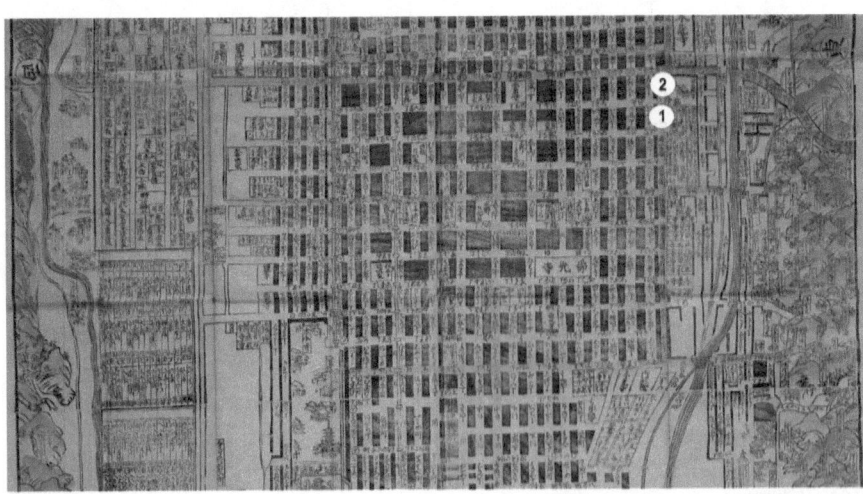

Figure 0.1 Detail from *Shinpan Heianjō narabi ni rakugai no zu*, 1680. Teramachi Street in Kyoto.

Courtesy of the National Diet Library, Tokyo

many works written in literary Chinese about medicine, Buddhism, and Confucianism, Akitaya issued texts in the vernacular starting with an abridged version of *Genji monogatari* (*The Tale of Genji*) in 1651 titled *Genji ko-kagami* (The little mirror to Genji). In his bookshop you could buy nonnarrative essays on Confucianism (e.g., *Tagami no ue* [The life of others; after 1657]), a guide to the annual festive days (*Annaisha* [The guide; 1662]), librettos of the Noh theater, and the chilling collection of ghost stories *Otogi bōko* (Hand puppets; 1666) by the best-selling writer Asai Ryōi 浅井了意 (d. 1691). Walking a few meters north, you would find the large compound of another temple, Seiganji (fig. 0.1, no. 2). Its architecture featured extensively in the lavish folding screens depicting Kyoto, and it was home to the famous storyteller Anrakuan Sakuden 安楽庵策伝 (1554–1642), father of the form of comic performance known as *rakugo*. In front of this iconic and lively temple was the shop of Nishimura Matazaemon 西村又左衛門 (dates unknown), whose oldest recorded publication dates to 1624. In addition to serious publications in Sinitic, which would probably have interested a chosen elite, Nishimura issued titles that would have appealed to a wider readership equipped with vernacular-only literacy. Much like his neighboring Akitaya, Nishimura wished to cater to the needs of those who had a couple of years of education in a *terakoya* school and were in the main trained to write and read the phonetic script. In 1634, for example, he released a conduct manual with letter templates (*Shogaku bunshō narabi ni yorozu shitsukekata* [Elementary letters and all forms of etiquette]; this work is discussed in chapters 4 and 5), which was an immediate hit and was reissued more than twelve times by him and other publishers, both in Kyoto and Edo, until the 1680s. You could have purchased it from his bookshop for the price of a bowl of steamed rice flavored with hot tea. Relatively low prices were one of the many pluses of the woodblock-printing technology. Nishimura's huge stock of books included, among other things, collections of medical recipes, cookbooks, arithmetic manuals, school textbooks, classics like *Ise monogatari* (*The Tales of Ise*), Buddhist sermons, poetry anthologies, and didactic books for women. He was also the first to issue, in 1662, the earliest printed work dealing with the tenth-century diviner Abe no Seimei (*Abe no Seimei monogatari* [The story of Abe no Seimei]), a figure who continues to inspire anime and video games. Nishimura's bookshop provided all sorts of readings to feed varied interests and deliver diverse pleasures. Nishimura was also one of the pioneers in publishing book-trade catalogues listing the titles available on the book market in Kyoto and possibly Edo. His catalogue dates to 1670 and gives us a clear idea of the magnitude of the contemporary commercial printing business, with a total of some thirty-eight hundred titles, out of which around eight hundred were in the vernacular (I return to this in chapter 2). Before the creation of publishers' guilds, Nishimura's ability to pull together information from the hundreds of publishers active in Kyoto speaks of his leading position in this world. If we consider that more than a thousand publishers are recorded in the colophons of books commercially printed in Kyoto between 1673 and 1688, we can grasp the impressive size of seventeenth-century commercial printing and the literary tradition that it brought to life. At the beginning of the eighteenth century, in the 1703 poetry collection *Fudanzakura* (Never-ending blossoms), the business of publishing was aptly described as a lush forest: "With the cutting of characters / the forest of books / luxuriantly bursts forth" (*Shokuji yori / fumihayashi wa / habikorite*).[7]

These figures tell a compelling story. It is the story of a considerable number of readers ravenous for books that suited their multifarious interests and addressed different literacies; the story of a profusion of printed books created by savvy publishers in response to this hunger. The handful of titles touched upon in our imaginary wander around bygone bookshops in Kyoto speaks of a literature created to feed curiosity and to gratify customers with printed products that engaged them at multiple levels: aesthetically, cognitively, and emotionally. To instruct and to delight—this is what the publications in the vernacular issued by commercial publishers in seventeenth-century Japan were attempting to do. The pleasure of reading was by no means relegated to entertainment: it was also sparked by interacting with transformative literature.

Sadly, we know very little of this story today. Of the numbers introduced here only a fraction have been included in literary histories. Over the past sixty years around twenty or twenty-five titles have been dealt with in some detail in English and only a handful have been deemed appropriate to be included in anthologies that have shaped the literary canon for undergraduate and graduate students. This is less than 1.5 percent of what seventeenth-century readers equipped with vernacular literacy could access, a tiny amount of what survives in the archives. We are not far from the "slaughterhouse of literature" lamented by Franco Moretti in his study of nineteenth-century English fiction.[8]

I wish in the present monograph to reconstruct the story of the Great Unread of seventeenth-century popular prose in Japan.[9] My research reflects a desire to understand which texts were in phase with a large group of seventeenth-century popular readers endowed with basic, vernacular literacy and how books shaped them as a community of fully-fledged human beings.[10] This publication is the first step into the forest of books that awaits (re)discovery. It is also an intellectual journey that urges us to alter our expectations vis-à-vis the literary, breaking down the wall that is traditionally perceived between enjoyment (the aesthetic) and knowledge (the didactic or the cognitive).

A (Literary) History of Exclusion

In 1957, and for the first time in English, the scholar and book collector Richard Lane introduced students of Japanese literature to the fiction produced between 1600 and 1682.¹¹ Lane's pioneering and now classic account of this literary production fully conformed to the findings and the interpretative stance favored by Japanese academia since the seminal work of Mizutani Futō.¹² In his examination of *kanazōshi*—the conventional label for the prose written in the vernacular after 1600 and before the publication of *Kōshoku ichidai otoko* (*The Life of an Amorous Man*; 1682)—Lane chose to focus mainly on fiction. For Lane literature is storytelling. Literature is narrative. While I concede that any distinction between narrative and nonnarrative is fraught with danger, I find Marie-Laure Ryan's reflections on narrative and narrativity of assistance in unraveling these concepts.¹³ Basic conditions of narrative (intended as story) include the representation of at least two events (actions and happenings) that entail a change, possess an internal time sequence, and occur in a world populated by intelligent individuals and objects (existents).¹⁴ Nonnarrative elements are identified in "extended descriptions, metanarrative comments, digressions, narratorial and authorial interventions, general considerations, and philosophical meditations."¹⁵ Narrativity is what allows us to grasp the complex, nonbinary relationship between narrative and nonnarrative, in that it "assesses the role of the story with respect to the whole of the text, taking both narrative and nonnarrative elements into consideration."¹⁶ When viewed through the lens of narrativity, Lane's work seems to evaluate positively those texts that push a story through and minimize any nonnarrative disruptions.

There is more, though, to Lane's intellectual position. Lane is in fact in search of the novel and identifies in realism the discriminating feature in his obsessive hunt for modernity and literary value. The nineteen works Lane selected for close reading are in one way or another narrating stories and are more or less successful in depicting the new age in realistic terms. References to Kabuki and pleasure quarters, kernels of psychological realism in the description of fictional characters, influences from classical literature such as *Ise monogatari* and *Tsurezuregusa* (*Essays in Idleness*), the presence of a coherent, well-structured story, and a hedonistic mood are conveyed as the watchwords of quality creative writing in seventeenth-century Japan. Lane is zealous in trying to neatly organize his selected titles into three categories: entertainment, enlightenment, and practical education/guidance. These categories, too, appear somewhat slavish in their adherence to the views propounded by twentieth-century Japanese scholarship. Once a title is associated with a particular category, Lane concentrates almost solely on the textual features that allow the text to fit that particular category. When he cannot silence the strident contradictions in some of the texts under discussion, Lane appears willing to blame seventeenth-century readers, who put up with such inconsistencies because they were "cut off from the mainstream of world literature."¹⁷ In all this, the real winner seems to be taxonomy. As readers of Lane's article, we are left with a slightly skewed view of a few titles of seventeenth-century vernacular fiction and the impression that these are the only titles that seventeenth-century

Japanese read. We are also reminded that we must wait for the genius of Ihara Saikaku 井原西鶴 (1642–1693) to witness what Lane sees as the highly notable results in creative writing of and for the masses: "The *kana-zōshi* are most important in the history of Japanese literature as a transitional form, bridging the gap between the medieval romance and the modern novel."[18]

Lane's study gave some impetus to a handful of English translations in subsequent years.[19] As praiseworthy and meaningful as they are, these translations have paradoxically contributed to molding the image of seventeenth-century vernacular prose as a tiny canon of around ten titles, the vast majority of which are fictional narratives. This image is fundamentally at odds with the nature of the forest of books that was created by commercial publishers as sketched at the outset of this study.

If one is keen to discover more beyond the set canon of a few works, the only resources to date that serve the purpose are in Japanese. Noda Hisao's study of *kanazōshi*, published as part of his multivolume *Kinsei shōsetsu shi*, remains a standard source in the field.[20] Organized chronologically with the division of works into categories that are reminiscent of Lane's 1957 article, Noda discusses around two hundred primary sources. His erudite annotations for each title are tremendously informative, containing plots, snippets of texts in transcription, insights into the publication history of select books, the mention of key scholarly articles, and interpretative remarks that together make Noda's work a solid starting point. Yet this learned companion to seventeenth-century prose falls into the same trap as Lane in its fixation with the novel (*shōsetsu*). Noda is admittedly more inclusive, as the sheer number of titles he examines suggests. When he touches upon texts that somehow lack in what I have identified as narrativity, however, Noda justifies their inclusion with defensive apologies.[21] As a result, he is reluctant to explore narrativity as a potentially generative framework that allows for a discussion about the degrees of the story's visibility and in turn provides the opportunity to study a variety of modulations of narrative and nonnarrative. His desire to include as many titles as possible is at odds with the perceived need to mention only novel-like texts that offer a clearly detectable story (and possibly a story with "literary" qualities).[22]

The two required readings for anyone keen to explore seventeenth-century vernacular prose by Richard Lane and Noda Hisao are thus plagued by the same weaknesses. Both trumpet an elitist notion of what literature should be; both launch an anachronistic quest for the modern novel in an age and a culture that had no knowledge of or need for the European novel; and both belittle the nonnarrative (and the nonfictional) as something unworthy of the attention of a literary scholar. The result is a history of exclusion, barring any work that does not adopt a belletristic and elitist view of literature. And this has sealed the fate of seventeenth-century prose as an embarrassment of Japanese literature: the black sheep no one wants to talk about. The dearth of articles and the absence of any book-length study on the subject speak loudly to this lamentable state of affairs. Indeed, Saikaku's imagination and his linguistic genius have been spared such a fate for reasons that are no less fraught with problems of cultural assimilation.

In seventeenth-century Japan, commercial publishers issued hundreds of titles that gained favor among what must have been a large constituency of readers. And these titles were as popular as Saikaku's prose. Clearly there was something in this rich outpouring of texts that struck a chord with contemporary readers and satisfied their fundamental cultural needs. My journey in retrieving the Great Unread of popular seventeenth-century Japanese prose begins with the gaps in Lane's account. Lane notes that a didactic strain is apparent to some degree in nearly all this corpus. Lane's contrast of didacticism with fiction seems to imply his belief that didacticism occurs primarily in nonfictional texts, endowed with little narrativity. This then suggests, albeit indirectly, the presence of much seventeenth-century prose as not concerned with recounting a story but with something else. What is this something else? Lane notes the existence of contradictions within a few of the texts he examines, but, as already touched upon, he readily repudiates them. But what if we decide to enter into dialogue with these contradictions and listen to their message(s)? Lane mentions that select fiction makes use of the information and knowledge provided in the practical genre of "courtesan critiques." This indicates that non-narrative texts (or texts characterized by a lower degree of narrativity) had the power to influence full-blown narrative texts. Lane justifies this interaction as meaningful because it infuses fictional stories with realism. Is this all that such an interaction can offer? Lane, as a book collector, includes in his article a few images from seventeenth-century books but does not discuss their materiality, as if it were irrelevant to the understanding of their contents. What happens if we take the materiality of books into account? While today we might see flaws in Lane's argument—after all, it was written in the nascent period of studies into popular seventeenth-century Japanese literature—it prompts us with thought-provoking questions that deserve examining in greater depth. My aim is to fully engage with what Lane (and Noda) have dismissed, silenced, trivialized, or discredited. As a result, I challenge the received view that most publications of the time were either poorly formed entertainment or dismal didactic things, waiting to be swept away by a brilliant development late in the century. Teleological considerations have no part to play in the story I wish to reconstruct.

Toward Inclusion

The time is ripe to address the questions prompted by the lines of inquiry disparaged by Lane and to envisage novel ways to look at commercial seventeenth-century popular prose. Three changes in literary studies by scholars working inside and outside Japanese studies drive this new research trajectory: the growth of new historical scholarship; a mature interest in popular and didactic literature; and the provocative intellectual considerations advanced by Nakano Mitsutoshi, one of the leading scholars of Japanese early modern literature and book history. Before I delve into an exploration of these three threads, I wish to clarify the use I make of analytical frameworks drawn from Western literary criticism or from studies on early modern European texts. I am fully aware that some might deplore this as an exercise in cultural hegemony, subsuming knowledge under existing Western paradigms. Yet that is by no means my intention. For me, theoretical remarks produced in a variety of contexts (cultural, temporal, and spatial) prompt questions that we might otherwise not be able to formulate. They make us aware of critical angles that we might not otherwise envisage.[23] I am not searching for any easy equivalence between early modern European and Japanese (popular) literatures. Texts are cultural products, firmly rooted in a specific time and space. Nevertheless, I am not ready to dispense altogether with the notion that the commercial desire to open up literature for a new kind of readership, one that possesses limited literacy and yet craves access to the written word, can undergo similar developments in different parts of the world and in different times. I seek to strike a balance between recognizing culturally specific choices and admitting universally applicable trends.

Beginning in the 1980s, the study of literature—that is, English-language literature—witnessed an exciting moment in the field when scholars of literature turned from working on the literary to an exploration of the social and cultural aspects that were once relegated to the contexts in traditional literary histories. The assumption that only a small number of texts were worthy of study because of an inherent literary value and their place in the elite ranks of the literary canon was called into question. The implications of such a shift are significant since we are left with no masterpieces. All texts are equal and should rightfully be treated as the object of investigation by scholars of literature.[24] While this approach does not come without its "burdens," as discussed by Lawrence Lipking, or without controversy, as noted by Catherine Gallagher, it also comes with a wondrous sense of liberation: the literary space has become richer and truly democratic.[25] In his study of what seventeenth-century readers in England enjoyed before the rise of the novel, Paul Hunter well sums up the excitement of this new approach:

> The past decade has brought new directions to literary study—interdisciplinarity, curiosity about generic issues, interest in theory for its typological potential and for its ability to sort among the strands of intention and outcome in texts, belief in history as a serious interpretive dimension for texts and in historiography as a means to analyze and recover cultures as wholes, pursuit of the

dimensions of desire in both readers and writers and concern with its communal and cultural forms as well as its individual and psychoanalytical ones, distrust of canonical categories and the disinterment of "minor" and "utilitarian" texts, replacement of strictly literary categories by cultural ones.[26]

Hunter adeptly describes the cultural turn in the study of literature and the positive results it generated. We are finally able to unearth those texts that traditional literary historians in the past eschewed.

In this light, Eco's identification of the literary tradition with texts produced "for humanity's own enjoyment" makes perfect sense.[27] The "enjoyment" of reading is not limited to the pleasure derived from the consumption of a beautifully crafted text or one that captivates because of its fictional nature. It is also the intellectual excitement derived from reading something that a reader finds interesting for all sorts of reasons. Eco's inclusion of "spiritual edification" and a "broadening of knowledge" also allows literature to encompass what we would normally view as didactic, or even transformative, literature—literature that appeals for its epistemic function. In line with this, exciting new territories and methodologies have been explored by scholars like Franco Moretti and Stephen Greenblatt.[28] Moretti views in what he terms distant reading a condition of knowledge that allows us "to focus on units that are much smaller or much larger than the text: devices, themes, tropes—or genres and systems."[29] We are invited to embrace skills like sampling and statistics as well as work with series and titles in order to make sense of the enormous number of texts released on the book market. Greenblatt and the New Historicism with which he is associated invite us to recover the marginal voices, those that have been suppressed or lost.[30] This is admittedly just one aspect of a much wider intellectual project, and it may appear that I am selectively choosing from New Historicism's rich basket, therefore risking oversimplification or misapprehension. I trust, however, that the idea of "culture as a text" and the resultant broadening of the literary field have great potential. In their introduction to *Practicing New Historicism*, Gallagher and Greenblatt explain,

> The notion of culture as text has a further major attraction: it vastly expands the range of objects available to be read and interpreted. Major works of art remain centrally important, but they are jostled now by an array of other texts and images. Some of these alternative objects of attention are literary works regarded as too minor to deserve sustained interest and hence marginalized or excluded entirely from the canon. Others are texts that have been regarded as altogether nonliterary, that is, as lacking the aesthetic polish, the self-conscious use of rhetorical figures, the aura of distance from the everyday world, the marked status as fiction that separately or together characterize belles lettres.[31]

It is in this democratic view of literature, one that expands beyond the boundaries of the canonical garden, that we are able to retrieve what literary histories have traditionally suppressed. Outcast texts, as Lipking calls them, can be reinstated as valuable objects of inquiry.[32] In this book I want to retrieve what readers in seventeenth-century Japan enjoyed reading (and why) centuries before any hint of the novel breached the horizon. Taking into full account texts that the canon has outlawed is the key. While I am anxious not to raise the expectation that my research might fall into the theoretical realm of New Historicism, I wish to point out that my attempt to embrace the democratic view of literature that New Historicism underscores is a fresh endeavor when it comes to seventeenth-century Japanese literature.

Research on popular literature and popular culture is seldom mentioned in the theoretical reflections around historical scholarship, and yet it seems to me that this research has, in its own way, set in motion a forceful challenge. In 1964, the historian Robert Mandrou published his work on the *bibliothèque bleue*, a corpus of blue-covered paperbacks that developed as early as the seventeenth century and were sold at a modest price by colporteurs.[33] It was not the first time that these materials were unearthed for scholarly treatment. In 1864, for example, the philologist and literary historian Charles Nisard issued two substantial volumes on the history of popular books (*livres populaires*), with others to follow.[34] Mandrou, however, remains the starting point for anyone curious about this literature.[35] An interest in cheap literature similarly emerged in the study of literary traditions other than the French one. Margaret Spufford's *Small Books and Pleasant Histories* is still regarded as a landmark publication for England and Scotland.[36] Jeffrey Brooks has shed light on the Russian literature of the *lubok*, Candace Slater on the Brazilian *literatura de cordel*, Francesca Orsini on popular literature in colonial North India; Cathy and Michael Preston have opened the field to American, Pakistani, and Egyptian chapbooks; and the *onitsha* market literature of Nigeria has been similarly discussed.[37] Research on commercial publishers in China across centuries has raised awareness of what kind of literature was produced to engage an ever-expanding readership.[38] We are also conscious of vernacular fiction and the development of the book trade in seventeenth-century Korea.[39] Whether conceived and marketed as book histories, literary histories, or cultural histories, these studies all pose the same questions, which Gary Kelly summarizes in the introduction to the Oxford Series of Popular Print Culture: "What did most people read? Where did they get it? Where did it come from? What were its uses in its readers' lives? How was it produced and distributed? What were its relations to the wider world of print culture? How did it develop over time?"[40] It is not within the remit of this introduction to provide a synopsis of the rich, manifold findings of the extensive work done over the years on popular literature around the globe. One point, however, does need to be singled out here as it resonates deeply with what historical scholarship and this monograph seek to achieve.

Each of these studies makes us aware that the contents of popular literature reflect the multifaceted interests of everyday life, urging us to include in our field of inquiry writings that are conceived for uses other than mere aesthetic appreciation. These studies thus showcase how important it is to work with titles that have traditionally been banned from literary histories. The French *bibliothèque bleue*, for instance, was much more than narrative fiction: cookbooks; manuals for health; divinatory books with prophecies, interpretations of dreams, and almanacs; religious books that included the lives of saints, select passages from the Bible, and manuals on the *ars moriendi*; fictional stories of love and war; conduct books for women on the pursuit of love and fostering a healthy conjugal life; and many others. English and Scottish chapbooks also display a parallel breadth in contents and scope. In her comparison of Samuel Pepys's collection of chapbooks at Magdalene College (University of Cambridge) with the *bibliothèque bleue*, Margaret Spufford discovered something strikingly similar, with titles including cookbooks, almanacs, books of prophecies, medical handbooks, letter manuals, books of instruction, and religious writings. Jeffrey Brooks has identified chivalrous tales, morally instructive tracts, tales about merchants, war and travel stories, humorous tales, and saints' lives as the preferred works commercially published as part of the literature of the *lubok* in Russia. In his investigation of Pakistani chapbooks, William L. Hanaway has uncovered traditional romances and adventure stories alongside religious stories, books of spells and charms, advice on marriage and family life, as well as humorous stories and jokes. In addition to these studies, mention should be made of the fascinating collection of books in the Fondazione Giorgio Cini on Venice's Isola di San Giorgio, which demonstrates that fifteenth- and sixteenth-century books printed in Italy were read not only by the period's cultural elite but also by the middle and lower classes. The many dimensions of human life are once again mirrored in the variety of these Italian works: manuals for intellectual and moral education, with printed versions of Aesop's fables occupying a prominent position; moral treatises about virtues; manuals of arithmetic; a range of religious booklets from missals to the lives of saints; verses, letters, and fictional tales teaching the art of love; books for entertainment, from manuals on gambling to tales of chivalry; and a vast selection of treatises on medicine, law, politics, and the art of war.[41] In her work on the book trade that developed in the Chinese area known as Sibao from the late seventeenth century to the early twentieth century, Cynthia J. Brokaw has identified a similar variety of printed products, including educational works; guides to good manners, health, and fortune; and fiction.[42] Yuming He has further expanded the textual typologies by looking at what she calls huckster or pulp scholarship, exploring Ming books of riddles, jokes, and drinking games, alongside nonfictional records of foreign countries.[43]

I could cite many more examples, but here I wish to reiterate the point suggested by these materials—that is, the probing of popular literature in print forces us to move beyond aesthetically pleasing fiction and to recover other voices that have been silenced in previous literary histories. It asks us to acknowledge and engage with what Maria Nikolajeva refers to as the epistemic value of literature, or how literature conveys knowledge of extraliterary reality—including factual, social, interpersonal, and metacritical knowledge.[44] Knowledge making, I argue, is a pivotal aspect of popular literature in print. The study of this field also prompts us to embrace a type of nonaesthetic reading, or what Louise M. Rosenblatt calls efferent reading, where the reader "concentrates on what the symbols designate . . . the information, the concepts, the guides to action."[45] When engrossed in aesthetic reading, our primary concern is "with what happens *during* the actual reading event."[46] But with efferent reading, we are interested in what comes after we have finished perusing a text. I disagree with Rosenblatt's claim that an aesthetic stance is essential to all literary art, but I find her idea that the same text admits both aesthetic and efferent reading tantalizing. As such, familiar dichotomies between fiction and nonfiction, narrative and nonnarrative, useful/didactic and aesthetic, literary and nonliterary cease to be relevant. And we are asked to move beyond belles lettres according to what historical scholarship of the past three or so decades has taught us.

As noted in the foregoing, a great proportion of popular literature around the world exhibits a strong penchant for the didactic, if not for the practical. In the introduction to *Didactic Literature in England, 1500–1800*, Natasha Glaisyer and Sara Pennell observe that the study of didactic texts still lacks "thorough and critically sophisticated treatment."[47] They suggest this is partly because of the academic judgments of what constitutes a valid text for study, which, in turn, takes us back to the problem inherent in traditional literary histories. Glaisyer and Pennell's work, in tandem with a few other publications, reclaims the importance and the centrality of didactic texts, and the efferent reading they invite, at the heart of the study of literature.[48]

An interest in didactic writings produced in early modern Japan—especially cookbooks, manuals for the tea ceremony, and texts on natural history—has similarly begun to surface in recent years.[49] This invaluable research has shed light on nonnarrative prose and allowed an appreciation of its historical, sociological, and cultural significance. At the same time, however, the fact that the great majority of these reflections position themselves outside the field of literary studies seems to be a missed opportunity for us to write a new literary history conceived from the perspective of what readers were actually interested in. What would happen if we integrated the study of didactic prose into the study of the literary?

The most recent thought-provoking (at times even provocative) articles by Nakano Mitsutoshi are germane to this discussion. In 1997, Nakano proposed, quite controversially, to shift the temporal boundaries of *gesaku* (literally, "playful writings") to before the conventionally accepted date of the 1750s, beginning in the seventeenth century and including the prose of Ihara Saikaku.[50] Some might object to Nakano's suggestion as nothing more than a cosmetic change in that he simply substitutes the umbrella term *bungaku* (literature) with the term *gesaku*. Others might find Nakano's writing overly dogmatic. Yet I would argue that Nakano's stance is cogent and aligned with the aforementioned developments in the field of literary studies (although unbeknownst to Nakano himself).

Nakano asks us to enter into dialogue with early modern texts once we have fully understood the intellectual world and beliefs of the Edo period. He speaks of fostering "two sets of eyes": a set of "Edo people's eyes" (*Edojin no manako*) complementing the second set of our modern eyes (*gendai no manako*).[51] I would rephrase this and state that Nakano in fact urges us to study Edo-period literature from within, on its own terms. This stance is strikingly similar to that advocated by Margaret Cohen in her study of nineteenth-century France and its forgotten novelistic context. Cohen's words seem to echo Nakano's:

> The great challenge confronting any excavation is to denaturalize these expectations and take forgotten literature on its own terms. What are a work's distinctive poetics; what are these poetics' aesthetic logic and ideological force? Without understanding that forgotten works are shaped by a coherent, if now lost, aesthetic, one simply dismisses them as uninteresting or inferior in terms of the aesthetics that have won out.[52]

What Nakano views as a set of Edo-period eyes is the retrieval of a lost early modern aesthetic. Nakano explains convincingly the drawbacks that arise when employing words that are intrinsically modern—therefore extraneous to the Edo period—when discussing early modern writings and highlights the dangers inherent in applying concepts such as literature (*bungaku*), literariness (*bungakusei*), and the novel (*shōsetsu*). He perceives unacceptable anachronism in the search for texts whose literary value resides in the resistance to and criticism of the dominant classes and their authority, arguing that early modern society had an unshakable faith in human beings and their intrinsic good nature. Nakano is also opposed to the view that Saikaku's interest in eroticism and the pleasure quarters transcends the ethics and logic of the real world, as traditionally viewed in received Japanese scholarship on Saikaku. He argues instead that eroticism and the pleasure quarters lay at the very heart of the early modern world and thus well within the borders of what was considered ethical at the time. In short, we are asked to study early modern texts in their historical context and without superimposing modern notions of literature. Ultimately, Nakano's decision to adopt the term *gesaku* accords with this point of view. Back in 1826, the *gesaku* writer Utei Enba II 烏亭焉馬 (1792–1862) wrote that "*gesaku* in Osaka started with Ihara Saikaku."[53] Nakano is looking at the Edo period through the lens of someone from the Edo period.

Having recalibrated his lens to the early modern era and espoused the historical concept of *gesaku*, Nakano continues by elucidating the key features of this prose, which (1) endorses the ideology of its epoch with no resistance, (2) shows a penchant for parodic playfulness and a keen interest in honing the language, and (3) combines humor with didacticism.[54] The point I find particularly relevant for my own work is Nakano's appreciation of the epistemic function of literature. For him, the literary-didactic split is alien to Edo-period prose (= *gesaku*), which results in the need for scholars of Edo-period prose texts to welcome didacticism as a pivotal quality. Nakano notes that "in pure literature a didactic stance [*kyōkun*] is viewed as a secondary, tertiary aspect. In other words, it is considered as something that should not exist in proper literature."[55] He claims, however, that "didacticism [*kyōkunsei*] is something intrinsically constitutive of Saikaku's work," therefore of *gesaku* and of early modern literature.[56] I contend that this equally applies to the seventeenth-century popular prose that I explore.

While a modern view of literature rejects didacticism, the view aligned with the early modern Weltanschauung fully embraces it. As Pierre Bourdieu observed, "Any cultural producer is irremediably placed and dated in so far as he or she participates in the same *problematic* as the ensemble of his or her contemporaries."[57] Nakano sees didacticism at the core of this problematic, which, in turn, allows us to unlock the aesthetic and ideological stakes of early modern literature. In accordance with historical scholarship and work undertaken on popular literature, Nakano's assessment asks us to move away from the canon and its dicta. It asks us to retrieve aspects of literature that have been relegated to the background or even negated by previous literary histories. It asks us to confront aspects of literature that have been buried in the modern process of canon making, aspects that are at the crux of the worldview of early modern literature.

Nakano tries to make this point crystal clear by explaining what didactic implies and maintains that early modern didacticism investigates how one should live as a human being.[58] He equates didacticism with beliefs or ideology (*shisōsei*)—in other words, early modern prose is interested in conveying ethical, societal, and interpersonal knowledge to form fully-fledged human beings who fit into contemporary society.[59] For Nakano, "in the early modern period it was universally accepted that prose had to profit morality."[60] Prose was expected to be of profit to its readers in the shaping of their morality; it was expected to instruct them. Humor could feature as well in order to make the teachings more palatable. The equilibrium between didacticism and humor, Nakano explains, could vary, at times leaning toward the former and at other times toward the latter. As noted, the expectation of early modern prose was to instruct and to delight.

It is not my aim to join in the debate about the origins of *gesaku*. Nakano asks if the beginnings of *gesaku* can be extended further back in time to the seventeenth-century prose before Saikaku. I do not wish to offer an answer, and I am not even convinced that this is the most meaningful part of the discussion. What interests me are the other issues ignited by Nakano's research. How can we approach seventeenth-century prose from within? How can we retrieve the didactic side of seventeenth-century prose? Should we restrict ourselves to narrative fiction, or should we also take into account nonnarrative texts? How are books designed to instruct readers? How is ethical and societal knowledge conveyed? Does this knowledge cross-pollinate with fiction? Does fiction only mirror society and its ethics, or does it participate in their construction? Are "profit" and "entertainment" antithetical? Or can pleasure be derived from profit? Whether we call it *gesaku* or something else, seventeenth-century prose invites us to confront these questions.

Working with the Popular

Galvanized by the sea changes in literary studies sketched in the previous section, my research aims at a reconstruction of the story of the Great Unread of seventeenth-century *popular* prose. A working definition of what I mean by "popular" is in order. Studies on popular culture and popular literature entreat us to ponder the meaning of "popular" as a complex entity.[61] Usually the term "popular" implies something that is liked and consumed by many people. When considered within historical periods for which statistics (such as sales figures or number of copies printed) are lacking—the early modern period is a case in point—any quantitative assessment of the notion of popular could be seen as almost impossible. Yet consideration of other aspects of the publishing industry can offer clues such as how many times a title was printed (or reprinted), how many different publishers were involved at different stages of the production, to what extent a work was printed or circulated outside Kyoto, and whether and how it was mentioned or appropriated in later works.[62] In this book I appraise the quantitative dimension of the popular in examining books that were in phase with a vast number of readers across society.

Linked to quantification is the understanding that popular culture deals with commerce and commodity. Scholars of popular culture often speak of "mass culture," a concept that is not devoid of traps.[63] Despite any skepticism we might feel vis-à-vis the use of this term, the idea of books produced by means of a technology that ensures circulation in large numbers and at cheap prices has been acknowledged as something useful when considering early modern popular literature.[64] Commercial printing and a commodified book trade can certainly be identified as key features in a discussion of the popular printed word in the Edo period.

One factor that had an important role in ensuring that commercial publications in early modern societies reached a high number of readers is the use of the vernacular. The choice of language is somehow overshadowed in the theoretical discourse regarding popular culture, in particular that on popular culture in contemporary societies. Peter Burke, however, has noted in the case of early modern Europe that the expansion of the vernacular into the domain of literature was intrinsically linked to the rise of lay, popular literacy and to the decline of the monopoly of knowledge by those who could master Latin.[65] Popular prose in seventeenth-century Japan was equally propelled by the adoption of the vernacular and by the promotion of what I call multiple literacies.

Another attribute traditionally attached to the popular is qualitative in the judgment of the aesthetic and literary quality of a product, in our case books. The popular is often associated with something that is lowbrow, not good enough to be elevated to the artistic, the literary, and the canonical. This then returns us to the intellectual stance championed by traditional literary histories. Qualitative judgment has led to the recognition of a striking contrast between lowbrow and highbrow culture, leading to a division into two clearcut spheres of the elite and the popular. For Japan, the well-trodden distinction between *ga* (elegance, refinement) and *zoku* (vulgarity, coarseness) is often invoked as fitting the dichotomies adopted in the West.[66] The intellectual lucidity of Peter Burke and his pioneering work on popular culture has clarified the complexities behind such a binary view of the popular.[67] He challenges the straightforward opposition between elite and popular, highbrow and lowbrow, the great tradition and the little tradition and encourages us to acknowledge osmotic boundaries between these seemingly antithetical poles. He believes that a dynamic "two-way traffic" exists between them: on the one hand, there is a process of "sinking," whereby elite culture is absorbed into and appropriated by popular culture through mechanisms of cultural translation, adaptation, and parody; on the other is a process of "rising," whereby popular culture is consumed by elite culture.[68] Put differently, the idea of circularity needs to be carefully addressed.[69] Rethinking the relationship between lowbrow and highbrow as a dynamic process is a matter of not only recognizing porosity but also accepting their relativity. In their introduction to *Literature and Popular Culture in Early Modern England*, Matthew Dimmock and Andrew Hadfield opine that objects associated with a low cultural status in one era can be raised to the status of canonical works in another, thereby entering the realm of elite culture and vice versa.[70] "High" and "low" are relative terms that need to be appropriately historicized to understand their contextual position in the contemporary cultural (and literary) panorama. This brings us back to the approaches espoused by historical scholarship relating to international developments and by Nakano Mitsutoshi in connection with Japan.

Research on popular culture has also been concerned with unraveling whether popular means produced *by* or *for* the people. This has led some scholars to work within the Gramscian idea of hegemony and to view popular culture as a site of struggle between dominant elites trying to impose culture on a subordinate class that resists.[71] Yet I contend that this line of inquiry is not especially fruitful when studying seventeenth-century popular prose. In her excellent study on Kabuki theater, Satoko Shimazaki seeks to shift the dominant view of this performance art as an "outlet for popular resistance to shogunal authority" to one of Edo Kabuki as a cultural site that "celebrated and drew on paradigms from samurai history and culture, gradually enabling a wider segment of Edo to internalize them both and thus contributing to the production of new popular culture."[72] The conclusions that Shimazaki draws are relevant for the corpus of texts examined here. Seventeenth-century popular prose does include texts that translate dominant ideologies for those who cannot access them in literary Chinese or via secret, orally transmitted traditions. For some this might be easily interpreted as an attempt to absorb subordinate groups into the dominant ideologies. We should not forget, however, that these texts were above all commercial products put on the market by publishers whose primary goal was to secure financial profit by giving readers what they demanded. In the chapters that follow, therefore, I explore the tension between strategies of domination and the inventiveness of appropriation, and I propose an alternative reading, one that calls attention to the empowerment that results from being granted entrance to previously precluded aspects of culture. I argue that much can be said about the satisfaction gained from the sense of agency and the pleasure derived from accessing fresh knowledge at one's leisure. Similarly, much can be said about the cognitive frisson at play when learning the skills necessary to become confident, successful members of a society. I also investigate the enjoyment derived from acquiring access to social universes removed from readers' everyday lives. At the same time, I discuss texts that uncover contentious societal problems and expose the wrongdoings of local administrations by invoking, quite paradoxically, the same ideology that had allegedly been forced upon the people. Moreover, I note how seventeenth-century printed books managed to raise controversial topics with virtual impunity. In doing so, I challenge the idea of "a despotic government that tolerated absolutely no public criticism of its policies and confiscated books that it found offensive."[73]

Foraging in the Forest

Where do we begin? This question has troubled me over the years, from the moment I discussed the inadequacy of *kanazōshi* as a meaningful paradigm to explore seventeenth-century popular prose.[74] As I have suggested elsewhere, the book-trade catalogues from commercial publishers active during this period with their categories for dividing and organizing their publications, which I call publishing genres, are the most appropriate starting point.[75] Having identified which segments of the forest of books to discuss, we are still left with a considerable number of publishing genres and a fairly large amount of titles. And this is part of the beauty of the story I hope to tell—that is, that diversity and quantity are key features of the Great Unread I unearth in this book.[76] This, in turn, explains the mention of a sizable number of primary sources. Because of the notable lack of translations and studies on these sources, as noted before, I have made a conscious decision to yield to the close reading of select texts, providing readers with copious details and textual snippets in translation. Ultimately, the hope is that readers will be in a position to get a feel for this prose and to indulge in the cognitive, emotional, and aesthetic responses it elicits. This volume thus fills a substantial gap in English scholarship on the subject and works in a similar fashion to the pioneering studies on popular literature in other cultures mentioned earlier.[77]

While acknowledging the virtues of a sampler approach, I also heed warnings against any attempt to be unreasonably inclusive. With this in mind, I have made specific choices based on the premise that seventeenth-century readers, in particular those who were for the first time in a position to access the written word, were full of curiosity and that commercial publishers saw a unique business opportunity in rewarding, and at the same time in fueling, that curiosity. But curiosity in what? Taking the lead from Alberto Manguel's investigation into curiosity, my answer would be in learning "about the world, and therefore be better equipped to cope with its pitfalls and dangers."[78] It is the epistemic curiosity defined by psychologist Daniel Berlyne as something intrinsically human and "aimed not only at obtaining access to information-bearing stimulation capable of dispelling the uncertainties of the moment, but also at acquiring knowledge."[79]

Books are undoubtedly one way of obtaining the answers we seek. They become vehicles of knowledge, engaging readers at a cognitive level, not only at an emotional or aesthetic one.[80] They satisfy curiosity and awaken more inquisitiveness, thus stimulating the infinite need for new publications. In this book I explore texts with different degrees of narrativity that provided seventeenth-century popular readers with knowledge about the relevant ethical and societal norms to become well-rounded human beings, suitably armed to fit into and thrive in contemporary society. By focusing on the process of knowledge making, the present study complements Mary Elizabeth Berry's landmark work on the "Library of Information."[81] I make a deliberate distinction between information and knowledge, drawing upon the work of Peter Burke: information is "knowing that," while knowledge is "knowing how"; information refers to "what is relatively 'raw,' specific and practical," while knowledge "denotes what has been 'cooked,' processed or systematized by thought."[82] Berry focuses on information and examines early modern maps, gazetteers, travel guidebooks, and rosters, including a small selection from the seventeenth century. She does so to put forward a compelling argument that the concept of nationhood already existed in early modern Japan and was constructed around the idea that national knowledge—with knowledge viewed as information—was made available to readers. This created a shared cultural literacy that encompassed "political and social geography, ritual and festival calendars, principal products and employments, conventional forms of self-cultivation and etiquette, histories focused on 'name and fame.'"[83] Berry's account does not encompass the type of knowledge that intrigues me and that overlaps with Nakano's notion of *shisōsei*.[84] How can I access, understand, and interiorize Buddhist teachings at a time when affiliation to a Buddhist temple has become the norm? How should I behave? How do I communicate better via letters in a stringently bureaucratic society? How can I improve my financial status? How can I cope with a land ravaged by disasters? How can I deal with the injustices perpetrated by the local administration? *Pleasure in Profit* culls from a variety of carefully selected primary sources in order to reveal answers to these questions.

In the process, my research diverges from Berry's on two more accounts. First, seventeenth-century sources seem to resist the idea of a national knowledge being pushed through. As I remark on several occasions in the chapters that follow, the underlying concern that emerges from these texts is in a desire to help forge human beings worthy of this appellation. There is no evidence that the same sources pitched this discourse around "our country," "our people," or "Nihon" (Japan), as noted by Berry in later materials.[85] Second, the present book is about *literature*. Berry seems to suggest a disjunction between texts of the information library and those that constitute literature, which she identifies solely in Saikaku's fiction. She talks of these two entities as "close cousins" but posits the information library outside and before fiction, as something that fiction (= literature) can mimic and use to entertain "knowing audiences."[86] My ultimate argument is to reclaim the place of knowledge-making texts at the very heart of literature. As noted at the outset, the network of texts that populate the seventeenth-century bookshop belongs to the literary tradition as broadly defined by Umberto Eco. I see no tension between the aesthetic and the cognitive. I see no dichotomy between pleasure and profit.

Pleasure *in* Profit

Commercially printed books sated and stimulated the curiosity for knowledge. Profit was the obvious outcome of this cultural transaction. Readers profited from learning how to become conscious of themselves and of the world around them. As mentioned at the beginning in touching on the titles issued by

Akitaya Heizaemon and Nishimura Matazaemon, commercial publishers were not so foolish as to publish only didactic prose aimed at the edification of its consumers. They were also quenching readers' thirst for pure entertainment. Pleasure would be gained by perusing stories full of delight. Instruction and delight. Profit and pleasure. These are the two pillars of seventeenth-century prose, in alignment with what Nakano defines as key features of *gesaku* and with what scholars of popular literature have identified in other cultures.

If I had wished to tell only this simpler story, the title of this publication might have been a more conventionally worded *Pleasure and Profit*. Intellectuals and psychologists, though, opine that feeding one's epistemic curiosity (learning) can involve enjoyment and lead to pleasure.[87] In this vein I opted for the title *Pleasure in Profit*: pleasure resides *within* profit, in particular in the profit gained from acquiring knowledge. In an attempt to erode any facile distinction, if not opposition, between pleasure and profit, this book also maintains that fictional texts were constructed to maximize and optimize their epistemic function, and I discuss how seventeenth-century popular fiction was designed to be transformative and deeply ethical. *Pleasure in Profit* does not claim that all seventeenth-century literature is by definition didactic. In chapter 7, for example, I deal with a number of texts of pleasure that celebrate plurality over unity, allowing for competing messages to cohabit the same textual space. Here, the pleasure is not derived only (or not so much) from the profit of learning. It is similarly derived from an appreciation of discontinuity and by relishing the power of choosing what to read at one's leisure. I am also eager to make it clear that my stance does not preclude that pleasure can be equally gained from a more traditional aesthetic reading of prose, where the reader delights in the thoughts and feelings generated *during* the very process of reading and by the words on the page. I argue, however, that the time is ripe to investigate the pleasure derived also from efferent reading, in particular when confronted with an impressive number of texts designed to prioritize this form of engagement with the written word. There is more. In the story I wish to reconstruct, there is an additional pleasure that needs to be appreciated: it exists with the publishers in their financial gains through the sale of popular books. We should hold in our minds that publishers were not moved by philanthropic aims. They required funds to enable the publication of these books in the first place. They required funds to run their businesses—cash to buy the wood for the wooden blocks, to pay for the woodblock cutter, to purchase the paper needed for printing, to remunerate the printer.[88] It is not a tremendous leap of imagination to assume that publishers received pleasure from their financial profit.

Where do I begin and when do I end my story? My starting point is around the Kan'ei era (1624–1644), when woodblock printing fully takes off in commercial publishing, and my story finishes roughly at the end of the seventeenth century. I often remark, however, that such cutoff points would have been meaningless for those who lived at this time. Seventeenth-century publishers were happy to reprint medieval texts as an integral part of their stock and to market their how-to manuals as books that provided knowledge traditionally transmitted from mouth to ear in previous eras. Similarly, many texts as well as several publishing genres introduced in the seventeenth century remained a regular feature of the publishing market until the end of the Edo period, if not after. That is why my work indulges in providing detailed information about the publication histories of the primary sources that I examine in close readings. While acknowledging the permeability of these boundaries, inevitably the story must have a beginning and an end.

Readers of my study will immediately notice the conspicuous absence of Ihara Saikaku. It has been tempting to include his prose because I am fundamentally convinced that Saikaku is an intrinsic part of the commercial publishing under discussion here and that he does not represent any watershed in seventeenth-century popular prose. Nakano's remarks on the didactic stance of Saikaku's prose and Yoshie Hisaya's view of Saikaku's work as "literature of the mind" (*hitogokoro no bungaku*) seem to suggest a similar viewpoint.[89] Nevertheless, I have chosen to keep Saikaku out of my study for three reasons. The first is pragmatic. Having welcomed warnings against an overly inclusive approach and being acutely aware that my project had to reach completion at some stage, I deliberately put aside any purposeful engagement with Saikaku's prose. The second is epistemological. Embarking on a project fully exploring how Saikaku forms an integral part of the seventeenth-century popular prose as I view it assumes a familiarization with a vast body of scholarly work produced specifically on Saikaku and demands an appreciation of the linguistic skills of this writer. My hope is that this monograph might entice scholars who are endowed with the required expertise to reassess Saikaku's prose with fresh eyes in terms of continuity with, not necessarily a break from, contemporary popular literature. The third, and for me the most significant reason, is methodological. Saikaku is relatively well known to English-language readers. Research on him and translations of his prose have been produced over the years.[90] While this scholarly work offers a tremendous contribution to the field of early modern Japanese literature, it has the regrettable disadvantage of having created a Saikaku-centered view of the seventeenth-century literary market and popular prose. Saikaku and his literary genius are portrayed as the exception that stands out from a century of mediocrity, mediocrity worth mentioning only as a preparatory phase to the true master. Thinking of Saikaku's prose as the pinnacle of the seventeenth century is the norm. As should be clear by now, I strongly disagree with this notion. What if we move away from this teleological narrative? What if we write a literary history of the seventeenth century that is not Saikaku centered? This is what my monograph aims to achieve.

Structure of the Book

The first two chapters set the stage, probing two preconditions for the emergence and success of a vibrant popular, commercial prose in the vernacular: the existence of a readership in a position to access such literature and the presence of a vigorous publishing industry that knew how to entice that body of readers to its products.

Chapter 1, "The Culture of the Written Word," explores how seventeenth-century Japan championed the ability to read and write as a new social must and witnessed an increase in people who could access the written word. I cull from several contemporary texts—printed books, handwritten diaries, and visual materials—to recover the powerful rhetoric behind this and to gauge how the written word began to permeate daily life across class and gender. I also present fresh considerations on the scope of the reading public at the time by grappling with the scant figures we have. In coming to terms with the thorny issue of literacy, and more specifically of popular literacy, I choose to move away from the question of who could read and ask rather, "Who could read what?" In this way, I provide an understanding of seventeenth-century literacy that differs from Richard Rubinger's in his now classic *Popular Literacy in Early Modern Japan*. This chapter examines the plurality of written languages and competence skills (paleographic, linguistic, and cultural) at play and postulates the existence of expert and novice readers who could move more or less freely across the spectrum of multiple literacies.

Having reconstructed the reading public and its complex identity, I continue with the study of the other major player in our story: the publisher-bookseller. Chapter 2, "The Publishing Business," investigates the commercial publishing market that emerged in response to a growing reading public and limns a vivid image of Japan's buoyant book industry in the seventeenth century. By gathering evidence from contemporary pictorial and verbal sources and making full use of Oka Masahiko's survey of seventeenth-century printed colophons, this chapter stretches received views on the subject. The second half of the chapter advances the notion of publishing genres and what it entails (something quite different from the modern understanding of genre). By scrutinizing book-trade catalogues issued beginning in the 1670s, this section discloses how publishers organized their products and identifies those book typologies that had the potential to spark interest in novice readers. Chapter 2 also discusses the marginal role played by authors during this period and puts forward the notion of a collective author as particularly fruitful in an examination of seventeenth-century popular prose.

Chapter 3, "Negotiating the Way," dissects two publishing genres—*kana bussho* and *kana washo*—and unveils how commercial publishers packaged ethical, religious, and civic knowledge associated with Confucianism and Buddhism for a wide readership. The close reading of selected primary sources uncovers how knowledge was decontextualized and translated to become comprehensible also to readers endowed with basic literacy and to guide them in becoming well-rounded human beings. In the process, I explore a few textual strategies that, I maintain, characterize contemporary didactic prose as a whole, including what I call the residue of aurality. This chapter appraises the power of unlocking knowledge and draws attention to the circular relationship between elite and popular cultures.

Chapter 4, "Civility Matters," is conceived as a journey to understand how publishers effectively exploited the idea of disclosing secret traditions in order to market an ample range of materials devised to teach conduct. The same materials consequently released a rich gamut of societal and interpersonal knowledge. The investigation into the publishing genre of *shitsukekata-sho narabi ni ryōri-sho*—encompassing manners and cookery—uncloaks a corpus of transformative literature that potentially assists readers in becoming successful individuals. Along the way, I challenge findings put forward in Eiko Ikegami's *Bonds of Civility*, including the notion of hierarchical civility and a nationalistic dimension to etiquette. This chapter embraces the porosity of publishing genres by expanding the study of civility literature to *nyosho* (books for women) and to the sexually explicit *Sanze aishō makura* (The pillow of affinities across three generations; 1687). I argue against any simplistic duality between efferent and aesthetic reading, introducing the idea of "narrative capital" and its use across texts that display different modes of narrativity.

Chapter 5, "Say It in a Skillful Letter," extends the inquiry of interpersonal and societal knowledge by exploring "letteracy," defined as the competency in the writing, reading, and interpreting of letters. It does so across publishing genres. The focus is on how nonnarrative manuals of epistolography did much more than teaching how to write missives. My contention is that they fueled the birth of a common (written) language and established culturally powerful literary tropes. The chapter first unearths the linguistic and aesthetic features of *sōrōbun* and *mairase-sōrōbun*, the two styles employed in letter writing. In this way it highlights a tension between the desire to ease communication notwithstanding gender or social status and the endorsement of hierarchical human relations. The chapter then examines the creation of the "*Usuyuki* master plot" and its ubiquitous reuse, as well as its visionary adaptations, in later epistolary fictions that engage readers cognitively, aesthetically, and emotionally. When zooming in on collections of love letters, in particular, I probe how manuals cleverly assembled all the essential features of fictional narratives.

Chapter 6, "A Commitment to the Present," continues to push us outside the boundaries of the publishing genres and concentrates on texts designed to help readers make sense of the contemporary world and what is topical in it. Money and disasters are foregrounded. The section on money explores the shift from a medieval to an early modern discourse on moneymaking. I indicate how several texts offered advice about how to accumulate wealth but simultaneously, almost contradictorily, upheld frugality and even justified poverty. Ultimately, I argue that under the veneer of how-to books, these texts hardly work as transformative literature. The analysis of disaster narratives reveals how they functioned as personal tales about history-making catastrophes while appeasing readers with the soothing hope of redress. In the process I claim that they work differently from the trauma narratives studied by Cathy Caruth. As a whole, this chapter aims to prompt a reflection on how popular literature was used to broadcast the news before the circulation of cheap broadsheets (*kawaraban*) and scrutinizes the pleasure derived from reading texts that operate like a compass in navigating society.

Chapter 7, "The Triumph of Plurality," invites reflection on how seventeenth-century popular prose elicits modes of reading that might be unfamiliar to the twenty-first-century reader. Drawing on Roland Barthes's discussion of "texts of pleasures" and "texts of bliss," I claim that in order to make full sense of seventeenth-century popular prose we need to embrace "discontinuous reading," as theorized by Peter Stallybrass and Eve Tavor Bannet. Failing to do so means that works designed as texts of pleasure and perceived as such in early modern times turn into challenging, inhospitable texts of bliss, with the consequent risk of their finding little or no place in discussions of Japanese literature. Utilizing a close reading of three primary sources, this chapter demonstrates that by adopting a reading strategy that satisfies both purposive and digressive curiosity we can rehabilitate texts almost entirely forgotten today and propose innovative critical venues for canonical works.

The 1703 verse "With the cutting of characters / the forest of books / luxuriantly bursts forth" captures the nature of Japanese seventeenth-century popular prose. *Pleasure in Profit* ventures into this lush realm, embracing its rich diversity, with the aim of retrieving what satisfied readers' epistemic curiosity and sparked the pleasure of knowing. The following chapters search the archive to reconstruct the story of seventeenth-century popular readers and the commercially printed books that encouraged them to live life to the fullest.

CHAPTER 1

The Culture of the Written Word

A peaceful world is maintained with literature,
a world in disorder is dealt with by the military arts.

—Kawachiya Yoshimasa, *Kawachiya Yoshimasa kyūki* (Old records of Kawachiya Yoshimasa)

Any project that seeks to investigate popular literature—where "popular" encompasses also a quantitative dimension—presupposes the existence of a readership wide enough to justify what would have been a significant financial investment on the part of commercial publishers. Can we safely assume that this was the case in seventeenth-century Japan?

Current scholarship lacks agreement in answering this thorny question. Konda Yōzō refuses to acknowledge that seventeenth-century commercially printed prose issued before Ihara Saikaku ever reached anyone other than samurai, Buddhist monks, and economically powerful merchants.[1] For him seventeenth-century prose never spoke to a truly popular readership, his argument tying the idea of popular with a specific segment of society—the *shomin*, or commoners. Nagatomo Chiyoji is equally skeptical of finding readers beyond townspeople endowed with financial substance.[2] By conducting fresh research on diaries of wealthy merchants, he seems to suggest that around the 1670s it is to affluent townspeople that we should look in discussing the readership of books produced for broad circulation.³ What both Konda and Nagatomo are saying is that commercial publishers were producing books—in considerable numbers, as this chapter reveals—for a negligible proportion of the population. A note on seventeenth-century Japanese society is in order here. In his foundational work on the status-system society of early modern Japan, David L. Howell takes us outside "the hierarchical social taxonomy of four estates" and introduces us to a number of status categories.⁴ There were the imperial family and the court nobility, who constituted a tiny fraction of society. There were Buddhist and Shinto clerics who, together with mountain priests (*yamabushi*), made up several hundred thousand. There were the samurai (or warrior class), which represented around 6 percent of the total population. There were the commoners, which included peasants (*hyakushō*) and townspeople (*chōnin*), most likely around 90 percent of the population. And finally, there were a number of marginal status groups (outcasts).⁵ With the warrior class making up 6 percent of the population, even if we were to add Buddhist monks and wealthy merchants, as Konda and Nagatomo suggest, we would still barely reach 10 percent of the total population.

Shibata Jun and Richard Rubinger have advanced a more inclusive account. Shibata claims that "at the beginning of the Edo period, skills such as writing, reading, and basic mathematics were quite advanced among commoners [*minshū*]."⁶ His reference to commoners subsumes peasants in charge of the village administration and merchants. He adds that after the 1660s a greater number of people must have mastered these same skills, hence suggesting that the reading public must have been wider than the one postulated by Konda and Nagatomo. Building on Shibata's research, Rubinger focuses on the state of literacy in villages during the Edo period and maintains that there were "high levels of functional literacy among the leadership of Japanese farming villages in the early seventeenth century and even before that."⁷ While acknowledging the difficulty in gauging the extent of administrative literacy beyond the elite group of village heads, Rubinger concludes that "by the end of the seventeenth century, some ordinary farmers had attained a significant degree of literacy" and recognizes "a high functional literacy to most landowning farmers, perhaps 50 percent of the farming population or even more."⁸ Through his work on signatures Rubinger also suggests that "the upper levels of the urban merchant class were highly literate early in the Tokugawa period and for decades before that" and that "illiteracy was generally much higher among women than men."⁹ Rubinger's compelling argument is somewhat problematized by the methodological suspicions raised around the merits in investigating "subscriptional ability," or the ability to sign.¹⁰ Even so, his findings, together with Shibata's, resonate greatly in that they prompt a question strongly entwined with the issue of readership: who could read what in seventeenth-century Japan?

It is the work by Yokota Fuyuhiko that explores this line of inquiry, leading to thought-provoking insights. Yokota has observed that beginning in the 1970s studies seem to agree that the ability to read and write was widespread among commoners (*minshū*) as early as the seventeenth century.[11] In his examination of the published works by the scholar and pedagogue Kaibara Ekiken 貝原益軒 (1630–1714) and based on the list of acquaintances that Ekiken himself compiled, Yokota posits a sort of two-tier corpus of Ekiken readership.[12] The first were those located near Ekiken and part of a closely linked network that included some sixty people, ranging from high-ranking samurai and doctors to Confucian scholars. This group would have been equipped with sophisticated literacy skills allowing them to read texts written in literary Chinese. The second were those geographically distant from Ekiken, outside his close network, and included more than two thousand names of low-ranking samurai, samurai attendants, merchants, village headsmen, and Shinto priests, among others. This group was characterized by the ability to read texts only in the vernacular. Yokota believes that Ekiken "discovered" these two different types of readers in 1688 and adjusted his writing style to appeal to both. Yokota applies his interpretation of a two-tiered Ekiken readership as a metaphor for early modern readership in general. Yokota's position is particularly generative when reflecting upon the notion of popular literacy. Readers are not classified on the basis of status but on that of who could read what. This leads us to problematize the very idea of literacy in the singular, pushing us to think instead in terms of literacies.

Building upon Yokota's methodological approach, this chapter maintains the existence of a spectrum of multiple literacies in seventeenth-century Japan and explores how readers could position themselves at one or more junctures on that spectrum. I start with an exploration of how basic literacy—or the ability to write and read the phonetic script (hiragana) and a few logographic characters (kanji)—was trumpeted as a new social must across the plurality of status categories. I then retrieve visual and verbal traces of how engagement with the written word started suffusing daily life. Subsequently, I offer figures on how many books in the vernacular were published during this period and how this number compares with the population statistics, arguing that only a sizable readership could justify and support such a buoyant industry. I end by considering the array of written languages of the seventeenth century, showing how the traditional dichotomy between literary Chinese and vernacular Japanese is reductive and misleading. In taking this approach I hope to suggest that readers endowed with basic literacy and some linguistic/cultural competencies, or what I call novice readers, were encouraged to move with some freedom across the spectrum of literacies.

Advocating Literacy

In seventeenth-century Japan the ability to write and consequently to read was promoted as a must-have skill across society and regardless of gender. One of the most powerful espousals of this stance comes slightly later, with Kaibara Ekiken's *Wazoku dōjikun* (Japanese traditional teachings for children; 1710):

> Of all things, knowledge of writing [*mono kaki*] and arithmetic should be taught to everyone, regardless of their status and across the four estates.... If you do not know how to write and read [*moji o shirazareba*], your speech will be broken, you will appear clumsy and uncultured; you will be looked down upon by others, the object of disdain and ridicule. How regrettable! Not only that. If you do not know how to write and read, you will not be conversant with the things and the words of this world. The result will be such that you will find it difficult to comply with all sorts of duties, and you will remain behind in many worldly affairs.[13]

Ekiken is clear in his message that the ability to write, and to read, is requisite for navigating this new world effectively and successfully.[14] Although Ekiken is writing at the beginning of the eighteenth century, he is not creating a new discourse regarding the importance of the written word. Rather, he is reflecting positions already advocated during the seventeenth century.

As early as 1662 there is evidence that basic literacy was promoted as something desirable among the peasants. Shibata Jun introduces the following evidence of this: "At the age of eight or nine, peasants' children should learn all sorts of things, regardless of their gender. They should be encouraged to learn how to write and to study the rudiments of arithmetic."[15] Shibata views this information alongside an ordinance issued in 1649 by the shogunate known as *Keian ofuregaki* (The Keian proclamation) to conclude that there was eagerness in educating peasants in an effort to ensure that they would respect the law and the authority of the shogun.[16]

In the 1690s, work by Namura Jōhaku 苗村常伯 (1674–1748) mirrored a similar stance. In his *Nan chōhōki* (A treasury for men; 1693) Namura enjoins men belonging to any of the four estates—samurai, peasant, artisan, merchant—to master writing and reading:

> Males of the four estates should comprehend that the art of reading and writing [*tenarai*], as well as learning [*gakumon*], should be cherished as the most essential skill.... If a samurai understands only archery, horsemanship, and fencing but is not literate, he will likewise be blind in the military arts. If he does not treasure the pursuit of learning, he will not have any success in the military arts.... For peasants, farming is just one part of their education.

Whenever a peasant has a respite from farming, he should devote himself to study.... Practical work is one facet of learning. It is only when one fully grasps the principles of things [ri] that discoveries in craftsmanship are possible.... Merchants ought to study and avoid being uncultured.[17]

The difference between *tenarai* and *gakumon* is discussed subsequently, but it should be noted here that Namura's *Nan chōhōki* devotes an entire section to the art of writing and reading in its second volume, giving details about Chinese characters, the phonetic hiragana and katakana syllabaries, calligraphic styles, paper, inkstones, and ink.[18]

Namura also wrote *Onna chōhōki* (A treasury for women; 1692), in which the division of women into social groups is more complex than the four-tiered hierarchy for men. Eight groups are identified: *kuge* (court aristocracy) *chōnin* (townspeople), *buke* (samurai), and *hyakushō* (peasant) refer to a woman's social status, whereas the remaining categories deal with the position of women vis-à-vis men or their occupation—that is, as concubines (*mekake*), prostitutes in the pleasure quarters (*keisei*), women (*kasha*) working in the houses of assignation (*ageya*) and teahouses (*chaya*) in the pleasure quarters, and widows (*goke*).[19] In the fourth volume the author affirms the importance of women's ability to write, at least in the phonetic hiragana syllabary: "Even uncultured women [*muchi no onna*] will be able to read poetry and books [*sōshi*] if they at least learn to write hiragana. They will become acquainted with the things of the past, will express their feelings, and will be capable of handling any business by writing letters."[20] Although Namura does not distinguish which groups or group of women is the subject of his treatise, it can be assumed that this remark on the importance of literacy targeted all women regardless of role or social position.

Further clarity about which type of women should engage with the written word can be gleaned from other earlier texts. For example, *Onna shikimoku* (Rules for women; 1660) devotes one of its two volumes to the writing skills that were considered necessary for women (further discussion of *Onna shikimoku* can be found in chapter 4). It maintained that women, regardless of their social class (*takaki hikiki ni yorazu*), should learn writing (*te o narai, mono kaki*) as the most vital of the cultural accomplishments (*gei*).[21] Merchants' wives (*akindo no nyōbō*) are singled out in this discourse: "In particular, this [writing] should come first and foremost for merchants' wives. Otherwise they will not be able to guide and teach their children, which would result in a shameful situation."[22] A similar stance is noted in *Onna kagami hidensho* (Book on the secret tradition of the mirror for women; 1650). The first volume lists each of the disadvantages facing women unable to write:

> From a tender age, girls must be forced to write. First, if they are not able to write letters, they will miss out on all sorts of things. Moreover, the inability to write means that one is stupid and unable to distinguish the west from the

east. For a woman who cannot write, turning to books [*mono no hon, sōshi*] is like a blind person turning to a wall. Similarly, even if she becomes intimate with a man of high rank, their relationship will not be deep. Once she is married, love will diminish. Moreover, even if she devotes herself to various forms of [artistic] training, she will be slow in learning.... Even lowborn women appear sophisticated if they can write well. This is all the more so for the wives and daughters of daimyo or from highborn families. It is inconceivable that they would be unable to write.... There is indeed no treasure that surpasses writing.[23]

These examples are intriguing not simply because they demonstrate the strong support of literacy across the highborn and lowborn but also for the emphasis they place on women. This creates a slight tension with Rubinger's findings: whereas Rubinger notes higher levels of illiteracy among women, the normative discourse produced for women at the time exhorted them to master *tenarai*.[24]

Above all, the ability to write and read is blazoned as a requisite for anyone to be regarded as a proper human being. For example, the 1681 *Nioi bukuro* (The scented pouch) explains the following:

No matter about the mastery of all arts: if you lack the ability to read and write, you are not worth being called a person [*hito to wa iwaremajiki koto*].... Those with knowledge have discernment and, as a result, they are not despised or laughed at by others. In their next life they will be born in paradise; in this life they will be protected by deities and Buddhas. Their lives will be long and their offspring will prosper—there is no doubt about this. And in any case, being able to read and write is to know good things. No matter how clear and talented one is, a lack of these two abilities means that it is difficult to be successful in life, regardless of whether you are from a high or low background.[25]

The educator Sasayama Baian 笹山梅庵 (dates unknown) takes an even harsher stance, and in his *Terako seikai no shikimoku* (Rules on the prohibitions for pupils of *terakoya* schools; 1695) condemns all those unable to write: "Those who are born as human beings and are not able to write are not worth consideration as human beings [*hito ni arazu*]. They are like blind people. They cast shame on their masters, on their parents, and on themselves."[26]

All this is circumstantial evidence that in seventeenth-century Japan there was a strong push for everyone to engage with the written word. Being able to write and read was framed as a new social must. Failing to do so meant not only jeopardizing one's daily life but also stigmatization and derision. In other words, writing and reading were seen as the key to social and personal success for everyone. Although this discourse might be seen, in part, as a mere posture, it cannot be denied that it was advanced and done so quite forcibly.

Traces of Literacy

Was the prescription that people of all sorts learn how to write and to read pure rhetoric? Previous scholarship has drawn attention to the existence of written documents regulating all aspects of daily life in early modern Japan.[27] Ishikawa Ken describes early modern Japan as a society that functioned based on written records.[28] He points to two main areas that were heavily dominated by the use of documents: business with its paperwork (e.g., contracts, records of financial transactions, orders, diaries) and the Tokugawa shogunate and local administrations, which greatly exploited the written word to exercise power and rule the country. Ishikawa mentions a diversity of documents containing rules and regulations (*gohatto*), official announcements (*ofuregaki*), notice boards or signs (*kōsatsu*), and record books for neighborhood associations (*goningumi-chō*). There are, in addition, other documents regulating daily life such as wills, family precepts (*kakun*), documents related to travel throughout the country, divorce papers, diaries, and so forth. It is quite plausible to assume that such documents were read aloud to those who could not read or written on behalf of those unable to write. But the sheer number of these documents and their importance in ensuring full participation in a newly emerging society equally suggest that there was a growing expectation that people would engage with the written word without intermediaries.

It is impossible to ascertain what level of literacy would have been attained in a seventeenth-century household, yet three accounts are particularly noteworthy in offering glimpses into how interaction with the written word impacted the lives of commoners—that is, farmers, artisans, and merchants. The first is from the village of Daigatsuka in Kawachi Province (present-day Osaka Prefecture). The Daigatsuka sake brewer Kawachiya Yoshimasa 河内屋可正 (also read Kōchiya Yoshimasa; b. Tsuboi Yoshimasa 壺井可正 [1636–1713]) compiled an ambitious diary today known under the title *Kawachiya Yoshimasa kyūki* (Old records of Kawachiya Yoshimasa).[29] Written over some years between 1693 and 1706, its nineteen volumes were handwritten, presumably by Yoshimasa, in vernacular Japanese using a mixture of logographic and phonetic scripts. The detailed records of local events, gossip about the area's many inhabitants, information about the family business, and household precepts show that Yoshimasa possessed enough knowledge to keep an extensive written account of any subject that interested him.

A reading of Yoshimasa's diary reveals that he was a sake brewer as well as the owner and cultivator of a large tract of land, which would have positioned him as a commoner, and he defines himself as a such (using the word *shojin*) in the introduction of his diary.[30] Moreover, we learn that he followed his father, Seiemon, in the study of Noh theater and haikai poetry composition, which is indicative of more than a simple interest in practical or vocational literacy.[31]

This diary reveals that a commoner like Yoshimasa was not only literate but also expected family members and residents in the region to share in the same standard of literacy by reading it: "What I am recording here are admonitions for the people living in this area, in particular my descendants. Those who create harmony in the household, exhibit good behavior, and enjoy peace should fully grasp the meaning of this book. Those who do not embrace the exhortations made here will certainly end up badly. There is no other note I shall leave behind after my death. My offspring should abide by this book."[32]

The possibility that members of the household or the village would gather for public readings of the diary cannot be rejected. But at the same time this can also be viewed as a declaration of expectations: anyone wishing to read Yoshimasa's diary would have needed basic literacy to decode the kanji, hiragana, and katakana in the text. Moreover, the ability to write and read is clearly stated as de rigueur in a merchant household:

> Writing [te o kaku] should be the first accomplishment [gei] for a man. Even good-looking men will be looked down upon if they have no writing [muhitsu] or bad writing [akuhitsu] skills. Those who cannot write are not able to send and receive letters and are barred from keeping diaries or account books. People who are economically well off as well as those who are in less-privileged financial situations should apply themselves to learning how to write [tenarai] whenever they have free time from business. Even ill-natured people will not be despised if they can write. Because it is difficult to excel in calligraphy, one should [at least] strive to master a standard level.[33]

While highlighting the benefits that await an individual and a household when they devote their free time to learning, Yoshimasa mentions that skills in writing and reading, together with training in Noh theater, can also prove helpful if a difficult financial situation arises. This is because one can use these skills to find an alternative way of living—namely, by instructing others in these skills.[34]

The second account is from Kawagoe near Edo. Enomoto Yazaemon 榎本弥左衛門 (1626–1686) was the grandson of a *shūgendō* monk who moved to Kawagoe from Kumano in Kii Province (present-day Wakayama and southern Mie Prefectures). He rose to prominence as a wealthy salt merchant, bequeathing the handwritten diary *Mitsugo yori no oboe* (Recollections from the age of three) and the handwritten record *Yorozu no oboe* (A myriad of memories).[35] Like Yoshimasa's diary, *Mitsugo yori no oboe* is a vernacular text written in a mixture of kanji and hiragana that presents diverse information about household and business matters, local personalities, and contemporary events. It also provides teachings to assist in developing ethical behavior, such as a commitment to hard work, filial piety, and more generally a respect for Confucian and Buddhist virtues. Unlike Yoshimasa's diary, there is no clear statement that these texts were composed for the benefit of his descendants or the local population. Nonetheless, it chronicles Yazaemon gifting his daughter Otake with a text of precepts—a copy of which is included in *Mitsugo yori no oboe*—when she was married at fourteen. This contained a list of texts that she should read daily and hints that she, too, was a capable reader.[36] We can easily imagine that Otake would have acquired basic writing and reading skills around the same age as her father when he studied with the teacher Moro Chōbee 毛呂長兵衛 between the age of eleven and twelve.[37] The text is, once again, about commoners, albeit here very wealthy, and their ability to write and read vernacular Japanese at the least.

The third example involves the Kōnoike 鴻池 family based in a village of the same name in the region of Itami near Osaka and reiterates the fact that literacy was part of the everyday life of a seventeenth-century merchant. By the end of the Edo period the Kōnoike had evolved into one of the most powerful and wealthy merchant families in the country. Its founder, Naofumi 直文 (also known as Shinroku 新六 [1570–1650]), was of samurai origins.[38] Following his coming of age at fifteen, Naofumi decided to renounce his high-ranking social background in order to enter into business. His desire to hide his origins was such that he changed his name to Shin'emon 新右衛門 and even kept the details of his background from his own children. His business initially (beginning in 1619) centered on the production and selling of sake, and in 1625 he soon moved into logistics, principally maritime shipping between Osaka and Edo. In 1637, he began a remunerative business in lending money to daimyo, and eventually his eighth son (1608–1693) assumed control of the family business and became the first-generation Kōnoike Zen'emon 鴻池善右衛門. In 1656, he expanded the business into another area—that is, as a money-exchange shop. The family continued to prosper even after the Edo period, with the thirteenth-generation Zen'emon inheriting in 1954. What characterizes each generation of the Edo-period Kōnoike family is the production of family precepts written down for the benefit of its descendants.[39] The first set of teachings, *Shison seishi jōmoku* (Articles with admonitions for the progeny), was recorded by Shinzaemon in 1614; the texts were regularly revised until 1723. As *kakun* they were produced to be read, understood, and implemented by the family's descendants, once again exhibiting clear expectations of a shared degree of literacy within the household.

The manuscripts compiled by the Kawachiya, Enomoto, and Kōnoike families constitute evidence that a mastery of writing and reading vernacular Japanese existed in farming and commerce households. These are wealthy, privileged families and so in a way not ordinary commoners. Admittedly, it would be difficult to draw conclusions about literacy levels of commoners who were not affluent from these documents. Yet when considered together with the exhortation that everyone master basic literacy, I would argue that they contribute to completing our picture and reinforce our understanding that people of all sorts were at least encouraged to engage with writing and reading.

The gradual assimilation of the written word in the daily lives of early modern Japanese is also reflected in visual materials of the period. The Chester Beatty Library in Dublin houses the hand scroll *Tohi zukan* (Scroll illustrating town and country), attributed to Sumiyoshi Gukei 住吉具慶 (1631–1705).[40] On the basis of the signature at the end of the scroll Sakakibara Satoru suggests a dating of the work to between 1691 and 1705.[41] This scroll takes us on a visual journey from the outskirts to the city of Kyoto. Three shops appear beyond the bamboo forest: from right to left they are vendors of umbrellas, house wares, and what appears to be rice (or salt?). The third shop has a wooden sign with a five-line inscription (fig. 1.1). Sadly, it is not an actual piece of writing, rather it simply mimics a written sign with indistinguishable curved lines. Nonetheless, it is a clear indication that the shop owner was conveying information through the written word with the intent of communicating with potential customers.

Figure 1.1 Detail from Sumiyoshi Gukei, *Tohi zukan*, ca. late seventeenth century. Salt or rice shop.

Courtesy of the Chester Beatty Library, Dublin

Figure 1.2 Detail from Sumiyoshi Gukei, *Tohi zukan*, ca. late seventeenth century. Man reading a document in a kitchen.

Courtesy of the Chester Beatty Library, Dublin

On the left and depicted as part of a mansion of a high-ranking family is a kitchen bustling with activity as men prepare food. A seated man (with a short sword) to the left faces the viewer and is engrossed in what appears to be a handwritten document such as a letter (fig. 1.2). The neighboring residence shows a genteel gathering of four men seated at tables with an opened book before each of them. This setting suggests a gathering to perhaps compose poetry or share readings (fig. 1.3). The attire of the men hints that at least three of them are court nobles. At the back of the same dwelling are the women of the household. They are surrounded by all sorts of delightful objects: a sumptuously decorated folding screen, toys on a veranda, and lacquered shelves with books. The woman with her back to the viewer reads a letter. The box on the floor was used to deliver the letter along with an inkstone and brush for the woman to write her reply (fig. 1.4). Beyond the outside wall and to the left are the busy urban streets. Immediately opposite the wall are two shops. One, probably selling ear picks, shows a Buddhist monk writing something down (fig. 1.5). In what appears to be a samurai residence on the left and behind the shops, a samurai writes a note that is perhaps meant to accompany the package being prepared by his servants (fig. 1.6). There is a money-exchange shop further along, where a clerk is busy with his abacus; the open ledger before him hints that he is in charge of

Figure 1.3 Detail from Sumiyoshi Gukei, *Tohi zukan*, ca. late seventeenth century. Possibly a poetry gathering or meeting to share readings.

Courtesy of the Chester Beatty Library, Dublin

Figure 1.4 Detail from Sumiyoshi Gukei, *Tohi zukan*, ca. late seventeenth century. Woman writing a letter.

Courtesy of the Chester Beatty Library, Dublin

Figure 1.5 Detail from Sumiyoshi Gukei, *Tohi zukan*, ca. late seventeenth century. Monk writing.

Courtesy of the Chester Beatty Library, Dublin

recording monetary transactions (fig. 1.7). Around the town are a variety of store signboards and *noren* curtains inscribed with characters. Altogether, this scroll can be read as a charming visual narrative of how the written word had become an integral part of the physical and cultural space of seventeenth-century Kyoto. Although we today must be careful in interpreting such a scene as an entirely realistic depiction of an actual urban space, there is enough to evince that writing was beginning to dwell the daily lives of people in Kyoto.

The spread of the written word in the landscape of everyday life is similarly echoed in printed works of the period, and *Kyō suzume* (The Kyoto

Figure 1.6 Detail from Sumiyoshi Gukei, *Tohi zukan*, ca. late seventeenth century. Samurai writing a note.

Courtesy of the Chester Beatty Library, Dublin

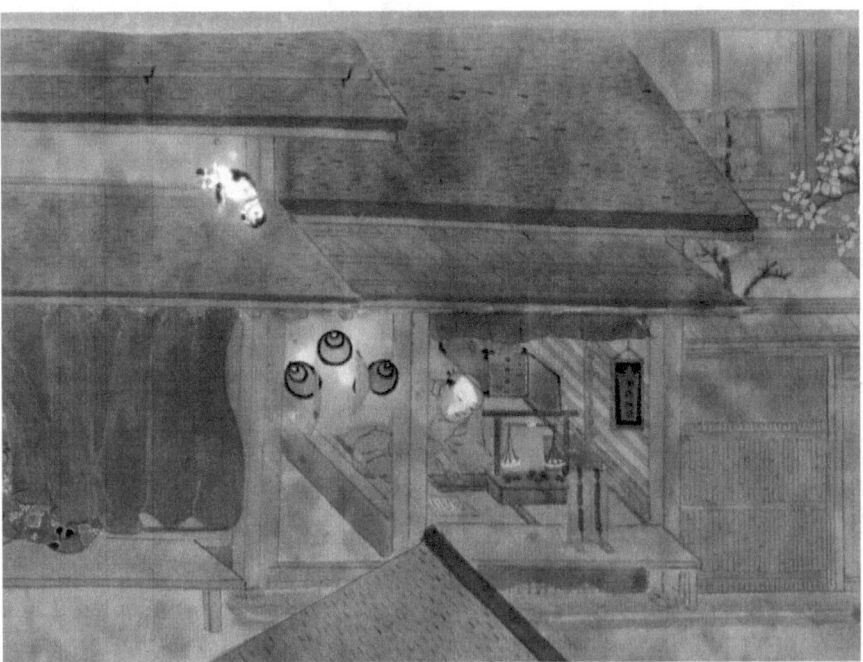

Figure 1.7 Detail from Sumiyoshi Gukei, *Tohi zukan*, ca. late seventeenth century. Shop clerk at work.

Courtesy of the Chester Beatty Library, Dublin

sparrow)—the first directory of Kyoto, issued in 1665 and ascribed to Asai Ryōi—is instructive.[42] The bulk of the text consists of an inventory of street names, followed by a list of shops and their trades. The illustrations center on the shops, and the written word is present though admittedly less so than in the Chester Beatty Library scroll. For example, the second volume includes a wholesale dealer on Gokōi-machi; ledgers are visible on the wall behind a merchant showing fabric to a young woman (fig. 1.8).[43] What is striking in the image of a timber merchant on Sakai-machi from the same volume (fig. 1.9) is the writing on many of the long wooden beams and planks.[44] Here the text comprises actual characters, listing either the measurement of the wood or indicating its superior quality. This kind of information would no doubt have been necessary in the sale of timber, thereby requiring the shop owner and his clerks to write and read, but also in the purchase of stock, thereby suggesting some form of client interaction mediated by the written word. The fifth volume depicts a place known as *fuda no tsuji* (literally, "street corner with notice boards") on Ichijō Avenue where government officials would affix their regulations, among other things, to wooden notice boards (fig. 1.10).[45] There is no evidence that all passers-by would have been able to read the notices on these boards. Nonetheless, the creation of a place devoted to the public display of diverse announcements indicates that some of the population would have been able to read them. And perhaps they read them aloud to those who lacked adequate literacy.[46]

The painted and printed materials of the seventeenth century confirm what I have noted for the three manuscripts examined earlier in this section: they attest to the dissemination of the written word among people of different statuses. When viewed together with the rhetoric promoting literacy as a new social must, these traces of literacy surfacing in both verbal and visual works suggest that basic literacy skills were acquired by an ever-growing number of people across society. Certainly, this change did not occur suddenly at the beginning of the seventeenth century, but it was a steady process that represented a prominent cultural feature of this century.

Numbers Talk

How helpful it would be to have statistics on literacy rates in seventeenth-century Japan. We know all too well how numerical data have the power to sway an argument in one direction or another. Numbers talk, and they talk convincingly. The desire for precise numbers, however, is challenged when we work on the seventeenth century and are faced with the dearth of reliable, consistent, and straightforward figures. Although I am acutely mindful that what I can offer here is at best a guesstimate, and that, as such, it might frustrate some readers, I trust that there is merit in letting the numbers we do have talk.

Figure 1.8 Asai Ryōi, *Kyō suzume*, 1665, vol. 2, 10r. Lower half, ledgers in a haberdashery.
Courtesy of the National Diet Library, Tokyo

Figure 1.9 Asai Ryōi, *Kyō suzume*, 1665, vol. 2, 12r. Timber merchant and the presence of writing.

Courtesy of the National Diet Library, Tokyo

Figure 1.10 Asai Ryōi, *Kyō suzume*, 1665, vol. 5, 9r. Upper half, *fuda no tsuji* on Ichijō Avenue.

Courtesy of the National Diet Library, Tokyo

The first set of numbers that needs consideration is the size of Japan's urban population in the seventeenth century.[47] There is some consensus for the figure of around twelve million for the population of Japan around 1600, with an increase to seventeen million by 1650 and twenty-eight million by 1700.[48] Rodrigo de Vivero y Velasco (ca. 1564–1636), a Spanish noble who served as interim governor of the Philippines from 1608 to 1609, was wrecked on the coast of Japan in 1609 and records that the population in Edo was 150,000.[49] Nakabe Yoshiko mentions the following numbers: 410,089 (1634), 362,322 (1661) in Kyoto; 148,719 (1634), 285, 814 (1657), 353,588 (1693) in Edo; and 279,610 (1625), 268,760 (1665), 287,891 (1679), 345,524 (1692) in Osaka.[50] Saitō Seiji estimates that in 1650 Edo had 430,000 inhabitants, Kyoto 430,000, and Osaka 220,000—that is, 1,080,000 people living in the main urban centers, with numbers changing by 1750: 1,220,000 (Edo), 370,000 (Kyoto), and 410,000 (Osaka).[51] Compare this with the end of the seventeenth century, when, according to Richard Rubinger, "Edo stood at close to one million, Osaka had 365,000, and the population of Kyoto was over 300,000."[52] The lack of accord in the figures presented by different authors may seem puzzling, but one point is certain: urban centers were clearly burgeoning.

The next set of numbers relate to how many printed books were circulating in seventeenth-century Japan. Comparing these against the size of the population can be revealing. If the quantity of commercially printed books versus the population numbers is significant enough, in fact, this would provide an indication that a fair-size readership must have existed to purchase books; otherwise, there would have been no need to publish them in any noticeable quantity. We should ever keep in mind that publishing was, above all, a commercial enterprise and as such was driven by financial gain.

Preliminary figures can be drawn from a study of book-trade catalogues (*shojaku mokuroku*), which were issued by commercial publishers as early as 1666–1667 and recorded titles that were printed by Kyoto and Edo publishers.[53] They differ from early modern European term catalogues in that they were not published at regular times during the course of a year and in that they did not limit themselves to listing only newly published titles. Rather, they recorded the stock of books in circulation at a given moment (i.e., the year of publication of the catalogue). Caution is needed when using *shojaku mokuroku*, and here we should remember that they were by no means comprehensive. As I discuss in chapter 2, the cheapest publications that began to emerge in the 1670s and certain titles published in Edo were not recorded in these catalogues (or anywhere else for that matter). For the purpose of my analysis, this implies that the numbers I discuss here are comparatively lower than the titles actually available on the market. Table 1.1 details the total number of books listed in the book-trade catalogues issued in the seventeenth-century.[54]

What about the number of copies that circulated for each title? This is where the figures become rather controversial. There seems to be little agreement about

TABLE 1.1 Number of titles in seventeenth-century book-trade catalogues

Kyoto book-trade catalogues		Edo book-trade catalogues	
Publication date	No. of titles	Publication date	No. of titles
1666–1667	2,713	—	—
1670	3,862	—	—
1671 (1672)	3,866	—	—
1673	3,998	—	—
1674	3,953	—	—
1675	4,049	1675	5,489
—	—	1681	4,925
1685	5,671	—	—
1692 (1698)	6,707	—	—
—	—	1696	6,408
1699	6,095	—	—
	—	—	—

Figures for the Kyoto book-trade catalogues are based on Laura Moretti, "The Japanese Early-Modern Publishing Market Unveiled: A Survey of Edo-Period Booksellers' Catalogues," *East Asian Publishing and Society* 2, no. 2 (2012): 199–308.

print runs. Nakano Mitsutoshi mentions that the first print run of early modern woodblock-printed books—those of interest in this study—would normally be in the range of the hundreds but refrains from giving more precise figures.[55] Nagatomo Chiyoji offers the much higher number of a thousand copies or more per print run.[56] For him this number is reasonable when compared with that of movable-type books, which were normally issued in figures close to one hundred or two hundred per print run. Hashiguchi Kōnosuke proposes a more nuanced understanding.[57] He explains that in order to make any profit at all a commercial publisher would have had to aim for at least three hundred copies to be sold and explains how publishers would set the price of books accordingly.

He adds that selling a thousand copies was celebrated as a particularly auspicious event known as *senbu furumai*, or "the feast of the one thousand copies." Hashiguchi's remarks also draw attention to the danger of thinking in terms of print runs only. After all, one of the many advantages of the woodblock-printing technology was that a publisher could store the blocks and print them upon demand at any point in time. That is why it is more productive to think in terms of copies being sold rather than print runs. Amid the uncertainty of the data we have at our disposal, it seems to me that thinking in the range of five hundred copies sold per title would allow us to account for both books that merely made the threshold of three hundred copies and those that hit the felicitous result of a thousand. What happens to the numbers of titles presented in table 1.1 when we take into consideration the number of copies? In 1666–1667, for example, the final number would be 1,356,500 copies of books in circulation. This is a small number when compared with the total Japanese population of approximately seventeen million in 1650. But if we consider that at this early stage books would not have traveled very far outside the main urban centers (there is no evidence to suggest otherwise), the same number is not negligible. When seen against the urban population in 1650 of just over a million in Kyoto, Edo, and Osaka, there was almost one book per head.[58] This becomes even more noteworthy if we remember that at this period books were circulating primarily in Kyoto—that is, a city with a population of about three hundred thousand (and I am using a total number that reflects the demographic trends quoted earlier in this section in a cautious manner). This suggests that there must have been a considerable amount of potential readers to justify the creation of a book industry of the size described here. As telling as these figures might be, they nonetheless prompt a question that is particularly relevant to this study: how do these numbers account for popular literature? They, in fact, encompass all sorts of books: those written in literary Chinese and those in the vernacular. In other words, they comprise books that appealed to both types of readers postulated by Yokota Fuyuhiko. Can we know the numbers of books in the vernacular issued in the seventeenth century?

Providing a convincing answer to this question by sifting out books in the vernacular is less straightforward than we might wish. Kyoto book-trade catalogues were organized around book categories. Unfortunately, though, any distinction in category between books in literary Chinese and those in the vernacular was not readily apparent, as I discuss in some detail in chapter 2. The Edo book-trade catalogues seem, at first glance, to better assist in identifying books in the vernacular, as each alphabetic entry contains a section for books in kana (i.e., in the vernacular). Yet these kana sections feature also *waka* poetry and Heian-period *monogatari*, which might have posed challenges at the level of vocabulary and cultural literacy for readers familiar only with seventeenth-century vernacular Japanese.[59] Table 1.2 and figure 1.11 offer some numbers for books in the vernacular reflecting these complexities.

TABLE 1.2 Estimated number of seventeenth-century books in the vernacular

Catalogue date	Kyoto book-trade catalogues						Edo book-trade catalogues	
	Vernacular	Gunsho	Vernacular + gunsho	Poetry	Nonvernacular		Catalogue date	Kana
1666–1667	388	107	495	306	1,912		—	—
1670	626	132	758	374	2,730		—	—
1671 (1672)	636	126	762	378	2,726		—	—
1673	664	126	790	411	2,797		—	—
1674	670	129	799	415	2,739		—	—
1675	720	127	847	447	2,755		1675	1296
—	—	—	—	—	—		1681	1254
1685	884	166	1,050	717	3,904		—	—
1692 (1698)	1,286	135	1,421	904	4,382		—	—
—	—	—	—	—	—		1696	1419
1699	927	169	1,096	455	4,544		—	—

Figures for the Kyoto book-trade catalogues are based on Laura Moretti, "The Japanese Early-Modern Publishing Market Unveiled: A Survey of Edo-Period Booksellers' Catalogues," *East Asian Publishing and Society* 2, no. 2 (2012): 199–308. The figures for the Edo book-trade catalogues are approximate and for reference only; they include poetry and *monogatari* but exclude

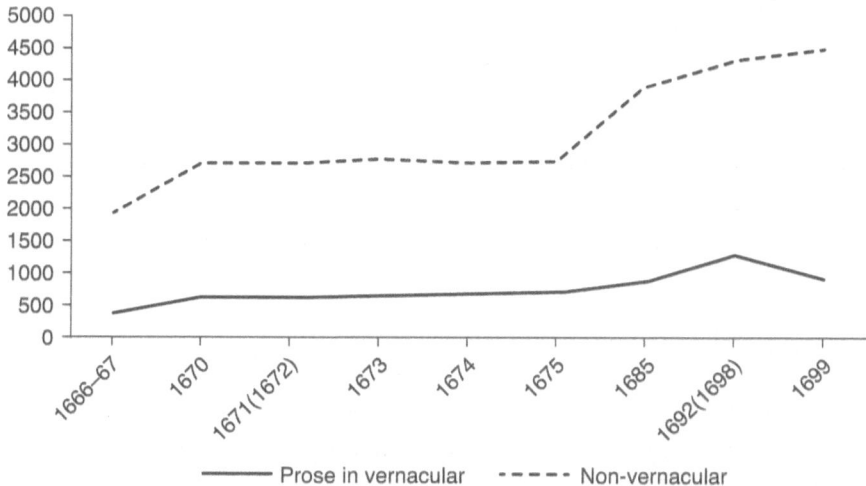

Figure 1.11 Prose in vernacular and nonvernacular in Kyoto book-trade catalogues. Based on table 1.2.

If we exclude poetry and even *gunsho* (military books and war tales) and consider vernacular prose alone, the results are nevertheless significant. For example, the 1666–1667 catalogue accounts for 388 titles of books in the vernacular, and if we multiply that by 500 copies, the total number of books in the vernacular circulating among a total urban population of around one million people is 194,000 copies. And if we then narrow this down to Kyoto, since as noted this was the primary center of printed book production and consumption at this time, it would mean that we are dealing with almost one book for fewer than two people. By the end of the seventeenth century, with the 1692 and 1698 catalogues, we are talking of more than a thousand titles in the vernacular, which can be converted in around half a million copies for the one million inhabitants in the three main cities.[60] It is also worth noting that the increase in vernacular prose did not effect a decrease in texts composed in literary Chinese, and this dovetails well with the idea of the existence of multiple literacies that I explore later in this chapter.

These numbers highlight a tension with Konda's and Nagatomo's positions summarized at the outset. If we suppose that only around 10 percent of the Kyoto population were readers, how could 30,000 (or even 40,000 if we choose higher estimates) readers justify the publication of 2,713 titles or 1,356,500 copies in 1666–1667? Each reader would have had to buy a very high number of copies to make this at all profitable for commercial publishers. Moreover, if only people with knowledge of literary Chinese—the majority of monks and to a certain extent samurai—were readers, why would publishers go to the trouble of producing and marketing 388 titles of vernacular prose (194,000 copies) in the same year? It is my contention that these numbers are a compelling piece of circumstantial evidence that the reading public—and within it readership of popular prose in the vernacular—must have been broader and more diversified than acknowledged to date. It is to be hoped that further research on the numbers we have will confirm, or maybe even correct, those presented here. Yet it is hard to avoid the preliminary conclusion that the received views on who engaged with reading in seventeenth-century Japan demand serious rethinking.

Between *Tenarai* and *Gakumon*

Any discussion around who could read naturally leads to the question of who could read what. Considerations of literacy in early modern Japan need to factor in a number of variables. The script was plural, with logographic characters (kanji) on the one hand and the two phonetic syllabaries on the other. It is also worth keeping in mind that each hiragana syllable could be represented by a number of graphic variants. The existence of noncursive, semicursive, and cursive calligraphic renderings of kanji and hiragana must also be acknowledged. And finally, there were a multitude of written languages that included literary Chinese and the vernacular but not exclusively. We are accustomed to think about literacy in the singular, but I suggest that it is far more productive to follow a better nuanced approach and embrace the idea of multiple literacies, as it allows us to give voice to all these variables.[61]

Before I discuss what I mean by multiple literacies in seventeenth-century Japan, it is important to grasp how literacy was conceptualized at this time. The early modern discourse on the ability to write and read postulates two components: *tenarai* and *gakumon*, the former referring to the basic skills of writing and reading and the second to something akin to advanced learning.

Kaibara Ekiken expounds *tenarai* in depth in his *Wazoku dōjikun*. At the age of six children were expected to learn how to write basic characters: those for numbers, those related to nature, family, Confucianism (e.g., the Five Relations, the Five Virtues), the four classes, the four directions, the five grains, the five senses, and the five colors.[62] He also mentions the existence of "characters required for daily life" that must be acquired at this stage, but no further details are given.[63] Ekiken carefully lists titles of teaching materials that should be used at this stage; they are mainly collections of kanji and their compounds.[64] At the same age, children should be taught hiragana.[65] Ekiken recommends teaching hiragana in the *a-i-u-e-o* order, yet there is evidence that the *i-ro-ha* order was widely applied at the time. Ekiken further specifies that pupils should practice writing and reading hiragana in both a vertical and horizontal orientation. For teaching materials, he suggests the use of hiragana texts included in the many textbooks circulating during the period in the form of copybooks (*tehon*).[66] It should be pointed out that these materials were normally written in a cursive script. Katakana is left for study at a later stage that remains unspecified.[67] Gender comes into play and accounts for further modulations. When outlining the curriculum for young girls, Ekiken mentions that they should begin at the age of seven with hiragana and only after that move on to kanji (referred to as *otoko moji*, "characters for males").[68] This order in learning is confirmed in *Onna chōhōki*, in which author Namura Jōhaku explains that girls should commence with writing the hiragana syllabary, then learn to construct sentences, and at a later stage study kanji.[69] Mastering the phonetic hiragana (in cursive) and being able to read and write a few basic kanji (probably in cursive) are the most basic form of literacy, what I refer to as basic literacy or kana-mainly literacy. The study of *tenarai* continued until the age of eight. This suggests that basic literacy was meant to be achieved within a couple of years.[70] Ekiken gives no indication of what status categories he was targeting when formulating the *tenarai* curriculum; however, in view of what I have discussed earlier, it is plausible that everyone was encouraged to master *tenarai* according to the steps outlined in the preceding.

How did children learn *tenarai*? There were at least three possible ways. One was to be taught at home, either by parents (a possibility suggested by the quoted passage from *Onna shikimoku*) or by a personal teacher (more likely in wealthier households). The existence of private tutors is confirmed in different sources. For example, Enomoto Yazaemon alludes to the existence of a teacher (*shishō*) in his diary.[71] Kawachiya Yoshimasa advises that a knowledge of Noh and haikai might create teaching opportunities if an individual encountered straitened circumstances.[72] And Shibata Jun explains that as early as 1648 a city ordinance (*machibure*) issued in Osaka mentioned "people who were taking pupils and taught *tenarai*" as the target of an investigation.[73] This suggests that teaching positions were taken by a number of people in seventeenth-century Japan, and this leads to the second way of learning basic literacy—in schools called *terakoya*.

Terakoya, also referred to as *tenaraisho* ("places to learn *tenarai*" or "writing schools") were established well before the seventeenth century and offered tuition in basic as well as vocational literacy. There is evidence to suggest that in the early modern period they catered primarily for the education of merchants.[74] A comparatively early pictorialization of a *terakoya* in Kyoto appears in Sumiyoshi Gukei's scroll *Tohi zukan* (or *Tohi emaki*) housed in Nara, which depicts a two-story building with a bookshop on the ground floor and a room on the second where pupils practice their writing (fig. 1.12).[75] The children, all males in this instance, are seated at low tables and are writing or looking at copybooks. Statistics on *terakoya* schools in the seventeenth century are unfortunately scant. But it is known that thirty-eight such institutions were in

Figure 1.12 Detail from Sumiyoshi Gukei, *Tohi zukan*, ca. late seventeenth century. Bookshop and *terakoya* school.

Courtesy of Konbuin, Nara. Licensed image provided by Nara National Museum, Nara

operation in the whole country between 1624 and 1680, and thirty-nine between 1681 and 1716.[76] These numbers are admittedly low compared with the 101 documented *terakoya* between 1781 and 1788 and the 4,293 between 1854 and 1868.[77] However, it does indicate that *terakoya* were becoming increasingly common in the seventeenth century and that they were vital in spreading literacy within a broad section of society.

The third option for studying *tenarai* was from printed books. The previously mentioned Sasayama Baian was involved in the publication of manuals that would assist with the study of *tenarai*, such as *Tenarai shiyō shū* (A collection to be used for learning to write; 1693).[78] Baian explains in the preface that he collected information about the "Way of the brush" from the teachings of his master, from what he heard from others, and from what he had written himself. He also explains that this work was printed for the benefit of children who had yet to begin their education. These days, he notes, even the children of humble and poor families (*shizu yamagatsu*) learn to write. When viewed in its entirety *Tenarai shiyō shū* is marketed as a substitute teacher for those who wished to learn basic literacy but did not have the means to employ a teacher. The price (3 *monme* in 1696) was affordable if we keep in mind that *Kōshoku ichidai otoko* was 5 *monme* in the same year. *Tenarai shiyō shū* starts with an illustration showing how to hold a brush and gives precise instructions about how to write characters. Baian offers very concrete teachings such as which lines to practice before writing kana and kanji, the types of calligraphic styles, as well as more philosophical remarks about the necessary mind-set needed in learning how to write.

Once a child had mastered basic literacy in the form of *tenarai*, he or she—most likely males—could aspire to something more advanced. The ultimate goal was *gakumon*. Translated as "learning," "study," or "scholarship," *gakumon* referred to the study of books written in literary Chinese and designed in such a way as to teach correct behavior—in other words, ethical knowledge. The writings of Kawachiya Yoshimasa and Kōnoike Shinroku, introduced earlier, provide some understanding of the notion of *gakumon*. In his family precepts Kōnoike Shinroku stipulates, "Whenever a person has spare time and energy away from their duties, they should apply themselves to learning [*gakumon*]. Learning serves to foster good behavior and creates harmony in the household. Yet duties should not be neglected in favor of learning."[79] Yoshimasa's writings repeatedly convey a similar message:

> A person with learning is like a tree with branches and leaves. Learning is not restricted to reading books. It refers to the acquisition of knowledge that is required for each individual's Way.... There are merchants and peasants who pay no attention to learning. As a result, they do not know the teachings of the ancient sages. A preference for ignorance causes a person to have many desires and to raise children thinking that there is nothing better. How can these people prosper for long? Is this not a sad thing?[80]

Yoshimasa further explains that his father was a model student of *gakumon*:

> While this might hardly be referred to as *gakumon*, [my father] Seiemon always read vernacular books [*kanagaki no shomotsu*] that explained the difference between good and bad as well as tales [*sōshi monogatari*] that discussed the principle of success and defeat in this world. This is why he developed a firm grasp of the principle of causality and understood the principle of the inevitable rise and fall of human beings. This, in turn, enabled him to observe frugality, to be prepared for any eventuality, to live quietly by putting others first, and to keep calm in all sorts of situations as he awaited the outcome of faith. By following the teachings of men of the past in this way, he enjoyed a tranquil life.... Unfilial are those who violate the spirits of the ancestors by saying that learning does not suit the people and the peasants and that it is a useless activity that only wastes time. They will be subject to divine punishment and their house will quickly fall into ruin.[81]

Ekiken also advocates *gakumon* as the next step in learning. He explains that at the age of eight, children—probably referring to boys—should advance further to the study of Chinese. But this does not simply mean writing and reading kanji. It encompasses the acquisition of skills in order to read and write literary Chinese:

> Eight years old is when children enter small learning [shōgaku]. . . . From the spring of this age it is appropriate to have children write kanji in both noncursive [shin] and cursive [sō]. It is advisable to have them use good copybooks written in a correct style. If they learn from bad examples, they will acquire bad habits and will not improve even if they shift later to good examples. At the outset, both noncursive and cursive characters should be written in large size. Writing small characters in the beginning will make the hand rigid and unable to move appropriately. Early on at this age it is also opportune to have them read. Books such as Kōkyō [The Classic of Filial Piety], Shōgaku [The Small Learning], and Shisho [The Four Books], with long and difficult sentences, are hard to read and memorize for beginners. They can cause the pupil to become bored and dislike learning. That is not good. Therefore, at the start pupils should be made to read texts with short sentences, which are easy to read and memorize; they should learn these by heart. . . . At the age of ten they should start studying under the guidance of a master [shishō]. At first, they must pay attention to the principle of the Five Virtues and the way of the Five Relations. They must read the books of the sages and engage with learning [gakumon]. . . . At this stage they should finally read Shōgaku, Shisho, and Gosho [The Five Classics]. . . . By the age of twenty they should have developed an understanding of these texts.[82]

These passages hint at a few salient features of early modern *gakumon*. First, the ultimate goal of *gakumon* was not to read difficult texts but to grasp the correct way of things and to master ethical conduct.[83] Suzuki Toshiyuki explains that *gakumon* was the best path to becoming a well-rounded human being and that it was the way to achieve the behavior required for one's social position.[84] This also implied a diversity in the types of *gakumon* catering to the needs of different status categories and professional activities. Nagashima Hiroaki, for example, distinguishes between "big learning" (*dai-gakumon*) and "small learning" (*shō-gakumon*).[85] The former refers to scholars' erudite activities related to textual typologies that included, most notably, the Confucian canon in Chinese, Chinese poetry, and Japanese classics of the Heian period (794–1185). "Small learning" is restricted to the studies necessary for the daily life of commoners.[86] This distinction takes us to the second feature of *gakumon*. In its purest form it required a much higher degree of literacy—namely, a knowledge of literary Chinese. This explains why Yoshimasa recounts that his father was not involved in what might be perceived as true *gakumon*. After all, he was reading books in the vernacular.

When viewed together, *tenarai* and *gakumon* can be positioned at opposite ends in the process of engaging with the written word. When learning *tenarai* individuals were required to master the phonetic syllabary and a few kanji, usually in cursive, so that they could write and read vernacular texts. As convincingly explained by Maryanne Wolf, a writing system that requires a limited number of signs increases cognitive efficiency.[87] Wolf explains that a "reduced number of symbols reduces the time and attention needed for rapid recognition; and thus fewer perceptual and memory resources are needed."[88] This gives time and space to be allocated to other mental processes. Needless to say, a syllabary like hiragana is different from an alphabet, but Wolf notes that when reading kana, Japanese readers use brain pathways similar to those utilized by alphabet readers (the posterior of the left hemisphere, with less bihemisphere activation) and that "the same words written in kana...are read faster than kanji."[89] *Gakumon* was more demanding. With *gakumon* readers were asked to master a plurality of scripts (phonographic and logographic), with thousands of signs, and in different calligraphic styles. Wolf notes that cognitive efficiency is equally achieved in reading logographs but also acknowledges that it involves "recruiting many areas for specialized, automatic processing across both hemispheres."[90] Moreover, learners of *gakumon* were also required to gain fluency in a different language: literary Chinese, or what Peter F. Kornicki has recently labeled as "Sinitic."[91] When viewed in this way, *tenarai* and *gakumon* coincide with what I see as opposite ends on the spectrum of literacies. On the one hand, there is vernacular Japanese (*wabun*) almost solely in hiragana, what I call *wabun* literacy. It corresponds to what I also name kana-mainly literacy. One the other, there is literary Chinese or Sinitic (*kanbun*), what I refer to as *kanbun* literacy. *Wabun* literacy can be seen as the lowest, most basic level of literacy. Its only demand was a knowledge of the contemporary mother tongue and a limited number of logographic characters in addition to the phonetic hiragana. Moreover, it could be mastered in two years of schooling. *Kanbun* literacy was the pinnacle of highbrow literacy. It necessitated a command of a substantial number of logographic signs, proficiency in a different grammar (Sinitic), and an ability to "translate" literary Chinese mentally or orally into Japanese.[92] As Ekiken informs us, several years were required to achieve an acceptable level, from when starting *gakumon* in earnest at ten years of age up to twenty.

Multiple Literacies

Traditionally *wabun* literacy (associated with *tenarai*) and *kanbun* literacy (linked to *gakumon*) are viewed as dichotomous, and so is their readership. As such, we might be tempted to postulate a straightforward, almost monolithic image of the popular reader: someone who has mastered basic literacy—because his or her social status does not allow for more than that—and is able to read vernacular but is barred from Sinitic texts. And yet closer engagement with the texts issued by the seventeenth-century commercial publishing industry complicates this view. Strategies were put in place to bridge these two opposite poles, creating in the process a spectrum rich in modulation.

Kanbun or Sinitic was indeed a foreign written language, but a variety of strategies could be effected to make it more accessible. These strategies come under the umbrella term of *kanbun kundoku*, or "reading Sinitic in the vernacular." I submit that such variety can be most effectively illustrated by inspecting a number of early modern editions of the primer *Jitsugokyō* (Teachings of the words of truth). I am mindful that what I present here are not seventeenth-century examples. Nonetheless, as the next chapters reveal, it should be understood that the textual strategies showcased by *Jitsugokyō* were already widely employed in the 1600s. Written in literary Chinese, *Jitsugokyō* is attributed to the Japanese Shingon-sect monk Kūkai 空海 (774–835) and became a best-selling title in the Edo period, assisted no doubt by the fact that it featured extensively in the curriculum of *terakoya*. Koizumi Yoshinaga mentions that *Jitsugokyō* was at the top of the top-ten teaching materials used in *terakoya* schools for the practice of *sodoku*, whereby pupils read the Sinitic aloud as vernacular and memorized the texts.[93] The pedagogical rationale behind *Jitsugokyō* is quite sound: short sentences in Sinitic that enabled pupils to learn kanji while memorizing teachings intended to shape a person's behavior. It translated exactly what Ekiken suggested was appropriate for an eight-year-old child in learning *gakumon*.

The first strategy that facilitated a vernacular reading of the Sinitic text was the insertion of reading marks (*kunten*) in the Chinese text, as evidenced in the 1792 edition of *Jitsugokyō* (fig. 1.13).[94] These marks allowed the reader to reorder words from the subject-verb-object sequence of the Sinitic to the subject-object-verb order of the Japanese. The reader would need to understand how *kunten* marks functioned, how the characters were read in Japanese, and how to conjugate parts of speech such as adjectives and verbs correctly. For example, the fourth character 不 in the first line (after the title) is followed by the fifth character 貴 (valuable). The reader would have to know that (1) the character 貴 is the adjective *tattoshi* in Japanese; (2) the character 不 is used in Chinese before another character to indicate a negative; (3) in Japanese the negative is the supplementary verb *zu*; (4) unlike Chinese syntax, in which the negative precedes a verb or an adjective, *zu* follows the adjective; (5) the adjective requires conjugation; and (6) *tattoshi* is read *tattokara*, conjugated in order to be followed by *zu*. The level of *kanbun* literacy required is therefore extremely high and the result is what Kornicki calls "bound translation."[95]

A later edition of *Jitsugokyō* (ca. 1843–1847 [fig. 1.14]) shows that there was ground for further negotiation and that commercial publishers fully exploited this.[96] Here the accessibility of the text is slightly enhanced by the insertion of *okurigana*, or suffixes in katakana following the kanji stems. These provide clues to the Japanese reading of the character and the conjugation of the word. For

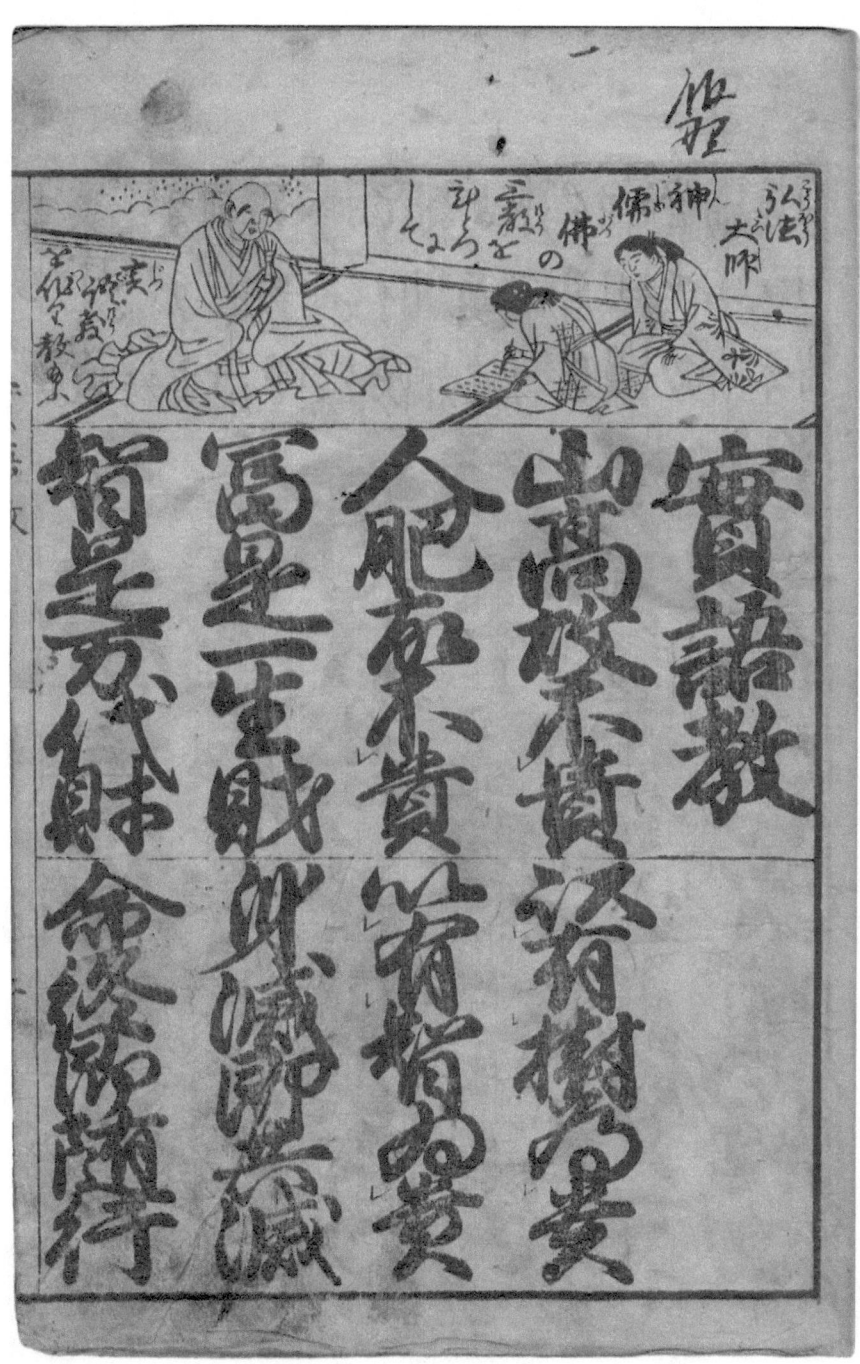

Figure 1.13 *Jitsugokyō*, 1792, 2r. Sinitic text with *kunten* marks only.
Author collection, Suzuran Bunko, Cambridge, U.K.

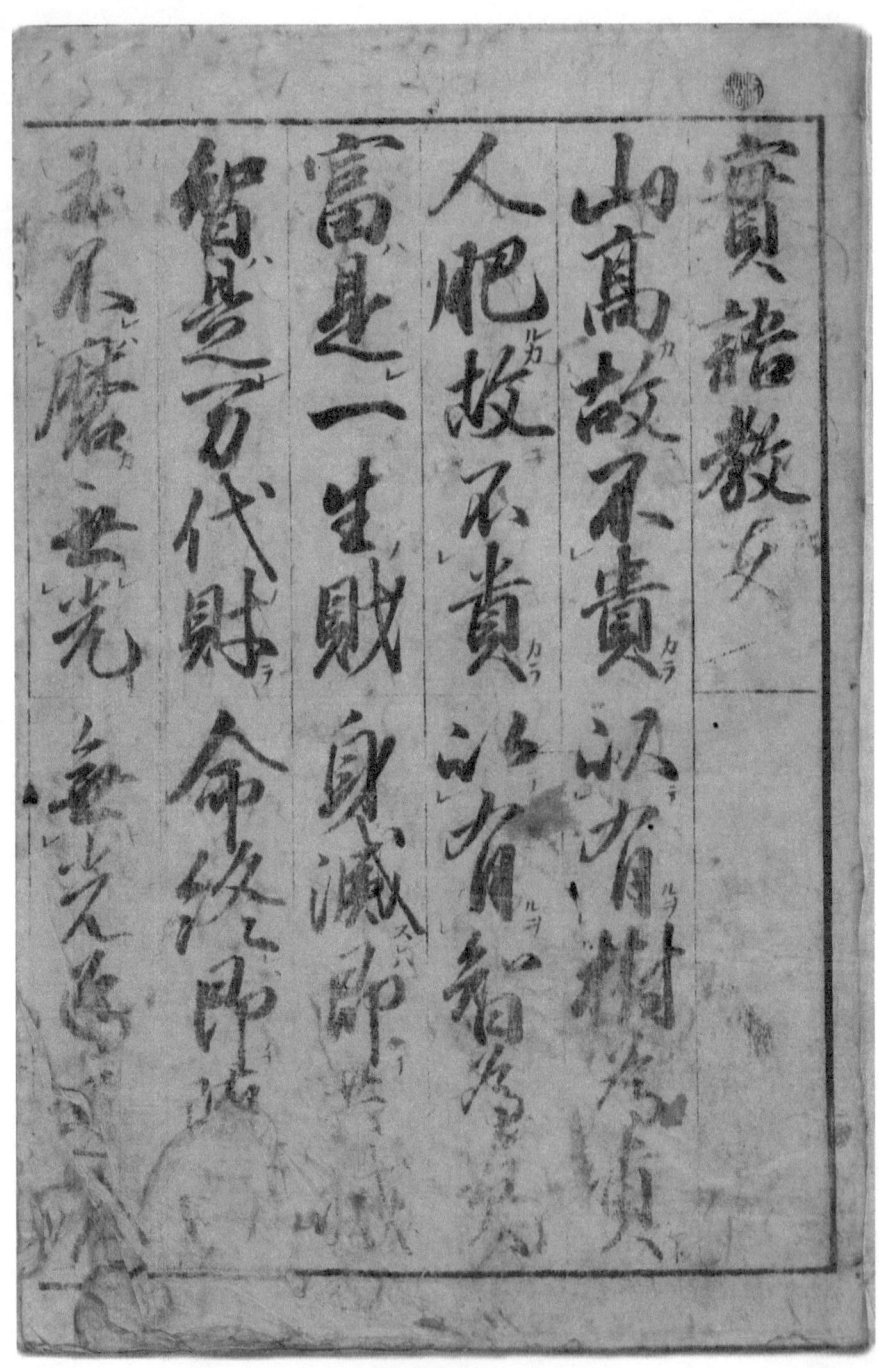

Figure 1.14 *Jitsugokyō*, ca. 1843–1847, 1r. Sinitic text with *kunten* marks and *okurigana*. Author collection, Suzuran Bunko, Cambridge, U.K.

example 貴 is followed by *kara* in katakana, indicating its reading as *tattokara*. The reader still has to make sense of the 不 that comes before with no further aid. The much later, 1863, edition (fig. 1.15) takes readability one step further, placing what approximates a Japanese interlinear translation to the right of the text in kana only (reading glosses, or *furigana*).⁹⁷ This can only *approximate* an interlinear translation because the order of Chinese grammar is retained. For instance, the kanji 貴 is glossed with the phonetic reading of *tattokara*. This phonetic reading presents the form of the adjective conjugated and ready for the addition of the supplementary verb *zu*. However, the phonetic reading *zu* is glossed next to the kanji for the negative 不, and they both precede 貴 *tattokara*. A knowledge of the Chinese characters is not essential since the reading in phonetic script (and in Japanese) appears in a parallel text. As Maryanne Wolf notes, background knowledge of vocabulary contributes to the speed and ease of decoding.⁹⁸ As a speaker of Japanese, I would know both words—*zu* and *tattokara*—and rearranging them in the right order would not be terribly demanding. Nonetheless, some engagement with the original Chinese and the *kunten* marks to sequence the words is still required. The 1812 edition (fig. 1.16) advances this "reader-friendly" approach.⁹⁹ To the right of the characters is the full translation in Japanese and in hiragana, which means that working with the Chinese text is no longer compulsory. In this case, even though the kanji are presented as 不貴, the Japanese on the right reads *tattokarazu*, with *zu* placed after the conjugated adjective. The reader need only read the Japanese translation provided on the right of the Sinitic text—in other words, anyone with *wabun* literacy could enjoy the contents of this text written in literary Chinese. Thus, readers might not achieve the goal of learning how to read Sinitic but were in a position to understand the teaching that was being conveyed. This, after all, was the true meaning of *gakumon*.

The aim here is not to examine when, why, or how these varied textual strategies were applied to the original *kanbun* or to decide whether these strategies constitute a form of translation. Rather, my intent is to show that the texts in figures 1.13 and 1.14 demanded a higher level of literacy than those in figures 1.15 and 1.16. The former required a knowledge of literary Chinese and an engagement with the Chinese characters, while the latter enabled readers conversant only with hiragana to comprehend the meaning of the text and learn its educational precepts. Of course, the presence of the vernacular, hiragana could also ease the study of the Sinitic for those readers who were eager to acquire some *kanbun* literacy. In other words, the first addresses the reader fully possessive of *kanbun* literacy, whereas the second extends to readers endowed with kana-mainly literacy. Both, however, bear witness to the possibility of accessing the same text using different literacies. As evinced in figure 1.17, even though we are in the realm of *kanbun* literacy, the modulations described here constitute a spectrum that seemingly moves toward *wabun* literacy.

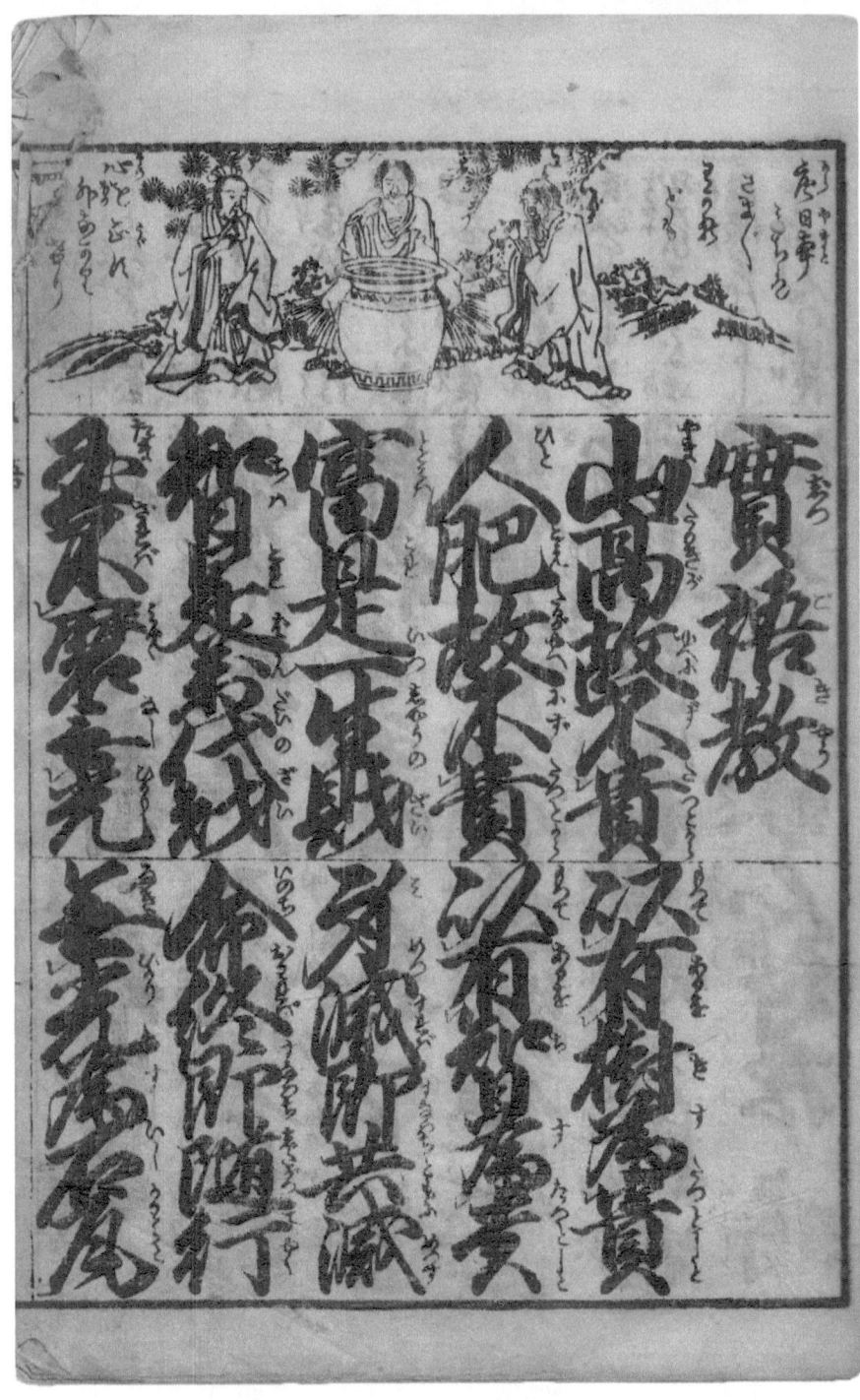

Figure 1.15 *Jitsugokyō*, 1863, 1r. Sinitic text with phonetic readings of single characters. Author collection, Suzuran Bunko, Cambridge, U.K.

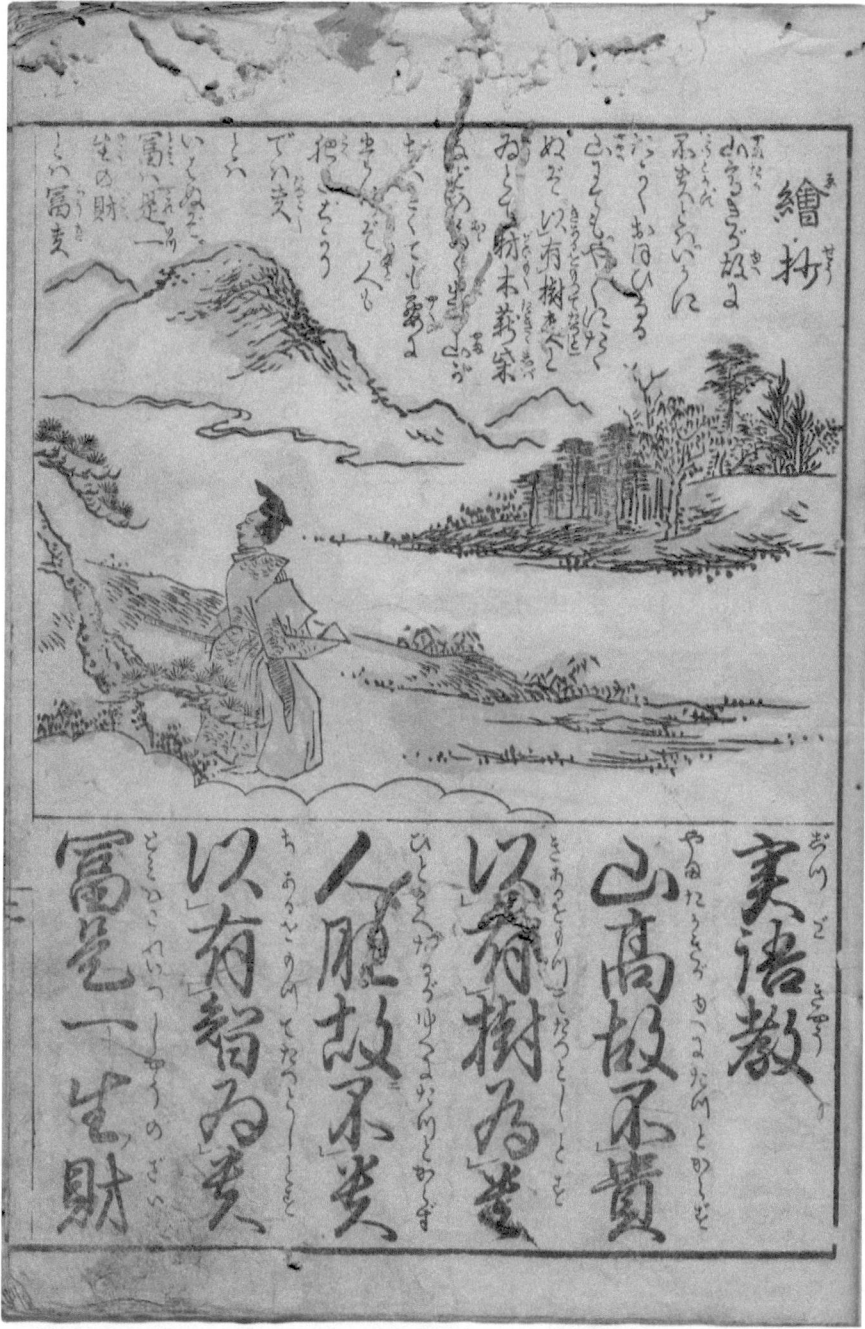

Figure 1.16 Kyokutei Bakin (author) and Okada Gyokuzan (illustrator), *Jitsugokyō eshō*, 1812, 2r. Sinitic text with interlinear vernacular translation in hiragana.

Author collection, Suzuran Bunko, Cambridge, U.K.

Kanbun literacy (Sinitic; logographic writing; cursive, semi-cursive, and non-cursive)					Wabun literacy (vernacular Japanese; logosyllabary writing; normally cursive or semi-cursive)				
No kunten No furigana	Kunten No furigana	Kunten No furigana With okurigana	Kunten Furigana (not in Japanese syntactic order)	Kunten Furigana (in Japanese syntactic order, interlinear translation)	Kanji-katakana no furigana	Kanji-katakana with furigana on characters	Kanji-hiragana no furigana on characters	Kanji-hiragana with furigana on characters	Hiragana mainly/only (with graphic variants for each syllable)

Sōrōbun and mairase-sōrōbun (hybrid kanbun; formulaic language)				
No kunten No furigana	Kunten No furigana Normally only for printed manuals	Kunten Furigana (not in Japanese syntactic order) Normally only for printed manuals	Kunten Furigana (in Japanese syntactic order, interlinear translation) Normally only for printed manuals	Kanji-hiragana no furigana on characters Normally only for printed manuals	Kanji-hiragana with furigana on characters Normally only for printed manuals	Hiragana mainly/only (with graphic variants for each syllable)

Higher degree of literacy ←————————————→ Lower degree of literacy

Figure 1.17 The spectrum of multiple literacies in early modern Japan.

Vernacular Japanese (*wabun*) displayed equal variety. The simplest type of *wabun* literacy was made up of texts written almost entirely in hiragana. The fewer the logographic characters, the easier the decoding. The insertion of *furigana* glosses alongside kanji would ensure that even readers who knew only a limited number of kanji could access a text; it was simply a matter of reading the phonetic gloss to grasp a word's meaning. Woefully little paleographic research has been done to date to understand how the modulation between hiragana and kanji was achieved in seventeenth-century texts in the vernacular, and this task is certainly beyond the ambit of my work. Having dealt over the years with a considerable number of primary sources from this century, I have preliminarily identified the 1660s (the beginning of the Kanbun era) as a possible turning point. I would argue that it is around this period that we witness a trend of moving away from texts written mainly in hiragana to texts with a higher number of kanji but normally accompanied by *furigana* glosses. It is to be hoped that continuing research will confirm or correct this estimate. For the time being I note that the greater the number of kanji without *furigana*, the harder for readers with kana-mainly literacy to comfortably decode any given text. Texts written in Heian-period Japanese might well be visually decodable to a reader with basic literacy—after all they were written mainly in hiragana—but, as mentioned, the linguistic and cultural competencies required to make sense of the text might have stood as an obstacle to such readers.

The next stage in vernacular prose includes texts written in a combination of kanji and katakana. As noted previously, katakana normally featured at later stages in the curriculum and therefore may have been unfamiliar to readers trained solely or primarily in *tenarai*. This writing style, moreover, was generally used in conjunction with what Kornicki describes as a specific practice of translating Sinitic texts whereby a bound translation, usually carried out silently or orally, was "transcribed and converted into written texts . . . usually for the benefit of those unable to read the Sinitic text accurately enough to grasp the meaning."[100] This style was also used when recording lecture notes or commentaries on Chinese classics or medical texts.[101] The result was that these texts did not necessarily sound like ordinary vernacular, rather as a sort of *kanbun tai*, or "translationese" from *kanbun*. Figure 1.17 illustrates that this was still within the realm of *wabun* literacy but moving increasingly toward *kanbun* literacy.

The picture is further complicated by the existence of a form of hybrid *kanbun* known as *sōrōbun*. *Sōrōbun* can be described as an artificial language that developed in the late eleventh century and came to full fruition in the Edo period.[102] On the surface it resembles literary Chinese because of its exclusive use of kanji. But grammatically it functions as a hybrid language positioned between Chinese and Japanese, with the supplementary verb *sōrō* 候 systematically applied to the end of each sentence.[103] It was customarily used in the Edo period for official records and letters, therefore with the functional literacy that Rubinger has identified in the case of village elders. Publishers also adopted this style in their marketing texts and paratexts used to address potential customers and readers.

Handwritten documents and letters in *sōrōbun* would, as a rule, be recorded entirely in cursive kanji, without any additional aid. This means that there was no inclusion of *kunten* marks or phonetic glosses. This was also true for the marketing materials issued by publishers, and it demonstrates that specific knowledge of how this other type of written language functioned was necessary if not expected. Nevertheless, when it came to printed manuals designed to teach letter writing or how to process administrative paperwork, *sōrōbun* was softened and negotiated for the reader who had yet to master this written language. The passage in figure 1.18 from *Shogaku bunshō narabi ni yorozu shitsukekata* (1647 edition), which I discuss in more detail in chapters 4 and 5, showcases how this was possible.[104] The passage that starts from the fourth line reads in translation, "It has been quite a while since we met and I miss you." If read aloud in Japanese the logographic characters 良久不懸御目御床敷存候 would be *yaya* 良 *hisashiku* 久しく *on* 御 *me* 目 *ni* に *kakarazu* 懸らず *on* 御 *yukashiku* 床しく *zonji* 存じ *sōrō* 候. The reader could process the passage 不懸御目, written according to the Chinese word order of negative + verb + object, because of the insertion of *kunten* marks to the left of the characters. These permit a reorganization of the order based on the rules of Japanese grammar (object + verb + negative), and the *furigana* offers clarification on the reading of single characters, a technique already mentioned for the 1863 *Jitsugokyō*. While learning how to read this form of hybrid Sinitic, readers were also introduced to the formulaic vocabulary required in this type of written correspondence. The ultimate goal in perusing this manual was for a reader to become independent in decoding and encoding *sōrōbun* in handwritten documents.

Sōrōbun offers an additional layer of complexity in that it also displayed a variation that I call *mairase-sōrōbun* and explore in some detail in chapter 5. On the page, be it handwritten or printed, *mairase-sōrōbun* appears to lean considerably toward *wabun* literacy because of the high percentage of phonetic script (see example, fig. 5.3). Yet it shares a few linguistic features with *sōrōbun*, including the use of *sōrō* (preceded by the additional supplementary verb *mairasu*), the formulaic nature of the vocabulary, and some syntactical elements. Although *mairase-sōrōbun* is customarily associated with women and the woman's hand (or brush), we must be aware that any easy distinction in terms of gender is fraught with danger. If a man intended to communicate in writing to a woman, in fact, he would normally apply the *mairase-sōrōbun* style and its conventions. Research is needed to fully understand what this linguistic variation of the *sōrōbun* style indexed beyond gender as well as to gauge the pragmatics and aesthetics it entailed.

What are we left with? Early modern Japanese men and women who engaged with writing or reading were positioned at different points on the complex spectrum of written languages described here and visualized in figure 1.17, depending

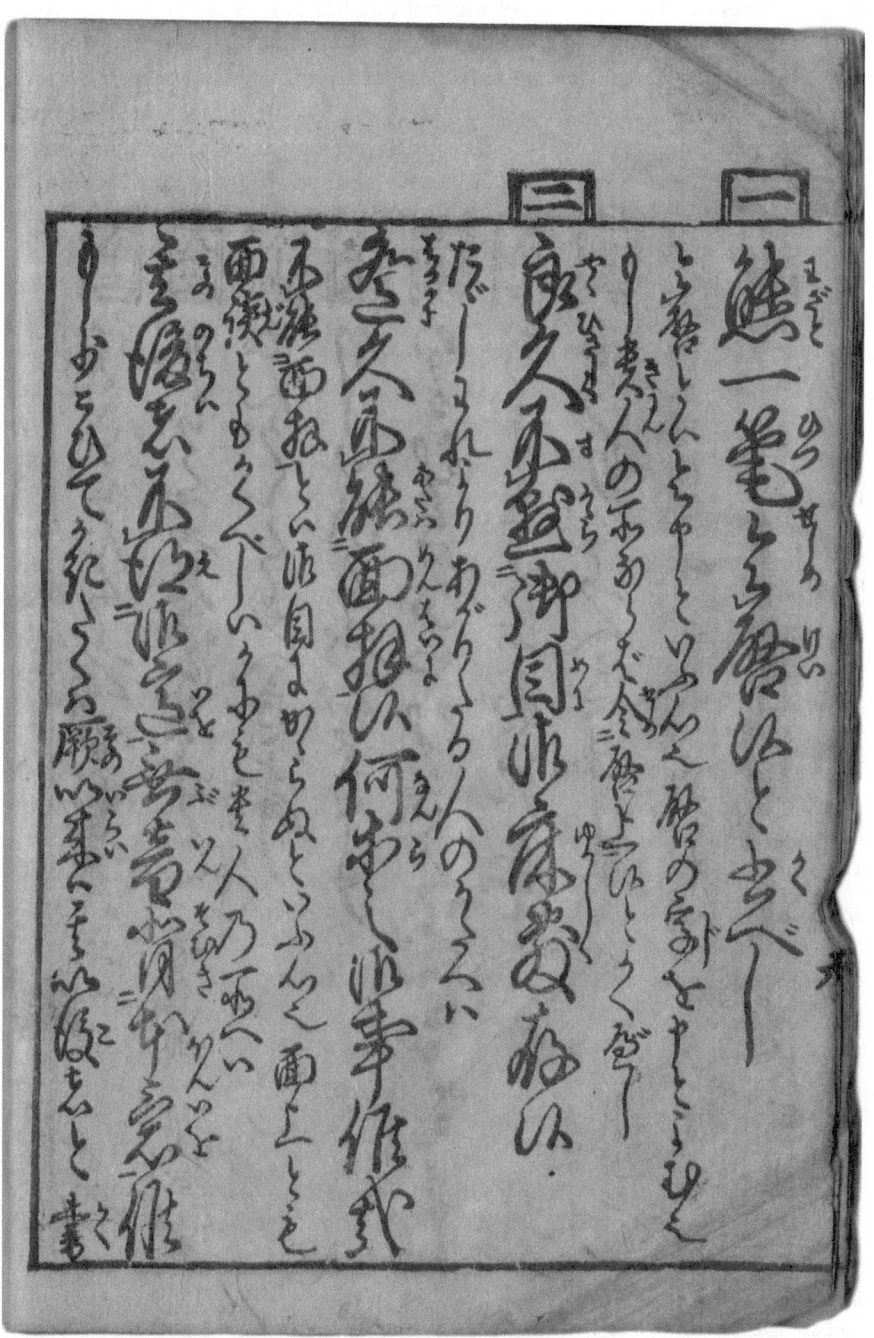

Figure 1.18 *Shogaku bunshō narabi ni yorozu shitsukekata*, 1647, 6v. Formulas for letter writing.

Author collection, Suzuran Bunko, Cambridge, U.K.

on their level of education. There was not one literacy, rather there were multiple literacies at play. An individual who had learned only basic *tenarai* could easily access vernacular texts written primarily in hiragana and in cursive, provided they were in contemporary Japanese. At the same time, that individual could potentially read other texts; for instance, vernacular books written with a predominance of kanji with phonetic glosses, or *kanbun* texts with *kunten* marks and interlinear translation, and perhaps even letters in *mairase-sōrōbun*. A person who had, for example, around nine years of education would probably have been conversant with *kanbun* displaying *kunten* marks only since one so educated would have acquired techniques like *sodoku*. Of course, this capacity would have potentially included other literacies on this spectrum, almost certainly *sōrōbun*. All in all, this indicates that in the case of early modern Japan it is as difficult to speak merely in terms of literate or illiterate as it is to speak of *kanbun* literacy or *wabun* literacy. We must acknowledge the full span of literacies and accept that a reader could master one or more of them.

This, in turn, makes it difficult to pinpoint popular literacy. As aptly noted by Heidi Brayman Hackel in her study of popular literacy in England, this concept is "slippery to define, impossible to quantify, misleading to characterize as singular."[105] It follows that talking about the popular reader can be equally problematic and eventually unproductive. That is why, for the purpose of my argument, I moot the idea of thinking in terms of novice and expert readers. Inspired by the use of these terms in, respectively, Maryanne Wolf's and Maria Nikolajeva's research, I define the expert reader as one who could move freely across the full spectrum of literacies as illustrated in figure 1.17.[106] Novice readers had mastered basic literacy and possessed a certain amount of linguistic and cultural competencies. They could move to a certain extent across the spectrum of literacies depending on the degree of their skills. The audience of the seventeenth-century popular prose under scrutiny in the present study encompassed both expert and novice readers, though my focus leans toward the latter.

Gakumon and Novice Readers

There is one more consideration that needs to be taken up once we have grasped the idea of multiple literacies. The modulations between the two poles of *wabun* literacy and *kanbun* literacy ensured that some bridging between *tenarai* and *gakumon* was possible. *Gakumon*, portrayed as the ultimate objective of study, as previously mentioned, was closely associated with books written in Sinitic and therefore presupposed expert readers with hard-core *kanbun* literacy. Novice readers with kana-mainly literacy would have been, in principle, cut off from *gakumon*, but commercial publishers ensured participation by putting in place the textual strategies explored with the example of *Jitsugokyō*.

The message of hope for novice readers is spelled out clearly in *Kiyomizu monogatari* (The tale of Kiyomizu; 1638).[107] It is structured as a dialogue between a pilgrim visiting Kiyomizu Temple in Kyoto and an old man there. The dialogue is allegedly witnessed and recorded by a first-person narrator, whose voice inevitably overlaps with that of the author, Asayama Irin'an 朝山意林庵 (1589–1664). In response to the pilgrim's queries about how to pray effectively, the old man stresses the importance of an honest heart. The ultimate quest for everyone is how to distinguish between *dōri* (the correct way of things) and *muri* (the absence of *dōri*). *Gakumon* is offered as the key to this quest, because it trains us to master such a distinction. The pilgrim is somewhat disheartened at hearing this: "For people like me, who are not literate [*moji mo naku*] and who cannot write, how could we all of a sudden possibly be presented with a book and learn from it?"[108] The old man's answer is reassuring: "So, do you think that only reading old books constitutes learning [*gakumon*]? I am not saying that this is not study [*manabi*], but to equate *gakumon* solely with reading is to miss the essence of *gakumon*."[109] The old man takes time to explore how *gakumon* evolved through history, from an era of no reading to one when only books can impart *gakumon*. In ancient times, when no writing existed, people would learn from the functioning of Heaven. During the subsequent age learning was possible through the oral accounts of people who had lived righteously. The next era abounded with both good and bad conduct, hence the need to start chronicling both good and bad deeds in written form. Once enlightened human beings had disappeared from mankind, it became essential to acquire *gakumon* through the activity of reading. The old man concludes, "Just because a person does not read books, this does not mean that he or she does not engage with learning. To learn simply means having a knowledge of the principle of things and bettering your behavior."[110] At the close of the passage the pilgrim expresses his gratitude and adds that the tale we are reading—that is, *Kiyomizu monogatari*—is itself a form of "quick *gakumon*" (*haya-gakumon*).[111] The message of hope is twofold. First, access to *gakumon* via aurality is still possible; after all, our pilgrim learns about *gakumon* in his conversation with a man. Even in a society that has embraced the culture of the written word, aurality remained a viable alternative to book reading. Second, by noting that *Kiyomizu monogatari*, which is written in the vernacular and uses a great many hiragana, becomes a form of quick *gakumon*, the possibility to engage with *gakumon* thanks to the mediation of vernacular Japanese becomes clear. This brings us back to Kawachiya Yoshimasa remarks on his father.

That novice readers were granted access to learning is lucidly reaffirmed in *Kashōki atooi* (Record that makes laughter possible, a follow-up; also known as *Zen'aku monogatari* [Tales of good and evil; 1670s]):

In between professional duties, people like to devote themselves to learning [*gakumon*]. It is beneficial to listen to the words of the people of the past, and it is even better if this is useful for a person's work.... They might find it discouraging that books describing the principles of learning are presented in a difficult way and cannot be read. But it should be remembered that there are as many other books that do explain the correct Way [*dōri*] in vernacular Japanese. *Gakumon* is not just about studying Chinese books. And if a person finds it difficult to read books even in Japanese, they should meet with contemporary scholars and pose all nature of questions orally—let's say about the Five Virtues and the Five Relations. This still counts as *gakumon*.[112]

Both expert and novice readers in seventeenth-century Japan were put in a position to join in the acquisition of *gakumon* and the ethical knowledge that went with it. Commercial publishers were invested in juggling the panoply of literacies involved in this process and were eager to explore ways in which *kanbun* literacy could be negotiated for the whole gamut of readers.

Seventeenth-century Japan was successful in fostering a culture of the written word. Admittedly, no statistics exist to offer an idea of what percentage of the population could write and read. Yet compelling circumstantial evidence suggests that engagement with the written word was in place for large sectors of society, stretching across the categories of status and gender. Discourses by contemporary intellectuals and pedagogues assert literacy as the key for everyone seeking to become successful members of society. Verbal and visual materials offer glimpses of how the written word began to percolate down into the daily lives of commoners. What is more, the soaring number of commercially printed books written in the vernacular speaks of an ever-growing readership.

The temptation in all of this is to identify in peasants, artisans, and merchants the readership of popular literature and to equate popular literacy with social status. Yet I have argued against this jejune interpretation. In its exploration of multiple literacies, this chapter has demonstrated that we can think more fruitfully in terms of a plurality of written languages as well as a span of competence skills (paleographic, linguistic, and cultural). My working definition of popular literacy espouses these complexities. I have postulated the existence of expert and novice readers who could move more or less freely across the spectrum of multiple literacies. Commercial publishers were cognizant of this plurality and deliberately packaged products appealing to a multiplicity of readers, bridging any polarity or binarity.

CHAPTER 2

The Publishing Business

Like the grains of sand on the seashore,
countless are the books published every year,
filling my shop up to the roof.

—Hōjō Dansui, *Chūya yōjinki* (On what to take care of day and night)

Seventeenth-century Japan fostered a culture of the written word that admitted multiple literacies and proactively encouraged people across society to engage with it. Merchants and craftsmen with entrepreneurial ambitions immediately saw a new and promising commercial opportunity in this. The production and sale of books catering to the full span of reading abilities became an exciting business prospect. The numbers of books that emerged throughout the seventeenth century show how successful this business was. But numbers are just one facet of a much more complex story, one this chapter is devoted to unraveling.

It would be misleading to claim that we know nothing about the seventeenth-century publishing industry. In his now classic monograph *The Book in Japan*, Peter F. Kornicki brings to the fore a few important features of the commercial book trade in the period. Kornicki mentions that "books became one of the visible commodities available in shops on the streets of Kyoto" and that they were also sold by book peddlers.[1] He touches upon the existence of "more than a hundred shops functioning in Kyoto as publishers of books" by the 1640s as well as on the existence of booksellers' catalogues.[2] There is mention of one specific Kyoto publisher, Murakami Kanbee, and of three booksellers based in Edo.[3] Kornicki also remarks that around the 1670s Japan discovered "an appreciation of the commercial value of authorship" and maintains that the prices of books were still high when compared with other commodities.[4]

The present chapter builds upon these findings while expanding and complementing them with a view to sketching a vivid portrayal of the seventeenth-century publishing business in Japan. I first draw upon contemporary visual and verbal depictions of publishers and booksellers to explore the physical and socializing space they created. It is important in this to be mindful that the printing and sale of books normally occurred in the same establishment. I next survey seventeenth-century publishers and suggest the existence of a large and vibrant community that surpassed the received number of one hundred. By zooming into a discussion of specific publishers and their products, this chapter touches upon the materiality of the books they released and reflects accordingly on the typologies of publishers in business. My analysis underscores the publishers' prominent role in shaping seventeenth-century books, arguing against the commercial value of authorship and advancing the idea of a collective author. After identifying who populated the publishing world, I look at their products. By looking at the concept of publishing genre as it emerges in book-trade catalogues, I map the varieties of books that publishers issued over the course of the century to identify which categories inhabited popular prose. The chapter closes with an attempt to gain some insights into the prices of books, arguing that publishers strove to cater not only to multiple literacies but also to diverse economic means.

The Anatomy of a Bookseller

In his delightful and deeply evocative journey through bookshops around the world, Jorge Carrión reminds us that we "need no passport to gain entry to the cartography of a bookshop."[5] That is certainly true when bookshops are physical entities existent in the world of the living. But what happens when we want to explore bookshops that belong to the world of the dead? Carrión himself notes how challenging it is to write a history of bookshops and how it "can only be written after recourse to photograph and postcard albums, a situationist mapping, short-lived links between shops that have vanished and those that still exist, together with a range of literary fragments and essays."[6]

A handful of scholars in Japan have taken up the difficult task of reconstructing the history of early modern booksellers.[7] While pointing readers to these studies for a systematic and comprehensive treatment of this topic, I discuss here a few examples that I deem particularly helpful in fashioning a mental picture of seventeenth-century bookshops.

As early as the Keichō era (1596–1615) images of bookshops appeared in the genre of folding screens illustrating "scenes in and around the capital" (*rakuchū rakugai zu byōbu*).[8] They continued to appear in visual materials depicting Kyoto and its people. Sumiyoshi Gukei's *Rakuchū rakugai zukan* (Scroll illustrated with scenes in and around the capital; late seventeenth century [fig. 2.1]) offers a charming example.[9] The shop owner is depicted as a merchant, with a patterned kimono and crest on his sleeves. He is pulling out a few books for his two customers, who appear to be Buddhist monks. Signboards advertise new publications, and titles are also inscribed on the wooden boxes used to store

Figure 2.1 Detail from Sumiyoshi Gukei, *Rakuchū rakugai zukan*, ca. late seventeenth century. Bookshop.

Courtesy of the Tokyo National Museum, Tokyo. Image: TNM Image Archives

Figure 2.2 Detail from Sumiyoshi Gukei, *Tohi zukan*, ca. late seventeenth century. Bookshop.

Courtesy of the Chester Beatty Library, Dublin

multivolume sets. Sumiyoshi Gukei's work introduces us to other examples of bookshops. The *Tohi zukan* in the collection of the Chester Beatty Library in Dublin examined in chapter 1 depicts a *noren* curtain displaying the character for *hon* 本 (books) (fig. 2.2).[10] Inside the shop another monk reads while the figure who appears to be the shop owner prepares other tomes. The *Tohi zukan* housed in Nara at the Konbuin (fig. 1.12) illustrates a two-story building with a *terakoya* on the second floor and, of special interest here, a bookshop on the first floor. The *noren* curtains outside the shop are inscribed with the character for books, and inside two monks browse through a few items; a man wearing a black kimono decorated with white crests on the sleeves selects books to show his customers. A third man in a light-blue kimono sits at the back of the shop intent on securing the covers to the book block. There is a panoply of books on the shelves: large-format *ōbon*, smaller-size *hanshibon*, scrolls, and rectangular concertina books.[11]

Together these pictorial materials offer an image of the bookshop as a lively space where customers are encouraged to interact with the books as well as with the shop owner, if not among themselves. The seventeenth-century Japanese bookshop, therefore, appears as a site of social interaction, not only of commerce. The number of books stacked on the shelves speaks of a thriving

Figure 2.3 Detail from Hishikawa Moronobu, *Shokunin zukushi emaki*, ca. 1682. Publisher and bookseller.

Courtesy of the British Museum, London

business, and the noticeable presence of signs outside the shops suggests a certain investment in publicity.

Hishikawa Moronobu 菱川師宣 (1618–1694), in his *Shokunin zukushi emaki* (Craftsmen of various trades; ca. 1682), sheds light on the production of printed materials as well as on a different business model in the sales of books (fig. 2.3).[12] In the shop the man on the right is engrossed in cutting a woodblock, while the one on the far left is intent on printing with his *baren*. The woman in the middle is responsible for sewing the covers onto the book block, and the stitches suggest that she is using the most common form of binding for early modern books, the *fukuro-toji* (literally, "bag bound"), whose appearance is close to a sleeve-shaped binding.[13] This is one of the earliest images illustrating how the workshop of a commercial publisher would have functioned.[14] The man in front of the shop is depicted in the act of carrying two wooden boxes full of books, balanced on a pole to allow transportation. I suggest that we are in front of an example of what Nagatomo Chiyoji refers to as *gyōshō hon'ya*, or an itinerant bookseller.[15] Whether this marked, as Nagatomo infers, the origins of lending libraries (commonly known as *kashihon'ya*), whether this man was delivering books to other retailers, or whether he was trading directly with customers can only be the object of speculation. Coeval depictions of other book peddlers introduced by Nagatomo seem to suggest that the man in Moronobu's scroll might be on his way to sell books to a number of households, perhaps even to the pleasure quarters.[16]

Judging from the book formats reproduced in all these images and from the kinds of customer included in some of the pictures, the sort of publisher-bookseller these visual fragments introduce us to is the so-called *mono no hon'ya* (also known as *shomotsuya* or *shomotsu doiya*). They are customarily associated with the publication of highbrow, learned materials, which might suggest a disengagement with the needs of a less-erudite public, our novice reader. Peter F. Kornicki, for example, explains the word *shomotsuya* as "dealers of more serious books, such as sinological texts."[17] Whether *mono no hon'ya* were interested only in the highbrow end of the publishing business is problematized by the image included in the 1669 *Inu Hyakunin isshu* (One hundred poets, one hundred poems: A bastard version), written by Yūsōan 幽双庵 (dates unknown) (fig. 2.4).[18] The owner, who looks to be a merchant, is opening books on the shop veranda so that, perhaps, potential customers (not seen) can have a look before going in. The signboard to the right of the scene reads *Shisho taizen* 四書大全, an annotated version of the Confucian Four Books in Sinitic, and that to the left states that this bookseller is investing in the publication of a new commentary on *Genji monogatari* (*The Tale of Genji*; the text on the signboard in question reads *Genji shō nyūgin* 源氏抄入銀). The two signboards suggest that this shop deals in books of a serious nature—a sinological text and a Heian-period tale—as we would expect from a *mono no hon'ya*. The detailed visual representation of the books allows us to appreciate that the volume the shop owner is holding in his right hand is an example of large-size *ōbon*. Larger-size paper inevitably meant higher costs, as elucidated by Hashiguchi Kōnosuke's research.[19] The presence of a half-folio illustration that breaks the written text suggests that we are moving away from texts in Sinitic, as a norm devoid of images, and dealing with something closer to *wabun* literacy. Whether this is a printed copy of *Genji monogatari* or any other book in the vernacular is impossible to ascertain. What complicates this seemingly straightforward picture of a *mono no hon'ya* is the poem inscribed in the blank space of the illustration. It mentions, in fact, a different type of publication available in the capital—namely, cheaply printed picture books and booklets related to the *jōruri* theater, here collectively referred to as *kusazōshi*. This verse, a parodic rewording of the *waka* by Fun'ya no Yasuhide, is titled "Booksellers' Cheap Sales" (Hon'ya no yasuuri) and reads, "As soon as they sell / even the cheap *kusazōshi* / drop in price / and this must be why, quite rightly, / their buyers are said to be happy" (*Uru kara ni / kusazōshi demo / yasukereba / mube kau hito no / ureshi to iuramu*).[20] This lively poem alludes to the existence of cheap books, here called *kusazōshi*, which would appeal to a wider range of customers, including readers with kana-mainly literacy.

The association of this poem with the image in question hints at the possibility that these lowbrow materials were part of the stock of the bookseller portrayed here. And yet this type of booklet is traditionally connected with a separate type of publisher-bookseller known as *sōshiya*.[21] *Sōshiya* would hardly have dealt with anything displayed in the illustration as analyzed here (i.e.,

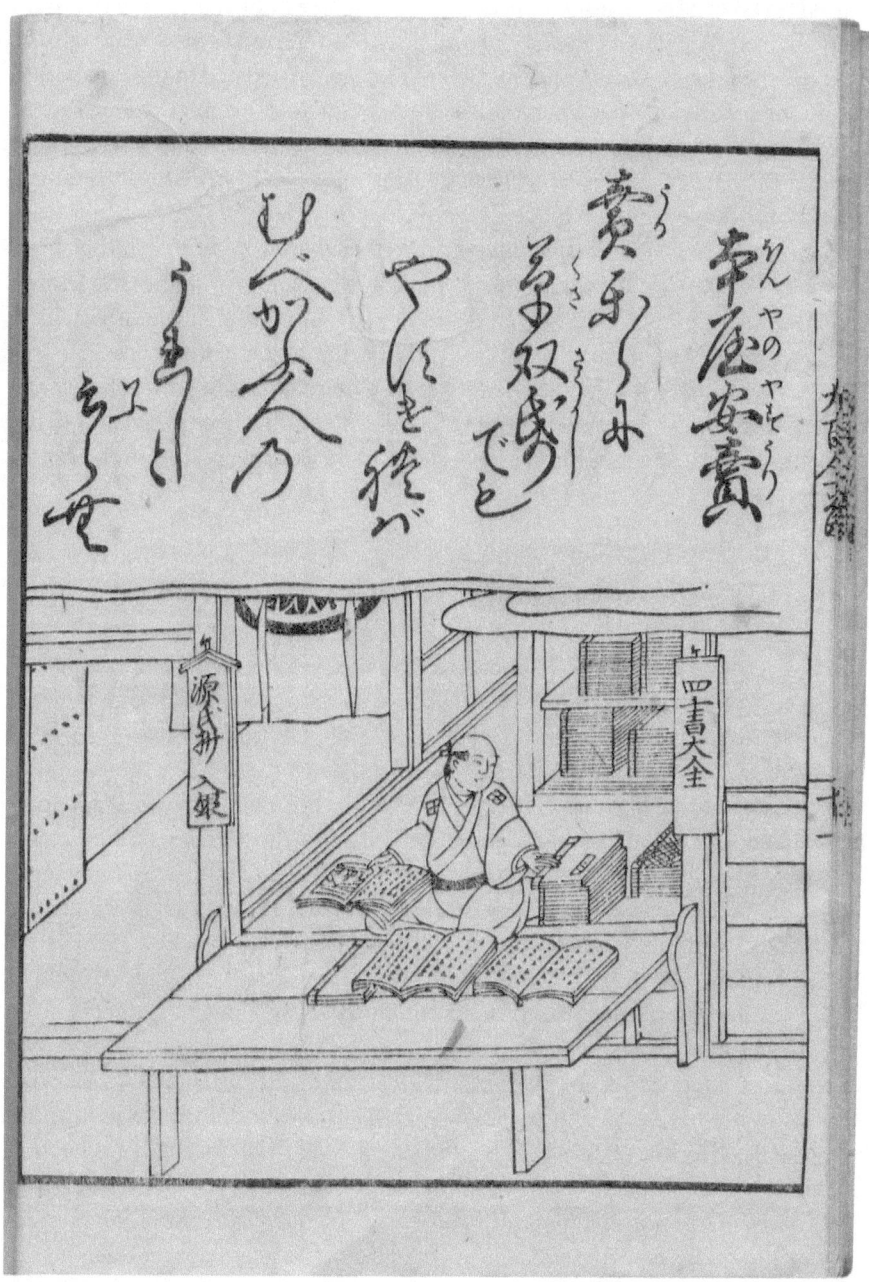

Figure 2.4 Yūsōan, *Inu Hyakunin isshu*, 1669 (1919 facsimile), 11v. Bookshop. Author collection, Suzuran Bunko, Cambridge, U.K.

Sinitic texts, Heian-period *monogatari*, and big-size books) but were the main publishers and dealers in the low-priced booklets referred to here as *kusazōshi*. That a distinction between *mono no hon'ya* and *sōshiya* existed in the Edo period cannot be readily denied: when booksellers' guilds were eventually constituted in the first half of the eighteenth century, *mono no hon'ya* and *sōshiya* kept independent from each other. Nevertheless, *Inu Hyakunin isshu* intimates a possible tension with the neat division that is portrayed in book histories, suggesting some overlap in the products marketed by *mono no hon'ya* and *sōshiya*. It is unfortunate that the illustration from *Inu Hyakunin isshu* does not show a customer, as this would have given a hint of the type of person who might have purchased cheap publications. It is only in the eighteenth century that illustrations of bookshops show customers from the merchant class and other social milieus seemingly interested in buying books. Also at this time publishers begin to speak about their shops in their own publications, the earliest recorded example to date being the 1719 *Yakusha kingeshō* (Actors' golden makeup).[22]

Mapping Seventeenth-Century Publisher-Booksellers

What was the size of publisher-booksellers in the seventeenth century in Kyoto? When confronted with this question *Genroku taiheiki* (Record of the great peace of the Genroku era, by Miyako no Nishiki 都の錦; 1702) is usually recommended as a reliable source of information.[23] In the sixth volume, in fact, there is mention of seventy-two booksellers active in Kyoto, who are all described as "notable publishers who have become well established in the recent past."[24] Among them, ten are identified as the top bookshops by virtue of being run by "exceptional people, known everywhere."[25] The Kyoto street directory *Kyō habutae* (Kyoto silk), originally issued in 1685 and compiled by Kojima Tokuemon 小嶋徳右衞門 (dates unknown), complements this information. The 1705 edition, in fact, includes ten names listed under *shomotsuya* (five overlapping with the top-ten veteran publishers in *Genroku taiheiki*).[26] By combining these two sources we understand, for instance, that Hayashi Hakusui 林白水 (d. 1704), also known as Izumoji Izumi no Jō 出雲寺和泉掾, and Murakami Kanbee 村上勘兵衞, also known under the shop name Heirakuji 平楽寺, were key figures in the publishing landscape at the time.[27]

Whereas *Genroku taiheiki* and *Kyō habutae* surface in research on the history of the book in early modern Japan as the must-go-to sources when estimating the number of booksellers, I maintain that they are equally revealing and misleading. They are revealing in that they contain firsthand information about contemporary Kyoto publishers but misleading in two ways: first, they narrow the scope of the publishing world to a number of publishers smaller than the actual one and, second, their choices give the false impression that the Kyoto publishing world focused entirely on highbrow publications. Konda Yōzō's work on the 1696 book-trade catalogue issued by Kawachiya Rihee 河内屋利兵衛 claims that the number of publishers by this time approximated four hundred shops, 90 percent of which were based in Kyoto.[28] Table 2.1 offers fresh figures that I have calculated by analyzing the data provided by Oka Masahiko in his survey of colophons dated between 1591 and 1704.[29]

Working with these data presents some challenges. First, Japanese names are complicated: different characters may be used to record the same name and, vice versa, names that appear very similar might well refer to different persons. Without in-depth research, it is difficult to make the necessary distinctions.[30] Second, some colophons list multiple publishers, some of which overlap with the names that appear alone in other colophons. I have decided to count these "teams" of publishers separately. Each of them contains a minimum of two publishers. Moreover, it must be kept in mind that there are many publications with colophons that record only the date of publication and not the name of the publisher, since no legislation before the 1720s required the presence of the publisher's name. I have examined Oka's data exercising the necessary prudence. Even so, the number of publishers who were active in the seventeenth century appears impressive and questions the received figures.

TABLE 2.1 Seventeenth-century publishers as recorded in contemporary colophons

	Total books inspected by Oka	Total titles	Total publisher names in colophons	Publishers publishing alone	Teams of publishers
1591–1658	5,782[a]	2,572[b]	837	793	—
1658–1673	4,251	ca. 3,133[c]	957	640	154
1673–1688	4,523	ca. 3,264[c]	1,333	808	402
1688–1704	4,560	ca. 3,572[c]	1,568	742	699

The data from 1591 to 1658 are based on Oka Masahiko et al., eds., *Edo jidai shoki shuppan nenpyō* (Tokyo: Bensei Shuppan, 2011). The figures for the later periods up to 1704 are based on unpublished spreadsheets compiled by Oka Masahiko, which he most kindly shared and allowed me to use for this publication. Oka also shared the spreadsheet that contains the raw data used for the publication of *Edo jidai shoki shuppan nenpyō*.

[a]Based on the number of entries in Oka's spreadsheet that matches *Edo jidai shoki shuppan nenpyō*.
[b]Based on the index in *Edo jidai shoki shuppan nenpyō*.
[c]I give an approximate number as it was not always possible to count the same title only once.

In table 2.1 I have recorded the number of titles gathered by Oka Masahiko. One might note that they largely confirm the figures for books listed in contemporary book-trade catalogues that I discuss in chapter 1, especially up to the 1670s. It is more difficult to use Oka's survey to gauge information about publications in the vernacular, since there is no indication of the language used. I have attempted some inspection of only the published data (until 1658). In doing so I have identified a minimum of sixty-five publishers of books in the vernacular.[31] Oka's comprehensive data lend themselves to a number of exciting investigations, but here I use them to study specific examples out of the sixty-plus publishers who were packaging reading materials for the novice reader.

One publisher that features prominently is the Nakano family. In *Genroku taiheiki*, Nakano stands out as one of the top ten publishers, and in *Kyō habutae* Nakano is recorded as a *shomotsuya*. When we consider the books that the Nakano family issued, we realize that they were also engaged in the publication of books with appeal for a broader public. The first-generation Nakano Kozaemon 中野小左衛門 (d. 1662; normally cited under the name Nakano Dōya 中野道也 in his colophons) is mentioned in *Kyō habutae* as the publisher of Buddhist texts of the esoteric Shingon sect.[32] Nevertheless, Oka Masahiko's survey reveals a degree of involvement with popular genres. These included several titles for *kōwakamai*, the texts of ballad dramas first performed in the Muromachi period and still in vogue during the sixteenth and seventeenth centuries.[33] Examples such as *Kagekiyo* (1632) show that the prose is written in the vernacular language and reveal an effort to package this material for novice readers with kana-mainly literacy.[34] Of the 183 characters (hiragana and kanji) on the verso of the first folio of the second volume, for instance, only 32 are logographic characters, and of those only 12 have no phonetic glosses (fig. 2.5). In terms of layout, the text is amply spaced on the page, with ten lines per half folio in a large-size book. The inclusion of half-folio, printed monochrome illustrations hand colored with red, green, and yellow would have further enhanced the appeal for anyone with a limited knowledge of the written word.[35] This type of page layout is confirmed in other *kōwakamai* from Nakano Dōya.[36] Nakano was also publishing other vernacular prose, including, for instance, a new version of the Muromachi tale *Fuji no hitoana sōshi* (The tale of the Fuji cave; 1632), as well as new prose like *Usuyuki monogatari* (The tale of Usuyuki; 1632).[37] The case of Nakano Dōya is revealing in showing how helpful Oka's data can be in dissecting the seventeenth-century publishing market. On the one hand, it is clear that Oka's survey confirms what the seventeenth-century primary sources disclose: in this case that the Nakano family was a prominent publishing firm. On the other hand, it becomes apparent that circumspection is needed when using the same primary sources: Nakano Dōya might well have been known primarily as a publisher of Shingon texts, as *Kyō habutae* records, but he was also active in the

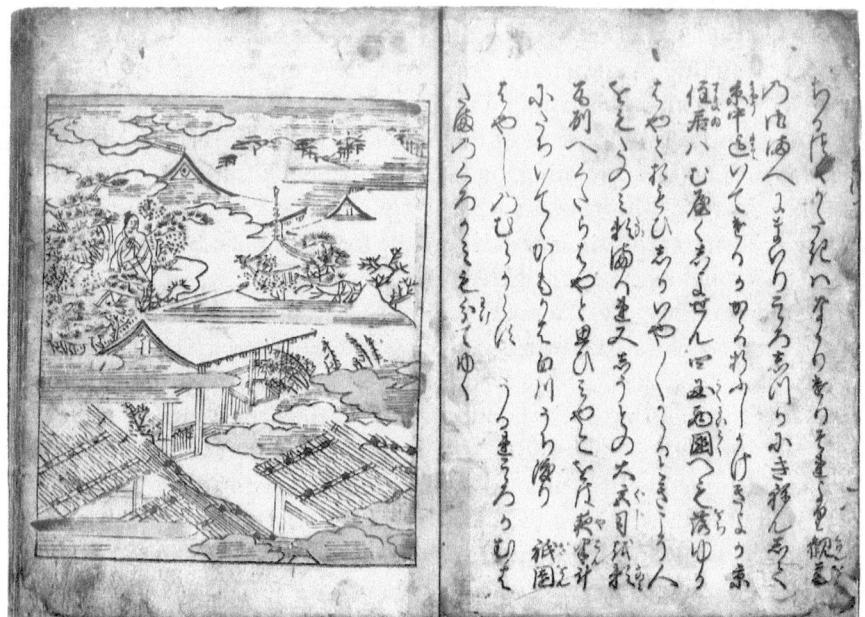

Figure 2.5 *Kagekiyo*, 1632, vol. 2, 1v. An example of a page printed by Nakano Dōya.
Courtesy of the National Institute of Japanese Literature, Tachikawa

kind of prose of interest in the present study. This, in turn, underpins the tension already pointed to when reflecting upon the typologies of publishers: we might well want to apply the more conventional, almost regimental distinction between publishers of serious materials (*mono no hon'ya*) and publishers of lighthearted booklets (*sōshiya*), but engagement with the publications they released shows that the former were not adverse to trying out issuing more popular products.

Oka's work is formidable in that it also points to publishers who were not mentioned in seventeenth-century sources like *Kyō habutae* or *Genroku taiheiki* but who nonetheless had a key role in pushing the business of printed books, in particular of books addressing a growing range of readers.

Nishimura Matazaemon 西村又左衛門 (dates unknown), located on Teramachi Avenue in front of the temple known as Seiganji, stands out. As with Nakano Dōya, the bulk of Nishimura's production included scholarly materials in Chinese, but he also published vernacular books intended for a broad readership. In 1643, for example, he issued a new edition of the best-selling calculation manual *Jinkōki* (Inexhaustible treatise).[38] Moreover, Nishimura issued two household manuals (discussed in greater depth in chapter 4): the aforementioned *Shogaku bunshō narabi ni yorozu shitsukekata* and the 1652 *Yorozu kikigaki hiden* (The secret tradition of things heard and recorded). It is worth noting that the latter also featured largely in the stocks of the Kyoto *sōshiya*, once again problematizing any strict, clear-cut division between *mono no hon'ya* and *sōshiya* in terms of the products they were issuing. Nishimura was also in charge of compiling the earliest dated book-trade catalogue (1670), which might hint at his role as a leading figure in the Kyoto commercial publishing industry at this time, well before the formation of a booksellers' guild (*hon'ya nakama*) in the early eighteenth century.

Equally significant was Yamada Ichirobee 山田市郎兵衛 (dates unknown), whose shop was located a little further north than that of Nishimura Matazaemon's on Teramachi and in front of the temple known as Honnōji. Until the 1650s he specialized in the publication of Muromachi-period tales, known in literary histories as *otogizōshi* or *Muromachi monogatari*, and in *kōwakamai*. Oka has identified twelve titles, all published in 1658, and what is particularly intriguing when we retrieve these materials from the archives is the attempt on the part of Yamada to print these texts in such a way that they looked similar to one another.[39] Yamada's collection of medieval tales are all the same size (ca. 26 × 18 cm). The titles are in hiragana only, a clear indicator to the potential customer that this is easily accessible reading material. The main text employs primarily phonetic characters, with a few kanji and frequently accompanied by phonetic glosses. There are fourteen lines for each half folio, and illustrations are interspersed throughout the text. Each folio includes an abbreviated title, and the folio number is printed on the inside of the recto toward the spine of the book. All of Yamada's books appear to have been issued in the ninth month of 1658 with colophons displaying a homogeneous calligraphic style. The endeavor put in place to give life to something akin to an integrated editorial series precedes by almost a century the better-known *Otogi bunko* (The companion library) published in Osaka by Shibukawa Seiemon 渋川清右衛門 (although Yamada makes no distinction between *otogizōshi* and *kōwakamai*).[40] Soon thereafter, Yamada Ichirobee began the publication of new types of material, including the guidebook to Kyoto by Asai Ryōi, *Kyō suzume*, mentioned in the previous chapter. Yamada Ichirobee, like Nishimura Matazaemon, issued, in 1671, a book-trade catalogue, suggesting that he, too, played a central role in the Kyoto publishing industry.

Oka's data also shed light on the existence of full-grown *sōshiya* in Kyoto as early as 1634. Sōshiya Tarōemon さうしや太郎右衛門 (dates unknown), whose firm was located in the Kyoto district of Nishi no Tōin between Nijō Castle and the Imperial Palace, released in that year the *jōruri* text *Hanaya*.[41] A *sōshiya* that features prominently in the records is Yamamoto Kyūbee 山本九兵衛 (also known as Sōshiya Kyūbee さうしや九兵衛 or Shōhon'ya Kyūbee 正本屋九兵衛; the name Kyūbee could also be read as Kuhee), with approximately ninety-five titles published between 1637 and 1704 (most likely over multiple generations). Originally located in the same area as Tarōemon, he then moved a little further east to Teramachi at the intersection with Nijō Avenue. His name appears for the first time in 1637 and is associated primarily with *jōruri* texts (earlier on) and *kusazōshi* picture books (beginning in the 1670s). Kyūbee's publication of *Nitan no Shirō* (The warrior Nitan no Shirō; 1667) is helpful in shaping our understanding of what visual features characterized the products issued by *sōshiya* based in Kyoto.[42] We are dealing with a vernacular text written with a predominance of hiragana and made visually appealing by the presence of discrete half-folio illustrations. Particularly striking is what I am tempted to call textual compression, which operates at a number of levels. First, the number of lines per half folio tends to increase (with seventeen lines in this specific instance). Second, we witness an attempt to cram the hiragana and the few kanji together into the vertical space. The detail in figure 2.6 reads *bonnin ni kawari* ぼんにんにかはり, with the two ん characters flattened between ぼ, に, and に, together with the か pushed into the empty space at the bottom of the second に. Why were these changes made? As I see it, much has to do with a reduced use of paper, which in turn meant less-expensive production costs and therefore a more affordable product.[43] This trend toward textual compression became a salient feature of the products of *sōshiya* in both Kyoto and Edo.[44]

Kyūbee's work is also revealing in that he contributed to the production of *kusazōshi* (the word *kusazōshi* being here used with a narrower meaning than that applied in *Inu Hyakunin isshu* and referring to a specific genre of picture books or graphic prose known in literary histories under this term).[45] Two of his picture books—*Ushiwaka sennin kiri hashi Benkei* (Little Yoshitsune slays

Figure 2.6 Detail from *Nitan no Shirō*, 1667, 4r. An example of textual compression in a page printed by Yamamoto Kyūbee.

Courtesy of the National Diet Library, Tokyo

a thousand, and Benkei on the bridge; 1667) and *Ikusa mai* (Dance of the armies; 1668)—feature among the collection owned by the little boy Obiya Chōkurō 帯屋長九郎, the son of the merchant Obiya Jirōkichi 帯屋次郎吉, which Okamoto Masaru discovered in the 1980s in a wooden statue of the bodhisattva Jizō in Matsusaka City (Mie Prefecture).[46]

The publishers discussed thus far were all based in Kyoto. But what about the other two burgeoning urban centers, Edo and Osaka? Oka Masahiko's survey singles out two publishers in Edo who were first active sometime around the second half of the 1600s. The first is Matsue Ichirobee 松会市郎兵衛 (also read as Shōkai Ichirobee), who started business in 1647 with the publication of scholarly books in Chinese. In the 1650s he began to produce works in the vernacular such as *Utai no hisho* (The secret book on Noh texts; 1652), a text on Noh theater performances, and *Nyohitsu Ono Otsū tehon* (Woman's brush: A copybook from Ono Otsū; 1652), a copybook with calligraphy by Ono Otsū 小野お通 (dates unknown), of the late Momoyama to early Edo period.[47]

Kashiwazaki Junko has conducted pioneering research into Matsue Ichirobee and has detected four phases in his business activity.[48] While the first generation issued facsimiles of works produced in Kyoto or, alternatively, bought and reused printing blocks from Kyoto publishers, the second generation (active between 1658 and 1674) moved ahead with the production of newly conceived materials marked by a page layout that aligns with that used by *sōshiya*. The *kōwakamai* text *Shida* (About Shida) and the Muromachi tale *Tengu no dairi* (The palace of Tengu), both dating to 1659, exemplify the traits that characterize the page layouts in books by this publisher.[49] The text is compressed on the page, with fourteen lines per page and an average of thirty characters per line. Half-folio illustrations in the style of Hishikawa Moronobu are inserted throughout the text. Kashiwazaki dates the third phase to between 1673 and 1684, when the Matsue firm either buys the blocks from Kyoto publishers or cuts facsimiles, thus reverting to the practice identified in the first phase. During the fourth phase the third-generation Matsue Sanshirō 松会三四郎 (also read Shōkai Sanshirō) assumes the helm. Although he rises to become a bookseller serving the *bakufu*, the firm's activity diminishes dramatically after the Genroku era.

The second publisher that Oka Masahiko singles out is Urokogataya うろこがたや (also written 鱗形屋), who started issuing titles in the 1660s, slightly later than Matsue Ichirobee.[50] Kashiwazaki Junko explains that the first-generation Urokogataya (Urokogataya Kahee 鱗形屋加兵衛) launched the business with the support of high-ranking members of the warrior class (*bushi*) based in Edo and asserts that he sought to have products differing from the Kyoto publications, an aspect that distinguishes him from the first-generation Matsue Ichirobee. Courtesan evaluation books and guidebooks to the pleasure quarters (often referred to as *yūjo hyōbanki*) appear to constitute the core of Urokogataya's output during this period. The second-generation Urokogataya Sanzaemon 鱗型屋三左衛門 and the third-generation Urokogataya Magobee 鱗型屋孫兵衛 continued their activity in specialized fields—namely, *jōruri* librettos and *kusazōshi* picture books. Urokogataya Magobee, in particular, emerged as a key figure in the *kusazōshi* genre.[51]

Only Matsue Ichirobee and Urokogataya stood out in the Edo publishing world during the 1660s, but by the end of the seventeenth century several publishers were operating in Edo. The 1687 street directory *Edo kanoko* (The Edo fawn) lists booksellers in two categories: *shomotsuya* and *jōruri hon'ya*.[52] The firms of Matsue (Shōkai) and Urokogataya are listed under the second category alongside three other publishers, who became influential in the second half of the seventeenth century. The first category includes sixteen publishers, whose names are linked with leading booksellers in the Kyoto publishing industry; for instance, Nakano Jinbee 中野仁兵衛 and Nishimura Mataemon 西村又右衛門. This suggests the emergence of a complex network of book entrepreneurs across Kyoto and Edo by the end of the century.

Publishing in Osaka developed slightly later, sometime in the 1670s.[53] Tajihi Ikuo explains that the first texts published there were anthologies of haikai and *kyōka* poetry, often joint publications between Kyoto and Osaka booksellers.[54] It was not until 1682 and the publication of *Kōshoku ichidai otoko* (*The Life of an Amorous Man*), by Ihara Saikaku, that Osaka commercial publishing witnessed a boom in the new genre of sensual *kōshokubon*. Osaka would become a thriving publishing center beginning in the early eighteenth century: the aforementioned *Genroku taiheiki* pays homage by portraying a Kyoto and an Osaka bookseller as the protagonists of the main narrative frame.

I began this section by touching upon the towering numbers of publishers in seventeenth-century Japan and highlighted a few among them. Although my account can scarcely claim to be exhaustive, it has hopefully revealed a few noteworthy findings. First, it shows how a sole reliance on seventeenth-century sources like *Kyō habutae* and *Genroku taiheiki* might lead to a misrepresentation and how Oka Masahiko's survey is valuable in redressing this situation. Second, I have identified around sixty-five publishers who were involved with the publication of prose in the vernacular in the 1660s. For this number to make sense (together with that of the books in the vernacular discussed in chapter 1) there must have been a growing demand for books that addressed the novice reader with kana-mainly literacy. These figures also reveal a tension with the visual materials examined in the previous section, where only monks, samurai, and wealthy merchants feature as the customers of bookshops. Third, the handful of publishers that I singled out and discussed in some detail prompt us to think carefully about any easy distinction between publishers of serious materials (*mono no hon'ya*) and publishers of lighthearted books (*sōshiya*). They might well have worked independently, but *mono no hon'ya* did not forgo participation in the production of books that appealed to novice readers with kana-mainly literacy. Fourth, engagement with the products issued by these publishers has shed light on some publishing strategies that were put in place to make books appealing as products accessible to a vast number of readers: the predominant use of hiragana and kanji accompanied by phonetic glosses; the insertion of illustrations; and efforts to curb the use of space on the page in an attempt to cut costs. It has also become apparent that the pioneers of the publishing business in Edo balanced two almost opposing trajectories, on the one hand preserving trends already explored by the Kyoto market and, on the other, experimenting with new contents and layouts. While the foregoing serves to sketch the outlines of a network of zestful publishers, in-depth research is much needed to produce a comprehensive study of the world of seventeenth-century commercial publishing. In the following chapters I strive to note the publishers, when known, of the books under discussion, and I do so in order to offer more data in this first foray at mapping seventeenth-century publishers and their achievements.

The Seventeenth-Century Author

Publishers were just one of the actors involved in the publication of texts in the vernacular. Other integral players were, as may be expected, the authors themselves. Yet the part played by authors in seventeenth-century Japan challenges our expectations about them as prominent figures and pushes us to think in terms of a type of collective author.

Let's begin at the end of the seventeenth century with *Genroku taiheiki*. This rich, multifaceted, and entertaining tale can be seen as an outstanding attempt of this period by a single author to sing his own praises and to seek celebrity. In the story, a boat leaves Fushimi for Osaka on an autumn evening in 1701. Onboard are two booksellers who remark how quickly the trends in the publishing market change. The only product that appears to have remained popular are erotic works known as *kōshokubon*. The Osaka bookseller lavishes praise on Ihara Saikaku, ending on a laudatory note: "When it comes to inventiveness in vernacular prose [*wabun*], no writer surpasses Saikaku."[55] In response, the Kyoto publisher admits that, "Needless to say, Saikaku is famous in all the provinces for his skill in witty humor [*karukuchi*] and for his erotic prose [*nurebumi*]," but he also accuses him of being ignorant in his knowledge of *gakumon*, making many mistakes in the use of words and quotations.[56] The criticisms aside, this exchange is a testimony to the perception and marketability of Ihara Saikaku as a "celebrity author." Even so, Saikaku is portrayed second to Miyako no Nishiki. It would not have been lost on the reader that the aim of the Kyoto bookseller was to place Kyoto above Osaka and more specifically to elevate the Kyoto writer Miyako no Nishiki as the rising star of vernacular prose: "In the capital, Nishimura Ichirōemon, a wizard of erotic literature [*kōshokubumi*], simply has to wield his brush to make Saikaku disappear. But he, too, is weak in learning [*gakumon*] and at times makes mistakes.... This spring in the capital Miyako ni Nishiki has come to the forefront, creating vernacular prose that will come to Saikaku's rescue."[57] We should not forget that the author of *Genroku taiheiki* is precisely Miyako no Nishiki and that he cleverly employs his own text to promote himself as the latest trendy author.

At this point in the tale, the Osaka bookseller tries his utmost at one-upmanship by accusing Miyako no Nishiki of being a nobody on the literary scene and a plagiarizer. He asserts that the quality of work by another Osaka writer, Nishizawa Ippū 西沢一風 (1665–1731), is far superior. The banter between the two booksellers continues, and the Kyoto merchant even introduces the tale of Saikaku in hell in his defense of Miyako no Nishiki. Ultimately, it matters little who the winner is. What does matter is the recognition that by the early eighteenth century certain names had emerged in literature as the period's literary icons.

Miyako no Nishiki's view of the author might appear comforting in largely aligning with our expectations vis-à-vis literature, with authors in charge of their own texts and selling their talent. This kind of notoriety is an aspect that Japanese authors of vernacular literature were beginning to fully enjoy for the first time at the end of the seventeenth century. This is perhaps not particularly surprising to any reader familiar with Japanese premodern literature. Before the seventeenth century, in fact, there had been little or no tradition of advertising the names of authors of vernacular prose. This situation remained largely unaltered at the beginning of the Edo period. It is only with the 1670 book-trade catalogue from Nishimura Matazaemon that the initial traces of authors of vernacular prose begins to surface. Yet while this catalogue offers a considerable number of names for publications relating to the sphere of *kanbun* literacy, only a handful of names were systematically attached to titles of books in the vernacular.[58] A few are worth mentioning here.

The first is Asai Ryōi 浅井了意 (d. 1691).[59] The son of a monk originally in service at Honshōji near Osaka, Asai Ryōi devoted himself to the study of Buddhist and Confucian texts from an early age. After taking the tonsure, Ryōi moved to Kyoto in 1644, entering the Zen temples of Shōganji and later Honshōji.[60] His corpus of works includes titles written in *kanbun* that dealt with the intellectual traditions of Buddhism and Confucianism, thus catering primarily to monks and scholars, alongside works written in *wabun* for novice readers. Ryōi was also a talented calligrapher and equally known as a skilled *hanshita-gaki*—that is, a person who produced the preparatory text used by block cutters to create blocks for printing.[61] The foreword written in 1693 by the writer and publisher Hayashi Gitan 林義端 (d. 1711) to *Inu hariko* (The papier-mâché dog), a work attributed to Asai Ryōi, describes the author as prolific and "gifted with exceptional knowledge and memory, a wizard of the art of writing."[62]

Despite his outstanding output, Asai Ryōi's name rarely appears in his texts or in contemporary sources discussing his prose.[63] For example, even though *Genroku taiheiki* mentions Asai Ryōi's *Otogi bōko* (Hand puppets; 1666) as one of three titles that "from the past until today continue to charm without anyone losing interest in them," the author's name does not feature anywhere.[64] It is not until much later, in the nineteenth century, that Asai Ryōi is described as an established author by professional writers like Santō Kyōden 山東京伝 (1761–1816) and Kyokutei Bakin 曲亭馬琴 (1767–1848). In 1810, Santō Kyōden published *Kabuki no hana botan dōrō* (Flower of Kabuki, the peony lantern ghost story) and traced the origins of this tale to *Mudan dengji* (J. *Botan tōki*, The peony lantern), recorded in the Chinese Ming-period text *Jiandeng xinhua* (J. *Sentō shinwa*, New stories under the lamplight).[65] He then notes the publication of Asai Ryōi's translation (under the title *Botan dōrō*) in easy Japanese in the Kanbun era (1661–1673) and recognizes Asai Ryōi's importance as an author. Similarly, Kyokutei Bakin also touches upon Asai Ryōi and his *Otogi bōko*—identified as an adaptation of *Sentō shinwa*—when discussing the origins of the genre known as *yomihon* in the second volume of his 1834 *Kinsei mono no hon Edo sakusha burui* (Early modern books and a taxonomy of Edo authors).[66] As I see it, they invest Ryōi with the status of author because of their own awareness of what being an author meant.

Multiple titles by Suzuki Shōsan 鈴木正三 (1579–1655) also appear in the 1670 book-trade catalogue. The son of a retainer of the Tokugawa family in Mikawa Province, Shōsan was fully committed to military activities as a younger man, fighting in the battles of Sekigahara (1600) and Osaka (1614/1615). At the age of forty-two he renounced a secular life to take the tonsure as a monk of the Sōtō sect of Zen Buddhism. He divided his time between traveling around the country overseeing the construction of temples and his intense efforts to expunge Christianity from Japan. The latter culminated in the treatise *Ha kirishitan* (Christian countered), which his disciples published posthumously in 1662.[67] Royall Tyler describes him as "a Zen teacher, moralist, and *kanazōshi* writer," adding that in Edo he "gave instruction, as was his habit, to people of every sort."[68] The names of other authors appear sporadically in the various vernacular publishing genres listed in the 1670 book-trade catalogue. There is Tsujihara Genpo 辻原元甫 (b. 1622), the son of a Confucian doctor well versed in the composition of Chinese poetry whose writings focused on the popularization of Confucian thought.[69] Nakagawa Kiun 中川喜雲 (1636–1705) was trained as a medical doctor and a student of haikai poetry under the tutelage of Matsunaga Teitoku 松永貞徳 (1571–1653). Both these activities enabled him to travel extensively around the country; this in turn fueled his prose production, primarily travelogues and guidebooks. He also issued collections of short, humorous stories that he allegedly performed to entertain his hosts.[70]

These writers, together with all the seventeenth-century authors of vernacular prose discussed in this study, hailed from a social and cultural background that would have equipped them with *kanbun* literacy. At the same time, though, they shared a desire to disseminate knowledge for the benefit of a less-erudite readership through the production of texts in the vernacular. Despite their efforts, none of them ever gained the status of a celebrity author during their lifetimes. Authors were unquestionably an integral part of the production of seventeenth-century books in the vernacular, yet the notion of authorial intention had little import. In other words, seventeenth-century Japanese popular prose advanced an idea of literature in which the author was not overly significant. I would contend that seventeenth-century Japanese authors of popular literature were substantially effaced from the publishing market and that the real players in the production of books were, in fact, the publishers.

This acknowledgment calls attention to some salient features of the literary production under scrutiny. In an age devoid of awareness surrounding intellectual property or copyright, publishers could (and did!) repackage the same text in different forms, making substantial changes over time. These "nonauthorial interventions"—to borrow the critical language of Jerome J. McGann—occurred at both the linguistic and bibliographical levels.[71] The following chapters discuss how textual production was often not so much the outcome of an individual author's efforts as the result of a collective author.[72] An individual writes a text (that person could easily be left unnamed), but it is the publisher who brings it to fruition (that name is often recorded despite the lack of any law requiring this). For books that sold well other publishers could and did appropriate the materials, modifying the text or paratext to ensure the product's continuous marketability. Illustrators were also employed, most likely by the publishers, and participated in the creation of popular books, but until the appearance of Hishikawa Moronobu they were not deemed particularly significant as individuals worth mentioning in the books. In other words, seventeenth-century popular prose was produced by a team of professionals and, apart from rare exceptions, the only name worth recording was that of the publisher alone.

Once the place of a collective author is recognized, another feature of seventeenth-century popular prose emerges: textual instability. Although it is always tempting to see commercially produced written texts as static entities delivered to readers as conceived by their author, the books examined in this study are, in fact, ever-changing entities. Publishers modified text, as well as paratext, to meet the needs of a continually evolving reading public, and readers were invited to fully enjoy these shifts as an integral part of their textual experience.

I have suggested that authors may have been motivated by a philanthropic desire to make knowledge available to readers. It is plausible to speak of philanthropy since there is no record of payment made to authors in seventeenth-century Japan. But publishers, the real trailblazers in this story, were interested in something different—financial profit. To ensure their business enterprises were viable, they had to issue books that would sell and would sell well. There were, then, economic reasons behind nonauthorial interventions, and we must fully engage with these in order to make sense of the popular prose examined here.

Publishing Genres and Popular Products in Book-Trade Catalogues

Up to this point I have identified a flourishing publishing business that was dependent on an ever-increasing hunger for reading matter that addressed both expert and novice readers. What products did publishers (and their authors) offer to meet the demands of a growing readership? Book-trade catalogues (*shojaku mokuroku*) provide a tentative answer. As previously noted, these catalogues first appeared around the mid-seventeenth century. The 1670 book-trade catalogue often cited in this study—jointly published by Nishimura Matazaemon (Kyoto) and Nishimura Mataemon (Edo)—was the first printed example with a complete colophon. As explained in my previously published work on the subject, these catalogues were regularly issued between 1671 and 1699, but not always annually.[73] They contained, or at least sought to contain, information on all the books then available on the market. There were two kinds of *shojaku mokuroku*. The first arranged titles under subject headings (or categories). The second type organized titles alphabetically (in *i-ro-ha* order), still maintaining some generic subject headings under each syllable—namely, Buddhist books, medical texts, and books in the vernacular. Catalogues of the second type also included maps (*zu*), stone rubbings (*ishizuri*), and erotica (*kōshokubon*; after 1691) as discrete categories. In essence, book-trade catalogues functioned as maps of the market of printed books.

The clusters or groups of texts found in these book-trade catalogues could be described as publishing genres.[74] The concept of a publishing genre is inherently different from the modern idea of genre.[75] For me one of the most effective expositions of what a genre, in the modern sense of the word, is can be found in the work of Japanese literature scholar Linda H. Chance:

> An author, we assert, chooses to write in a certain genre—chooses as from a menu, no less—setting the task of conforming to the rules, or deciding to push the limit of a given genre (the latter choice is a minimum necessity for a

masterpiece, most would argue). A title or another signal early in the work tips off the audience to its status as sonnet, romance novel, elegy, science fiction.... The reader then brings a set of implicit, common sense, culturally bound, generic characteristics to the table and navigates the text accordingly; genre is a property of the text, put there by the author and read there by the reader. It is a tool by which to raise the creation and apprehension of form to a more conscious level, or rather the mechanism by which form is both created and apprehended.[76]

Seventeenth-century publishing genres were formulated solely by publishers with a view to alerting their clientele about the existence of texts that arguably shared similar contents. The ultimate goal was to entice potential buyers to purchase more of the same, or at least what on the surface was signposted as more of the same by the use of a unified label. There is no evidence that authors were aware of where their texts would be placed among the several publishing genres. To use Chance's metaphor, there was no menu that authors were asked to conform to when writing. Moreover, as the following chapters reveal, the boundaries of publishing genres were often porous, with titles traveling from one category to another over time.[77] What is more, the study of individual publishing genres displays an appreciable lack of core features characterizing all the texts inscribed under the same heading. As such, publishing genres were meaningful epistemological tools, not at the moment of the creation of or the perusal of a text but rather when a book was put up for sale. In short, publishing genres were devised as convenient marketing tools. They can consequently be viewed as the means chosen by publishers to impose some order on a publishing space that otherwise would have been utterly chaotic. It should be pointed out that early modern Japanese publishers did not employ any specific term for what I call publishing genres and that there is no trace of any systematic a priori thinking around these clusters of texts. However, publishers did repeatedly use the same labels to highlight similarities within a group of titles. These publishing genres, therefore, offer an insider view of the publishing products released and marketed by seventeenth-century publishers. They enable us to organize the forest of books commercially produced in the seventeenth century, in full respect of the early modern sensibility around genre and without imposing any ahistorical constructs.[78] As I see them, publishing genres are the best epistemological tool we have to gain what Nakano Mitsutoshi calls "Edo people's eyes."[79] We should never lose sight, though, of the fact that they were convenient labels and marketing tools, not genres in the modern sense of the word.

Our quest in unearthing the publishing genres that inhabited seventeenth-century popular prose begins with the oldest surviving documented book-trade catalogue, published sometime around 1666–1667. Table 2.2 lists the publishing genres identified by the unnamed publisher of this catalogue.

TABLE 2.2 Publishing genres in the 1666–1667 book-trade catalogue

	Publishing genre	English equivalent	No. of books
1	Kyō 経	Buddhist sutras	76
2	Tendai narabi ni Tōshū 天台并当宗	Texts related to Tendai-shū and Nichiren-shū	360
3	Hossō 法相	Texts related to Hossō-shū	10
4	Risshū 律宗	Texts related to Risshū	28
5	Kusha 倶舎	Texts related to Kusha-shū	12
6	Shingon 真言	Texts related to Shingon-shū	188
7	Zen 禅	Texts related to Zen-shū	267
8	Jōdo narabi ni Ikkō 浄土并一向	Texts related to Jōdo-shū and Ikkō-shū	245
9	Geten 外典	Confucian texts	247
10	Shi narabi ni renku 詩并聯句	Poetry in Chinese	67
11	Jishū 字集	Dictionaries	38
12	Shinsho 神書	Shinto texts	45
13	Rekisho 暦書	Calendars	28
14	Gunsho 軍書	Military books and war tales	107
15	Isho 医書	Medical texts	272
16	Kasho 歌書	Poetry in Japanese	133
17	Washo narabi ni kanarui 和書并仮名類	Japanese books and books in kana	198
18	Renga 連歌	Renga poetry	17

	Publishing genre	English equivalent	No. of books
19	*Haikai* 俳諧	Haikai poetry	156
20	*Mai narabi ni sōshi* 舞并草子	*Kōwakamai* and booklets	162
21	*Ōraimono narabi ni tehon* 往来物并手本	Textbooks and copybooks	28
22	*Tsurimono narabi ni ezu* 釣物并絵図	Hanging scrolls and pictures	29
			2713

Based on data in Laura Moretti, "The Japanese Early-Modern Publishing Market Unveiled: A Survey of Edo-Period Booksellers' Catalogues," *East Asian Publishing and Society* 2, no. 2 (2012): 267–68. Note that the wording for the same publishing genre could change slightly from catalogue to catalogue as well as within the same catalogue. I have made them consistent with the wording in this table for the sake of comparison.

The first step in identifying the typologies germane to this study is differentiating between the categories addressing readers equipped with kana-mainly literacy and those that were likely to appeal to an elite readership with a high level of *kanbun* literacy. In earlier research, I concluded that book-trade catalogues made a distinction between texts written in Japanese (*wabun*) and those in *kanbun*, and that the choice of the calligraphic style used for the titles was instrumental in signaling this division. More precisely, the titles of texts in *kanbun* were recorded in noncursive script (*kaisho*) and those in Japanese in cursive script (*sōsho*).[80] Using this criterion, the following publishing genres appear related to the sphere of *kanbun* literacy: texts dealing with Buddhism (1–8), Confucianism (9), Shintoism (12), poetry in Chinese (10), as well as dictionaries (11), calendars (13), military books (14), and medical texts (15). (The parenthetical numbers correspond to the typologies listed in table 2.2.)

Such an easy differentiation is, however, far from being straightforward. First of all, table 2.2 shows that these elite publishing genres incorporate a great many titles. This demonstrates that a vast, well-established market existed for them, thus raising questions regarding the actual size of the elite group supposedly able to read them. Furthermore, it is clear that these publishing genres also included vernacular publications. Medical books (*isho*) are a case in point. This category certainly included texts in Sinitic. *Igaku nyūmon* (Introduction to medicine), composed by the Ming-dynasty doctor Li Chan 李梴 (J. Ri Ten [dates unknown]), for example, was published in *kanbun* by Murakami Kanbee and dutifully appears in several book-trade catalogues under the *isho* section. Yet, *Shokushō nōdoku* (Bad and good properties of food; also known as *Nichiyō shokushō nōdoku*) and *Nichiyō shokushō* (Properties of everyday food) by Manase Gensaku 曲直瀬玄朔 (1549–1631) are also in a number of catalogues, their titles sometimes accompanied by the words "kana" or "hiragana." The archive confirms the variety of languages and scripts used for Gensaku's work. For example, the 1642 edition of *Nichiyō shokushō* issued by Fūgetsu Sōchi 風月宗知 in Kyoto displays a mixture of kanji and katakana, whereas the 1673 edition by Matsue offers a combination of kanji and hiragana.[81]

Gunsho (military books and war tales; 14) are equally problematic, but for different reasons. The titles in this category are systematically recorded using the noncursive script, suggesting an inherent link with *kanbun* literacy (although they were not necessarily written in *kanbun*). And yet there is evidence that *gunsho* enjoyed great popularity in seventeenth-century Japan, progressively diffusing into early modern printed culture in a number of fashions.[82] For example, the medieval *Heike monogatari* (*The Tales of Heike*) inspired a number of popular products for centuries.[83] The inclusion of *gunsho* in later materials describing the development of Japanese history suggests that eventually they became used by early modern scholars as the bedrock of historical evidence and historical narrative.[84] How the seventeenth-century publishing industry constructed Japanese history is a fascinating question that awaits further research. But what is clear is that *gunsho* captivated readers well beyond any defined elite.

While acknowledging the complexity of attempting to create a neat division between books of *wabun* and those of *kanbun* literacy, the study of seventeenth-century catalogues is nonetheless revealing of the contours of popular-prose literature. So, what are these contours? *Waka* (16), *renga* (18), and haikai (19) are clearly poetic forms written in the vernacular, and certainly the latter two had an important role in the development of early modern popular culture at the time. The category of *tsurimono narabi ni ezu* (hanging scrolls and pictures [22]) subsumes visual materials such as maps, medical charts, and the board game *sugoroku*. The remaining publishing genres are *ōraimono narabi ni tehon* (21), *mai narabi ni sōshi* (20), and *washo narabi ni kanarui* (17). They each combine two categories, as indicated by the insertion of the conjunction *naribi ni* (and).

Ōraimono narabi ni tehon (textbooks and copybooks) are at the center of what Matthias Hayek and Annick Horiuchi refer to as "popular learning."[85] Koizumi Yoshinaga defines *ōraimono* as "an elementary written medium for teaching children to read and write," and the term *tehon* further reinforces the link between books and practical learning in their role as copybooks.[86] The publishing genre of *ōraimono narabi ni tehon* is thus relatively self-explanatory, containing printed books catering to *tenarai* and "small learning," as defined in chapter 1.

Mai narabi ni sōshi (*kōwakamai* and booklets) is a more elusive grouping. *Mai* books can be easily identified as a distinct genre—that is, the aforementioned *kōwakamai*. But *sōshi* (booklets) are more difficult to characterize. A large portion of *sōshi* are *honji mono*, a term still used in literary histories to describe a narrative structure begun during the Muromachi period that involves the appearance of a deity on earth who seeks to aid the salvation of humankind. After *honji mono* is a broad group of fictional tales originally composed during the Muromachi period of the same type as those discussed in relation to Yamada Ichirobee. It is, as a result, tempting to view *sōshi* as a publishing genre typified by fictional tales that were in circulation as early as the Muromachi period and later inherited (and appropriated) by early modern publishers. That would be misleading, however. In fact, *honji mono* and *otogizōshi*-type books are interspersed with fictional tales that are thought to have been composed at the beginning of the seventeenth century. Also subsumed within *sōshi* are *hyōbanki*, or "critiques," which are intrinsically early modern, nonfictional, and substantially nonnarrative prose materials. They serve as guides to two types of entertainment created in the seventeenth century: Kabuki theater and the licensed pleasure quarters (*yūjo hyōbanki* were previously mentioned in connection with the Edo publisher Urokogataya). It is worth pointing out that while today we tend to make a clear-cut distinction between medieval and early modern prose, such a differentiation cannot be retrieved from early modern book-trade catalogues.

A similar composite nature is recognizable in *washo narabi ni kanarui* (Japanese books and books in kana). The *washo* and *kanarui* categories, in fact, subsumed a great variety of texts without further categorization into subgenres; there was no distinction between fiction and nonfiction, narrative and nonnarrative, or between didactic, practical, and entertaining materials. My own research has shown that this category consisted of sixteen types of texts.[87] If we remember that publishing genres were inserted in book-trade catalogues in an effort to list similar books under the same heading with the aim of suggesting comparable titles to prospective buyers, the existence of a category like *washo narabi ni kanarui*, which brings together all sorts of unrelated materials, would seem to defeat the purpose.

Seventeenth-century publishers must have perceived both *washo narabi ni kanarui* and *sōshi* as inefficient, unworkable publishing genres, since beginning in 1670 these two categories underwent a major reorganization. *Washo narabi ni kanarui* was renamed *kana washo*, with the contents identified as "Books on the Five Virtues" (*gojō-sho*), "Books on Filial Piety" (*kōkō-sho*), "Books on Learning of the Mind" (*shingaku*), and "Educational Books" (*kyōkun-sho*). As a result of this renaming, texts that did not fit into this description were removed and regrouped into new independent publishing genres (see table 2.3).

TABLE 2.3 *Washo narabi ni kanarui* as it had evolved in the 1670 book-trade catalogue

Publishing genre	English equivalent	No. of books in 1670
Kana washo 仮名和書	Japanese books in kana	88
Nyosho 女書	Books for women	19
Utaibon 謡本	Librettos for the Noh theater	30
Sansho 算書	Arithmetic books	18
Banjō-sho 盤上書	Books for board games	12
Cha no yu sho narabi ni kasho 茶湯書并華書	Books for the tea ceremony and flower arranging	7
Shitsukekata-sho narabi ni ryōri-sho 躾方書并料理書	Books on manners and cookery	11
Meisho zukushi 名所尽	Books on famous places	28
Kyōka-shū narabi ni hanashibon 狂歌集并咄本	Collections of *kyōka* poetry and jestbooks	14

Based on data in Laura Moretti, "The Japanese Early-Modern Publishing Market Unveiled: A Survey of Edo-Period Booksellers' Catalogues," *East Asian Publishing and Society* 2, no. 2 (2012): 269–72. The wording of the categories is based on the table of contents of the 1670 catalogue. Note that the wording for the same publishing genre could change slightly from catalogue to catalogue as well as within the same catalogue. I have made them consistent with the wording in this table for the sake of comparison.

These, I argue, constituted the bulk of the popular products issued by publishers that now sought to cater to the needs of an expanding readership equipped with kana-mainly literacy. The sorting of *sōshi* did not occur until 1685, when the book-trade catalogue for that year added *monogatari-rui* (*monogatari*-type books). Many titles—interestingly, not all—including the word *monogatari* were moved from *sōshi* to the *monogatari-rui* category, while titles containing the word *sōshi* tended to be retained in this typology. The few titles dealing with sexually charged material appearing in *sōshi* before 1685 became a completely independent publishing genre in the form of *kōshoku narabi ni rakuji* (erotica and diversions). These were an equally intrinsic part of the world of popular prose.⁸⁸ While a degree of reorganization was thus ensured, the haphazard and protean nature of these publishing genres never entirely disappeared, confirming what I mentioned earlier: they inherently lacked the systematicity we would expect from a modern genre. *Sōshi* and the other categories born from its sorting add to those in table 2.3 in providing us with the contours of seventeenth-century popular prose, the kind of prose that had the potential to engage novice readers with kana-mainly literacy.

A note of caution needs to be sounded at this point. It would be incorrect to assume that the publishing genres in *shojaku mokuroku* constitute the entire corpus of literature available to the seventeenth-century reader. First, titles published in Kyoto by the same publishers that feature in book-trade catalogues can be missing from the catalogues, although it is not entirely clear why this happens. For this reason the following chapters examine also titles that were not listed in book-trade catalogues. Second, other important text typologies of seventeenth-century vernacular literature are omitted in book-trade catalogues, most notably the already mentioned picture books (*kusazōshi*) and *kawaraban* news sheets.⁸⁹ This was most likely because they were printed and issued by *sōshiya* publishers who were not part of the network involved in the making of book-trade catalogues. Even though I have chosen not to consider these titles as part of my analysis—*kawaraban* from this century have hardly survived and the few *kusazōshi* picture books issued in this timeframe have already been examined in some detail—we must consider them as an integral part of seventeenth-century popular prose.

A Range of Book Prices

Were these types of books affordable? Sadly, no prices are listed on the covers, in the colophons, or elsewhere in the books. It is in the 1681 book-trade catalogue issued by the Edo publisher Yamada Kihee 山田喜兵衛 that book prices were indicated for the first time. The presence of prices became a feature of alphabetically ordered Edo and Kyoto catalogues well into the eighteenth century.⁹⁰ They are to be viewed as retailers' prices, which helps to gauge how much a single buyer would have had to pay in order to purchase a specific title.⁹¹ But their nature is relative, as explained by Yamada Kihee: "The addition of the prices applies only to books that are of inferior quality. The prices of medium-quality and high-quality books vary according to the quality of the paper. Therefore, I have not included them here."⁹² Kawachiya Rihee 河内屋利兵衛, in his 1696 catalogue, reiterates the point, adding a brief remark about shipping costs: "I have listed the prices. Since they vary according to paper quality and shipping costs to distant provinces, it is difficult to give any exact price. I have listed them approximately."⁹³ As these observations suggest, catalogues provide us with the most basic prices, and we must accept that fluctuations would apply on the basis of type of paper and a book's destination. To this we must add the intrinsic complexity of the Edo-period monetary system, as aptly noted by Peter F. Kornicki.[94] While fully acknowledging the many pitfalls in trying to gain meaningful information about the cost of books in the seventeenth century, I think that some preliminary estimates can help in forming our view of the commercial book market at this time.

A sense of what constituted the actual value of money during the seventeenth century is not an easy task because the information about prices is scant and far from systematic. We do have a few records around the Meireki era (1655–1658), but it must be kept in mind that prices escalated as a result of the Great Meireki Fire that destroyed much of Edo in 1657. The *bakufu* issued an edict specifying the cost of labor (*temachin*): three silver *monme* a day for high-quality tradesmen, including carpenters, roofers, and masons, and two silver *monme* for qualified sawyers.[95] Albeit slightly later, we know that the daily payment for tradesmen (the type of which is unspecified) was one *monme* five *fun* (silver) in Kyoto in 1710 and two *monme* four *fun* (silver) in 1715 in Edo.[96] We also have a sense of how much a maidservant, responsible for tasks such as cooking rice, fetching water, and repairing clothes, would earn annually: half a gold *ryō* (about twenty-five silver *monme*) in the Kan'ei era (1624–1644), one gold *ryō* (approximately fifty silver *monme*) in the years 1661–1673, and one and a half *ryō* (ca. 75/80 silver *monme*) in the Hōei era (1704–1711).[97] Commodities such as one *koku* of white rice (ca. 180 liters = 125 kilos) was priced at eighty *monme* six *fun* in the spring (Edo, 1710) and sixty-nine *monme* nine *fun* in the autumn (Edo, 1710). And the same quantity of salt was thirty-eight *monme* three *fun* (Edo, 1710), while one *kan* 貫 (3.75 kilos) of miso was one *monme* three *fun* (Edo, 1710).[98] We also know that a bowl of *chazuke*, steamed rice seasoned with hot tea, in a shop near Asakusa Temple was five silver *fun* in around 1693, while slightly earlier in the Kanbun era a bowl of soba was sixteen copper *mon* (later increased to twenty and twenty-four *mon*).[99] In 1688, a Kyoto resident could purchase a whole sea bream (*tai*)—certainly not an everyday food—for two *monme* and four or five *fun*.[100]

These prices of various commodities provide a benchmark against which we can try to make sense of book prices as recorded in catalogues. For instance, the 1681 catalogue records the price for the Confucian text in *kanbun* titled *Shisho taizen*, which we saw publicized in *Inu Hyakunin isshu*. An ambitious work in twenty-two volumes, it was priced at fifty-five silver *monme* (I assume that all prices are in silver). Later, in the 1696 catalogue, there are two different version of *Shisho taizen*: one in eighteen volumes for thirty-five *monme* and another in twenty-two volumes for sixty *monme*. Even though this type of work would probably have held little interest to a tradesman or maidservant, it would have cost the former at least one month of wages, if not more, and the latter almost a year's income. This is not to say, however, that all the books in *kanbun* were expensive. For example, *Kōkyō* (*The Classic of Filial Piety*) was available in the 1681 catalogue in different formats and at different prices. A single volume of the Chinese text without annotations was as little as eight *fun* (decreased to five *fun* in the 1696 catalogue). It was as much as a bowl of *chazuke* in Asakusa. The version with katakana was slightly higher (one *monme*), and the annotated commentary *Kōkyō taizen* (The great collection of *The Classic of Filial Piety*) in ten volumes was priced at twenty-five *monme* (sixteen *monme* in the 1696 catalogue). Similarly, *Daigaku* (*The Great Learning*) was available at five *fun* without reading marks, at seven *fun* if you wanted reading marks by the leading Confucian scholar Hayashi Razan 林羅山 (1583–1657), and up to eight *monme* for the five-volume version with explanations added in the vernacular (in katakana; the so-called *zokkai* version).

Books in the vernacular equally offered a range in prices. For instance, in 1681 the Kyoto guidebook *Kyō suzume* (The Kyoto sparrow), mentioned in the previous chapter, was available in seven volumes for seven *monme*, with the price decreasing to four *monme* five *fun* in 1696. The two-volume 1638 *Kiyomizu monogatari* (The Kiyomizu tale), mentioned in chapter 1, was priced at one *monme* seven *fun* in the 1681 catalogue and one *monme* five *fun* in 1696. Two other popular books in the Edo period, *Chikusai* and *Ikkyū banashi* (Stories about Ikkyū) were even cheaper: the two-volume *Chikusai* was one *monme* eight *bu* (one *monme* five *fun* in 1696), while the four-volume *Ikkyū banashi* was two *monme* (one *monme* seven *fun* in 1696). We are talking about one or two days of work for a tradesman in Edo soon after the Meireki fire. If we keep in mind that Ihara Saikaku's best-selling *Kōshoku ichidai otoko* in five volumes was priced at five *monme* in the 1696 catalogue, we realize that the texts mentioned here were relatively cheap.

Prices dropped further for other types of books. The previously mentioned *Shogaku bunshō narabi ni yorozu shitsukekata* sold for five *fun* for one volume (reduced to three *fun* in 1696). Muromachi tales and *kōwakamai* were within the same range. *Kagekiyo*, for example, was sold for eight *fun*, as was *Shida*, *Fuji no hitoana sōshi*, and *Tengu no dairi* in the 1681 catalogue. Single-sheet, poorly printed *kawaraban* were at the very bottom of the price ladder, and at the end of the seventeenth century their cost was reportedly around five or six *mon*.[101] In sum, books in the vernacular were available for a range of prices.

In-depth research on the cost of books in the Edo period is much needed, and the figures proposed here—based on several assumptions—might well be challenged. Yet my core argument should stand: the publishing market offered diverse materials for every taste and every pocket. A reader might have thought twice about spending a weekly wage on a book, but there may well have been less hesitation in purchasing a useful household manual for less than the cost of a bowl of *chazuke*. Hoping that future research will shed more light on this complex topic, I provide in the following chapters (in notes) indications of the cost of the books I have chosen for my close-reading analysis.[102]

Publishers and booksellers saw a unique business opportunity in printing and selling books catering to a broad spectrum of needs of a society that encouraged engagement with the written word. As early as the first half of the seventeenth century, Kyoto witnessed the flourishing of a considerable number of commercial publishers active in producing books in the vernacular. It might be a *shomotsuya*, such as Nakano Dōya or Nishimura Matazaemon, active in issuing highbrow books in *kanbun* as well as lowbrow materials in Japanese, or a *sōshiya*, such as Yamamoto Kyūbee, who focused almost exclusively on the publication of cheaper items often related to the world of *jōruri* theater. Over time, their shops became an integral part of the urban landscape celebrated in text and image, and a testimony to the central role they played in city life. Edo and Osaka would shortly follow in joining this new commercial and cultural trend.

During an era when writers of books in the vernacular were yet to be elevated to the status of celebrity authors and had very little or no consciousness of their intellectual rights over the written word, publishers were the real movers and shakers. Books were packaged and repackaged with linguistic and bibliographic variations in response to the ever-changing tastes and needs of a growing public.

In an attempt to organize their products and stimulate readers' interests, publishers in the second half of the seventeenth century issued book-trade catalogues that organized titles into what I refer to as publishing genres. Mapping these publishing genres, while adding to them other categories (namely, *kusazōshi* and *kawaraban*) excluded from the catalogues, has enabled us to grasp the contours of popular literature at this time. Publishers set prices of printed matter that would appeal to a diverse clientele, and books were available to suit all sorts of incomes. Despite the fact that sources of the period do not depict commoners browsing in bookshops, the sheer number of publishers and books that catered to the interests of both expert and novice readers, as well as the range in prices, attests to a printing industry that was opening up to a growing and diversified readership.

CHAPTER 3

Negotiating the Way

*On the strength of their studies, good people rely on
the echo of the waves initiated by the wise men of the past
and clean themselves in the pure stream of those waves.*

—Katayama Naotsugu, *Makura no hibiki* (Pillow's echoes)

Book-trade catalogues underscore the centrality occupied by Buddhism in the cultural universe of seventeenth-century Japan. In an age when the affiliation to a Buddhist temple was turned into a must and individuals became embedded in something akin to a parish system, the publishing market was inundated by scholarly publications dealing with Buddhism.[1] Of the 2,713 titles included in the first *shojaku mokuroku* of 1666–1667, 1,186 are Buddhist texts in *kanbun* (see table 2.2). In other words, some 43.7 percent of the books published in Kyoto during this period were Buddhist related, and this percentage is confirmed in the 1670 book-trade catalogue in which 1,688 (43.7 percent) of the 3,862 titles pertain to Buddhism. It is only later—in the 1692 catalogue—that the figure starts decreasing, to around 39 percent.[2] These titles were organized in separate categories labeled according to Buddhist schools, thus echoing the new sense of sectarianism fueled by scholasticism, which Richard Bowring asserts characterizes early modern

Buddhism.³ The "Confucian turn" and the increasing interest in Chinese learning were equally mirrored in the publishing business.⁴ *Geten* or *jusho* were the labels used for Confucian texts written in *kanbun*. It should also be noted that the percentages they occupied in the grand scheme of things were considerably smaller: 247 (1666–1667; 9.1 percent), 136 (1670; 3.5 percent), and 353 (1692; 5.2 percent) titles.

When summed together, Buddhist and Confucian texts in literary Chinese made up more than half of the book market. This towering figure suggests the existence of a stable readership of this kind of erudite texts. It is easy to imagine that the clientele depicted in the images discussed in the previous chapter—made up mostly of monks and samurai—would have been the ideal target for these publications. It is difficult to envisage any appeal for readers equipped with kana-mainly literacy, though, simply because of the linguistic barrier of literary Chinese. Yet it is equally hard to imagine complete disengagement with these two Ways that so greatly shaped devotion and morality in daily life. After all, vernacular Buddhism had already infused the life of a vast number of people in medieval times, and Chinese learning was championed not only as the Way of the Sage but also as the Way of Man.⁵ This is not so different from the situation in early modern Europe, where religion (i.e., Christianity and its many forms) played a central role in the lives of men and women from all social backgrounds; however, Latin hindered many from accessing sacred texts. The solution was in the development of "popular piety," in which religious readings written in vernacular languages and using a variety of textual devices to enhance accessibility and understanding were produced in the hundreds.⁶ Vernacular translations of Buddhist and Confucian texts were an important phenomenon across East Asia.⁷

Seventeenth-century Japanese publishers saw a business opportunity in marketing Buddhist and Confucian texts packaged to negotiate the Ways for the benefit of a wider range of readers. *Kana washo*, or "Japanese books in the vernacular," appeared as a stand-alone category for the first time in the 1670 book-trade catalogue and was accompanied by headings identifying the contents as "Books on the Five Virtues" (*gojō-sho*), "Books on Filial Piety" (*kōkō-sho*), "Books on Learning of the Mind" (*shingaku*), and "Educational Books" (*kyōkun-sho*). In other words, *kana washo* referred specifically to didactic texts that focused on teachings usually associated with Confucianism.

For Buddhist works, publishers issued *kana bussho*, which also appears as a stand-alone category beginning with the 1670 catalogue. The choice of the word *kana* advised the reader that these Buddhist texts (*bussho*) were written in the vernacular. Interestingly, no mention is made of specific Buddhist schools, which suggests that the treatment of *kana bussho* was transsectarian, possibly an echo of medieval popular Buddhism.⁸ Another term used interchangeably in the same catalogue, and in later ones, for this category is *hōgo* (or *kana hōgo*). The oldest-known title with this term is *Yokawa hōgo* (Dharma talks at Yokawa; probably composed between 985 and 1017), written by the Tendai monk Genshin 源信 (942–1017). As *Yokawa hōgo* exemplifies, *hōgo* were vernacular texts that explained Buddhist thought in a manner that a broad readership could easily digest.[9] Although *hōgo*, which developed as a genre beginning in the eleventh century, might be perceived as corresponding to medieval Buddhist literature, I argue that its popularity continued well into the Edo period and that it was marketed as a publishing genre geared at early modern popular readers. It is worth mentioning that the contents of *kana hōgo* (as I call them in the following) are described in the 1670 catalogue as follows: *shoshū hōgo* (vernacular Dharma talks for all schools), *inga monogatari* (tales of karmic causality), and *jubutsuron* (debates between Confucianism and Buddhism).

Inasmuch as these two publishing genres have probably been judged too prosaic to be examined as part of the history of Japanese religion and too dry to be discussed as a form of literature, we know virtually nothing about them. Yet as I see it, they must have occupied an important place in the cultural imagination of readers to justify publishers' investment in the publication and marketing of such works in the first place.

This chapter explores the aesthetics of appropriation at play in the commodification of Buddhism and Confucianism. By conducting a close reading of selected primary sources across *kana washo* and *kana hōgo* I map the techniques employed in this corpus of didactic literature to make a plurality of knowledges accessible to and engaging for a public that also includes novice readers with kana-mainly literacy. In the process I reflect on the creative methods put in place to "translate" the Buddhist canon, in a way that enhanced comprehension over performativity. I also highlight the synergies that put these two publishing genres in dialogue, probing how at a popular level Buddhism and Confucianism were interpreted with a view to promoting a nonconfrontational, harmonious view of social morality. The motif running through the chapter is a desire to forge "people worth being called human" (*hito taru mi*), to employ an apt expression from the 1688 *Makura no hibiki*.[10] Described in book-trade catalogues as "a tale about the Five Virtues," it well summarizes the wisdom unlocked by the texts analyzed in this chapter. "The attitude of a person worthy of being called human is careful not to go against the path of the correct Way. Those who, without fail, do not put into place the correct behavior will not perform the role that is expected from a human being."[11] The knowledge that *kana washo* and *kana hōgo* embody is not framed as "national" knowledge. It is not a matter of forging "Japanese people" or "Nihon," as claimed by Mary Elizabeth Berry with regard to other publishing genres at the time.[12] It is rather a matter of assisting readers in becoming well-rounded human beings.

Mirrors for a Righteous Life

As part of the Confucian turn that characterized seventeenth-century Japan, scholars of Chinese learning engaged in activities designed to popularize Confucian (and neo-Confucian) thought and texts. A scholar of the caliber of Hayashi Razan, for example, was active in the production of *genkai* (vernacular explanations) versions of Chinese texts.[13] In these, he normally provided the original wording in *kanbun* with *kunten* marks and added the text in Japanese after it, using a mixture of kanji and katakana. In other adaptations known as *waji kai* or *waji shō*, katakana was replaced in favor of the easier hiragana. Yet the fact that the majority of these titles were available only in manuscript form makes us wonder how much Hayashi Razan intended his efforts to reach a wide readership.[14] In order to explore more radical forms in the popularization of Confucianism we must therefore look elsewhere. Two fascinating examples written in the vernacular, *Mi no kagami* (A mirror for yourself; 1659) and *Rihi kagami* (A mirror of right and wrong behavior; 1664), by Ejima Tamenobu 江島為信 (1635–1695), are particularly revealing.[15]

Originally from Hyūga Province in Kyushu, Ejima Tamenobu was a ronin until 1668, when he became an officer in the Imabari domain in Shikoku. He signed his works produced before this official appointment as *hyōhaku yajin*, or "wandering countryman," a reflection of his peripatetic life during these years.[16] It is reported that he studied the art of war (*heihō*) in Kyoto before moving to Osaka, where he lived in the vicinity of a sword smith named Inoue Shinkai. His publications generally mirror interest in the military arts, and of the ten titles attributed to Ejima to date, five relate to *heihō* and more generally *gunsho*, including *Kokon gunri mondō* (Dialogues on the principles of warfare past and present; 1665). He was also conversant with the world of haikai, composing poetry under the name Ejima Sansui.

His writing demonstrates an extensive knowledge of Chinese learning. Unfortunately, no record remains as to where, how, and under whose guidance he mastered this specific field, but it is clear that he was a committed Confucianist resistant to any form of syncretism. He condemns Buddhism as heresy and urges his readers to choose Confucianism over Buddhism.[17] Ejima not only was a purist in his belief that the two traditions should not be combined but also advocated a line of thought that appears in perfect unison with neo-Confucianism. On more than one occasion he homed in on a concept central to neo-Confucianism: the nature (*sei*, *honshō*, or *hontai*) of human beings is fundamentally good, "with no clouds whatsoever," because Heaven (*ten*) and human beings share the same "pattern" or "principle" (*ri*).[18] This, however, is influenced by materiality (*kishitsu*). It depends on which way materiality leans whether a person remains good or becomes bad. "If one draws one's heart toward the good, virtue [*zenshin*] will be generated. If one draws one's heart toward the bad, greed [*yokushin*] will be generated."[19] And because good is like a foul-tasting medicine and evil is like a sweet poison, humans tend to choose the latter. In all this, desire (*butsuyoku*) plays a hugely detrimental part. To make this concept more palatable, Ejima uses an apt analogy:

> [In the beginning], the sun and the moon are not clouded. But from time to time floating clouds cover their bright light. Because neither the sun nor the moon is intrinsically overcast, once the clouds have disappeared, they resume shining. Similarly, the nature of human beings is also extremely radiant. Occasionally desire covers that radiance. Because light is intrinsic to human nature, if only one cleanses desire and throws it away, the good of one's nature will shine again.[20]

The project undertaken by Ejima in his vernacular writings aims at assisting people to find ways to cleanse materiality and regain the original brightness of a good nature. The focus is unmistakably on the here and now. While Buddhism encourages people to pray for the afterlife, or so at least Ejima maintains, he urges his readers to take action on their present life.[21] His books are there to guide readers in this quest. They are framed as transformative literature.

The choice of the word *kagami* (mirror) in both titles is not coincidental—looking at other people's examples offer the opportunity for self-reflection.[22] Ejima writes these two mirrors in vernacular Japanese and has them commercially published at an affordable price. The presence of half-folio, ancillary illustrations serving to intersperse the verbal text is also significant.[23] As Maria Nikolajeva observes in her work on Western children's literature, research on how the brain functions has shown that "visual perception is evolutionarily hard-wired in our brain," enabling a visual stimulus to be quicker and stronger than a verbal one.[24] Although children do not make up the readership dealt with here, the presence of something as direct and immediate as images could have been used as a gimmick to beckon the less-experienced readers.[25] Ejima and his publishers fully exploited the technology available at the time to dress up scholarly contents in a way that would have attracted readers beyond those already au fait with Confucian knowledge in literary Chinese. Ejima's motivation in this enterprise lay in an aversion to secret traditions and a desire to open up knowledge to everyone. His belief that knowledge should be made available is advocated quite forcibly in *Rihi monogatari*:

> In today's world people want to keep secret [*hiji himitsu*] even the smallest things. This is because they want to be considered knowledgeable by everyone. But this is not the right Way [*daidō*]. When one knows something that is good,

one should teach it to others. Likewise, one should learn about good things that other people know. It is by being honest and sympathetic [*chūjo*] that one can be successful in all sorts of things.²⁶

What textual structures does Ejima employ in his mirrors to make knowledge (Confucian knowledge) accessible to a broad readership and to engage his readers? First, texts are made digestible by chopping them down into snippets that can be perused at one's leisure. *Mi no kagami* is divided into thirty-eight short, independent sections and *Rihi kagami* into thirty-two. Both are accompanied by a handy table of contents that puts readers in a position to pick and choose. The loose structure of both mirrors calls to mind that of *zuihitsu* (miscellanies), and the intertextual effort is revealed by Ejima in the closing section of *Mi no kagami*, where he rephrases the opening of *Tsurezuregusa* by stating, "In moments of idleness, I made my inkstone sing, I dipped my brush in the ink and have thus composed this draft."²⁷ The choice of the miscellany format is significant also because it is a key feature of many of the texts discussed in my study. Second, in *Rihi kagami* Ejima offers what I read as an attempt to prompt emotional engagement in his readers by employing an almost autobiographical register. Terms like *yo* and *yatsugare*, both denoting the first person, punctuate the text to remind the reader that what is being read is nothing more than Ejima's own experiences recounted through Ejima's voice. Readers are invited to adopt the perspective of the first-person narrator and experience his memories not only by listening to his voice but also by viewing him in action in the illustrations. The anonymous illustrator has tried his very best in the third volume to make Ejima's figure identifiable by giving him individual physical and facial features as well as by furnishing him with a kimono that always displays the same crest.²⁸ The decision to portray him as a young boy in two instances—as a seven-year-old boy who has survived an encounter with two thieves in the second volume and as a child of four to five, depicted together with his pet turtle and conversing with his mother in the third—has the potential to heighten viewers' empathy.²⁹ The third strategy lies in a rather nonconventional use of the dialogical format.³⁰ In *Rihi kagami* Ejima's narrative persona is frequently depicted in dialogue with family, friends, guests, and strangers. In the mainstream didactic dialogical format, as I discuss later in this chapter, interlocutors were normally used as a tool for the author to pose a series of questions and the main character as the voice of the author dispensing knowledge while answering them. In *Rihi kagami*, however, everyone is entitled to a voice and Ejima is not hesitant in presenting himself as less learned than the other characters. In my view this is a powerful choice advocating knowledge as something created by everyone for everyone and not something imparted from above. Ejima's world allows all sorts of people to be the teachers, and he learns himself about *ri* from all types of people: beggars, an old woman, and an old man whose name he does not know.³¹ Whether this is fictional or autobiographical is a matter of speculation. Yet the intellectual implications of this choice are intriguing. While Ejima does not push any overt political agenda in his two mirrors, the decision to endow people of all sorts with a didactic persona suggests a rather titillating idea of egalitarianism. Finally, Ejima opts for a vernacular prose that incorporates a few quotations in Chinese (in *kanbun* with *kunten* marks) from Confucian texts. While making sure to draw upon textual authority, Ejima is true to his own teachings and strives to make these sources comprehensible to all levels of readers. He does so by providing quasi-interlinear translations in vernacular Japanese (with reading glosses appended to single characters), full interlinear translations, or a mixture of the two, as can be seen, for example, in *Mi no kagami* (fig. 3.1). (These are techniques that I have examined in some detail in chapter 1.) Whenever he thinks it appropriate, Ejima even adds an easier paraphrase of the same passage.

What teachings do we gather from *Mi no kagami* and *Rihi kagami*? They are rooted in the idea of *gakumon*, which is presented as a person's most important endeavor. Ejima's view of *gakumon* confirms what I described in the first chapter: it is not merely a matter of erudition; rather, knowledge must be acquired in order to behave correctly within society: "The Way of learning [*gakumon no michi*] implies what follows. By discovering what is good for people and in people, you take that good, make it your own, look back on your evil, and throw it away. You serve your parents and are devoted to filial piety. You undertake your duties toward a master without any negligence. You mingle with friends with honesty. This is what *gakumon* entails."³² Learning can begin at any age and should take prominence over other activities, including poetry composition.³³ While advocating the importance of study in the pursuit of virtuous behavior, Ejima does acknowledge how difficult this can be. In *Mi no kagami* he notes that at the outset *gakumon* can be tedious. He strives to create an emotional bond with his readers by recalling his own experience as a young boy:

> When confronted with books at a tender age I would yawn and succumb to a headache. For that reason, I did not do any studying, spending my time singing the latest songs, wandering around aimlessly, and generally having fun. Afterward this resulted in terrible mistakes. Also, I would feel embarrassed whenever I had to appear in front of people. A certain man gave me a lesson: "By all means do study!" But because of my chronic headaches and because I would get dizzy, I gave up. He reproached me by saying, "By all means do study, even if that means putting your life in jeopardy!" At that point I had an epiphany. Day and night I would fight back the headaches and the dizziness, applying myself to the study of books. With time, even the headaches disappeared.³⁴

The underlying message is clear and full of hope: endure the initial hardship and you will become accustomed to studying. It worked for Ejima and so could work for anyone. Readers not used to studying are put in a position to understand Ejima's feelings by connecting them to emotionally charged memories of their own, and the positive message is likely to resonate deeply.[35] We are at the intersection of two modes—the experiential and the exemplary, where the former almost seamlessly turns into the latter. Ejima offers another warning, which is that *gakumon* must be pursued with the right attitude, not simply because one wants to become famous and respected.[36] For him the worst mistake that one can make is to preach one thing and do another, or to feign knowledge when there is none: "To feign knowledge when one does not know is truly despicable. . . . Pitiful are those who do not understand the principle whereby wisdom is 'to recognize what you know as what you know, and recognize what you do not know as what you do not know.'"[37] Because *gakumon* must be undertaken with a view to embracing good and rejecting evil, Ejima also encourages his readers to mingle with good-hearted people and to imitate them. The key is to do this with a truthful heart.[38]

Another prime teaching for Ejima is to avoid excess. For example, while love is what distinguishes sentient beings from wood or stones and should thus be cherished, lustful behavior will only cause greater misfortune. This begins with being negligent in your own duties and spending all your fortune.[39] As the saying goes, "One should not give in to alcohol or women."[40] Yet if alcohol is consumed in small amounts, it does have certain merits. It warms you up on a cold winter's day and helps you to forget the heaviness in your legs during a long, tiring journey. To drink in moderation is therefore fine, but excess leads to dangerous behavior and misfortune. Similarly, a knowledge of poetry also has its merits—in particular, it enriches a person's vocabulary. Although not as severe an obsession as prostitutes and gambling, a preoccupation with poetry is equally bad.[41] Compared with *Ukiyo monogatari* (Tales of the Floating

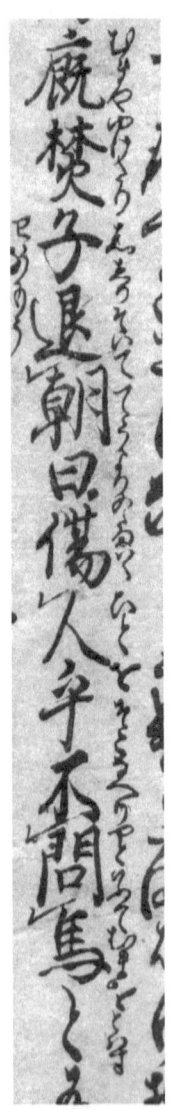

Figure 3.1 Detail from *Mi no kagami*, undated edition, 8v. A quotation from Confucius's *Analects* with Sinitic text accompanied by a mixture of a quasi-interlinear and full interlinear translation.

Author collection, Suzuran Bunko, Cambridge, U.K.

World), written by Asai Ryōi around 1665 and speaking, at least at first glance, to a new hedonistic approach to life, Ejima's message is cautionary:

> Eight or nine out of ten wealthy people are self-indulgent [*ogori*]. Without applying themselves even to study, they spend all their days going out. In spring, they go and enjoy the flowers. In the autumn they are preoccupied with moon viewing. They make sure to have delicious food and delectable sake. They devote themselves only to these kinds of foolish endeavors. When they do get down to studying, they chatter away, saying, "Amid the difficult teachings of old sages, lousy books, and the principle of impermanence, today's fun is the only happy thing in our uncertain life. How on earth can the teachings left by Chinese such as Confucius be of any help? Drinking and singing: this is what matters!" It is pitiful that people such as these do not understand the teaching "Having heard in the morning that the Way was being put into practice, I could die that evening without regret." What is worse, they give in to self-indulgence, they allure friends and drag them onto the same bad route.... Those who go against the pattern of Heaven [*tenri*] will be detested by Heaven, and they will not prosper for long.[42]

The knowledge of one's limits (*mi no hodo o shiru*) is key to achieving harmony with the pattern (*ri*) of Heaven, which in turn will bring happiness and prosperity.[43]

The pursuit of true learning and living life according to moderation are inward looking in that they imply enrichment of heart and mind. Yet Ejima also stressed the importance of mastering etiquette, since an individual should know how to greet people and, most notably, how to distinguish formal from informal situations.[44] When going to see Kabuki and *jōruri* one should not forget the social graces required to behave correctly as a member of the audience—namely, a spectator should remain quiet during the performance, neither shouting at unskillful actors nor engaging in fights with others.[45] In *Rihi kagami* Ejima recounts a colorful incident he witnessed firsthand as a way to illustrate the value of etiquette.[46] It is midsummer and very hot. When her husband is out, a mother of a toddler unties the sash of her kimono and lies down, with her child sleeping on her naked belly. This serene domestic scene is interrupted by her husband, who enters all of a sudden with a group of friends. The shame he feels at his wife's disheveled appearance being revealed to others is such that he writes a letter of divorce because he maintains that his wife is guilty of not knowing how to behave properly (*busahō*). The situation is saved by the intervention of an old man, who cites a tale in which Mencius was also going to leave his wife for having committed the same mistake, but his mother reminds him that a man should always announce himself upon entering a house. In this case, Ejima not only supports the significance of knowing the forms of etiquette but also demonstrates the potential inherent in the Confucian classics for helping to regulate social life.

While all these teachings constitute the substance of Ejima's mirrors, other advice is equally offered here and there. Funerals, for instance, seem to intrigue him. It is not the afterlife that interests him, since he believes this is the domain of the heretic Buddhists. It is instead the practical issue of ensuring a decorous funeral in accordance with a person's social obligations. A woman who has just lost her husband laments the fact that she was able to provide only a pitiful funeral. Ejima offers her comfort by explaining that the etiquette surrounding funerals depends on the financial circumstances of a household and that she should be content to have had a funeral within the means at her disposal.[47] He also clarifies that, as Confucius states, providing a burial for your parents is an act of filial piety.[48] But the burial rites must be accomplished according to one's finances. This agrees with what Sakai Tadao identifies as a basic principle of prescribed rituals in Confucianism and is a concrete application of the broader teaching of "knowing one's limits."[49]

Filial piety (*kōkō*) features together with compassion as two key virtues. They both emerge in two autobiographical passages (or so claimed) in *Rihi kagami*, where Ejima explores a more personalized didactic mode, imbued with experience. In the first volume Ejima recalls intimate moments spent with his mother as a young boy.[50] One evening, he chats with his mother about his favorite activities: singing and fighting with other boys. His mother reprimands him for the latter and tells him to stop playing in such a manner. Although he promises to relinquish these bad ways, he does not and keeps this secret from his mother. His father and older brother then begin to tell him to concentrate solely on his studying, but as a young boy he felt great bitterness toward what he perceived to be a stifling lifestyle. And when he was adopted into another family, he preferred spending time with his stepfather because he was less strict. It was only later in life, after having lived many years far away from his real parents, that he realized how foolish he had been in leaving his parents alone, and he deeply regretted his lack of filial piety. That explains why he strongly advocates the importance of being filial. Filial piety is not only about ensuring that your parents have food and drink; it also means that you should never disobey your parents, raise your voice against them, or become angry with them.[51] And what about compassion? Again Ejima's mother seems to have played a central part in teaching him the importance of being kind to all creatures.[52] In *Rihi kagami*, Ejima recalls catching a turtle to keep as a pet. One rainy night, his mother urges him to release the turtle, as its own mother would be worried about it. Ejima is, for the first time, awakened to feelings of compassion for a living creature and immediately sets the turtle free. These examples offer a glimpse into how parents could and should have an active role in equipping their children with the right education to follow the Way of *ri* (interpreted here as "right behavior") and reject *hi* (wrong behavior).⁵³ Ejima teaches his readers on the strength of his personal experience and in the process depicts his mother as a perfectly suitable didactic authority. Once again, learning (*gakumon*) is presented as something that can (and should) be acquired outside books, in the interaction with people. On this occasion *gakumon* is anchored not only to the world of interpersonal interaction and aurality but also to that of domesticity.

While insisting upon key teachings of Chinese learning, Ejima engages also with more mundane interests. For example, he includes gripping episodes, such as how as a child he had managed to escape an awkward situation when journeying alone in a forest and encourages travelers to be alert.⁵⁴ He also reminds us that animals should be considered less significant than human beings, no matter how attached we might be to our beloved pets.⁵⁵ Much in the vein of *Makura no sōshi* and its early modern rewritings—namely, *Inu makura* and *Mottomo no sōshi*—he offers a list of despicable things.⁵⁶ Reading is turned into a rewarding activity, where the pleasure lies in both the acquisition of knowledge, which can be translated into righteous action, and in the enjoyment of a plurality of topics. In this way, efferent and aesthetic engagements work in tandem to make the reading experience gratifying.

Altogether, the reader can peruse Ejima's mirrors to gain grounding in the ethical, social, and interpersonal knowledge deemed necessary for responsible human beings. Ejima's writings not only package Confucian teachings to suit less-expert readers but also try to create an emotional bond with his readers by acknowledging their weaknesses and by investing them with a meaningful voice.

Confucianism and Buddhism in Dialogue

While Ejima championed Confucianism and rejected Buddhism as heresy, other seventeenth-century books conveyed an interest in comparing, contrasting, and evaluating these two intellectual traditions. This resulted either in the promotion of one tradition to the detriment of the other or, more often, in the celebration of harmonious syncretism. The dialogical format was an ideal structure for both. Yet these texts move away from an inclusive conversation that entitles everyone to a voice, as we have seen in Ejima's work, to a more traditional structure in which an inexperienced interlocutor asks questions of a wise, learned, and enlightened person.

A revealing example of a dialogue comparing Buddhism and Confucianism is the extremely popular *Kiyomizu monogatari*, first published in 1638.⁵⁷ The structure of the two volumes is based on a series of dialogues, which the first-person narrator appears to have witnessed. The first dialogue occurs between a pilgrim visiting Kiyomizu Temple and an old man. The pilgrim is eager to learn and asks a series of questions to assist him in achieving enlightenment.[58] The old man alerts his interlocutor to the value of other teachings. While the Five Virtues and the Five Relations, inherently Confucian in nature, are immutable, laws (*okite*) must change as society advances. The primary duty is to "improve one's bad heart," and the first step in this direction reverts to *gakumon*. At the same time, those who are worthy to be called human beings (*hito taru hito*) must master the Way of Man (*hito no michi*). Familiarity with concepts like *honmatsu zengo* (knowing who is above and who is below in the Five Relations) and *sōō* (harmony) are pivotal in this process. We are constantly reminded that the key to all this resides in a willingness to improve oneself and to pursue learning with the main purpose of distinguishing between virtuous (*ri*) and inappropriate (*hi*) behavior. Reading extensively is not important per se. What is important, however, is to develop morally acceptable behavior. The consonance with the teachings offered in Ejima's mirrors should be immediately evident, and the decision to frame them in a Buddhist context suggests a penchant for syncretism.

The dialogue pauses briefly when the pilgrim suggests eating something. The text mentions the delicacy of grilled rice cakes filled with bean paste (*yaki mochi*) that could be purchased around Kiyomizu Temple. Even an apparently innocent act like buying and consuming food is used as an opportunity to dispense teachings. The old man deplores the fact that the bean paste is so thick and the rice so thin, making the point that they should not be called rice cakes but instead "bean paste": "Since there are many lies regarding something like this, which can be purchased for a coin, imagine how much deception is around us in all sorts of things," he says, crying.[59] Hearing this, everyone around him bursts into tears. The humor that derives from the exaggerated reaction to the thin rice cakes helps to register the underlying teaching that mendacity is unacceptable.

The dialogue resumes with a discussion about *yūmin*, those numerous idle people who are in all the four estates (samurai, peasant, artisan, and merchant) and who jeopardize the quality of society as a whole. The social criticism continues with reflections upon teachers, friends, and courage until dawn breaks and both the old man and the pilgrim depart.[60] During the course of this discussion we lose sight of the first-person narrator.

The second volume is titled *Gekō* (On the way home), and we assume that the narrator (*yo*, or "I") is heading home. In this volume the unnamed narrator operates like a video camera that moves and captures snapshots of people engaged in various conversations that take place at different locations, including a tea shop, Kyōkakudō, and Gion-bayashi.[61] Among the highlights of the many topics debated is the practice of following one's master into death (*oibara-kiri*), which once again echoes Ejima's work, and the social issue of masterless samurai (ronin) is also touched on.

Emoto Hiroshi considers the entire text as one that "explains how each person should correct their behavior, advises about the differences in lifestyles and bravery of country leaders, chief councillors, military commanders, teachers, friends, and takes up problems specific to samurai."[62] In other words, *Kiyomizu monogatari* operates as an instruction manual for people on how to live successfully in society, very much in the vein of Ejima's mirrors. What stands out is the decision to evaluate Buddhism vis-à-vis Confucianism in the short passage that opens the second volume.[63]

The text introduces a Buddhist monk among the crowds of pilgrims going to the temple in the morning as the first-person narrator is leaving. This monk, perhaps an abbot, delivers a sermon as he makes his way:

> There are many teachings that are part of the traditions of learning outside Buddhism [*geten*], but they are limited to the Three Bonds and the Five Virtues [*sankō gojō*]. The Three Bonds are those of ruler-subject, father-child, and husband-wife. The Five Virtues—benevolence, righteousness, propriety, wisdom, and trustworthiness—should be exercised within those bonds. All this pertains to realm of the here and now [*kono yo ni aru uchi no koto*].[64]

What jeopardizes the validity of these teachings, the monk explains, is the realization that everything is impermanent: the fate of those who engage in reading books and in composing Chinese poetry—a reference to hard-core Confucians—is no different from everyone else's in that they will be buried, their voices will be unheard, and they will face the terrifying king of the underworld, Enma, and his book of reckoning. The warning that emerges is clear, "In this transient world there is no point in polishing one's heart. Apply yourself to ensure a positive future after death and pray for the afterlife."[65] The monk launches into a tirade against the value of the Three Bonds and the Five Virtues since they are all meaningless when seen in the context of a life as precarious as a candle in the wind. "Just pray that the long life [after death] be a happy one."[66]

In a text like *Kiyomizu monogatari*, which embraces an intellectual stance similar to Ejima's, it is hardly surprising to see the monk's position challenged. An unidentified voice offers an effective analogy to express dissent: to simply hope for the afterlife is like trying to cross a river without a bridge or to sail on the sea without a boat. There is no point in thinking about the life to come if there is no way to head to tomorrow. The same voice defends the Three Bonds. Without the ruler-subject bond, this world will be chaos. Without the father-child bond, we would be no different from beasts. Without the husband-wife bond, there would be no human beings, including those who take the tonsure.[67]

The monk naturally feels enraged by such declarations and takes up the same metaphor of the boat to champion the Buddhist worldview:

> Reading sutras, building temples, and giving offerings to monks are the best types of boats and bridges to become a Buddha. There are no benefits for the afterlife, even if you know about the Way of this world [*kono yo no michi*]. The sutras explain that in moments of need we receive the Buddha's mercy, as when a boat comes to our rescue when crossing a river. This is referred to as "the boat of the pledge to aid human beings" [*guzei no fune*]. It is thanks to *kudoku* [meritorious acts and their blessings] that we receive assistance for the next life.[68]

At the core of the monk's worldview is faith in the Buddhas and in their pledge to help us. And faith manifests itself in specific acts, including the reading and recitation of the sutras (*kyō o yomu*). Embedded in the idea of *kudoku* are both meritorious acts, which people need in order to receive the mercy of the Buddhas and to secure the right to a happy afterlife, and the miraculous blessings bestowed upon those who act in this way. Central to the monk's view of the world is the concept of faith:

> If you just believe [*shinkō*] in Buddha, you will live a peaceful life in this world [*genze an'on*], you will avoid calamities, you will gain matchless comfort, and you will receive blessings from the Buddhas so that your family will happily prosper. In your afterlife you will go to the land of the Seven Treasures, where pillars are covered in gold and silver leaf. This is what we refer to as "the comfort in both lives" [*nise anraku*]. For those who have committed sins it is simply the case of reciting the *daimoku* [*namu myōhō rengekyō*] or the *nenbutsu* [*namu Amida butsu*] in order for their sins to be erased and to become good people. There is no need to follow the Way of this world. It is sufficient to entrust oneself to the means taken by Buddha to lead people [*hotoke no hōben ni makase*] and to have an honest heart [in doing so].[69]

By combining the different strands of Buddhist thought—namely, those of the Nichiren tradition and Pure Land Buddhism—the monk offers an easy recipe for happiness in this world and the next: believe in the Buddhas and their mercy.

The dialogue—close to a debate—between the monk and the man in *Kiyomizu monogatari* escalates into an impassioned exchange, in which the Confucian's supporter accuses the monk of being a hypocrite. After all, money and rice are needed in order to erect temples and to provide offerings to monks. But money and rice are nothing but treasures of this world and therefore should be jettisoned to focus instead on the next world. Nonetheless, Buddhist monks take full advantage of these worldly comforts. Criticism of Buddhism as nothing more than a moneymaking venture surfaces in other texts, often *kana hōgo*, and appears particularly strident in the 1659 *Minu kyō monogatari* (Tales of the unseen capital).⁷⁰ The section titled "A Dispute between Confucianism and Buddhism" (*jubutsu no ron*) stages a heated quarrel between a young Confucian scholar intent on delivering a lecture on the *Analects* and a monk accusing him of being ignorant of the principle of impermanence.⁷¹ The Confucian scholar fights back, accusing Buddhism of being organized as a clever way to secure donations. First, he blames Kumarajū (Kumārajīva) for turning to the translation of the Buddhist sutras from Sanskrit to Chinese as simply a way to make money.⁷² Then he criticizes Buddhist monks for cashing in on death by offering services to help dead people escape the horrors of hell and reach the joys of paradise. He goes even as far as to accuse Buddhism as comparable to the fake money that was circulating at this time.⁷³ The point I wish to make here is that overt social criticism inhabits these texts, alongside moral, social, and interpersonal knowledge.

In *Kiyomizu monogatari* the argument between the monk and the man has an unexpected, humorous outcome. The man unsheathes his sword and challenges the monk to prove that by invoking the name of the Buddha he will be saved from being killed. But the monk simply runs away, leaving the narrator to express his disappointment in not being able to witness the Buddhist promises of saving human beings in action. Although we might share the narrator's frustration that the prose does not turn into narrative action, it might be instructive here to reassess the view of Buddhism advocated in *Kiyomizu monogatari*. Buddhism fuels faith in the Buddhas and their miraculous blessings and this, in turn, ensures happiness in this life and the next. In *Kiyomizu monogatari*, this teaching is rejected in favor of the Way of Man.

Kiyomizu monogatari initiated a trend of dialogical texts comparing and evaluating Buddhism and Confucianism or different Buddhist schools of thought. *Gion monogatari* (The tale of Gion) is the first such text and is particularly interesting as it was conceived as a response to *Kiyomizu monogatari*.⁷⁴

Once again we are presented with a first-person narrator who reports what he hears, this time at Gion Shrine. Catching a glimpse of a private party that includes seven or eight monks, samurai, and townsmen, he decides to stop and listen to their conversation. The text reenacts the dialogue between a monk who has read *Kiyomizu monogatari* and another who asks to hear about the contents of this famous book that "people in the prime of their life [*sakari no hito*] are used to reading day and night."⁷⁵ The first monk ends up quoting verbatim all the passages of *Kiyomizu monogatari*, while the other comments on it. From time to time the samurai in the party joins in, but, interestingly, the townspeople are not given a voice.

Emoto Hiroshi remarks that *Gion monogatari* on the whole supports the teachings offered in *Kiyomizu monogatari*.[76] At the end of the first volume the second monk summarizes the contents as follows:

> Now that I have heard this tale I have not changed my mind at all from my original position: this shows understanding by someone who has vast knowledge and broad skills. At the beginning he speaks about how the distinction between right [*ri*] and wrong [*hi*] behavior constitutes the merits of knowledge [*chi no toku*]. Toward the middle he talks about how the Three Bonds and the Five Virtues, together with *honmatsu zengo*, constitute the merit of benevolence [*jintoku*]. If you are not a benevolent person the Three Bonds and the Five Virtues will not be correct. At the end, he discusses the difference between small and great courage—in other words the merit of courage [*yōtoku*]. To compose something based on these three merits [*toku*] means that the writer has the knowledge of a sage.[77]

For the most part *Gion monogatari* reinforces the teachings found in *Kiyomizu monogatari*, but the perspective changes when it comes to the passage about Buddhism versus Confucianism. While *Kiyomizu monogatari* creates an oppositional stance between the two schools of thought, *Gion monogatari* claims that such a distinction reveals a lack of understanding and champions the fact that these two religious and intellectual traditions share the same core values. The monk in *Gion monogatari* begins the commentary by presenting the main points of the Buddhist teachings. The roots (*konpon*) of Buddhism lie in encouraging virtue and punishing evil (*kanzen chōaku*). Evil is not tolerated because the next life is determined by whether good or bad deeds are done in this life. Confucianism shares the same fundamental teaching; however, Buddhism goes farther in encouraging virtue and punishing evil. It is nothing more than a matter of degree, we are told.[78] The monk then details the similarities. The Five Precepts (*gokai*), for example, mirror the Five Virtues: not killing equals benevolence (*jin*); not stealing implies justice (*gi*); not indulging in sexual misconduct matches propriety (*rei*); not lying is sincerity (*shin*); and the avoidance of drink is wisdom (*chi*). He also makes clear that Buddhism does not demand that believers dismiss the Three Bonds and the Five Relations. Rather, it asks that caution be observed to prevent any obsessive attachment.[79] A long passage explains how the Five Relations feature prominently in the Buddhist sutras.[80] The monk continues his commentary by reinforcing the basic principle shared by both Buddhism and Confucianism in teaching followers how to pursue virtue and good. This serves for this life and the next. Quotations in the vernacular from Buddhist and Confucian texts add a scholarly element that was less developed in *Kiyomizu monogatari* and display equal knowledge of both intellectual traditions on the part of the anonymous author.

This call for syncretism characterizes much of the dialogical texts inspired by *Kiyomizu monogatari* and *Gion monogatari*.[81] For instance, the 1644 *Daibutsu monogatari* (Tales of the Great Buddha) reconciles Buddhist traditions with both Confucianism and Shintoism, as does the best-selling *Tadasu monogatari* (Tales of Tadasu), which stages a dialogue among women in the precinct of Shimogamo Shrine.[82] Syncretism also imbues the work of Suzuki Shōsan, one of the most prolific writers of *kana hōgo* and one of the few authors identified as such by publishers of the period. Royall Tyler, who has translated key texts by Suzuki Shōsan, describes him as someone who "believed himself to be the first truly to proclaim that the Buddha's teachings and the world's teaching are one and the same."[83] Although Shōsan may not have been the first, as the examples discussed here reveal, his teachings nonetheless reinforce the penchant for intellectual syncretism. One example, *Mōanjō* (A staff to guide the blind; composed in 1619 and first published in 1651) is useful in understanding Shōsan's approach.[84] Very much in accordance with Ejima's mirrors, the text is structured around ten chapters, clearly titled in the table of contents as well as at the beginning of each passage. This text takes us to a set of behavioral teachings focused on what Bowring defines as "the importance of selfless acts."[85] By using a vernacular prose that strives to reach readers of all literacy levels and by including systematic phonetic glosses in hiragana for kanji for the few passages quoted from Chinese sources, *Mōanjō* promotes an ethical behavior that centers on sincerity (*makoto, shin*), compassion (*nasake*), kind acts (*on*), loyalty (*chū*), filial piety (*kō*), and dedication to household matters (*kashoku*). The text's message is straightforward: actions that go against proper comportment (*higagoto*) must be avoided, and if a person is not able to manage this unaided, he or she must pray to the Buddhas for liberation from desire. The Buddhist tone in *Mōanjō* is never underestimated. Yet the focus is not solely on the afterlife. *Mōanjō*, in fact, proves instructive in generating socially responsible conduct. This shows that *kana hōgo* had the potential to function as manuals for civic consciousness as well as guidebooks to Buddhist concepts. In turn this underscores the porosity of the two publishing genres considered in this chapter, *kana washo* and *kana hōgo*. At their heart was the promotion of different religious and intellectual traditions as vehicles to channel consonant social and interpersonal knowledge. As mentioned in the preceding, they also operated as mirrors of their time, highlighting aspects that were considered to be sensitive social issues.

Commodifying Faith

As the monk in *Kiyomizu monogatari* reminds the reader, recitation of the Buddhist sutras was an important activity for any believer, and this was done with a very specific desire—namely, not only to secure a happy afterlife but also to live peacefully in this life. This brings us to the question of faith and devotion.

Sutras were available on the commercial market during the second half of the seventeenth century, as demonstrated by their presence in book-trade catalogues. While everyone could purchase woodblock-printed copies of sutras, they were not easy reading, and ultimately, it can be argued, they were not even designed for reading as such. Sutras were meant to be recited. As Charlotte Eubanks explains, to recite (in Japanese, *ju*) "indicates the devotional act of chanting a sutra aloud and suggests that the chanter is doing so from memory, without looking at the physical, external object of the written text."[86] Eubanks notes that recitation could also happen at the intersection of memory and reading from a book, a practice called *dokuju*. Either way, a sutra would be written in *kanbun*, demanding the reciter to vocalize the Chinese characters by using their Sino-Japanese readings. While the Japanese reading of Chinese characters functions as a form of vernacular reading (or vernacular translation), the Sino-Japanese reading does not give any hint of the meaning of the word; it merely adapts the original Chinese sound to the Japanese phonetic system. This, in turn, meant that unless one knew the meaning of the character itself, one would not be in a position to grasp it by producing or hearing its vocalized reading. In short, this form of recitation was designed to allow people to chant the text but did not enhance any understanding of its contents. Performance was the essence, while comprehension of the meaning was secondary.

Seventeenth-century publishers, ever keen to expand their readerships, devised ways to package sutras into cognitively exciting products that had the potential to appeal to diverse readerships. In the process they reshaped sutras into reading materials that engaged readers at multiple levels, not only as tools for recitation. Admittedly much later than the period we are interested in here, the publicity blurb created for a later edition of the 1739 *Kannon-gyō hayayomi eshō* (The Kannon Sutra for easy reading and with illustrations) provides us with insights that are helpful to unpack the publishing endeavors scrutinized in this section:

> This text [*Kannon-gyō hayayomi eshō*] makes the Kannon Sutra easy for children and women to read. It does so by adding the phonetic reading to the main text [the Sino-Japanese reading for recitation as well as the Japanese reading for grasping the meaning], it uses vernacular Japanese [hiragana] and images to explain the meaning in a detailed, clear manner, and it adds comments [*kōshaku*] by using notes indicated with *i-ro-ha*. It truly allows everyone, including children and women, to know about the miraculous efficacy [*riyaku*] of this sutra. Also, it allows people who live in the remote countryside with no access to a teacher [*shishō*] to memorize the sutra quickly and benefit from the grace it dispenses. With this in mind we have published this volume. We hope it will spread through the country.[87]

We read about the desire to appeal to all readers, embodied here in the trope of "children and women," and to provide a text that readers could read by themselves. We learn that the goal is not only to teach how to recite the sutra but also to make the contents understandable. This is done with a view to elucidating the blessings obtained by engaging with this sutra. I maintain that publishers in the seventeenth century applied similar techniques in shaping what they called *wadan shō* versions of the sutras, where *wadan* means "to explain in a friendly manner" and *shō* can be translated as "commentary." The main difference with *Kannon-gyō hayayomi eshō* lies in a lack of interest in the devotional recitation of the sutra. *Kannon-gyō wadan shō* (The Kannon Sutra explained and commented upon) offers an excellent example of what *wadan shō* are and how they function.

Initially published in 1661, *Kannon-gyō wadan shō* remained a popular best seller throughout the seventeenth century and beyond.[88] As the title suggests, it offers a version of the Kannon Sutra, which is nothing but the twenty-fifth chapter of the *Hokekyō*, or the Lotus Sutra. It was also known by the title *Kanzeon bosatsu fumon bon*. The Kannon Sutra is retained in *kanbun* and stands out on the printed page because it is written in the noncursive *kaisho* calligraphic style (fig. 3.2, right). The sutra is turned into something less daunting by being divided into discrete and brief segments, for a total of seventy-five. In this way the reader is able to engage with short, self-contained textual portions averaging three lines each. Reducing texts into manageable units appears to be a technique widely applied in seventeenth-century didactic prose and should be noted as such. Accessibility is further enhanced by adding *kunten* marks and phonetic glosses to the classical Chinese. They are not meant for recitation, though. They are instead designed for the comprehension of the meaning. On the recto of the tenth folio of the 1661 edition, for example, the citation from the original sutra reads, 若為大水所漂称其名号即得浅処 (fig. 3.2, first line). The glosses translate the single characters into words that were part of the vernacular language in seventeenth-century Japan: 若 *moshi* (if), 為 *tame ni* (because of), 大水 *ōmizu* (big water, large waves), [no character] *no* (particle for noun modification), 所 *saren nimo* (auxiliary verb *ru* to make the verb passive, followed by the auxiliary verb *mu*[*n*] for conjecture, and particles *ni* for "when" and *mo* for "also"; the initial *sa* belongs to the next character), 漂 *tadayowa* (to be tossed about; here the transitive verb *tadayowasu* conjugated as *tadayowasa*), 称 *shōseba* (when you invoke), 其名号 *sono myōgō* ([Kannon's] name), [no character] *o* (object particle), 即 *sunawachi* (promptly), 得 *en* ([one] will obtain), 浅処 *asaki tokoro* (shallow places), [no character] *o* (object particle). Different from what we have seen in Ejima's work, these vernacular readings are not rearranged in the order of Japanese syntax and thus require some engagement with the *kunten* marks to become a fully-fledged interlinear translation. Once the Japanese glosses are reordered (*moshi ōmizu no tame ni tadayowasaren nimo sono myōgō o shōseba sunawachi asaki tokoro o en*), the meaning of the sentence is

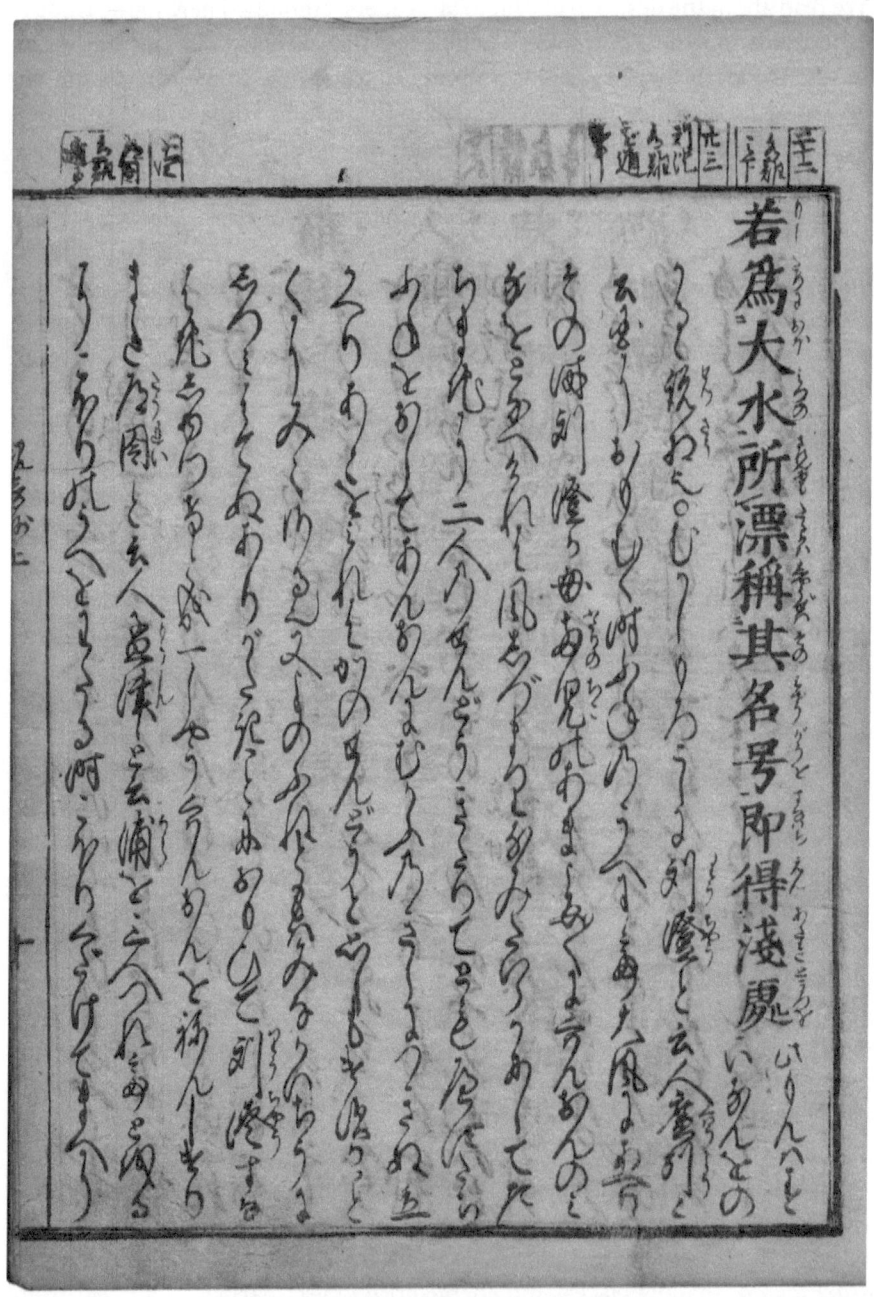

Figure 3.2 *Kannon-gyō wadan shō*, 1661, 10r. Example of how the Kannon Sutra is "translated" for a novice reader.

Author collection, Suzuran Bunko, Cambridge, U.K.

clear: "Even when you are tossed around by large waves, if you invoke Kannon's name you will find shallow places [and stop being tossed about]." I argue that this technique is very close to a form of translation.

Vernacular reading glosses must not have been deemed sufficient to help the novice reader fully grasp the meaning of the sutra, though, since additional commentaries are appended after each of the quoted segments of the Kannon Sutra. They stand out on the page by being written in vernacular Japanese, mainly in hiragana, and in the more conventional cursive calligraphic style (fig. 3.2, text after the first line). They are designed to equip the reader with a clearer, at times more in-depth, understanding of the source text, and they do so by applying several strategies. First, they provide explanations of words that are considered too difficult even with the aid of the phonetic glosses. For instance, when commenting on the title *Kanzeon bosatsu fumon bon*, the text devotes some space to the following elucidation of the term "Kanzeon" (i.e., Kannon):

> The bodhisattva Kanzeon [観世音] is the bodhisattva of the Amida Nyorai of the Pure Land. Originally he attained Buddhahood as Shōbōmyō Nyorai but refused the position of the Enlightened and became a bodhisattva in order to save human beings from the suffering of their unenlightened condition. The meaning [*kokoro*] of the name Kanzeon is [literally] "to see [*miru* 観] the voice [*oto* 音] of the world [*yo* 世]," but what does this expression signify? When human beings invoke the name of Kanzeon, this bodhisattva hears their voices and saves them. Nevertheless, because it is by "hearing" the sound of the people invoking the bodhisattva's name that the bodhisattva helps them, the term "to listen," not "to see," should be employed. So one might find the expression "to see" odd. Let's understand this by considering what happens when children call their parents. When parents walk in front of their child and when the child calls out for them, they will immediately turn back, look at the child, and show love and compassion. In the same way, when Kanzeon hears voices reciting her name, she will look with eyes full of compassion and save them. And that is why the name is Kanzeon—"to *see* the voice of the world."[89]

We are not dealing with erudite notes but with friendly remarks conceived to turn complex concepts into something palatable. To this end, the comparison between calling Kannon and calling one's parents is effective in reducing the alien, challenging notion subsumed under the name Kannon to a familiar scene drawn from life experience. Even a novice reader, with limited cultural literacy, is likely to understand and possibly perceive an emotional bond with this domesticated image of Kannon.

The second type of commentary featuring in *Kannon-gyō wadan shō* takes the form of short narrative anecdotes that provide readers with concrete examples of what is to be gained when someone invokes Kannon's help. The passage that describes how Kannon will save you from drowning is instructive.[90] Following the fragment of the sutra discussed at some length in the preceding are two narratives. The first recounts the story of Ryūchō (C. Liu Deng) heading toward the province of Kōshū (C. Guangzhou) when a strong wind strikes his boat. Kannon's name is invoked, and suddenly two boatmen appear and guide the boat to a safe port. Once off the boat, Ryūchō looks behind and notices that the two boatmen have disappeared. Upon realizing that all the other boats were destroyed, he decides to take the tonsure and devote the rest of his life to his faith in Kannon. The second example mentions another Chinese man, Dōrei (C. Dao Ling), who is walking on a frozen bay with three other men. When the ice starts to break, making it impossible to move either backward or forward, he is saved by praying to Kannon. The mysterious and supernatural presence of the bodhisattva remains tangible throughout the night, when rays of vermilion light emanate from the heads of Dōrei's children while he intently expresses his gratitude in prayer. These emotionally gripping stories translate the teaching of the sutra into concrete examples. They thus promote a life-to-text strategy: the reader uses the knowledge of the actual world to make better sense of the teaching promoted by the sutra passage that has been explained.[91]

The presence of illustrations should not be underestimated. The 1661 edition by the *shomotsuya* Akitaya Seibee does not contain images, but those published by *sōshiya* do. Let's consider, for example, the depiction of the preceding passage concerning drowning. The later edition published by Urokogataya Magobee and Nishimuraya Yohachi has a double-page illustration accompanying this passage (fig. 3.3).[92] The scene on the left (vol. 1, 10r) depicts Ryūchō's story. Ryūchō is shown with his hands clasped in prayer, surrounded by three other men; Kannon has just appeared in the sky. The trail of mist from the upper-left corner forms the cloud on which Kannon is seated to suggest movement: the bodhisattva has floated down from Heaven in response to Ryūchō's prayer. The inclusion of two goblins on the shore, whose presence is reinforced by the gaze of the people and of Kannon directed toward them, is at first sight puzzling since it is at odds with the verbal narration. Could they be the two boatmen, having revealed their true nature? If so, does this mean that Kannon has subjugated them to help Ryūchō? Or are they there to symbolize a different peril? Readers are left with a few open questions that tickle the imagination and keep them engaged beyond the printed page. On the right (vol. 1, 9v) there is a rendition of the tale of Dōrei. He stands on ice as he invokes the name of Kannon, who once again appears in the sky. While the verbal text does not specify who is rescued, the iconotext suggests that Kannon will be compassionate only toward those who invoke her name. Of the other men, two are seen drowning through cracks in the ice. What happened to the third one mentioned in the narrative is not clear. Once again we are left speculating on an image that asks our imagination to fill in the blanks. Nothing in these visual texts suggests the emotional state of the protagonists.

Figure 3.3 *Kannon-gyō wadan shō*, edition by Urokogataya Magobee and Nishimuraya Yohachi, n.d., vol. 1, 9v–10r. Illustration accompanying the passage concerning drowning.

Author collection, Suzuran Bunko, Cambridge, U.K.

It is only in the 1833 *Kannon-gyō wadan shō zue* (The Kannon Sutra explained, commented upon, and illustrated), a new and expanded edition of the text published by the Kyoto publisher Sakaiya Jinbee, that the human drama of Ryūchō's story is enhanced visually (fig. 3.4).[93] The upper part of the page is covered in sharp, black lines that convincingly convey the power of the wind. At the same time, the bottom half of the composition is dominated by the curvilinear forms of the waves. Nature, not expressed in the previous images, becomes the focus of this scene. Therein three men are captured at the moment their boat is almost totally destroyed by the water. Their facial expressions are witness to their pain and fear. For the first time we are confronted with basic emotional states, which are hardwired in our brains and therefore can easily be recognized by even the most inexperienced readers/viewers.[94] This encourages an empathic identification with these characters and pushes the reader to *feel* the danger of not having faith in Kannon. Two of the three drowning men look to the right, where, miraculously, a boat survives the elements and the tiny form of the bodhisattva Kannon is visible on top. Illustrations like this demonstrate they serve a larger purpose than as eye-catching additions to the text. They have the capacity to transform the story. While seventeenth-century illustrations

Figure 3.4 Hirata Shisui and Tsujimoto Motosada, *Kannon-gyō wadan shō zue*, 1833, vol. 1, 10v–11r. Illustration accompanying the passage concerning drowning.

Author collection, Suzuran Bunko, Cambridge, U.K.

confirm that Kannon and her compassion are at the heart of the story, the nineteenth-century image here relegates Kannon to the background, pushing the human drama to the fore.

Being saved from drowning is only one of the many blessings we are promised by *Kannon-gyō wadan shō* if only we nurture our faith in the bodhisattva Kannon. Altogether the text offers sixteen embedded stories that detail a variety of benefits to be gained. The first volume tells us of how we can avoid the seven disasters (*shichinan*), including being spared life when caught in a fire or upon arrest, and even being saved from goblins and demons. The second volume focuses on yet another miraculous benefit bestowed upon us by Kannon: the birth of a son will be granted to those who worship and give offerings to her. This teaching is used as an occasion to move away from the sutra itself and develop some reflections on the status of women in Buddhism and in society. While women are described as intrinsically sinful and are not destined to be saved, the commentary elaborates on the dreadful problems encountered by not having children, including being divorced, being despised by other women in the household, and being mocked by others. Unsurprisingly, the solution lies in having faith in Kannon. This is the key to gaining a male child, which in turn is the only way through which a woman can win enlightenment. To illustrate the principle *Kannon-gyō wadan shō* recurs once again to a fairly long narrative that engages readers at an emotional level by recounting the story of an abandoned child and the quest for his mother.[95] After a discussion of the ways in which offerings should be made to Kannon, the third volume is dominated by twenty-six poems in praise of Kannon.

Viewed in its entirety *Kannon-gyō wadan shō* is a multifarious text that engages readers cognitively on a multitude of levels. It is not a straightforward translation of the Kannon Sutra, yet it provides what is close enough to an interlinear translation of the Buddhist canonical text. From this point of view the *performance* of the sacred text, which would have been enabled by the presence of Sino-Japanese readings of the *kanbun*, is pared down to maximize the *comprehension* of the text. At the same time *Kannon-gyō wadan shō* is fashioned as an easily intelligible guide to understand Kannon's miraculous power. It is no coincidence that the text was also known under the variant title of *Kannon riyaku monogatari* (Tales of the miraculous power of Kannon).[96] This mirrors well the nature of *Kannon-gyō wadan shō* as a collection of narratives that account for the miraculous benefits to be obtained from the compassion of the bodhisattva Kannon. The focus is not so much on how to reach enlightenment and escape the cycle of rebirth, although inevitably this is an underlining concern. Rather, it centers on this life and on the quest for happiness. And happiness can be bestowed upon any of us, provided we invoke Kannon's name. It is a form of devotion and religiosity that echoes what we have seen articulated in *Kiyomizu monogatari*: faith in Buddha (or, in this case, in a bodhisattva) leads to a peaceful and comfortable life here and now. *Kannon-gyō wadan shō* is a tool to assist any believer in this endeavor. Yet there is more to it. While fueling understanding of the sutra and appreciation of its miraculous power, it provides readers with engaging narratives packed with action and infused by the supernatural. The images added in some editions further contribute to the emotional and cognitive engagement with the narrative world that is disclosed in between the quotations from the sutra.

The blurb that Sakaiya Jinbee produced to publicize his 1833 edition—the aforementioned *Kannon-gyō wadan shō zue*—well crystallizes the multifaceted nature of the text and can be retrospectively applied to grasp the nature of the seventeenth-century *Kannon-gyō wadan shō*:

> This text [*Kannon-gyō wadan shō zue*] explains the sutra in such a way that it can be readily understood, even by children and women. There are miraculous instances from the past of people who, through faith in Kannon, avoided all sorts of disasters, such as fire, robbery, and illness. People unable to have

children [prayed to Kannon and] were blessed with good sons. People in all the provinces were receiving Kannon's miraculous power. This text records many good things and illustrates them with pictures. It is a text that seeks to be of assistance to the believer.[97]

Kannon-gyō wadan shō is one of many *wadan shō*, even though the only one to appear in *shojaku mokuroku*. *Amida kyō wadan shō* (The Amida Sutra explained and commented upon), published in 1672 and 1685, offers something very similar, as the afterword to the 1685 edition succinctly reveals:

> This *Amida kyō wadan shō* has been written in Japanese [hiragana] with the inclusion of illustrations for the benefit of fools and the ignorant. Consulting this book one will develop the right disposition to achieve enlightenment. Indeed, this book is a seed from which Buddhist fruits will sprout in the future. Reading this book is akin to listening to the sermon of a sage, so do read it when you have some spare time. It will allow you to develop the heart [required] to reach enlightenment on your own. We have printed this book, distributing it to the world in the hope that it will aid the salvation of human beings.[98]

The *kanbun* is glossed with vernacular readings, in the same manner as *Kannon-gyō wadan shō*. Other examples included *Hannya kyō wadan shō* (The Perfection of Wisdom Sutra explained and commented upon), first issued in 1648 and reprinted in the Enpō era (1673–1681), and *Hokekyō wadan shō* (The Lotus Sutra explained and commented upon), published in 1696.

By offering a form of translation of the sutras, *wadan shō* not only alert us to a type of text cherished by seventeenth-century readers but also ask us to rethink what we know about the translation history of Buddhist sacred texts. For example, Peter F. Kornicki remarks that in the seventeenth century "Japanese transcriptions of vernacular reading of the *Lotus sutra* and the *Essentials of rebirth* became available in commercially printed editions" but that this method of presenting Sinitic texts in Japanese transcription was limited mostly to these two texts and that we must wait for the twentieth century for mature translations of the Buddhist canon.[99] In this regard, Kornicki contrasts Japan and Korea: "The reluctance to translate Sinitic texts in Japan has gone largely unremarked: it applies to Buddhist and Confucian texts alike and stands out in marked contrast with translation practice in Korea."[100] *Wadan shō* can hardly be labeled as full-scale translations, yet they adopt specific strategies designed to translate the Sinitic text for novice readers and to keep them engaged with the text. From this point of view I argue that *wadan shō* constitute an important aspect of the history of cultural translation in early modern Japan that awaits investigation.

Bringing Moral Instruction Alive

The texts examined so far are straightforward with the moral teaching spelled out directly either by means of a narrator who exposes the principles at stake as if he were delivering a sermon or by means of a narrator who reports a dialogue in which one of two interlocutors exposes the precept. Exempla could be inserted here and there, as seen in *Kannon-gyō wadan shō*. And exempla can be a very compelling tool in didactic literature, not only in Japan but across different cultures and eras: "Exempla revolve around a perceptive principle or 'moral' that is brought to life by the vividness of the story told. By embodying in fictional characters the thoughts, emotions, and behaviors under scrutiny, exempla take readers from the abstract and general to the concrete and particular, making their lesson more tangible."[101] Medieval Japan had a long tradition of narratives embodying moral teachings in the genre of *setsuwa*. This tradition remained buoyant in early modern Japan, with *Inga monogatari* (Tales of karmic causality) being a useful example.

Ascribed to Suzuki Shōsan, *Inga monogatari* is a collection of anecdotes concerning the Buddhist concept of causality (*inga*). The text was circulated at the time in two different versions: one written in a mixture of kanji and katakana, known in Japanese secondary literature as *katakana-bon*, and the other in a mixture of kanji and hiragana, usually labeled *hiragana-bon*.[102] The circumstances that led to the existence of these two formats is explained in the preface, by a certain Unpo, to the katakana version:

> [Suzuki Shōsan's] disciples kept the text strictly secret and did not circulate it because it contained the names of living people. Nonetheless, someone was able to copy the text and unscrupulously had it printed. Moreover, he added his own preface. There are many things that will please people since he freely added spurious stories. It was for this reason that [Suzuki Shōsan's] disciples felt obliged to print the correct version [*shōhon*] of their master's work, in the hope that this would put to rest the doubts created by that evil book [*jahon*].[103]

The "evil book" to which Unpo refers is the hiragana version first issued by the Kyoto publisher Yamada Ichirobee (or by another Kyoto publisher, Zeniya; which came first is unclear), probably around 1658–1659.[104] Unpo's account points to the existence of an original, secret copy, probably a manuscript that circulated only among Suzuki Shōsan's students. It appears that an unidentified individual—described as "unscrupulous" (*okasumono*) by Unpo— obtained the manuscript and had it printed in a fashion that would more widely appeal to readers. To counter the existence of this "pirated" commercial edition, Shōsan's followers decided to publish the "authenticated" version in

1661. The version by Shōsan's students was initially issued privately (the sponsors are named in the colophon, here, unusually, included at the back of the second volume). It was later released commercially and appeared in book-trade catalogues beginning in 1670.

I pause at this juncture to consider the cultural significance of these two different versions of *Inga monogatari*. In his now classic work on a sixteenth-century miller from Friuli, Carlo Ginzburg cautions us against what he views as "stereotyped and saccharine" images of popular culture and not to fall into the trap of seeing in popular culture "a passive accommodation to the cultural sub-products proffered by the dominant classes," "partly autonomous values in respect to the culture of the latter," or "a state prior to *culture*."[105] We are urged to consider "Bakhtin's hypothesis of a reciprocal influence between lower class and dominant cultures."[106] I would argue that the publication history of *Inga monogatari* exemplifies this circularity. Shōsan's text was originally conceived for the small elite circle of his disciples and as belonging to a rarefied cosmos of secret traditions. But profit-conscious publishers such as Zeniya and Yamada Ichirobee realized that this manuscript (how it reached them is unclear) represented a tremendous business opportunity. They repackaged the text such that it would appeal to inexperienced readers, an aspect I explore subsequently, and released the book for the price of a delicacy like sea bream. This, in turn, prompted Shōsan's students to release their own version of the text, claiming its "purity" and thereby acknowledging its genuineness and quality. But this version was also released commercially and for a similar price. Thereafter, the popular reader could enjoy both texts: the one pirated (or creatively appropriated) from a highbrow tradition of secrecy by commercial publishers and the other produced by members of the highbrow tradition of secrecy who were forced, quite paradoxically, to break the vow of secrecy and publish what they viewed as the pure text. How the seventeenth-century popular reader actually read these two versions, however, is difficult to prove, as to the best of my knowledge we lack materials similar to those studied by Ginzburg.

The hiragana version and the katakana version of *Inga monogatari* are intrinsically different, although they package what is assumed to be the same text. From a linguistic point of view, they both use Japanese. But the Zeniya and Yamada editions apply the easily accessible mixture of kanji and hiragana, whereas the "correct" version reverts to the less-friendly katakana. In other words, the hiragana version makes knowledge fully accessible, while the katakana version appears to resist this drive, even while it has indeed been printed for publication.

The variant nature of the two versions is mirrored in the range of differences in their materiality and textuality. The three-volume katakana version has seventy-seven topics constituting titled sections; each section is further divided into two or more stories dealing with the same topic. The hiragana version has eighty-four tales spread over six volumes, but no further internal divisions. A comparative study by Yoshida Kōichi shows that there are twenty-four passages in the fourth, fifth, and sixth volumes of the hiragana version that are absent from the katakana version. What changes occurred to the text between the katakana and hiragana versions? The tale that opens the hiragana version proves helpful in answering this question:

A WOMAN WHOSE DEEP ATTACHMENT CAUSES HER
TO TURN INTO A SNAKE

A man from the neighborhood of Kitsunezaki, in the area of Innai-machi in Fuchū, Suruga Province, went to Shinano. During his stay, he courted a woman and had no choice but to exchange love vows with her. Time passed and when he returned to Suruga, the woman he had courted in Shinano followed him all the way back to Suruga. [When she met the man's wife] she said, "Where is he? Is he here? I am from Suruga but came here because of the pledge exchanged with him." Since her appearance was indeed frightening, the wife ran inside and reported this to her husband. He went out and managed to persuade her to come inside. He kept her in their house.

One day, he accompanied the woman to the bay with the ruse of showing her Miho no Matsubara. Once in the boat, he paddled toward the middle of the bay and threw the woman overboard. All of a sudden she transformed herself into a snake that coiled itself around his waist. The man, unsure about what to do, tried to pull and cast off the snake, but to no avail. There was nothing he could do.

He thought seriously about how to resolve the situation and came to the conclusion that he should go to Mount Kōya. Since women are not allowed on this mountain, he believed the woman-snake would leave him once there. He climbed Mount Kōya and, as expected, on the Fudō slope, the snake detached itself from his body, moved back, and remained behind.

The man was happy about this. He stayed three years on the mountain, thinking that by this point her attachment [*shūshin*] to him would have vanished. He was resolved to return home, but as he passed the Fudō slope, the same snake wrapped itself around him as before, squeezing his waist.

Dispirited, the man headed home. He boarded the ferryboat at Yabase in Ōmi Province. The boat stopped moving when it was offshore. The boatmen and the passengers all grew suspicious, saying, "There must be someone on the boat who is facing circumstances that cannot be revealed." This said, they began to search the boat and discovered that the man's waist was strangely oversized, the shape of the snake visible. They said, "We have never heard of anything so wretched. It is such a pitiful thing! Nonetheless, we cannot endanger the lives of many people because of this," and they threw the man into the sea. The boat reached the shore with no further ado.

The karmic repercussions of his unreasonable behavior [*hibun*] lasted three years. This event took place in the seventeenth year of the Keichō era [1612].[107]

The illustration that accompanies the text (fig. 3.5) shows the man on the boat at Miho no Matsubara.[108] It captures the moment when the woman has turned into a snake and has wrapped around his waist. The snake is shown in the act of dangerously confronting the man, its head raised against him. The body language of the man highlights his state of mind described in the text by the word *meiwaku*, or finding oneself at a loss. The sense of bewilderment and confusion that we witness on the man's face helps elicit an empathic bond between the reader and the protagonist.

The tale is presented as a nonfictional record of real events. The factual, almost journalistic nature of this narrative is suggested by the inclusion of specific place-names and a precise date. Other stories even include the names of the protagonists. The chronicle-like nature of the text is heralded in the preface of the hiragana version: "This text collects events supported by certain evidence [*shōko tadashiki mono*], and they have been written down as advice to people living in the latter days of the Buddhist law [*masse*]."[109] In this way the paratext asks readers to believe that each story in the collection is based on facts. The world thus created appears as a credible one. Yet the supernatural permeates this seemingly factual prose, following narrative conventions typical of *setsuwa*.[110] All of a sudden a plausible, even familiar world turns into an eerie one. I maintain that rather than drawing our attention to fictionality and generating cognitive skepticism, the presence of something mysterious, at times even uncanny, stimulates cognitive activity, with the reader trying to make sense of what is on the page. Order is regained once we appreciate the Buddhist teachings that justify the narrative actions. In this case we are dealing with attachment (*shūshin*) and unreasonable behavior (*hibun*). They work as the plot engine that reconciles the factual with the supernatural and as the ultimate goal of the reading experience—namely, gaining moral instruction. What about the rendering of the same story in the katakana version? We need to turn to the fifth section in the first volume, which contains three tales, to find the same story. The thread that runs through all three tales is spelled out in the title of the section, "A Woman Full of Jealousy, Her Death, and How She Kills a Man; Followed by How a Dead Woman Turns Herself into a Snake and Coils Around a Man" (fig. 3.6).[111] In all three stories it is attachment, interwoven with the idea of jealousy, that triggers the vengeful rancor of the woman's spirit. The first tale concerns Yoshida Sakubyōe, who leaves his wife and children in Shinano to take up an appointment as a local magistrate in Ōnuma County, Echigo Province. The disappearance of one of his wife's maidservants

Figure 3.5 Suzuki Shōsan, *Inga monogatari*, hiragana version, publication details unknown, vol. 1, 3v. Illustration accompanying the opening tale.

Author collection, Suzuran Bunko, Cambridge, U.K.

二番ヲサセ置タルヲ見タリト。本秀愡ニ語リ給フ。鈊樹刀山ト云
フ明カナルフ也。○江州佗和山ニテ去人下女ヲ炬火ヲ以灸殺
ケリ。然ニ彼人火ノ病ヲ受テ。総身燒也。早ク水ヲクレヨト云間
イソギ水ヲ持來レバ是更ニ水ニテナレト云テ。呑ト不叶。尤有バ
トテ大半切ニ水ヲ入篠ノ葉ナドニテ。露ヲ掛テ見ケルニ滴リ
身ニ落ルヽ其モ欠也ヤレアツヤ堪難ヤイカニモ皆不知総身火
ニ燃ルトテ。悲ムホドニ祈念ニ名ヲ得タル真言坊主ヲ頼犬法秘
法ヲ行樣々加持シケレ圧水呑ノ不能尺水ヽト云ニテ七日
ニ燒死ケリ。愡ニ知人語也寛永十七年ノフ也
五妬深女死ノ男ヲ取殺スノ付女死ノ蚯ト爲男ヲ巻事
越後國大沼郡ノ代宮吉田作兵衛ト云者信濃善光寺ノ
者ニテ。妻子ヲ善光寺ニ置ケリ。或時妻召使シ。下女失去

serves as a prelude to the drama. The wife discovers the illicit relationship between her husband and the maidservant and that the mistress had been invited to Ōnuma. The realization of her husband's affair causes such intense resentment (*urami*) that she becomes extremely ill. She contracts her trustworthy friend Buhyōe to murder the mistress. Yet despite the satisfaction she feels at seeing the mistress's head, the wife's condition worsens and she dies. Her spirit, unsettled and still vengeful, haunts the husband; she appears before him and strangles him. The feelings of resentment (*urami*), anger (*shin'i*), and obsession (*mōshu*) are openly condemned in the story. The image of death by strangulation leads to the second and third tales, which are relevant here because they both feed into the above hiragana tale:

[SECOND TALE OF THE FIFTH SECTION IN THE FIRST
VOLUME OF THE KATAKANA VERSION]

In the Kan'ei era there was a Buddhist monk named Nyoō. When asked about the reasons that gave rise to his faith, he offered the following explanation. He was a carpenter in Kyoto, and when his wife died he married his wife's niece. One day while he was napping, a snake descended from the sky and flicked its tongue. He grabbed the snake and cast it off. But this was all done in vain, since the snake kept coming back and eventually wrapped itself around his neck. There was no way to detach it.

Left with no other choice, he decided to take the tonsure. He shaved his head and went begging for alms, but the snake would still not leave him. Then he climbed Mount Kōya, and the snake disappeared on the Fudō slope. He rejoiced, but when he came down from the mountain after three years, the snake again wrapped itself around his neck on the same slope. He placed a towel around his neck, so that people will not be afraid.

Many years elapsed before he confessed everything to Abbot Gon'yo of the temple, Hōdoji, located in front of Shōkokuji in the upper district of Kyoto. He created a bond with the Buddha Amida by reciting Amida's name ten times. While reciting the *nenbutsu* the snake disappeared before he realized it.

[THIRD TALE OF THE FIFTH SECTION IN THE FIRST
VOLUME OF THE KATAKANA VERSION]

Two or three years before the Battle of Osaka, a person living four or five *ken* from Harada Jirōzaemon's dwelling near Kitsunezaki, in the area of Inreimachi [*sic*], in Fuchū, Suruga Province, went to Shinshū [Shinano]. He found a wife and lived there, but after a while he returned to Suruga. The woman from Shinshū followed him. Her appearance was frightening, and at her sight the Suruga wife ran away to tell her husband. The man persuaded the other woman to go with him to Miho no Matsubara, where he killed her by throwing her into the sea. The dead woman immediately turned into a snake and wrapped itself around his waist. No matter how many times he tried to dislodge it, the snake would return as before. He had no other choice but to move to Mount Kōya.[112]

It should be fairly self-evident that the hiragana version offers a pastiche of the two stories. The katakana version has much drier prose. A comparison of the two texts reveals that the hiragana version uses direct speech to give the protagonists a distinct voice, in a sort of dramatization that has the potential to better engage the reader.[113] It also introduces short comments by the narrator that function as verbal representations of emotions, or as "emotion ekphrasis," to borrow a term coined by Maria Nikolajeva.[114] This results in enriching the story with greater depth as a story and serves to make the characters come alive, inviting the reader to develop an empathic response to them. All this is absent from the katakana version. Moreover, the gripping scene of the boat and the fateful ending in the hiragana version offer an additional thrilling note to the story line. As for the Buddhist concepts underlying the narrative events, they are spelled out in the hiragana version but are almost left unvoiced in the katakana one. This might suggest that the katakana version records a text that was, or had the potential to be, delivered vocally as part of a sermon and that when it was recounted aloud by the storyteller, most likely a monk, he would clarify the necessary didactic apparatus. By contrast, the hiragana version was conceived to be read silently or aloud but not performed as part of a sermon. It incorporated everything that was necessary to instruct while holding the reader's attention.

Inga monogatari, more specifically in the hiragana version, situates itself at the intersection of at least two textual strands. It is a collection of *setsuwa*, showing how this medieval genre was still popular in the seventeenth century. It also absorbs literary fashions that were making inroads into the publishing market, in particular a taste for ghost stories.[115] The didactic value of *Inga monogatari* is highlighted in the introduction added to the abridged version titled *Shokoku inga monogatari* (Tales of karma across the provinces).[116]

> It is said that water adapts itself to the shape of the container and that human beings are molded on the basis of their relationship with good and evil. This principle is easily applicable to all sorts of things. When a person commits misdeeds, being distanced from good people and in the company of evil people, that person will suffer misfortune, and on occasion misfortune extends beyond them and strikes their descendants. When one does good deeds, the entire household will undoubtedly enjoy good fortune and its heirs will prosper. The Way of Heaven does not lie. It is exactly the same when one plants seeds. When

they are ready, they will bloom and produce fruits. It creates awe. There are many forms of retribution [*mukui*] from the past. But since people also question what is before their eyes, all we have recorded here is mainly recent events supported by certain evidence. We have entitled this the *Mirror of Good and Evil* [*Ayame kagami*]. This will hopefully make the reader move away from evil and move toward the good.[117]

Inga monogatari is portrayed as a "mirror of good and evil."[118] This brings us back to the idea of mirrors for a righteous life that began this chapter. Whether underpinned by Buddhism, Confucianism, or a harmonious combination of the two, both *kana hōgo* and *kana washo* offer models for correct behavior.

Through a close reading of chosen primary sources, this chapter has dissected two core publishing genres—*kana washo* and *kana hōgo*—of Japanese seventeenth-century popular prose. The analysis has focused on how commercial publishers negotiated the plurality of knowledge associated with Confucianism and Buddhism for the benefit of the novice reader. Several findings have emerged. The cultural negotiation of the Way was carried out by decontextualizing knowledge from its original linguistic context (i.e., *kanbun*) and from its primary milieus (i.e., temples, sermons, lectures) and engaging with the translation of Confucian and Buddhist concepts to make them comprehensible to readers equipped with kana-mainly literacy. Infused with inherent syncretism, the texts scrutinized in the preceding operated as mirrors of morally acceptable behavior. Readers were presented with a corpus of transformative literature that encouraged the study of—and therefore the assimilation of—virtues including sincerity, harmony, frugality, filial piety, and patience. This corpus also offered soothing hope. Readers were assured of fulfilling, happy, and comfortable lives when embracing the righteous path illustrated in these texts and when developing the rather straightforward faith in Buddhism promoted in them. Altogether, *kana washo* and *kana hōgo* embodied the desire to commodify moral, religious, and to a certain extent civic knowledge.

This chapter has also thrown light on a handful of textual strategies that, I argue, characterize didactic prose of the time. First, quotations from Confucian and Buddhist sources were used as seals of authority, but they were also made accessible thanks to the addition of phonetic glosses that approximated a form of interlinear translation in the vernacular. Second, analogies were cherished as an apt means of domesticating complex ideas. Third, exempla and pictures punctuated the drier, nonnarrative explanatory prose. They both provided the reader with narratives that were at times packed with action and at times emotionally captivating, ensuring sustained cognitive engagement.

Fourth, as the popularity of the dialogical format suggests, there was a fascination with filling texts with *voices*. This problematizes the very act of reading with what I call a residue of aurality: while reading the written page we are asked to listen to someone speaking. In a way, this builds upon the oral (or vocal) tradition with which popular readers had been familiar since medieval times. What is exciting in seventeenth-century texts is that we are confronted with a panoply of voices: it can be one authoritative voice that stands for a single truth, or it can be a plurality of voices that promote debate as well as intellectual syncretism.

It might be tempting to disparage *kana washo* and *kana hōgo* as examples of a dominant culture wishing to inculcate norms top-down. Yet I strongly argue for the thrill that opening up knowledge for everyone must have allowed for. For the first time, people of all sorts could access the Way(s) through books that were designed and marketed to appeal to the novice reader. It was not simply the case of listening to a short sermon or of asking questions, two oral practices that were adopted in popularizing the Way(s) and that existed alongside the printed word. Rather, it involved a fairly cheap written record packaged in an easy and enticing way for readers to engage with intensive reading whenever they wished or could spare time. Moreover, with *Inga monogatari* we have appreciated how a fruitful circular relationship could be ignited between different cultures: the commercial book appropriated secret traditions for the benefit of the popular reader, and this forced those who had access to the secret traditions to disclose them to a wider public. Indeed, all kinds of readers were introduced to the worldview of those well *au fait* with *gakumon*. But they also partook in shaping the popularized Way(s). Profit-driven, commercial publishers acted as middlemen. How and if readers used the power of knowledge advanced by *kana washo* and *kana hōgo* to challenge the system in which they lived is a chapter yet to be written.

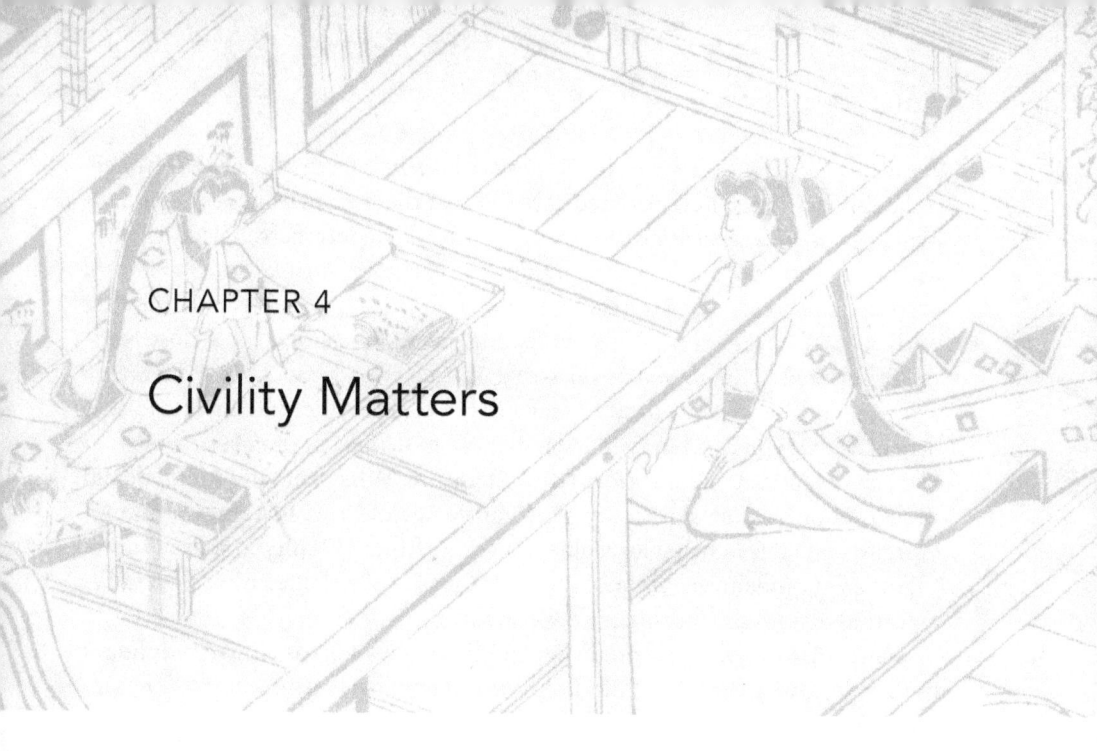

CHAPTER 4

Civility Matters

The need for etiquette is in everything. It softens your disposition, it always improves your appearance, and your speech will not be bad. It is said that when you have the truth within, it shows on the outside. If it were not for etiquette it would not be possible to distinguish between high, middle, and low.

—Tō Mitsunaka, *Shorei tōyō shū* (The collection for all immediate needs on etiquette)

The analysis of *kana hōgo* and *kana washo* in chapter 3 demonstrated that commercial publishers were active in packaging the basic principles of Buddhism and Confucianism in such a way to make them accessible to a potentially broad range of readers. Mastery of these teachings was framed as the way in which an individual—regardless of social position, age, or gender—could grow into a fully-developed person. This, in turn, ensured fitting into society in a successful way. In other words, *kana hōgo* and *kana washo* were conceived as publishing genres that aided readers to build their humanity by conveying ethical, religious, and civic knowledge. Yet as Ejima Tamenobu declares, to behave appropriately in all types of human interactions was not just a matter of morality or ethics. It was also a matter of etiquette, manners, and comportment. The word that Ejima uses for this is *sahō*, but terms such as *shitsukekata* and *rei* were largely interchangeable. Commercial publishers must have realized early on that there was business potential in issuing easily accessible books that taught societal and interpersonal knowledge, inasmuch as the 1670 catalogue contains the category *shitsukekata-sho narabi ni ryōri-sho* (books on manners and cookery). This chapter is conceived, first of all, as an examination of this publishing genre. By conducting a close reading of selected primary sources, I strive to understand how civility literature was packaged in such a way as to make secret oral traditions accessible for the benefit of everyone and invited its audiences to delight in the reading of what had the potential to be transformative literature. What were the fundamental standards of *sahō* or *shitsukekata*? What values did this literature promote? Were these codes of behavior stable or ever shifting? Whom did they address? Was there a gender orientation? What was the pleasure elicited by nonnarrative texts that expounded norms of deportment?

Some might view my desire to explore these questions as almost redundant in light of the existence of Eiko Ikegami research on the subject.[1] Yet I maintain that engagement with seventeenth-century sources, which Ikegami largely overlooks, is valuable in that it leads to findings that are at variance with what we know to date on the subject of civility in early modern Japan.

It might be useful to call to mind Ikegami's core arguments. Civility is defined by Ikegami as "the cultural grammar of sociability that governs interactional public spaces."[2] By working primarily on eighteenth- and nineteenth-century sources, Ikegami notes the existence of what she calls "hierarchical civility," wherein codes of etiquette emphasized "status differentials between the interacting parties" and, in doing so, were "compatible with the operative ideology of the Tokugawa state, namely rule by status."[3] Ikegami views a top-down process: "As a result of continued samurai domination, the Tokugawa Japanese adapted and popularized vertically structured codes of civility to govern formal social interactions."[4] In order to support her position of civility as "differentiated idioms for expressing differences," Ikegami focuses on the 1809 *Ogasawara shorei taizen* (The complete book of Ogasawara school manners).[5] She looks at specific codes of etiquette, including bowing, the use of fans, clearing the nasal passages, and table manners. She also reflects upon the meaning of *shitsukekata* and *rei*, stating that, "This convergence of the two terms suggests the nature of the emerging standard of good behavior for all classes during this period—an ideal of physical elegance expressive of politeness and simultaneously sensitive to the recognition of status differentials."[6] Ikegami stresses the contrast between a "vocabulary of manners" mirroring "hierarchical boundaries" and the "comparatively horizontally structured grammar of sociability that prevailed in the aesthetic enclaves," which is the focus of her work.[7] While the former confirmed the social status quo, the latter offered an alternative.[8] She views this as a "curious social paradox."[9] Ikegami relaxes her avowal of a hierarchical civility when she notes that the readership of handbooks of manners must have exceeded an elite readership and that commoners striving to move upward could acquire the necessary cultural conventions by reading books.[10] Ikegami also makes the claim that books on civilized knowledge are preoccupied with creating a specific image of Japan, exhibiting a desire for self-identification and for the construction of a "Japanese tradition."[11] One striking point in Ikegami's argument is the ready rejection of any connection between manners and morality.[12]

Ikegami's work remains invaluable for the study of civility in early modern Japan as a whole, but the seventeenth-century publishing genre under scrutiny here problematizes the idea of hierarchical civility and prompts a reconsideration of the nexus between manners, morality, and the creation of a protonational identity. My inquiry in these directions is guided by methodological questions that emerge from studies pursued on civility in other parts of the world, with specific reference to the work of Anna Bryson and Keith Thomas, among others.[13] Although firmly anchored in the Western world, these studies offer what seems to me a more nuanced approach to an examination of conduct books and elucidate important complexities.

First, while acknowledging that civility was bound up with the existence of social hierarchy, they prompt considerations about the somewhat counterintuitive link with egalitarianism, as lucidly expounded by Thomas: "This assumption that people should be treated differently according to their social position was an enduring strand in the concept of civility. But it has to be reconciled with the almost equally tenacious, and potentially egalitarian, notion that the well-mannered person should extend to everyone the polite deference which had originally been reserved for superiors."[14] Thomas reflects upon the existence of "*parvenus* who successfully acquired the social polish of their superiors" within a social structure that was hierarchical but also relatively fluid.[15] His final position on this intricate matter is subtle: "Civility is as important in an egalitarian society as in a hierarchical one."[16] Could we apply this approach to seventeenth-century Japanese conduct books? If so, what kind of findings would we gather?

Second, the studies in question encourage reflections on how civility played an active part in promoting social harmony. In assessing Erasmus's *De civilitate morum puerilium* (1530), Norbert Elias remarks that "Erasmus did not see his precepts as intended for a particular class. He placed no particular emphasis on social distinctions."[17] Elias identifies the cause for this lack of social orientation in the underlying social process that typified Erasmus's time:

> The old social ties were, if not broken, extensively loosened and were in a process of transformation. Individuals of different social origins were thrown together. The social circulation of ascending and descending groups and

individuals speeded up.... People, forced to live with one another in a new way, became more sensitive to the impulses of others. Not abruptly but very gradually the code of behaviour became stricter and the degree of consideration expected of others became greater. The sense of what to do and what not to do in order not to offend or shock others became subtler, and in conjunction with the new power relationships the social imperative not to offend others became more binding, as compared to the preceding phase.[18]

This passage indicates, albeit indirectly, that social conduct is seen as a way to ensure the harmonious coexistence of human beings in a rapidly changing society that brings together people of different backgrounds into the same space (a type of society that calls to mind seventeenth-century Japanese urban centers). In somewhat clearer terms, Bryson notes an "elaborate, self-conscious connection made between good manners, 'courtesy,' 'civility,' and other virtues perceived to promote social harmony and the overall peace of the community" when discussing English sources.[19] Is this a stance that can also be identified in the Japanese materials under examination in this chapter? If so, how does this change our understanding of early modern civility in Japan?

The remark made by Bryson on civility being associated with "virtues" suggests a third point of interest: morality comes into play when thinking about conduct. Thomas reaches similar conclusions in noting that civility and morality were closely linked in early modern British society, implying the "religious duty to live 'honestly and civilly.'"[20] Is this a valid line of reasoning when confronted with Japanese materials?

If the application of conceptual frameworks alien to the Japanese context might cause some uneasiness in readers, it is worth noting that concerns similar to those raised by Thomas, Bryson, and Elias were voiced in early modern Japan. For instance, in 1770 the Osaka publisher Katsuoya Rokubee 勝尾屋六兵衞 (dates unknown) reflects as follows on his *Ogasawara-ryū shitsukekata hyakka jō* (One hundred articles on the Ogasawara-style etiquette):

> It is said that etiquette [*rei*] highlights the distinction between the high- and lowborn. As a human being [*hito to shite*] one must be conversant with etiquette. To attend one's parents and to serve one's master are both Ways that imply the mastery of etiquette. That is why the wise men of the past revered etiquette above all else and also why etiquette is first among the Six Arts [*rikugei*]: ceremonies, music, archery, horsemanship, calligraphy, and mathematics.[21]

This short passage underscores the knotty nature of etiquette as a concept. Katsuoya's words point to a tension between civility as a means to reinforce social hierarchy on the one hand and, on the other, civility as something that fosters everyone's "humanity." He also stresses the link with two ethical teachings deeply ingrained in Confucianism—filial piety and loyalty—hence alerting us to conduct and morality as being to a degree interrelated. This, in turn, justifies his preference for the word *rei*, which was strongly tied to Chinese learning. At the same time, however, the title of his publication uses the synonym *shitsukekata*, thus making its appeal resonate beyond Confucian constraints. Mention of the Six Arts, a normal part of warrior upbringing, calls attention to the fact that etiquette has deep roots in this specific social group. In probing *shitsukekata-sho narabi ni ryōri-sho*, and more specifically its role in civility literature, my aim in this chapter is to come to terms with these complexities. I do so by a close reading of *Ogasawara hyakka jō* (The hundred articles of the Ogasawara school), which proved particularly popular during and after the 1600s.

The study of etiquette pushes us outside the confines of a single publishing genre, however, highlighting once more the porosity of the categories conceived by seventeenth-century publishers and booksellers. When reflecting on whether seventeenth-century discourse on manners was gendered, I focus on two conduct books that were marketed as *nyosho* (books for women): *Onna kagami hidensho* (Book on the secret tradition of the mirror for women) and *Onna shikimoku* (Rules for women). The textual analysis leads to an acknowledgment of forms of social differentiation other than status hierarchy and an exploration of the associations between civility and morality.

I then return to *shitsukekata-sho narabi ni ryōri-sho* to understand how and why publishers combined cookery books with manners. As the analysis unfolds, I point readers to another tension that emerges from the study of books that deal with etiquette and food culture—namely, that nonnarrative conduct manuals could be read aesthetically as sources of narrative enjoyment inasmuch as texts normally considered literature or art fulfilled a cognitive function in tandem with an aesthetic and emotional one. I thus call into question the argument put forward by Mary Elizabeth Berry concerning cultural literacy and its use by Ihara Saikaku.[22]

Breaking Secrecy: Etiquette for Everyone

My exploration of manuals of manners—the *shitsukekata* component of the publishing genre *shitsukekata-sho narabi ni ryōri-sho*—starts with the Ogasawara school.[23] This school existed long before the seventeenth century, laying claim to a history that dates to the Kamakura shogunate (1185–1333). Its teachings traditionally belonged to an oral and secret tradition that was the strict reserve of the warrior elite. This is a crucial element when investigating the publication of conduct manuals in the seventeenth century: publishers were determined to commit to print social and interpersonal knowledge that had been orally transmitted for centuries in an attempt to break away from secrecy, an endeavor that would have surely been applauded by Ejima Tamenobu (discussed in chapter 3). Michael Kinski identifies Mizushima Bokuya 水島卜也 (1607–1697), his job in Edo as a teacher of etiquette and his written work—circulated mainly in manuscript form and dating to the second half of the 1600s—as crucial agents in the dissemination of Ogasawara-style etiquette to a broader public.[24] I would suggest, however, that all started with the anonymous work *Ogasawara hyakka jō*: it was the first serious bid to disclose the secret tradition of this school of manners to a wider readership.[25]

The oldest documented printed version of *Ogasawara hyakka jō* is a movable-type edition written in a mixture of noncursive kanji and katakana.[26] The slim, horizontal format suggests the practical nature of a booklet that could easily have been carried around in one's kimono sleeves. The printing technique, lack of involvement by a commercial publisher, and the writing style position this text somewhat outside the world of popular literature. What about the contents? Without any paratextual aids or the insertion of any fictional narrative to frame the didactic message, the movable-type *Ogasawara hyakka jō* delivers discrete sections that are identified by the diacritic mark *hitotsu* 一, which functions like a bullet point. Their contents can be retrospectively organized around the following topics. The first consists of a handful of sections that explain specific words. For example, we learn that the first day of the year is also referred to as *ganzan* (literally, "the three firsts") because it is the first day of the New Year, the first day of the first month, and the first of all the days in a year.[27] The second group deals with the requirements of dress. The garments featured in the text clearly refer to the military class, with formal trousers (*hakama*) being discussed as the first item: in spring they should be green, in summer light blue, in autumn gray, and in winter black.[28] There are a great number of points in the third group about how the master of a household should entertain his guests and how to eat properly. For example, the guest should not be in shadow when candles are used, water should be poured over dry rice (*kareii*) and mixed, it being consumed after any accompanying dishes have been eaten.[29] The fourth group involves numerous detailed instructions for servants on how they should interact with their masters. Mention of objects like swords, saddles, horses, and bows are clear indicators of the social class and gender of the implied reader—that is, those belonging to the warrior class.[30]

It is useful to pause and reflect on a publication that seems at best puzzling. As the analysis of the contents has shown, the appeal of the movable-type *Ogasawara hyakka jō* seems to lay solely within the purview of males of warrior houses. And yet, why was it necessary to fix on the printed page teachings that they could have accessed as mouth-to-ear advice under the tutelage of a master or by emulating peers in their household? Could it be that the warrior class did not necessarily have ready access to the secret tradition and found it useful to have reference books to consult at leisure? Or could the publication of this book be justified as part of a more general fascination with books related to the world of warriors (referred to as *gunsho*) that were characteristic of the first half of the seventeenth century?[31]

The dry tone of the prose, together with its rather elitist worldview, might suggest that it was unlikely for *Ogasawara hyakka jō* to become a best seller with a wide readership. And yet commercial publishers of the period must have seen great potential since they went ahead to reinvent its contents in such a way that it would appeal to people outside the military elite. This, I would argue, is the beginning of the popularization of civility.

Ogasawara hyakka jō is transformed into a new textual entity under the same title in 1632.[32] The Kyoto publisher Nakano Ichiemon 中野市右衛門 (d. 1639) explains the drive behind this publication: "The sections in this book are part of the secret tradition of the Ogasawara school. They are exactly the same in the text known under the title *Shitsukekata chikuba shō* [A treatise on etiquette and wooden horses]. There have been repeated pleas [for access to the text] for many years, and therefore we have decided to make it available. Be diligent and do not show this book to any third party."[33]

Similarly to what we saw in the previous chapter, Nakano Ichiemon declares to be unlocking secret traditions for a larger readership. The mention of "repeated pleas" might simply be a cunning marketing strategy, or it could reflect a historical reality; it is impossible to determine. But the cultural significance of this statement should not be too readily discarded. It also signals another aspect associated with novice readers at the time: they were not privy to knowledge that was transmitted and circulated orally within private enclaves. Yet they yearned to access such knowledge. Nakano's final remark—"Be diligent and do not show this book to any third party"—may at first glance seem paradoxical: Nakano has placed this secret text on the market but expects his readers to keep it hidden. By doing so, however, he entices his readers with the promise to become part of an exclusive, secret tradition. In effect, when buying this book a reader is given the chance to join in an otherwise inaccessible corpus of social and interpersonal knowledge. Nakano is disseminating a form of know-how whose value depends on its exclusivity.

Who are the readers Nakano envisages? The desire to appeal to a greater readership is spelled out in the heading of the foreword: "Here Is What All People, High and Low, Need to Be Careful Of" (Jōge banmin tashinamu beki shidai). Be they high- or lowborn, *banmin* (all people, or people of all sorts) are identified as the target readership.[34] Nakano (the absence of any other name leads to the assumption that he is the author of this introduction) suggests that this edition of *Ogasawara hyakka jō* is taken out of its original restricted milieu of the warrior class in order to reach out to everyone. As such, Nakano seems to infer that all individuals, regardless of social background, should (and could) master the behavioral code inscribed in this text. This pledge for the democratization of the text—with "democratization" used here to mean the action of making something accessible to everyone—is somewhat toned down in the introduction, in which Nakano seems to confine the definition of *banmin* to servants (*hōkōnin*), whereby servants under no circumstances should displease their masters (*shujin*) and hence the need to master etiquette.[35] The word *hōkōnin* can refer to servants in a military household, thus bringing us back to the warrior sphere after promises of a more democratic appeal to *banmin*. But it is worth noting that the same word could also apply to merchant households. This might explain the need to publish this text in the first place: if it were only servants of military households, they could have received some form of training within their households. But this would have been difficult in a merchant's household. Ultimately, though, we are left wondering how exactly Nakano intended the word.

The paratextual elements of the 1632 *Ogasawara hyakka jō* speak of a tension between a desire to make known secret traditions beyond the warrior elite, on the one hand, and, on the other, the decision to address mainly those who work in military households. I would interpret this as a more substantial tension between a drive to democratize knowledge beyond any social hierarchy and a seemingly opposite choice to uphold social hierarchy in the training of servants that do not offend their masters with rude behavior. While the paratext reveals this tension, the text seeks to unlock social and interpersonal knowledge for the benefit of a broader readership. The text is packaged in a relatively accessible manner. It is woodblock printed, it appears in book-trade catalogues, and the price is comparatively cheap. The shift from noncursive to cursive and from katakana to hiragana confirms the desire to reach out to novice readers with basic literacy.

What happens to the contents? The first part of the text, from the first folio to the seventh, displays a sound-bite list of teachings, once again arranged in "bullet-point" format with each instruction listed on a single line (fig. 4.1). The contents break free from the rarefied world of the military elite to embrace all sorts of advice on how to behave in a thoughtful and polite manner. It begins with five items dealing with toothpicks. The reader is advised not to use a toothpick in front of people, not to clean teeth or tongue with a toothpick in the presence of others, not to talk with a toothpick in the mouth, and not to use a large toothpick regardless of rank.[36] These details all pertain to the realm of bodily cleanliness undertaken in a manner showing respect for others. The notation that the size of a toothpick must be commensurate with a person's rank is the only detail that ties deportment to the idea of hierarchy. Yet what that hierarchy is remains unsaid, as if the author of the text were taking for granted an understanding of hierarchy beyond the written text. Bodily propriety is

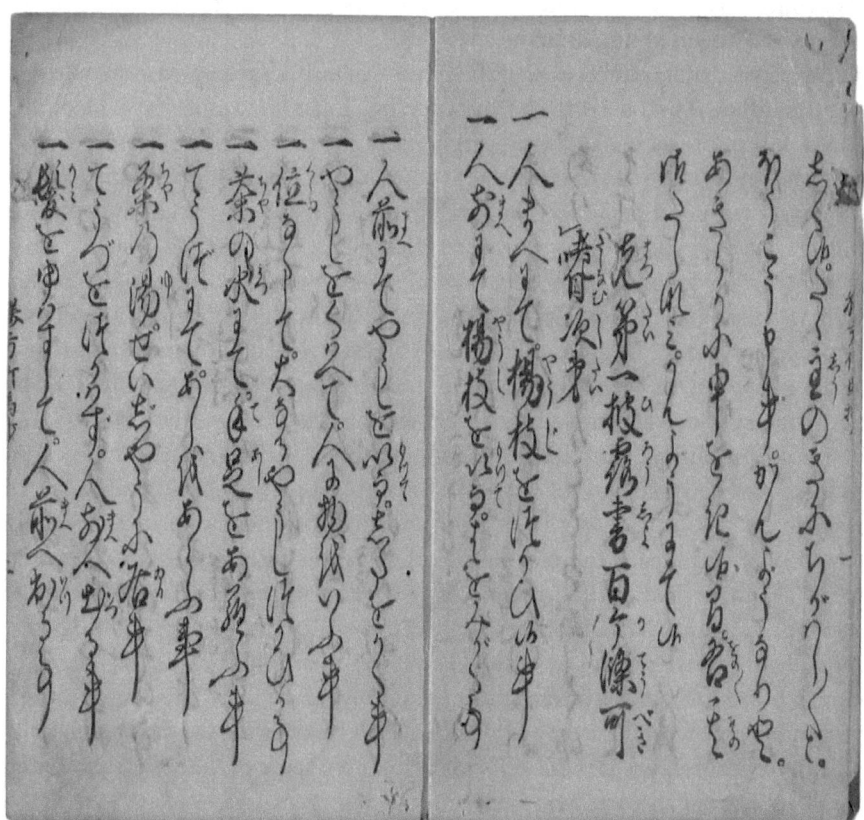

Figure 4.1 *Ogasawara hyakka jō*, 1632, 1v–2r. Beginning of "Here Is What All People, High and Low, Need to Be Careful Of."

Courtesy of the National Diet Library, Tokyo

covered in the five points that follow, including the need to wash and to coif the hair before meeting people.[37] The mention of formal trousers (*hakama*) is the only detail that discloses the male-centered, relatively high-status background of the text.[38] The next five items teach the reader that a person should not be noisy, bang doors and stamp, yell, or blow the nose loudly.[39] These remarks seem to suggest that correct deportment implied a high degree of bodily control. Respect for others continues to feature in the items that follow, advising to avoid using objects that belong to third parties or to guests, including their water basins, towels, and fans.[40] One should refrain from treading on other people's footwear and bedding and from placing feet on desks or *kotatsu* heaters.[41] The list then takes up the matter of respecting other people's possessions, including tangible objects such as writing implements but also concepts and actions like looking at another man's wife or reading correspondence intended for someone else.[42]

Equally important is the need for propriety in interacting with people one is intimate with (*jin taru hito*): for instance, one must avoid entering somebody's house without reserve or talking about sex in the presence of a friend's wife.[43] Sex was not an issue. It should be remembered that erotic and sexually explicit titles were included in book-trade catalogues as an integral part of the publishing genre known as *kōshoku narabi ni rakuji* (erotica and diversions).[44] What is identified as problematic in *Ogasawara hyakka jō* is speaking about sex in a woman's presence. It is not a matter of status as much as of gender. Reference to proper conduct in watching kickball games as well as in handling the bow and horses returns the reader to a more specific warrior-class context.[45] The many instructions about writing letters emphasize the importance of written communication.[46] Miscellaneous teachings punctuate the text summarized up to this point and also end the list.[47] We learn that a person should not be late in welcoming guests, should refrain from showing his underwear in public, cutting nails in front of others or using other people's knives to cut their own nails.[48] Equally disdainful is the use of another's footgear without asking or of wiping one's body with another's *yukata*.[49] Once again, respect for the other, regardless of their social status, which is never mentioned, as well as a certain degree of inhibition, are offered as key teachings in civility. This seems to suggest a more general concern with the need to be considerate, not necessarily within the household. It is not difficult to imagine some of the advice presented in the first seven folios as being relevant in a number of social situations: when sharing a room while traveling, when living with other people in a merchant's house, or when visiting someone else's dwellings, for instance.

Overall the first seven folios of *Ogasawara hyakka jō* are true to the publisher's intention to speak to all people, be they highborn or lowborn. However, the remainder of the text comprises longer teachings that would interest primarily those of warrior houses. Advice on how to behave when visiting other people's residences, including stables, rock gardens, and private rooms, is followed by instructions on how to handle all sorts of objects, including swords, bows, birds, books, and writing implements.[50] The text seems to mirror the friction noted in the publisher's introduction between a wish to engage all sorts of readers, regardless of their status, and a tendency to revert to the highborn. This echoes what Anna Bryson has noted in English late-medieval courtesy literature: she talks about a "striking disjunction" between "the comprehensive claim made for 'courtesy' . . . and the restricted aristocratic environment with its technicalities at service, which are then presented as the primary focus of the value."[51]

Instructions on how to eat—what we might refer to as table manners, although early modern Japan did not have tables as we might imagine them—occupy one-third of *Ogasawara hyakka jō*.⁵² Clearly, eating was viewed as a social act that needed to be regulated as any other activity of the body. The desire to appeal to both the highborn and the lowborn is confirmed here once more: rice dumplings or cooked rice might have been relevant to all sorts of readers, while delicacies like sweets to go with tea or meat might have resonated with only a few. The instructions are quite precise and focus primarily on forms:

> How to eat broth [*suimono*]:
> Take up your chopsticks. While holding your chopsticks take the bowl in your right hand, then pass it to your left and eat the pieces of food in the soup. Under no circumstances should you begin by drinking the soup. After [you have finished eating the piece of food], drink the soup and lay the bowl back down.⁵³

Interestingly, this section does not dwell on issues of hierarchical precedence in eating food when in a party of people. Consuming food is fundamentally an individual act: you are asked to control your body according to codified gestures, regardless of whom you are sitting with. Ceremonies also feature as yet another important aspect of civility. Rituals such as those held when a warrior returns from or leaves for the battlefield were surely a concern of those belonging to the warrior elite, while they likely had little or no practical application in times of peace.⁵⁴ Weddings, however, might have possessed more universal appeal. Occupying six out of sixty folios, weddings come across as a salient moment of a person's life that needs to be regulated as to form.⁵⁵ *Ogasawara hyakka jō* indulges in details that presume a degree of affluence, including tatami mats with white borders, folding screens decorated with faint ink and subdued colors, and white garments for the bride. The bridal procession is depicted in comparably lavish terms. Yet the same section contains information that might have been helpful for any newly wedded couple, such as the list of words that should be avoided during the first night together. The *sansan kudo* (literally, "three times three for a total of nine") celebration occupies pride of place, accompanied by a helpful visual representation of the *hikiwatashi* tray that displays the sake to be drunk and the festive, symbolic foods, together with precise instructions on how to use them.⁵⁶ Because the *sansan kudo* was by no means restricted to the upper echelons of society, it had the potential to resonate with the interests and needs of a wide range of readers.

Ogasawara hyakka jō is formidable in its decision to free interpersonal and social knowledge from the cultural tyranny of elitist secret traditions and to democratize it for the benefit of the novice reader. And yet the text never fully escapes the power of orality. On several occasions, in particular when it comes to the more formal ceremonies, readers are referred back to oral traditions (*kuden*) for further details. All of a sudden, the publisher jettisons his mission to make secret teachings available in print for the low price of a few coins and instructs readers to access the information that is orally transmitted within the exclusive circle of the Ogasawara school if they want to learn more. We thus realize that *Ogasawara hyakka jō* scratches the surface of the complex universe of etiquette, something much vaster than what can be covered in sixty or so folios. As a result, those who do have access to the oral tradition constitute, de facto, a privileged group, thus bringing us back to an intrinsically hierarchical view of the world. Written, printed culture enabled readers to access orally transmitted traditions. But the egalitarian printed word never fully replaced the more elitist orality.

Ogasawara hyakka jō remained hugely popular until the nineteenth century, suggesting a wide and variegated readership.[57] This despite the fact that almost half of the text seems somewhat removed from the daily lives of the *banmin*. The favor encountered by a conduct manual should not come as any surprise. After all, we might recall the popularity enjoyed for centuries by Castiglione's *Cortegiano* in Europe.[58] Yet the question remains: why would people, irrespective of their social background, relate with this text in the first place? It might be tempting to see a passive cultural subjugation to the warrior stratum, in line with the top-down process identified by Ikegami. I think that this is a very reductive, if not reactionary, reading, however.

To answer the question, we could perhaps place all this in a modern context. Let's say I purchase a copy of the famous *Debrett's Handbook*, enticed by the promise delivered by the subtitle that I will master "British style, correct form, and modern manners" and assured that manners "make everyday life easier, removing anxiety and minimizing social difficulties and awkwardness."[59] It is unlikely that I would consult the sections that teach me how to communicate with the queen or how to invite members of the royal family, but I might find pertinent sections such as "Social Kissing," "Driving," and "Table Manners" among many others. Undoubtedly they can all be extremely useful in my daily life. There might be items that I would never have thought might interest me—such as the grace before a meal, high tables, or loving cups—and yet life in a British college unexpectedly demanded I come to terms with a number of stuffy formalities. *Debrett's* helped no end. I may never have the opportunity to mingle with the peerage, let alone acquire a title, but, if I wanted, I could learn to behave *as if* I belonged to that rarefied sphere. And in moments of idleness I can pick up my copy of *Debrett's* just to sneak a look into things that I would never dream of actualizing—having bridesmaids at my wedding or entertaining royalty, among others. An apparently sterile conduct manual provides me with manifold pleasures: edification, broadening of knowledge, or maybe just a pastime (quoting, once more, Umberto Eco on literature).[60] There is no doubt that *Debrett's Handbook* does not intend to abrade status hierarchy. After all, the queen and the long list of peers are mentioned at length in the handbook and are a fact of British society. But enforcing social hierarchy is hardly the point of interest in this book.

I contend that all this can be applied retrospectively to *Ogasawara hyakka jō* and may well explain its popularity. Seventeenth-century readers from all sorts of backgrounds (*banmin*) were first and foremost encouraged to peruse this conduct manual efferently, as a piece of transformative literature, choosing what they deemed relevant for their own lifestyle. By mastering (if only a few, freely chosen) etiquette rules recorded in this text, readers, regardless of social status, could learn how to behave in order to evade embarrassment, criticism, and scorn.[61] They were also given a chance to master behavioral codes that were useful in situations where they had to mingle with people of higher status. As Eiko Ikegami has shown in the case of poetry gatherings and Rebecca Corbett for tea ceremonies, such was in fact the case for a number of wealthy commoners in early modern Japan.[62] On those occasions "commoners found it increasingly important to learn the appropriate modes of communication, both verbal and nonverbal, with which to communicate with their social superiors."[63] But there is more. By adopting proper behavior everyone in society was given a chance at least to "appear" equally as genteel and civilized as those at the top of society. This is no different from what Cynthia J. Brokaw notes in the case of the guides to social interaction that were issued by commercial publishers from the area known as Sibao in Qing-dynasty China. For example, the preface to the 1802 newly cut version of *Chousi jinnang* (Precious guide to social exchange) argues for the usefulness of the book for those who do not pursue an official career taking examinations but wish to practice "the reality of living as a *shi*," or in other words becoming a scholar in name.[64] As such, seventeenth-century etiquette can be viewed as a form of what Pierre Bourdieu called "embodied cultural capital"—that is, "long-lasting dispositions of the mind and body" that are acquired through work of self-improvement and that carry a "symbolic logic of distinction."[65] Comportment adhering to the rules of etiquette endorsed by the prestigious Ogasawara school would have created an aura of social respectability around anyone who had mastered them. Yes, one's clothes might have given away one's status were one to slavishly follow the sumptuary laws.[66] But proper manners would have elevated a person above those who did not possess the same embodied cultural capital. It is interesting to note that the paratext of other editions of *Ogasawara hyakka jō* had an active role in suggesting social inclusiveness. The much later 1843 edition issued in Edo by Wan'ya Ihee 椀屋伊兵衛 (dates unknown) under the title *Ogasawara-ryū shitsukekata hyakka jō*, for example, mixes together illustrations of warriors (fig. 4.2) with others that appear to be generic males, potentially belonging to the merchant class (fig. 4.3).[67] Does this mean a challenge to social order? Hardly, but by the same token social equality is not altogether denied. If one adopts

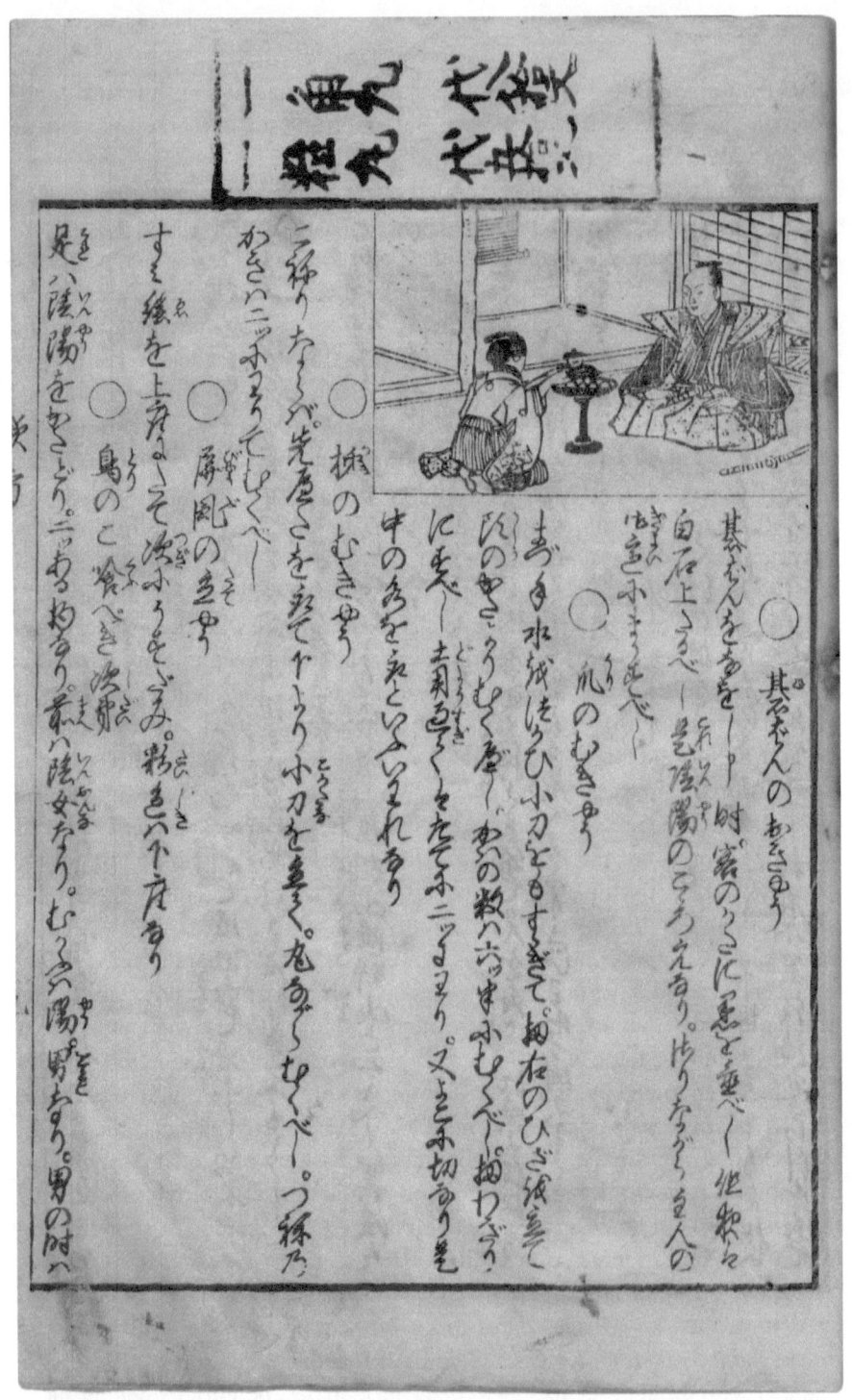

Figure 4.2 *Ogasawara-ryū shitsukekata hyakka jō*, 1843, 9r. A warrior being served.
Author collection, Suzuran Bunko, Cambridge, U.K.

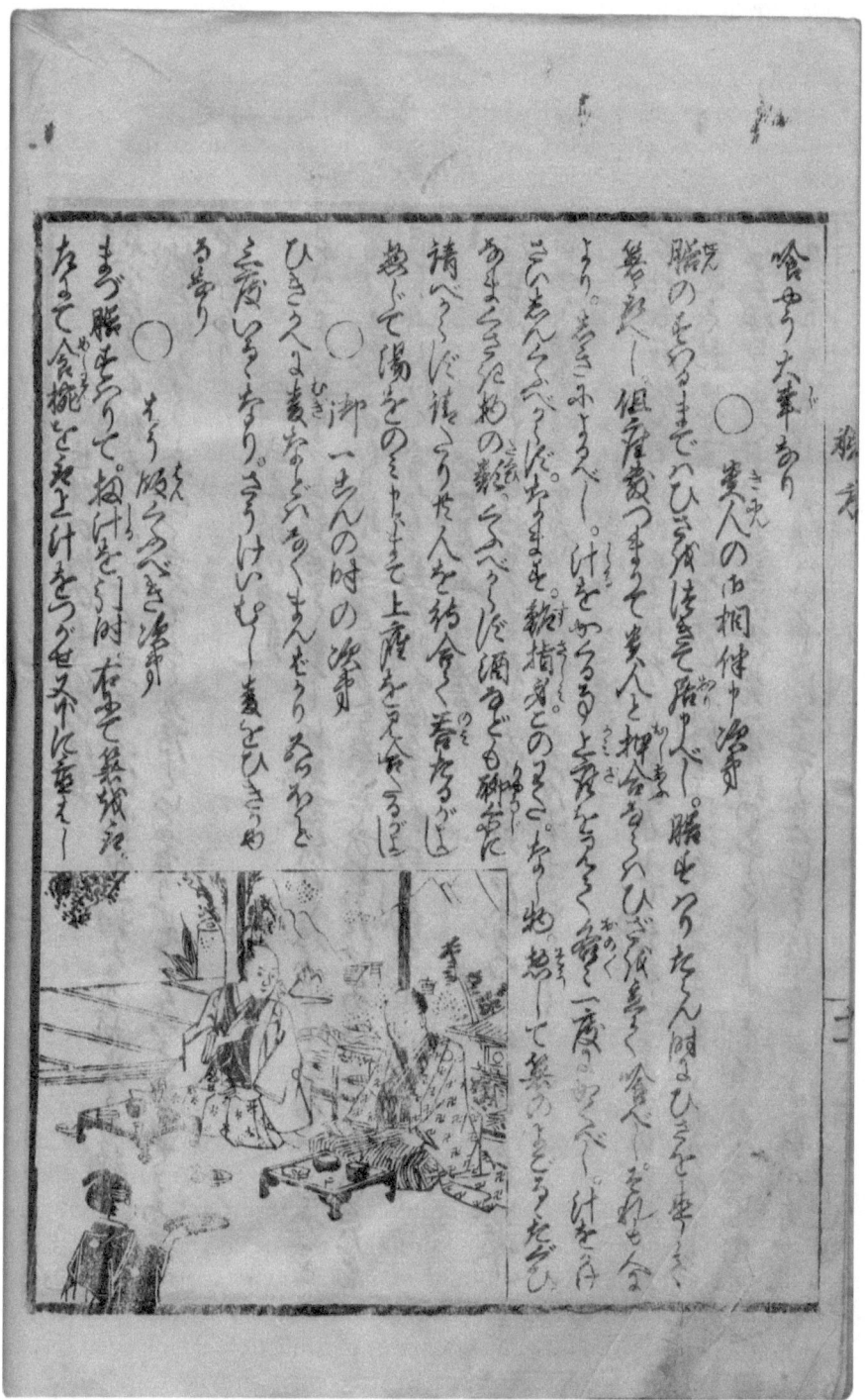

Figure 4.3 *Ogasawara-ryū shitsukekata hyakka jō*, 1843, 11v. Commoners being served.
Author collection, Suzuran Bunko, Cambridge, U.K.

civilized comportment one will be able to not only interact with superiors in an appropriate manner but also begin to appear, albeit superficially, like them. The illusion of social equality was promoted within a discourse that endorsed social differentiation. While today this might appear as a paradox, it worked for the seventeenth-century Japanese reader. For those who were desperate to try to climb the social ladder this kind of embodied cultural capital would have endowed them with the suitable tools.

The promise of transformation after the act of reading is not the only reason for the sustained popularity of *Ogasawara hyakka jō*. I maintain that by balancing contents that related to the daily life of all sorts with those that were clearly meaningful for members of the warrior elite or the wealthy only, *Ogasawara hyakka jō* opened a window onto worlds other than one's own. As a result, the dry, nonnarrative prose was transformed into a spectacle of lifestyles that were not necessarily visible or accessible to all in society. It would have been an almost voyeuristic desire to peep into others' lives—especially if they were higher in status and part of a remote, almost exotic universe—that drew the novice reader to this conduct manual. When approached in this fashion, the pleasure of *Ogasawara hyakka jō* resides in the very act of reading, in making the most of the imaginative stimulation provided in images of unfamiliar ways of living. Readers may have well conceded that being blessed with a similar station might have been implausible, but the text nonetheless enabled them to fantasize about this world.

Whether read efferently, aesthetically, or in both ways, civility literature remained in phase with readers throughout the seventeenth century and beyond. *Shogaku bunshō narabi ni yorozu shitsukekata* (Elementary letters and all forms of etiquette) was originally published in 1634, and its second half offers something akin to *Ogasawara hyakka jō*.[68] "Good Manners That People of All Sorts Should Cherish" (Banmin tashinamu beki shitsukekata) repeats a great deal of the instructions examined in the preceding.[69] The almost identical image of the *hikiwatashi* suggests familiarity on the part of Nishimura Matazaemon (the publisher of *Shogaku bunshō*) with the work of Nakano Ichiemon (the publisher of *Ogasawara hyakka jō*). Whenever it was deemed appropriate, new conduct rules were added. This shows a twofold commitment, on the one hand to perpetuate etiquette as something immutable that transcends time and space and, on the other, to make updates according to new needs and fashions. Conduct manuals continued production throughout the Edo period, with many of them being published (at least on the surface) under the auspices of the Ogasawara school.[70] A small number of rules of etiquette were included also in encyclopedic materials that developed after the eighteenth century.[71] And the Ogasawara school endures in the twenty-first century (very much like *Debrett's*, which started in 1769).[72] The current head of the Ogasawara school, Ogasawara Keishōsai 小笠原敬承斎 (b. 1966)—the first female head in the school's history—has released a number of books that teach basic civility for daily life.[73] How to greet, how to sit, how to open sliding doors, how to eat and drink, how to speak, and much more. The new buzzwords to market civility in the new millennium are "beauty" and "Japaneseness." The message is clear: do you wish to come across as a "true Japanese"? Do you want to appear as a beautiful person? If so, buy these books to grasp the standards of comportment. Illustrations, easy explanations, and plain language will help you in this quest. This is remarkably close to the aims of seventeenth-century publishers in perpetuating social distinctions fueled by appearance while, almost paradoxically, allowing everyone to appear sufficiently genteel.

In sum, seventeenth-century civility literature did not attempt to repress people through subjugation to a strictly hierarchical society. Rather, it provided individuals with modes for pleasing self-representation and with means to express themselves in ways beyond their social status. It also allowed novice readers to enjoy the spectacle of manners and ceremonies that had hitherto been kept secret. It also needs to be stressed that *Ogasawara hyakka jō* and *Shogaku bunshō* do not attempt in any way to advance any discourse on national consciousness. Etiquette is not something uniquely Japanese; rather, its practice promises attainment of being fully human. This plays havoc with later sources, those that Ikegami focuses on.

Constructing Femininity Through Conduct

As noted earlier, *Ogasawara hyakka jō* (and *Shogaku bunshō*) refers to *banmin*, but the contents seem to restrict the reference of this word to men. Does this mean that civility standards did not apply to women?[74] In order to answer this question, we must move away from the publishing genre of *shitsukekata-sho narabi ni ryōri-sho* and turn to another publishing genre known as *nyosho* (books for women). It encompasses a wide variety of educational titles designed specifically for women, and this area has been comparatively well researched in both Japanese- and English-language scholarship.[75] In seventeenth-century *nyosho*, moral education, examples of virtuous behavior by Chinese and Japanese women in history, and letter templates are the main contents. What is of interest here is that etiquette also features in these books. The inclusion of norms of conduct in a publishing genre different from *shitsukekata-sho narabi ni ryōri-sho* and in a category that targets women is in itself revealing. On the one hand, it confirms the permeability of such book typologies in book-trade catalogues. On the other, it signposts that masculinity and femininity were perceived as a meaningful differentiation in norms of behavior.

Onna kagami hidensho (also known simply as *Onna kagami* [The mirror for women]), first published in 1650 by the Kyoto publisher Noda Yahee 野田弥兵衛

(dates unknown), offers a compelling case study.[76] I examine it in tandem with a similar book printed a decade later, in 1660, titled *Onna shikimoku* (Rules for women).[77] The reference to "secret tradition" (*hiden*) echoes the rhetoric examined in *Ogasawara hyakka jō* of divulging knowledge that had traditionally been a prerogative of chosen people. The use of the word "mirror" indicates that we are dealing with transformative literature: ideally, reading leads to adjustments in our life, and the book in question is nothing but a mirror that shows what change to implement.

The centrality of etiquette is revealed in the 1670 *shojaku mokuroku*, where *Onna kagami hidensho* is identified as a book especially designed for conduct (*shitsukekata*). And yet *Onna kagami hidensho* opens with a passage focusing on morality.[78] The initial section of the first volume explains the Buddhist view of the Five Hindrances (*goshō*) and the disadvantaged position of women.[79] It then expounds the Confucian concept of the Three Obediences (*sanjū*), according to which women are required to obey their fathers in childhood, their husbands after marriage, and their sons in old age.[80] A religious tone is retained in the second section, where women are encouraged to profess faith in the deities and Buddhas.[81] *Onna shikimoku* confirms the importance of morality: it urges women to adhere to both Confucian teachings (i.e., the Five Relations and the Five Virtues) and key Buddhist teachings such as the Five Precepts, among others.[82] As such, women's civility is framed as a facet of ethical behavior. Comportment is subsumed by virtue and virtue is defined alongside the syncretic lines discussed in chapter 3. From this perspective, *Onna kagami hidensho* and *Onna shikimoku* challenge Ikegami Eiko's claim that "most of the handbooks were clearly detached from any sort of moralizing," with the exception of Kaibara Ekiken.[83] Clearly that is not the case.

Having set precise ideological parameters, *Onna kagami hidensho* then turns to more practical teachings. The reader is reminded that nothing can be done about physical appearance since one is born either pretty or ugly.[84] Yet a woman should always be vigilant about bodily propriety. Black hair and white skin are the main traits of womanhood, and a woman should always keep her nails clipped, wear clean clothes, and wash body and hair so that they do not stink.[85] Etiquette (*shitsuke*) is crucial beginning with the age of seven.[86] The key word for appropriate behavior is *yawaraka*, or "softness."[87] Dispensing with any heavy physical work (*chikarawaza*), a woman should concentrate on writing, composing poetry, music, and reading.[88] A woman should achieve proficiency in correct behavior by the time she is twelve or thirteen, with a clear view to becoming an ideal wife.[89] Sixteen folios into *Onna kagami hidensho* we start realizing that at the very heart of the discourse on female civility is the wish to produce a desirable woman, one who is shaped in such a way as to attract men and gain married status. The reader gathers instruction about how to sit, how to stand, how to wear and take care of clothing, how to deal with hair, nails, makeup, and body odor, and how to greet others properly.[90] The decision to include a section on how to display filial piety to one's parents-in-law evinces the real point of interest: proper deportment leads to married life.[91] Teachings on how to laugh, how to speak, and how to treat others conclude the first volume, indicating that a woman was expected to interact with several people within as well as outside the confines of the household.[92] The passage on how to speak underscores the complexities at play in terms of gender and social distinctions:

> When speaking, a woman should first of all make sure not to speak too much. Too many words lead to countless mistakes and are ostentatious. Men are also warned against speaking too much. Even more so, a woman should refrain from having a big mouth and from lying. As mentioned before, when scolding your servants you should do so without raising your voice. Softness [*yawaraka*] and elegance [*yasashiki*] are paramount. Wives and daughters of military or court aristocracy should avoid being taciturn. The key is to reach a happy medium. All this needs to be mastered within the first three years of marriage.[93]

The contrast between men and women is not as straightforward as we might expect. Some sort of distinction is made regarding women occupying the highest social ranks, but the exhortation to find the right balance between extremes seems to apply to all.

The second volume zooms in on proper comportment in all aspects of married life. After an initial section dealing with written correspondence (which I examine in chapter 5), we share in a moment in a woman's life when she receives a marriage proposal.[94] Sections 2–20 offer a systematic treatment of the marriage ritual and does so more than forty years before the well-known *Onna chōhōki* (1692).[95] First is the acceptance ceremony of the wedding proposal (*iire no shūgi*), then the celebration of the woman leaving her own house (*kadoide no iwai*), the procession carrying the bride and her dowry, the ceremony known as *shiki sankon*, the changing of clothes after the *shiki sangon* (*ironaoshi*), food rituals (*zōni* soup with *mochi*, *kyōzen*, *hikiwatashi*, *shichi go san*), the appearance of the parents-in-law, the consumption of an ordinary meal (*tsune no zen*), the first night and the morning after, and finally the ablutions on the second day after the wedding. Some of the details of this long passage are drawn from *Ogasawara hyakka jō*. This suggests a certain amount of overlap in conduct norms as presented to a male and to a female readership as well as a fruitful circulation of knowledge across publishers and publishing genres. For example, the description of how one should consume food from the *hikiwatashi*, together with an illustration of the tray and its contents (two pieces of dried *konbu* seaweed on the right, four dried chestnuts on the left, and the three cups of sake in the middle), recycles what was already included in *Ogasawara hyakka jō* and *Shogaku bunshō*. Here again the reader is given guidance on what should be done.⁹⁶ The information is retained almost verbatim, but an interesting change occurs at the linguistic level. While the previous two male-centered conduct manuals apply plain language in the choice of verbs, such as *nomu* for "to drink" and *kuu* for "to eat/hold in one's mouth," the anonymous author of *Onna kagami hidensho* uses the humble form *mairu*, placing the woman in a lower position vis-à-vis the husband with whom she shares the room.

The importance of the wedding ceremonies in the sphere of women's civility is confirmed in *Onna shikimoku*.⁹⁷ It begins with a description of how a marriage is administered in China and then deplores the fact that the standards in Japan are not equal. *Onna shikimoku* is one of the very first texts to bring the notion of Japan into a discussion of conduct. Rather counterintuitively, however, it does not promote Japan as civilly superior; instead it praises China as the more civilized land. It then strongly advises men to look for women who come from a lower-status household and women to look for men from a higher-status family, hence underscoring social hierarchies. The passage ends with a mention of the *shiki sankon* and the *shichi go san* but refrains from giving details and points readers to other, unspecified books. An unmarked allusion to *Onna kagami hidensho* is sufficiently plausible here. In doing so, *Onna shikimoku* appears less friendly toward its readers and forces them to buy or borrow other books in order to get the full picture of how to administer a wedding.

Following information on the wedding ceremony, *Onna kagami hidensho* outlines the essentials of married life. While jealousy need not be totally eliminated—something that stands out from the mainstream discourse on jealousy at the time—it should be kept in check, especially if the husband is short-tempered.⁹⁸ A good wife should acquire the same interests as her husband, be well disposed toward the servants, and exercise filial piety toward the mother-in-law.⁹⁹ It becomes more and more apparent as the text progresses that, for a woman, civility is closely linked with marital conduct. If a wife conforms to the rules of proper behavior, the relationship with her husband will bloom and they will be blessed with children. And the first half of the third volume focuses on sexual hygiene, pregnancy, childbirth, and child rearing.¹⁰⁰

This is not to say that etiquette did not cover areas of the universe of male civility. In the third volume, from sections 27 to 41, the text abruptly moves away from writing about women as mothers and focuses on table manners.¹⁰¹ What is striking here is that table manners for women are somewhat different from those of men. When speaking about how to consume broth (*suimono*), for example, the text instructs as follows: "Put your chopsticks down and drink by holding [the cup] in your right hand. It is good to leave some and not drink all of it. Unlike men, you should not eat pickles."¹⁰² Whereas the descriptions of how to eat dishes are the same in *Ogasawara hyakka jō* and *Shogaku bunshō*, it is notable that women are required to follow different rules. In the context of seventeenth-century Japan, table manners are an important element in books targeting both men and women, but there is clearly an attempt to distinguish between female and male patterns of behavior. This offers a different picture of what Anna Bryson has noted in the English context: "Advice on education and duties of women ... contains very little technical advice on manners," suggesting that "it seems plausible that the code of elementary civility formulated in works such as *De Civilitate* in many ways applied equally to boys and girls."[103]

The third volume of *Onna kagami hidensho* includes counsel on health and aging, ending with advice for dealing with daughters-in-law and grandchildren.[104] Seen altogether this mirror reflects the ideal life that a woman should aspire to. As such it can be read not only as an ensemble of practical teachings but also as a conceptual grammar of womanhood. At the same time, the structure of the text—in one hundred twenty discreet sections clearly numbered, titled, and preceded by a handy table of contents—enables readers to pick and choose what they wish to read efferently: ethics, social knowledge, bodily civility, and manners.

Who would have read this kind of conduct manual? *Onna shikimoku* offers a preliminary answer, albeit indirectly. It organizes the teachings around four main groups: high-ranking women (*ueue no jōrōgata*); townswomen and the like (*chōnin nado no nyūbō*), with a specific reference to merchants (*shōnin*); women in service to high-ranking women; and women in service in townsman households. This intimates that women of all sorts were conceptualized as the target readership and encouraged to peruse this text, very much in line with the idea of *banmin* discussed previously. This also confirms the paradox noted before: civility literature makes etiquette accessible for the benefit of everyone, but social hierarchy is never dispensed with. Different from what has been noted in the manuals for men, *Onna shikimoku* does mention different standards for different social constituencies. Key for upper-class women, for instance, is compassionate and just behavior in the household, with a strong call for staying at home as much as possible and following the Three Obediences. For townswomen, compassion is still noted, but other virtues are stressed: frugality, hard work, and deference for one's husband. Honesty, respect, and complete dedication to work are expected from servants.[105] Unfortunately, *Onna kagami hidensho* does not specify at any point what kind of women it implies. It is safe to argue that its contents have the potential to appeal to all. Perhaps a woman born into a household not that affluent might not be able to compose poetry, devote herself to music, or pay great attention to clothing. Yet as chapter 1 in this study demonstrates, reading and writing were a must across society. Similarly, bodily cleanliness, which features prominently in the first volume, as well as childbirth-related matters, which occupy much of the third volume, among other topics, have the potential to appeal to a

154 Civility Matters

large segment of the female readership. Altogether *Onna kagami hidensho* comes across as completely disengaged with any form of social differentiation and so works differently from *Onna shikimoku*. We must accept that popular civility literature did not necessarily offer any coordinated and systematic approach but worked as a welter of diverse and at times diverging views.

In keeping with what we have seen regarding male-oriented conduct manuals in the tradition of the Ogasawara school, the teachings offered by *Onna kagami hidensho* were inherited and reshaped as one aspect of the encyclopedic materials for women until the end of the Edo period.[106]

Maximizing Profit

Read efferently, *Onna kagami hidensho* had the potential to teach a woman correct behavior that would have ensured a successful marriage and a harmonious household, thus a fulfilling life. Publishers, though, attempted to do something more with this manual, and the six-volume edition issued sometime after 1652, possibly by Yamamoto Chōbee, is revealing.[107] The verbal text is for the most part a new impression of the 1652 blocks, but a number of images are added anew. This combination of old and new blocks was by no means unheard of and was easily accommodated by a convenient use of pagination numbers: illustrations would occupy a complete folio, verso and recto, and the folio number would simply repeat the previous one preceded by the word *mata* (again). In this way publishers were able to minimize production costs—they had to cut new blocks only for the folios with images; this, in turn, meant that they were maximizing financial profit. This went hand in hand with marketing the book in a way to beckon more invitingly potential customers: the title slip advertised the new visual component using the word *e-iri* (pictures inserted).

Something very clever goes on in the illustrations. The first of the six volumes (covering half of what was the first volume in the 1652 edition) is nothing extraordinary, the illustrations being a visual translation of the contents—we find, for example, a depiction of a woman engrossed in learning (*tenarai* [fig. 4.4]). In the second volume (which covers the second half of the first volume in the 1652 edition) the correspondence with the contents weakens and the intertextual use of other sources becomes more apparent. We find, for instance, sixteen images of *kosode* (short-sleeved kimono) hung on kimono stands (fig. 4.5).[108] The text inscribed within the illustrations links the kimono to a specific month or occasion and explains in some detail the design and color scheme. What is especially intriguing is that the images and the descriptions are not new: they are borrowed from *Onna shorei shū* (Compendium of

Figure 4.4 *Onna kagami hidensho*, later reprint of the 1652 Yamamoto Chōbee edition, with additions, vol. 1, 10r (*mata*). A woman engrossed in *tenarai*.

Author collection, Suzuran Bunko, Cambridge, U.K.

156 Civility Matters

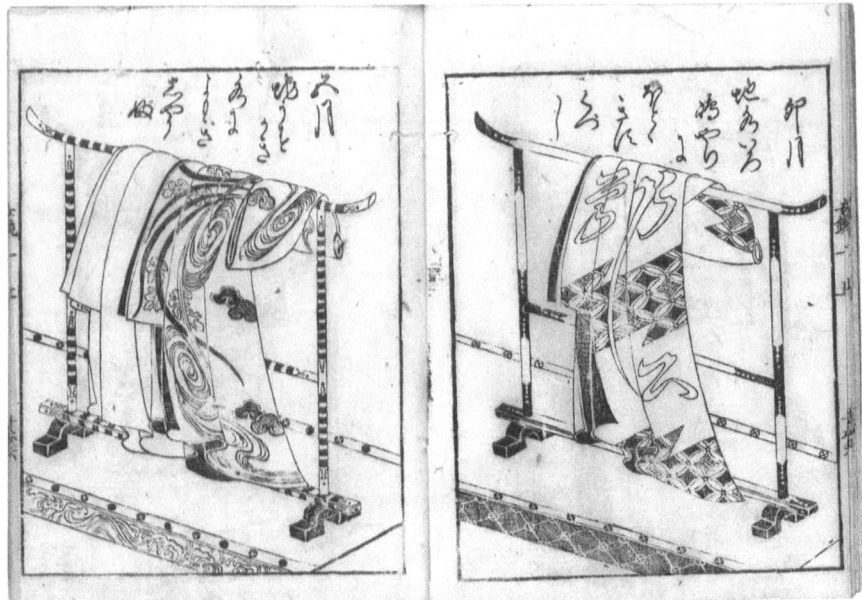

Figure 4.5 *Onna kagami hidensho*, later reprint of the 1652 Yamamoto Chōbee edition, with additions, vol. 2, 16/5v–16/6r. Kimono on display.

Author collection, Suzuran Bunko, Cambridge, U.K.

the complete etiquette for women; first published in 1660), another influential etiquette book for women.[109] While further research is needed to ascertain which edition of *Onna shorei shū* was used and whether the blocks were cannibalized or recut, I would like to pause on the significance of this intertextual, visual borrowing. In *Onna shorei shū* the presence of these sixteen images was justified by their inclusion after a section dealing in detail with what a woman should wear depending on the season. Therefore images of clothing for specific times of the year were a natural visual choice to complement the verbal text. In *Onna kagami hidensho* these images follow section 15, which instructs on how to wear a *kosode*. No mention in the verbal text is made of seasonality. Consequently, the illustrations, in this case, *expand* the verbal text by providing fresh information. As a result, suddenly *Onna kagami hidensho* moves away from being simply a manual of etiquette to become a book of kimono patterns. The title slip attached to this volume of *Onna kagami hidensho* foregrounds this new function by advertising the contents as "*kosode* patterns" (*kosode no moyō*). The inclusion of images borrowed from *Onna shorei shū* enables *Onna kagami hidensho* to multiply its functions: a book of conduct offers snippets of what would normally have been referred to as a *hinagata* book (or book of kimono patterns) and, at the same time, features morsels from another popular book, *Onna shorei shū*. The pleasure of the text expands. Readers could now combine the efferent reading of conduct norms with the aesthetic enjoyment of the beauty of kimono patterns, as they would do with a *hinagata* book. They could also read the same illustrations efferently in case they had the financial means to buy the necessary fabrics and maybe commission the manufacture. Furthermore, they were given the thrill of accessing some of *Onna shorei shū* without the need to purchase this other title (of course assuming that they were aware of the intertextual borrowing).

This strategy is further amplified in the remaining four volumes of this illustrated edition of *Onna kagami hidensho*, and the title slips are used to publicize the expanded contents: "Shūgen no ezu" ("Images of the Wedding Ceremony," vol. 3), "Mizushi kurodana" ("The Shelves with the Bridal Possession and Dowry," vol. 4), and "San'ya no ezu" ("Pictures About the Ceremony of the Third Day After Giving Birth," vols. 5 and 6). The space constructed by the images is not of any ordinary household but one of affluence. The twelve *kosode* on display, the cornucopia of food and gifts for the wedding ceremonies, and the lavish interiors (fig. 4.6) speak of a world that would have been out of reach for most readers. As a result, this edition of *Onna kagami hidensho* turns a piece of transformative, nonnarrative literature teaching civil

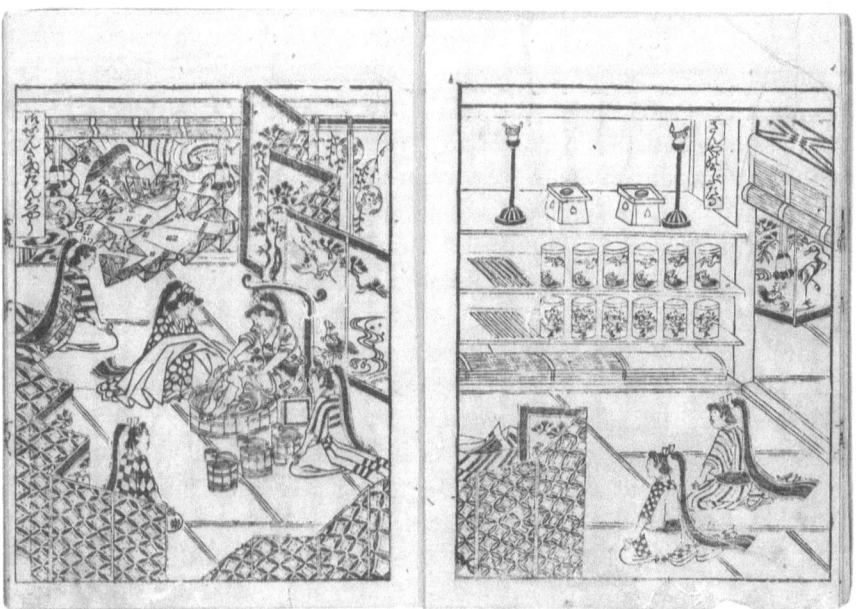

Figure 4.6 *Onna kagami hidensho*, later reprint of the 1652 Yamamoto Chōbee edition, with additions, vol. 6, 15v–16r. Ceremony of the third day after birth.

Author collection, Suzuran Bunko, Cambridge, U.K.

behavior into a tale of the life of a wealthy woman, one that any ordinary woman could fantasize about just by paying the relatively low price of approximately four *monme*. This brings us back to one of the arguments I put forward when discussing *Ogasawara hyakka jō* and its popularity: the profit derived from reading practical advice, which endows a reader with the necessary embodied cultural capital, is matched with the pleasure of reading a story of a world one could dream of and—why not—aspire to.

The Birth of a Communal Food Culture

In seventeenth-century Japan cookery books were marketed as something associated with civility literature, as the choice of the label *shitsukekata-sho narabi ni ryōri-sho* (books on manners and cookery) suggests. To the best of my knowledge, the discourse on civility in early modern Europe did not emphasize any such connection with food culture. In Japan, however, this combination had already been fostered in medieval Japan. Eric C. Rath writes that medieval culinary writings by professional chefs included "not only information about knife ceremonies (*shikibōchō*) but also recipes, description of model banquets, information about table manners."[110] By featuring table manners extensively, seventeenth-century conduct manuals were clearly concerned with regulating eating as a social practice. Cookbooks, for their part, were equally shaping a culinary culture in ways that I explore in this section. Together *shitsukekata-sho narabi ni ryōri-sho* can be seen as a publishing genre that fueled the creation of a communal food culture, sharing a desire to release food-related knowledge from the world of the few privileged.

The starting point of what developed into a buoyant production of all sorts of early modern cookery manuals is *Ryōri monogatari* (Food tales).[111] The democratizing attitude identified at the heart of the conduct manuals examined in the previous sections is confirmed in the afterword to *Ryōri monogatari*:

> The present volume on food is not based on the etiquette followed by professional chefs [*hōchō kirikata no shikihō*]. Rather, it records the cooking of ordinary people [*tadabito no tsukuri shidai*] and therefore does not prescribe any fixed way of cooking. It is what has been passed down orally [*kikitsutaeshi koto*] from the past and the tales [*monogatari*] of people until the present time. That is why we titled it *Ryōri monogatari*.[112]

This suggests that *Ryōri monogatari* breaks from the constraints of the culinary schools of professional chefs that proliferated in medieval Japan.[113] The anonymous author and the publisher wish to empower the common people by giving them a voice and by recording their "food tales" in print for the benefit of anyone reading this written record. In this regard, it seems to me that this work is not so removed from the attitude displayed by Hannah Glasse in her groundbreaking cookbook *The Art of Cookery Made Plain and Easy*, first published in England in 1747 and intended to be an instruction manual for servants, "the lower sort."[114] The author of *Ryōri monogatari* (most likely a man) did not look for the imprimatur of a specific school, which is at variance with the case of conduct manuals for men. Yet there is still an attempt to market the book as a text that makes known a secret tradition, as indicated by a 1643 edition in the Ōei Bunko that has the cover title *Ryōri hidenshō* (A commentary on the secret tradition of cookery).[115] Whether recording information gathered from the common people or disclosing a secret tradition, *Ryōri monogatari* marks the first step in the creation of a shared, popular culture of food in Japan. In this respect it is similar to *Ogasawara hyakka jō* and its desire to commodify the teachings of the Ogasawara school.

Ryōri monogatari is organized into twenty sections, which can be broken down into three main groups. The first concerns ingredients and the best methods to cook them. The first seven sections of the book arrange ingredients according to the following categories: ocean fish, seaweed, river fish, fowl, large animals (red meat), mushrooms, and vegetables. Harada Nobuo argues that there is a certain logic in the order of the ingredients, with those appearing first endowed with greater value.[116] An inventory of ingredients is included in each category, and they are accompanied by a list of the most delicious ways to eat them. It appears that the king of the kitchen at this time, at least in the popular imagination, was the sea bream (*tai*), because it is the first ingredient in the first section. The passage delineates how this fish might be prepared: broiled whole (*hamayaki*); grilled on cedar wood (*sugiyaki*); made into a seasoned paste, steamed, and processed (*kamaboko*); pickled (*namasu*); à la *shimofuri* (blanched in hot water, then placed in cold water); in a soup; on a skewer with miso sauce (*dengaku*); marinated in seasoned sake (*sakabite*); fermented (*sushi*); and so forth.[117] No information is actually given on how to prepare the sea bream in these ways. For that we need to move on to the second group: "ways of cooking," or recipes.

Recipes, the second group in my analysis, are arranged according to the following broad categories: soups (*shiru*), fish salads (*namasu*), sashimi and fish marinated in seasoned sake (*sashimi sakabite*), simmered dishes (*nimono*), grilled dishes (*yakimono*), and broths (*suimono*).[118] The order is meaningful as it mirrors the organization of items on a menu (*kondate*), a practice that continues today. Different from the easily navigable conduct manuals examined earlier in this chapter, here readers must patiently wade their way through each section to identify the desired ingredient.[119] For example, if a reader wished to know how to make the sea bream soup suggested in section 1, it would be necessary to go to section 9. In this second group, the ingredients are arranged in roughly the same order as in the first group, and sea bream appears in pole position. Three recipes for sea bream soups are then given.¹²⁰

The third group deals with specific types of dishes: sauces and stock (*namadare dashi irizake*), various types of cooking sake (*ryōrizake*), side dishes (*sakana*), and food to be served after the main meal (*godan*; including sweets and tea).¹²¹ *Ryōri monogatari* concludes with the section "Yorozu kikigaki no bu" (Section that records all sorts of things heard and recorded) and takes the form of a miscellany of random culinary knowledge, including instructions on how to preserve food.¹²² In the aforementioned *The Art of Cookery Made Plain and Easy*, recipes for preserving food were similarly included in the "Additions" at the end of the book.

It is also worth noting that the 1670 and the 1684 abridged editions of *Ryōri monogatari*, published under the title *Ryōri hidenshō*, both begin with a one-folio section on the food to be prepared for wedding ceremonies, and this choice signals a close link with conduct books in which, as explained, wedding ceremonies feature extensively.¹²³ If in the conduct manuals readers learned how to eat the celebratory food, in these editions of *Ryōri monogatari* they understood how

Figures 4.7 *Ryōri hidenshō*, 1670, 1v–2r. Wedding ceremony.

Courtesy of the National Institute of Japanese Literature, Tachikawa to prepare the tray. A double-page illustration depicts the wedding party (fig. 4.7). It takes the reader away from the moment of food preparation to that of the ritual consumption and therefore back to the realm of etiquette.

Culinary Manuals and Storytelling

The dry, nonnarrative, and instructional prose of *Ryōri monogatari* aptly conveys the utilitarian character of this culinary manual, which clearly invites efferent reading. Eric C. Rath maintains, however, that we cannot be certain of the extent to which readers at the time actually used this text as a cooking manual: "All Edo-period culinary books could be read and enjoyed without having to create the dishes within them."[124] This stance aligns with the argument I put forward for conduct manuals: readers could use them to acquire the embodied cultural capital needed to appear well mannered, or they could peruse them to fantasize about worlds other than their daily reality. Putting knowledge to practical use and exploiting knowledge to quench the thirst for entertaining stories were two sides of the same coin. What is interesting about *Ryōri monogatari* is the proactive attempt on the part of publishers to package a potentially arid list of ingredients and recipes as entertaining reading.

The undated edition of *Ryōri monogatari*, released by the Edo publisher Matsue Ichirobee as a later reprint of his 1664 edition, is instructive for understanding what I mean by "entertaining."[125] Its illustrations are the key. In a cookbook one would expect the presence of what Francesca Bray labels "technical images" (C. *tu*, J. *zu*) in the Chinese tradition—that is, "graphic images or layouts which encoded technical knowledge ... instructive images conveying skilled specialist knowledge" and "templates for action."[126] This was certainly the case in other seventeenth-century cookbooks; for instance, *Ryōri kirigata hidenshō* (Secret writings on culinary slicing; 1642).[127] Advertised in book-trade catalogues as a book containing the "secrets of the knife" (*hōchō himitsu*) as well as a "treatise on the etiquette of cooking" (*ryōhō shitsukeshō*), as I see it *Ryōri kirigata hidenshō* is opposite to *Ryōri monogatari* in that it falls back on the authority of the secret tradition instead of giving a voice to ordinary people. The reference to Takahashi Gozaemon 高橋五左衛門 (dates unknown)—of the Takahashi house of chefs in service to the emperor—is used as a stamp of authority.[128] Eager to focus solely on the secrets of highbrow culinary practices, *Ryōri kirigata hidenshō* includes a number of technical images on how to cut raw fish and game fowl. However, when Matsue Ichirobee publishes his edition of *Ryōri monogatari*, he surprises us with the illustration on the recto of the third folio (fig. 4.8).[129] We are in the middle of a kitchen. Two men are preparing the dishes; two women, sporting the *hyōgo* hairstyle much in vogue during the Kanbun era (1661–1673), are in charge of carrying food and drinks to another room.

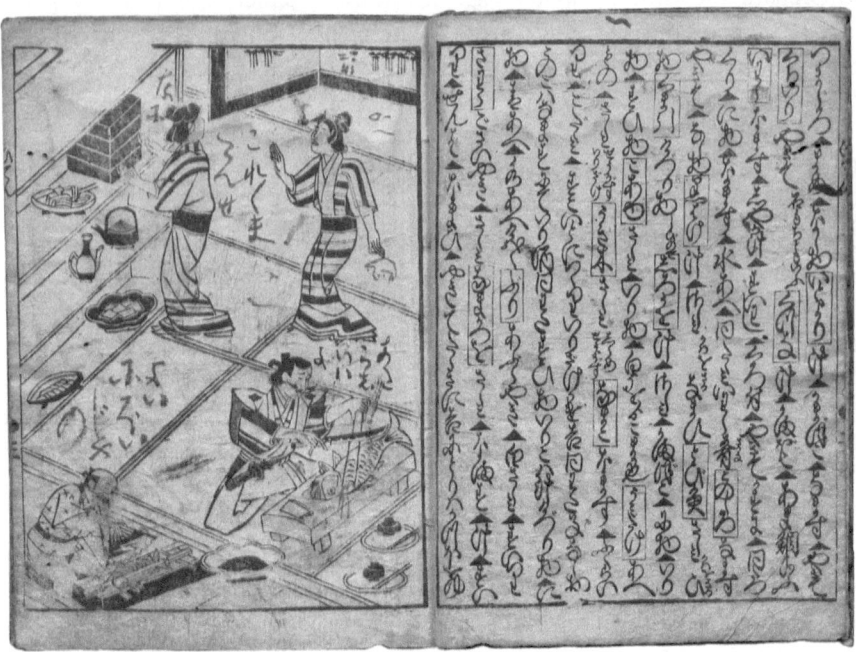

Figure 4.8 *Ryōri monogatari*, published by Matsue [Ichirobee], 2v–3r. Kitchen scene.
Courtesy of the National Institute of Japanese Literature, Tachikawa

There are three points of interest in this illustration. First of all, we are dealing with a case of "intervisuality"—that is, visual intertextuality.[130] It is my contention that Matsue Ichirobee adapted this image from *Onna jingi monogatari* (Tales of female virtue) (fig. 4.9). First published in 1659 by Yamamoto Kyūbee, all the editions include the image in question.[131] It is also worth noting that Matsue Ichirobee himself published *Onna jingi monogatari*, first in 1664 as a facsimile of the Yamamoto edition and then as a later reprint of his own edition but without date.

A comparison of the two compositions reveals that *Ryōri monogatari* uses the right side of the double-page spread in *Onna jingi monogatari*. It retains the scene of a man cutting the fish and the woman with her back turned to the viewer who is about to grab the stacked trays of food. In *Ryōri monogatari*, however, we find a second chef (or a kitchen servant) who fans another fish on a grill, while in *Onna jingi monogatari* a woman sits in front of the main chef. There is a second standing woman in both. In *Ryōri monogatari* she is seen calling the other woman, while in *Onna jingi monogatari* she holds a tray with a bowl and walks into the adjoining room, where a party is under way. This borrowing might at first sight appear rather puzzling as *Onna jingi monogatari* has

Figure 4.9 *Onna jingi monogatari*, publication details unknown, vol. 2, 2v–3r. Kitchen scene with adjacent party.

Courtesy of the National Institute of Japanese Literature, Tachikawa

nothing to do with food. It is a dialogue delivered in a nonnarrative, nonfictional mode that elucidates a woman's duties and behavior, most notably the Five Virtues and the Five Relations. The inclusion of this image in *Onna jingi monogatari* is self-explanatory. The verbal text depicts two young women, a mature married woman and an old man in conversation. The illustration on the recto of the third folio translates visually the moment of the verbal exchange: the cartouche on the left identifies the woman as the elder figure and the cartouche on the right introduces the old man. The kitchen scene on the right suggests that food will be served to the party, a narrative detail that is suggested in the image but never developed in the text. The way in which the three women in the kitchen are drawn (looking or walking in the direction of the room where the dialogue is taking place) helps guide the reader to the left side of the double-page spread, indicating that this is the center of the scene.

The meaning of the image changes when it migrates to *Ryōri monogatari*. The choice of a kitchen harmonizes well with the nature of *Ryōri monogatari* as a culinary manual, but the iconotext does not translate the contents of the verbal text into graphic signs. Instead, it provides us with a space populated by individuals at work. This leads to the second point I wish to make regarding this illustration. By portraying figures in action (or agents in narratological terms), this illustration suggests that there is potential for a story to be developed. A narrative as such is not brought to life on the printed page, but there is enough on the printed page to stimulate the reader's creativity in inventing a story. In other words, the reader is put in a position to play with the image, using the culinary space as a springboard for narrative imagination. This possibility is confirmed by the handwritten jottings added by an anonymous reader to the copy in the National Institute of Japanese Literature (fig. 4.8). Captions have been added to the various characters. They are now given a distinct voice. The cook preparing the fish says, "It is fresh!" (*atarashii yo*), and the cook grilling the fish titillates our sense of smell, exclaiming, "Oh, it smells lovely!" (*yoi nioi ja no*). The woman on the left acknowledges that the other is calling her and simply asks, "What is it?" (*nani*), to which the other replies, "Hey, hey! Wait a moment" (*kore kore matanse*). The use of *matanse*, with the verb *matsu* followed by the supplementary verbal ending *-nsu* to denote a slightly honorific register, creates another twist. This supplementary ending, in fact, is believed to have originated in the pleasure quarters. As such, we are persuaded to imagine that we are in no ordinary kitchen but maybe inside Yoshiwara. What appears to be a simple half-folio illustration has empowered the anonymous reader to turn a nonnarrative, how-to manual into a charming snippet of a tale created outside the printed page.

A third element in this illustration needs to be highlighted. A closer look at the man cutting the fish—most likely a sea bream—reveals that he is dressed in very formal attire, with a stiff, sleeveless ceremonial robe (*kataginu*) and *hakama*. He sits before a low wooden table (*manaita*), skillfully using a long knife and metal chopsticks to carve up the fish. This rendition must have triggered in the minds of readers of this period (at least of some) an immediate connection with the knife ceremonies performed by professional chefs.[132] By employing the visual trope of the *hōchōnin* (literally, "man of the carving knife") in action, this image is at odds with the essence of *Ryōri monogatari* as a cookbook recording the recipes of ordinary people (*tadabito*). The illustration takes the reader away from the world of the average person cooking and back to the elite world of secret traditions. It reinforces the character of a secret tradition and therefore elevates the text to the respected lineages of professional chefs, imbuing it with authority.

A Recipe for Everything

The publishing genre of *shitsukekata-sho narabi ni ryōri-sho* stretches our expectations further by subsuming manuals that take us outside the kitchen and into the household more broadly defined. *Yorozu kikigaki hiden* (The secret tradition of things heard and recorded; also known as *Kikigaki hidenshō* [The commentary on the secret tradition of things heard and recorded]), a title that echoes the final section of *Ryōri monogatari*, is instructive.[133]

The book is organized into fifty-four sections, which can be divided conceptually in two main parts. The first concerns clothing, with sections 1 to 13 explaining the different ways of dyeing cloth and 14 to 19 containing information about how to clean and preserve cloth. The remaining sections make up the second part and focus on activities in the household and in the kitchen, with recipes and handy tips for all sorts of domestic things:

14

HOW TO REMOVE ALL KINDS OF STAINS

If oil has stained your kimono, boil together one *shō* [ca. 1.81 L] of water and one *gō* [ca. 0.181 L] of salt; let cool for a while and then rinse the stained area. The more water used, the more salt should be added. The stain will also be cleaned if you wash it in urine. When oil has stained your tatami floor, you should utilize lime [*ishibai*]. Sprinkle lime powder on the stain and let it stand overnight. The lime will remove the stain. You can also use lime for things that are colored. Also, you can use rice paste to remove oil from tatami. Smear the rice paste on some paper and place the paper on the stain. If you leave it there overnight, the stain disappears.[134]

Instructions are also given for a series of basic dishes: miso, assorted pickles, dried food, sake, vinegar, and soy sauce. These recipes complement the slightly higher-level culinary culture dealt with in *Ryōri monogatari*, covering the essentials in an everyday diet as well as the basics of cooking. The volume closes with recipes for the preservation of various foods, together with tips for growing trees. Seen in its entirety *Yorozu kikigaki hiden* was a handy manual for household management that focused on dispensing practical knowledge to assist readers in their daily life.

As always it is difficult to pinpoint the implied reader, but the nature of the advice given in *Yorozu kikigaki hiden* suggests an appeal for anyone dealing with rather humble tasks in potentially all sorts of households. A partially extant copy of the 1651 edition at the Waseda University Library reveals how an early modern reader translated the knowledge contained in this book into action.[135] There is a handwritten note on the verso of the last folio by a certain Kobayashi Sōemon 小林速右衛門 from the village of Yajima in Saku County, Shinshū Province (present-day Nagano Prefecture), which indicates that the book traveled as far as northern Japan. The colophon printed on the recto of the same folio is copied by hand, but the inside of the back cover is dated the twelfth day of the seventh month of 1675. It is unclear whether the same person wrote this, but if this is the case it would imply that someone engaged with the book more than twenty years after its publication and far removed from Kyoto, where it was printed. Moreover, there are also some marginalia, probably written by the same hand. Placed along the top of the section dealing with how to make vinegar, for example, are various ingredients in different measures, most plausibly intended to achieve the same result.[136]

I wish to reflect briefly on how the traces left by early modern readers point us to different forms of pleasure cohabiting the intellectual space of manners and cookery. The jottings in *Ryōri monogatari* examined in the previous section showcase the potential of useful books to be appropriated by readers and turned into sources of narrative entertainment. For the anonymous reader of *Ryōri monogatari* who gave voices to the figures in the illustration of the Matsue (Shōkai) edition, the pleasure derived from indulging in storytelling fantasies. The comments added to this copy of *Yorozu kikigaki hiden* demonstrate how the practical instructions delivered by the book could lead to actions in real life as well as serving as a prompt for readers to formulate their own recipes. For the reader of *Yorozu kikigaki hiden* the pleasure was in learning something useful and recording notes that complement the culinary knowledge printed on the page.

Food and recipes were by no means limited to the publishing genre under consideration here, signaling once again the permeable boundaries existing between these categories. *Waka shokumotsu honzō* (Food and medical herbs in poem form) is a representative example in understanding how commercial publishers catered to the need for recipes. Originally published in 1630 and listed in the category of medical texts in book-trade catalogues, *Waka shokumotsu honzō* was well received.[137] The popularity of this text is proclaimed in the 1642 edition printed by Yasuda Jūbee 安田十兵衛, as the following printed remark before the colophon makes clear: "*Uta honzō* is widely circulating in society. The spelling of some words is not correct and there are other mistakes. For that reason, we are releasing a new edition that addresses these issues."[138] There is nothing new in an attempt to promote a current edition as the most reliable. Yet it would not be unreasonable to take the remark about the wide circulation of *Waka shokumotsu honzō* at face value. After all, having an entire set of new blocks recut would have involved a financial investment on the part of the publisher, Yasuda Jūbee.

What would have enticed readers to buy this book? It is organized alphabetically according to the *i-ro-ha* poem. The text is further divided under each *i-ro-ha* syllable into sections devoted to diverse food types: herbs and vegetables (*kusa*), red meat (*kedamono*), sweets (*kashi*), game birds (*tori*), fish (*uo*), insects (*mushi*; containing also crustaceans), and grains/rice (*koku*).[139] Although the text deals with food, here we are not guided as to how to cook, preserve, or even eat it. Instead, the book cites these foods as sources for maintaining good health. In other words *Waka shokumotsu honzō* dispenses instructions on how to have a healthy lifestyle. And it does so in an effective and enjoyable manner through verse.

Easy-to-memorize *waka* are offered to assist in conveying the curative properties of the foods in question: "Apples stop pains in the belly as well as thirst"; "Mice are a good medicine for deafness. One must ingest mice once they have been cooked well"; "*Mumeboshi* [pickled plums] stop nausea and dissolve phlegm. They are good for all this, including a sore throat."[140] Not all the ingredients listed are beneficial, and *Waka shokumotsu honzō* likewise warns of the dangers of certain substances: "Do not eat too much raccoon dog [*tanuki*]. It affects the circulation of the blood and will cause swelling and pustules"; "Green tea is forbidden to people who are too slim. It sucks up the liquid in one's body"; or "Don't eat garlic for too long. It damages lungs and liver; it causes phlegm."[141]

Food culture, as it surfaces from the investigation of the primary sources examined here, appears truly multifaceted. Cooking as such emerges as a complex concept. Delicacies and ceremonial food occupy the same space as ordinary dishes, while secret traditions of knife ceremonies compete with the quotidian of the household. A broader domestic dimension also comes to the fore, suggesting that people craved all sorts of recipes to regulate an efficient and healthy existence. Ingredients normally used in the kitchen are redeployed to assist in various daily-life chores. All this was part of the communal food culture that entered the world of commercial printing.

The Complex Interplay of Narrative and Nonnarrative

Thus far this chapter has demonstrated that the pleasure readers of seventeenth-century civility literature gained was twofold. First, there was the thrill of acquiring new social and interpersonal knowledge and with it embodied cultural capital that permitted the successful navigation of the world as fully developed human beings. Second, there was the pleasure derived from indulging in fantasies about real or fictional worlds, on or outside the printed page. The former is pleasure derived from the practical profit earned through the act of efferent reading, the latter is pleasure obtained from aesthetic reading and imaginative fictionalizing, which I see as a form of storytelling (or story making).

What about narrative texts—that is, texts interested primarily in telling a story (often a fictional one)? Were they at any point connected with the cultural capital generated by nonnarrative civility literature? The contents, or the "raw materials," of conduct manuals and cookbooks became an integral part of a shared, communal knowledge, what Mary Elizabeth Berry calls "cultural literacy" or "cultural fluency."[142] Berry defines "cultural literacy" as a form of "core learning," ranging "across the history, institutions, and mundane civility of Nihon" and equates it with "national knowledge."[143] She discusses how Ihara Saikaku's fiction is "a close cousin of the text of the information library" and argues that Saikaku's fiction "presumes cultural literacy."[144] Saikaku is perceived as a writer who "mimics the content of standard texts from the information library" and "rehearses the well-established categories of gazetteers and the like to limn a field of common knowledge."[145] The result is what Berry views as the "entertainment of knowing audiences," mentioning Saikaku's ability to play with the language—"puns, syntactical breaks, poetic reversals, lexical and metaphorical linkages"—at the heart of his art and of the enjoyment that readers derived from it.[146] I do agree with Berry's assertion that the raw materials of nonnarrative, educational prose form a bedrock of shared knowledge that writers can use to infuse their texts with realism, thereby expecting readers to recognize allusions to this shared knowledge. I question Berry's stance on two points, though. First, by disregarding anything that precedes Saikaku, Berry seems to suggest that Saikaku was the first in seventeenth-century fiction to make creative use of nonnarrative texts. This, I maintain, is problematic not only because it does not reflect the historical reality but also because it runs the risk of fueling the already widespread academic belief that Saikaku was achieving something extraordinary within the literary panorama of this period. Second, through the use of verbs such as "mimic" and "rehearse," Berry seems to imply that narrative fiction echoes information but does not partake in shaping new knowledge and, while appearing to recognize aesthetic value in narrative fiction, finds no real epistemic value in it.[147] I contend that seventeenth-century narrative prose *complements* nonnarrative prose, rather than mimicking or rehearsing it, prompting in readers not only an aesthetic response but also cognitive engagement. Reading narrative can be as much for learning as reading nonnarrative can be for entertainment.

Two examples serve to illustrate my twofold premise here. The first example is an episode from the Kanbun-era (1661–1673) *Ikkyū shokoku monogatari* (Tales of Ikkyū from all the provinces), which adapts a section of the Kan'ei-era (1624–1644) *Chikusai*.[148] Abbot Ikkyū was renowned in his early modern fictional persona for being an extremely witty character.[149] In the passage in question, a certain man visits Ikkyū and asks for some medications to help his grandmother, who suffers from eye problems. Ikkyū not only treats the woman but also writes down a list of foods that should help the cure. The list is laid out as follows: *tobi no yakimono* (grilled kite); *suzume no sushi* (sushi of sparrow); *taka no suiri* (hawk boiled in vinegar); *karasu no misuzuke* (pickles of crow with miso); *gobō no maruyaki* (burdock roasted whole); *fukurō no sashimi* (sashimi of owl); *kujira no yakimono* (grilled whale); *kawauso no maruyaki* (otter roasted whole); *namako no yakimono* (grilled sea slug); *yokata no aburaage* (fried nightjar); *dojō no kamaboko* (loach served as *kamaboko*); *kaminari no manako* (eyes of thunder); *sennin no shirami* (lice of a holy man); and *tengu no nashimono* (salty *tengu*). The man cherishes this note until someone else sees it and reacts by bursting into laughter.

The humor underpinning the episode can be appreciated only when seen against the knowledge dispensed to contemporary readers in the first seven sections of *Ryōri monogatari* and in *Waka shokumotsu honzō*. Sparrow, for instance, is listed in section 4 of *Ryōri monogatari* as an edible bird, so there is nothing unusual here, but as sushi was not one of the recommended ways of eating it. Similarly, whale is listed in section 1 but not as a grilled dish; loach appears in section 3 but not as *kamaboko*. Other food items in Ikkyū's list are not recorded as edible, such as kite, hawk, and sea slug. And of course the fantastical "eyes of thunder," the lice of a holy man, and a mythical *tengu* are not remotely related to food—unless they were code words for other foods. None of the items prescribed by Abbot Ikkyū feature in *Waka shokumotsu honzō*. The reader laughs, together with the unnamed fictional character at the end of the story, at the nonsensical nature of this list, and at the naivete of the protagonist, who is unaware of what he should know. But laughter on the part of the reader of *Ikkyū shokoku monogatari* can be expected only when we assume that the reader had absorbed the communal food culture that was being shaped by books like *Ryōri monogatari* and further exploited in *Waka shokumotsu honzō*. Like Saikaku's fiction, but twenty or so years earlier, this episode presumes a reader's grasp of cultural literacy. At the same time, it also offers readers an element of surprise in testing and twisting their knowledge of fake food. Qualities of burlesque and parody spice up the reading experience, very much in keeping with what Saikaku does at a later date with his prose. Does this episode share Saikaku's genius for language? Perhaps not. Nonetheless, it must have resonated with its readers at the time since it not only traveled across thirty years from *Chikusai* to *Ikkyū shokoku monogatari* but also inspired adaptation well into the 1680s.[150] It should also be stressed that a comical fictional tale such as this works fully only when we embrace nonnarrative, nonfictional prose as an integral part of the literary panorama. It seems to me that the embodied cultural capital created by prose was successfully turned into textual capital that authors and publishers of fiction actively used in adding extra layers to their narrative worlds. I am tempted to call this "narrative capital."

The episode from *Ikkyū shokoku monogatari* has shown how the narrative capital generated by nonnarrative manuals could infuse all sorts of narrative texts and lead to aesthetic pleasure, much before Saikaku used a similar technique in his prose. The 1687 *Sanze aishō makura* (The pillow of affinities across three generations) prompts reflections on how narrative texts engaged readers at a cognitive level and further contributed to the creation of knowledge and narrative capital.¹⁵¹ The attribution of *Sanze aishō makura* is disputed: Hayashi Yoshikazu ascribes the text to Hishikawa Moronobu, while Shirakura Yoshihiko and Asano Shūgō attribute it to Sugimura Jihee 杉村治兵衛 (active ca. 1681–1703).¹⁵² What appears to be on firm ground, amid the scant research produced on this text, is its appreciation as a piece of erotic art (*shunga* or *shunpon*). The presence of sexually explicit pictures from the verso of the tenth folio of the first volume onward certainly justifies this approach. But it is my contention that the opening ten folios serve a different purpose; namely; the rehearsal as well as the production of knowledge about the civility surrounding the wedding ceremony. I also argue that, in doing so, *Sanze aishō makura* complements the knowledge offered by nonnarrative manuals and, more specifically, *Onna kagami hidensho*.

The first of the three volumes opens with a table of contents, which creates specific expectations about the nature of the text as a whole: we anticipate it being a manual of divination that instructs readers about the compatibility between a man and a woman (*aishō*) in the past, the present, and the future (*sanze*, "the three generations"), based on variables such as the year of birth, past deeds, and so forth. Yet as soon as we turn the page, we are confronted with something unexpected: a series of double-page spreads describing the various steps of marriage celebrations. After a brief eulogy on the spiritual power of the union between men and women, the text turns into a narration where the son of a wealthy man is looking for a suitable wife, and an intermediary identifies the daughter of a respectable family as the ideal match. In the next scene the boy and girl are given the opportunity to catch a glimpse of each other under the ruse of a pilgrimage to Asakusa Temple. Love blossoms between the two.

The third double-page spread captures the moment when marital vows are exchanged (*yuiire* or *iiire*). This is where the narrative capital starts coming into play. In *Onna kagami hidensho* this specific moment of the celebrations focuses in detail on how a woman should prepare her toilette for the occasion.¹⁵³ We learn that her attire should be a white-lined kimono, on top of which is a colored kimono and another white kimono, and she wears the appropriate headgear. *Sanze aishō makura* translates this information into images, depicting the woman donning appropriate clothes (fig. 4.10).¹⁵⁴ At the same time, though, *Sanze aishō makura* provides us with additional details. The verbal text advises about which gifts are to be displayed: kimono with golden threads and intricate patterns, money, delicacies, and sake casks. The illustration visually confirms this in part and also includes other items such as the *yuiwata*, or cotton sheets, fastened on one side, seen in the top right. The text (both visual and verbal) keeps us engaged on a cognitive level by providing us with new knowledge about the etiquette to be followed—new when compared with *Onna kagami hidensho*—while further developing the fictional story. We learn more about the character of the young woman (left unnamed), who claims to be very young

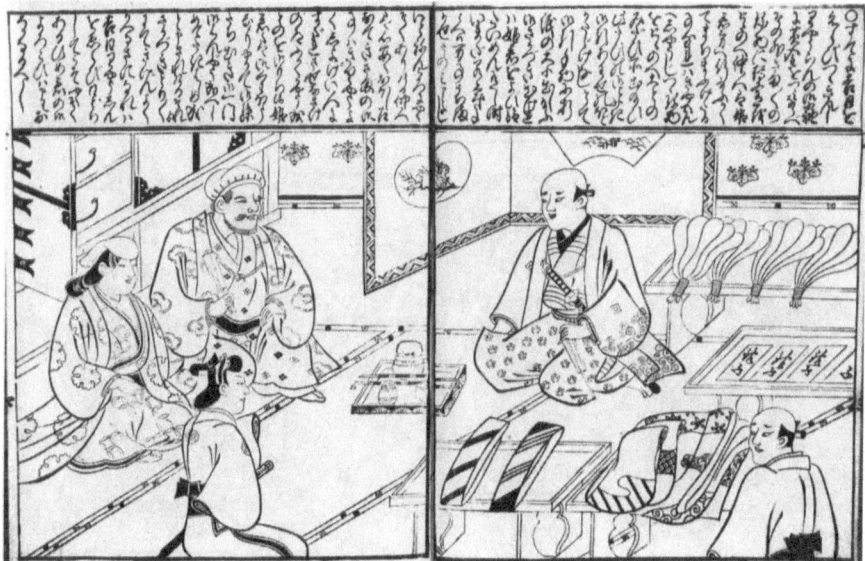

Figure 4.10 *Sanze aishō makura*, 1687, vol. 1, 3v–4r. Marital vows exchanged.
Courtesy of Kawade Shobō Shinsha, Tokyo

and inexperienced. She therefore entrusts herself to the intermediary and her future husband, being reassured that the prospective husband not only is handsome but also possesses an unrivaled knowledge of the various arts and a profound understanding of the Way of love (*nasake no michi*).

The following double-page spread (fig. 4.11) takes us behind the scenes and to the middle of a kitchen in a visual composition that brings to mind the one examined in the Matsue (Shōkai) edition of *Ryōri monogatari* (fig. 4.8).[155] While the iconotext infuses new life in the visual trope of a professional chef at work, the verbal text lists in great detail all the dishes prepared for the banquet. Once again *Sanze aishō makura* provides us with particulars not found in previous civility literature. The reader who can afford duck, crane, and foreign delicacies (among a few other exotic ingredients mentioned in the text) gathers useful information, and the one who is in no position to afford any of this can enjoy the wonders of an extraordinary wedding. Mention of the decorations needed for the event, including a painting of a Kano-school artist, helps to conjure up the mental picture of a magnificent celebration.

The ceremony of the bride leaving her house (*kadoide*) is briefly mentioned in the fifth double-page spread, which swiftly zooms in on the procession from the bride's to the groom's home (fig. 4.12).[156] Once again *Sanze aishō makura* appears complementary to *Onna kagami hidensho* in terms of generating new

Figure 4.11 *Sanze aishō makura*, 1687, vol. 1, 4v–5r. Preparations for the wedding ceremony.
Courtesy of Kawade Shobō Shinsha, Tokyo

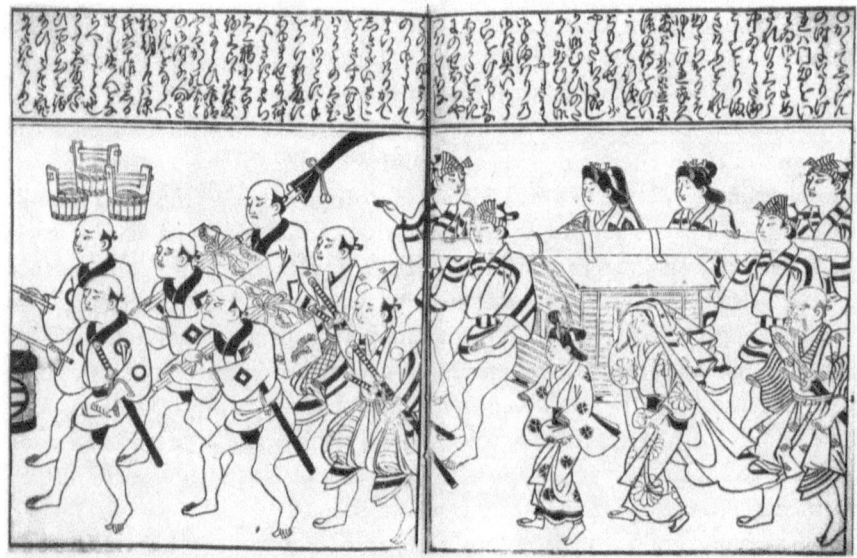

Figure 4.12 *Sanze aishō makura*, 1687, vol. 1, 5v–6r. Bridal procession.
Courtesy of Kawade Shobō Shinsha, Tokyo

Figure 4.13 *Sanze aishō makura*, 1687, vol. 1, 6v–7r. Wedding ceremony.
Courtesy of Kawade Shobō Shinsha, Tokyo

knowledge about this ceremony. *Onna kagami hidensho* details the *kadoide* ritual and describes who goes first in the procession (e.g., where people step on and off the palanquin).[157] *Sanze aishō makura* focuses on the transport of the belongings and dowry of the bride to the groom's house. We read that the older members of the bride's household had to brush up on their knowledge of rituals in the tradition of the Ogasawara school, a reminder of the existence and importance of oral teachings. Both texts offer the detail of the soon-to-be husband touching the palanquin before the bride is taken into the house. The sixth double-page spread outlines the climax of the wedding ceremony and not surprisingly mentions that it consists of the *sansan kudo* ritual.[158] The intermediary first drinks three cups, followed by the groom and the bride. No food is mentioned here, giving the impression that the *sansan kudo* is nothing more than a *shiki sangon*. Although the illustration reinforces the visual trope associated with this ceremony (fig. 4.13), the verbal text emphasizes the auspiciousness of the occasion and stresses the great joy: "Everyone, high and low, rejoiced and congratulated the newly wedded. This kind of happiness is indeed something to be envious of."[159] The closing remarks of this scene offer an unexpected narrative twist.

> In the past the two gods Izanagi and Izanami began the exchange of love vows between a man and a woman standing on the floating bridge of Heaven. Since

then love between the two sexes has thrived. Now, starting with those of the high class [*uetsukata*] and going down to everyone [*banmin*] the vows of love and intimacy exchanged by men and women are deep. Because the ceremony took place in the eleventh month [known as *shimotsuki*, the "frost month"], a certain man composed a *hokku* [seventeen-syllable verse] that said, "Below the belly button / some white hair; white as the frost / this is marriage" (*heso no shita / chito shimotsuki no / yomeri kana*). Everyone laughed.[160]

The allusion to Izanagi and Izanami and their sexual encounter together with the indirect mention of the genitalia as the hairy area below the belly button works as a springboard to the next double-page spread showing the couple having sex (fig. 4.14). *Onna kagami hidensho* is extremely coy about what happens once the couple withdraws from the party.[161] It explains that following the ceremonies, the newlyweds enter the bedroom, where more sake and snacks are consumed. Then the women attendants help the bride lie down while the husband takes care of his ablutions. The wife positions her head toward the north, without undoing her sash, and refrains from speaking. The text is then vague about what happens next: "After that, things change depending on the people, so it is difficult to record this in writing."[162] This is

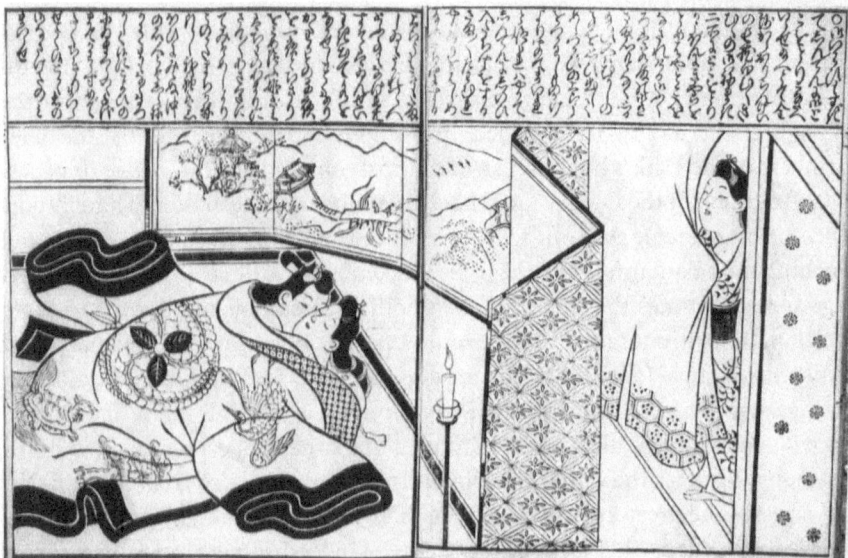

Figure 4.14 *Sanze aishō makura*, 1687, vol. 1, 7v–8r. Newlyweds' first night.
Courtesy of Kawade Shobō Shinsha, Tokyo

where *Sanze aishō makura* once more complements our knowledge by making explicit what happens during the first night. On the visual level the couple is depicted in a voluptuous embrace, wrapped in sumptuous bedding hiding their bodies. Yet the picture leaves little room for doubt: what dominates this phase of the wedding celebration is the physical union of the man and woman. The verbal text refrains from providing further details and proceeds to strengthen the titillating nature of the scene. The narrator, in fact, explains that a maidservant has been sent by the mother-in-law to keep an eye on the couple and that she becomes wet to the point that the hem of her kimono is completely soaked. Here is where *Sanze aishō makura* starts moving away from civility literature toward a sexually explicit work. The outcome of this night of lovemaking is revealed in the next scene, with the woman having just given birth to a child. The remark that closes the recto of the ninth folio, and with it the part of the text of interest in this chapter, reflects on the word *sanze*: "The bond of a couple is a wondrous one. On the basis of past karma, a man and a woman are joined in matrimony in this life, and this will be the same in their future life."[163]

Much transpires in the confined space of the first folios of *Sanze aishō makura*. Indeed, it reenacts the social and interpersonal knowledge appearing in a nonnarrative text such as *Onna kagami hidensho*. The reader already possessing that knowledge is able to fully enjoy the first part of *Sanze aishō makura* in both the repetition of that knowledge and the surprises that unfold as the story progresses. This is no different from what we have seen in the episode from *Ikkyū shokoku monogatari* or from what Berry has noted in the case of Saikaku's fiction. At the same time, however, the 1687 title operates as a text with a strong epistemic function: it rewrites the wedding rituals with a view to supplying practical information that complements conduct manuals. Novice readers—in this case those who have yet to acquire the necessary social knowledge—can approach this section of *Sanze aishō makura* as if they were perusing a conduct manual, while expert readers can use it to hone and extend their knowledge. The fictional story of the couple develops alongside and invites the audience to enjoy the love story as it unfolds. The story is told in such a way as to inspire the reader with awe: we are made to dream about such a perfect marriage, but at the same time the narration reveals little by little the true nature of this text as a book concerned with sex. All is packaged in an exquisite picture book that provokes pleasure for its intrinsic, visually aesthetic qualities. Put differently, the fictional narrative deployed in this text engages both the expert and the novice reader at a cognitive, as well as emotional and aesthetic, level. For us twenty-first-century readers and scholars, the many facets of *Sanze aishō makura* make sense only if we have acquired sufficient knowledge of the narrative capital accumulated in seventeenth-century nonnarrative prose.

A generative understanding of this fictional, narrative text is possible only when we view it as an integral part of a vast corpus of didactic, nonnarrative literature.

If individuals wished to be successful members of seventeenth-century Japanese society—whether they were high- or lowborn, male or female—it was imperative they come to terms with civility. The societal and interpersonal knowledge embedded in etiquette complemented the ethical, religious, and societal knowledge explored in the previous chapter in casting responsible, happy individuals. Commercial publishers were there to cater to these needs. In effectively exploiting the rhetoric of disclosing secret traditions, they issued a wide range of materials designed to teach civility and marketed them under the label of *shitsukekata-sho narabi ni ryōri-sho*. Easily navigable, relatively cheap, and readily accessible manuals of conduct promoted the gradual creation of a shared set of socially acceptable behaviors sanctioned, at least on the page, by the authority of the Ogasawara school. Our journey into nonnarrative civility literature has brought to light a tension between a desire to democratize civility for people of all sorts and a commitment to underpin social differentiation. In my analysis I have argued against any attempt to reconcile what we may perceive as a contradiction and probed how an illusion of social equality was promoted by popular prose that fostered the acquisition of embodied cultural capital. This chapter has also tried to unravel the publishers' decision to market etiquette alongside cookbooks. I have identified a shared democratic drive in the choice to empower the common people, by consecrating their own oral tradition of cookery to the written page. A communal food culture, household tips, and domestic medicine featured with etiquette to promote a well-mannered and healthy lifestyle inside and outside the kitchen.

This chapter extended beyond the boundaries of the publishing genre of *shitsukekata-sho narabi ni ryōri-sho* to investigate how civility assumed different contents when addressing women. Working with two *nyosho* packaged as conduct manuals for women—*Onna kagami hidensho* and *Onna shikimoku*—I have noted how civility was deployed to construct femininity primarily within the framework of married life. The comparative study of conduct manuals for men and for women has led to the conclusion that in terms of social differentiation femininity and masculinity appeared more relevant than status categories.

By examining the publishing history and reception of select best-selling titles, I have challenged any simplistic duality between efferent and aesthetic readings of these materials. First, I have located a significant part of the success of civility literature in its ability to satisfy, and at the same time fuel, readers' voyeuristic desire to spy on the world of the warrior class (or the wealthy) and its ingrained association with the teachings of the Ogasawara school. Second, I have studied how conduct manuals were appropriated as a source of aesthetically pleasing storytelling, with illustrations offering fertile ground for readers to create their own tales beyond the constraints of the printed page. Third, I have discussed the complex interbreeding between nonnarrative and narrative prose. In particular, by conducting a close reading of the sexually explicit *Sanze aishō makura*, I have shown that stories lent themselves to being read efferently as practical manuals, complementing social and interpersonal knowledge for the benefit of both expert and novice readers. In the process I have advanced the idea of narrative capital: a bedrock of raw materials that could be and were reimagined and reshaped in fictional, narrative texts. I argue that without an adequate knowledge of the nonnarrative reading materials printed in the seventeenth century our understanding and enjoyment of contemporaneous narrative materials are severely limited.

This chapter has also shown that these books were undeniably commercial in nature. Publishers sought ways to dress up their products in an effort to maximize profits, at times even cannibalizing other books to do so. Readers did not protest, however; they were given the opportunity to enjoy books that contained snippets from other relevant titles and reveled in the anticipation that a book might metamorphose into something totally unwonted. In an era predating the formation of booksellers' guilds when intellectual property, let alone copyright, was not an issue, this was all carried out without guilt. A further aspect of popular print culture has emerged from the sources examined here. Despite the claims made in the texts and their paratexts that the printed word anchors the oral tradition, thus freeing knowledge from elitist secrecy, if not from cultural amnesia, the same texts nonetheless continuously refer back to a world of oral teachings. Civility literature in print makes knowledge open to all, but for those seeking further details, depth, and instruction there was still the need to turn to actual teachers. Civility, as well as the printed word, did not supplant oral traditions (a notion examined also in chapter 3)—it coexisted harmoniously with them. Finally, I have emphasized the porosity that characterized publishing genres at the time. While the chapter started as an examination of a specific publishing genre, the journey undertaken to explore civility as part of seventeenth-century book culture has taken us beyond its confines.

CHAPTER 5

Say It in a Skillful Letter

> *Writing letters might appear trivial and yet it is something of great importance. After all, what you record in writing remains for the days to come and will be seen by other people. Therefore you must apply yourself in earnest when writing and sending letters.*
>
> —*Onna shikimoku* (Rules for women)

In seventeenth-century Japan letter writing constituted a salient aspect of interpersonal and societal knowledge, complementing the other features investigated in the previous chapter on civility literature.[1] We are dealing with what Roger Chartier calls the "civility of correspondence."[2] The know-how required for writing letters is not to be underestimated, to the point that scholar of English literature Eve Tavor Bannet has coined the term "letteracy," meaning "the collection of different skills, values, and kinds of knowledge beyond mere literacy that were involved in achieving competency in the writing, reading and interpreting of letters."[3]

Letteracy, literacy, and learning were tightly entwined in the Japanese cultural imagination well before the Edo period, and their association is tangible in *ōraimono* (literally, "things going and coming"). As Markus Rüttermann notes, this term is employed in modern scholarship to refer to a broad range of educational materials.[4] Rüttermann demonstrates that medieval and early modern *ōraimono* often took the shape of epistolary correspondence—one letter going out, the other coming in as a response—or the form of a single missive. Still, they were not designed so much to instruct on how to write and read letters as to teach vocabulary. In other words, they were intended as manuals for basic literacy (*tenarai*; discussed in chapter 1). They also imparted moral instruction, thereby approximating a form of learning (*gakumon*), complementing the ethical knowledge that Buddhist and Confucian texts promoted (taken up in chapter 3). Added to these were textbooks that offered education in certain professions. Seventeenth-century booksellers pointed to an additional link with calligraphy when conceiving the publishing genre of *ōraimono narabi ni tehon* (*ōraimono* and copybooks). It appeared as early as the 1666–1667 book-trade catalogue and encompassed three types of books. First are titles that feature the word *ōrai* (or the almost synonymous *jō*). They are precisely the kind of books that Rüttermann discusses. Second, we find albums of exemplary calligraphy.[5] Third are texts whose titles end with the word *bunshō* (writing). These are full-scale manuals for letter writing, which are of interest in this chapter.[6] The foreword to *Shoshin bunshō*, published sometime before 1670 and listed in this category, elucidates the conceptual frame surrounding letter writing.

> Texts [*fumi*] are a tool to adhere to the Way [*kandō*]. Human beings must learn how to write and read [*moji o narau*]. This is the same now as in the past. Yet there are only few who can study under the supervision of a teacher; there are very few who know how to use the brush correctly, despite their wholehearted and devoted attitude. Moreover, the style of writing epistles [*shōsoku*] is particularly difficult and yet applies to all sorts, highborn and lowborn, monks and laymen.[7]

Both literacy and letteracy are identified as skills that all people must possess. In accord with the rhetoric examined in the two previous chapters, the desired result lies in forging fully-equipped human beings. This passage also acknowledges the difficulty in finding suitable teachers and stresses the intrinsic complexity of letteracy. Hence the response of seventeenth-century commercial publishers: they issued manuals to assist in the study of letter writing. *Shoshin bunshō* itself is structured as an anthology of specimens of letters, from seasonal greetings to congratulatory notes for weddings and letters of condolence.

This chapter explores how seventeenth-century letteracy was shaped by commercial publishers and examines their products across a number of publishing genres, thus filling a conspicuous gap in current scholarship.[8] It starts with an examination of nonnarrative manuals of epistolography. What were the contents of published materials that taught letteracy? What do they tell us about epistolary codes, practices, and ideologies? The textual analysis includes a detailed examination of the language promoted by these manuals in the hope of shedding light on how they played a significant part in the creation of gendered, artificial languages shared across society. I argue that these manuals thus complicate any facile opposition between highbrow Sinitic literacy and lowbrow vernacular literacy, as already mentioned when putting forward the idea of multiple literacies. At the same time, this chapter deals with how the promotion of such a shared language almost paradoxically endorsed social hierarchy. The conclusions reached in chapter 4 about civility emerge as equally relevant for the discussion of letteracy here.

This chapter is interested not only in seventeenth-century letter manuals, however. It also investigates how publishers throughout the seventeenth century used the narrative capital generated by their letter miscellanies and letter-writing compendia to fuel the creation of fictional narratives and powerful tropes. I discuss the 1630s *Usuyuki monogatari* (The tale of Usuyuki) and how it was marketed as both a story and practical manual for the composition of love letters. The chapter then explores how these two facets were imaginatively appropriated during the second half of the century, first by looking at how the 1659 *Usugumo monogatari* (The tale of Usugumo) bent what I call the *Usuyuki* master plot in order to problematize power relations between genders. Second, I study how the 1661 *Nishikigi* (The winged spindle tree) used love-letter templates to write about love typologies. I conclude with a study of the 1680s erotic book *Nasake no uwamori* (Heightened feelings) to call into question once more any easy differentiation between the aesthetic and epistemic functions of prose. I also demonstrate how influential *Nishikigi* was by the end of the seventeenth century and hope to prompt reflections on how works that are today excluded from the canon were at the heart of the popular imagination.

Teaching Letteracy

In the previous chapter I discussed at some length the second half of *Shogaku bunshō narabi ni yorozu shitsukekata* (hereafter *Shogaku bunshō*).[9] Here I wish to explore the first half as it represents an early attempt at equipping readers with basic letteracy. The wording *shogaku bunshō* alerts readers that these are texts (*bunshō*), or more specifically, letters, that can be studied when a pupil is at an elementary stage (*shogaku*). The table of contents and the main body are meant to be used in tandem: while the latter offers a selection of epistolary formulas, the former clarifies in what kind of letter a specific formula can be used.[10] Number 1 in the table of contents, for instance, tells us that the corresponding section deals with "Sending a Letter When One Has Some Business to Attend To."[11] Once we move to number 1 in the main text (fig. 1.18, first three lines) we are not given a specimen or a template for the whole letter, as I have mentioned happens in *Shoshin bunshō*. What appears in front of us is a text-constitutive formula that we can use to open our letter.¹²

You should write *wazato ippitsu kei seshime sōrō* (I am writing to you with a specific purpose). The expression *kei seshimu* connotes *mōsashimu* ("to say" in humble speech). The character 啓 should be understood as 申 (to say, to speak). If you write to a noble you should use the expression *keijō seshime sōrō* 令啓上候.¹³	態一筆令啓候と書くべし 令啓とは令申といふ心也啓の字を申とよむ也 もし貴人の所ならば令啓上候とかくべし

The text of the formula employs a writing style that is normally referred to as *sōrōbun*, a highly formulaic hybrid Sino-Japanese form (discussed in chapter 1). In the Edo period *sōrōbun* became an "artificial" language used only for written correspondence, including letters, contracts, laws, and so forth.¹⁴ As the English translation of the passage selected here suggests, the introductory formula is followed by notes about the vocabulary that should be used. It clarifies the meaning of the word *kei* 啓, providing the example of the more common, synonymic variation *mōsu* 申. It then focuses on the linguistic register and the lexical variation that must be employed when addressing individuals of a higher social status. Letteracy is framed as a skill that helps regulate interpersonal relations, including hierarchical ones.

Although *Shōgaku bunshō* hardly discards its formulaic nature, it moves from short formulas that form only part of a letter to longer, ready-made texts for specific contents. There is, for instance, a short thank-you text in response to an invitation to visit a person's home (section 3), notes to be sent with gifts (sections 5, 8), and texts that can be used when lending and returning things (sections 10, 11, 12, 13), among others. The list continues and covers an extensive range of social occasions. This means that a manual teaching letteracy also nourished the necessary social know-how. The notes that accompany these content-oriented formulaic templates are more than explanations of chosen words, providing further insights into how these lengthy formulas could and should be applied. Section 10 is instructive in this regard. The title provided in the table of contents reads "What to Send When Borrowing Something That Was Promised." The specimen is as follows (fig. 5.1):

I would like to borrow the Noh libretto that we agreed upon earlier. I shall return it to you promptly. The word *keiyaku* (promise, agreement) has the same meaning as *yakusoku*; it can also be substituted with *yakudaku*. "Noh libretto" can be changed to "copybook" (*tehon*) or the name of any object agreed to be borrowed.[15]	先度契約申候謡之本借用申度候 頓而返進可申候 契約とはやくそくと おなじ事なり約諾やくだくとも書かへべし 謡の本手本其外何なり共 其かり物の名をかくべし

While the letter sample gives us a ready-to-use text, thus fostering mere repetition, the notes assist the reader in breaking away from formulaic patterns and provide suggestions for individualistic variation. We can choose between two synonyms for "promise"—*keiyaku* and *yakudaku*—and we are encouraged to substitute "Noh libretto" with anything else we wish to borrow. Notes abound in *Shogaku bunshō*. They mostly provide hints for linguistic variation, but they also give suggestions about other aspects of letter writing, with remarks on the ink and the paper to be used, for example, or the use of additional parts added to the main body of a missive.

Section 35 contains a template that is complete in all its parts (fig. 5.2).[16]

The sample includes the title of the document (A), the amount of money received (B), a statement that the sum has been received (C), the date (D), the

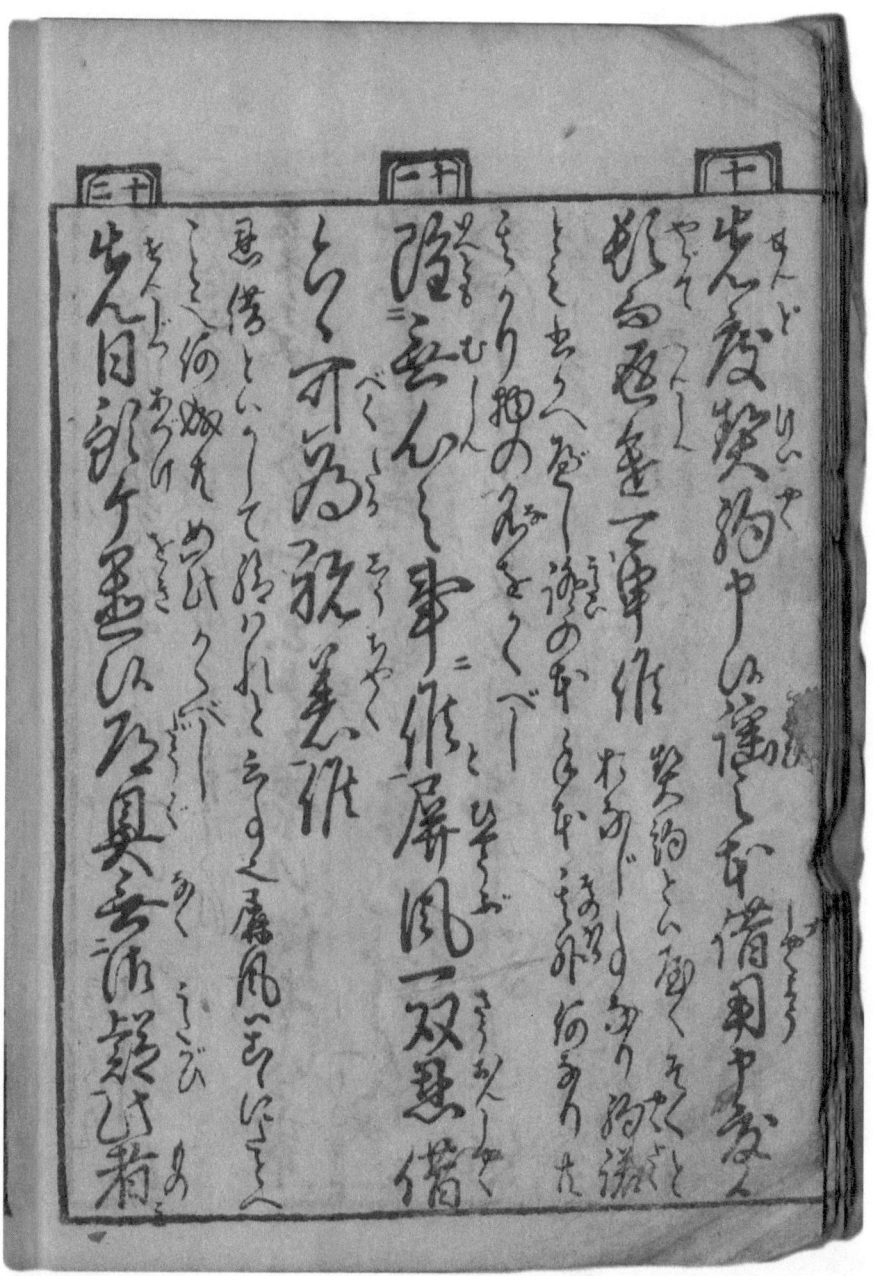

Figure 5.1 *Shogaku bunshō narabi ni yorozu shitsukekata*, 1647, 9v. Formulas for letter writing.

Author collection, Suzuran Bunko, Cambridge, U.K.

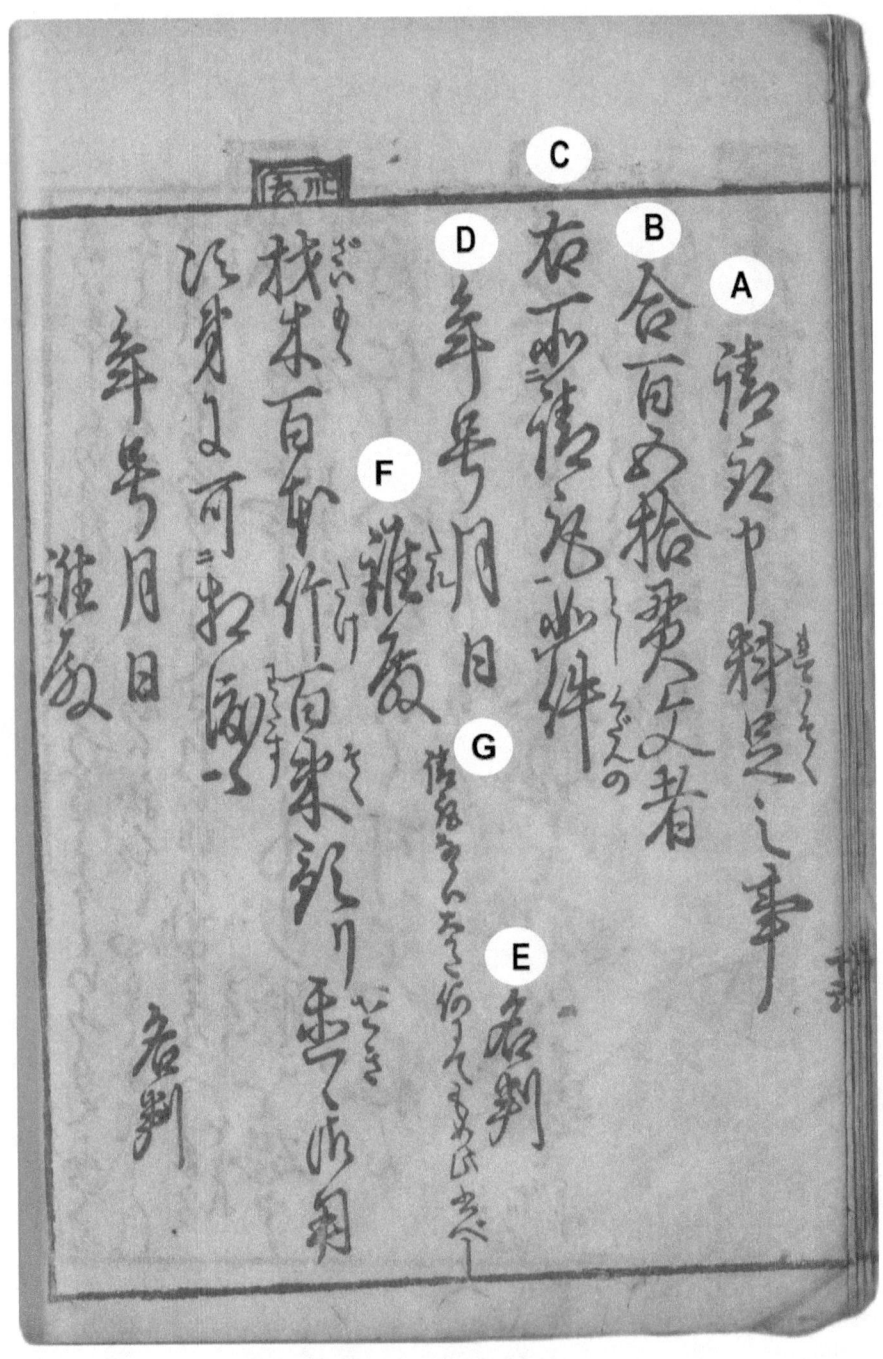

Figure 5.2 *Shogaku bunshō narabi ni yorozu shitsukekata*, 1647, 16v. Letter template.
Author collection, Suzuran Bunko, Cambridge, U.K.

name with stamp of the person who has received the money (E), and the name of the addressee (F). It then adds, "When something is received, no matter what it is, this is how to write the document in question in the majority of cases" (G). Variation is possible and indeed required for B, D, E, and F. Other than that, one can simply copy the text as it is. The same strategy is applied in templates for borrowing money and selling land.[17]

When seen in its entirety, the first half of *Shogaku bunshō* functions as a letter-writing manual that combines a formulary with a commentary.[18] As a commentary, it adds notes that explain some practicalities involved in writing and sending missives and discuss to a degree some theoretical aspects of letter writing. As a formulary, it offers model letters and documents, although it is not complete enough to enable the reader to reproduce the entire text and to have it function as a complete letter (with the few exceptions examined in the preceding). Moreover, it does not give adequate formulas for individual phrases or letter parts for a reader to assemble a letter.[19] But at the same time it clearly shows that defined forms and fixed formulas were the touchstone of letter writing in seventeenth-century Japan. Originality was not discouraged in that an alternative lexicon was suggested and letter writers were allowed to employ words that best suited the situation. From this perspective, imitation rather than mere reproduction was promoted as a meaningful use of this formulary.

The idea of a formulary of letter specimens with commentary will be widely explored during and beyond the seventeenth century. For example, Namura Jōhaku, already mentioned several times for his *Nan chōhōki* and *Onna chōhōki*, published an extensive collection of letter templates under the title *Yorozu anshi tegata kagami* (A mirror for ten thousand letter templates, 1693).[20] This mirror offers letter samples for all sorts of social interaction: from receiving money to adopting a child, from drawing up contracts to apologies for a quarrel, and much more. All the letter templates come complete, like the last example from *Shogaku bunshō*. Phonetic readings are appended systematically to the characters that compose the *sōrōbun* text so that the reader can easily understand the meaning and master reading letters aloud if necessary. Rich headnotes provide readers with all they need to understand when using these templates, as well as tips for linguistic variation. Hundreds of these mirrors continued to be produced as part of the commercial book culture of early modern Japan and await a systematic study.

Back to *Shogaku bunshō*. What was the target readership? The contents and the language strongly suggest that it would appeal primarily to male readers, from members of the warrior class to wealthy merchants, confirming my previous findings on this text (see chapter 4). So what about women? Marcia Yonemoto offers an insightful overview of self-cultivation for early modern women in Japan in a process that she defines as involving "the active development of both moral values and practical skills," which subsumed reading and writing, sewing, speech, appearance, and the arts.[21] Drawing on the work of Koizumi

Yoshinaga, Yonemoto describes calligraphy models and manuals on letter writing as "a major subcategory of instructional manuals for women."[22] She opines that "becoming a competent and perhaps even an accomplished writer of formal correspondence was considered a skill that women ought to possess."[23] Yonemoto emphasizes these materials as calligraphic models, but here I concentrate primarily on their contents as letter manuals with a view to clarifying how they shaped what I preliminarily call gendered translations of letteracy.

The 1660 *Onna shogaku bunshō* (Elementary letter writing for women) is particularly revealing.[24] The title, in fact, frames this text as a female version (*onna*) of the aforementioned *Shogaku bunshō narabi ni yorozu shitsukekata*. Not only is this a text marketed *for* women. It is also a text produced, at least partly, *by* a woman, as indicated in the afterword, signed by Yasu やす. Sadly, we know very little about her. She identifies herself as the daughter of a certain Kubota Muneyasu 窪田宗保 from Ōtsu, not far from Kyoto.[25] Book-trade catalogues as early as 1670 confirm that Yasu produced the calligraphy for this text, but her name appears together with that of Ikkadō 一花堂 (also known as Ikkadō Setsurin 一華堂切臨 [b. 1591]), a male poet and intellectual active in Kyoto around the mid-seventeenth century who was known for his commentaries on Heian-period texts. He might have been in charge of the contents of *Onna shogaku bunshō*, but nothing in the text specifies his role.

As the three tables of content that open each volume of *Onna shogaku bunshō* suggest, Ikkadō and Yasu were most probably aware of *Shogaku bunshō*: it covers the same typologies of letters and even follows the same order.[26] There is, however, a rather striking metamorphosis in the passage from male- to female-gendered letter-writing practices. The example for "What to Send When Borrowing Something That Was Promised" is instructive (see next page and fig. 5.3).

The English rendering fails to convey the intricacies of what I call a gendered translation from the male language and aesthetics of letter writing to the female counterparts. This entails, first, the visual presentation of the text. While the male version of this letter was written in the usual manner of a text running in parallel vertical lines—that is, from right to left—the female version exhibits what is known as *chirashi-gaki*, typically translated as "scattered writing."[28] In this case, the text is arranged in four "layers." It begins with the larger characters in the center of the page (underlined in the translation); we then move back to the beginning and to the middle-size text, commencing with the short section positioned on the right between the upper and the lower layers (underlined in the translation), only to turn to the upper layer and read until the end of the letter (underlined in the translation), at which point we return to the start and read the bottom layer (underlined in the translation). By infusing new life into a calligraphic style in vogue since the Heian period, the printed page offers an explosion of aesthetic, visual pleasure.[29] Yasu's calligraphy, with the diagonal patterns and spatial variation it creates, brings to mind what the American violinist and conductor Paul Zukofsky names "dispersed calligraphy" and describes as "a most extraordinary example of artifice."[30] It is chiefly the prominence given to this aesthetic dimension that translates letteracy for the female reader and writer.

A second aspect of this gendered translation lies in the language. The language used is as artificial as that in the male version, and yet it does differ. This is seen, for example, in the frequent use of the humble form *mairase* followed

10. Letter to Send When Borrowing Something That Was Promised

<u>I would like to borrow the book agreed upon. It displays an especially refined brush and I know you treasure it, but I would like to look at it. I would never dream of showing it to any third party. May I have a quick look this evening (?). Yours sincerely.</u>

[Upper Notes]
- The word *mizuguki* means "brushwork" (*fude no ato*)
- The word *yume* has the same meaning as "not even in my dreams" (*yume yume*)
- 3. The word *koto hito* means "another person" (*bechi no hito*)
- 4. The word *hime* means "to treasure" (*hisō suru*)
- 5. The word *hikudari* means "evening" (*higure*)[27]

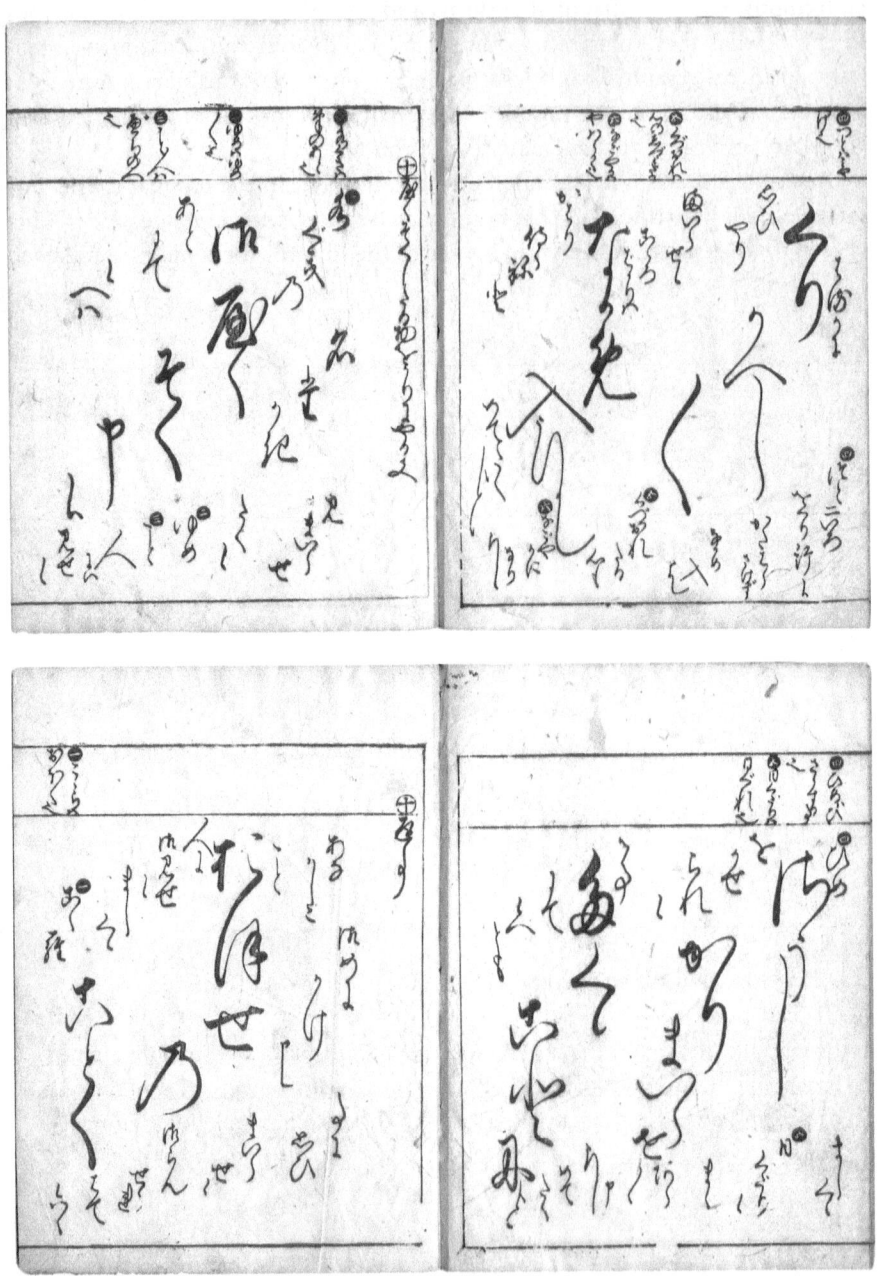

Figure 5.3 Kubota Yasu, *Onna shogaku bunshō*, 1660, 19v–21r. Letter template. Of interest here 20r (upper left half) and 20v (lower right half).

Collection of Koizumi Yoshinaga. Courtesy of the owner

by the more conventional *sōrō*. This combination of two supplementary verbs—the first to convey respect and the second as a standard feature of the *sōrōbun* style—became such a fixed formula in the language of women's correspondence that it was rendered with what looks like a symbol (fig. 5.4, A). I refer to this linguistic variant of the *sōrōbun* style as the *mairase-sōrōbun* style. This leads to a third trait of the female epistolary language: a tendency to include visual elements that operate almost like abstract and conventional signs. This can be verified in *mairase-sōrō* but also in the closing word *kashiku* (fig. 5.4, B). Finally, the change from a Noh libretto to a more generic book (*sōshi*) and the mention of a "refined brush," which recalls the calligraphic quality of the very book we are reading, might be interpreted as a subtle distancing from a male-centered cultural sphere to a more feminine one.

Notes accompany the sample letter, in conformity with the format of the male version, and appear in a separate section at the top of the page. In the passage translated here, for instance, each note explains the meaning of the words. The notes accompanying other letter templates, for example a letter of condolences, concern other practical aspects, such as how a missive should be sent. Following this letter, as for all the letters in *Onna shogaku bunshō*, is a sample reply.

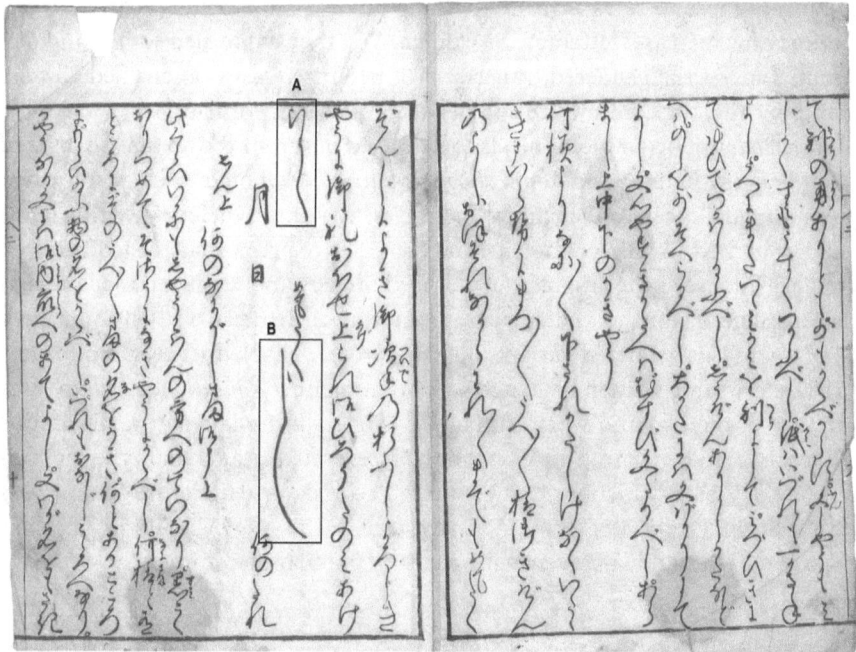

Figure 5.4 *Onna shikimoku*, publication details unknown, vol. 2, 10v–11r. Letter template. A = symbol for *mairase-sorō*; B = symbol for *kashiku*.

Author collection, Suzuran Bunko, Cambridge, U.K.

Overall, *Onna shogaku bunshō* is a letter-writing manual that combines a formulary with commentaries. Yet its role as a formulary is more enhanced than that of *Shogaku bunshō*, and except for information on how to insert the name of the addresser, the addressee, and the date, the reader would find a wide range of ready-to-use examples in this text. *Onna shogaku bunshō* also functions as a copybook for the calligraphic rendering of scattered (or dispersed) writing. What appears less developed than in the male version, however, is the inclusion of notes that provide synonyms. This, in turn, makes the text less flexible in the creative imitation of the templates and seems to suggest a rather passive reproduction of the samples. As research by Koizumi Yoshinaga has shown, there were hundreds of this kind of text produced throughout the Edo period.[31] They might confirm or challenge the findings drawn from *Onna shogaku bunshō*. But the cultural significance of this title should not be underestimated: it marks the beginning of an important type of early modern popular prose.

A note of caution is in order at this point. So far I have suggested a polarized view of a male and a female hand. Indeed the type of letter writing showcased in *Onna shogaku bunshō* is normally referred to as *nyohitsu*, or "the woman's brush." Yet as this chapter describes, men were expected to adopt feminine letteracy, with its aesthetic and linguistic features, when writing to women, thus encouraging us to refrain from applying any easy, binary division between letteracy for men and letteracy for women. Yes, they embodied something different, and yet the gendered translation of letteracy was what enabled, almost paradoxically, the communication between men and women.[32]

One last, important point needs to be teased out from the textual analysis of both *Shogaku bunshō* and *Onna shogaku bunshō*. As noted in chapter 1 when presenting the spectrum of multiple literacies, these kinds of letter-writing manuals positioned themselves outside the competitive arena that existed between literary Chinese as the language of cultured literacy and vernacular Japanese as the language of vernacular literacy by promoting an artificial written language.[33] *Sōrōbun* and its gendered variant *mairase-sōrōbun* enabled writers and readers to share the same written language, which was neither *kanbun* nor *wabun* but a mixture of the two and which displayed a strong formulaic nature. From this perspective, these letter samples might be interpreted as a textual type that fulfills one of the key functions that Umberto Eco assigns to literature—namely, as an aid in the creation of a common language.[34] This alone should justify their inclusion in the study of seventeenth-century popular literature.

Hierarchical Letteracy

It might be tempting to view the adoption of a shared artificial language (*sōrōbun* and *mairase-sōrōbun*) as tantamount to a push for a democratic view of social relations, in that it enables people to communicate by using standardized formulas regardless of their social and educational backgrounds. However, a distinction between high-, middle-, and low-ranking addressees is equally acknowledged and regulated in these manuals. We are very close to the paradox noted by Bannet in the European context: "On the one hand, the popularization of polite letteracy and the democratic extension of polite manners to everyone above the laboring poor, and on the other hand, insistence on observance of the customary, deferential, non-egalitarian forms."[35]

Social deference in letter writing emerges as a paramount concept in two examples of civility literature for women that I discussed in the previous chapter, *Onna shikimoku* and *Onna kagami hidensho*.[36] The second volume of *Onna shikimoku* is a tribute to the art of writing intended both as literacy and letteracy. It commences by stressing that writing (*tenarai*) is de rigueur for all women, be they highborn (*takaki*) or lowborn (*hikiki*). Particular emphasis is placed on the wives of merchants: for them literacy was to be viewed as the most important art. The explicit reference to merchant households deserves a brief observation. Drawing on Richard Rubinger's work on literacy in early modern Japan, Marcia Yonemoto notes that "it seems reasonable to postulate that the female readership for instructional texts was extremely limited until at least the early eighteenth century" and stresses the importance of other forms of oral and informal circulation of information in schools and within the household.[37] However, the focus that *Onna shikimoku* places on the need for merchant-class women to be able to write suggests that authors and publishers of these educational materials strove to target a larger body of readers than we might have thought of.

Letteracy teams up with literacy, occupying half of the second volume of *Onna shikimoku*. Here letteracy is conceptualized around one specific golden rule: "letters change depending on the addressee," and the title of the entire passage reads, "How to Write Letters Distinguishing Between High-, Medium-, and Low-Ranking Recipients" (Fumi kaki tamau beki jō-chū-ge no koto).[38] The opening section of the second volume of *Onna kagami hidensho* shares an almost identical title.[39]

Following a brief discussion of the aesthetic features of letter writing—with *Onna shikimoku* recommending, for example, that the brushwork should be swift and light and *Onna kagami hidensho* suggesting that women use mainly kana—both texts offer sample letters. Unlike *Onna shogaku bunshō*, however, we are provided with only one type of letter, which is rewritten in a number of different ways depending on the social level of the addressee. In both cases the content of the letter is rather generic, beginning with thanks for the receipt of a letter or gifts, then expressing joy over the addressee's good health, and ending with an expression of gratitude. *Onna shikimoku* is attentive to re-creating a calligraphy that is visually appealing (fig. 5.4) and as such may function to a certain extent as a copybook. *Onna kagami hidensho* pays less attention to the aesthetic dimension. Both, it must be acknowledged, fall short of *Onna shogaku bunshō* and the delights of Yasu's hand.

Notes follow each letter template, clarifying when and how it should be used. For instance, at the end of the first example, *Onna shikimoku* explains,

> This kind of text is indeed for high-ranking addressees. It must be written carefully and with an ink-laden brush. You must write the name of the high-ranking person to whom you are addressing the letter in place of "Mr./Ms. So-and-so" [*nanisama*]. You must also substitute the word "something" [*nani*] with the thing you have received. The principle is the same. This letter is suitable for nobility [*miuchishū*]. [At the end of the letter] you should write your name to the side in a smaller size. This is to show respect to the addressee. There are many other rules, but this is roughly what you should know. All of you may already be aware of all this, but I have listed the main points for the benefit of those who may have no previous knowledge.[40]

Everything—from the choice of words and honorifics in the template to the ink and the page composition—is regulated to give a visual shape to social deference. *Onna kagami hidensho* similarly starts with a specimen intended for the highest echelons of society, mentioning the imperial court and nobility as the addressee and daimyo or high-ranking families (*kōke*) as the sender. In both texts the remaining variant samples for the same letter are organized in such a way as to move from high to low. However, hierarchy is not a matter of any straightforward distinction in social classes. The second variant for both *Onna shikimoku* and *Onna kagami hidensho* is presented as something to be "readily sent" (*sugu ni yaru*), slightly lower in formality than the previous one.[41] Yet we are left to wonder who the addressee might be, although the mention of parents, parents-in-law, and men in *Onna kagami hidensho* suggests that we are moving away from social status and dealing more with issues of age and gender. At the bottom of this hierarchical pyramid are people from the same household, thus suggesting a divide between familiarity and unfamiliarity. Altogether ranking, as it emerges in these two texts, subsumes a complex network made of social hierarchy, age difference, and kinship or its lack. This, in turn, complicates any discussion on early modern Japanese hierarchy: popular literature suggests that status categories were just one side of a more complex equation.

Onna shikimoku provides additional instructions on how to visually translate rank. First is the use of cursive. The higher the status of the addressee, the greater is the care needed in writing each sign intelligibly, as the example of the character for the honorific *on*, 御, shows (fig. 5.5). Less cursive, at the top in the figure, indexes more deference. More cursive, as we progress down, indexes less deference. Second is the selection of words. The third section in the second volume of *Onna shikimoku* assumes the form of a minidictionary for letter writing. Each of the fifty entries groups together synonymic words. There are, for instance, four options for the term "letter": *on-fumi* 御文, *on-tamazusa* 御玉章, *on-mizuguki* 御水茎, and *on-hineri* 御捻.[42] The closing remarks mention that this is just a small selection of a much vaster lexicon and that each of the variants has a specific positioning (high, middle, low). Once again the reader is told that all choices depend on and give shape to the rank of the addressee.

Both *Onna shikimoku* and *Onna kagami hidensho* yield to the complexity of letteracy by noting that there is much more to it and that it is simply impossible to record in detail all that is needed. It is again clear that the printed word can only complement other cultural forms employed in the transmission of knowledge. Still, these two civility manuals make every effort to provide readers with a compass for navigating the social dimensions of letter writing.

Breaking Formulas and Shaping Love

The manuals examined thus far offer formulaic patterns that individuals can employ when composing letters. The pleasure in perusing such materials lies almost entirely in the acquisition of a set of practical skills that help establish successful interpersonal relations in a society heavily regulated by written documents. To appreciate letter writing and letteracy solely for their intrinsic heuristic value, though, would be misguided. Fiction appropriated and broke formulas to celebrate creativity, engaging readers on at least three levels: cognitive, emotional, and aesthetic. Among all the letter types, love missives were a privileged form in this regard.

Collections of Japanese love letters were not a new invention in early modern Japan; the tradition is deeply rooted in the country's cultural history and dates back to the late Heian period with *Horikawa-in enjo awase* (The collection of love

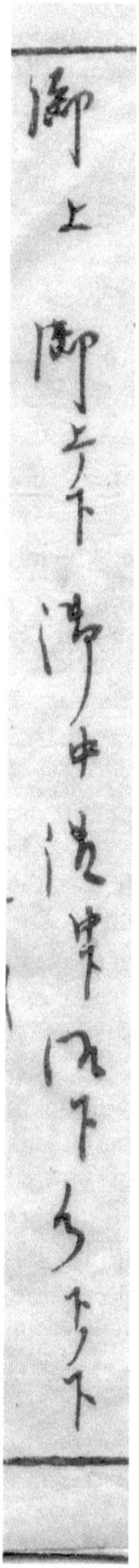

Figure 5.5 Detail from *Onna shikimoku*, publication details unknown, vol. 2, 12v. How to write 御 on the basis of the addressee's social status.

Author collection, Suzuran Bunko, Cambridge, U.K.

letters of Horikawa-in; 1102).[43] Ogawa Takeo has argued convincingly that by the fifteenth century the writing of love letters had become a highly formalized practice thanks to the production and wide distribution of manuals that included sample letters and instructions on how to compose them. *Shika kenro shū* (Anthology of beautifully crafted words) was one such well-received title in the late Muromachi period, and it remained influential into the early modern period.[44] A hallmark of these manuals is their absorption and adaptation of language, aesthetics, and rhetoric from the classical world of *waka* poetry and Heian-period tales. It is therefore no surprise that Edo-period booksellers listed them under the category of "books of poetry and *monogatari*" (*kasho narabi ni monogatari*; as per the title given to this category in 1670).

Meanwhile love stories constructed around epistolary exchanges flourished in the medieval period.[45] In the seventeenth century undoubtedly the most successful publication of this type was *Usuyuki monogatari*. First issued as a movable-type edition at the very beginning of the Edo period, *Usuyuki monogatari* was popular until the Meiji era, undergoing an impressive number of editions over the course of almost three centuries.[46]

Whether medieval or early modern, the fictional texts revolving around letters often function as variations of the same master plot or story skeleton.[47] A man and woman visit a temple or shrine; one sees the other (or they both see each other); one falls deeply in love with the other and asks the deity enshrined at the temple or shrine for assistance in realizing his or her burning passion; the request for help is granted in a dream or by introducing a key person to track down the identity of the other; letters are exchanged, generally with the man initiating the epistolary correspondence; this exchange fuels the love on both sides, despite the initial reticence of the woman; and the lovers manage to spend one night, or a short period, together. Yet their fate is doomed, with one dying prematurely and the other taking the tonsure, or both dying.

In the case of *Usuyuki monogatari*, the narrative action centers on this master plot and occupies very little space—for instance, a total of four folios out of twenty-six in the 1636 edition and two and a half folios of thirteen in the 1664 edition.[48] Sonobe no Emon catches a glimpse of the seventeen-year-old Usuyuki within the grounds of Kiyomizudera. Usuyuki's beauty is limned in a highly stylized manner, compared with beauties across Japanese and Chinese history. This hyperbolic tone also continues in the description of the passion ignited in Sonobe no Emon. He asks Kannon to exercise compassion and facilitate his love to blossom. Rather miraculously and clearly as a result of Kannon's intervention, Sonobe no Emon happens upon Usuyuki's maidservant, who agrees to deliver his letter to her mistress. The text then moves into the first of the twenty-four letters that are employed to heighten the emotional crescendo of the tale, and it is only in the second volume—for example, the twenty-third folio in the 1636 edition and the eleventh folio in the 1664 one—that the narrative resumes with the lovers spending their first night together. The relationship continues for nine months, at which stage the man is required to visit a sick friend in Ōmi Province. Sonobe no Emon returns home after a month and learns that Usuyuki has died after a sudden illness. Stopped just before taking his own life, he decides to become a Buddhist monk and dies at age twenty-six.

Framed within this formulaic plot, the core of *Usuyuki monogatari* is a virtuoso of literary allusions interwoven into the structure of love letters. While they apply the artificial language established in the letter templates, the *mairasesōrōbun* examined in the preceding, they break formulas by offering a refined texture that Joshua S. Mostow aptly describes as a "true 'cento pastiche.'"[49] Each letter is a gem of epistolary rhetoric that makes extensive use of poetic allusion and displays a skillful appropriation of an array of previous tales. The letters are organized as an escalation of desire. Sonobe no Emon never ceases to express his enduring love for Usuyuki while she, initially rebuffing his advances because she is married, gradually warms to him.

Mostow presents an intriguing reading of *Usuyuki monogatari* as a tale that showcases adulterous love as its main theme. Drawing on the numerous allusions to the Heian-period *Ise monogatari* in the first volume, along with the fact that an illustration from episode 23 of *Ise monogatari* opens one of the two movable-type editions, Mostow demonstrates convincingly that at this early stage *Usuyuki monogatari* was probably read as a tale of fidelity and rejection that ultimately encouraged unfaithful liaisons.[50]

I would like to suggest an alternative reading of *Usuyuki monogatari*, one that focuses on how this work was refashioned and reconceptualized beginning in the 1660s. I do so by investigating the twofold identity of the text as a love story on the one hand and, on the other, as a practical collection of letter templates. The essential components of the narrative recipe employed by *Usuyuki monogatari* are highlighted in the illustrated editions produced around the 1660s. Starting with the 1664 edition, they dispense with visual allusions to Heian- and Muromachi-period prose to illustrate the key narrative moments of the love story between Sonobe no Emon and Usuyuki.[51] Four visual tropes emerge in the process: the lovers' first encounter at a temple; the act of reading a letter; the morning after the first night the lovers have spent together; and the tragic denouement of death and seclusion (fig. 5.6). Whereas the verbal text devotes less than 14 percent to the development of the love narrative, 100 percent of the images deal with the love story. This balance can be viewed as a conscious attempt by the publishers to frame *Usuyuki monogatari* as a gripping and dramatic love story, with the potential to attract a broader readership. At the same time, this choice serves to highlight the key moments of the story and assists in their being fixed in the reader's memory. Thus, the basic plot of *Usuyuki monogatari* becomes a "culturally common story."[52] It is no coincidence that

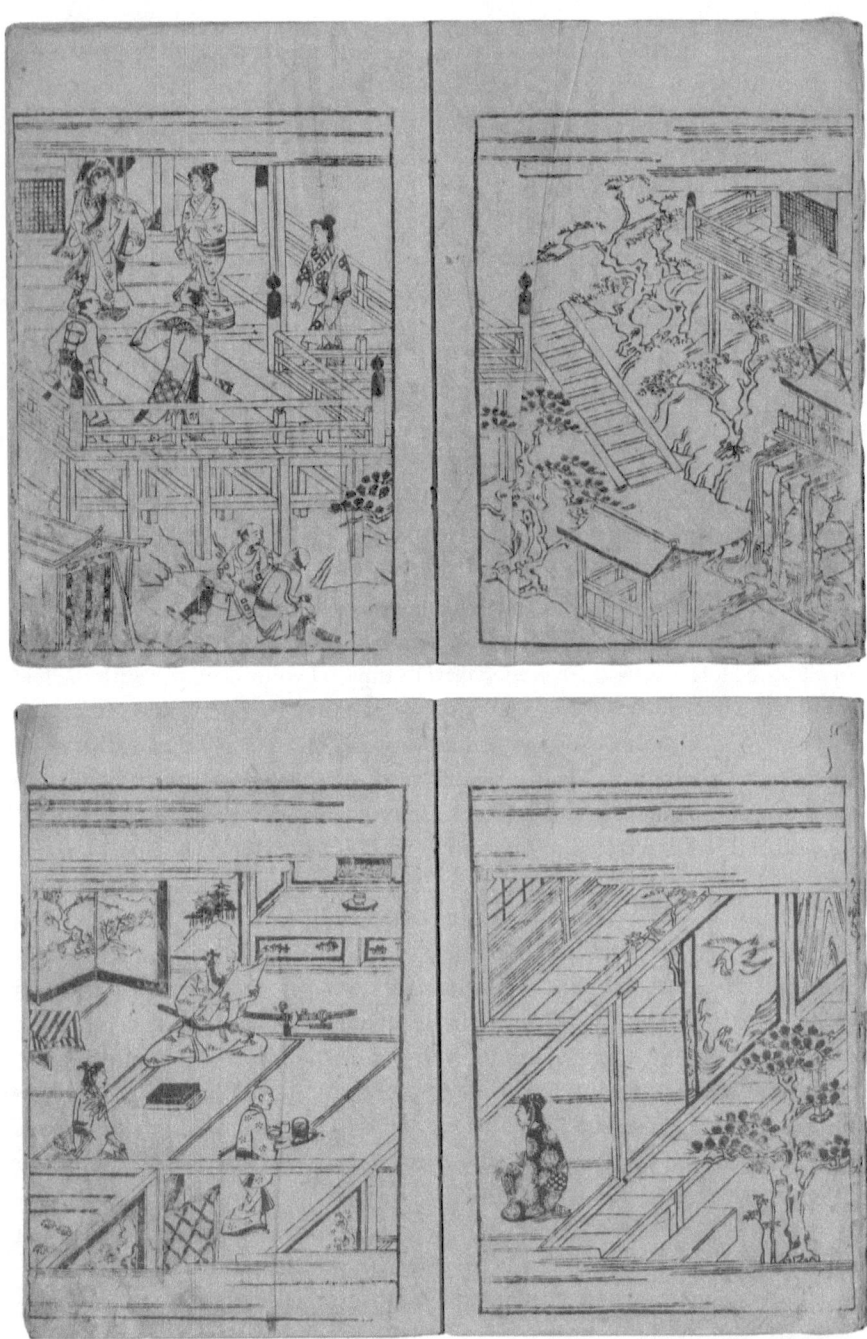

Figure 5.6 Composite image of four double-page spreads with illustrations from *Usuyuki monogatari*, 1664. Respectively vol. 1, 3v–4r, 9v–10r; vol. 2, 3v–4r, 9v–10r.

Courtesy of the National Diet Library, Tokyo

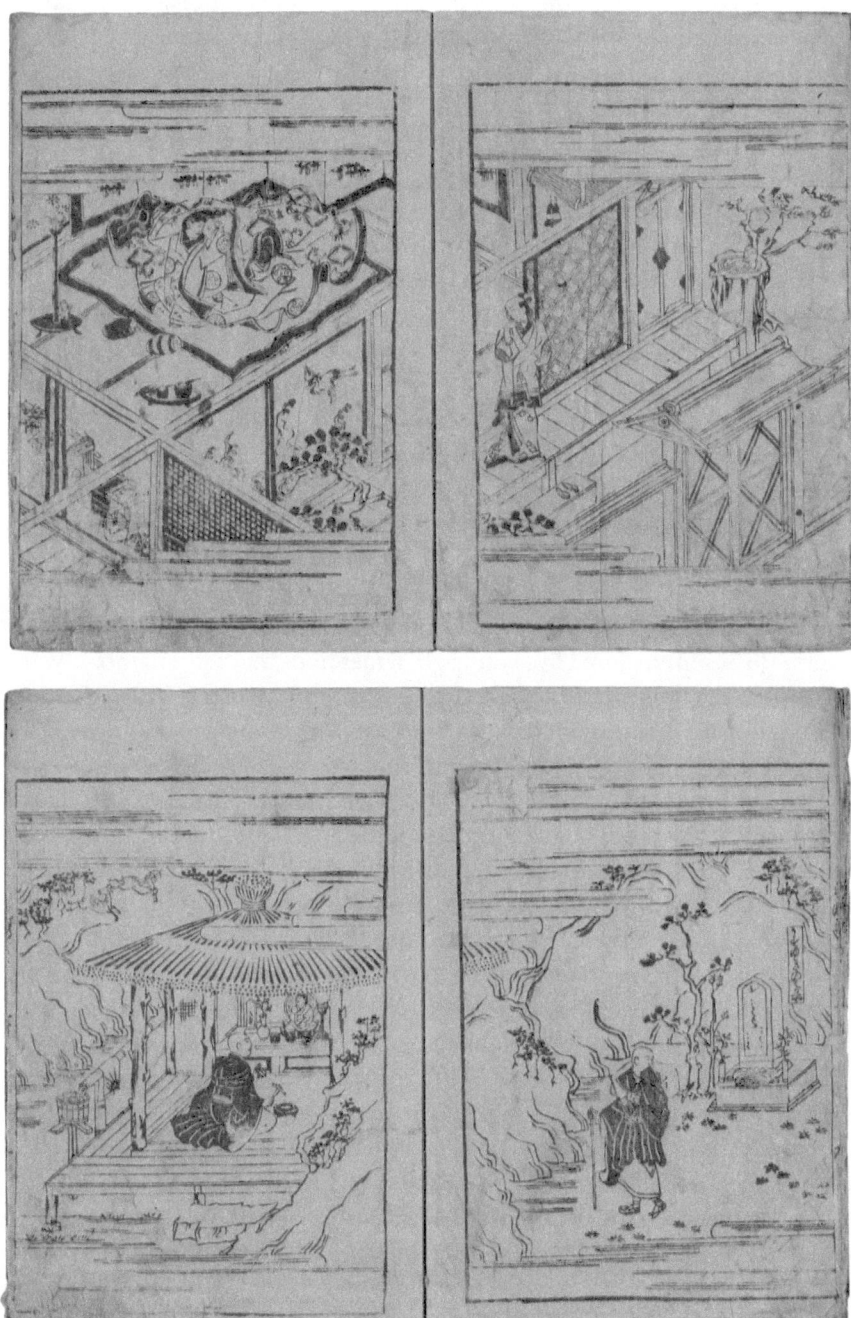

Figure 5.6 (Continued)

subsequent editions adopt the same pattern for the illustrations. For instance, when Izumoji Manjirō 出雲寺万次郎 (dates unknown) reissues the text as late as 1895 (using blocks originally cut probably between 1716 and 1736), the four scenes are retained but updated in style. The introduction added in this Meiji-era edition describes the tale as "writing words of passion [*nasake*] in which deep feelings, as deep as luxuriant grass, have unexpectedly melted away the light snow in the recesses of the valley."[53] These words help market the book as an emotionally involving love story, in the same vein as Edo-period booksellers had done since the Kanbun era (1661–1673).

While being marketed as a striking love story that encourages readers to develop an emotional involvement with the characters and their fate, *Usuyuki monogatari* also served an epistemic function in operating as a manual of love letters. Noda Hisao has shown that by the first half of the eighteenth century *Usuyuki monogatari* was being portrayed in coeval fiction as a manual used to master the art of love letters.[54] In the third story of the second volume of the 1686 *Shokoku shinjū onna* (Women's double suicides around the provinces), for example, the male protagonist, Kitarō, manages to sway the heart of a girl by sending "a letter that he learned from the illustrated tale [*ezōshi*] *Usuyuki*."[55] Equally, the opening story of the second volume of the 1735 *Sakiwake gonin musume* (The multicolored five young girls) mentions that a girl named Oyotsu learned the art of writing love missives (*nurebumi*) by using *Usuyuki monogatari* and its compilation of letters (*fumi-zukushi*) as a copybook (*tehon*).[56] A concrete example of how *Usuyuki monogatari* was reinterpreted as a copybook for letter writing is seen in the 1700 *Onna sewa yōbunshō taisei* (Collection of letters useful for women's daily business).[57] The core of this multipurpose book consists of letter templates written in the calligraphy of a woman named Sawa さわ from the Maeda family. In the introduction Sawa stresses that the book is striking because it presents unusual words and texts alongside useful materials for women. Not surprisingly, the majority of the space on each page is occupied by letter templates written in the *chirashi-gaki* style much like *Onna shogaku bunshō*. The sections in the upper register of the work contain other materials: the first volume recounts the story of Urashima Tarō, while in the second and third volumes the text of *Usuyuki monogatari* appears under the title *Imayō Usuyuki monogatari*. Despite the label *imayō* (in vogue, fashionable), the text remains substantially unchanged.[58] It cannot be denied that this part of the work could have been used as an educational text, instructing women on the affairs of the heart but also warning them against adultery. At the same time, however, the other materials in *Onna sewa yōbunshō taisei* seem eminently useful. This can be read as a hint that *Usuyuki monogatari* itself might have been read on a practical level to understand how to formulate a particular type of letter—the love letter. As such, it would complement the letter templates in the remainder of the book.

The practical nature of *Usuyuki monogatari* as a copybook is certainly enhanced when, in 1716, an adaptation of the text was published under the title *Shin Usuyuki monogatari* (New *Tale of Usuyuki*; subtitled *Miyako kenjo kagami* [The mirror of a virtuous woman from Kyoto]).[59] Two of the letters—the first sent by the man to Usuyuki after their initial night together and the second sent by Usuyuki before dying—are written in the *chirashi-gaki* calligraphic style and by the strikingly elegant hand of the female calligrapher Rankeishi 蘭渓子 (dates unknown [fig. 5.7]). I submit that this was an attempt by the publishers of *Shin Usuyuki monogatari* to market this book also as a copybook for love letters.

Usuyuki monogatari is an intriguing example of how letter templates in the *mairase-sōrōbun* style were used as narrative capital to develop a fictional text full of complexities. Originally conceived as a story of adulterous love, we have seen that *Usuyuki monogatari* was rebranded during the Edo period as a tragic love story that follows a master plot emerging as early as the medieval period. The popularity of *Usuyuki monogatari* allowed for this story skeleton—what I label the *Usuyuki* master plot—to be further fixed in the popular imagination and to become a part of the stock of raw materials available to create new

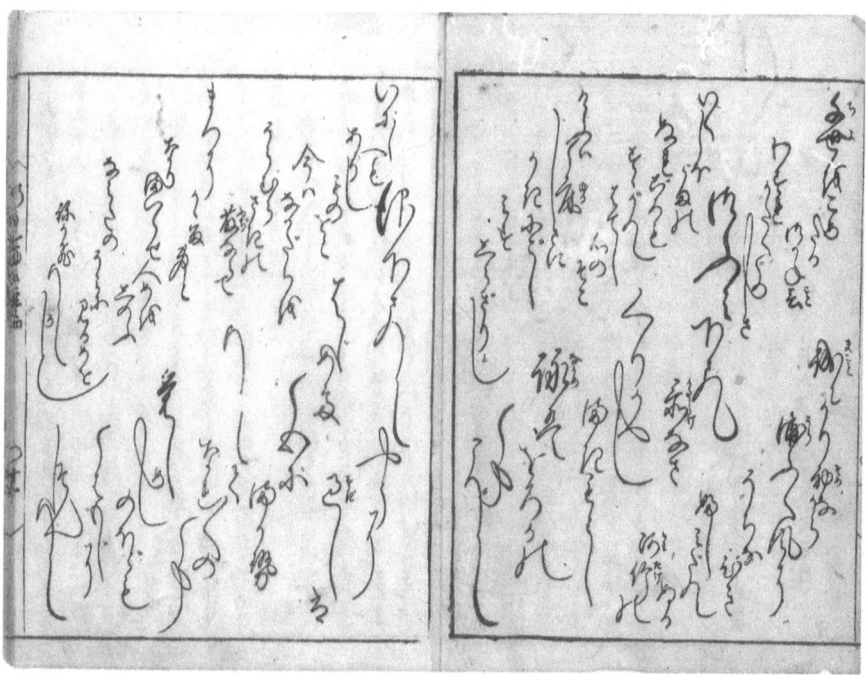

Figure 5.7 Rankeishi (calligrapher) and Ōmori Yoshikiyo (illustrator), *Shin Usuyuki monogatari*, 1716, vol. 4, 10v–11r. Letter sent to Usuyuki after the first night with her suitor. Author collection, Suzuran Bunko, Cambridge, U.K.

texts.⁶⁰ At the same time, early modern publishers tried to stress the practical prospects of *Usuyuki monogatari* as a collection of exemplary love letters that could be used as templates. One question emerges: to what extent could the average reader imitate epistolary texts conceived as a clever pastiche of source texts drawn from the classical tradition? While this remains a challenging point of issue that needs to be answered, it is clear that *Usuyuki monogatari* profoundly influenced Edo-period popular literature.

Adapting the *Usuyuki* Master Plot to Empower Women

In 1659, the Kyoto publisher Mizuta Jinzaemon 水田甚左衛門 (dates unknown) released *Usugumo monogatari* (The tale of Usugumo).⁶¹ Noda Hisao has underrated this work as an unimaginative replica of medieval prose, yet I would assert that this text showcases the extent to which the story skeleton popularized by *Usuyuki monogatari* and the narrative device of love-letter correspondence could be cunningly reappropriated and imbued with new meanings—namely, a powerful play of gender inversion.⁶²

On the surface *Usugumo monogatari* functions as a pastiche of master plots and narrative tropes known from medieval literature. The text starts with the image of a son who works relentlessly to support his elderly parents, a stellar example of filial piety.⁶³ The setting is Muro no Tsu village in Harima Province, where a certain Kanaoka makes a living by fishing. The narrator commends his behavior with an allusion to the *Twenty-Four Paradigms of Filial Piety* (*Nijūshikō*): "Because he was such a virtuous man [*seijin*], the neighbors used to praise him as an example surpassing the *Twenty-Four Paradigms of Filial Piety* from China."⁶⁴ Kanaoka's commitment to filial piety is rewarded. An old man of around eighty appears in front of Kanaoka's wife on thin clouds in the skies, declaring, "Because your husband is such a filial son, Heaven takes pity on him and bestows you with this jewel. You must rejoice.... When you pray in the direction of this jewel there is nothing that will not be granted to you."⁶⁵ The effect of this precious gift extended not only to the accumulation of wealth—Kanaoka is portrayed as a millionaire in the first line of the tale—but also to the birth of a girl. This is where the second literary motif comes into play. Kanaoka's daughter, Usugumo, or "Thin Clouds" (also referred to as Usugumo no Mae), was not conceived naturally but arrived as a divine gift.⁶⁶ We learn from the old man's words that he is the manifestation of the deity known as Muro no Myōjin (connected to Kamo Shrine in Kyoto). In line with the generally miraculous tone that perfuses the narration, within a few lines Usugumo is a girl of fifteen. During the rainy season of the fifth month, Kanaoka decides to take the young girl to Kyoto and pay homage to Kamo Shrine, as was promised to Muro no Myōjin. The mention of a pilgrimage to a shrine in the capital must have triggered specific expectations—that is, a man will see Usugumo and become enamored of her. This is because readers at the time would probably have been familiar with the master plot of *Usuyuki monogatari*, one of the culturally common stories stored in their collective memory, as demonstrated in the previous section. But does this occur in *Usugumo monogatari*? Yes and no, and this is where the novelty of this work is effected.

Sakura no Miya, the nineteen-year-old son of the aristocrat Chief Councillor Takei no Arizumi, and Usugumo do indeed meet at Kamo Shrine. This proceeds as expected. Yet here the gaze is inverted. While Sonobe no Emon glimpsed Usuyuki as she stepped out of the palanquin, in *Usugumo monogatari* "the multitude of people, high and low, kept staring at him [Sakura no Miya]—all were captivated."[67] Why? Because of his extraordinary beauty. Whereas *Usuyuki monogatari* opens with a description of Usuyuki's charming countenance, *Usugumo monogatari* celebrates Sakura no Miya. The description of him echoes that of Usuyuki: "her [Usuyuki's] features are alluring, a spring flower, the fragrance of which diffuses the mist, and her elegance is like branches of green willow trees moved by the spring wind" becomes "his [Sakura no Miya's] appearance can be compared to the graceful branches of a green willow tree, among the fragrance of the plum blossoms and the cherry in bloom. And still this does him little justice."[68] Usugumo has finished praying and is descending the steps on her way home when she happens across Sakura no Miya, who is just arriving to pray. His refined beauty beguiles her. The illustration reinforces this shift from a male to a female gaze: Sakura no Miya faces the altar, while Usugumo is looking backward, with the text cartouche in the lower right stressing the action of "looking back" (*mikaeshi tamau*).

The inversion of which character looks at whom is accompanied by an equally transposed emotional outcome. Usugumo is "ecstatic" at the sight of Sakura no Miya, while he is moved only by curiosity at seeing this girl. There is no tumultuous love, no feelings compared to "smoke emanating from the heart and higher than Mount Fuji" that overwhelmed Sonobe no Emon.[69] It is simple curiosity. Sakura no Miya sends someone to discover the identity of Usugumo, who is then described to him as "a person from the distant countryside."[70] Not surprisingly, Sakura no Miya's reaction to this news is not disclosed, but Usugumo is flattered to hear that she is the object of inquiry. For her, "the seed of love" germinates as soon as she understands Sakura no Miya's aristocratic origins. The stage is now set for a powerful inversion in the gender dynamics at play in the *Usuyuki* master plot. Women take action and men remain passive.[71]

Usugumo returns to her village and passes the time wallowing in her lovesickness: "If only a letter from him would arrive, the sadness would not be so great."[72] Whether this is the narrator's voice or we are in fact party to Usugumo's thoughts is difficult to establish, yet this sentence voices the expectations of all, readers included, who are nurtured by a familiarity with the master plot. The reader anticipates a letter from Sakura no Miya, but it never arrives.

Izayoi, Usugumo's maidservant, is the first to take action. Using an excuse, she convinces Usugumo's mother to let them both go to the capital. But her underlying motive is clear: she intends to resolve Usugumo's love problem.[73] Fate, as it turns out, is on the side of these proactive women since their lodgings on Gojō Avenue in Kyoto are near Sakura no Miya's wet nurse, Aoyagi. Izayoi recounts the events to Aoyagi, and Aoyagi then becomes a useful ally in the plan to have Usugumo's love fulfilled. There is no divine intervention, only a ploy that is successful thanks to the determination of the two maidservants. A letter finally is delivered, but this time from Usugumo to Sakura no Miya, from woman to man, and not the other way around.

Yuasa Yoshiko acknowledges that *Usugumo monogatari* depicts "a proactive female protagonist" but underplays its significance by ascribing it to a mere intertextual impulse to reuse the plot of the medieval *Hanyū no monogatari* (The tale of Hanyū). In it the love between a princess and a young Buddhist acolyte blossoms thanks to the actions of the people around the princess.[74] This link is certainly plausible, but to what extent would the average reader have identified and enjoyed an intertextual reference to a medieval text never published in the Edo period and surviving at that time in only a handful of manuscripts? Even if narrative details from *Hanyū monogatari* were drawn upon, I would argue that what most resonated with readers is the gender inversion of the *Usuyuki* master plot.

The forceful attitude of women continues into the second volume, where the exchange of love letters finally occurs. This is another noticeable difference with *Usuyuki monogatari*. While in *Usuyuki monogatari* only a fraction of the tale was devoted to the narration of the plot, in *Usugumo monogatari* it dominates one of two volumes. Once Aoyagi's support has been guaranteed, Usugumo writes the first missive that is entrusted to Aoyagi.[75] In *Usuyuki monogatari* it is the narrator who describes Usuyuki's beauty at the outset; here, however, it is Aoyagi's voice that is used to praise Usugumo with Sakura no Miya. A comparison with the usual suspects—the stereotypical beauties of China and Japan—is followed by an inflated commendation of her refined disposition. Aoyagi's words convince Sakura no Miya to open the letter. The narrator does reveal at this juncture that Sakura no Miya had missed Usugumo in the past months and that he is struck by the beauty of her calligraphy (as manuals teach, refined calligraphy is important!). After reading the letter, he applauds her feelings as refined, but his only concern is the "scorn of people," presumably in connection with his social position as the son of a court nobleman vis-à-vis that of Usugumo, the daughter of a rich fisherman.[76] The letter exchange that takes place in the second volume, in the relatively confined space between 18r and 25v, is a verbal battle between a relentless woman driven by an enduring passion and an ever-reticent man who displays coldhearted social snobbery.

Usugumo's frustration at the repeated rejections leads her to take the initiative, and she lurks outside the man's room in an attempt to convince him of the merits of a relationship. This is not a dignified *kaimami* (stolen glimpse), rather a blatant love pursuit. But a happy ending is still possible, thanks to the divine intervention of Muro no Myōjin. The conclusion of *Usugumo monogatari* avoids the tragic fate of the *Usuyuki* master plot when a diviner interprets mysterious events at Kamo Shrine as a sign that requires the appointment of Usugumo's father, Kanaoka, as a military governor in the capital. In the end, Usugumo marries Sakura no Miya, and he is promoted to chief councillor.[77]

There are only four letters in *Usugumo monogatari*, a drastic decrease relative to the twenty-four in *Usuyuki monogatari*. Sakura no Miya's epistles are pitifully short and almost entirely void of any significant literary allusion, but Usugumo's are replete with masterfully crafted intertextual overtones similar to those identifiable in *Usuyuki monogatari*. While they both apply the *mairase-sōrōbun* style, Usugumo's prose displays a degree of aesthetic sophistication absent from Sakura no Miya's. Once again *Usugumo monogatari* celebrates women over men, in this case women's cultural literacy and sophistication. The second letter by Usugumo aptly showcases the intricate brocade of literary allusions as Usugumo challenges Sakura no Miya's fears of derision for a socially mismatched relation.[78]

Usugumo starts with a brief allusion to the tale of Princess Mano and Emperor Yōmei originally included as an embedded narrative in the *kōwakamai* text *Eboshi ori* (The fold of the *eboshi*). In the story Emperor Yōmei falls in love with the daughter of a wealthy family in Bungo Province, but her father repeatedly turns down his proposals of marriage. The emperor decides to travel to Bungo in disguise and serves for three years in the woman's household looking after oxen. Once his identity is revealed, the father acquiesces and permits his daughter to marry him.[79] This love story perfectly illustrates Usugumo's point: love transcends social differences and even a man of high status, like an emperor, can marry a woman of lower status who belongs to a wealthy household. Yet Usugumo does seem to gloss over the fact that it is in fact the emperor who is the active agent in the tale and not the woman.[80]

Usugumo's second example is elucidated in greater detail. Susuki no Mae, the daughter of Ono no Yoshihiro and the cousin of the famous Ono no Komachi, lives in distant Dewa Province in northwestern Japan. Her beauty is surpassed only by her generosity of heart. The lieutenant general (*chūjō*) Shii Masamichi, son of Chief Councillor Ōhashi Masashige, is sent to Dewa. She is immediately smitten and sends him love letters, but no reply is forthcoming. Usugumo, who recounts the tale in her letter, even adds that Masamichi is exactly like Sakura no Miya—"a man with a hard heart [*kokorozuyoki hitosama*]."[81] Susuki no Mae then decides to visit her beloved; she stands quietly outside his quarters and gently persuades him to open his door, and his heart, to her. This story, narrated in Usugumo's letter before she herself behaves exactly like Susuki no Mae, works as a perfect *mise en abyme* of the main narration, a foretaste of what both the male protagonist and readers might expect. Usugumo ends the letter with the celebrated story of Fukakusa no Shōshō and his enduring love for Ono no Komachi. She quotes verbatim from the Noh play *Kayoi Komachi* when speaking about Fukakusa no Shōshō as the "dog of earthly passions" (*bonnō no inu*).[82] We are cautioned that Usugumo's attachment does not differ from Fukakusa no Shōshō's, but readers are enjoined, once again, to invert the gender dynamics.

Usugumo monogatari adapts the *Usuyuki* master plot to develop the tale of a passionate woman ready to take initiative in order to satisfy her love. By flipping the gender dynamics at play in the story skeleton, this text alerts us to a much more complex relation of power between men and women in early modern Japan. The step to extreme behavior taken by other strongheaded women in the name of love portrayed in Japanese early modern literature and theater is a natural outcome.

Taxonomies of Love

As seen thus far, the cultural legacy of *Usuyuki monogatari* as a love story is inherited and creatively appropriated by *Usugumo monogatari*. *Usuyuki monogatari*'s nature as a compendium of love letters is also used as a direct source of inspiration, this time in the 1660 *Nishikigi*.[83] The title tells us more than the name of a tree known as a winged spindle, in Japanese *nishikigi*. It refers, in fact, to a tradition of courtship of the Michinoku region whereby in lieu of a love letter a man would place a tree painted in a variety of colors in front of the house of the woman he was in love with. If the woman reciprocated, she would take the tree inside; if she did not, the man would keep bringing trees until they reached a thousand. The title not only indicates that the book deals with love affairs but also implies a connection with poetry inasmuch as *nishikigi* was used as a poetic word in both *waka* and haikai. The stage is set: *Nishikigi* promises to be a book concerned with love pursuits and the art of poetry. The introduction gives additional explanations about the nature of *Nishikigi*: it is a book that contains instruction on formulating letters and poems that give an appropriate voice to individual feelings. The same introduction makes a bold, didactic claim: love letters and love poems should not be used to encourage love and sensuality (*kōshoku*). Even works like *Genji monogatari* and *Ise monogatari*—celebrated as early as *Shika kenro shū* as the primary sources of reference in writing love letters—offer no teachings about love (*irogonomi*). Rather, they admonish in an attempt to rectify behavior and steer the heart. *Nishikigi* allegedly does the same. We could take this avowal at face value, or we could exercise some caution. After all, as Bradin Cormack and Carla Mazzio have pointed out in the case of early modern European books, "such warnings could function as an invitation, a guide to the book's own abuse."[84] In *Nishikigi*, the oblique invitation is for the reader to acquire skills in writing love letters, which should, in turn, lead to sensual pleasures.

But how is this done? The text is not organized according to a teleological structure that follows the development of a specific love story between a man and a woman from start to finish through their epistolary exchanges. Instead, it assembles letters under different taxonomies of love. For example, the table of contents for the first volume starts with "The Very First Love: Approaching a Young Girl" (Hatsu no koi yōjo yosuru), then moves on to "Love After the First Night Spent Together" (Nochi no ashita no koi), "Love for a Woman Just Encountered" (Misomuru koi), and finishes with "Love That Goes and Comes Back Empty" (Yukite munashiku kaeru koi). The second volume returns to the theme of "The Very First Love" (Hatsukoi), then "Doubtful Love" (Utagau koi), continuing on with seven other typologies. The fourth volume is devoted entirely to love letters sent to women in the pleasure quarters, and the fifth concludes with "Love That Is Thrown Away" (Suteraruru koi). Yuasa Yoshiko maintains that this style is reminiscent of the tables of contents found in *waka* poetry anthologies centered on a common theme (known in Japanese as *ruidai shū* or *ruidai waka shū*) and thus functions as useful didactic material for poetic composition.[85] On the one hand, this strengthens the link between *Nishikigi* and poetry, as announced in the title and introduction; on the other, it highlights the text's educational nature. At the end of the fifth volume, *Nishikigi* includes a short section with supplemental information in what appears to be a dictionary of poetic, love-related vocabulary. This glossary is topped by a list of the six types of love, accompanied by simple explanations of their natures and poems.[86] A collection of specific words used in love exchanges and their meanings follows.[87] All in all, *Nishikigi* is packaged as a miscellany of letters that can be used when dealing with a particular typology of love, together with a list of useful words. All is imbued with the aesthetics of *waka* poetry.

It is only by engaging in a close reading of a specific section that we can fully appreciate the textual strategies at play in *Nishikigi*. I have chosen "Love for a Woman Just Encountered" to complement the analysis conducted in Japanese on other sections.[88] This letter is written by a man and starts with a reference to the moment when he first glimpses the woman on a pilgrimage to Inari Shrine on the third day of the second month. The mention of the pilgrimage would likely trigger in readers an association with the *Usuyuki* master plot. The letter then launches into a description of the man's feelings. First, he reveals to the woman that her image is indelibly etched in his memory. The quotation of a poem from *Goshūi waka shū* (Collection of gleanings continued) lyrically evokes his emotional state: "That the opening / in the beautiful blind could freeze. / How can I convey / the feelings developed / from today?" (*hima tomete / ikade shirasen / tamasudare / kyō yori kakaru / omoi ari to wa*).⁸⁹ The text goes on to mention the emotional distress of the man: "I wanted to conceal [my feelings] [*shinobu to suredo*] but they keep appearing [*hitasura ni ho ni arawarete*] and I cannot stand them anymore. *Hence I shall let you know what I feel in my heart.*"⁹⁰ This brief passage is a gem of sophisticated poetic rhetoric, packed with skillful intertextual allusions. My translation might capture the feelings the man wishes to express but hardly conveys the linguistic complexity at play. When translated literally, the sentence that I have highlighted in italics reads as follows: "I shall let you know of the robe dyed with the indigo of Hatsuyama together with the color of my heart" (*hatsuyama no ai no someginu ya kokoro no iro o shirase mairase sōrō*). I maintain that it displays a deft reuse of a *waka* from the poetry anthology *Shin Senzai waka shū* (New Collection of a Thousand Years): "Soon, soon / I would like to show the depth / of the love that I have felt for the first time / dyed of the same distinct color / of the indigo of Hatsuyama" (*itsushika to / hatsuyama ai no / iro ni idete / omoi sometsuru / hodo o miseba ya*).⁹¹ The words *hatsu* and *some* in the prose text are generated from the poem and they function as pivot words (*kakekotoba*) to connote "first" and "starting." As such they serve to underpin the idea that we are dealing with a type of love regarding someone whom the man has seen for the very first time: *misomuru* in the title of this section resonates in the choice of *hatsu* and *some*. Moreover, the word *some*, meaning "to dye," encourages the reader to reconsider the meaning of the word *shinobu* used in the previous sentence and translated as "to conceal [one's feelings]." Any cultured reader familiar with *Ise monogatari* would have recalled the first section of this tale and the irregular, tangled pattern on Narihira's robe, referred to as *shinobu-zuri*, employed in Narihira's poem to express his disconcertment when he first sees the women in Kasuga Village.⁹² This, in turn, discloses more about the feelings of the man in this passage of *Nishikigi*, suggesting that he is as puzzled as Narihira had been. Finally, the expression *ho ni arawarete* (translated here as "they keep appearing") is interesting because it uses one of the words discussed at some length in the brief poetry/love dictionary at the end of the fifth volume, showing how this section of *Nishikigi* could be used to complement the perusal of the letters themselves.⁹³ The letter closes with the request for a reply: "If not to you, to whom should I address [these feelings of mine]? In the hope that you will be moved by compassion and will at least send me a few words, I have entrusted this missive to the moonlight that glows through the wind. *Kashiku*."⁹⁴ As in *Usuyuki monogatari* and *Usugumo monogatari*, here, too, the man's written language follows conventions already established in letter manuals for women, with the use of the *mairase-sōrōbun* and the closing *kashiku*. As previously noted, men were expected to embrace the conventions of what I have called gendered translations of letter-writing manuals when encoding texts intended for women. The letter in its entirety engages the reader on a plurality of levels. First, it fulfills its epistemic function by teaching us how we should compose a love letter sent in similar circumstances. Whether any practical application of such knowledge was feasible—considering the amount of cultural literacy subsumed by the letter—remains to be proved. The cognitive engagement is complemented by an aesthetic response to a text that displays mastery of poetic and intertextual techniques. On top of this, the letter opens a window onto the man's feelings, eliciting an emotional reaction.

The woman's open rejection has the effect of piquing the reader's curiosity.[95] Usuyuki, if we remember, had initially sent a negative response to Sonobe no Emon, and this became the inception of a poignant love story that blossoms in further letters. A similar negative response in this context might well have fostered the hope for a passionate love story. *Nishikigi* does not betray this expectation. The letters listed under this section tender a brief love story that concludes with a one-night liaison. To reinforce the narrative nature of the text is the surfacing of a narratorial voice at the end of "Love for a Woman Just Encountered" that explains, "The first night when the man and the woman met things were flurried and the man went home early."[96] Notwithstanding its brevity, this storylike passage naturally leads to the following section containing letters for "Love That Goes and Comes Back Empty," as if it were a logical, narrative development. However, while the brief narratorial voice asks us to see this section as nothing more than the next step in the lovers' exchange, and as such part of a story, the new title nudges us to distance ourselves from the narrative and return to reading a compilation of taxonomies of love with sample letters.

The first half of the second volume further intensifies the interplay between narrative fragments that build the skeleton of a story and letter specimens that reveal the emotional universe of its protagonists. It begins, again, with a letter a man sends to a woman he has just seen. The contents adopt a similar pattern as previously discussed: the man is on a pilgrimage to Kitano Shrine in the second month, on the day of the shrine festival, when he notices a woman of matchless beauty. Consumed by a burning passion he writes to her, trying to appeal to her compassionate nature for a reply. This time, however, the narrator appears soon after the first letter to explain that the woman was annoyed and therefore sent no reply.[97] The text resumes with yet another missive from the man, to which the woman reluctantly replies. The narrator reenters, noting that "the man sent another reply, as the woman's letter was showing signs of some acceptance but ended with a poem that cast some doubt on his being 'over the moon' [*wa no sora*]."[98] This leads to a new category of love, "Doubtful

Love." At this point, we can follow the story line by skipping the letters and jumping to the narrator's comments, to be read in conjunction with the titles of the typologies of love described. The woman's parents hear of the exchange of letters and instruct the intermediary to stop the correspondence; this leads to "Love Halted by the Intermediary" (Nakadachi taetaru koi). The next morning the man sends a letter, which implies that the couple have spent a night together despite parental opposition, taking us then to "Love After Separation" (Wakarete kaerishi koi). The woman decides to become a nun, and the man cries "tears of blood" before proceeding to "Pining Love" (Shitau koi). As with the editions of *Usuyuki monogatari* produced after the 1660s, the illustrations here highlight the salient moments in the narrative. While the images assist in conveying, albeit rather simply, some of the feelings of the protagonists, it is ultimately the letters that lay bare the emotional world of these two lovers. The tale thus developed ends in the middle of the second volume.[99] Once it ends, the text proceeds to the next tale, commencing once again with the trope of a man who has seen a woman and confides his innermost feelings in a letter ("Secret Love" [Shinobu kokoro no koi]).

Noda Hisao claims that it is only in the fourth volume that the text exhibits an interest in storytelling—or what he calls a "novel-like" penchant.[100] Yet the textual analysis here has revealed that this movement between narrative and nonnarrative, between a story and a letter manual applies more or less throughout the text. *Nishikigi* tantalizes with snippets of unadorned stories that embody a particular typology of love, and these stories are outlined by the short narratorial comments inserted at times between the letter samples. They gain in emotional depth through the letters themselves. This problematizes Noda Hisao's more general criticism of *Nishikigi* as merely a practical text and echoes some of the findings put forward by Yuasa Yoshiko.[101] It also corroborates Roger Chartier's intuition that manuals of love-letter templates could be read as fictional stories.[102] *Nishikigi*, however, does not rely on the reader's imagination to fill in the narrative gaps left between occasions for writing, as Chartier explains, because it deploys an overt narratorial voice that constructs a story line on the printed page.

There are two more aspects of *Nishikigi* that engage us, this time at a cognitive level. First, it offers multiple letters for the same occasion. This repetition represents a striking difference not only from *Usuyuki monogatari* and *Usugumo monogatari* but also from subsequent compendiums of love letters. The multiplicity of models for the same occurrence makes it possible for the reader to gain a clearer understanding of the imagery to be used on given occasions and encourages a creative mix and match. Repetition and difference thus work in tandem to make *Nishikigi* a potentially effective mirror for writing proficient love letters. Second, it contains illustrations that help us to understand how letters were produced and consumed. The adoption of specific,

Figure 5.8 *Nishikigi*, publication details unknown, vol. 5, 14r. Woman writing a letter.
Author collection, Suzuran Bunko, Cambridge, U.K.

recurrent visual tropes allowed readers in the seventeenth century to understand how to write, send, and read letters. Those who peruse the text learn, for instance, about the need for fairly sizable sheets of paper on which to write either by holding a sheet in the hands or placed on the knees (fig. 5.8). The presence of a second person suggests that letters were delivered by messengers. Nothing indicates that letters were read aloud for the recipient.[103]

Nishikigi must have enjoyed the favor of readers at the time as it inspired a handful of early modern rewritings. A *Zoku Nishikigi* (*Nishikigi* continued; undated) is recorded, but no copy seems to have survived, while extant works include *Kōshoku Nishikigi* (The amorous *Nishikigi*; 1692) and *Shin Nishikigi monogatari* (The new *Nishikigi*; 1758).[104] The subtitle of the latter, *Azuma kenjo kagami* (The mirror of a virtuous woman from Edo), clearly links *Shin Nishikigi monogatari* with the 1716 *Shin Usuyuki monogatari*, subtitled *The Mirror of a Virtuous Woman from Kyoto*. Early modern readers were enticed to buy this new *Nishikigi* with the promise that it would complement the new *Usuyuki*, suggesting the cross-breeding of these two texts.

Letters for Sex

The conceit of using love letters to write about taxonomies of love, explored for the first time in *Nishikigi*, is taken to new levels of creativity in the 1680s with the three-volume *Nasake no uwamori* (Heightened feelings) by the Edo publisher Urokogataya and illustrated by Hishikawa Moronobu.[105] To suggest a synergy between what has been viewed to date as a dry manual for letter writing—*Nishikigi*—and a sexually explicit *shunpon* appreciated for the genius of its illustrator—*Nasake no uwamori*—might be viewed as a bête noire in more traditional approaches to literary history. Yet in the following I strive to demonstrate how the complex layers of *Nasake no uwamori* can be fully appreciated in light of its appropriation of the narrative capital disclosed by *Nishikigi*.

The introduction at the beginning of the first volume of *Nasake no uwamori* unlocks what is to be expected from it:

> From the past the great connoisseur of love, Lord Ariwara [Ariwara no Narihira], visited Takayasu because he loved a woman. Full of envy, I have used him [as inspiration] for the pictures [in this book] and jotted down without any specific reason trivialities that move the heart. Hoping that it will become a copybook [*tehon*] for those who want to embark on the path of love, I have added words in the upper register of the page that can actually be used [*mono ieru gotoku no kotoba*], but the important secret tricks are represented in the illustrations. I hope that it will inspire those who look at it. *Ana kashiku*.[106]

Whereas *Nishikigi* discouraged using love letters to embark on love pursuits and claimed its usefulness as a poetic and epistolary manual, *Nasake no uwamori* is framed as a copybook for sensuality. The reference to Ariwara no Narihira comes as no surprise. By this time, in fact, he had been turned into a well-trodden trope in books belonging to the publishing genre of *kōshoku narabi ni rakuji* (erotica and diversions), including those illustrated by Moronobu.[107] The use of *ana kashiku* at the end makes us realize that what we have been reading is in fact a letter. The "words in the upper register" are also letter samples. On the whole, the introduction of *Nasake no uwamori* alerts the reader to its multifaceted nature: an erotic picture book and a copybook for love and letters.

Unlike the other titles analyzed in this chapter, *Nasake no uwamori* neither possesses a unitary narrative frame that adapts the *Usuyuki* master plot nor offers a systematic collection of letter samples. Each double-page spread functions as a discrete tale embodying a specific type of love and normally includes a letter. The role of letters in facilitating romance and sex is spelled out in the section "Inferior Love" (Shita no koi), describing the love that hatches secretly in one's heart and remains unrequited. Letters are described as vehicles to "permit flowers, at least, to blossom with words," even though no bond at first materializes.[108] Yet the text explains that by fueling an exchange of love letters, marriage is possible without any intermediary and eventually leads to playful sex. And it is sex that dominates the visual component of the scene. "Inferior Love" showcases how *Nasake no uwamori* as a whole is fashioned. It is an anthology of examples of love stories—labeled as typologies of love very much in the fashion of *Nishikigi*—and the majority are developed with the aid of written correspondence. With few exceptions, the illustrations celebrate the fulfillment of love in the form of sexual intercourse.

The letters included in *Nasake no uwamori* appeal on three levels, as seen in the other texts discussed in this chapter: epistemic, aesthetic, and emotional. A close reading of the section "Assessment Made on the Basis of a Letter" (Fumi ni yoru shinadasame) reveals how this is achieved.

> A certain man saw a beautiful woman and since that moment thought, "In all likelihood she is a married woman. It is my responsibility as a man to court her and win her heart." And he sent a letter.
>
> Since I first saw you sometime ago, the image of your beauty rises like a wave in my mind—it stays with me day and night. Of course, my wish is that we share pillows, even if for only a night, as if we were sleeping on stone pillows during the journey that turned Fortune's wheel, enabling us to meet. But at least I would like my thoughts to reach you in a letter carried by the wind that slips through the crevices. New leaves sprout from the earth in a remote mountain:

I am burning under the surface. It is dreadful to think that the smoke might ultimately soar high and vanish. What would I become?

ima zo shiru	Now I know
uki Musashino no	in the floating Musashi Plain
yukari to wa	ties among the gromwell
omoisomenishi	new feelings tinged
murasaki no iro	with purple.

Beneath the sleeves that hold my tears, I talk to myself but am unable to endure the pain of my heart any longer, so I have written to you. *Kashiko*.

The beautiful woman read the letter; unable to curb her feelings of excitement, she met him secretly.[109]

As expected, the text presents an intricate tapestry of poetic rhetorical devices and literary allusions. Very similar to what I have noted for the letters included in *Usuyuki monogatari*, *Usugumo monogatari*, and *Nishikigi*, we are asked to relish in unraveling the intertextual echoes while delighting in the cognitive thrill provided by solving what appears as a complex puzzle. In this way we discover that the pillow word *tatsu nami no* (rising waves) is used, according to convention, to introduce the word *yoru* (night). The same expression follows *omokage ni*, conveying the meaning that the thought of the woman "rises" as an image in the man's imagination. *Oguruma* combines the meaning of "wheel" (in turn leading to the word *meguriawase*, "fortune" or "fate") with that of a small carriage, thereby kindling the idea of the journey. The latter is necessary to introduce the word *iwamakura* (stone pillows). The reference to "pillows" consequently alerts us to the message that the man wants to sleep with the woman. At the same time, the use of this specific word—and not the more common *niimakura* (new pillows)—evokes the Tanabata legend, in which Orihime and Hikoboshi are permitted to meet only once and are characteristically portrayed sleeping together on the rocks (*iwamakura*) on the Heavenly Plain. *Hatsu warai* is generally connected to the first month and indicates the first smile or laugh of the year. The merging of *yama* and *warai* in the form of *warau yama* appeared in haikai poetry in around the late 1670s to indicate a mountain in early spring bedecked in the light green of new leaves. Whether there is already an association of *warai* with the sexual (as in *warai-e*, or "erotic pictures") is not clear, as the use of *warai-e* for sex-related materials is usually ascribed to the late eighteenth century. But the image of "new leaves" imbues the word *shitamoe* with a double meaning: *shitamoe* 下萌え (a sprout shooting up from the soil) and *shitamoe* 下燃え (burning under the surface). The second nuance relates to the man's burning passion.

The Musashi Plain mentioned in the *waka* poem further fuels the connection with fire, as an allusion to the twelfth section of *Ise monogatari* when

Narihira abducts a woman and carries her off to the Musashi Plain. The provincial governor orders that they be followed, and at the moment when the pursuers are about to set the grass on the plain alight the woman composes a poem, pleading with them to stop.[110] Plain and grass coalesce, eliciting the word *yukari*. The meaning of "relation" is doubled up with that for *yukarigusa*, another label for the purple gromwell known as *murasaki*, and this invokes the purple in the closing line of the poem. The mention of *murasaki* might equally have triggered a link with the first section of *Ise monogatari*, which we have already seen in a similar type of letter in *Nishikigi*. *Omoisomenishi* and the embedded *somu*, denoting both "beginning to" and "to dye," also echo the same letter from *Nishikigi* analyzed in the previous section. The letter closes with a reference to the well-hewn imagery of sleeves moist with tears. But the detail of "beneath the sleeves" (*tamoto no shita*) and the reference to "talking alone" (*hitorigoto*) might suggest an autoerotic act. The outcome of the letter contradicts the expectation that a woman would initially deflect a man's courtship. Here the woman expresses no reticence, no rejection as she is delighted to receive the letter and to take pleasure in meeting the man.

As the image clarifies, meeting (*yarikuri*) implies having sex (fig. 5.9). The reader is invited to enjoy the striking visual composition dominated by the black, round-shaped cartouche inscribed with the characters 風圖 in white. This

Figure 5.9 Hishikawa Moronobu, *Nasake no uwamori*, ca. 1680s, vol. 2, 3v–4r. "Assessment Made on the Basis of a Letter."

Courtesy of Kawade Shobō Shinsha, Tokyo

could be read *kaze no zu*, or "a picture of the wind," perhaps in association with the letter that the man has entrusted to the wind, as explained in the verbal text. The style of the calligraphy recalls the hand of Hikkaidō 筆海堂 (Masaki Seishin 真幸正心 [1608–1674]), therefore proffering a form of intervisuality that elicits an aesthetic response.[111] The gaze of the three people in the composition prompts us to move our eyes away from the genitalia to appreciate the pastiche of calligraphy and images that adorn the wall on the left. While taking pleasure in the aesthetic and emotional world evoked by both the text and the illustration, we are given a letter that can be copied in the hope of securing someone's heart (and body). Whether the reader might also enjoy sexual stimulation in the act of reading and viewing this scene remains, of course, a possibility.

In shaping a text that stimulates composite pleasure, *Nasake no uwamori* makes extensive use of *Nishikigi*. The first two double-page spreads of the first volume of *Nasake no uwamori* well illustrates how *Nishikigi* is adapted (fig. 5.10). "Love That Grows with Poetry" (Uta ni sosoru koi) starts with the mention of the daughter of a wealthy family who falls in love with a young boy (*wakashu*). The text, however, soon switches to the male's perspective, stating that "he

Figure 5.10 Hishikawa Moronobu, *Nasake no uwamori*, ca. 1680s, vol. 1, 1v–2r. "Love That Grows with Poetry."

Author collection, Suzuran Bunko, Cambridge, U.K.

caught sight of the woman through an opening in the *noren* curtain made by the wind."¹¹² This remark creates an intertextual allusion to *Genji monogatari* and the episode of Onnasan no Miya in the first part of the "Wakana" chapter. Moronobu's illustration, with the girl peeping out of the door in contrast to what the verbal text explains, could be viewed as a visual allusion to the illustration of the first part of the "Wakana" chapter as illustrated by Moronobu in his *Genji Yamato e kagami* (The mirror of Japanese pictures of *The Tale of Genji* [fig. 5.11]).¹¹³ The text continues with a description of the young man's being too timorous to send a letter, thus his resort to poetry. After exchanging four poems, the woman suggests that any scandal arising from their relationship would be undesirable and proposes a secret liaison. While the illustration alludes to *Genji Yamato e kagami*, the verbal text of this double-page spread takes inspiration from the fifth volume of *Nishikigi*. In "Love That Has Been Concealed for a Long Time" (Shinobu hisashiki koi), *Nishikigi* recounts that a man, long lovesick for a woman but weary of the judgment of others, refrained from sending any message. For a while, this allowed him to keep his feelings hidden, but when he was unable to endure his emotions any longer he

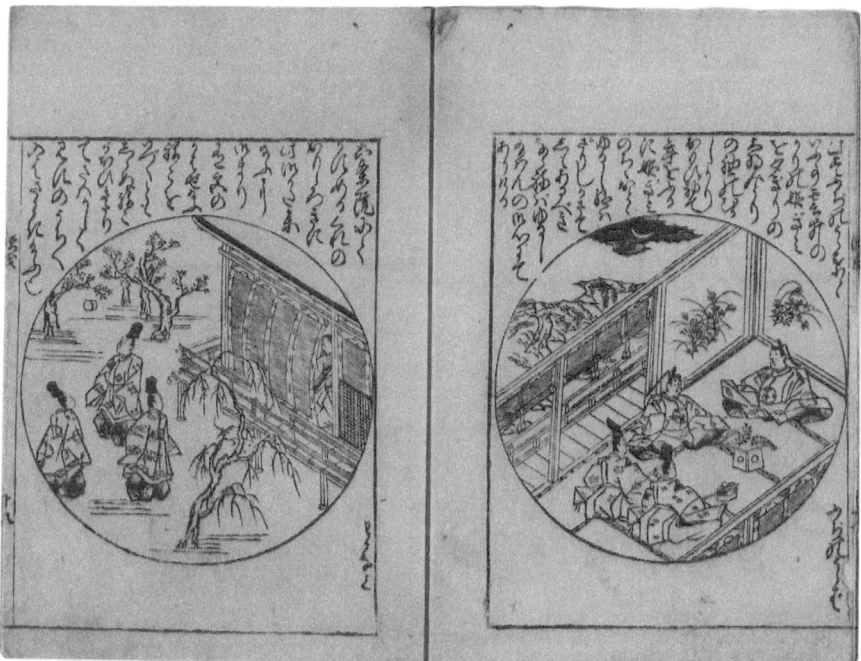

Figure 5.11 Hishikawa Moronobu, *Genji Yamato e kagami*, 1685, vol. 1, 17v–18r. "Wakana" chapter (*left*).

Private collection, Ebi Bunko, U.K. Images courtesy of Art Research Center, Ritsumeikan University

dispatched a letter in which he explains that "wind that slightly opened the bamboo blinds" (*tamadare no hima moru kaze*) prompted him to compose the letter.[114] The woman begins her reply with the same motif of the blowing wind. The exchange of the two letters concludes with a passage that appears to be an addition by the woman, "I am not against it, but to have people know and rumors spreading [*ukina no tatan koto*] is bad for both of us. So let's share vows in secret."[115] The same words appear almost verbatim in the closing of "Love That Grows with Poetry" in *Nasake no uwamori*, with the woman writing, "I am not against it, but to have rumors spreading [*ukina no tachinan koto*] is bad for both of us. So let's share vows in secret."[116]

The second double-page spread in *Nasake no uwamori* picks up from the passage that closes the previous opening and is titled "Love That Causes a Great Stir" (*Na no tatsu koi* [fig. 5.12]).[117] This story begins by reiterating the point that concluded the previous double-page spread, employing it as a springboard for the development of a new episode. As in the previous scene there is a young boy (*wakashu*) and a young girl treasured by her parents (*hizō musume*). But in this second scene it is the boy who is in love with the girl. He has the courage

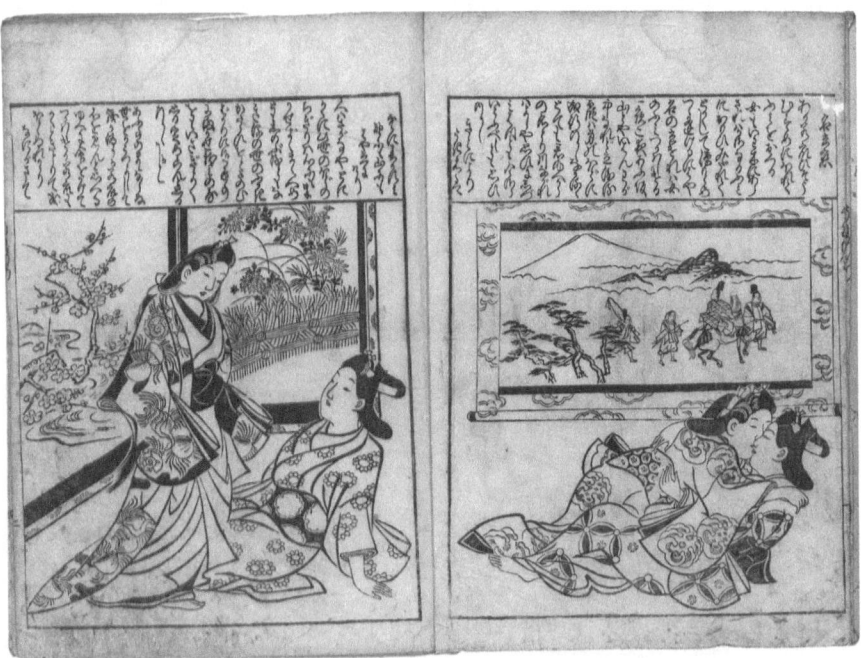

Figure 5.12 Hishikawa Moronobu, *Nasake no uwamori*, ca. 1680s, vol. 1, 2v–3r. "Love That Causes a Great Stir."

Author collection, Suzuran Bunko, Cambridge, U.K.

to send a letter (the text is omitted) and the story unfolds: "As she was neither rock nor wood, the girl's feelings were increasing letter after letter. Somehow she managed to escape her parents' control and met the boy. It was not long before rumors spread and the girl sent a letter to the boy."[118] The text of this letter is given in full, and, echoing the previous scene, it takes inspiration from "Love That Causes a Great Stir" in *Nishikigi*. Both *Nasake no uwamori* and *Nishikigi* mention the poetic place-name Natorigawa as a device to introduce the idea that their secret relationship has created a sensation (*na o toru*). With its associations to spring and use in poetry as a pillow word for the verb *tatsu*, the motif of mist dominates the two passages, enabling the evocation of the expression *na no tatsu* that is central to the type of love under discussion. Both letters finish with the same entreaty, almost identical in formulation: "Our pledge of love in this world is not fulfilled. I ask only for a deep promise for the next world. I will decide upon your answer . . . *kashiku*."[119] At this point in *Nishikigi* the narrator appears and adds, "She lamented the fact that they cannot meet as they desire. Because she wanted to test the sincerity of the man's heart, she sent these words at her own peril."[120] Even this passage is retained in *Nasake no uwamori*.

Nasake no uwamori also makes creative use of the final part of *Nishikigi*, turning what might be perceived as a dry dictionary of words into what is presented by Moronobu as "The ABC of Love" (Koi no tenarai).[121] While emphasizing the importance of *tenarai* in women's education, as celebrated early on in *Onna shikimoku*, for instance, this is no ordinary *tenarai* book. The first half of the section lists a variety of love typologies and defines them briefly with each conveniently divided into a stand-alone descriptive line: "The first love [*hatsukoi*] refers to the very first experience of love. No matter how you look at it or hear about it, it is the first time that someone feels love"; "Secret love [*shinobu koi*] is used when you nurture love within yourself, without showing it and without having people know about it." The list contains three further types that cover "Love Heard" (Kiku koi), "Love Upon Seeing but Not Meeting" (Mite awazaru koi), "Love Met but Feelings Not Shared" (Ōte awazaru koi). For all of these the wording is similar to that used in *Nishikigi*, although abbreviated in places and omitting the *waka* poems.[122] The remaining half of the double-page spread offers a list of words employed in love, followed by their meaning:

isasame means "temporary"
isayou means "to rest"
imose means "couple"
iwahashi means "the relationship ends"
inase means "no"
imokari means "to go visit a woman"
hatenaki means "to reveal one's feelings"

hahakigi means "not meeting"
niimakura means "to meet for the first time"
nishikitori means "to act as intermediary"
nishikigi means "indifferent"
tokiwa no iro means "that your heart does not change"
chiiro no soko means "to fall in love"
nurekinu means "that rumors spread"[123]

Six of these fourteen entries are taken verbatim from *Nishikigi*.[124] Needless to say, the creative touch of *Nasake no uwamori* is to have reconceptualized the list into the *i-ro-ha* of love. Once again the text captivates us also at a cognitive and heuristic level: we take delight in acquiring knowledge of the vocabulary for the affairs of the heart.

Nasake no uwamori appropriates *Nishikigi* to infuse life into a work of art that served multiple purposes: as an anthology of erotic stories involving different typologies of love; as a collection of letters to be employed in a variety of contexts related to love pursuits and leading to sex; as a highly self-referential picture book depicting sex; and as a grammar and dictionary of love that offers a lexicon as if instructing the reader on how to write. All this is achieved in a book that came to full fruition thanks to the narrative capital accumulated around letter writing in *Nishikigi*.

Letteracy was a skill that men and women in seventeenth-century Japan were urged to master in order to fit into their society. As such, it was another facet of the societal and interpersonal knowledge explored in the previous chapter. While promoting a close connection between literacy and letteracy, commercial publishers worked to disseminate the notion that everyone, regardless of class, could (and should) be able to write and read letters. Publishers accomplished this, first and foremost, by issuing user-friendly manuals that taught the basics of epistolography. These offered text-constitutive and intersubjective formulas to be inserted ad hoc in a letter. Yet they also provided readers with full-fledged letter samples ready to be re-created (or imitated) on social occasions or for business transactions. Imitation with added individual touches was often encouraged by an apparatus of notes that listed synonyms for selected words.

The legacy of these manuals continued throughout and after the early modern period. Manuals teaching letteracy became a regular product in early modern commercial publishing, with works spanning a range of situations, from more private publications that regulated social interaction between individuals and households at key points annually or during a lifetime to more public publications dealing with business and administration. Letter manuals addressed to women likewise held their place in Japan's early modern book industry. Twenty-first century Japan is no different, and numerous letter miscellanies are published as books or online to allow Japanese (and foreigners!) to wordsmith their written correspondence, aware of the subtle hierarchy governing epistolary exchanges. As this chapter has shown, all began in seventeenth-century popular prose.

In addition to their practical function, seventeenth-century manuals of letteracy also fostered the creation of an artificially written style that operated like a shared language. *Sōrōbun* and *mairase-sōrōbun* permitted men and women to speak the same language by spreading letteracy in a democratic manner, across gender and society. And yet, almost paradoxically, they played a large part in reinforcing hierarchical civility in that they instructed readers to discriminate words and their calligraphic rendering on the basis of an addressee's status. We have noted how the hierarchical view of the world embraced and fostered by letteracy complicates the distinction in social classes with other parameters.

Letter manuals were, however, not the only course for commercial publishers to promote letteracy. A fictional tale constructed around the exchange of love letters like *Usuyuki monogatari* well exemplifies the multifaceted nature of early modern epistolary prose. On the one hand, it adapted a master plot already in circulation in medieval fiction, planting it firmly in the popular imagination as a culturally common story. This in turn enabled the same story skeleton to be appropriated in later texts and in ways that challenged gender dynamics, as seen in *Usugumo monogatari*. On the other hand, *Usuyuki monogatari* operated as a resourceful manual of letters, showcasing how love letters could be crafted as gems of intertextual allusions to poetry and *monogatari*. Emotionally engaging love stories combine with aesthetically pleasing prose to teach readers how to write in an effective manner. Whether the knowledge acquired in this way was ever put into practical use awaits research. Moronobu's work demonstrates how the narrative capital generated by letteracy manuals and epistolary prose could be adapted to forge visually striking multimodal texts that tickled readers on many levels.

When viewed together, the seventeenth-century letter manuals and epistolary tales examined in this chapter reveal that all was in place for Ihara Saikaku to *join in* this rich tradition. Saikaku's *Yorozu no fumi hōgu* (A miscellany of old letters), for instance, is just another example of how the format of a miscellany of letters could be used to develop narratives.[125] Each of the twenty stories in the five volumes of *Yorozu no fumi hōgu* consists of a single letter. Through these snapshots of epistolary correspondence Saikaku offers a rich *comédie humaine*: financial problems, parties, revenge, suicide, debts, and much more. The prose makes full use of the artificial language that characterizes seventeenth-century letteracy and its idiosyncratic codes, thus exploiting and reinforcing the necessary knowledge in letter writing. Virginia Marcus praises Saikaku's endeavors as something extraordinary. "In the hands of a master such as Saikaku, epistolary fiction developed even further," she opines, praising the "development" in realism introduced by Saikaku and the variety created beyond the constraints of love exchanges.[126] While *Yorozu no fumi hōgu* does have the merit of deploying a multitude of human affairs exceeding those of the heart, I might caution against the teleological trajectory that Marcus's comment seems to encourage. *Usuyuki monogatari* may not have had the characteristics expected of a modern novel—and why should it!—but it certainly struck a specific chord in early modern readers since it was used repeatedly as a source text and survived well into the Meiji period. All the titles discussed in this chapter, *together with* Saikaku's *Yorozu no fumi hōgu* and other texts I did not have space to consider here, constituted different facets of early modern letteracy and its role in popular literature. Each deserves appreciation in its own right, without forcing any judgment of a presumed literary value. I would also argue for the need to study the mechanisms whereby epistolary prose conveyed not only aesthetic knowledge but also epistemic value (i.e., teaching letteracy). The pleasure of the text was multifarious and strongly tied to the profit gained by the act of reading—the profit being the acquisition of the necessary letteracy skills.

I would like to conclude with a wider, methodological consideration prompted by this chapter. Once more I have explored how porous the boundaries between nonnarrative and narrative can be. A text celebrated for being a fictional story such as *Usuyuki monogatari* was viewed in the Edo period as a manual for letter writing. By the same token, a letter miscellany like *Nishikigi*, overlooked in literary histories because of its allegedly practical character, was replete with narrative potential. Once again, it is the reader who has the power to unlock the full potential of each text. By questioning the strict, artificial boundaries that modern scholarship has constructed as a way to divide genres, this chapter has examined the intricate *réseau* of textual borrowings that existed in relation to epistolary prose.

CHAPTER 6

A Commitment to the Present

Greed and immoral desire are evil thoughts that go against the Way. To despise wasting money and embrace frugality are to be honored as the Way of Heaven.

—Katayama Naotsugu, *Makura no hibiki* (Pillow's echoes)

There are many who put on a happy face when hearing good things about others, but deep down the majority do not give it much thought. This is because good deeds are known and people don't feel the need to talk about them. On the other hand, bad things may well cause distaste for a split second. And yet this sort of thing travels great mileage in people's accounts.

—Yamaoka Genrin, *Tagami no ue* (The life of others)

The previous three chapters have discussed how seventeenth-century commercial publishers issued books that encouraged readers to effect change in their lives. The aim was not simply the acquisition of knowledge through reading but also to be in a position to translate that knowledge into concrete action with a view to better fitting into contemporary society. How could someone in the seventeenth century embrace an ethically correct lifestyle? How could a person behave according to what was viewed as proper conduct? How could one communicate effectively through the written word? With books unlocking knowledge for the benefit of all, the answers to these questions could be gained by reading the printed word. Seen in this light, the works examined in the previous chapters could be interpreted as how-to books, for which a text-to-life reading strategy was encouraged. In other words, what these texts called for was efferent reading above all. As Bradin Cormack and Carla Mazzio note for early modern European how-to books, "by positioning readers as actors, by requiring them to actualize knowledge by performing it, these books promised a transformation of identity."[1] Naturally, readers were free to choose not to translate their newly acquired knowledge into action. After all, as Roger Chartier notes, "readings are always plural" in the sense that "they construct the meanings of texts in different ways, even if texts are inscribed with the meaning they want to be attributed to themselves."[2] By the same token, however, readers were given the possibility of a transformation through reading. The previous chapters also probed the process whereby these kinds of instructional materials turned into what I call narrative capital. I examined a selection of fictional narratives that employed narrative capital to connect readers with the experiential aspects of the reading act while contributing further to the knowledge-making process. In viewing these materials as part of the same continuum, we appreciate how efferent reading led to the pleasure gained from satisfying one's epistemic curiosity, while aesthetic reading and the pleasure generated by savoring the words, the page layout, the calligraphy, and the illustrations contributed to making efferent reading more efficient.

In this process I have also reflected on the nature of publishing genres as ad hoc categories, which lack the programmatic character of genre as we know it. I have explored how commercial publishers organized titles as part of specific book categories (e.g., *kana washo, kana hōgo, shitsukekata-sho narabi ni ryōri-sho,* etc.) so that potential readers would be enticed to consume more of the same. But I have equally noted how pervious the boundaries between publishing genres were and how we must expand our investigation beyond a specific category in order to identify thematic and stylistic synergies in the publishing market.

The present chapter follows this line of inquiry, moving across publishing genres and broadening the analysis of the gamut of knowledge that was made available by printed books. So far it has been shown how seventeenth-century publishers appeared to assist readers in becoming successful individuals. To assume, however, that this was the only way in which they created literature designed to generate knowledge and to engage readers at a cognitive level would be misleading. Publishers, authors, and illustrators also addressed what was topical in contemporary society and packaged it as profitable products. Travel, for example, was an important new feature of Edo-period society.[3] As previous research has shown, early modern publishers issued diverse materials that aimed to assist readers in learning how to move in the newly designed urban spaces and across the country.[4] Other topics were also prominent in seventeenth-century Japanese commercial publishing, with money and disasters standing out among others. In the following I examine a range of prose texts that were concerned with these two themes and positioned across publishing genres. On the surface the books under discussion here might be identified as how-to books, providing readers with answers to some apparently simple yet persistent questions that apply to human beings well beyond early modern times. How do I make money? How do I cope with disaster? Yet I argue that when examined in detail these books, while certainly informative about what was current, were hardly transformative, in that there was little a reader could do to translate knowledge into action. Money, for example, mattered in Edo-period society. Select titles discussed in this chapter might give the impression that they were manuals on how to make money, but equally they informed their readers that society is made up of rich and poor, a reality that could not be avoided. Natural disasters were a part of life in Japan, then as now. Moved either by a genuine desire to gather news about a catastrophe or by a morbid interest in gruesome details, readers were hungry for accounts of famines, fires, and earthquakes. The books that responded to this demand even suggested strategies on how to make sense of the unthinkable and to cope with trauma. But ultimately they could not change the status quo of a land hit by calamities. This chapter therefore offers a sampling of those texts that enabled readers to become au courant with those things that mattered in seventeenth-century society. Readers could not necessarily change themselves or the world around them by reading these books, but at least they could perhaps make sense of the world in which they lived. One could untangle the present as well as construct it, a phenomenon I call present-mindedness, borrowing a term coined by Daniel Woolf in his treatment of early modern England and the publication of news.[5]

The Power of Money

At the beginning of the Edo period, Japan was developing an economic view of value and a money economy.[6] A variety of factors encouraged the economization of Japanese society in the seventeenth century, including a rapid expansion of agricultural production, an explosive increase in (urban) population, and a demand for qualified labor necessary to realize the public works that local lords had to conduct in exchange for tax revenues.[7] Akira Hayami observes that "the expansion of demand stimulates production, raises the level of technology, lowers costs and raises purchasing power."[8] The rise in purchasing power is at the very heart of the consumer society that Penelope Francks describes as burgeoning in urban and rural early modern Japan.[9] The salient point here is that this purchasing power took the form of cash since, according to Ethan Segal, "the government began issuing its own currency for the first time in centuries... the Edo bakufu issued gold and copper coins and took active steps to control and support the value of its tri-metallic currency."[10] The monetary system established by the Tokugawa shogunate led to the minting of gold and silver coins as well as copper coins.[11] And wealth was instrumental to anyone wishing to sate an appetite for material culture and an enjoyable life.

Paradoxically, the government made attempts to bridle the temptations now available to this consumer society through the issuance of sumptuary laws. Donald H. Shively argues that these regulations were implemented as a means to maintain the sociopolitical order of early modern Japan—an order that was beginning to be challenged by the emerging economic conditions—the underlying motive being the avoidance of revealing "the disparity between social rank and the distribution of wealth."[12] Shively stresses the fact that frugality was promoted as a principle to be followed by *hatamoto*.[13] He further notes that in this case frugality was conceived as something different from "parsimony," in that *hatamoto* should refrain from extravagance but at the same time spend money in order to live according to what was required of their status. By contrast, he argues that in the laws targeting townsmen (*chōnin*) there is little suggestion of frugality being a virtue or even something that allows savings.[14] In the following pages I problematize such a view, however. The edicts, Shively concludes, were intended to force townspeople to live a more austere lifestyle, with no ostentatious or presumptuous display, thereby circumventing any "disruptive effect on the morale and discipline of the samurai class."[15]

The paradox of a market economy fueled by consumption and a government trying to curb excessive consumption in the name of a political agenda does not seem to have undermined the power of money. By the end of the seventeenth century, wealth was celebrated in popular publications as the real driver of society. A rather cynical, yet lucid, account of this view is seen in the text *Jinkyōron* (On the mirror of human beings), also known as *Kanemochi chōhōki* (The treasury of wealthy people) or *Kingin mannōgan* (The almighty medication for money).[16] It was reportedly composed as early as 1487, with the addition of an introduction by the high-ranking court noble Saionji Kinfuji 西園寺公藤 (1455–1512) in 1503. Whether this was merely an attempt to give authority to a text composed in the Edo period is beyond the scope of this study, but it is clear from the text's publishing history that it resonated with the popular readership beginning in the 1680s.[17] And everything in the text is redolent of the early modern: the language, the style and, above all, the contents.

The first thirteen folios conform to the dialogic literature discussed in chapter 3. Hagiwara no Chūjō, a man who has mastered the Way of Shinto, meets with the Buddhist monk Ichinyo Shōnin and the Confucian Shōshi. They are joined by a certain Dōmusai (Mr. Without a Way), who is described as an eccentric who lives without a care in the world.[18] Not surprisingly, and in keeping with the textual tradition begun with *Kiyomizu monogatari*, the text turns into a verbal jostle about which Way is better. Within the opening thirteen folios the text condenses a brief history of Buddhism, Confucianism, and Shinto, ending with Hagiwara no Chūjō convincing Ichinyo Shōnin and Shōshi that Japan is the Divine Country and that the native religious tradition of Shinto should be regarded as superior to all others. En route to Ise Shrine, Dōmusai gives a lengthy speech whose ultimate goal is to convince that money is superior to any other Way. His opening remarks are lucid:

> The only thing that sounds truly interesting and inspiring is gold [*ōgon*; i.e., money]. There is nothing entertaining or interesting in looking at the maple leaves on Mount Hie, the brocades of Nagara, or the moon at Yokawa if you have no money. The world is made, quite simply, by money. It is thanks to money that Heaven and earth have come together, and it is money that moves everything. Money is the most pressing business for human beings.[19]

The remaining twenty-eight folios are taken up by the glorification of money and its power. By regaling his intradiegetic audience, and the extradiegetic reader as well, with stories of specific people, Dōmusai harps on about the fact that everything is determined by wealth. Buddhism, Confucianism, and Shinto are deeply intertwined with monetary profit. Ascendency to the upper social echelons of *buke* and *kuge* circles, marriage, scholarship, health, craftsmanship, medicine—there is nothing in this world that cannot be obtained when one has money. For example, Tokudayū in Osaka hails from humble origins but is extremely rich. As the eldest son, he is entrusted with the family's finances and properties, and he manages to marry the daughter of a court aristocrat. His second son is successful in becoming a samurai, as a result of Tokudayū's buying him the requisite training and bribing the necessary people. The third son becomes a Buddhist abbot, the fourth is adopted by a samurai in the eastern region, and the fifth becomes a Shinto priest. The three daughters are all married off to high-ranking members of the military and court aristocracy.[20] In another tale, the only daughter of Izumiya Yosaburō had only one eye and was crippled. Her parents ensured that even such a repugnant girl would find a husband by distributing cash around the capital as a ploy to get men to consider marrying her. Dōmusai cannot refrain from remarking how startling, sad, and ludicrous he found this when there are so many fine girls.[21] The conclusion reached by Hagiwara no Chūjō, the one who so far had championed Shinto, sums up the issue: "Japan, known for being a land of respect and morality, is no different from the countries of the Southern Barbarians . . . people live only for the love and desire of profit [*riyoku*]."[22] The last three folios employ the medieval trope of a divine revelation in the form of a dream to prompt all four protagonists to champion Shinto as the true Way. This occurs, however, without putting forth any convincing argument to the reader, who at this point in the text has been brainwashed by the various discourses on the power of money. On occasion, the fictional protagonists betray feelings of dissatisfaction at this state of affairs, yet as paradoxical or cynical as this might be, this is the way of the world: "a floating world that is in love with money" (*kanezuki no ukiyo*).[23] When dealing with a society so enamored of wealth, the natural question for readers at the time (but also for us) would be, how can we make money?

From Medieval to Early Modern Millionaires

The image of millionaires (*chōja*) already existed in medieval vernacular prose.[24] The discourse related to wealth that developed in medieval popular tales was characterized by a degree of determinism. It was the Buddhas or deities who bestowed wealth in a form of remuneration for praiseworthy moral behavior—in other words, poverty and wealth were described as being determined by the karma accumulated in previous lives.[25] That did not mean that a person was unable to influence his or her destiny: refining one's behavior according to Buddhist teachings would bring miraculous intervention despite what might have been dictated by karma. What actions are necessary, then, to redress the karmic balance? The first is faith in the Buddhas and deities.[26] The second is filial piety.[27] The third is altruism, admittedly rather counterintuitive in the larger scenario of amassing wealth![28]

The part played by karma does not completely disappear from the seventeenth-century Japanese literature interested in the topic of moneymaking. Wealth as a reward for some meritorious behavior also features as a motif. *Ichimori chōja*, for example, revolves around the idea of filial piety.[29] This is not unexpected since both filial piety and karma were core teachings of Buddhism and Confucianism. There are, however, a few interesting twists in the repetition of these tropes, which are of interest here. The first is the 1655 *Kanninki* (The chronicle of patience), a work attributed to Asai Ryōi.[30] It inherits the medieval tradition of *setsuwa* as a collection of short stories that aim to teach the importance of patience (*kannin*), and the structure is reminiscent of the katakana version of *Inga monogatari* (discussed in chapter 3): the eight volumes are divided into twenty-five topics with each topic containing brief exempla that elucidate the key teachings.

The thirteenth topic in *Kanninki* is "Patience to Be Shown to Parents," and the fifth story therein is relevant.[31] It is set in China during the Wanli era (1573–1620); a peasant faces a bad season yet must care for his aged mother. On his way home from the market, where he purchased some rice, he encounters one of the many tigers that roam the countryside. He pleads with the tiger to let him deliver the rice to his mother, promising to return to the tiger (and be devoured by it) once his filial duties are done. He is rewarded not only with the tiger's sparing his life but also with a large sum of money so that he can continue to care for his parent. The narratorial voice that closes the tale stresses the significance of filial piety, regardless of a person's economic circumstances. And nothing stops the reader from interpreting the tiger's generosity as the result of the man's filial devotion. But one word surfaces repeatedly in the conversation between the man and his mother—"promise" (*yakusoku*). The man wishes to keep his word to the tiger, even at the expense of his own life. His sincerity, combined with his filial piety, is paid back as a monetary reward. The text thus inherits the trope of financial reward as a recognition of filial piety, but it also suggests a new moral aspect to moneymaking in the form of honesty. And the notion of honesty will become a refrain in early modern literature in its advice about how to aspire to wealth.

Similarly, the 1662 *Iguchi monogatari* (Foolish tales), a collection of short educational stories covering a kaleidoscopic range of subjects, offers a new take on the relationship between karma and wealth.[32] In the sixth volume a wise boy questions a millionaire as to how to become rich.[33] The man cannot gloss over the significance of "karma brought over from past good deeds," with karma being compared to a stone and a millionaire to a jeweler: "When a skillful jeweler polishes a good-quality stone over a long period, it will, without fail, become a precious gem. There is no jewel as such at the outset. But if the stone is an ordinary one, it does not matter how much and how well you polish it, it will not have iridescence. This is the most important teaching [to become rich]."[34] The millionaire expands upon this teaching by recounting the tale of a Chinese peasant whose land was rich with precious stones that required simply skillful polishing to transform them into shining jewels. For two generations, he entrusted these precious stones to kings, whose jewelers failed to make them shine. Only King Cheng of Chu (671–626 BCE) succeeded in unlocking their precious nature: "The Way of the millionaire is very similar. If one polishes a stone without the right skills, no good results will follow, no light will be revealed, and it will be difficult to become rich."[35] On the one hand, we are counseled that good deeds in previous lives do matter. But it is not enough to behave well. In order to turn this potential into actual economic gain, one must be devoted to fine-tuning that potential, and this is, I contend, where seventeenth-century materials break from the medieval approach to a popular discourse on money. Fatalism is gradually supplanted by pragmatism; but in more practical terms, how do you transform a stone into a jewel?

How to Make Money

Chōjakyō (The millionaire's doctrine; 1627) represents a starting point in answering this question, one that a young boy poses to three millionaires.[36] The first key word introduced in their response is *shimatsu*, or "frugality," framed as the need to economize on a regular basis. We are alerted to the centrality of this concept once we take into account a later, revised edition of *Chōjakyō*, issued in 1762.[37] In it "frugality" (*shimatsu* or *ken'yaku*) is heralded in the newly added introduction. This foreword announces that the book aims to save people from the world of poverty by spreading knowledge of the meaning of the word *ken'yaku* and even concludes with the signature of a certain "Mr. Be Sparing with Fun, Amid the Way to Frugality [倹道中興惜之子]." This revised edition also starts with a newly conceived passage that features Hiki no Tōheiji from Kamakura, who teaches that *ken'yaku*, frugality, is a must across the four classes and asserts that peasants, artisans, and merchants should not pursue luxury and extravagance.[38] This might suggest that frugality was conceptualized very much in accordance with the sumptuary laws mentioned earlier. And yet I would maintain that frugality in *Chōjakyō* and in the other materials examined here offers a different facet—namely, that frugality has a practical, positive side, since a fortune can be amassed by saving. This logic is outlined plainly in another source, the 1681 *Nioi bukuro* (The scented pouch): "One copper coin [*sen*] is difficult to gain, but ten coins are easily wasted. We say that dust collects to become a mountain and that pebbles increase in size to become rocks. Similarly, a copper coin might be light but when copper coins pile up, they become a heavy treasure."[39] The cautioning against indulgent overspending is not used for political reasons as a means to maintain social order, at least on the surface, as was the case with the sumptuary laws. Instead, it is sold as a pragmatic, sound piece of advice, a universal and timeless notion shared across cultures and eras—put money away and you will be better off.[40] *Chōjakyō* makes a distinction between frugality and avarice. The words of the God of Poverty clearly resonate therein: the wealthy who begrudge spending because they are obsessed with a desire to accumulate money are the target of derision.[41]

While the idea of economizing might seem not particularly sophisticated in terms of economic thought, *Chōjakyō* equally recognizes the importance of money circulation. Both Kamadaya and Nabaya, for example, discuss how they saved money and then invested through interest loans. Both stress that this is a long, painstaking process that requires time and patience. We might welcome some concrete details about how to invest money, but *Chōjakyō* fails to dispense any practical advice, and what we are left with is a series of ethical precepts. Patience is not the only moral virtue linked to moneymaking: honesty, humility, and hard work are also promoted as necessary in moneymaking endeavors. The list of the ten sons of the God of Wealth mentions other necessary virtues, ranging from rising early (*asaoki*) and keeping accounts (*san'yō*) to the more abstract attitudes of kindness (*eshaku*) and good-naturedness (*kokorodate*). And there are some old friends under "things that are necessary to practice"—"writing, arithmetic, the ability to discriminate, medicine, etiquette, and cooking."⁴² *Chōjakyō* is framed as a how-to book on making money, constructed as a text that responds to the question, how can I become rich? And yet there is very little practical guidance about how to achieve this. One can save money, yes, and one can attempt to reinvest savings. But the reader is not taught exactly how to achieve this. Rather, the text seems more concerned with reinforcing the ideal of human nature fashioned in other coeval texts—namely, *kana washo* (discussed in chapter 3). Efferent reading is encouraged, but any transformative reading seems difficult.

What is more, *Chōjakyō* concedes that the teachings put forward offer no infallible recipe. Kamadaya acknowledges that a person may not necessarily accumulate as much as he or she wishes. Izumiya, one of the other millionaires in the story, notes that karma alone does not necessarily lead to wealth and that one must work hard to become rich. But what about if an individual's karmic fate is bad? This question is not asked or answered, but the reader well aware of the power of past deeds cannot but wonder. And the God of Poverty offers a panegyric of how true wealth is embedded in poverty. It matters little that the narratorial voice continues to promote money as the most desirable thing at the end of the text since readers are nonetheless made aware that there is merit in living even if they fall short of becoming millionaires. On the surface *Chōjakyō* might well appear as a manual that teaches how to become rich. But when examined in detail, it becomes evident that this is not a text that "posits direct and infallible links between frugal behavior, moral rectitude, and economic success," as David Atherton has suggested.⁴³ Frugality and morality can lead to wealth, but ultimately there is no guarantee.

In Praise of Frugality

While texts on the theme of money and the desire to make money continue to surface throughout the seventeenth century, they lose sight of what economic history might view as the most crucial factor: the need to keep money in circulation. Their focus is instead on the call for frugality and the avoidance of expenditure beyond one's station.

Iguchi monogatari offers a good vantage point on this matter.⁴⁴ In the fourth volume (section 14) money is celebrated as the best medicine for human beings.⁴⁵ But, like any other medicine, it can work as a miraculous drug or a terrible poison. It must therefore be prepared and taken carefully. The text adapts the instructional prose typical of manuals for homemade remedies to discuss money. It starts with a list of the medicine's benefits: the eradication of the hardships of poverty, the lifting of the spirits and the alleviation of anguish, as well as the strength to avoid being exploited by others, the removal of greediness and evil thoughts, the fulfillment of hope, the birth of pleasure, the curing of stupidity, the enhancement of intelligence and wisdom, and the prolongation of life.[46] In the case of the medicine's acting as a poison, the deleterious effects include vanity, arrogance, lust, and the loss of sexual fluids, among others.[47] The text then details what ingredients to add or subtract to augment the benefits. In order to wipe out poverty, for example, one needs to cut out useless expenses (*tsuie*), self-indulgence (*ogori*), and luxury (*karei*). The recipe—with very strong Buddhist overtones—stresses the need for self-restraint, and the call for frugality is taken to the extreme in the third section of the seventh volume:

> In the place called Wakamatsu in Mutsu no Oku [Michinoku] Province there was a very rich man celebrated for his military prowess. He had a son, aged four, whom he greatly cherished. The child suffered from smallpox, and when it became clear that the end was nigh, the child expressed the desire to eat a large pear [*kamenashi*; turtle-shaped pear from Yamanashi]. His father was thrifty, even with the smallest copper coin, and did not fulfill his son's request. In the end, the son died. Family and friends gathered together, and when they heard this story, they frowned on him saying, "Why are you amassing treasures? Money is worth less than rocks. It is very hard for us to understand why you spared such a small amount of money for the child who just died. Even animals and birds have deep feelings for their children. You are worse than any beast! You are no human being!" They scorned and insulted him. The man said, "It is not so that I begrudged spending money. It is just that, without losing my sound judgment, I warned my child against unnecessary expenses [*muyaku no tsuie*]. If one has sound judgment, it does not matter if it is your own child or someone else's. Even if it were someone else's child, I would have spent thousands, even millions, but only if by eating this food the child's life would have been prolonged. If there was the chance for the child to live even one more day, I would have had no choice. But to spend even a little money on a child who is going to die is simply useless. That's why I did not fulfill his request." So he said, and there was no one who criticized him.[48]

Cutting back on nonessential expenses is also a teaching apparent in the tale of a millionaire from Saga, who features in two passages in the second volume.[49] He is introduced as an individual who enjoys activities that do not cost him any money: tending the fire to cook rice in the morning and evening, sweeping the garden, cleaning the ditches, simply dressed in his paper-cloth kimono and a handkerchief on his head. When asked why he does not behave like other wealthy people in the capital, indulging in poetry gatherings and outings, he launches into long-winded praise for a simple lifestyle that requires no money: "If you do not use your assets," he explains, "you will not cry over their loss."[50]

Whereas *Chōjakyō* championed frugality as a way of producing money, *Iguchi monogatari* stresses its importance as a method to maintain wealth and associates it with an adage that surfaces in different sources during this period: "There is no second generation to a millionaire" (*chōja nidai nashi*). An apt example of this teaching can be found in the 1673 *Shison kagami* (The mirror for posterity).⁵¹ While Noda Hisao readily repudiates this text for what he believes is its lack of a narrative dimension, *Shison kagami* makes perfect sense in the context of seventeenth-century popular literature by being a gold mine of teachings that could prove beneficial for future generations.⁵² One section in the second volume deals with the issue of the second generation's frittering away the family fortune.⁵³ A townsman and a masterless samurai chat about how the sons of people who have amassed treasures think that they have plenty and spend without restraint. The results are naturally disastrous: "They are left stranded and end up making a living by engaging in bad activities such as gambling or thieving or simply by becoming beggars."⁵⁴ While they ascribe this to karma, another man joins the discussion and accuses parents as the real cause: "The future of households in which the parents were lowborn and poor but then earned money and acquired a small fortune is grim. This is because those parents soon forget the past, raise their children by indulging them, giving them all they want and letting them enjoy various arts. This shows a lack of insight regarding what will happen in the future."⁵⁵ The same principle dominates a good portion of *Zeraku monogatari* (The story of Zeraku; ca. 1655).⁵⁶ While spinning a gripping tale about the love obsession of a wealthy man named Tomona, the dangerous jealousy of his wife, and the rapport of trust built with his confidant, the penniless and eccentric Zeraku, *Zeraku monogatari* uses the second volume to stage a series of dialogues that take place at the Arima hot spring. Zeraku plays the part of the wise man; he is asked questions and dispenses knowledge, very much in keeping with the dialogic structures examined in chapter 3. It is there that he answers the question regarding the proverb *chōja nidai nashi* by telling the story of the Chinese statesman Tao Zhu Gong (otherwise known as Fan Li [sixth century BCE]), celebrated as one of the wealthiest men in China and author of *Jing shang bao dian* (Golden rules of business success). Zeraku's tale is borrowed from Chinese sources and focuses on the episode of Tao Zhu Gong's middle son, who is accused of murder. In order to prevent him from being executed, Tao Zhu Gong is prepared to send money as a sort of bribe and wishes to entrust the money to his youngest son, who, born after the family had become wealthy, is totally unaware of the hardships encountered in making money: "He considers treasures lighter than rubbish."⁵⁷ This is where the teaching lies: those who have inherited wealth without knowing how hard it was to amass it in the first place are prone to give it away in a lighthearted manner. In the case of Tao Zhu Gong, the family's assets are saved by the eldest son, the one who in the end is tasked with delivering the money. Because he is old enough to know how difficult it was for his father to become wealthy, he is unwilling to waste any money on the convicted brother. The result is the tragic death of the middle boy.

In seventeenth-century popular prose frugality is depicted in a twofold manner: on the one hand saving is necessary for a small fortune to turn into conspicuous riches; on the other, it is celebrated as a means to maintain the wealth acquired by the previous generations.

Rich and Poor

On the surface the texts examined so far proclaim the power inherent in the Way of money and appear infused with helpful pragmatism. Yet as the preceding analysis has shown, there is little to turn these texts into compelling how-to manuals to become rich. We might all be parsimonious, but how many of us can turn into millionaires? What is more, the same texts are equally keen to convey a different, almost opposite and self-contradictory, message. Yes, you may desire to become rich, but the coexistence of rich and poor is an inescapable reality. This is something already noted in *Chōjakyō*, but *Iguchi monogatari* is unwavering on this point:

> Poverty and wealth simply depend on who you are born as, not on your mental disposition. It is something that is decided at the outset while you are in your mother's womb. And this is all the doing of Heaven. From past to present, this does not depend on whether you are a virtuous sage or a flattering wrongdoer. It does not depend on whether you are high- or lowborn, or on whether you have knowledge or not. There are rich and there are poor.[58]

The notion of inevitability contradicts what the text notes elsewhere and alerts readers to the fact that not everyone can be rich. *Kanninki* reinforces this message: "Everyone wants to become rich, but, when this is not possible, trying too hard is a recipe for disaster and regret."[59] So what can we do? *Kanninki* harks back to the idea of behaving according to one's station using the metaphor of "digging a hole that matches the shape of one's shell."[60] In other words, we return to the idea of frugality, but this time not to generate or preserve wealth but to be content with what one has. This teaching echoes "the knowledge of one's limit" that we have seen in Ejima Tamenobu's work (chapter 3). *Iguchi monogatari* elaborates on this point:

> A certain man said, "When a person does not know the limitations of their status [*waga mi no bungen*] bestowed by Heaven, they become obsessed with securing fame and wealth, desiring luxury and stretching the boundaries of behavior. In this way, they end up suffering a lack of wealth. Instead of craving for what other people have, a person should apply frugality and refrain from ostentatious extravagance. There is nothing better in avoiding a lack of wealth than by being frugal with what has been given by Heaven."[61]

This passage seems to revert to the idea of frugality as sketched in the sumptuary laws of the time. There is even an attempt to advise readers that there is merit in being poor: "If you remain humble, do not envy other people's luxury, exhibit no interest in partying or eating well, do not adorn yourself, and follow the Way, you will avoid poverty."[62] Poverty, in other words, is not so much a matter of lacking money: you may have no wealth but if you behave according to the Way and not above your station, you will be content with what you have. Although never stated openly in *Iguchi monogatari*, we can infer that this is meant as true wealth.

Seventeenth-century popular texts not only urge readers to accept the existence of poverty and find some value in it but also promote a culture of mutual acceptance between the rich and the poor. *Shison kagami*, for example, warns that wealthy people should not be arrogant and poor people should not curry favor. A word of caution is also leveled against any tendency of the rich to despise the poor and the poor to envy the rich.[63] And this is a subtle way to promote mutual respect in a society in which everyone—both rich and poor—have their place. Wealth matters but not at the cost of social harmony.

Before the publication of works by Ihara Saikaku, whom David Atherton aptly describes as "one of the first Japanese authors to write extensively about economic subject matter" and to play "with economic material—both at the level of plot, and at the level of language," readers were aware that money was a powerful social drive.[64] They would have had access to materials offering straightforward instruction on how they might gain or retain wealth. At the same time, however, readers knew that money was accompanied by great sacrifice, and they understood that not everyone could become rich. This was perceived as the natural way of society. Seventeenth-century popular literature encouraged the acceptance of both rich and poor, in what is portrayed as a salubrious harmony. These texts thus might well have been framed as how-to-get-rich guides, but they hardly functioned as effective how-to books. In fact, their efficacy was in declaring the sway of money, portraying the complexities of moneymaking, and eventually justifying the status quo in which rich and poor coexist. It would only be in the eighteenth century that more economically sophisticated reflections on the money and the Way of the merchant would appear.[65]

The Voices of Disaster

As a preoccupation with one's financial status emerges as a significant theme in seventeenth-century popular prose, publishers also show awareness that disasters were an equally pressing concern for their readers. This is hardly surprising. Famines were a regular occurrence, with those of 1641–1643 and 1680–1682 particularly tragic.[66] Conflagrations and earthquakes were equally destructive: a fire ravaged Edo for three days in the first month of 1657 and a few years later, in the fifth month of 1662, Kyoto was struck by a catastrophic earthquake. In an era when the cheap news broadsheets known as *kawaraban* were yet to take off, commercial publishers devised ways to broadcast the news while providing their readers with enthralling narratives of suffering and atonement.[67]

Disaster narratives, as I call them, were not unified in one publishing genre, and four texts stand out as representative of the publishing trend under scrutiny here: *Yakushi tsūya monogatari* (The tale of the wake of the Buddha Yakushi; 1643), *Musashi abumi* (Stirrups of Musashi; 1661), *Kanameishi* (The keystone; 1662–1663), and *Inu Hōjōki* (The bastard *Hōjōki*; 1682).[68] It might be tempting to also include *Hinin taiheiki* (The paupers' chronicle of peace; 1688), since it is set against the backdrop of the 1681 famine. Its character as disaster narrative is, however, fairly thin, the text focusing instead on the social conflict that erupted in the summer of that year between two groups of outcasts.[69]

It would be difficult to discuss seventeenth-century disaster narratives without acknowledging their intellectual debt to Kamo no Chōmei's *Hōjōki* (*An Account of My Hut*; 1212), which was issued in a movable-type edition in the early 1600s and later made available in woodblock-printed form by commercial publishers (1647, 1658, 1675, and 1690). Asai Ryōi praised the "extraordinary textual power" (*hissei obitadashiku shiruseri*) of *Hōjōki* and made extensive use of linguistic borrowings from it.[70] The ultimate homage to the medieval text was paid by *Inu Hōjōki*. Even though the title has prompted scholars to label *Inu Hōjōki* as a burlesque rewriting, no mocking or polemical intention vis-à-vis Kamo no Chōmei's work can be found at any point.[71] *Inu Hōjōki* intersperses passages that retain the source text verbatim with others that rework it minimally while presenting also sections that do not mirror *Hōjōki* in any way.[72] As I see them, these intertextual choices convey a precise message: Kamo no Chōmei's work provides writers of all times with effective linguistic and narrative tools tailor-made to give voice to the human drama amid disaster. Yet adjustments need to be put in place to make the recounting compelling for the readers of a different epoch. The word *inu* was meant to signal that this was a modernized version of *Hōjōki*.[73]

In what follows I concentrate on four lines of inquiry in the study of seventeenth-century disaster narratives. First, I explore how the four aforementioned texts were interested in reporting the news in a factual manner, amplifying a textual feature of *Hōjōki* and initiating patterns that will become recurrent in later *kawaraban* broadsheets. Second, I probe how these disaster narratives attempted to characterize these destructive events as epoch- and history-making ones. This leads to the third point of interest, the ghoulish nature of despair and horror marking these narratives. In this last, I intend to look at what Nicholas Daly has identified as a relatively undertheorized aesthetic element in the case of nineteenth-century European disaster narratives: "the pleasure of the reader or viewer in destruction—of people, of property, of hopes."[74] Although *Hōjōki* does not spare graphic descriptions of human suffering, I maintain that seventeenth-century materials intensify this textual penchant and indulge the morbid curiosity of their readers. Finally, I investigate how the same narratives are quasi therapeutic in that they provide strategies for coping with the trauma and for regaining normalcy. Whereas *Hōjōki*, at least on the surface, suggests reclusion and detachment as the only solution, early modern texts celebrate full engagement with the here and now.

Broadcasting the News

The texts under examination here are reportages of different typologies of disasters—famine, fire, and earthquake—that share specific choices in broadcasting the news. They all convey a desire to present as many facts as possible on the event in question. Dates are recorded, with a degree of accuracy, spanning from the more generic information about the year(s) down to the precise hour. *Yakushi tsūya monogatari*, for example, mentions the "recent years" of famine and then designates the period from the end of 1641 to the spring of 1643 as particularly crucial.[75] *Inu Hōjōki* adopts a less-orderly chronological style in reorganizing the 1680–1682 famine, but the anonymous author meticulously orders the events into the precise season. It starts with the epidemic that began in 1681, returns to the crop failure in the autumn of 1680 and to the windstorm that wreaked havoc on the twentieth day of the seventh month of 1681. It then fast-forwards to the first month of 1682, when the famine is in its third year. In *Musashi abumi*, Asai Ryōi pinpoints the outbreak of the fire at the hour of the dragon (7–9 a.m.) on the eighteenth day of the first month of 1657.[76] The reader is thereafter updated about significant changes hour by hour: at the hour of the sheep (1–3 p.m.) a fire started at Honmyōji, at the hour of the cock (5–7 p.m.) the wind shifted to the west, at the hour of the snake (9–11 a.m.) on the nineteenth day a second fire broke out, with the wind changing from a northerly to westerly direction at the hour of the monkey (3–5 p.m.), and the fire finally stopped at the hour of the dragon (7–9 a.m.) on the twentieth of the same month.[77] Similarly, in his *Kanameishi* Asai Ryōi informs the reader that the 1662 earthquake struck at the hour of the snake (9–11 a.m.) on the first day of the fifth month and that a second, equally strong tremor struck at the hour of the sheep (9–11 p.m.) on the fourth day.[78]

An almost obsessive need to record precise details is evident when disaster narratives report on losses. In this regard *Musashi abumi* stands out from the other texts. *Musashi abumi* systematically lists all the buildings impacted by the conflagration. In the first volume we read that at the hour of the snake, two hours after the fire had started, the Nichiren temple Honmyōji was reduced to ashes while the wind fueled the flames that burned Yushima Shrine to the ground. The blaze then jumped to the districts of Hatagoya-chō and Suruga-dai; Asai Ryōi chronicles five daimyo residences affected there, starting with Lord Nagai of Shinano.[79] This textual strategy dominates the first half of the second volume. Hundreds of place-names are listed in describing the areas damaged by the second fire (ordered according to the direction): the obliteration of the areas north of Kichijōji occupies almost two folios, and with the change of wind to the west we read about the twenty blocks (*chō*) south and north of Nakabashi and Kyōbashi being destroyed by flames.[80] When the direction of the wind changes again, this time to the south, the text records all the places ravaged, beginning with Shinbashi, and this list continues for almost three folios.[81] A summary of the total number of losses follows: more than 500 *chō*, more than 500 alleyways used by daimyo, more than 500 daimyo residences, more than 600 accommodations for lower-ranking daimyo.[82] A list of the Buddhist temples and Shinto shrines destroyed is also provided.[83] *Musashi abumi* additionally attempts to assign the number of dead: more than 9,600 when the fire struck the temple Reiganji, more than 450 at Nishi-Honganji, more than 23,000 around Asakusa, and so forth.[84] The total exceeded 102,000 people.[85]

I contend that there is more to these passages than a documentary-like quality: they inaugurate a style that will be embraced in later *kawaraban* that report on fires. For the 1852 blaze in Osaka, for example, the *kawaraban* produced immediately thereafter (fig. 6.1) applies textual strategies identical to those identified in the preceding.[86] The fire broke out at the hour of the rat (sometime between 11 p.m. and 1 a.m.) of the second day of the second month

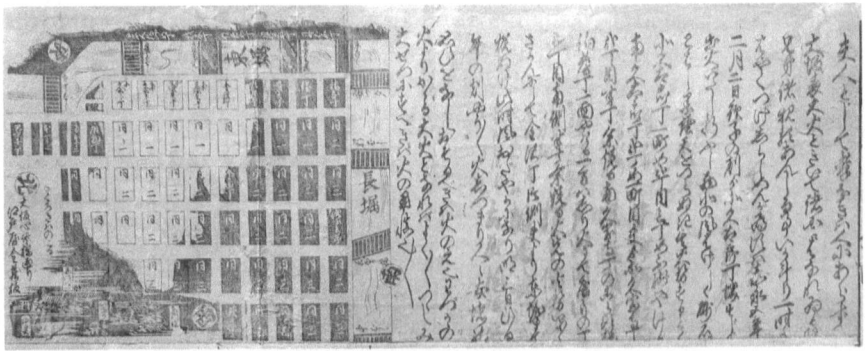

Figure 6.1 *Kawaraban* on Osaka fire, 1852. From album titled *Shūkojō*.

Author collection, Suzuran Bunko, Cambridge, U.K.

of 1852 at the intersection of Kyūtarō-machi and Sakai-suji. The fierce northwest wind swept through a vast portion of the city, and the buildings damaged are recorded in a list that ends with the observation that the wind calmed down the next day at the hour of the ox (1–3 a.m.). The text is accompanied by a map with a visual account of the affected areas, the black sections representing those that survived the tragedy and the white ones indicating those that had burned.

Another aspect shared by narratives like *Musashi abumi* and later *kawaraban* is the desire to provide readers with firsthand information. In the narrative frame that opens *Musashi abumi*, we learn that the Edo monk Rakusaibō, originally from the area around Yushima Shrine, visits Kitano Shrine in Kyoto and meets a haberdasher. Rakusaibō reveals that he is in a wretched state owing to being in disgrace in Edo at the time of the 1657 fire. When asked whether he knows about the fire, the haberdasher replies, "This is a famous event that everyone knows about. In that disaster young kids from Kyoto who had moved to Edo for work died as well, and there are many parents and siblings who are grieving. The amount of secondhand information [*kikitsutaetaru arisama*] is massive. So please, as a form of confession, do talk about what happened."[87] Asai Ryōi himself might not have been a witness to the fire, but Rakusaibō, who becomes the narratorial voice in recounting the catastrophe, is introduced as a firsthand spectator. A Kyoto readership was probably not emotionally detached from the event: after all, they have lost their own young people in the calamity, as the intradiegetic character, the haberdasher, explains. *Musashi abumi* is therefore conceived as a witness's reportage that allows readers to gauge how their loved ones perished (or survived) depending on their location in Edo. A similar concern is shared by the aforementioned *kawaraban*: "Lacking in filial piety means that you are not worth being called a human being. Having heard of the large fire that hit central Osaka, we know how worried parents, brothers, and relatives living elsewhere must be. This broadsheet was printed with the intention of letting them know what happened."[88] Viewed in this light, *Musashi abumi*'s accuracy in detailing the geography of the disasters might be interpreted as a desire to offer readers a map—albeit a mental one and not a physical one as in the *kawaraban* mentioned here—not so much of Edo as a cityscape as much as of a space afflicted by death. What stands in striking contrast between *Musashi abumi* and later *kawaraban* is the timing of their publication vis-à-vis the catastrophe: while single-sheet prints were issued in a timely manner, immediately after the events, *Musashi abumi* is published as late as four years after the fire. This undermines, to a certain extent, its validity in broadcasting the news. But this is not to deny that it could bring some closure to the relatives of those who were lost to the flames: at least they could access what was delivered as firsthand, accurate information about what happened to the space inhabited by their beloved.

Constructing a Historical Catastrophe

An interesting tension emerges from the seventeenth-century disaster narratives: on the one hand they are committed to delivering authentic, accurate reports; on the other they stress the exceptionality of the disasters being recounted.[89] *Musashi abumi*, for example, spells this out clearly toward the end of the book: "The figure of several thousands of people who perished in this fire is unprecedented."[90] A similar remark appears in *Kanameishi*: "Such upheaval was unparalleled in Kyoto."[91] The voices recorded in *Kanameishi* also note that "an earthquake of such extraordinary proportions is something that we have never experienced before in our lives."[92] To give more credibility to such statements is an effort to position the calamity in question as part of a longer history of corresponding disasters. *Yakushi tsūya monogatari*, for example, enumerates the major famines in Japan from 889 to the date of its publication in 1643.[93] The author of *Inu Hōjōki* claims to have consulted the four-volume historical source *Nendaiki* (Chronicles) for a list of famines and associated events from the era of Emperor Kinmei (510–571) until 1675.[94] *Musashi abumi* makes clear that fires have an extended history in both China and Japan.[95] *Kanameishi* mentions earthquakes from 416 to the 1660s, with an additional short reference to China.[96] These works sketch a transnational history of disasters, while framing the calamity under discussion as something different—the ultimate catastrophe that appears different from anything before."[97] It is the unprecedented magnitude of the event that seems to justify the need to record it with a new publication. In this respect seventeenth-century disaster narratives work not only as news reports but also as accounts of history-making moments.

Different textual strategies are applied to underscore the exceptional nature of what is perceived as unrivaled catastrophes. There is a tendency to spotlight the fact that the damages are greater in scale and what was avoided in previous disasters was now unavoidable. The example of the Mimizuka tomb given in *Kanameishi* is representative of this trend. Located south of the gate to Daibutsu Hall in Kyoto, this tomb was built when Toyotomi Hideyoshi undertook his foreign campaigns. Up to a point the information provided in *Kanameishi* about the origins of this place mirrors what is found in the 1658 guidebook *Kyō warabe* (Denizens of Kyoto).[98] The illustration also uses the image included in this guide to famous places, here with a twist—that is, of destruction. *Kanameishi* (fig. 6.2) splits the image from *Kyō warabe* (fig. 6.3) in two. One is from almost the same angle for Daibutsu Hall that depicts the moment of its destruction, suggested by the somewhat diagonal vertical lines, by the toppled stone lanterns, and by the people fleeing. Mimizuka dominates the second scene, with the detail of the pagoda's fifth story missing and a large chasm at its base.[99] The power of destruction changes the verbal text from an innocuous account of a touristic

Figure 6.2 Asai Ryōi, *Kanameishi*, ca. 1662–1663, vol. 1, 11v and 13r (next page). Earthquake at Daibutsu Hall.

Courtesy of the National Diet Library, Tokyo

Figure 6.2 (continued)

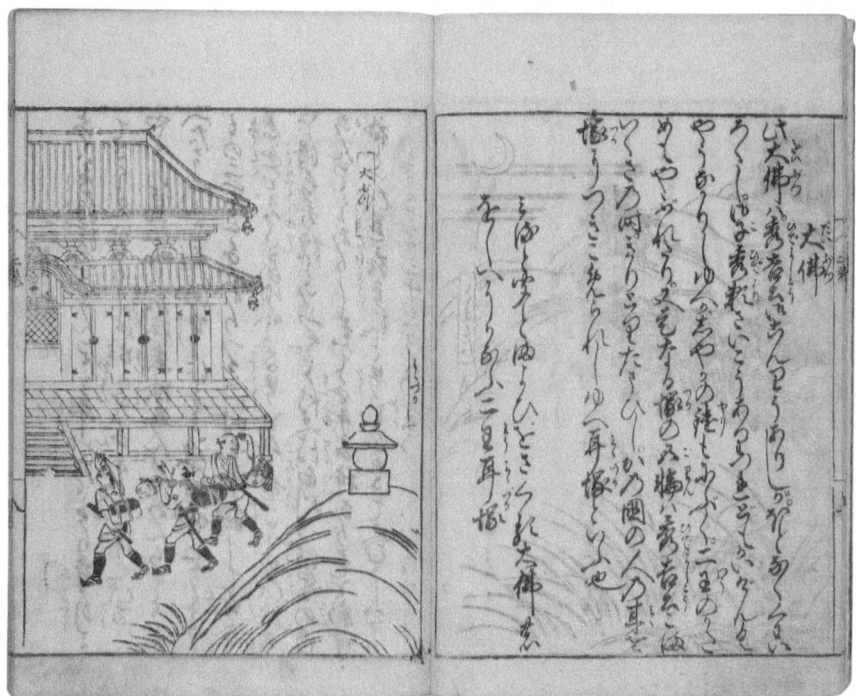

Figure 6.3 Nakagawa Kiun, *Kyō warabe*, 1658, vol. 2, 8r. Daibutsu Hall.
Courtesy of the National Institute of Japanese Literature, Tachikawa

spot into documentary evidence in the aftermath of this earthquake. Asai Ryōi notes that during the 1614 earthquake the pagoda was unscathed. But during the 1662 earthquake, the top of the pagoda fell off because of the force of the quake, thereby creating a large hole in the mound. And a humorous poem, echoing the structure of the *waka* poem concluding the first section of *Ise monogatari*, reinforces the point of such an unprecedented disaster: "Tomb of the ears / let me ask something / of the many ears: / have you ever heard / of such an earthquake?" (*mimizuka no / ōku no mimi yo / koto towan / kakaru jishin o / kiki ya tsutaeshi*).[100]

The second strategy employed to highlight the epoch-making nature of these disasters centers on the use of apocalyptic images. In *Kanameishi* people begin to speak about the end of the world: "The world will soon be destroyed and everything will turn into a sea of mud"; "This is nothing ordinary. The world will be destroyed and human beings wiped out."[101] The portent of the drama even challenges the ability of the writer to keep track of the losses against the desire for factual coverage of the event already identified in the same sources.

In *Kanameishi* the author notes that the mountains, the houses, and the sacred buildings destroyed outnumber what can be recorded in writing—it is all too much, he suggests, to be expressed in words.[102] In *Musashi abumi* Asai Ryōi speaks of the "sadness and pain difficult to put into words" when describing people's reactions as they stand before the common grave created in the temple compound of Muenji.[103]

The ultimate hyperbole resides in the narrative choice to turn a familiar space into a living hell, and *Musashi abumi* showcases this technique masterfully. Toward the end of the second volume, Rakusaibō captures his audience—the aforementioned haberdasher as well as us, the extradiegetic readers—with a more personal account. At the end of the first day, he is so relieved that he and his family are spared that he drinks himself into unconsciousness. A new fire breaks out and his family decides to evacuate him from the house by locking him in a chest. They drag the chest up to Shibaguchi and then abandon him. Opportunistic thieves try to smash the lock and open the chest in the hope that there might be something valuable inside, at which point Rakusaibō wakes up but thinks that he has since died and the chest is his coffin. He walks stupefied through the burning city, believing that he has been plunged into a Buddhist hell, and indeed the scenes he encounters correspond to the Six Paths of the Underworld.[104] It is only when he bumps into an acquaintance that Rakusaibō realizes his delusion and awakes to the harsh reality that in fact his life has been spared, even though he has lost everything and everyone.[105]

In his discussion of this passage Peter F. Kornicki highlights the entertaining nature of a narrative that uses a well-trodden literary topos—that of *jigoku meguri*, or a "descent into hell"—and plays with the topography of hell familiar to seventeenth-century readers through oral storytelling.[106] Kornicki concludes that this passage functions as a "metaphor for the horrific aftermath of the fire."[107] Michael A. Levine reaches a similar interpretation, stating that the author of *Musashi abumi* creates "for the reader an experience that brings horror and humor together."[108] Levine further suggests that the reader might have laughed at a man who was so drunk that he mistook the real world for the afterlife or might have realized that witnessing a conflagration of this magnitude must be like hell. Henry D. Smith and Steven Wills mention Rakusaibō's "entertaining (if not particularly plausible) experiences."[109] I would argue that this passage also suggests a different line of inquiry. The key word in untangling the passage is the verb *urotayu*, which denotes a state of confusion or disorientation generated by something unexpected. Rakusaibō is described in this emotional state. In Shibaguchi he mistakes a statue of Enma for the real King of Hell; he then knocks on a door, thinking that he is in the presence of the bodhisattva Seishi and asks to be saved. The people inside laugh and say, "Here comes someone who got confused [*urotaete*] by the fire and lost his mind."[110] When Rakusaibō ends his tale, the haberdasher observes, "This kind of catastrophe has few precedents. When confronted with something so unrivaled, it is inevitable that you would lose your mind [*urotaete*], and it could happen that you end up behaving so foolishly. You should not feel so ashamed, however."[111] The words of the unidentified person on whose door Rakusaibō knocks and the haberdasher lead to the same conclusion, albeit with different degrees of compassion: the trauma experienced when confronted by such an unexpected, unimaginable, and terrifying experience of catastrophic proportions is such that it would be impossible to function normally. The haberdasher invites Rakusaibō, and us the readers, to recognize that acting doltishly during such confusion is normal within the abnormality of the circumstances. The worst that can happen is that someone will laugh at you; at the very least you are not dead and can recount your story of survival. And in doing so, you reconnect with society, and those who listen to you will absolve you from what is most likely your greatest source of guilt: having been spared while others have perished. Rakusaibō's personal tale invites us to laugh and to acknowledge the horror of a fire experienced as a living hell but also to accept that any behavior otherwise considered deviational in normal circumstances is in fact the norm in such exceptional times.

In framing Rakusaibō's human tragedy as the unsettling experience of unprecedented abnormality, *Musashi abumi* embraces a narrative attitude that aligns with the twentieth-century earthquake narratives introduced and discussed by Regina Bendix.[112] Students in her class at the University of California were invited to share personal experiences of the 1989 Loma Prieta earthquake, and one student recounts a tale with similarities to Rakusaibō's story. After having watched a Disney cartoon (*Chip and Dale*) to recover from the stress of studying for his midterms, he fell asleep only to be awakened by the bed's shaking. He woke in a state of confusion and was under the impression that Chip and Dale were shaking the bed. He even got up in an effort to find these tormentors. It was only when he realized that the bed was not the only thing moving that he understood "there was something larger and worse than two invisible chipmunks."[113] The student, now acting as a storyteller, punctuates the account with laughter and the class joins in. Bendix explains that "this individual awoke to earthquake consciousness out of a dual un-reality: his own dream and a fictional TV cartoon embedded into it."[114] Similarly, Rakusaibō wakes up from the deep sleep caused by too much drinking in celebration of life the day before to a new fire. His state of incoherence from the effects of a hangover and a catastrophic fire cause him to connect with the unreality of the underworld, codified in his cultural memory by oral literature, as if it were real, until he is brought back to reality and becomes aware that he is alive but has lost everything. It is by recounting his tale that he is absolved by the haberdasher, and we, the extradiegetic readers, are equally ready to forgive him. Regardless of the age—seventeenth-century

Japan or twentieth-century America—tragic circumstances of unprecedented proportions lead to unpredictable behavior. It could happen to any of us at any point in history.

The Horrific Human Tragedy

In shaping accounts of epoch-making disasters, the texts examined here dwell on the ghastly nature of the events. Horror is evoked to a great degree by means of sounds, as evinced in *Musashi abumi*. The flames at Reiganji push the population toward the sea; some die in the freezing waters, others are consumed by the blaze: "The groans and screams of those being burned [alive] cannot but inspire abiding compassion."[115] The terrible sounds that reach our ears make us aware of the human tragedy before us:

> The shrieks of the thousand or several thousand people added to the screeching noise of wheels and the cracking sound of things burning to the ground. It was just like the roar of a thousand thunderstorms. The portent of all this is beyond words.... While it was moving [at Asakusa] to hear voices chanting the *nenbutsu*, the screams of the people who were surrounded by the flames were so audible that they would echo to the upper realms of the highest Heaven and could be heard at the bottom of the Golden Wheel that sustains the earth from below. It was such that I had goose pimples all over.[116]

The sense that we are witnessing an unspeakably dreadful scene is conveyed through the use of yet again hyperbolic language. The screams are such that they resemble "a thousand thunderstorms," and their intensity is such that they can be heard in the remotest parts of the imagined Buddhist universe. And, once more, the image of hell is used as a powerful metaphor: the screams of sinners burning in hell must be like the voices heard in Edo during the fire.[117]

Added to the soundscape of the events are the depictions of the physical space and the loss of life. After the fire in Asakusa had subsided, "the next day, the sight of dead bodies piling up on top of one another in all directions from Bakurō-chō and Yokoyama-chō was unbearable."[118] Amid the tears of the survivors calling out for their families, amid those rejoicing to find their loved ones alive, and amid the screams of despair of those who have lost everyone is the image of the carnage:

> Not wanting to listen to the reality, some gathered around the piles of burned bodies and pushed their way through the cadavers searching for parents, children, siblings, and spouses. Some of the bodies had their hair completely burned by the fire, and with their blackened bodies they looked like nuns and

monks. Others had their clothes completely destroyed, their muscles and bones exposed, their flesh split open in all directions, as if they were grilled fish.[119]

The intensity of the drama is heightened by unexpected comparisons. Asai Ryōi does not spare his readers from reports of how people died: engulfed by the flames, crushed by the fleeing crowds, used as shields against the approaching fire, killed by throwing themselves off burning buildings, or drowned by plunging into the water in the hope of being spared.

In *Kanameishi* the human drama takes center stage because of Asai Ryōi's decision to zoom in on how the tragedy impacted certain individuals. Levine speaks about the use of verisimilar "vignettes" that are structured in such a way as to "allow the reader to take in a mosaic of simultaneous experiences" of the earthquake.[120] And these vignettes expose the atrocity of the situation. The effects of the quake on the village of Katsuragawa, for example, evoke horror and commotion. The reader is first presented with the facts: a mountain collapses on the houses and fills in the valley in front of the settlement. The river water, with nowhere to go, turns into a rising pool of water. Almost all the inhabitants end up being buried alive: "For two, three days the faint screams of men and women were audible from the earth. Because they were buried deep down, there was no way to dig them out. Those who heard their voices could only shed tears. And then after four, five days even the voices stopped."[121] *Kanameishi* displays a tendency to turn horror into the more gruesome, possibly catering to the sensationalism demanded by readers. In Shimogoryō, for example, the two sons of Kotoya and Mariya were praying in the shrine precincts when the earthquake struck. They attempted to survive by clinging on to a stone lantern, unaware of the tragedy about to unfold when the lantern falls on them. As if this unfortunate detail was not enough, the text dwells on the disintegration of their bodies: "From head to toe, there was no point where the flesh was not torn apart," and "their faces were crushed and unrecognizable."[122] Their parents hurried to the scene and could identify them only by their blood-soaked clothing. Similarly, on Muromachi Avenue, the pregnant wife of a certain Mukadeya dies in a vain attempt to help other women: "Tragically crushed [under the warehouse], the woman's belly was wide open and the baby inside, just five months old, had been pushed out, wrapped in her intestines, disfigured and covered in blood."[123] Readers are forced to confront death in its most graphic and disturbing aspects, while enjoying a text that feeds their morbid curiosity. At this point, what was a factual account is transformed into a horrific spectacle that keeps readers engaged at an emotional level with its macabre details.

Accounts of famine participate in constructing the human drama, and *Inu Hōjōki* brings before our eyes harrowing images of death. Unidentified corpses of the Edo fire were at least given a proper burial at Muenji. But for the poor who die in a famine, even that was not an option. *Inu Hōjōki* explains that the unidentified bodies were dumped on riverbanks, and an even worse fate awaited those who died in open fields, as their corpses would be torn apart by ravenous dogs and wolves.[124] The sight of this human hell was encapsulated in recounting mothers dead on the ground, their babies still suckling at their breasts, and mothers carrying around the corpses of their children as they beg for food.[125] The soundscape of horror is enlisted: "Parents abandoned their children; children were left alone, and on every street, at every corner the screams sounded just like the torments of the sinners in hell. One could not but feel sorry at the realization that this was the ultimate sorrow."[126]

Inu Hōjōki keeps its readers gripped at an emotional level by highlighting the psychological distress that accompanies famines. Different from a fire or an earthquake, which are limited in time, famines can endure and those affected can spiral into a situation of despair, losing all sense of shame. *Inu Hōjōki* recounts that, for instance, when the government intervened with food relief during the 1669 famine, people would openly jostle for a place in line with no embarrassment.[127] After two years of famine in 1682, people were "without any sense of embarrassment . . . and dragged their feet to beg at every house."[128] Theft was another means of survival, and the topic is given equal treatment in *Musashi abumi*, *Kanameishi*, and *Inu Hōjōki*. The last justifies theft in desperate situations: "When beasts are facing death they kill and when people are confronted with hunger they steal" and "to poor people theft is as natural as poems to people in love."[129] If your parents, wife, and children are starving, do you not become a thief to save them? In extraordinary circumstances abnormal behavior becomes the norm and people accept all sorts of fates to survive through the unimaginable.

Seventeenth-century disaster narratives show a desire to report the news in a factual and informative manner while portraying the human drama as it emerges from destructive events of unprecedented scale. In the process they bring readers as witnesses to the horror and the emotional despair but also teach them how to condone otherwise unacceptable behavior. These are no mere documentary accounts. The physical, social, and emotional magnitude of these disasters, as well as the tsunami of the trauma they release, made it possible for these events to begin inhabiting Japanese history.

Coping with Trauma

Is it at all possible to regain order out of the chaos inflicted by disasters? Can the trauma occasioned by calamities be overcome? I maintain that seventeenth-century disaster narratives propound four strategies to survive trauma: first-person storytelling, humor, didacticism, and redress.[130]

The four texts examined here are all conceived as stories that survivors recount and share with us (and possibly an intradiegetic readership). As noted by Regina Bendix, psychoanalytical research has been undertaken to learn the power of storytelling in dealing with traumatic experiences.[131] Of the four texts examined here, *Musashi abumi*, is comparatively straightforward. The haberdasher prompts Rakusaibō to give an account of the fire he witnessed and that of his own personal experience.[132] As noted, by relating his own story he is forgiven for his foolish behavior and, eventually, for having survived. *Kanameishi* is more challenging from this point of view. Until the third volume, in fact, we are confronted with a third-person, effaced narrator. In is only at the beginning of the third section in the third volume that we are introduced to the monk Atarashibō.[133] He is described wandering around Kyoto on the fourth day of the fifth month, with aftershocks still being felt, calling for the apocalyptic end of the world through a fiery shower. At this point the text seems to move to an unrelated, comical episode of a wealthy merchant. Despite his attempts to put on a brave face during the disaster, he panics and flees to survive the predicted end of the world. He thinks he has grabbed his wife's hand, but in the commotion he drags with him a Kumano nun instead of his wife. It is only when he reaches Shichijō that he realizes his witless mistake. This is again another instance of foolish behavior when confronted with fear. We might be willing to forgive him, but his wife is not. Once safely back home, she is so outraged that she demands a divorce, and the man, who has been adopted into the family, is thrown out. Having lost everything, the man suddenly decides to become a monk, and the tale closes with these remarks: "The sixth and the seventh months passed, but the painful memory of the earthquake had not dissipated. While wandering around the country through the various provinces he continued to recount in detail the destruction of and the losses from this earthquake." [134] That this man is Atarashibō is implausible from a narrative point of view since Atarashibō is the one who predicted the end of the world that frightened the unnamed merchant. However, the final remarks quoted here suggests that the merchant is doing exactly what Atarashibō is doing—going around the country and narrating what has happened. In the fourth, and final, section of this last volume, the narration imperceptibly shifts to a first-person perspective, with the narratorial voice explaining the origins of the title *Kanameishi*. This could be Atarashibō's voice or that of someone who listened to Atarashibō's tale of the 1662 earthquake and decided to inscribe it under the title *Kanameishi*. Either way, the impression is that the text is indeed the product of Atarashibō's keen desire to keep the memory of the disaster alive.

Inu Hōjōki uses a strategy that is not dissimilar. Until the second volume the identity of the narrator remains concealed. At this point we are introduced to Ima Chōmei, whose name could be translated to mean a modern Chōmei and who perfectly fits with the fact that we are reading an appropriation of Kamo no Chōmei's *Hōjōki*. The reader is initially told about his past: a spendthrift who wastes his father's money; he conforms perfectly to the cliché of the second-generation millionaire discussed previously in this chapter. Bad luck forces him to move initially to a hut in a sort of relief center behind the temple, Hiden-in, and later to a beggar's room (*kojiki no heya*) in the same district.[135] The reader with knowledge of the medieval *Hōjōki* can fully enjoy a beautifully crafted word-by-word rewriting of the source text: everything that was familiar about the two dwellings that Kamo no Chōmei occupied in the *Hōjōki* tale when he was thirty and then sixty is adapted to a space that suits a pauper.[136] In search of spiritual enlightenment, Ima Chōmei embarks on a journey that will take him to Nagasaki, Osaka, and back to Kyoto; along the way he will discover how relief is dispensed to those impacted by the famine. It is only at the end, when he has returned, that the text records, "Toward the end of the third month of the second year of the Tenna era [1682], Ima Chōmei, back in his hut at Hiden-in, wrote this," after which is presented a poem.[137] The pronoun "this" (*kore*) has two possible interpretations. It could quite innocently point to the closing verse that immediately follows, or it could refer to the entire text. The second is a possible reading because the text copies the ending of *Hōjōki* in which Kamo no Chōmei states that he finished writing "this" (i.e., *Hōjōki*) in his hut in the second year of the Kenryaku era (1212). This makes the text that we are reading a narrative account by Ima Chōmei, notwithstanding the use of third-person narration.

Yakushi tsūya monogatari stages multiple narrators who have survived the 1641–1643 famine. At the outset the reader is introduced to a quack doctor named Fukusai who visits Inabadō in Kyoto and prays to Yakushi, the Buddha of healing and medicine.[138] Fukusai's story, though, is left untold. After two folios, in fact, this character is relegated to the role of a witness to a supernatural event that takes place at Inabadō. At that point the true protagonists of the story make their entrance: Yakushi's Twelve Heavenly Generals appear in the guise of old men, wearing on their heads the image of the zodiacal animal with which they are associated. They are the voices that narrate about the famine. Kubira, here represented by a rat, introduces some basic facts about the famine. We then hear that Kubira and the rats he leads are among the victims—there is nothing for them to eat—and we realize that the Twelve Heavenly Generals are not above the tragedy. In fact, they are narrating a catastrophe that has directly affected them. But they are not the only narrators. They are replaced by the God of Wealth, Daikoku, who becomes their spokesman and who has the remit to request Yakushi to stop everything that is happening. He appears, emaciated, before Yakushi and admits that he has used up all the contents of his bag and has even had to pawn the bag itself! The dialogue between Daikoku and Yakushi reveals new facets of the famine and at the same time empowers also the paupers to recount their own personal stories.

Witnesses and survivors of a disaster narrate their own experience of it, on the one hand perpetuating the memory of this tragedy and, on the other, seeking closure. This technique, as I see it, serves to personalize the accounts of the four disaster narratives. At the same time they offer a message of hope. Here are individuals who have survived an unparalleled catastrophe and are able to share their stories. The unthinkable is not unspeakable, and to speak about it is the first step toward both personal and social healing.

Humor also has a significant role in the seventeenth-century disaster narrative, a penchant that is particularly evident in Asai Ryōi's work. Similar to what I have examined for *Musashi abumi*, in *Kanameishi* the humor derives principally from foolish behavior prompted by the inability to respond in a rational and composed manner to the sudden catastrophe. For instance, a group of youngsters has climbed to the top of Yasaka Pagoda to help with roof repairs. They think that the movement of the building during the quake is nothing more than a prank by other youths shaking the base of the pagoda. When they overhear people talking about an earthquake and the fate of the pagoda, they scramble down in complete mental confusion.[139] This passage invites laughter, but, as noted previously, the humor helps to recast unusual behavior as normal in stressful situations.

The accounts of famine seem to allow less room to express humor, although on occasion the emotional strain caused by reading about such great human misery is relieved by comic touches. The very fact that figures such as the Twelve Heavenly Generals and Daikoku are stripped of their divine nature and are themselves the victims of the famine would invite a reader to smile. No creature, be it god, human, or animal, is spared the consequences of famine (or any other disaster), prompting in readers the somehow comforting realization that misfortune happens to everyone, regardless of social status. It is social satire, though, that features prominently in the accounts of famines. *Inu Hōjōki* offers scorning amusement in pinpointing societal flaws when a disaster hits. The narrator does not spare anyone—doctors, monks, the sick—in describing the wave of epidemics that struck the capital in 1681 and the result of the endemic poverty caused by the famine.[140] *Kanameishi* voices particular disdain against superstition. At the end of the first day, as the tremors continued people were convinced that the end of the world was nigh, so the Imperial Palace dispatched someone with a poem that was believed to halt the earthquake if attached to front doors and gates. It had, of course, no effect, and the population had to endure forty-seven aftershocks. The narrator explains that "these kinds of poems are a bunch of nonsense, with no foundation."[141] The narrator acknowledges the foolishness of such beliefs but recognizes that these sorts of things can act as a sort of tonic to alleviate people's fears. And foolish behavior is (again) excusable. In a similar vein *Kanameishi* sneers at similar events like the sudden devotion to Toyokuni Shrine after years of neglect simply because the earthquake left it unscathed.[142] The message clearly cautions against falling prey to such simplistic beliefs, even though they are commonly encountered in times of crisis and disaster.

The same texts offers also what comes across as practical advice to cope with, or even avoid, such tragedies. *Kanameishi* is the only text that provides, albeit in a relatively short passage, a how-to manual with practical advice on what to do in case of an earthquake. Do not place stones on your roof to stabilize the eaves, because they will fall; prop them up instead. If the earth under your feet opens up, lay down a board. Sliding doors might get stuck, so leave them open day and night. When small children are paralyzed by fear, give them some medication and comfort them. If the house looks like it might collapse, flee. Be especially careful when you are in front of a tiled roof or an earthen warehouse, and be mindful of fire.[143] Although blandly factual, such a list, I would argue, could have had a powerful and positive effect on readers. An earthquake of this size might well appear unbeatable, but by applying this set of simple rules, one might actually find a way to survive.

Other texts call for a need to behave appropriately, focusing not so much on any practical action as on ethical teachings that echo what we have seen thus far in other coeval publications. For instance, the didactic approach dominates *Yakushi tsūya monogatari*, in which the roots of the famine are identified in inappropriate social behavior. Yakushi explains that people are still suffering from hunger despite the abundance of rice for two reasons. The first is the samurai class, which is guilty of cornering the market and selling the rice at inflated prices: "Because samurai delight in making money, people in this world greatly suffer and die. They are guilty of murder."[144] The second, most serious, cause lies in excessive expenditure. And this returns to the notion of economizing explored earlier in this chapter: "The present famine is the punishment of Heaven since Heaven abhors people's extravagant lifestyles."[145] It is here that the paupers give their personal narratives. Each admits that they have indulged in a lifestyle above their station and have now become outcasts. This goes across social strata: a farmer, a son of a renowned Kyotoite, and a sixty-year-old man from the distant provinces.[146] The final storyteller includes three similar tales from the past regarding China and Japan:

> Those who thrive in luxury [*ogori*] and comfort [*raku*] are despised by Heaven. The Buddhas and the deities leave behind those who are despised by Heaven. Those who are turned down by the Buddhas and deities go through this kind of life [struggling for food and health]—there is no hope for them even in the next life. What a sad floating world ... those who indulge in

excessive expenses [*ogori*] are despised by Heaven, and they will find it difficult to escape divine punishment.¹⁴⁷

The need to be frugal is at the core of this passage: famine and illness can be avoided, but you must be frugal.¹⁴⁸ Daikoku reinforces the teaching by quoting a miraculous story about a poor boy who lives in Kagamiishi-machi, west of Ichijō. The story employs the trope of filial piety as a way to wealth but then updates it to correspond with the current era of famine. The young boy sells all his possessions and, to care for his parents, works on the riverbed dispensing food to others affected by the famine. This act of compassion, combined with his extraordinary filial piety, leads to a reward: he finds gold and thereafter is able to provide for his parents. The didactic message continues, stating that a person should not only avoid excessive expenditure but also be morally correct. This is, of course, not surprising and is in keeping with texts discussed in chapter 3. Kubira's rats join in and impart the further teaching that a person should not steal. Why? Because this, too, offends Heaven and is a negation of the Way.¹⁴⁹ Abhorring stealing as something that leads to tragedy and condoning stealing when in the midst of that tragedy are two sides of the same coin in these texts. Disaster narratives encourage an aesthetic reading centered on the emotional experience gained in the reading event. At the same time, these narratives invite an efferent reading from which the reader is to take away teachings to be applied in real life. Admittedly their efficacy in preventing disasters is questionable, and the temptation might be to discard them as mere indoctrination, but the message of hope they carry is undeniable: if we behave according to the Way we have the hope that Heaven will spare us from tragedy.

Hope dominates seventeenth-century disaster narratives, with *Musashi abumi* and *Inu Hōjōki* eager to explore the theme of redress, especially in terms of the relief for victims. Once the fire in Edo is under control, survivors are faced with new challenges of having no rice, no shelter, and the onset of winter.¹⁵⁰ People are dying from both hunger and cold. Compassionate magistrates build temporary huts as shelters from the cold and distribute rice porridge. In the process, the narrative focus moves slightly away from detailing human despair to the more reassuring image of regaining normalcy. *Musashi abumi* describes how Edo was reconstructed such that a disaster of these proportions could be avoided in the future.¹⁵¹ What was thus far a description of a devastating fire becomes an account of the opportunities that the city now had to be rebuilt more efficiently, in a manner designed to save lives in case a similar disaster hits again. The government is even ready to pay compensation to landowners for areas earmarked for protective embankments. Furthermore, the government offers payment to merchants in an effort to encourage them to return to business. It is apparently thanks to "the mercy of the shogun" (*kimi no on megumi*) that life returns to normal.¹⁵² Whereas David Atherton interprets this as a move away from a medieval worldview of *ukiyo* (sorrowful world), where calamities were presented as a sign of tainted rulers, to the early modern one of *ukiyo* (floating world), where Edo's destruction is made use of to display the authority and sagacity of Tokugawa rule, I wish to stress the shift from a narrative focused around trauma to one that celebrates life.[153] *Musashi abumi* undoubtedly sketches a faithful history of a destructive event and depicts a traumatized individual whose life becomes purposeful in recounting the catastrophic experience and, therefore, in repeating the trauma. Yet in the end, the collective and individual trauma is overcome by the description of life going back to normal. It is no mere survival: life as was known before the horror is not only regained but also improved, with the cityscape upgraded to avoid the repetition of trauma.

The government is not the only body to be praised for its aid. *Inu Hōjōki* devotes almost the entire second volume—once Ima Chōmei has set out on his journey around the country—to the celebration of the relief offered by Buddhist temples.[154] Named Buddhist institutions in Nagasaki, Sakai, and Edo offer rice porridge, to which was added a daily allowance of twelve copper coins per person. Buddhist monks encouraged rich people to participate and share their wealth with the needy. As a result, Heaven could not leave such righteous behavior unrewarded:

> In this way, people's hearts were alleviated and the wheel of Heavenly Fortune must have once again begun to spin. The crops began to grow as hoped, and by the middle of the second month the price of rice decreased day after day. The epidemics gradually came under control. Everyone [*banmin*] flourished and was in high spirits. Those paupers who had left their houses went back home. Those who were famished and tired were able to stand. Those who were ill were healed. Abandoned children were returned to their homes. Parents met their children and children nurtured their parents in return. The happy sight of merchants singing in the market and of farmers working in the fields is comparable to fish meeting with the water and a dark evening growing light. Everyone was rejoicing and celebrating boundlessly at the fact that by being born in such an era of peace one could benefit from such mercy.[155]

Whether it is the local or central government, Buddhist temples, or Heaven, if human beings act in the name of mutual support and compassion, any catastrophe can be overcome—if not even avoided—and traumatic emotional wounds healed. We cannot completely deny that this might simply represent a form of lip service to the shogunate. But by the same token we cannot reject the message of hope that these narratives contain. People do survive the tragedy, in spite of its unprecedented, apocalyptic nature. They not only survive the tragedy but also can give firsthand accounts of their harrowing experiences.

And storytelling becomes in itself a form of therapeutic treatment of the trauma. Storytelling encourages acceptance and forgiveness vis-à-vis silly behavior. Humor, at times bordering on social satire, helps alleviate emotional distress. Righteous behavior is invoked as a powerful tool to inspire Heaven to bestow its mercy and end the catastrophe. Relief offered to the survivors and the reconstruction of the wounded space give hope that a return to normalcy is possible. Ultimately seventeenth-century disaster narratives are designed as narratives of hope. Hope in life. Hope in compassion. Hope that something better can and will rise from the ashes. From this perspective, these texts, I argue, differ greatly from the trauma narratives explored by leading scholar Cathy Caruth. Caruth acknowledges that at the heart of trauma narratives is "a kind of double telling, the oscillation between a *crisis of death* and the correlative *crisis of life*: between the story of the unbearable nature of an event and the story of the unbearable nature of its survival."[156] In the texts analyzed here trauma is a wound inflicted upon the mind but is represented as lacking the complexity acknowledged in the twentieth century.[157] It is true that narrators do relive their trauma while recounting it, but it is also true that their stories label the disaster as past history while at the same time celebrating the present as the moment when wounds are healed and hope for the future fostered. These narratives fight against the idea that trauma has endless impact on a life. Research is needed to ascertain whether such straightforward optimism infuses disaster narratives across the early modern period.

Scattered across the publishing genres in the 1600s were books that focused public attention on the present moment. When perusing seventeenth-century popular prose in search of what I have called present-mindedness, money and disasters emerge as pressing concerns.

Money is characterized as central for any human being in a floating world that is in love with cash and its power. We might gain the impression that several texts taught readers how to make or retain money. And yet my analysis has shown that they offered little meaningful practical advice. While fueling a fascination for wealth, they provided readers with an understanding that not everyone in society could become a millionaire. The paradox that emerges in texts that instruct readers about money is a comforting one: you need to be au courant with how money works, but you are excused if you do not yourself succeed in improving your financial situation. The greatest teaching is to be accepting of differences in a society that, if asked to choose, values social harmony over material riches. At the same time, the popular discourse on money does not stigmatize it as something intrinsically bad. If you are determined to put into action what these texts suggest and if you are lucky enough to become a millionaire, that is equally welcome. Popular prose is there to assist you either way in the celebration of an epoch that pushes everyone to aspire for a better life.

Disaster narratives ultimately teach universal lessons about fate and death, those that Umberto Eco identifies at the core of literature.[158] They do so, however, moved by a desire to report the local news in factual terms—a penchant for journalism that emerges in an epoch when news broadsheets were yet to be printed. But the focus on the contemporary is balanced by an eagerness to gauge these disasters as part of history (both Chinese and Japanese) and to frame them as epoch making in their exceptionality. In this way, disaster narratives report the present to construct history. The same narratives also encourage a therapeutic treatment of trauma: foolish behavior is condoned as normal in moments of heightened distress; virtuous behavior is promoted as one way to gain Heaven's favor and survive; and optimism is sparked by the celebration of aid from governmental and religious institutions. A cynical reader, now as in the seventeenth century, might be nauseated by what may well be read as blind subservience to the shogunate. Yet the message of hope that these narratives convey cannot easily be underestimated.

These books keep readers engaged at both a cognitive and an emotional level. The profit gained by the reader is different from what I explored in the previous chapters, in that there is little in these texts that could be translated into concrete action. This is not to say, however, that these books offered no intellectual profit. They empowered readers with an understanding of how the present was shaping up while providing them with the pleasure of narratives that kept them abreast of what mattered in the here and now. Travel literature, prose dealing with the pleasure quarters, books on medicine designed for the sickly reader, and many more equally helped constructing the present as it was unfolding. Seventeenth-century popular prose can be read as a celebration of present-mindedness.

CHAPTER 7

The Triumph of Plurality

Thus, what I enjoy in a narrative is not directly its content or even its structure, but rather the abrasions I impose upon the fine surface: I read on, I skip, I look up, I dip in again.

—Roland Barthes, *The Pleasure of the Text*

Dichotomies are somehow presented as a reassuring truth in literary histories, and this is certainly the case for histories of early modern Japanese literature: narrative versus nonnarrative, fiction versus nonfiction, unitary versus fragmentary, for instance. In some way we feel better when these categories are kept separate and left unreconciled. After all, divisions facilitate labeling, and labeling allows the positioning of a text within a specific box in anthologies and textbooks. Yet taxonomies are often home to what seem to me rather unproductive critical venues. When confronted with a text that challenges our comforting dichotomies and classifications, we feel a certain degree of uneasiness and often opt to suspend any engagement with the unwieldy object. As a result, the text is removed from critical engagement, literary histories, and cultural memory. Alternatively, we try and repress any oppositional forces at play within that text, reducing it to something homogeneous and molding it into something that it is not. We end up with a wrought unhistorical construct.

Roland Barthes, admittedly discussing a corpus of literary works that are very different from those of interest here, has produced a theoretical framework that I personally find quite compelling.

Barthes distinguishes between what he calls "texts of pleasure" and "texts of bliss":

> Text of pleasure: the text that contents, fills, grants euphoria: the text that comes from culture and does not break with it, is linked to a *comfortable* practice of reading. Text of bliss: the text that imposes a state of loss, the text that discomforts (perhaps to the point of a certain boredom), unsettles the reader's historical, cultural, psychological assumptions, the consistency of his tastes, values, memories, brings to a crisis his relation with language.[1]

For us, Western readers of Japanese literature (or more generally of early modern popular prose) in the twenty-first century, most of the texts examined in the previous chapters come across as alien as they unsettle our assumptions and expectations of literature. In fulfilling primarily an epistemic function and providing us with ethical, social, and interpersonal knowledge, these texts bemuse those readers who expect literature to serve only an aesthetic function that appeals to emotions rather than reason. This, to a certain degree, is true for any form of didactic literature, where pleasure derives primarily from the cognitive engagement and the profit (= knowledge) we gain.[2] From this point of view I do not think it is too much of a stretch to see in these texts something that *discomforts* the modern reader—that is, something akin to Barthes's texts of bliss. And yet the same texts back in the seventeenth century perfectly met the expectations and demands of an increasing number of readers: they were published repeatedly, enjoying sustained popularity, and created powerful cultural tropes that resonated deeply across publishing genres. In other words, they were texts of pleasure for seventeenth-century readers. Therefore, what may appear to us as texts of bliss might well have been texts of pleasure when they first circulated. Once we accept this argument, we are in a position to embrace and enjoy the stance advocated by Franco Moretti: "You enter the archive, and the usual coordinates disappear; all you see are swarms of hybrids and oddities, for which the categories of literary taxonomy offer little help. It's fascinating, to feel so lost in a universe one didn't even know existed."[3]

The writings chosen for discussion in this chapter prompt us to move beyond what we feel comfortable with, in that they challenge the dichotomies between narrative and nonnarrative, fiction and nonfiction, unitary and fragmentary. They comprise the narrative as well as the nonnarrative, are fictional but also embrace the nonfictional. They lack unity, or, if they appear to have some sort of unity, it crumbles into fragments upon careful reading. Together these elements make for uncomfortable reading, with the result that these literary oddities have been either excluded from literary histories or reduced to something they are not.

This chapter argues that key for an appreciation of how these texts can work (and worked) as texts of pleasure is the retrieval of what made the act of reading pleasurable in the first place. As noted in previous chapters, there are little or no traces left by popular readers of the time. Yet I would contend that the manner in which books are textually and materially organized can offer some preliminary answers regarding their reading experience. After all, as leading scholars in the history of reading Roger Chartier and D. F. McKenzie have asserted, the material form shapes the production of meaning by the reader.[4] My ultimate argument is that seventeenth-century, commercially printed Japanese texts were constructed in a way that fostered a form of reading that aligns with Barthes's remarks: we "read a text (of pleasure) the way a fly buzzes around a room."[5] By accepting that the pleasure of reading, or at least part of it, lies in a form of drifting that does not necessarily respect the whole, we acknowledge that texts can deliver a multiplicity of messages and fulfill a number of functions. Reading means applauding plurality.

Barthes's sophisticated language appears, at least to me, consonant with the concept of "discontinuous reading" as conceived in studies on early modern European literature. Building on the foundational work of Peter Stallybrass, Eve Tavor Bannet notes that eighteenth-century books were constructed in such a way as to encourage a form of reading that is discontinuous—in other words a form of reading that allows the reader to skip, look up, dip in and out of the text.[6] Bannet notes that this form of reading does not apply only to books composed as miscellanies, what she calls "discontinuous writing," but was also practiced spontaneously by readers in their perusal of, for example, novels.[7] In the following I submit that, in the Japanese context, popular books of the seventeenth century also nurtured this form of reading, be they constructed as piecemeal and miscellaneous writings or as apparently coherent units. I develop my argument through a close reading of three primary sources: *Jigabachi monogatari* (The tale of a sand wasp), *Ukiyo monogatari* (*Tales of the Floating World*), and *Chikusai*. *Jigabachi monogatari* is a comparatively unknown text, an example of what is left out of literary histories.[8] And although *Ukiyo monogatari* and *Chikusai* have already been widely discussed in Japanese and Western scholarship, in my analysis I question their current place in literary taxonomies and challenge received views.

The Power of the Fragment: *Jigabachi monogatari*

In 1661, the Kyoto publisher Nakano Gorōzaemon 中野五郎左衛門 (dates unknown) issued the six-volume *Jigabachi monogatari*.[9] The *jigabachi* in the title is a type of hunting wasp commonly referred to as a "thread-waisted wasp" or "sand wasp" (*Ammophilinae*). In the West there is little romanticism attached to this insect that typically catches prey in order to feed its larvae. While the reading *jiga-jiga* in Japanese captures the buzzing sound of the wasp, the characters used for *jiga*, 似我, mean "resemble me." Japanese folklore embellishes the meaning of *jiga* to describe how the prey reemerges from the wasp's nest after a few days, having assumed a wasplike form. The anonymous author of *Jigabachi monogatari* borrows the image of the wasp to shape his own authorial persona and to identify himself as the ultimate teacher: "This wasp takes the children of other insects, places them in its own nest, teaches them good things, educates them, and raises them with affection."[10] *Jigabachi monogatari* is the very embodiment of the caring teachings of a wasplike author. We the readers are promised a new life after emerging from his nest at the end of our contact with the text. This, it seems to me, is a clever variation on the metaphor of the mirror employed in several texts examined previously in this study and a clear promise for a piece of transformative literature.

Jigabachi monogatari adopts several educational strategies to stimulate cognitive engagement with its readers. First, the voice of the first-person narrator is constructed as if it were *speaking* directly to the reader, thus encouraging the type of emotional bond discussed previously (chapter 3) in connection with Ejima Tamenobu's writings. Along the way, we hear more about the identity of the authorial persona: he is of warrior-class background, is highly educated with a knowledge of court literature and command of Chinese texts, and has embraced the ascetic life of a Zen Buddhist. It is plausible to assume that all this functioned as some sort of quality assurance: this voice is that of a highly suitable teacher. The oral and aural quality of the text is reinforced by the introduction, where the author-narrator explains, "I have recorded in writing what I have heard over the years."[11] Readers are equally encouraged to perform the text orally for the benefit of other people, as section 14 in the fifth volume suggests. At the end of a tale of karmic retribution, whereby a man who tries to sell the same dog three times to the same person ends up looking like a dog himself, the authorial persona asks us to take this story back into the world of orality: "Do recount this story to your grandmother, your servants, your daughters, and children."[12]

This first-person narrator reveals in full his educational agenda at the end of the first volume. "I" wants to provide readers with "entertainment" (*waraigusa*) and "amusement" (*okashiki koto*). And yet the ultimate gain is not solely pleasurable diversion but rather multifaceted "profit" (*eki*). The reader is promised historical anecdotes (*koji*), poetry (*uta* and *renga*), and tales of love (*koi no kotoba*). The presence of love is justified as something that human beings are besotted with—hence desirable from the reader's point of view—but also as a means that leads to Buddhism. In turn, *Jigabachi monogatari* promises to introduce readers to the Buddhist Way of compassion (*jihi*) and Way of truth (*shin* or *makoto*). *Jigabachi monogatari* offers also more "useful" (*yaku ni tatsu koto*) means for meeting needs, from spells to recipes.[13] The result is a "miscellarian repository of instruction and entertainment," to borrow from Eve Tavor Bannet's description of eighteenth-century English popular texts.[14] In other words, *Jigabachi monogatari* is shaped as an example of miscellaneous, fragmentary, and discontinuous writing, where nonnarrative and narrative, fictional and nonfictional are combined to captivate readers with pleasure (aesthetic and emotional) and profit (knowledge and instruction). In this light, *Jigabachi monogatari* could very well be considered a *zuihitsu* (miscellany) that displays the fragmentary nature typifying this genre. The tribute paid by the author to *Tsurezuregusa* and Sei Shōnagon certainly suggests familiarity with the existence of this genre.[15] However, *Jigabachi monogatari* lacks a key feature of *zuihitsu* identified by literary scholar Linda H. Chance as an "unfixed mode" that espouses the aesthetic of impermanence.[16] Buddhist teachings do feature in many of the 138 sections of the text, including karma and death. Yet the discontinuity in *Jigabachi monogatari* is a celebration of everyday life, a triumph of the here and now. Noda Hisao holds that it is difficult to justify the inclusion of such a miscellarian anthology in the history of seventeenth-century Japanese "novels."[17] This is, after all, not a unitary piece of narrative fiction and contains far too many nonnarrative, nonfictional passages, as the analysis that follows shows. For Noda, the only redeeming feature of *Jigabachi monogatari* is the presence of fairly long narrative passages, and he concentrates solely on these in his analysis. He goes as far as labeling this text as a collection of *setsuwa* stories included in a *zuihitsu*. Richard Lane decides on a different classification: he mentions the title of *Jigabachi monogatari* in a note listing examples of didactic tracts.[18] I maintain, however, that exclusive focus on circumscribed textual aspects of *Jigabachi monogatari* is nothing but a denial of its intrinsic nature, one that thrives precisely *because* of its variety.

How, then, can a discussion of *Jigabachi monogatari* do justice to its fragmentary and miscellaneous nature? Exploring this text as an example of an early modern *zuihitsu* might help, as I have discussed elsewhere.[19] Here, though, I would like to hazard a different, riskier comparison: *Jigabachi monogatari* is not so different from modern magazines in that it includes a little of everything to feed the curiosity of all sorts of readers. Variety was a shrewd way to broaden a potential readership and ensure economic profit for the publisher.[20]

A number of sections in *Jigabachi monogatari* quench the thirst for amusing passages in the vein of contemporaneous jestbook (*hanashibon*), to the point that in book-trade catalogues at the time it was listed as a jestbook.[21] The fourth volume, for example, entertains us with the story of an inept quack:

> There was a quack in the countryside. A person who cared for him said, "Come for a while to Kyoto. If you aim to be a doctor, you will find many opportunities. Do come by all means." And they exchanged promises on this. At the

beginning of the New Year, our quack went up to the capital with only his case of medicines. His friend was very kind and initially rented a place on Shijō. At that time Kabuki was very popular in the Shijō Kawara area—it was truly spectacular. It happened that a young actor of seventeen or eighteen had a stomachache and was completely at a loss as to what to do. He had heard of our doctor, so he asked his landlord to contact him: "That's no problem. I'll go see him right away," he said. The doctor followed the landlord to the actor's house, and as might be expected the actor was wearing a gorgeous kimono, embellished with gold and lined with red silk. Perhaps because his stomach hurt and to keep his head warm, he still had on the headgear that was used on the stage [for playing the female part]. It was at this time that the doctor arrived. Since he was a provincial countryman he knew nothing about Kabuki actors taking female roles [*kabuki ko*]. Judging from the beauty of the nightwear, he believed that the person before him was a woman who had just given birth. He promptly took the actor's pulse and offered the diagnosis: "You are suffering of postpartum bleeding and your pulse is irregular. The pain in the abdomen is probably because of the fact that you have caught a cold. I will give you some medicine. Also, do have some warm miso soup." He then returned home.[22]

The humor quite clearly lies in the quack's inability to distinguish a man from a woman, a comic situation that will be picked up by later comic literature.[23] At the same time it expects readers to be *au fait* with the world of Kabuki theater—namely, with the presence of men taking female roles—to fully enjoy the story. This leads to the second layer of humor, which ridicules people from the countryside because they are not accustomed to urban lifestyles and fashions. Poking fun at the other—those who do not belong to the urban space—will become a leitmotif in Edo-based *gesaku* almost a century after the publication of *Jigabachi monogatari*.

The humorous stories in *Jigabachi monogatari* can show more sophistication, as is apparent from the following passage:

"Guess the answer to this riddle: What is *i-ro-ha-ho-he-do*?"

The person beside him said, "The answer is 'chicken' [*niwatori*]."

"What a great job in solving the riddle! I'll now recount a strange story about a chicken."

There was a man who had bred chickens since his youth in the area of the Fudō Pavilion on the avenue Abura no Kōji in the seventh ward. He used the chickens differently; for example, he sold their eggs and butchered them for their meat. With the passing of years, his mouth became pointed like a chicken's beak, and somehow his face became chicken shaped. In the mornings he would announce the dawn like a chicken, and he woke up early and stayed in the garden. He never stayed inside the house. In effect, he became a chicken. One should not be surprised that the realm of beasts is just here, right before our eyes. This man will certainly be reborn into the realm of beasts, but his sins are such that he has now turned into a chicken. At least those who pray for the next life will not fall victim to such consequences. It must be quite common to get medications when ill, even without realizing that one will die soon after. Those who live their life experiencing many illnesses, not doing anything to improve and passing the time idly, are deserving of the punishment of Enma, the King of Hell.[24]

The intradiegetic audience and the extradiegetic reader are initially challenged with a riddle (*nazo nazo*), an example of what Suzuki Tōzō classifies as a *nidan nazo*, in which only the question and answer are given.[25] This riddle plays with the *i-ro-ha* poem that was used in *terakoya* schools to learn the hiragana syllabary. The usual opening of the poem is *i-ro-ha-ni-ho-he-do*, but the riddle here uses *i-ro-ha-ho-he-do* such that the particle *ni* has been "removed" (*tori*). The answer—*ni-wa-tori* (*wa* is added as a particle for emphasis)—is homophonic with the word for chicken (*niwatori*). The riddle then leads to a short story that stimulates the reader's imagination by liking a man to a chicken. The man's bizarre form and the juxtaposition of zoomorphic transformation becomes the object of laughter, but it also alerts the reader to the potential negative repercussions of bad karma. The protagonist's profiting from butchering chickens, in fact, is what seals his unfortunate, yet comical, fate, since Buddhist doctrine dictates that the taking of life leads to bad karma. Altogether, the reader benefits from this entertaining, yet moralizing, tale. Once having read this combination of riddle, story, and teaching, the reader comes out having learned something new, like the insect reemerging from the wasp's nest.

Other narratives in *Jigabachi monogatari* include tales that lead to a forthright moral teaching.[26] Love stories feature among them—as promised in the introduction. It should be no surprise to see the *Usuyuki* master plot (discussed in chapter 5) at play. For instance, the five folios of section 6 in the third volume rework the story skeleton of *Usuyuki monogatari* to talk about a wealthy, amorous (*kōshoku*) man.[27] The female protagonist is introduced as an elegant princess aged around seventeen who, the text explains, would not have appeared out of place in "A Branch of Plum" (Umegae), a reference to chapter 32 of *Genji monogatari*. Needless to say, it is at Kiyomizu Temple that the male protagonist gets a glimpse of the woman. Unable to forget her, he returns to the temple to pray for his love to be fulfilled. The connection with the world of *Genji monogatari* is evoked once more, with the amorous man being compared to Genji when he first caught glimpses of Murasaki no Ue. A taste for intertextuality suggests the style of *Usuyuki monogatari*, and the story continues in a predictable way—needless to say predictable for those who are aware of the *Usuyuki* master plot. The longing of the amorous man for the princess is such that he falls ill. His friends summon a proper doctor (not a quack this time!), who fully understands the situation; they need to identify the girl. The man's reaction injects a note of unexpected humor: "He was so happy that he dribbled."[28] At this point the master plot is twisted, leading to an auspicious ending with both sets of parents delighted at the possibility of the couple's marriage. The doctor is showcased as the true hero, and the passage closes with the man's composing a poem ad hoc. The teaching, expressed in it, is straightforward—one needs a sincere prayer to be united in happiness.

Altogether narratives represent a fraction of *Jigabachi monogatari*. Approximately 88 percent of the total text consists of nonnarrative passages on diverse topics. Social criticism and political commentary appear in a few passages and deserve attention inasmuch as they signal an important feature of this miscellany: it allows for conflicting views to occupy the same textual space.

Section 45 in the fourth volume offers a dialogue between a poor monk and a peasant who launches himself into a bitter attack against the current administration. The point of controversy lies in what is perceived as an unreasonable economic gap between peasants and those in local administrations, from daimyo to high-ranking public servants (*kōi kōkan*). Those in power are accused of squeezing peasants, and as a result peasants teeter on the brink of starvation. This is despite the fact that they are responsible for producing the nation's rice. Local administrators, on the other hand, live a lavish life made up of all sorts of excesses, unappreciative that the money they spend and the rice they eat are thanks to the arduous labor of others. This leads the peasant to question, "What kind of age do we live in?"[29] We are close to the criticism of the samurai class advanced in *Yakushi tsūya monogatari* (see chapter 6). He then enters into a long historical account of the eras when rulers displayed great compassion toward their subjects. Emperor Godaigō is named as the ultimate example of the ideal leader, ready to give the populace his own clothes on bitterly cold nights. The present era, though, is different: those at the top thrive and those at the bottom suffer. The tone of the peasant's words leaves no doubt: it is a harsh criticism of the local government. It is tempting to see the author as the figure of the peasant and to assume that his stance is antiestablishment, but section 58 in the fourth volume reveals a completely different viewpoint. Another monk is engaged in a discussion about recent judiciary cases: two thieves and three men involved with the trafficking of children are crucified, whereas two men involved in gambling are set free. Opinions are divided over the issue. The monk believes that the gamblers should have been executed, too. But a man from the intradiegetic audience, a gambler himself, tries to downplay any offense caused by gambling: "It is not that you kill someone or that it goes against your lord. It is just the offense of going against an ordinance proclaimed by the shogun."[30] At this point the monk launches into a panegyric to the shogun, noting that he is like a Buddha wishing to aid all human beings and the ordinances are in place to eradicate the evil in us all. What until this point was a text centering on the value of legal ordinances issued by a Buddha-like shogun becomes a nonnarrative, sermonlike passage on the merits of living an austere life:

> Even a powerful medication like ginger is toxic when taken in excessively high doses. When there is too much money, it also is poison. Going out every day becomes boring and is poison. Moon-viewing and flower-viewing parties become poison if done often. Sex is also poison. Nothing surpasses abstinence from sex.... Good things are good but when done in excess they turn bad. So how can a bad thing like gambling be good when done in excess?[31]

The style and message of this final passage resonate deeply with the didactic prose explored in chapter 3. Back to the point: is *Jigabachi monogatari* pro or anti *bakufu*? The text is designed so as to accommodate both stances, encouraging a plurality of views. The peasant criticizes the present government and praises the imperial power, whereas the monk applauds the figure of the shogun, who embodies the very essence of the present government. The format of a miscellany, where the authorial persona claims to be jotting down things heard from third parties, is ideal to give voice to competing opinions, and this in turn has the potential to please different groups of readers. In selecting discontinuous writing the author, with his publisher, encourages free thinking.[32] This is in itself a compelling finding that fights against the prevailing view that seventeenth-century literature was highly censored. For instance, Donald Keene wrote of "a despotic government that tolerated absolutely no public criticism of its policies and confiscated books that it found offensive."[33] More recently E. Taylor Atkins has espoused a similar stance when writing about censorship in the 1660s: "Criticisms and even depictions of the Tokugawa or *daimyō* families, official policies, and recent incidents in the news were forbidden."[34] Edicts that advised booksellers to seek guidance from the city's commissioner's office when publishing materials concerning the politics of the *bakufu* or materials that might cause inconvenience to daimyo and high-ranking samurai did exist.[35] That is undeniable. A text like *Jigabachi monogatari*, however, asks us to think carefully whether the regime was really as harsh as it is generally portrayed. After all, the author gives voice to what comes across as open criticism of the local authorities. There is no camouflage employed to soften the message. And yet the text was published without being censored and, as far as we know, did not lead to any punishment. So much so that it even went through reprints well into the eighteenth century.

While addressing current societal and political issues, the authorial persona seems eager to instruct readers on Buddhist knowledge and how it infuses aspects of daily life.[36] Put differently, a number of sections in *Jigabachi monogatari* employ the rhetoric of *kana hōgo* (described in chapter 3). Section 18 in the fifth volume, for instance, elaborates on the relationship between karma and social status.[37] We are reborn as a noble, a high-ranking person, or a daimyo if in our previous life we underwent the correct training, honing our compassion and respecting the Buddhist law. Once more a comparison is introduced to expound the concept in a clearer manner: we are like an arrow shot into the sky that will eventually fall to the ground. In other words, even if an individual is born a daimyo the effect of past deeds will eventually play out; any indulgence in bad acts, such as killing or bullying retainers, as well as an excessive lifestyle will adversely impact the next life. The authorial persona particularly condemns hunting and reinforces this view in two more stories in *Jigabachi monogatari*, explaining how the mistreatment of animals causes bad karma—and does so almost twenty years before the Edicts for the Compassion Toward All Living Beings.[38] This, in turn, also occasions the explanation that being born a human being is a blessing and carries with it the message that karma influences a person's social status in this life. Yet the key is to never stop practicing a righteous life until rebirth into the Pure Land. It is noteworthy that the writer, who is closely associated with Zen Buddhism, would mention teachings associated with Pure Land Buddhism; this espouses the syncretic view of Buddhism encountered in seventeenth-century *kana washo* and *kana hōgo*. Ultimately Buddhism is portrayed yet again as instrumental in molding sensible human beings.

Keeping the reader constantly engaged at a cognitive level and nurturing the manifold joys of learning is a constant concern of *Jigabachi monogatari*. The text's author is eager, for example, to teach about poetry in Japanese and Chinese or to introduce readers to brief anecdotes from the Chinese tradition. By systematically glossing the Chinese text with interlinear vernacular translations (as described in chapter 1), it shows a willingness to adapt to different levels of literacy. It is left up to the reader how to process these twenty-six passages. They could be memorized, used as a springboard for further study, or simply discarded if deemed too difficult. The author is likewise enthusiastic in offering useful tips with practical, how-to information on homemade medications (fifteen sections), food preservation (six sections), the growing of plants and vegetables (five sections), spells and divination (four sections), horse riding and archery (four sections), and other, miscellaneous matters (eight sections). In this way, *Jigabachi monogatari* becomes a dispensary of recipes that shares much with some of the household manuals examined in chapter 4. *Yorozu kikigaki hiden*, for example, included tips about how to remove stains, and in *Jigabachi monogatari*, too, there is a brief section that suggests using lime powder or daikon radish juice to remove oily stains.[39] The reader also learns about such things as how to prevent metal rust, treat skin conditions, keep miso fresh, preserve Japanese pepper, and stop underarm odor, among many others.[40] There are even instructions on how to get your kitten to return home: "When your kitten has run away, recall when it went missing and cancel that day on the calendar using black ink. Your cat will return promptly."[41] The text covers everyday preoccupations of the seventeenth-century Japanese and shows that they are in essence not unlike our own in the twenty-first century.

As a piece of discontinuous writing, *Jigabachi monogatari* functions like a modern magazine and is constructed so as to ensure that there is something for everyone. We find love tales that prompt an emotional, if not an aesthetic, response, but there is also humor that solicits a good laugh while making us think, together with more somber nonnarrative didactic passages aimed at dispensing ethical teachings, but also sections openly critical of contemporary society and politics. All this is spiced up with bits of practical knowledge and snippets of a more refined culture. To amalgamate this potpourri of contents that celebrate plurality is the claim made by the narrator that the text is a sort of scrapbook of things he has heard over the years. The oral and aural dimension justifies the inclusion of *Jigabachi monogatari*, at least initially, in the publishing genre of *hanashibon*: early modern jestbooks collected stories that were used as a springboard for oral performances. But for us this text remains a multifarious body that escapes any taxonomy, a text that demands to be appreciated precisely for its eclectic nature.

How are we supposed to read *Jigabachi monogatari*? Nothing prevents us from reading it from beginning to end. In this case continuous reading allows us to enjoy the lack of unity and almost paradoxically foster an appreciation of the discontinuous nature of the text. But nothing prevents us from perusing the text in a discontinuous manner, navigating it freely in search of what we are most interested in. The handy table of contents, included as early as the first edition, enables and encourages our freedom in skipping and jumping from one topic to another, very much like Barthes's fly buzzing around a room. By exercising our right to discontinuous reading we can select passages that share a common thread, and we thus end up transforming a piece of discontinuous writing into continuous writing, imposing uniformity onto plurality. A reader could, for example, use *Jigabachi monogatari* to collect stories about the provinces since a number of such segments are included: on Tosa (sec. 3, vol. 1), Sagami (sec. 10, vol. 1), Arima (sec. 33, vol. 2), Gōshū (sec. 23, vol. 6), and others. Another reader could decide to focus solely on the recipes in *Jigabachi monogatari*, employing it as any other household manual. While this is a prerogative of any reader, it should not become the way in which we talk about *Jigabachi monogatari* in literary histories: pigeonholing this text, as Noda and Lane have tried to do, in a specific category betrays its inherent discontinuous nature and reduces it to something it is not.

The Pleasure of a Broken Narrative: *Ukiyo monogatari*

The fragmentary structure of *Jigabachi monogatari* naturally invites readers to enjoy discontinuous reading since there is nothing in the text that demands the seeking of a common thread. This changes when a fictional character is positioned in a miscellany and signposted as the protagonist of a fictional story, as exemplified in *Ukiyo monogatari*.

Seventeenth-century book-trade catalogues ascribe *Ukiyo monogatari*, published in Kyoto around 1665, to the prolific author Asai Ryōi (discussed in chapter 2).[42] It is often cited in modern studies of Japanese literature as the manifesto of the early modern floating world (*ukiyo*), with the art and literary historian Richard Lane praising it for what he calls "the first conscious expression of the hedonistic mood of the new age."[43] In his unpublished English translation of *Ukiyo monogatari*, Daniel Lewis Barber notes that the "overall tone" of the work needs to be identified within the construct of *ukiyo* as a world of pleasure.[44] Donald H. Shively talks about the "first expression of the hedonistic abandon of the floating world and the odyssey of the rake," praising the tale as something that anticipates by two decades Ihara Saikaku's *Kōshoku ichidai otoko*.[45]

The opening section of *Ukiyo monogatari* does focus on a definition of *ukiyo*, with the prose assuming the form of a dialogue between three undefined voices. The first voice explains the medieval view of *ukiyo* by quoting songs that espouse the idea of this world as a place where nothing takes place as expected. The second voice rejects the idea of *uki* as suffering caused by the transience of this earthly existence and instead asserts the need to embrace a carefree attitude to a life full of pleasure. The third voice steps in to advocate an epicurean interpretation of the word *ukiyo* as the correct one.

The second section introduces the figure of Ukiyobō, who is described as "a monk who 'floats' oblivious to any cares in the world and is droll."[46] The language employed to describe Ukiyobō tells the reader that he may represent the ultimate personification of the concept of *ukiyo*. "A monk who 'floats' oblivious to any cares in the world," in fact, repeats the expression *uki ni uite* that appears in the first section, introduced by the second voice to delineate how we should enjoy this world. The adjectival noun *hyōkin* 瓢金, translated here as "droll," also connects Ukiyobō with the first section. The reading of *hyōkin* 瓢金 calls to mind the homophonous word *hyōkin* 剽軽, which connotes something thoughtless, funny, facetious, and droll. The author chooses, however, an unconventional logographic compound, with the first character, *hyō* 瓢, suggesting the image of a "gourd" (*hyōtan* 瓢箪). This, in turn, links with the image of the gourd used in the first section as the metaphor for how to live *ukiyo*: "like a gourd bobbing along with the current." The manner in which Ukiyobō is introduced creates a precise set of expectations for the reader, that *Ukiyo monogatari* recounts the tale of Ukiyobō, the embodiment of the floating world and its gay, careless aesthetic. In other words, the reader is left with the impression that what follows will be a unitary narrative constructed around the life of Ukiyobō and his lighthearted attitude to life.

The second section focuses exclusively on Ukiyobō and his early life. His father is a low-ranking samurai, an adept liar and flatterer, traits that facilitate his move up in society and fuel his intense desire for wealth that he achieves by accepting bribes. His cowardice is unparalleled, and he eventually decides to give up his military career to become a rich merchant. He is blessed with a son, and the text summarizes the son's childhood and youth in just a few lines. He is portrayed as a sort of defective child who could not stop crying at night, with a lump on his head resulting from an infection while in the womb; he also contracts smallpox and measles. Having survived all these afflictions, he is introduced to the military arts and *tenarai*, but with little success. Instead, he becomes a drifter (*ukaremono*) who wanders around in search of pleasure. Nothing in how Ukiyobō is introduced offers the prospect of a realistic, three-dimensional character endowed with psychological depth. Instead, Ukiyobō is portrayed as a two-dimensional figure with humorous shortcomings and as a caricature of a human being. It is therefore not surprising that Ukiyobō's story can be condensed in just a few lines despite the work being in five volumes.

As an adult he chooses the name Hyōtarō 瓢太郎, the *hyō* 瓢 stressing his "gourdlike" nature, and he enjoys gambling and visits to the pleasure quarters. After he has spent all his money on prostitutes, he undergoes a personality change and becomes Hyōtarō 兵太郎, the new character *hyō* 兵 in his name connoting military activities. Once he has mastered the requisite skills to become a low-ranking samurai—namely, the ability to be an unscrupulous accountant who helps his master increase his profits!—he is hired by his master as a type of councillor. He also works as a jester (*o-hanashi no shu*) and adviser to a daimyo. At this point he seems to have become a carbon copy of his father; his acts of greed force other retainers and peasants into poverty and starvation. When confronted by an angry samurai, Hyōtarō opts for a career change: he takes the tonsure and changes his name to Ukiyobō 浮世坊 (or 浮世房). With the exception of a brief and unsuccessful attempt at making a living as a quack, Ukiyobō settles down in his life as a monk and is pictured as a mendicant priest, traveling through Kyoto, then to Osaka and environs. His personality undergoes a dramatic turn as he regrets having neglected his duties to indulge in gambling and prostitutes. He then is invited to stay at a samurai's residence, the location of which remains undisclosed. At this point in the tale, Ukiyobō becomes a voice, more precisely the voice of wisdom that reflects on current affairs and dispenses teachings. Ukiyobō's voice, often appearing in dialogue with his employer and a doctor named Tsūsai, is the only trace of him in the last three volumes. His character resurfaces only in the final section when he mysteriously disappears from this world, leaving the reader to ponder about what happened to him and whether all this was just a dream. This, in turns, conjures up the view of *ukiyo* as a transient realm rather than a floating world of pleasure, thus, almost counterintuitively, taking us back to the medieval take on the word.

Ukiyobō's story represents only a small fraction of the entire text. A large segment of the prose consists of a series of nonnarrative fragments that deal with a variety of topics and are mixed with a handful of narrative passages. Ukiyobō might or might not make his appearance in them. While the verbal text gradually reduces the significance of Ukiyobō by turning him into a voice, the visual text in the form of half-folio illustrations clearly pictures him as the central character. The illustrations in the first two volumes faithfully depict him undertaking specific activities mentioned in the text. Even in the last three volumes, when he is presented as the voice offering nonnarrative contents, he still features in the illustrations as part of a group of people in conversation. Ukiyobō is conspicuous in the images with his black kimono and shaved head (fig. 7.1).[47] The reader is able to enjoy the gap between the verbal and the visual text. While the former discourages readers to focus on Ukiyobō, the latter reshapes the nature of *Ukiyo monogatari* as the story of Ukiyobō.

Literary scholars have harshly criticized (and still do) *Ukiyo monogatari* as something near to a literary aberration. In 1940, Noda Hisao wrote that *Ukiyo monogatari* was an attempt to move away from what he called "utilitarianism" (*jitsuri shugi*) toward an interest for life and human beings but fiercely condemned Asai Ryōi's inability to master psychological introspection and a unitary structure. This is seen as the ultimate failure in creating a novel in the modern definition of the term.[48] Writing almost sixty years after Noda, the literary scholar Taniwaki Masachika expresses the same disappointment, although Taniwaki is careful to avoid any mention of the term "novel." Rather, Taniwaki sees *Ukiyo monogatari* as an example of a "full-length prose structure" (*chōhenteki kōsō*) that attempts to harmonize all the traits of coeval prose (*kanazōshi no sho yōso*).[49] He does not directly express this view in the prefatory matter to his critical edition of *Ukiyo monogatari*, but it slowly emerges in the brief comments added at the end of or as part of the headnotes for each section. By the end of the first volume, Taniwaki bemoans the fact that Asai Ryōi's initial idea of creating a full-length narration of Ukiyobō's life is not realized. Taniwaki defines the structure as one that "crumbles" and points out the "disintegration" of the full-length prose to the point that the structure is lost.[50] Taniwaki even accuses Asai Ryōi of "sloppiness" in handling compositional strategies and of a "deficiency in creative powers."[51]

The negative judgment leveled by Japanese scholars at *Ukiyo monogatari* for more than fifty years is echoed in the assessment by Donald Keene, who viewed the plot as "primitive." He did acknowledge the text's "episodic nature," but

Figure 7.1 *Zoku Kashōki*, later undated edition of *Ukiyo monogatari*, vol. 3, 9r. Ukiyobō in his black kimono.

Author collection, Suzuran Bunko, Cambridge, U.K.

downplayed it as something done for "readers whose attention could not be kept very long."[52] He believed that the humorous and frivolous scenes were what enticed readers to buy the book in the first place. Daniel Lewis Barber is unreserved in speaking about these elements as "defects" of *Ukiyo monogatari*; however, he does praise the ability of *Ukiyo monogatari* to "incorporate some idea of the gaiety and light-heartedness of the time," which is assessed as a "development of Japanese fiction towards a more modern novel."[53] Richard Lane is willing to discuss *Ukiyo monogatari* outside a teleological quest for the modern novel. Lane consequently views the text as a series of "didactic and informative essays" that are "interspersed here and there between the stories."[54] Despite his recognition that "Ryōi succeeds in being both didactic and entertaining at the same time," Lane nonetheless categorizes the text as a "genre tale of didacticism."[55] The short essay that precedes the partial translation included in *Early Modern Japanese Literature: An Anthology, 1600–1900*, edited by Haruo Shirane, describes *Ukiyo monogatari* as a collection of "didactic narratives that have Confucian and Buddhist underpinnings and satirize contemporary society, particularly the *rōnin* and the pleasure-loving townsmen," while recognizing a "mixture of entertainment, humor, and moral purpose."[56] And yet the omission of this translation in the abridged edition of this anthology seems to suggest—at least to our busy undergraduate students—that *Ukiyo monogatari* can be dispensed with when discussing the canon of Japanese early modern literature. Shively casts a negative judgment over any didactic penchant: "His [Asai Ryōi's] moralizing overwhelms the plausibility of his main character."[57]

How would we interpret *Ukiyo monogatari* were we to let go of the search for a cohesive and coherent narrative built around Ukiyobō—or even simply a collection of narratives—and read the text instead through the lens of discontinuous writing and reading? *Ukiyo monogatari* offers a compelling miscellany of varied contents, very much like *Jigabachi monogatari*. It contains stories that echo the humorous nature of jestbooks, passages that share features of contemporary travel literature (the publishing genre of *meisho zukushi*, also referred to as *meisho michi no ki* or, more commonly, *meishoki*), and an imposing number of nonnarrative sections with teachings as well as critical reflections on society. What is absent, compared with *Jigabachi monogatari*, is an interest in practical sections designed as how-to manuals. This, however, does not alter the fact that *Ukiyo monogatari* is ultimately a pastiche of diverse contents that would have resonated in one way or another with disparate readers at the time. Ryōi worked as other authors of miscellanies, compiling a text that could engage his readers at multiple levels and that facilitated discontinuous reading.

Let's assume that as a reader I am after humorous stories as I like a good laugh. I can navigate the table of contents of *Ukiyo monogatari* and identify what I wish to read. In that case I would be struck by the title "Administering the Wrong Medication" and move on to section 2 of the second volume.[58] Ukiyobō is there, having just assumed the identity of a quack. The tale plays off what could be expected from a charlatan. After boasting about his abilities, he is summoned by a patient. He confidently takes the patient's pulse and then launches into a minilecture on medicine. His lack of medical knowledge, however, is exposed when the patient complains of fever and shivering (*gyahei* 瘧病). Ukiyobō, who has probably learned the medical art from popular books written in the vernacular and in phonetic script, confuses this word with the Buddhist term *gyatei* 揭諦. What follows is a series of misunderstandings that parody the closing lines of the *Hannya shingyō* (Heart Sutra). The reader is encouraged to savor the linguistic humor by getting the jokes as they unfold on the written page. Failing to do so spoils the full potential of this passage. Humor—not necessarily linguistic—is at the heart of other sections in *Ukiyo monogatari*: an account of how the penniless Ukiyobō dupes a seller of *mochi* cakes and runs away without paying; a dialogue over Ukiyobō's religion that degenerates into puns about his belonging to the "drinking religion"; and a tale about a quack named Tsūsai who mistakes the author's name of a medical treatise because he has seen only its vernacular version in phonetic script.[59] Ukiyobō features in many of these humorous stories, and in some he becomes the object of laughter.[60] The character of Ukiyobō is also witty, as episodes based on puns clearly demonstrate, and in his droll resourcefulness he is analogous to the monk Ikkyū.[61] The point I wish to make here is that whether Ukiyobō is present or not in these passages is of little concern to the reader. What we are offered are short humorous passages that can be enjoyed on their own, independent of the story of Ukiyobō. When read discontinuously, *Ukiyo monogatari* becomes just another of the many jestbooks circulating at the time.

Ukiyo monogatari is also a trove for any reader interested in travel literature.[62] As I see it, *Ukiyo monogatari* employs textual conventions of contemporary guidebooks to ground the physical reality of the geographical space while conceptualizing the same space in both intellectual and human terms. For instance, the descriptions of the visit to Kyoto as well as the journey from Kyoto to Osaka present a condensed encyclopedic knowledge of the physical space. We accompany Ukiyobō and partake in his journey, learning in the process forty-five place-names. In both cases the space is defined as a physical, navigable entity and exposes what Mary Elizabeth Berry calls the "basic urban anatomy."[63] *Ukiyo monogatari* does not aim at any sort of comprehensiveness, however, and in this light does not function as a street directory. Instead, it uses a basic geographical anatomy to offer readers useful itineraries that can be taken from the printed page and translated into action. These sections have the potential to invite readers to march into adventure. It is also noteworthy that in stylistic terms Asai Ryōi almost completely forgoes the *michiyukibun* style, a frequently encountered form of journey narration in 5-7-5-7 syllables that predates early modern literature.[64] Ryōi's choice to part from this established literary tradition possibly conveys a strong message that the poetic quality of the journey and the language employed to describe it are not of particular interest here. Rather, the reader is invited to enjoy a prose text delivered in a factual, practical, and useful manner: pleasure comes from the benefit derived when reading (efferently, not aesthetically) about a route that we might choose for a future trip.

While grounding the physical space as a practical itinerary through which one can travel, *Ukiyo monogatari* also conceives the same space in cultural terms, as the passage about Gojō Tenjin showcases:

> There is a shrine for the worship of Tenjin, on Gojō along the avenue Nishi no Tōin. It is said that this is where Sukunabikona no Mikami appeared. Poor and rich from the capital all come here once a year on the evening of the *setsubun* festival, when they buy *okera* and *mochi* and purify themselves against epidemic illnesses for the entire year. Visitors are rare during other times of the year. The main shrine is dilapidated, and I heard that they are collecting money to rebuild it.[65]

By presenting the history and folk rituals of a specific place, *Ukiyo monogatari* reads just like a tourist guidebook of the time. The striking similarity with the section titled Gojō no Tenjin in the 1658 *Kyō warabe* suggests that Asai Ryōi may even have drawn inspiration from this guide.[66] After all he was himself the author of such a guidebook with *Tōkaidō meishoki* (Record of famous places along the Tōkaidō; ca. 1658–1661).[67] Once we apply discontinuous reading to *Ukiyo monogatari* we appreciate that some of its sections function like any other practical guidebook of the period. For the reader, the pleasure is derived from the benefits of gathering practical information about the physical space and the enjoyment of textual segments that appropriate the popular genre of guidebooks. These segments halt the narrative. This is fine; ultimately our pleasure is derived from the very cracks in this broken narrative.

The narrative is also interrupted by a considerable number of nonnarrative parts, either entire sections or long segments within a section, and these represent the bulk of *Ukiyo monogatari*. The discontinuous nature of these passages allows for the diversity of contents. It is possible to identify a common thread that emerges from the various fragments. This common thread has nothing to do with the "plebeian ideal . . . of living the pleasure of the moment."[68] It rather transforms *Ukiyo monogatari* into what I would refer to as a mirror for politicians.

It is with the opening section of the fourth volume that the reader is instructed on the characteristics of the ideal statesman: "Those who rule a province or a county should have compassion for their people, they should be merciful to their farmers, and their government should be upright."[69] This statement appears after a long discussion on how all living beings, in particular human beings, differ from one another, a discourse that is deeply rooted in Buddhist and Confucian teachings. In contrast to this is the harsh reality of rulers who have no compassion, no mercy, and no sense of righteousness. The text continues by singling out the beastlike nature of local authorities: "Despite a bad harvest they demand the full payment of taxes. They show no compassion for those [retainers and farmers] who are forced to sell their wives and children to get some money. They feel no mercy for the fact that the imposition of taxes causes bankruptcy and the complete ruin of their people."[70] Scattered throughout *Ukiyo monogatari* are a number of passages that elaborate upon bad governance—bad governance not as a theoretical possibility but in the here and now. We are faced with a reality that clashes with the ideal, and in this regard *Ukiyo monogatari* is relentless in its harsh criticism of what is a deplorable state of affairs in the country. The text depicts the local administration as deeply inhuman and corrupt. The daimyo who employs Hyōtarō is in effect the embodiment of an evil politician, and he is interested in the following tactics:

> How to squeeze taxes out of the rice stipend given to retainers in such a way that half of it would come back; how to get money out of those farmers who had been forced to sell their wives and children, leaving behind their dwellings and running away. They would not be able to pay their annual tax and yet no allowance would be made. How to charge taxes on the farmers' personal belongings and how to levy additional tariffs on anything else they could. The basis for everything was simply greed. He knew no compassion, he had no understanding of the Way. There was no consultation apart from how to squeeze everything out of retainers and farmers.[71]

The result is that retainers are choked by debt and driven to starvation. The subsequent section compares these appallingly treated retainers to a horse bought because of its potential and yet so malnourished that it is incapable of functioning as a steed in battle. How can retainers effectively and efficiently support their masters if treated so dreadfully?[72]

In his advisory role, Hyōtarō personifies the individuals close to daimyo who do nothing but fuel such immoral behavior. Taniwaki Masachika, in one of the headnotes to his critical edition, finds fault with this negative depiction of Hyōtarō: while serving as a preparation for his tonsure, it is at odds with the redemption of the character in the subsequent volumes. This is seen by Taniwaki as a shortcoming in the construction of a full-length narrative.[73] This passage can be evaluated differently, however, if we acknowledge that Ryōi is playing with miscellarian prose. This fragment focuses on a depiction of what is interpreted as corrupt government, and the character of Hyōtarō is used effectively to showcase the corruption of not only a daimyo but also an entire administration that allows the inhumane treatment of its people. Whether this accords with the protagonist's overall identity is of little concern.

Ukiyo monogatari therefore depicts a local government motivated by greed, what elsewhere in the text is referred to as the vice of money (*zeni no kuse*):

> Those in high social positions [*kunshi*] are not at all without greed. [In principle,] they take what they should take and refrain from taking what they should not. There are those, however, who have a habit [*kuse*] of grabbing what is not their due, motivated by greed and employing coercion. They are petty people who have no understanding of the Way. If these kinds of people become daimyo, peasants will be squeezed to the point that they will be ruined. And if these kinds of people become senior councillors [*otona*], attendants [*shuttō*], or magistrates [*bugyō*], personal interest will drive their unscrupulous behavior, and this will perpetuate juridical injustice. This is the cause of a country's despair.[74]

Retainers and farmers reduced to poverty, families destroyed, and social injustice—these are the immediate, deleterious outcomes of a local administration motivated by greed. There is another, further social issue imputable to bad government, and that is the extortionate prices of commodities. Following the comparison between retainers and a badly treated horse in section 8 in the first volume the voice of the third-person narrator explains the unbearable inflation that is crippling Edo:

> During the year they are required to spend in Kamakura, the retainers are forced into extreme poverty. They end up depleting all their assets and are reduced to being penniless.... Kamakura is buzzing with all sorts of people coming and going from throughout the entire country, and for this reason the price of rice, firewood, food, and drink is incredibly high. People's livelihoods are consequently in jeopardy. And this broad world appears all of a sudden as small and dangerous as a bridge made with only one log—this is how people live.[75]

The reference to Kamakura might appear incongruous, particularly when mentioned together with the practice of alternate attendance (*sankin kōtai*) introduced by the Tokugawa shogunate in 1635 that forced daimyo to live in Edo during alternate years. As Taniwaki Masachika opines, we need to read this as a form of camouflage put in place to avoid any clash with the censors.[76] This would suggest that the author or publisher of *Ukiyo monogatari* was conscious of the controversial nature of parts of the text. At the same time I would like to echo what I have already noted for *Jigabachi monogatari*. In the passages examined so far, the attack on the local government is relentless and carried out in heated tones. It is not so much a satire as an overt criticism of politicians. Would a device as simple as naming Kamakura in lieu of Edo be enough to deflect the censor's sharp eye from the core message of *Ukiyo monogatari*'s criticism? If so, we might question how sharp the censors' eyes were!

The last passage quoted here brings in a new social issue: overpriced goods, beginning with rice, are seen as a major social problem. And here what I call the rice problem becomes relevant.

In the second volume, after a description of how to travel from Kyoto to Osaka and before a visit to Tennōji (section 4), the narrator places Ukiyobō in dialogue with a rice wholesaler as a means to launch a fairly lengthy condemnation of the high price of rice. Yet the passage touches only tangentially on the avarice of merchants and points the finger instead at the local administration. Ukiyobō quotes a Chinese poem, glossed with a quasi-interlinear translation, that sets the stage for a discussion of government storehouses (*kansō*).[77] He then explains the underlying motive of a greedy local government. Daimyo wish to make huge profits from their rice and therefore refrain from selling it; the rice piles up in their storehouses, each grain becoming as precious as a jewel. This prompts a vicious cycle, a consequence of which is that increasingly greater quantities of rice are left unsold. Rice accumulates, people starve, and the mice rejoice. Ukiyobō quotes another Chinese poem to reinforce his point, but this time he additionally speaks about the issue of bad crops. Drought, flood, and insects ruin the crops, and yet the local administration continues to charge exorbitant levies. While there is ample rice being stockpiled in the daimyo warehouses, it is not being circulated; a remark that recalls what we saw in *Jigabachi monogatari* and *Yakushi tsūya monogatari* (in chapter 6). Ukiyobō is strident in his accusations, comparing landlords to rice weevils. It is only at the very end of the passage that merchants are brought into the discussion, with Ukiyobō accusing them of rejoicing as they benefit from drought, flood, and typhoons because they can increase the price of their rice. They are, as Donald Keene described, "rapacious merchants," even though it is difficult to agree with Keene's assessment in seeing *Ukiyo monogatari* as nothing more than an echo "of the Confucian philosophers who despised the money-grubbing of the townsmen."[78] The message in this section, as in the others probed earlier, is clear: it is the local administration and its greed that are the root of the problem. Avaricious merchants may not be different, but they are in second place. This remark equally problematizes the view that ronin and pleasure-loving townsmen are the main object of satire in *Ukiyo monogatari*.[79]

A similar rhetoric is adopted regarding the rapaciousness of merchants in section 1 in the fourth volume that began my analysis of the political discourse in *Ukiyo monogatari*. Merchants wish for poor harvests since they can set their prices with impunity and without compassion or pity, ultimately dictating the fate of others. Yet merchants are not entirely discredited. There are those who go into business with little capital and are unable to turn a profit and so are vulnerable to the same fate as farmers: "They sell their children, they part from their spouse, and become beggars."[80] In other words, it is not a question of social status, rather one of greed, and this turns people into tigers and wolves. Be it daimyo or merchant, greed pushes them to act in the same way. The text, however, is more sympathetic toward merchants, who are given the benefit of the doubt, while daimyo are not. In the end it is the current age that is to blame: "This is not the fault of merchants. It is because those who happen to be born in this age are endowed with little luck."[81] The question that a peasant asks in *Jigabachi monogatari*—"What kind of age do we live in?"—resonates here, but why the entire age is at fault is not explained, nor does the reader understand why Heaven does not favor those born at this time. This leaves the reader to speculate upon the cause most likely to be playing the greatest part, including the government.

Ukiyo monogatari does not shy away from identifying problems in other sectors of society. From this standpoint, the text in its entirety offers fragments that cover social issues in addition to bad governance. The reader learns, for example, that there are genuine Buddhist monks who have realized the impermanence of things (and therefore enlightenment) and strive to assist others along this path, and fake Buddhist monks who took the tonsure only to make a living.[82] Readers may recall a similar criticism of money-grubbing Buddhists in chapter 3. The same applies to samurai. Sincere samurai possess qualities of filial piety, loyalty, compassion, and a love for truth; disingenuous samurai are the opposite and are considered worse because they mask their shortcomings through the use of flattery.[83]

Ukiyo monogatari also informs the reader that there are samurai so obsessed with the tea ceremony that they fall into financial ruin through the purchase of items for it.[84] Eccentric dandies (*kankatsumono*), plentiful among the ranks of samurai and townsmen, are depicted as foolish in a passage that borders on the satirical. These figures are pictured as conceited and arrogant until they meet a person with actual power, at which point they become coyly submissive.[85] The author Asai Ryōi is not the first to write about human and societal flaws. Taniwaki Masachika points out, for instance, that these sections are based on *Kashōki* (Record that makes laughter possible [see chapter 1]). Ryōi's familiarity with this work is clear from the fact that just a few years earlier, in 1660, he had issued a commentary on it titled *Kashōki hyōban* (*Record That Makes Laughter Possible*: An evaluation). Ryōi's reuse of *Kashōki* is telling: it so aptly expresses the malaise with the current age that Ryōi chooses to borrow it almost verbatim rather than crafting his own prose. Savvy early modern publishers did not overlook this link between *Ukiyo monogatari* and *Kashōki*, as evinced by an edition of *Ukiyo monogatari* published probably in 1757 under the title *Zoku Kashōki* (*Record That Makes Laughter Possible*: A sequel).[86] The Kichimonjiya family of Osaka and Edo used blocks originally cut probably by Matsue Ichirobee and then acquired by Taharaya Heibee 田原屋平兵衛 (dates unknown) and changed the title to Zoku Kashōki. The new title clearly underscored its nature as a miscellany dealing with social issues, just like *Kashōki*.

In addition to supplying social criticism, *Ukiyo monogatari* provides readers with practical teachings, as in the case of greed, which is portrayed as an undesirable trait. The advice proffered in *Ukiyo monogatari* is to accept one's own limitations. Section 3 of the fourth volume, titled "Knowing When One Has Enough," begins with the humorous tale of a man who is so inebriated that he falls on the way home; once home he collapses onto his bed and he is scolded by his wife.[87] Holding this man up as an example, who ultimately becomes "consumed by alcohol," Ukiyobō's voice is adopted to offer a long nonnarrative passage about how we should be content with what we have and not desire more. The similarities with the philosophy of life discussed in chapters 3 and 6 are striking. The opening section of the fifth volume reinforces this message in an account about frogs who pray to the bodhisattva Kannon for the ability to walk like human beings.[88] Their wish is fulfilled, but the result is tragically comic: they are able to walk on two legs, but their eyes are placed at the back of their heads. Ukiyobō's voice warns readers that human beings are no different, and in a lengthy passage that calls for an orderly, unchanging society they are told that they should be content with their lots in life. The irreverence leveled against local government in other sections in *Ukiyo monogatari* is now tempered with a more conciliatory attitude that echoes the sumptuary laws mentioned in chapter 6. The inclusion of conflicting views in the same textual space finds parallels in *Jigabachi monogatari* and is one of the characteristics of discontinuous writing. Section 9 in the second volume demonstrates how competing views can blend without obvious clashing.[89] Here, the text quotes the famous Chinese politician and scholar Sima Guang 司馬光 (J. Shiba Onkō 司馬温公 [1019–1086]) on the Six Causes for Regret (*rikukai no mei*).

> First. Senior councillors, attendants, and magistrates succumb to greed, act according to selfish desires, perpetrate injustices, promote evil, and cause peasants to suffer. They receive not only repeated complaints from everyone but also heavenly punishment, struck by all sorts of catastrophes and ruin. At that point they will regret their actions. Second. The rich indulge in luxury and deplete their fortunes as they wish, without realizing how much they are spending. In this way they are acting against the will of Heaven; they will be abandoned on this earth, end up penniless, and ruined. At that point they will regret their actions. Third. Those who are proud of being wealthy flatter daimyo and are taken under the wings of senior councillors, magistrates, and assistant headmen. Exploiting their power, they disregard laws and ordinances, they are reckless, and they belittle those at the top of society [*kōgi*]. They will regret their

actions when they are finally prosecuted. Fourth. When one is young and in the prime of life, one does not study and neglects to learn what is required. Such people embarrass themselves on public occasions. It is when they have aged that they will regret their actions. Fifth. One drinks too much, loses composure, speaks nonsense, and behaves improperly. Once sober, these people will regret their actions. Sixth. When becoming ill, one does not take prompt action while the illness is minor. It is when the condition worsens that one's actions are regretted.[90]

This passage condenses, to a degree, the nature of *Ukiyo monogatari*. The list proffers a series of teachings, ranging from a discussion of politics to practical advice. *Ukiyo monogatari* as a whole achieves the same: its fragmentary nature presents readers with a variety of topics that move between harmless didacticism to polemical social criticism. The beauty of *Ukiyo monogatari* lies in its plurality, I contend.

A twentieth-century critic such as Donald Keene, who I might argue has little faith in the seventeenth-century reader, expects this to be "a work intended primarily for entertainment" and presumes that readers "found his [Ryōi's] criticism ... the least interesting part of the stories."[91] And yet early modern book-trade catalogues list this work under the publishing genre of *kana washo*, thereby positioning *Ukiyo monogatari* in the same intellectual space as *Kashōki*, *Mi no kagami*, *Rihi kagami*, and many other works discussed in the present volume. However, to define *Ukiyo monogatari* as a purely—or primarily—didactic work would be misleading since it contains narrative sections that are characteristic of jestbooks and nonnarrative segments that echo touristic guidebooks, as I have demonstrated. And while it is true that book-trade catalogues of the period pigeonholed *Ukiyo monogatari*, today we are no longer constrained by such categorizations and do not need to compartmentalize the text. We can appreciate the miscellarian nature of this example of discontinuous writing. Nothing prevents us from reading *Ukiyo monogatari* as a tale of Ukiyobō's life, from beginning to end; after all, the illustrations suggest this as a possible reading. Yet the analysis in this chapter has established how narrow a teleological quest for a novel centered on a fictional protagonist and his psychological depth can be. While the figure of Ukiyobō is certainly a part of the text, he is also used as a narrative tool to encourage the development of diverse discourses. We are exhorted to enjoy every twist and turn in what is constructed as a multifaceted text.

A Harmonious Collection of Parts: *Chikusai*

Few early modern fictional characters had a literary career as successful as Chikusai.[92] Appearing in popular literature as early as the 1620s, the character of Chikusai surfaced in a variety of genres and media until the Meiji period.[93]

The rich intertextual serialization ignited by the eponymously named book *Chikusai* is rivaled by only a few other texts. What was the secret behind the success of *Chikusai*, one may ask. I contend that the answer lies in a story line that pauses to allow for the insertion of new materials that, in turn, enable the book to become something unexpected. The story line is at once unified but diverse, comprising an array of narrative fragments. It sets precise expectations on the identity of the character and on how his story might unfold; then quite abruptly the story line stops and the text evolves into something else as the protagonist takes on a new persona or even disappears. Expectations are raised, then dashed, but the reader is invited to enjoy such moments not as narrative oddities rather as moments replete with narrative resonance. It is precisely because *Chikusai* is filled with diverse narrative possibilities and is characterized by a protagonist who has multiple personas (quack, traveler, and a gifted poet of mad verse, or *kyōka*) that this text became the source for numerous sequels and adaptations.

Eve Tavor Bannet's thought-provoking discussion of eighteenth-century English novels assists our understanding of how we can approach *Chikusai*. Bannet outlines two modalities in what she calls "the pleasures of curiosity," in that the novel

> fed the *purposive curiosity* which followed a character into the hidden recesses of private life and shadowed him/her through the events determining his/her fate to their unknown conclusion; and they fed the *digressive curiosity* which delighted in variety, multiplicity, and whatever strange, uncommon, new or chance-met characters, narratives and events that were encountered along the way. This may also be why novels proved so popular with readers—and so unstoppable by philosophical critics—and why they lived on, constantly renewing themselves, long after other genres went out of fashion.[94]

On the one hand we as the readers are moved by purposive curiosity, drawn by a desire to discover Chikusai's fate. Nothing stops us from reading *Chikusai* continuously, from beginning to end. But a more effective reading strategy for anyone moved by purposive curiosity would be to skip passages unrelated to Chikusai and his story in order to learn as quickly and economically as possible what happens to the protagonist. This form of discontinuous reading ignores variety and favors a single story line that progresses teleologically. In other words, discontinuous reading allows us to experience *Chikusai* as a coherent piece of continuous writing. On the other hand, the construction of *Chikusai* as a collection of different parts, as I explain in the following, fuels digressive curiosity. When the story line pauses to introduce a noncontiguous element or passage, the reader is attracted by the novelty and is ready to almost forget about the main character while enjoying the unexpected twists. In this case the reader exercises continuous reading, which, almost counterintuitively, fosters appreciation of *Chikusai* as a piece of discontinuous writing. This can be retrospectively said to be true also in the case of *Ukiyo monogatari*, even though we must acknowledge a higher degree in its miscellarian nature than *Chikusai*, as this section seeks to explain.

It might be instructive to outline the publication history of *Chikusai* before I undertake a close reading. The author is thought to be the physician Isoda Dōya 磯田道冶 (also known as Tomiyama Dōya 富山道冶 [1585–1634]).[95] Yet the identity of the author is of comparatively little significance in the age of the collective author (as described in chapter 2). *Chikusai* could be, and was, appropriated by later publishers, undergoing not only cosmetic changes but also important structural transformations. The first two documented editions were produced in movable type in the Genna era (1615–1624), and apart from minor differences they are the same text. At some point in the Kan'ei era (1624–1644) the first woodblock edition in two volumes was published anonymously in Kyoto. Several half-folio illustrations were added, and of more interest here is the interpolation of a lengthy narrative passage of twenty-three folios (out of eighty-one) that signal a brand-new story line completely unrelated to Chikusai. This and other changes in the contents flag a willingness on the part of the publisher(s) to alter the source text into one that loses textual unity in favor of textual multiplicity. *Chikusai* as one story becomes *Chikusai* with multiple stories.

This new textual identity must have charmed contemporary readers since it was retained in later editions.[96] In the Kanbun era (1661–1673) the text surfaced probably in Edo. New double-page illustrations were inserted, which replaced those in previous editions and are notable for the richness in detail. In the Enpō era (1673–1681) Urokogataya had a new set of blocks cut, a sign of the title's continuing popularity, and had Hishikawa Moronobu, one of the most popular book artists of the time, illustrate the work. The existence of a 1683 facsimile of this edition, also an Urokogataya publication, testifies to *Chikusai* as a best seller. The text, in three or four volumes, was sold under three variant titles: the printed title slip *Kudari Chikusai banashi* (The story of Chikusai moving east) appears on the copy in the Richard Lane Collection (Honolulu), that of *Chikusai kyōka banashi* (The story of Chikusai's mad poems) is in the copy housed in Tōyō Bunko, Tokyo, and that of *Chikusai shokoku monogatari* (Tales of Chikusai in the different provinces) on the cover of the copy in the Akagi Bunko. This was patently a clever marketing strategy, but at the same time the phrasing of these variant titles reflects the diverse nature of the contents of *Chikusai*. It can be seen as a text that offers a travelogue from Kyoto to Edo (*kudari*), that can be read as a collection of short stories constructed around humorous poems (*kyōka*), or viewed as a series of narratives concerning different provinces (*shokoku monogatari*).[97] The publication history of *Chikusai* underlines the popularity of this text throughout the seventeenth century. It also demonstrates how authority gradually shifted from authors to publishers, thereby confirming that seventeenth-century authorship was more collective than individual. More germane to this chapter, however, is that the most popular edition was the Kan'ei-era woodblock edition that reshaped *Chikusai* as a seemingly unitary ensemble of diverse narrative materials.

What parts made up the richly diverse tapestry of *Chikusai* and how are they organized to appear, and be readable, as one story? Different from *Ukiyo monogatari*, *Chikusai* is fashioned not as a miscellany of singularly titled sections but as a narrative structure known in literary jargon as a chiastic or palistrophic structure, which presents a series of ideas and then repeats them in the opposite order. The following shows how all of *Chikusai* exhibits a symmetrically reversible pattern:

> A(1): Chikusai decides to leave Kyoto and his old life (life-changing turn of events)
>> B(1): Chikusai and his servant, Niraminosuke, visit Kyoto (sightseeing of urban space)
>>> C(1): Chikusai and Niraminosuke travel from Kyoto to Nagoya (travel between two places)
>>>> D: Chikusai settles down temporarily in Nagoya and opens a medical practice
>>> C(2): Chikusai and Niraminosuke travel from Nagoya to Edo (travel between two places)
>> B(2): Chikusai and Niraminosuke visit Edo (sightseeing of urban space)
> A(2): Chikusai starts his new life in Edo (life-changing turn of events)

This structure is fairly widespread in Western literature, and recent studies have demonstrated its presence also in old Chinese literature.[98] This means that at least for us, Western readers in the twenty-first century, *Chikusai* appears on the surface as a fairly comfortable text.

The schematization here not only exemplifies how a palistrophe functions but also sketches the main plot. It begins in media res with Chikusai being described as a poor quack who feels alienated in Kyoto and therefore sees little benefit in remaining there. This is, quite clearly, an intertextual reference to what is known as the *azuma kudari* section in *Ise monogatari*, where Narihira travels to the east. Chikusai consults with his servant, Niraminosuke, about what to do and decides to move to the east in search of a better place to earn a living. The reader follows Chikusai in order to find out what transpires once he reaches the eastern provinces, and in the process we partake in his multiple identity as a traveler, a quack, and a poet gifted in *kyōka*. Chikusai visits different places, but very little happens to him that occasions any change in his personal story. Even when he works as a pseudodoctor in Nagoya, nothing really happens. The poem that closes the text leads us to believe that Chikusai will resume his medical profession in Edo, with hopes for a better outcome: "When encountering / such an upright age/ as upright as a giant black bamboo even a quack / can be filled with hope" (*kuretake no / sugu naru miyo ni / ainureba / yabu kusushi made / tanomoshiki kana*).[99]

While the basic structure of *Chikusai* appears compact, a closer inspection reveals the multifaceted nature of the text. I would like to start with probing part B(1), when Chikusai and Niraminosuke visit Kyoto. In this segment, which constitutes all of the first volume and continues into the first six folios of the second volume in the woodblock-printed edition of the Kan'ei era, Chikusai's significance as a character is minimal. The figure of Chikusai is in fact employed to introduce humorous *kyōka* poetry and embedded stories in the narrative, in which he functions either as an active agent in the poetical creation or as a passive observer in witnessing other people's stories. For the reader, the pleasure is not so much in following Chikusai's story as in enjoying humorous verses or reading about the lives of people other than Chikusai. At the same time, it would be misleading to treat this section of *Chikusai* as a guidebook, as suggested by Richard Lane, and more recently by Sumie Jones and Adam L. Kern, or what Laurence Bresler describes as "chapters of Baedeker."[100] A list of famous places (*meisho*) does appear in this section, and yet we learn almost nothing about each of these celebrated beauty spots.

Chikusai's initial foray in Kyoto exemplifies how the text does not revolve around Chikusai or the places he visits:

They [Chikusai and Niraminosuke] crossed the Sanjō Bridge, walked through Gionbayashi, and went first to see Kiyomizudera. They struck the gong and prayed with fervor: "O merciful Kannon, don't forget your promise to protect us all. It is said that you, The Thousand-Armed Kannon [Senju Kannon], have promised to make even withered trees blossom—we are full of confidence in our future. If we fall ill, please cure us quickly." He composed a few verses:

Chikai nao	Because of your promise,
Kiyomizudera no	like the waterfall
taki no ito no	at Kiyomizudera,
kurikaeshitsutsu	ceaseless
inoru yuku sue	are our prayers for our future.

Chikusai prostrated himself before Kannon. He said, "It is said that you appear in the world in different forms and that you protect human beings, in particular, from the calamities caused by the anger of kings [*ōnan*]" and then chanted the prayer: "If someone is going to die on an execution site because of a king's fury, then confiding in Kannon's strength will foil the executioner's sword."[101]

In this passage Chikusai and the temple of Kiyomizu are of little significance; instead, the focus of the passage is on Kannon and this bodhisattva's miraculous powers. Chikusai quotes verbatim an incantation that deals with the Kannon's pledge to save all human beings that is included in the *Kannon-gyō* (Kannon Sutra). Chikusai's voice is used to allude to one of the Seven Calamities—namely, that caused by the anger of kings—and is followed by the incantation. This brings to mind the 1661 *Kannon-gyō wadan shō* discussed in chapter 3. Interestingly, in *Chikusai* the incantation is given only in *on'yomi* readings and entirely in hiragana, which permits readers with different literacy levels to vocalize it. A comparison with the passage about Kiyomizu Temple in the guidebook *Kyō warabe* indicates how this fragment in *Chikusai* does not attempt to give readers any guidebook-like prose.[102] *Kyō warabe* mentions Kannon's miraculous powers, and the narrator's request to Kannon to intervene in his life accords with *Chikusai*. However, *Kyō warabe* provides extensive information on the origins of this temple, the deities enshrined there, the geography of the temple compound, and its main festival. All this is systematically missing in *Chikusai*.

The visit to Toribe Plain, Toyokuni Shrine, Daibutsu Hall, Sanjūsangendō, Seiganji, Izumi Shikibu's tomb, and Takoyakushi are noteworthy for the obvious lack of descriptive details. Each place is reduced to merely a name used for Chikusai to compose humorous verses. For example, *Kyō warabe* explains in some detail why Eifukuji is called Takoyakushi, but in *Chikusai* all that is presented is a comic poem: "O, holy Yakushi! / I thought you were holding / a lapis lazuli vessel / but when looked at closely / it is an octopus pot" (*Namu Yakushi / ruri no tsubo to zo / omoishi ni / yoku yoku mireba / takotsubo zo kashi*).[103] Chikusai's *kyōka* gently pokes fun at the standard iconography of the Buddha Yakushi, with the vessel that the Buddha generally holds in his left hand being recast as a pot used to catch octopuses. Ultimately, nothing is learned about Chikusai or Takoyakushi. The inclusion of humorous poems makes this section of *Chikusai* analogous to collections of stories constructed around *kyōka* (mad poems), such as the 1669 *Inu Hyakunin isshu* mentioned in chapter 2, or the well-known minimal parody of *Ise monogatari* titled *Nise monogatari* (The fake *Tales of Ise*).[104]

To view part B(1) of *Chikusai* only as a narrative exploitation of Chikusai and his visit to Kyoto to introduce *kyōka* would be, however, reductive and misleading. At Kitano Shrine, in fact, *Chikusai* becomes something else. The location is used as a stage to display the types of leisurely activities, as follows:

1. People in carriages and allusion to stories of love at first sight narrated in *Genji monogatari*

2. A session of *renga* poetry followed by the master's didactic discourse
3. A *kemari* (kickball) match
4. A lively party with popular songs sung to the accompaniment of shamisen
5. A Noh performance
6. Gambling
7. Incense ceremony
8. A sumo match
9. A party of women serving at court
10. The visit of these women to a Buddhist temple and their conversation with a lustful monk
11. The infatuation of a rough man for a young and refined samurai

Chikusai plays almost an irrelevant role in these vignettes. Although he composes a few *kyōka*, he acts mainly as an *ante litteram* camera—that is, he is the focalizer of the tale. Each of the eleven sketches of the passage at Kitano Shrine commences with the third-person narrator recounting how Chikusai is now looking in a different direction, and the prose moves on to a description of what he sees.[105] In all but the last two vignettes the third-person narrator, and the reader, knows what Chikusai knows, can see or hear what Chikusai sees and hears, and perceives what Chikusai perceives. Chikusai's point of view is ubiquitous, and the text employs what is known as internal focalization. This, in turn, gives the impression that *Chikusai* has transformed into what Laurence Bresler describes as a catalogue of "the many varieties of recreation taking place in the perennial holiday atmosphere of the shrine."[106]

Chikusai is, however, much more than a cataloguing of recreations. Each vignette suspends the main narration; Chikusai, after all, is the lens through which we view the scenes. Some slip into didactic and informational nonnarrative snippets, as exemplified by the passage on *renga* (no. 2), where we peruse a nonnarrative speech delivered by a *renga* master that explains the fundamentals of this poetic form and echoes some of the ethical teachings investigated in chapter 3.[107] The tenth and eleventh sketches further problematize Bresler's idea of a catalogue of recreation. Earlier, in the ninth sketch, Chikusai catches sight of a party of young ladies-in-waiting, and together with Chikusai we hear them singing the latest popular songs. There is also a woman decrying the fact that ladies-in-waiting are so busy with their court duties that they have no time to devote to Buddhism. This prompts the idea to go to an unspecified temple and speak with a monk.[108] At this point, when the ninth vignette moves into the tenth, Chikusai completely disappears, even in the role as a focalizer. The text suggests that Chikusai does not follow the women to the temple since at the end of the tenth sketch he is still at Kitano, about to guide the reader in another direction. Chikusai's place is taken by a third-person narrator who, for the first time in the text, becomes what I call an omnipresent narrator.[109] The narrator directs us to the temple, where he introduces us to the monk, who is the real protagonist of this vignette.[110] We learn not only what the monk is wearing but also where and why he bought his clothes, with a narrator who starts intimating we are dealing with a lustful man obsessed with women. When the monk invites the ladies-in-waiting to his bedchamber, we expect that the story will turn into a short, humorous passage that satirizes Buddhist monks trapped in carnal passion. And yet for almost five folios the narration is suspended to allow for the insertion of a lengthy sermon delivered by the monk. In the same vein as the *kana hōgo* examined in chapter 3, the monk's detailed sermon offers multiple teachings centered on the place of women in Buddhism. The serious tone of this nonnarrative didactic passage is softened by the mention of *Ise monogatari* as if it were a legitimate Buddhist source and functions to direct the sermon back to the story of the lustful monk. He suggests, in fact, that women can recover from their piteous nature only by cherishing mercy and compassion, and then pushes this legitimate Buddhist concept beyond any orthodox interpretation to mean that a woman should never refuse a man's advances. In response to the question about whether he would accept a woman's courtship, he replies, "If bad actions are done by a saintly man they will ultimately be good."[111] The oldest woman soon grasps the monk's true aim and promises to return in the middle of the night to satisfy his needs, including his laundry. Only at that point does Chikusai reappear, leaving the reader with another humorous *kyōka*: "The laundry / in a tub / will be washed; the law explained / amid stinky /humors" (*sendaku wa / hidarai nite ya / arauramu / toku nori made mo / namagusaki kana*).[112]

These ten folios of *Chikusai* are an impressive example of a prose text that continuously, and unexpectedly, shifts and turns, thriving in its multiplicity. Chikusai's visit to Kyoto stops to allow room for the depiction of the culture of leisure staged at Kitano Shrine. This description is then jettisoned, together with Chikusai, to introduce a short narrative centered on a lustful monk. This comic, risqué short story is very much in keeping with jestbooks and develops fully after a fairly long and serious Buddhist sermon as a *kana hōgo* would have done. Readers could enjoy all this as a pastiche of various textual elements but could also decide to skip these ten folios, since they do not, after all, tell us anything about Chikusai. The reader could equally choose to read this story as a standalone text. It could be read aloud or recounted to friends as an independent narrative or could even be used as a sermon to expound teachings to women. The organization of the prose effectively facilitated a multiplicity of readings.

Before departing Kitano, Chikusai prays to the Heian-period courtier-poet Sugawara no Michizane to protect him from false accusations once in Edo. The mention of the eastern provinces hints that the prose might shift to the main topic of Chikusai's travel from Kyoto to Edo. This hope—at least the hope of the reader moved by purposive curiosity—is yet again frustrated: at this point

Chikusai is intrigued by the sad news of a man trying to commit suicide on the grounds of Kurodani Temple. In woodblock-printed editions beginning with the Kan'ei era the text takes an unwonted twist at this point, and in the following twenty-three folios the reader is thrown into a dramatic tale of male-male love (*nanshoku*).[113] Once again we have an omnipresent narrator who knows everything about the story—its past, present, and future—and busies himself recounting the emotionally gripping story of an unidentified samurai from Harima and a samurai named Sasaki Uneme. Why would a reader decide to come to terms with a passage that forgets about Chikusai's story despite the fact that it occupies almost one-fourth of the text? Three are the reasons. First, this love story functions as a superb rewriting of the *Usuyuki* master plot, which I have explored in chapter 5, moving it from different-sex to same-sex love.[114] Second, it gives readers what was trendy in the book market. *Nanshoku*, in fact, sold in the hundreds during the first half of the seventeenth century.[115] It did so by moving away from the medieval interest in male-male love in temples and opening it up to the world of the warrior.[116] Third, as research done by Shibayama Hajime and Hanada Fujio suggest, it might have been a story based on a piece of sensational news, thus feeding an interest in what I refer to, in the previous chapter, as present-mindedness.[117] As readers we have at least two options when reaching this passage. We can choose to read the story, momentarily forgetting about the traveler and quack Chikusai, or skip it in order to remain focused on the figure of Chikusai. Both readings are somehow discontinuous—the first disconnects us from the main narration of Chikusai's story, making it feel like a form of discontinuous writing, whereas the second is more discontinuous as we act like Barthes's fly. Both readings are possible and equally pleasurable. The pleasure differs, though. In case we decide to enter into this love story, we are engaged emotionally, with a tragic story of love and death, but also cognitively, with a narrative that plays with and reinforces literary tropes and publishing fashions. In case we skip it, we fulfill our desire to stick to Chikusai and his adventures.

The main narrative resumes with Chikusai meeting an old acquaintance and Chikusai's servant, Niraminosuke, urging him to continue his journey. Chikusai's travel in parts C(1), C(2), and B(2) differs once again from commercial guidebooks (*meishoki*) or road directories (*dōchūki*), despite the fact that both Western and Japanese scholars generally place *Chikusai* into one of these two categories. Chikusai journeys to actual sites, and in this regard the narration was potentially a source for information on the seventeenth-century space. I would argue, however, that what is meaningful in *Chikusai* is its textual, not its physical and geographical, nature. In other words, the space through which Chikusai travels is merely a pretext to play with the literary tradition, in particular with the *michiyukibun* style and the topos of the *azuma kudari*.

Unlike *Ukiyo monogatari*, *Chikusai* employs the *michiyukibun* style: a poetic prose constructed on the basis of the rhythm of 5-7 syllables and relying heavily on pivot words. Nevertheless, it transforms the imagery called up by the pivot words and therefore presents a skillful revisioning of the *michiyukibun* style. How? For example, we read, "Crossing Sanjō Bridge at <u>Awata</u> they <u>met</u> a sick person. When they inquired about the illness at <u>Seki Temple</u> [*Sekidera* 関寺] they learned that it was a <u>cough</u> [*seki* 咳]."[118] In mentioning Awata-guchi *Chikusai* follows the tradition of the *michiyukibun* style and employs the sound *awa* to conjure associations with the verb "to meet" (*au* 会ふ, conjugated as *awa*). What is dramatically different is the object normally associated with this verb, which traditionally would refer to meeting a lover. Here, however, Chikusai does not meet a lover but someone who is ill. Similarly the word *seki* is used as a pivot word, but the connection between the temple known as Sekidera and the cough would have undermined the poetic expectations inherent in the traditional *michiyukibun* style. This technique is applied to shape the journey from Awata-guchi to Moriyama as dominated by vocabulary related to medicine and the stretch from Moriyama to Hagiwara as eliciting the image of a pitiful traveler. *Chikusai* is not intended to undermine the *michiyukibun* style and its conventions. In fact, they are made the most of in the work, and what might have been a rather dull travelogue is now enlivened to become an example of humorous literature. The space ceases to be a geographical category and becomes instead a literary, textual entity that is further enriched by a human dimension. In effect, the space becomes an extension of Chikusai the quack and the wretched traveler.

Humor remains the key for appreciating part B(2). This time the humor lies in the parodic treatment of the *azuma kudari* topos, which, as mentioned, is associated with *Ise monogatari*.[119] Chikusai's journey from Nagoya to Edo, as well as his visit to Edo, morphs into a journey of cultural memory. Titular allusions (e.g., *Narihira shū*, "that tale") and onomastic allusions (e.g., Ariwara, known as the "man of the past," "that man of the past," Narihira) punctuate the prose and reveal the source text. The juxtaposition of *Ise monogatari* and *Chikusai* is reinforced through quotations that provide verbatim citations or paraphrases of the source text. This is not a simple overlapping of Narihira and Chikusai, however, as there is a twist that leads to the creation of a trivialized and almost burlesque duplicate of Narihira: Narihira the lover is turned into Chikusai the lonely, miserable traveler. For instance, in the source text at Utsu Narihira meets an itinerant priest and gives him a message for his beloved, but Chikusai encounters no one and has no reason to send a message because he has left no lover behind.[120] Moreover, Narihira addresses the *miyakodori* (bird of the capital) in an effort to procure information about his lover in Kyoto, while Chikusai addressed the same bird, pleading that it would not disclose his pathetic state to his acquaintances back in the capital.[121]

Chikusai's travels, as well as his identity as a traveler, did not go unnoticed in the seventeenth century. The ultimate homage is seen in the work of the poet Matsuo Bashō 松尾芭蕉 (1644–1694) in the prose passage and *hokku* (seventeen-syllable opening verse) that begin the 1684 poetic sequence titled *Fuyu no hi* (The winter day) and composed for a haikai session organized for him in Nagoya:

> The rains of the long journey have torn my hat, and my coat has become crumpled in the daily storms. Accustomed as I am to extreme poverty, I feel sorry for myself. Suddenly remembering that master of mad verse who traveled long ago to this province, I wrote:

> | *kyōku kogarashi no* | Mad verse: in the withering gusts |
> | *mi wa Chikusai ni* | a wanderer—how much like Chikusai |
> | *nitaru kana* | I have become![122] |

The city of Nagoya, where Bashō visited in 1684, had associations with Chikusai, as he spends almost three years there (part D). The allusion to Chikusai in Bashō's *hokku* suggests that by the end of the seventeenth century *Chikusai* had successfully become part of the collective memory. The perception of *Chikusai* as an example of travel writing is likewise confirmed by the 1685 *Chikusai ryōji no hyōban* (*Chikusai*: An evaluation of its medicine): "This booklet recounts the story of the quack Chikusai. When you look through it you will find that it is indeed a source for tales [*hanashi no tane*]. It is a travelogue [*kikō*] of the journey between the capital and the eastern provinces; it offers *hokku* at famous places, temples and shrines, and it contains 'mad verse' [*kyōka*]."[123] This quote from *Chikusai ryōji no hyōban* is relevant also because it reinforces my argument as a whole: *Chikusai* is not one text but an ensemble of many. The last piece of our puzzle is hinted at by the fact that *Chikusai ryōji no hyōban* treats *Chikusai* as a fictional piece that discusses medicine. In part D *Chikusai* loses, once more, its unity, and the narration fragments into nine short stories that focus on Chikusai performing as a doctor, or at least one sui generis, in Nagoya.[124] The thread running through the text relates to Chikusai and his inept medical treatments, but, beyond that, each story can be enjoyed as an independent tale. Metaphorically speaking, the real protagonist of these nine passages is humor, presented in forms typical of contemporary jestbooks.

The first of the nine stories offers an interesting case study. Chikusai hangs out his sign, the inscription of which boasts that his skills are akin to legendary Chinese and Indian doctors. In the dead of winter he is summoned by a samurai who lives in the neighborhood and has a fever. Chikusai approaches the patient:

Chikusai began his visit by taking the patient's pulse.

"You don't have a fever?" he asked.

"Indeed, I have," replied the patient.

"Well, isn't that what I just said?" remarked Chikusai, and he jumps with joy at these long-awaited words.

"You don't have a headache?" he asked again.

"Yes, my temples hurt," answered the man.

"Well, isn't that what I just said," replied Chikusai boastfully.

"You don't have worms?" he inquired again.

"I always have worms," he said.

"Well, this is as it should be," said Chikusai, looking as if he had expected this answer.[125]

On the surface it appears that Chikusai has behaved exactly in the manner expected of a doctor by performing what was known as the four operations (taking the pulse, checking the complexion, listening to the voice and cough, and asking about symptoms). For this reason, the patient is not suspicious and happily takes the medicine prescribed by the quack Chikusai. Yet a seventeenth-century reader would have understood this passage differently because it employs a comic technique already exploited in the jestbook titled *Seisuishō* (Laughter to banish sleep), probably compiled around 1628:

> There was a doctor who did not know about the different types of pulse and did not possess even the most basic medical knowledge. After taking the pulse it was his custom to ask the patient about their condition.
>
> "Do you have chest pains?"
>
> "Yes indeed."
>
> "That's as it should be. I saw it from your pulse! And do your legs feel cold?"
>
> "No, they feel fine."
>
> "That's as it should be. I saw it from your pulse! And does your head ache?"
>
> "No, it's not aching."
>
> "That's as it should be. I saw it from your pulse!"
>
> And to think that even these fellows are considered "doctors"! What a dreadful thing to fall ill and to have to seek treatment.[126]

This story was inserted in the section that gathers jokes on the theme of false pretenses titled "Moji shirigao" (To pretend to know characters). Any reader *au fait* with this passage in *Seisuishō* would have perceived immediately that Chikusai has no idea what he is talking about but has devised a cunning way of feigning knowledge.[127] The adaptation of a story from a contemporary jestbook also suggests that this passage from *Chikusai* could be read as a discrete tale, independently from the rest of *Chikusai*, because jestbooks invited this type of discontinuous reading. At the same time, however, the presence of Chikusai as the quack on duty anchors the story as an integral part of the whole of *Chikusai*.

The nine stories in this section repeat a specific narrative pattern: Chikusai is summoned by a patient, tries a cure, usually fails, and covers up by using his wits. Except for the second story, in which Chikusai cites titles of actual medical texts to give the impression of a learned doctor, these stories are not designed to instruct us on seventeenth-century medicine but to provoke laughter. Repetition of the same pattern without any difference, though, would have proven rather uninspiring for the reader. Therefore *Chikusai* ensures variety by changing *what* is humorous. In some stories the humor lies in the use of ingredients that were not meant to be used as medications. Reducing old tatami mats to powder and administering it as a medication, as suggested in the first episode, is as bogus as treating a man with a fever by adding pickled eggplant to a soup.[128] In some other stories, we encounter a more Rabelaisian, earthy comicalness that indulges in grotesque realism. For instance, Chikusai loves using his magnet, after it proved effective in treating some iron dust stuck in the eyes of a blacksmith.[129] But when he applies it to extract a plum from a woman's throat, his actions lead to gruesome consequences: the woman's face is horribly disfigured, with the eyeballs and nose being squashed together.[130] It is even worse when the same treatment is used for childbirth: the fetus of a pregnant woman is pulled up to her chest, thereby leading to a delivery so violent that it catapults the baby several meters.[131]

Regardless of how the humor works, each of the nine vignettes that form the central part of *Chikusai* can be enjoyed as independent passages. A few were already known in earlier jestbooks, while others would be taken up in later examples. Therefore, we are entirely justified in reading them as self-contained short stories, and yet, at the same time, they are organized into a masterful whole. When read together they reveal a crescendo in the nonsensical nature of Chikusai's treatments, which goes hand in hand with the increasing number of errors he makes and in the horrifying consequences for the patients.

When *Chikusai* is read through the lens of the textual analysis proposed here, it is clear that any attempt to categorize and pigeonhole this work influences our pleasure of the text because it diminishes the way we can appreciate all its myriad facets. *Chikusai* is a travelogue, a jestbook; it is one story, but also many stories. It is constructed as a unitary piece of fictional writing, and yet it is narrated in such a way that it easily fragments into a multiplicity of potentially self-sufficient narratives. The text can be read in its entirety as if it were a well-designed puzzle, or readers can skip the parts that halt the main narration and distract from Chikusai's own tale. A reader might choose to read only the tragic story of the Harima samurai or pick up just the second volume to enjoy a condensed jestbook involving a quack. The pleasure of reading derives from all these possible approaches—a rejection of the book's plurality is to deny the very nature of this patchwork text.

As this chapter has discussed, seventeenth-century popular prose at times confronts us with texts that challenge our expectations and takes us out of our comfort zone. Traditional scholarship has shown some resistance in coming to terms with them. *Jigabachi monogatari* is a full-scale miscellany with a fragmented, incohesive structure where narrative and nonnarrative compete in engaging readers with a multiplicity of contents—from love stories to recipes—that masterfully bring to life some of the textual tropes examined in the previous chapters. But rarely is it mentioned in scholarship on this period, let alone in literary histories. *Ukiyo monogatari*, Western and Japanese scholarship tell us, is the story of Ukiyobō and celebrates the new hedonistic approach to life, admittedly presenting some didactic passages. And yet the text has much more to it, with an array of nonnarrative passages that present a harsh criticism of the government while entertaining with sections akin to jestbooks and instructing about travel with prose that borrows from contemporary guidebooks. *Chikusai* is at first sight comforting with its well-designed fictional account of a wandering quack. And yet labeling it as an example of travel literature quashes the plurality that is untethered underneath the surface in a profusion of narrative passages that halt Chikusai's story to introduce other, unrelated tales.

If we insist on viewing these works as some sort of unitary fictional narrative, a great portion of the text makes little sense. And frustration takes the place of any pleasure: after all, we want to follow a story that keeps being interrupted and does so for fairly lengthy portions. But the longevity and popularity enjoyed by these texts during the early modern period suggest that the reading experience of readers at the time could not have been such a painful one. Once we stop looking for unity and accept these texts as variations of discontinuous writing, we partake in the pleasure of the text. I hope that this chapter has sketched something akin to an alternative methodology for reading texts that celebrate plurality. I have shown how both purposive and digressive curiosity have their place. I have also discussed how these texts are designed to encourage both continuous and discontinuous reading. We can read from beginning to end. For texts that have a story—*Ukiyo monogatari* and *Chikusai*—we embrace the halts in the story and we keep suspending our desire to know how the story unfolds by savoring every new twist. For miscellarian texts—like *Jigabachi monogatari*—we enjoy how every section takes us to unexpected topics and styles. We can equally skip all the bits that do not interest us. In texts with a story this means giving the text a unitary, linear trajectory that allows us to focus solely on the main protagonist and his story. In miscellanies, this means that we can bring together passages that we view as somehow connected. Either way, we are able to appreciate what Roland Barthes praises as a textual "success": "narrativity is dismantled yet the story is still readable: never have the two edges of the seam been clearer and more tenuous, never has the pleasure been better offered to the reader—if at least he appreciates controlled discontinuities, faked conformities, and indirect destructions."[132]

This is not to claim that all the popular Japanese texts commercially produced in the seventeenth century were constructed to be read in this way. In the previous chapters I examined a variety of texts that make perfect sense as coherent units. By the same token, I do not see this as something that characterizes seventeenth-century prose alone, and I trust that research on early modern Japanese literature will test whether the idea of discontinuous writing and discontinuous reading can be applied to other textual traditions. Probably some readers might be tempted to see this as a prerogative of premodern Japanese literature as a whole. Personally I am not interested in any generalization, as that becomes in itself a taxonomic exercise. What I am interested in is to apply the methodology used in this chapter to other early modern texts to gauge what can be discovered about a specific title once we welcome plurality.

I wish to conclude with a final remark. My earlier research on *Chikusai* opined that it can be viewed as a form of genre hybridism.[133] The research I have conducted for the present volume has prompted me to redefine my position. Two elements are necessary in any discussion of genre hybridism: genres, which are so established that they become a set of conventions shared by both authors and readers, and the desire to blend them, thus creating something worthy of the appellation "hybrid." Chapters 2, 3, 4, and 5 have shown that seventeenth-century Japanese readers might have been aware of the publishing genres created by the publishers as part of their marketing strategies, but, as I have noted on several occasions, the boundaries of these publishing genres were permeable. These genres were in fact convenient labels to market books and to entice readers to purchase more of the same type (although they were not necessarily the same!). Nothing suggests that authors consciously created works in compliance with these publishing genres, and readers probably did not make a differentiation in genre types. In effect, it is too early to detect any programmatic—or modern—view of genre since authors and readers were still finding their way in the production and consumption of popular prose. And how can there be any conscious blending of genres if there is no genre consciousness? Even more so when we consider that genre hybridism is often connected to a transgressive desire to destabilize genres.[134] We might then ask how there can be transgression when a familiar form is barely sketched. How can there be a desire to challenge when authors, publishers, and readers are in the process of finding their feet? The texts examined in this chapter evince that the seventeenth century was an exciting period of "way finding" in popular publishing—authors, publishers, and readers were all experimenting in the creation, production, and consumption of popular prose.[135] There was no concern regarding textual unity, neither was there a requirement to separate the narrative and the nonnarrative. There was, however, the need to understand the market and to experiment, and this resulted in texts often celebrating a triumph of plurality.

Epilogue

Wayfinding

A book outside the constellation in which it makes sense is an orphaned book.

—Gabriel Zaid, *So Many Books*

Imagine yourself as a reader in seventeenth-century Japan. Your gender or social status are not so relevant; what matters is your level of literacy. You have learned the hiragana syllabary and a few basic characters at a *terakoya* school, or perhaps in the household where you are employed. You can now write and read vernacular Japanese. There is so much that you need to know to become an integral, successful part of society, and books are one of the ways in which you can find the answers you need. Commercial publishers are invested in packaging books even for you, a novice reader. Their shops are part of the cityscape and entice you to the kaleidoscopic universe of the printed word. Admittedly, books have not supplanted traditional oral practices (sermons, lectures, or face-to-face instruction), but they are a valuable source of knowledge. If you cannot afford to buy books—although prices are quite varied—you may be able to borrow them. If your reading ability is still weak, you can always join someone—a more expert reader—who can read them aloud for you.

Books reveal a multifaceted world. Key teachings of Buddhism and Confucianism move from the rarefied sphere of literary Sinitic and are translated into something more palatable. Sincerity, harmony, frugality, filial piety, and patience are some of the qualities you can acquire through the perusal of such materials. The essentials of proper conduct are transported from the exclusive world of the warrior and made available to all in user-friendly manuals, which target men and women respectively. You learn, for example, about body cleanliness and consideration for others, among many other things. If you manage to follow some of these rules of conduct, you will begin to resemble those higher up in the social hierarchy. But if you think that such deportment is of no interest to you, you can still enjoy these how-to books as a window onto other people's lives, somewhat like entertaining fiction. Handbooks for letter writing assist you in dealing with all sorts of human interactions: from business transactions to love affairs. The same compendiums also teach you the artificial idioms applied in written correspondence, *sōrōbun* and *mairase-sōrōbun.* Placed at the intersection of literary Chinese and vernacular Japanese, these work as a shared language. And, why not, you also get to enjoy love stories packed with gripping emotions. If you are lucky, you may even develop techniques that help you in winning the heart of the person you are besotted with. Books also assist you in other ways. Making money is de rigueur. You can find tips on how to become rich, but, paradoxically, you also understand that rich and poor are both necessary for a society to function. Disasters, you learn, are an unavoidable part of life. There are accounts of horror and trauma, but they come with soothing messages of hope. All in all, bookshops are a trove of precious tools for you to make sense of the present and to become a well-rounded individual.

Texts with a low degree of narrativity that unlock knowledge of all sorts, and for all sorts, constituted the core of what seventeenth-century novice readers in Japan enjoyed reading. We are talking about prose that appeals primarily for its epistemic function. Accessing this knowledge, I have suggested, endowed readers with an empowering form of cultural capital that helped them to fit into their society, if not advance in it. Pleasure lay in the cognitive profit gained by feeding one's thirst for knowing. By reinstating this type of transformative writing at the very heart of the literature of this period, *Pleasure in Profit* has explored a fresh definition of popular prose for early modern Japan, one that enters into dialogue with research done on other forms of popular literatures around the globe. In the process, I have challenged any facile dichotomy between efferent and aesthetic reading, claiming that all the texts analyzed in this book belong firmly to the sphere of the literary. Therefore *Pleasure in Profit* encourage readers to reappraise the understanding of literature and to approach the study of literary history in a more democratic manner.

This is not to claim that narrative texts played no role in seventeenth-century popular prose. Quite the opposite. I have explored a number of fictional tales in which I have identified two marked features. First, they are shaped in such a way as to engage readers at a cognitive as well as emotional and aesthetic levels. Narrative texts absorb the ethical, social, and interpersonal knowledge we find in nonnarrative texts—what I have called narrative capital—with a view not only to rehearse the same knowledge but also to generate new knowledge. Their object is not simply to please but to please through instruction. Second, many of these narratives unsettle our present literary (or cultural) expectations: they appear to us as Barthesian "texts of bliss." But this is to impose our values on a culture and a time that had different values and needs. If we adjust our vision to fit that of early modern Japanese readers, we should be able to appreciate these same texts as "texts of pleasure." I have also argued that discontinuous reading is a way to celebrate the plurality of texts that interweave the narrative and the nonnarrative.

Publishing genres, as I have called them, have also featured extensively in this account. I hope to have demonstrated their usefulness as a starting point in the task of unraveling the Great Unread of seventeenth-century popular prose. Publishers devised them as convenient categories in advertising books of a similar nature and in enticing customers to find more of the same. As such, they allow us to explore the seventeenth-century book market from within. At the same time, however, I have called attention to their limitations as an epistemological tool. In chapters 3 and 4, I examined selected publishing genres, with a view to understand how they worked. What has emerged is that they operated differently from genres, at least in the modern sense of the word. Coherence and consistency within a given book category were of almost no concern. There was as yet no concept of an author writing in accordance with the rules of a particular genre, or for a reader to expect a piece of writing to adhere to specific generic conventions. Many seventeenth-century texts begin in one category and end up in another. This is not because of a wish to transgress. Simply, there were no clear-cut genre boundaries. This realization has led me to wander also outside the publishing genres. In doing so, I probed fruitful connections between texts that were placed by publishers in different categories and managed to retrieve titles that never made it into book-trade catalogues despite their popularity. This has resulted in an appreciation of the fact that many seventeenth-century texts resist any taxonomic endeavor. Rather than viewing this as a drawback, we should embrace it as a key feature and look for other approaches to make sense of this corpus.

This brings us to what I see as another core finding of my research. Seventeenth-century publishers started to discover the existence of a new public that, for the first time, could access the written word without an intermediary. They began to experiment to see what might work with this potential readership, what would sell in good numbers, what got readers excited, what generated more curiosity, and consequently more demand. Authors, illustrators, and readers all participated in this invitation to invention. Publishing was finding its way, inventing as it went. It was a new world of popular publishing that preceded the creation of genres and literary conventions. It was made of plurality, instability, and porousness.

To a certain extent, this book has also been an exercise in way finding, in that it sought a way to read seventeenth-century popular prose on its own terms. For me that path was the search for texts that quenched readers' thirst for knowledge and their curiosity about the world they belonged to. The search was fruitful as the Archive confirmed that texts appealing for their epistemic function were extremely popular. Nevertheless, I do not wish to give the impression that a penchant for knowledge making and didacticism was the be all and end all or that it was the hallmark of a *kanazōshi* genre that I claim never existed. Humor, for example, was equally germane. There is a profusion of humorous texts from this period that wait to be discovered. The three texts examined in the final chapter all share a penchant for comedy and could easily become the starting point for a study on laughter in seventeenth-century popular prose. As I briefly mentioned in chapter 2 in conjunction with the publication of war tales and military books (*gunki* and *gunsho*), exploring the past was another aspect that fascinated publishers and readers in this century. Several titles that discussed the origins of things and that retold tales of battles enjoyed popularity. There was a clear interest in history and historical narratives, which remains to be investigated. Sex was also, maybe unsurprisingly, another hot topic. The study in chapters 4 and 5 of two sexually explicit books drew attention to the existence of a publishing genre that dealt in one way or another with sex. How such a category functioned in the seventeenth century still needs to be fully understood. Seventeenth-century popular literature was made of all these strands, and possibly more. They coexisted in the same publishing space, across books, and often within the same book. The previous chapters have also identified lines of inquiry that await further investigation. We have discovered a publishing industry that was more developed than scholarship has suggested to date. We have encountered strident criticism of the ruling class and a willingness to lambaste the flaws in contemporary society in a virtually unpunished defiance of censorial regulations. We have enjoyed narratives that empower women over men. We have come across savant uses of the narrative voice and have identified an almost ubiquitous trace of orality/aurality in print. We have appreciated how adaptation was cherished by publishers as an apt strategy to give second, if not third, life to best-selling titles. My hope is that future research on this century will shed light on this and much more.

My book concludes at the end of the seventeenth century, but I do not wish to suggest that this marked any particular change. Many of the publishing genres described here continued to thrive throughout the Edo period. Booktrade catalogues exhibit continuity well beyond the turn of the eighteenth century, and we must wait for the 1754 catalogue to see a substantial change in the way books were categorized. Conduct and letter-writing manuals, with cookery books, survived well into the twenty-first century. Some texts, such as *Usuyuki monogatari*, continued to be published in the nineteenth century. They clearly struck a chord that was not specific to the 1600s. Some texts, such as *Chikusai*, gave life to thriving intertextual serializations that allowed these texts to migrate across media and to be constantly adapted to new needs. It would not be an exaggeration to say, for example, that twentieth-century Japanese children enjoyed the cleverness of the little monk known as Ikkyū in picture books, anime, and TV dramas thanks to the fact that this charismatic protagonist appeared in print back in 1668. There remains much work to do on the legacy of seventeenth-century popular literature to gauge whether there was any significant change and at what point. Above all, we need to find out when, if ever, early modern Japan discovered the concept of "genre" as we understand it.

While I have strived to point to similarities between the texts investigated here and popular literature commercially published in other cultures around a similar time frame, I have made a conscious choice to retain my focus on Japan. It is to be hoped that scholars whose research interest is transregional will complement my findings by studying synergies born of commercial and cultural exchanges across East Asia and will refine any comparison we can draw between Japan, China, and Korea.

For now, imagine yourself transported back again in time to Kyoto. You are on Teramachi Street, standing in front of the shop of the prolific publisher and bookseller Nishimura Matazaemon. His stock is rich and diverse. I hope you are now better equipped to start foraging into the forest of books that he, and hundreds of other publishers, are growing. Keep your mind open to read a wide range of texts that will provide you with both intellectual profit and cognitive pleasures. And fully enjoy this journey into dazzling plurality.

Notes

Introduction

1. The comparison between bookshops and a condensed version of the world is suggested by Jorge Carrión, *Bookshops*, trans. Peter Bush (London: MacLehose Press, 2016), 20.
2. Gabriel Zaid, *So Many Books*, trans. Natasha Wimmer (London: Sort of Books, 2004), 24.
3. Robert Macfarlane, *The Gifts of Reading* (London: Penguin Books, 2017), 13.
4. Umberto Eco, *On Literature*, trans. Martin McLaughlin (London: Vintage Books, 2006), 1.
5. Eco, *On Literature*, 1.
6. *Shinpan Heianjō narabi ni rakugai no zu* ([Kyoto]: Itsutsuya Kichibee, 1680), National Diet Library, Tokyo (shelf mark: WB39-5).
7. This is one of the *maeku* verses included in *Fudanzakura* and composed on the subject "Their Species Increase More and More." See the manuscript at the Tenri Central Library (Wataya Bunko), transcribed in vol. 11 of *Mikan zappai shiryō*, ed. Suzuki Katsutada (Okazaki: Suzuki Katsutada, 1961), 20v. The term *shokuji* 植字 was used in the 1690 *Jinrin kinmōzui* (An illustrated encyclopedia of human affairs) to designate movable-type printing; Makieshi Genzaburō, illus., *Jinrin kinmōzui* ([Kyoto]: Heirakuji; Osaka: Murakami Seizaburō; Edo: Murakami Gorobee, 1690), critical edition in *Jinrin kinmōzui*, ed. Asakura Haruhiko, Tōyō bunko 519 (Tokyo: Heibonsha 1990), 145–46. I think that here it refers to woodblock printing, since by the beginning of the eighteenth century movable type was being employed sparingly. The choice of the word *shoku* 植, meaning "to plant," well suits the context where the action of "planting" characters as if they were trees give life to a "forest" of books (*fumihayashi* 書林). This word, in turn, brings to mind booksellers, as one of the ways to refer to them in the Edo period was precisely with the compound 書林, read *shorin*. I thank Ellis Tinios for suggesting this interpretation.

8. Franco Moretti, "The Slaughterhouse of Literature," *Modern Language Quarterly* 61, no. 1 (2000): 207–27. Reprinted in Franco Moretti, *Distant Reading* (London: Verso, 2013), 63–90.
9. The idea of the Great Unread is inspired by Margaret Cohen, *The Sentimental Education of the Novel* (Princeton, N.J.: Princeton University Press, 1999), 23. See also F. Moretti, "The Slaughterhouse of Literature."
10. I am indebted to George McFadden, "'Literature': A Many-Sided Process," in *What Is Literature?*, ed. Paul Hernadi (Bloomington: Indiana University Press, 1978), 55, for the idea of "books being in phase" with readers: "I should argue that a definition of literature ought to include especially those works which are actually living in the sense that some readers are currently making concretizations of them. . . . The term *literature*, I suggest, out to include every work which is 'alive' by being in phase with one or more of these (reading public, academic scholars or critics, the writers) groups of readers."
11. Richard Lane, "The Beginnings of the Modern Japanese Novel: *Kana-zōshi*, 1600–1682," *Harvard Journal of Asiatic Studies* 20, no. 3/4 (December 1957): 644–701.
12. Mizutani Futō, *Kinsei retsudentai shōsetsu shi*, 2 vols. (Tokyo: Shun'yōdō, 1897). For a synopsis in English of how the Japanese critical discourse developed after Mizutani's work, see Laura Moretti, "*Kanazōshi* Revisited: Reconsidering the Beginnings of Japanese Popular Literature in Print," *Monumenta Nipponica* 65, no. 2 (2010): 297–356.
13. Marie-Laure Ryan, "The Modes of Narrativity and Their Visual Metaphors," *Style* 26, no. 3 (Fall 1992): 368–87.
14. Ryan, "Modes of Narrativity," 371. For a more in-depth discussion of what Marie-Laure Ryan calls a "fuzzy-set conception of narrative," see Marie-Laure Ryan, "Toward a Definition of Narrative," in *The Cambridge Companion to Narrative*, ed. David Herman (Cambridge: Cambridge University Press, 2007), 22–35, and Marie-Laure Ryan, "Narrativity and Its Modes as Culture-Transcending Analytical Categories," in "Narrativity and Fictionality in Edo-Period Prose Literature," ed. Laura Moretti, special issue, *Japan Forum* 21, no. 3 (2010): 307–23.
15. Ryan, "Modes of Narrativity," 375.
16. Ryan, "Modes of Narrativity," 369. In the same article Ryan discusses at length a number of "modes of narrativity," including simple narrativity, multiple narrativity, complex narrativity, diluted narrativity, and so forth. For how Ryan's theoretical positions can be expanded when studying early modern Japanese literature, see Ryan, "Narrativity and Its Modes," 321–22.
17. Lane, "Beginnings," 656.
18. Lane, "Beginnings," 699.
19. Edward Putzar, trans., "*Chikusai Monogatari*: A Partial Translation," *Monumenta Nipponica* 16, no. 1/2 (April–July 1960): 161–95; Edward Putzar, trans., "*Inu Makura: The Dog Pillow*," *Harvard Journal of Asiatic Studies* 28 (1968): 98–113, Jack Rucinski, trans., "A Japanese Burlesque: *Nise Monogatari*," *Monumenta Nipponica* 30, no. 1 (Spring 1975): 1–18; Daniel Lewis Barber, "Tales of the Floating World: The *Ukiyo monogatari* of Asai Ryōi" (master's thesis, Ohio State University, 1984). Partial translations of *Chikusai*, *Ukiyo monogatari*, and *Tōkaidō meishoki* are in Laurence Bresler, "The Origins of Popular Travel and Travel Literature in Japan" (PhD diss., Columbia University, 1975). More recently, excerpts from *Inu makura*, *Nise monogatari*, *Kinō wa kyō no monogatari*, *Ukiyo monogatari*, *Otogi bōko*, and *Oan monogatari* are included in the unabridged edition of Haruo Shirane, ed., *Early Modern Japanese Literature: An Anthology, 1600–1900* (New York: Columbia University Press, 2002). Partial translations of *Inu tsurezure*, *Kinō wa kyō no monogatari*, *Kyō warabe*, *Musashi abumi*, *Tōkaidō meishoki*, and *Zeraku*

monogatari are available in Sumie Jones and Adam L. Kern, with Kenji Watanabe, eds., *A Kamigata Anthology: Literature from Japan's Metropolitan Centers, 1600–1750* (Honolulu: University of Hawai'i Press, 2020). Snippets from *Seisuishō* and *Otogi bōko* are available, respectively, in the episodic festschrifts for Howard Hibbett, H. Mack Horton, trans., *Laughs to Banish Sleep* (Hollywood, Calif.: Highmoonoon, 2001), and Maryellen Toman Mori, trans., *The Peony Lantern* (Hollywood, Calif.: Highmoonoon, 2000).

20. Noda Hisao, *Nihon kinsei shōsetsu shi: Kanazōshi hen* (Tokyo: Benseisha, 1986).
21. Noda employs a variety of words—*monogatarisei, monogatariteki ishiki, shōsetsuteki keitai, setsuwa*—for what I refer to as narrativity.
22. For other studies on *kanazōshi*, a good starting point, albeit slightly dated, is the following bibliography: Fukasawa Akio and Kikuchi Shin'ichi, eds., *Kanazōshi kenkyū bunken mokuroku* (Osaka: Izumi Shoin, 2004). Useful reprints of key articles and books can be found in Fukasawa Akio and Kikuchi Shin'ichi, eds., *Kanazōshi kenkyū sōsho*, 8 vols. (Tokyo: Kuresu Shuppan, 2006).
23. A similar position is been noted, for example, in Julia K. Murray, "Changing the Frame: Preface and Colophons in the Chinese Illustrated Book *Dijian tushuo* (The Emperor's Mirror, Illustrated and Discussed)," *East Asian Library Journal* 12, no. 1 (Spring 2006): 24. Thought-provoking also is the remark by Jan Baetens and Hugo Frey concerning what they call "retrospective reading": "The very existence of the label 'graphic novel' enables modern readers to reinterpret works and models of the past that had not been read as such but that clearly belong to the same universe" (*The Graphic Novel: An Introduction* [Cambridge: Cambridge University Press, 2015], 22–23).
24. The publications of the Modern Language Association geared toward students of literature clearly show this shift by substituting the entry for "Literary History" with that for "Historical Scholarship." See Annabelle Patterson, "Historical Scholarship," in *Introduction to Scholarship in Modern Languages and Literatures*, ed. Joseph Gibaldi, 2nd ed. (New York: Modern Language Association of America, 1992), 183–200; Catherine Gallagher, "Historical Scholarship," in *Introduction to Scholarship in Modern Languages and Literatures*, ed. David G. Nicholls, 3rd ed. (New York: Modern Language Association of America, 2007), 171–93. For a discussion of this shift, see Lawrence Lipking, "A Trout in the Milk," in *The Uses of Literary History*, ed. Marshall Brown (Durham, N.C.: Duke University Press, 1995), 1–12.
25. Lipking, "Trout in the Milk," 3–8, and Gallagher, "Historical Scholarship," 171.
26. J. Paul Hunter, *Before Novels: The Cultural Contexts of Eighteenth-Century English Fiction* (New York: Norton, 1990), xvii.
27. Eco, *On Literature*, 1.
28. Franco Moretti, *Graphs, Maps, Trees: Abstract Models for a Literary History* (London: Verso, 2005); *Atlas of the European Novel: 1800–1900* (London: Verso, 1999); and Moretti, *Distant Reading*. For reactions to and critical views regarding Moretti's intellectual position, see Jonathan Goodwin and John Holbo, eds., *Reading Graphs, Maps, Trees: Responses to Franco Moretti* (Anderson, S.C.: Parlor Press, 2011). See also Stephen Greenblatt, *Shakespearean Negotiations: The Circulation of Social Energy in Renaissance England* (Oxford: Clarendon Press, 2001); Michael Payne, ed., *The Greenblatt Reader* (Oxford: Blackwell Publishing, 2005); and Stephen Greenblatt, "What Is the History of Literature?" *Critical Inquiry* 23, no. 3 (Spring 1997): 460–81.
29. F. Moretti, *Distant Reading*, 49.
30. "Works that have been hitherto denigrated or ignored can be treated as major achievements, claiming space in an already crowded curriculum or diminishing the value of

established works in a kind of literary stock market.... This unsettling of the hierarchies does not seem revolutionary... but it does feel democratizing, in that it refuses to limit creativity to the spectacular achievements of a group of trained specialists" (Catherine Gallagher and Stephen Greenblatt, *Practicing New Historicism* [Chicago: University of Chicago Press, 2000], 10–11). Like Greenblatt, Gallagher is a well-known advocate of New Historicism. For an introduction to New Historicism and key concepts other than the one discussed here, see Mark Robson, *Stephen Greenblatt* (London: Routledge, 2008).

31. Gallagher and Greenblatt, *Practicing New Historicism*, 9.
32. Lipking, "Trout in the Milk," 4.
33. Robert Mandrou, *De la culture populaire aux 17e et 18e siècles: La bibliothèque bleue de Troyes* (Paris: Imago, 1999); first published in 1964.
34. Charles Nisard, *Histoire des livres populaires; ou, De la littérature du colportage* (Paris: Dentu, 1864).
35. Further contributions to the field include, in chronological order, L. Andries et al., *La "Bibliothèque bleue" nel Seicento; o, Della letteratura per il popolo* (Bari: Adriatica; Paris: Nizet, 1981); Giovanni Dotoli, *Letteratura per il popolo in Francia (1600–1750): Proposte di letture della "Bibliothèque bleue,"* Biblioteca della ricera 4 (Fasano: Schena, 1991); Roger Chartier and Hans-Jürgen Lüsebrink, eds., *Colportage et lecture populaire: Imprimés de large circulation en Europe, XVIe–XIXe siècles*, Actes du colloque des 21–24 avril 1991, Wolfenbüttel (Paris: IMEC, 1996); Nicolas Petit, *L'éphémère, l'occasionnel et le non livre à la bibliothèque Sainte-Geneviève (XVe–XVIIIe siècles)* (Paris: Klincksieck, 1997); Lise Andries and Geneviève Bollème, *La bibliothèque bleue: Littérature de colportage* (Paris: Laffont, 2003), which includes transcriptions of a wide range of primary sources.
36. Margaret Spufford, *Small Books and Pleasant Histories: Popular Fiction and Its Readership in Seventeenth-Century England* (Cambridge: Cambridge University Press, 1985). See also, in chronological order, John Ashton, *Chapbooks of the Eighteenth Century* (London: Skoob Books, 1992) (first published by Chatto and Windus in 1882); William Harvey, *Scottish Chapbook Literature* (Paisley, U.K.: Alexander Gardner, 1903); Roger Thompson, *Samuel Pepys' Penny Merriments* (London: Constable, 1976); Victor E. Neuburg, *Popular Literature: A History and Guide, from the Beginning of Printing to the Year 1897* (London: Woburn Press, 1977); Victor E. Neuburg, *The Batsford Companion to Popular Literature* (London: Batsford Academic and Educational, 1982); Barry McKay, *An Introduction to Chapbooks* (Oldham, U.K.: Incline Press, 2003); Edward J. Cowan and Mike Paterson, *Folk in Print: Scotland's Chapbook Heritage, 1750–1850* (Edinburgh: John Donald / Birlinn, 2007); Kobayashi Akio, *Chappu bukku no sekai: Kindai Igirisu shomin to renkabon* (Tokyo: Kōdansha, 2007); and John Meriton and Carlo Dumontet, *Small Books for the Common Man: A Descriptive Bibliography* (London: British Library, 2010).
37. Jeffrey Brooks, *When Russia Learned to Read: Literacy and Popular Literature, 1861–1917*, Studies in Russian Literature and Theory (Evanston, Ill.: Northwestern University Press, 2003); Candace Slater, *Stories on a String: The Brazilian Literatura de Cordel* (Berkeley: University of California Press, 1982); Francesca Orsini, *Print and Pleasure: Popular Literature and Entertaining Fictions in Colonial North India* (New Delhi: Permanent Black, 2009); Cathy L. Preston and Michael J. Preston, eds., *The Other Print Tradition: Essays on Chapbooks, Broadsides, and Related Ephemera*, New Perspectives in Folklore (New York: Garland Publishing, 1995); Emmanuel Obiechina, *An African Popular Literature: A Study of Onitsha Market Pamphlets* (Cambridge: Cambridge

University Press, 1973). I am grateful to Peter Burke for alerting me to the *onitsha* market literature.
38. Lucille Chia, *Printing for Profit: The Commercial Publishers of Jianyang, Fujian (11th–17th Centuries)*, Harvard-Yenching Institute Monograph Series 56 (Cambridge, Mass.: Harvard University Asia Center for the Harvard-Yenching Institute, 2002); Cynthia J. Brokaw, *Commerce in Culture: The Sibao Book Trade in the Qing and Republican Periods*, Harvard East Asian Monographs 280 (Cambridge, Mass.: Harvard University Asia Center, 2007); Cynthia J. Brokaw and Kai-wing Chow, eds., *Printing and Book Culture in Late Imperial China* (Berkeley: University of California Press, 2005); Lucille Chia and Hilde De Weerdt, eds., *Knowledge and Text Production in an Age of Print: China, 900–1400*, Sinica Leidensia 100 (Leiden: Brill, 2011); Joseph P. McDermott, *A Social History of the Chinese Book: Books and Literati Culture in Late Imperial China* (Hong Kong: Hong Kong University Press, 2006); Yuming He, *Home and the World: Editing the "Glorious Ming" in Woodblock-Printed Books of the Sixteenth and Seventeenth Centuries*, Harvard-Yenching Institute Monograph Series 82 (Cambridge, Mass.: Harvard University Asia Center, 2013).
39. An introduction can be found in Kim Hŭnggyu and Peter H. Lee, "Chosŏn Fiction in Korean," in *A History of Korean Literature*, ed. Peter H. Lee (Cambridge: Cambridge University Press, 2003), 273–87. See also Kim Hŭnggyu, *Understanding Korean Literature*, trans. Robert J. Fouser (New York: Routledge, 2016), 176–92.
40. Gary Kelly, "General Editor's Introduction," in *Cheap Print in Britain and Ireland to 1660*, ed. Joad Raymond (Oxford: Oxford University Press, 2011), The Oxford History of Popular Print Culture, vol. 1. To date only the first, fifth, and sixth volumes of this set have been published.
41. Marino Zorzi, *La vita nei libri: Edizioni illustrate a stampa del quattro e cinquecento dalla Fondazione Giorgio Cini* (Gorizia: Edizioni della Laguna, 2003).
42. Brokaw, *Commerce in Culture*, 305–512.
43. He, *Home and the World*.
44. Maria Nikolajeva, *Reading for Learning: Cognitive Approaches to Children's Literature* (Amsterdam: Benjamins, 2014), 21. I am indebted to Elena Follador for alerting me to this study.
45. Louise M. Rosenblatt, *The Reader, the Text, the Poem: The Transactional Theory of the Literary Work* (Carbondale: Southern Illinois University Press, 1978), 27.
46. Rosenblatt, *Reader*, 24. Emphasis in original.
47. Natasha Glaisyer and Sara Pennell, eds., *Didactic Literature in England, 1500–1800: Expertise Constructed* (Aldershot, Hants., U.K.: Ashgate Publishing, 2003), 1.
48. See, for example, Juanita Feros Ruys, ed., *What Nature Does Not Teach: Didactic Literature in the Medieval and Early-Modern Periods* (Turnhout, Belg.: Brepols, 2008).
49. For example, Eric C. Rath, *Food and Fantasy in Early Modern Japan* (Berkeley: University of California Press, 2010), examines culinary writings; Rebecca Corbett, *Cultivating Femininity: Women and Tea Culture in Edo and Meiji Japan* (Honolulu: University of Hawai'i Press, 2018), looks at manuals for the tea ceremony; and Federico Marcon, *The Knowledge of Nature and the Nature of Knowledge in Early Modern Japan* (Chicago: University of Chicago Press, 2015), considers books of natural history.
50. Nakano Mitsutoshi, "Gesaku no han'i: *Ichidai otoko* shushō o rei ni shite," in *Kinsei bungaku fukan*, ed. Hasegawa Tsuyoshi (Tokyo: Kyūko Shoin, 1997), 77–92. This essay was reprinted with the new title "Gesaku no kakuritsu: *Ichidai otoko* shushō o rei ni shite," in *Jūhasseiki no Edo bungei: Ga to zoku no seijuku* (Tokyo: Iwanami Shoten, 1999), 123–42. He further expanded on his original thesis in 2000 in "Tōsho sakki

setcho Jūhasseiki no Edo bungei shoka hyō ni," *Ga zoku* 8 (2000): 70–93; "Jūnanaseiki no shōsetsu shi: Watakushi no gesakuron josetsu," in "Saikaku chōhatsu suru tekisuto," ed. Kigoshi Osamu, special issue, *Kokubungaku kaishaku to kanshō* (March 2005): 19–27; and "Saikaku gesakusha setsu saikō: Edo no manako to gendai no manako o motsu imi," *Bungaku*, 15, no. 1 (January 2014): 140–57. For a study of *gesaku* by Nakano, see *Gesaku kenkyū* (Tokyo: Chūō Kōronsha, 1981). I am indebted to Thomas Gaubatz for alerting me to some of these articles.

51. Nakano, "Saikaku gesakusha setsu saikō," 148.
52. Cohen, *Sentimental Education*, 21.
53. Nakano, "Gesaku no kakuritsu," 124.
54. Nakano, "Saikaku gesakusha setsu saikō," 150–51.
55. Nakano, "Saikaku gesakusha setsu saikō," 151.
56. Nakano, "Saikaku gesakusha setsu saikō," 151.
57. Pierre Bourdieu, *The Rules of Art: Genesis and Structure of the Literary Field*, trans. Susan Emanuel (Cambridge: Polity Press, 1996), 236; emphasis in original.
58. Nakano, "Saikaku gesakusha setsu saikō," 152.
59. Nakano, "Saikaku gesakusha setsu saikō," 153, talks about didacticism that nurtures interiority (*kyūshinsei*) and sociability (*shakaisei*). Nakano, "Jūnanaseiki no shōsetsu shi," 24, draws upon Yoshie Hisaya's work on Saikaku to further develop his view of didacticism and how a person should behave. See also Yoshie Hisaya, *Saikaku: Hitogokoro no bungaku* (Osaka: Izumi Shoin, 1988), 34–68, and Yoshie Hisaya, *Saikaku: Shisō to sakuhin* (Tokyo: Musashino Shoin, 2004), 19–28.
60. Nakano, "Jūnanaseiki no shōsetsu shi," 21.
61. A thoughtful account of how popular culture has been defined in several key studies on the subject is found in Holt N. Parker, "Toward a Definition of Popular Culture," *History and Theory* 50 (May 2011): 147–70. I have also referred to E. Taylor Atkins, "Popular Culture," in *A Companion to Japanese History*, ed. William Tsutsui (Malden, Mass.: Blackwell Publishing, 2007), 460–76, and E. Taylor Atkins, *A History of Popular Culture in Japan: From the Seventeenth Century to the Present* (London: Bloomsbury, 2017), 17–32.
62. Reflection on how to judge the popularity (wide circulation) of a title in early modern Japan has been prompted by Thomas R. Adams and Nicolas Barker, "A New Model for the Study of the Book," in *A Potencie of Life: Books in Society*, ed. Nicolas Barker (London: British Library, 2001), 28–29. The set of indirect measures discussed here, however, is in part different from those mentioned by Adams and Barker as it fits the specific case of printing in early modern Japan.
63. See Parker, "Toward a Definition," 152–53.
64. Joad Raymond, in reflecting on the meaning of popular in the context of early modern England, identifies "cheap print" as a key factor ("Introduction: The Origins of Popular Print Culture," in *Cheap Print*, 4–7).
65. Peter Burke, *Languages and Communities in Early Modern Europe* (Cambridge: Cambridge University Press, 2004), 62.
66. Atkins, *History of Popular Culture*, 29–30. This distinction is repeatedly invoked by Suzuki Sadami in his study of the word *bungaku* (literature); *The Concept of "Literature" in Japan*, trans. Royall Tyler (Kyoto: International Research Center for Japanese Studies, 2006), 19, 70–71, 78–82, 115–17, 217.
67. Peter Burke, *Popular Culture in Early Modern Europe*, 3rd ed. (London: Routledge, 2017); first published in 1978. The part played by Peter Burke in "writing history from below" and in crafting the new field of cultural history is highlighted in "Pītā Bāku

[Peter Burke] no shigoto: Bunkashi kenkyū no genzai," special issue, *Shisō* 1074 (October 2013).
68. Burke, *Popular Culture*, 24–29, 58–64.
69. Carlo Ginzburg, *The Cheese and the Worms: The Cosmos of a Sixteenth-Century Miller*, trans. John and Anne Tedeschi (Baltimore: Johns Hopkins University Press, 2013), xx, reaches similar conclusions and explains that "between the culture of the dominant classes and that of the subordinate classes there existed, in preindustrial Europe, a circular relationship composed of reciprocal influences, which traveled from low to high as well as from high to low." This idea of the interaction between elite and popular cultures as opposed to a simple opposition between the two has been reiterated in more recent studies; see, for example, Robert Darnton, *The Case for Books: Past, Present, and Future* (New York: Public Affairs, 2009), 204.
70. Matthew Dimmock and Andrew Hadfield, eds., *Literature and Popular Culture in Early Modern England* (London: Ashgate Publishing, 2009), 3–6.
71. Parker, "Toward a Definition," 153–57, and Atkins, *History of Popular Culture*, 25–29.
72. Satoko Shimazaki, *Edo Kabuki in Transition: From the Worlds of the Samurai to the Vengeful Female Ghost* (New York: Columbia University Press, 2016), 22. It is worth noting that Atkins fails to engage with Shimazaki's fresh perspective in his account of how Kabuki navigated censorship; *History of Popular Culture*, 62–68.
73. Donald Keene, *World Within Walls: Japanese Literature of the Pre-modern Era, 1600–1867* (New York: Columbia University Press, 1999), 159, offers this view in discussing seventeenth-century fiction.
74. L. Moretti, "*Kanazōshi* Revisited." The misguided desire to see in *kanazōshi* a fully-fledged and somehow comforting "genre" persists. See, for example, Jones and Kern, *A Kamigata Anthology*, 13. The description of the contents of *kanazōshi* as "a wide range of how-to books, including travel guides, as well as romantic tales, battle histories, courtesan reviews, and fantasies" (14) is also restrictive.
75. Laura Moretti, "A Forest of Books: Seventeenth-Century Kamigata Commercial Prose," in *The Cambridge History of Japanese Literature*, ed. Haruo Shirane and Tomi Suzuki, with David Lurie (Cambridge: Cambridge University Press, 2016), 396–402. In reorganizing the literary field of the nineteenth-century French novel, Margaret Cohen adopts a similar approach: "In reconstructing the contours of early-nineteenth-century sentimentality, for example, I found booksellers' catalogs from the Restoration useful because they organize works in generic categories, even if these categories were completely unscientific" (*Sentimental Education*, 22n53).
76. The idea of diversity (in Japanese *tayōsei*) is something that Japanese scholarship has also tried to underscore; see, for example, Suzuki Ken'ichi, "Jūnanaseiki no bungaku: Sono tayōsei," in "Jūnanaseiki no bungaku," special issue, *Bungaku* 11, no. 3 (May–June 2010): 32–43, and *zadankai* in the same volume, 2–31.
77. In addition to the Japanese scholarship on *kanazōshi* briefly discussed in this introduction and in my previous work (Moretti, "*Kanazōshi* Revisited"), two other works have been published recently on seventeenth-century literature in Japanese: Suzuki Ken'ichi, *Jūnanaseiki no bungaku*, vol. 1 of *Kinsei bungaku shi kenkyū* (Tokyo: Perikansha, 2017); Wiebke Denecke and Kano Kimiko, eds., *Nihon bungaku shi*, vol. 2 (Tokyo: Bensei Shuppan, 2017). Both volumes offer important insights on poetry, prose in literary Chinese, medical texts, and more generally on genres far detached from popular prose in the vernacular. Atkins, *History of Popular Culture*, promises to consider Japanese popular culture beginning in the seventeenth century but unfortunately does not cover much of what precedes Saikaku's prose.

78. Alberto Manguel, *Curiosity* (New Haven, Conn.: Yale University Press, 2015), 3. Manguel formulates this definition of curiosity drawing on Richard Dawkins, *The Selfish Gene* 30th anniversary ed. (Oxford: Oxford University Press, 2006), 63–65.
79. Daniel E. Berlyne, "Curiosity and Exploration," *Science* 153 (July 1966): 31; quoted also in Jordan A. Litman, "Measuring Epistemic Curiosity and Its Diversive and Specific Components," *Journal of Personality Assessment* 80, no. 1 (February 2003): 75–86, and in Celeste Kidd and Benjamin Y. Hayden, "The Psychology and Neuroscience of Curiosity," *Neuron* 88, no. 3 (November 2015): 449–60.
80. This is an important point of cognitive studies, as explained in Nikolajeva, *Reading for Learning*.
81. Mary Elizabeth Berry, *Japan in Print: Information and Nation in the Early Modern Period* (Berkeley: University of California Press, 2006).
82. See Peter Burke, *Social History of Knowledge: From Gutenberg to Diderot* (Cambridge: Polity Press, 2000), 11. Peter Burke, *Social History of Knowledge: From the Encyclopédie to Wikipedia* (Cambridge: Polity Press, 2012), 50–84, defines the steps by which information is processed into knowledge as follows: classifying, deciphering, reconstructing, evaluating, dating, counting and measuring, describing, comparing, explaining, interpreting, narrating, and theorizing.
83. Berry, *Japan in Print*, 243.
84. Berry mentions "conventional forms of self-cultivation and etiquette," but her book does not elaborate on this issue.
85. Berry, *Japan in Print*, 209–13.
86. Berry, *Japan in Print*, 214–17.
87. The connection between learning and pleasure is by no means a new discovery. For example, Samuel Johnson, man of letters in eighteenth-century England, states, "The gratification of curiosity rather frees us from uneasiness that confers pleasure; we are more pained by ignorance than delighted by instruction" (*The Rambler* [London, 1794], 2:281–82). For more on curiosity in early modern Europe, see also Barbara M. Benedict, *Curiosity: A Cultural History of Early Modern Inquiry* (Chicago: University of Chicago Press, 2001), 1–24. The seventeenth-century Confucian writer Ejima Tamenobu (1635–1695), whose work I discuss in detail in chapter 3, explains that study might at first appear dull and daunting, but once the first hurdle is overcome "learning is more interesting [entertaining] than Kabuki or puppet theater" (*Mi no kagami* [1659], critical edition in *Kanazōshi shū*, ed. Watanabe Morikuni and Watanabe Kenji, Shin Nihon koten bungaku taikei 74 [Tokyo: Iwanami Shoten, 1991], 276). More recently, discoveries in psychology and neuroscience are showing how and why acquiring knowledge can indeed be pleasurable; see, for example, Jordan A. Litman, "Curiosity and the Pleasures of Learning: Wanting and Liking New Information," *Cognition and Emotion* 19, no. 6 (2005): 793–814.
88. Hashiguchi Kōnosuke, *Zoku wahon nyūmon: Edo no hon'ya to hon zukuri* (Tokyo: Heibonsha, 2007), 83–132, gives a rich account of all the expenses involved in the business of woodblock printing in early modern Japan.
89. See note 59.
90. For recent scholarship on Saikaku, see Jeffrey Johnson, "The Carnivalesque in Saikaku's Oeuvre," in *Bakhtinian Theory in Japanese Studies*, ed. Jeffrey Johnson (Lewiston, N.Y.: Mellen Press, 2001), 19–51; Jeffrey Johnson, "Novelness in Comical Edo Fiction: A Carnivalesque Reading of Ihara Saikaku's *Kōshoku ichidai otoko* (PhD diss., University of Washington, 1994); and David J. Gundry, *Parody, Irony and Ideology in the Fiction of Ihara Saikaku*, Brill's Japanese Studies Library 58

(Leiden: Brill, 2017); for a comprehensive bibliography of the translations of Saikaku's prose, see 8–12.

1. The Culture of the Written Word

1. Konda Yōzō, *Edo no hon'ya san: Kinsei bunkashi no sokumen*, Heibonsha raiburarī 685 (Tokyo: Heibonsha, 2009), 43.
2. Nagatomo Chiyoji, *Kinsei no dokusho*, Nihon shoshigaku taikei 52 (Musashimurayama: Seishōdō Shoten, 1987), 21.
3. Nagatomo, *Kinsei no dokusho*, 21.
4. David L. Howell, *Geographies of Identity in Nineteenth-Century Japan* (Berkeley: University of California Press, 2005), 24. The four estates, as Howell calls them, are known as *shi-nō-kō-shō* (samurai, peasants, artisans, and merchants). They were prescribed by Confucian thinkers and referred to at the time as the four estates (*shimin*). Status is defined as follows: "Status in Tokugawa Japan referred both to membership in a group (usually based on the occupation of the head of the household) and to the formal duties (*yaku*) that accompanied such membership" (28).
5. Howell, *Geographies*, 28.
6. Shibata Jun, "Kinsei zenki ni okeru gakumon no rekishiteki ichi," *Nihonshi kenkyū* 247 (March 1983): 116.
7. Richard Rubinger, *Popular Literacy in Early Modern Japan* (Honolulu: University of Hawai'i Press, 2007), 41.
8. Rubinger, *Popular Literacy*, 41.
9. Rubinger, *Popular Literacy*, 62, 68.
10. For example, Wyn Ford, "The Problem of Literacy in Early Modern England," *History* 78, no. 252 (February 1993): 31, notes that "the term 'subscriptional ability' implies the qualitative difference between the ability to sign and literacy proper." Similarly Keith Thomas notes, "But what do these totals of marks and signatures really tell us? In any individual case a mark does not necessarily mean that the person concerned could not write.... Conversely someone who wrote his name could not necessarily write anything else" ("The Meaning of Literacy in Early Modern England," in *The Written Word: Literacy in Transition*, ed. Gerd Baumann, Wolfson College Lectures 1985 [Oxford: Clarendon Press, 1986], 102).
11. Yokota Fuyuhiko, *Nihon kinsei shomotsu bunka shi no kenkyū* (Tokyo: Iwanami Shoten, 2018), 28.
12. Yokota, *Nihon kinsei shomotsu*, 126–50.
13. Kaibara Ekiken, *Wazoku dōjikun* (Osaka: Shibukawa Seiemon, 1710), critical edition in *Yōjōkun, Wazoku dōjikun*, ed. Ishikawa Ken (Tokyo: Iwanami Shoten, 1961), 220. On Kaibara Ekiken, see Mary Evelyn Tucker, *Moral and Spiritual Cultivation in Japanese Neo-Confucianism: The Life and Thought of Kaibara Ekken, 1630–1740*, SUNY Series in Philosophy (Albany: State University of New York Press, 1989), and Inoue Tadashi, *Kaibara Ekiken*, Jinbutsu sōsho (Tokyo: Yoshikawa Kōbunkan, 1989).
14. It is worth nothing that in early modern Japan writing was taught before reading. This was noted, for example, in 1585 by the Portuguese Jesuit missionary Luís Fróis (1532–1597). He observed a pattern of instruction that set Japanese education apart from practices in the West—that is, Japanese children learned to write before reading, whereas Western children practiced the reverse. See Luís Fróis, *Tratado das contradições e*

diferenças de costumes entre a Europa e o Japão (Macau: Instituto Português do Oriente, 2001), 60.
15. Shibata, "Kinsei zenki," 133.
16. Shibata, "Kinsei zenki," 131–34. It seems to me that Shibata's argument parallels that of Keith Thomas in his research on early modern England: "Literacy thus appeared to the authorities as a route to obedience and docility. It enabled the government to penetrate more deeply, saturating the country with proclamations, injunctions, homilies, and visitation articles; and it helped the clergy to bring the population to a new type of religion based on the book. . . . On the whole, the consensus in this period was that literacy should be encouraged because it did more to support the social order than to subvert it" (Thomas, "Meaning of Literacy," 118–19).
17. Namura Jōhaku, *Nan chōhōki* (Kyoto: Nakagawa Hikosaburō and Yamatoya Kanshichirō, 1693), critical edition in *Onna chōhōki Nan chōhōki*, 203–7.
18. Namura, *Nan chōhōki*, 235–42.
19. Namura Jōhaku, *Onna chōhōki* (Edo: Yorozuya Seibee; Osaka: Itan'ya Tarōemon; Kyoto: Yoshinoya Jirobee, 1692), critical edition in Nagatomo, *Onna chōhōki Nan chōhōki*, 14–15, 18–20.
20. Namura, *Onna chōhōki*, 118.
21. *Onna shikimoku* ([Kyoto]: publisher unknown, 1660), diplomatic transcription in vol. 11 of *Kanazōshi shūsei*, ed. Asakura Haruhiko and Fukasawa Akio (Tokyo: Tōkyōdō Shuppan, 1990). The reference is to vol. 2, 2r; *KS* 11:161. Note that hereafter *Kanazōshi shūsei* is abbreviated as *KS* throughout the notes.
22. *Onna shikimoku*, vol. 2, 2r; *KS* 11:161.
23. *Onna kagami hidensho* (Kyoto: Noda Yahee, 1650), diplomatic transcription in vol. 10 of *Kanazōshi shūsei*, ed. Asakura Haruhiko and Fukasawa Akio (Tokyo: Tōkyōdō Shuppan, 1989). The quotation is from vol. 1, 8r–9r; *KS* 10:10–11.
24. Rubinger, *Popular Literacy*, 68. Peter F. Kornicki has convincingly argued that women were very much involved in reading activities in the seventeenth century; "Women, Education, and Literacy," in *The Female as Subject: Reading and Writing in Early Modern Japan*, ed. P. F. Kornicki, Mara Patessio, and G. G. Rowley (Ann Arbor: Center for Japanese Studies, University of Michigan, 2010), 7–38.
25. *Nioi bukuro* (Kyoto: Nagaharaya Magobee, 1681), diplomatic transcription in vol. 55 of *Kanazōshi shūsei*, ed. Hanada Fujio et al. (Tokyo: Tōkyōdō Shuppan, 2016), 113–36. It must have enjoyed some popularity since it was later reprinted, as *Shorei kyōkun kagami* (The mirror of etiquette and morals), by Kikuya Shichirobee, also a Kyoto publisher, most likely in the first half of the eighteenth century and sometime after 1738; original in the British Museum (shelf mark: 1979,0305,0.31). The quotations are from vol. 2, 33v and 36v; *KS* 55:133, 136.
26. Sasayama Baian, *Terako seikai no shikimoku* (Osaka: Kawachiya Shinjirō and Kawachiya Tasuke, 1835), posthumous printed edition; Tottori Kenritsu Toshokan, Tottori; digital version, National Institute of Japanese Literature, Tachikawa (shelf mark: DIG-TOKT-11), 1r.
27. Takahashi Satoshi, *Edo no kyōiku ryoku* (Tokyo: Chikuma Shobō, 2007), 19. Rubinger elaborates on the profusion of records and regulations as proof of "power being directed downward by means of written documents" (*Popular Literacy*, 19, and, more generally, 18–43).
28. Ishikawa Ken, *Terakoya: Shomin kyōiku kikan*, Nihon rekishi shinsho (Tokyo: Shibundō, 1960), 59–63.

1. The Culture of the Written Word   309

29. The diplomatic transcription of the manuscript of *Kawachiya Yoshimasa kyūki* is available in *Kawachiya Yoshimasa kyūki*, ed. Nomura Yutaka and Yui Kitarō, Seibundō shiryō sōsho 1 (Tokyo: Seibundō Shuppan, 1970). Additional materials known as *Kashō zakki*, in the private collection of the Tsuboi family, have been made available in diplomatic transcription in *Kashō zakki*, vol. 41 of *Ōtani Joshi Daigaku Shiryōkan hōkokusho*, ed. Ōtani Joshi Daigaku Shiryōkan (Tondabayashi: Ōtani Joshi Daigaku Shiryōkan, 1999), 1–87.
30. *Kawachiya Yoshimasa kyūki*, 3–8, 26.
31. On the reference to Noh theater in Yoshimasa's diary, see Sado Emi, "Nōson shakai ni okeru Genroku bunka no juyō keitai," *Tachibana shigaku* 14 (1999): 26–50.
32. *Kawachiya Yoshimasa kyūki*, 242; see also 252, 293, 363, and 371. Kawachiya sets forth his teachings in sections referred to as *shoseikun* (the guiding principles for one's life).
33. *Kawachiya Yoshimasa kyūki*, 124.
34. *Kawachiya Yoshimasa kyūki*, 42, 124.
35. *Mitsugo yori no oboe* and *Yorozu no oboe* are owned by the descendants of the Enomoto family and on permanent loan to the Kawagoe City Museum. The diplomatic transcriptions are available in *Enomoto Yazaemon oboegaki: Kinsei shoki shōnin no kiroku*, ed. Ōno Mizuo, Tōyō bunko 695 (Tokyo: Heibonsha, 2001), 15–120, 121–352.
36. *Enomoto Yazaemon oboegaki*, 72–74.
37. *Enomoto Yazaemon oboegaki*, 154.
38. On the Kōnoike family, see Miyamoto Mataji, *Kōnoike Zen'emon*, Jinbutsu sōsho (Tokyo: Yoshikawa Kōbunkan, 1986). *Mitate banzuke* (ranking charts) issued toward the end of the Edo period rank Kōnoike Zen'emon as the wealthiest man in the country.
39. For a study of the Kōnoike family *kakun*, see Miyamoto Mataji, "Kōnoike Zen'emon ke no kakun ni tsuite," *Kokumin keizai zasshi* 110, no. 3 (September 1964): 36–58.
40. Sumiyoshi Gukei, *Tohi zukan*, manuscript without colophon, ca. late seventeenth century, Chester Beatty Library, Dublin (shelf mark: CBL J 1120).
41. Sakakibara Satoru, "Sumiyoshi Gukei hitsu *Tohi zu* kaidai," *Kobijutsu* 88 (October 1988): 60–61.
42. Asai Ryōi, *Kyō suzume* ([Kyoto]: Yamada Ichirobee, 1665), National Diet Library, Tokyo (shelf mark: 京乙:252). Hereafter cited as *Kyō suzume*.
43. *Kyō suzume*, vol. 2, 10r.
44. *Kyō suzume*, vol. 2, 12r.
45. *Kyō suzume*, vol. 5, 9r.
46. Keith Thomas notes this phenomenon in early modern England: "When notices and posters were displayed, a little group would gather and one would read the contents aloud to the others.... So long as they had access to someone who would read, therefore, there was no reason why others needed to be cut off from the culture of the written word" ("Meaning of Literacy," 106–7).
47. I am indebted to David Howell and Amy Stanley for their assistance with information about the urban population in seventeenth-century Japan. Because the shogunate did not attempt to estimate the national population until 1721, when the first census was conducted (and every subsequent six years), gauging the numbers for seventeenth-century Japan is no easy task. It must also be kept in mind that two status categories, the court aristocracy and the warrior class, were always excluded from the census. Also excluded were Buddhist monks, Shinto priests, and outcasts.
48. Miyamoto Matao, "Quantitative Aspects of Tokugawa Economy," in *Emergence of Economic Society in Japan, 1600–1859: Early Modern*, ed. Akira Hayami, Osamu Saitō,

and Ronald P. Toby, vol. 1 of *The Economic History of Japan: 1600–1990* (Oxford: Oxford University Press, 2004), 36, 38, 84. Kitō Hiroshi provides similar numbers: a total population of 12,273,000 in 1600 and 31, 278,500 in 1721; *Jinkō kara yomu Nihon no rekishi* (Tokyo: Kōdansha, 2000), 16–17. Kitō, *Jinkō kara yomu Nihon*, 80–84, also explains the complexities around calculating figures for the seventeenth century. For in-depth research on demographics in premodern Japan, see William Wayne Farris, *Daily Life and Demographics in Ancient Japan*, Michigan Monograph Series in Japanese Studies 63 (Ann Arbor: Center for Japanese Studies, University of Michigan, 2009).

49. Roderigo de Vivero, *An Account of Japan, 1609*, trans. Caroline Stone (Edinburgh: Hardinge Simpole, 2015), 129.
50. Nakabe Yoshiko, *Kinsei toshi no seiritsu to kōzō* (Tokyo: Shinseisha, 1967), 637.
51. Saitō Seiji, "Edo jidai no toshi jinkō," *Chiiki kaihatsu* 9 (September 1984): 48–63.
52. Rubinger, *Popular Literacy*, 78. He bases his figures on James L. McClain, *A Modern History of Japan* (New York: Norton, 2002), 51–54.
53. For a detailed study of these catalogues, see Laura Moretti, "The Japanese Early-Modern Publishing Market Unveiled: A Survey of Edo-Period Booksellers' Catalogues," *East Asian Publishing and Society* 2, no. 2 (2012): 199–308.
54. To the best of my knowledge there is no searchable, digital edition of the book-trade catalogues. It is to be hoped that such a database will be released at some point, which would allow for more precision in gathering data. Counting from a facsimile can lead to mistakes. I ask readers to be fully aware of this as they go through the data.
55. Nakano Mitsutoshi, *Shoshigaku dangi: Edo no hanpon* (Tokyo: Iwanami Shoten, 1995), 10. Nakano also specifies that subsequent print runs would normally entail thirty copies at a time.
56. Nagatomo Chiyoji, *Edo shomin no dokusho to manabi* (Tokyo: Benseisha, 2017), 33.
57. Hashiguchi Kōnosuke, *Zoku wahon nyūmon: Edo no hon'ya to hon zukuri* (Tokyo: Heibonsha, 2007), 120–21.
58. There is a trace of circulating libraries disseminating books, but evidence of people in the countryside buying books is scant. Yokota Fuyuhiko, for example, discusses the case of Yoda Nagayasu 依田長安 (1674–1758). Born into a samurai household that served the Tokugawa family, Nagayasu was given the status of peasant in Yamanashi County in Kai Province. The location is along the Tōkaidō highway not too far from Edo. Yokota has gathered information about the books Nagayasu owned between 1730 and 1732 and has identified where the books were bought. Yokota's research brings us back to booksellers mainly in Kyoto and Edo. See Yokota, *Nihon kinsei shomotsu*, 151–78.
59. In my research on *Ise monogatari*, for example, I noted that translations in "modern" (i.e., seventeenth-century) Japanese were produced in the second half of the 1600s; see Laura Moretti, "Kinsei shoki, zenki no sanbun bungaku ni okeru *Ise monogatari* no kakinaoshi, parodi oyobi shin tenkai," in *Ise monogatari sōzō to hen'yō*, ed. Yamamoto Tokurō and Joshua Mostow (Osaka: Izumi Shoin, 2010), 269–301. For discussion on how *Genji monogatari* (*The Tale of Genji*) and *Makura no sōshi* (*The Pillow Book*) were adapted for early modern readers, see, respectively, Michael Emmerich, *The Tale of Genji: Translation, Canonization, and World Literature* (New York: Columbia University Press, 2013), and Gergana Ivanova, *Unbinding* The Pillow Book: *The Many Lives of a Japanese Classic* (New York: Columbia University Press, 2018).
60. The drop of book numbers in 1699 should be seen against the background of a new expanding market based in Edo not acknowledged in these book-trade catalogues.
61. In his discussion of literacy in early modern England, Keith Thomas introduces the idea of multiple literacies. Thomas points out that "there were so many kinds of

written word, such as diversity of scripts, typefaces, and languages, that a simple contrast between 'literacy' and 'illiteracy' fails to register the complexity of the situation" ("Meaning of Literacy," 99). Eve Rachele Sanders and Margaret W. Ferguson echo this position: "Factors such as these—varieties of script forms and type fonts, kinds of language instruction ranging from English-only to classical Latin and Greek, variable access to kinds of books and tiers of educational institutions—all helped the emergence of multiple literacies in this period: reading-only literacy, scribal-literacy, English-only literacy, vernacular foreign-language literacy, Latin-literacy, scriptural literacy, heraldic literacy, legal literacy, etc." ("Literacies in Early Modern England," special issue, *Critical Survey* 14, no. 1 [2002]: 3). Heidi Brayman Hackel points to the link between the idea of multiple literacies and that of popular literacy: "The very concept of popular literacy, however, presupposes other levels of literacy—elite, high, clerical, classical—and popular literacy itself was surely various" ("Popular Literacy and Society," in *Cheap Print in Britain and Ireland to 1660*, ed. Joad Raymond, The Oxford History of Popular Print Culture, vol. 1 [Oxford: Oxford University Press, 2011], 97).

62. The first instance of this teaching is in the third volume (Kaibara, *Wazoku dōjikun*, 240). In his research regarding the age considered appropriate to begin *tenarai*, Koizumi Yoshinaga collected information from several Edo-period texts; *Edo no ko sodate yomihon* (Tokyo: Shōgakukan, 2007), 125.

63. See Kaibara, *Wazoku dōjikun*, 240 and 256. Other contemporary sources specify different categories of kanji requiring mastery after basic hiragana. These normally include the kanji for village, province, and family names. For details, see Takahashi, *Edo no kyōiku ryoku*, 37–45, and Koizumi Yoshinaga, "Learning to Read and Write—A Study of *Tenaraibon*," in *Listen, Copy, Read: Popular Learning in Early Modern Japan*, ed. Matthias Hayek and Annick Horiuchi, Brill's Japanese Studies Library 46 (Leiden: Brill, 2014), 103–4.

64. Kaibara, *Wazoku dōjikun*, 262.

65. It is noteworthy that the use of multiple variants for the same hiragana (today known as *hentaigana*) was the norm for both handwritten and printed texts. This choice did not create an obstacle to text accessibility, as is often conjectured. See Peter F. Kornicki, review of *Novel Japan: Spaces of Nationhood in Early Meiji Narrative, 1870–88*, by John Pierre Mertz, *Journal of Japanese Studies* 31, no. 2 (Summer 2005): 504.

66. Kaibara, *Wazoku dōjikun*, 256–57. Textbooks were also circulating in printed format, and the genre is normally referred to as *ōraimono*. Koizumi Yoshinaga defines *ōraimono* as "an elementary written medium for teaching children to read and write" ("Learning to Read and Write," 91). Markus Rüttermann offers a sophisticated analysis of the term *ōraimono* as a genre and challenges the most common view of *ōraimono* as referring to schoolbooks; "What Does 'Literature of Correspondence' Mean? An Examination of the Japanese Genre Term *ōraimono* and Its History," in Hayek and Horiuchi, *Listen, Copy, Read*, 139–60. While his work is insightful, extensive research in Japanese has shown that *ōraimono* were actually used for the education of children. *Ōraimono* and *tehon* were identified by seventeenth-century publishers as a specific category that featured regularly in their book-trade catalogues.

67. Kaibara, *Wazoku dōjikun*, 256.
68. Kaibara, *Wazoku dōjikun*, 268–69.
69. Namura, *Onna chōhōki*, 118.
70. The account of the wealthy salt merchant Enomoto Yazaemon records that he studied *tenarai* between the ages of eleven and twelve. Although this is later than what Ekiken proposes, it nonetheless confirms that the rudiments of writing and reading could be

mastered in a couple of years. An analysis of the curricula adopted for students in the *terakoya* called Tsukumo-an in the later nineteenth century by Koizumi and Takahashi confirms the approximate time frame included here. See Koizumi, "Learning to Read and Write," 108; Takahashi, *Edo no kyōiku ryoku*, 52–56.

71. *Enomoto Yazaemon oboegaki*, 154.
72. *Kawachiya Yoshimasa kyūki*, 124.
73. Shibata, "Kinsei zenki," 117. The same piece of information is quoted in Rubinger, *Popular Literacy*, 37.
74. On *terakoya* schools in medieval and early modern Japan, see Ishikawa Ken, *Terakoya*, 40–59; for a focus on the education of commoners, see 74. For an introduction to *terakoya* in English, see Ronald P. Dore, *Education in Tokugawa Japan* (London: Routledge and Kegan Paul, 1965), 252–92.
75. Sumiyoshi Gukei, *Tohi zukan* (also known as *Tohi emaki*), manuscript without colophon, ca. late seventeenth century, owned by Konbuin, Nara, housed in the Nara National Museum, Nara (no shelf mark).
76. Umihara Tetsu, *Kinsei no gakkō to kyōiku* (Kyoto: Shibunkaku Shuppan, 1988), 294. The figures are based on Ishikawa Ken, *Terakoya*.
77. Umihara, *Kinsei no gakkō*, 294.
78. Sasayama Baian, *Tenarai shiyō shū* (Osaka: Kichimonjiya Ichizaemon, n.d.), Sakata Shiritsu Toshokan, Sakata; microfilm copy, National Institute of Japanese Literature, Tachikawa (microfilm number: 26-153-16), 1r.
79. From Kōnoike Shinroku, *Shison seishi jōmoku* (Precepts for the progeny; 1614), quoted in Miyamoto, "Kōnoike Zen'emon ke," 40. The same call to dedicate free time to learning (reading books and listening to lectures) is made in the 1716 list of precepts compiled by the third-generation male head of the Kōnoike family; see, Miyamoto, *Kōnoike Zen'emon*, 171.
80. *Kawachiya Yoshimasa kyūki*, 278, 294. For other references to *gakumon*, see *Kawachiya Yoshimasa kyūki*, 28, 35, 41, 42, 124, 166, 202, 224, 278, 288, 294, 305, 366, 367, and 377.
81. *Kawachiya Yoshimasa kyūki*, 283–84.
82. Kaibara, *Wazoku dōjikun*, 240–42. Koizumi, "Learning to Read and Write," 103–5, gives other examples of texts that discuss at what age children should learn which discipline.
83. The view of *gakumon* as something that should lead to virtuous behavior is confirmed in other, coeval sources such as *Kashōki* (Records that make laughter possible; 1636), a best-selling title written by Nyoraishi 如儡子 (d. 1674). While the term *gakumon* appears in a few passages, there is unfortunately no attempt to define it. Brief remarks, however, indicate that the aim of learning is a practical one—to pursue the Way (*michi ni itaran*; vol. 1, sec. 8) and to become a good person (*yoki hito*) through learning (vol. 4, sec. 1); Nyoraishi, *Kashōki* ([Kyoto]: publisher unknown, 1642), diplomatic transcription in vol. 14 of *Kanazōshi shūsei*, ed. Asakura Haruhiko and Fukasawa Akio (Tokyo: Tōkyōdō Shuppan, 1993), 131–376. Groundbreaking work on *Kashōki* and Nyoraishi has been done by Fukasawa Akio; see, for example, Fukasawa Akio, *Saitō Chikamori (Nyoraishi) denki shiryō* (Tokorozawa: Kinsei Shoki Bungei Kenkyūkai, 2010).
84. Suzuki Toshiyuki, "Gakumon to bungei to seikatsu to: Kinsei kōki minshū no gakugei sekai," in "Bungaku to gakumon no aida: Kinsei bungaku," special issue, *Bungaku* 8, no. 3 (May–June 2007): 39–50.
85. *Zadankai* led by Nagashima Hiroaki in "Bungaku to gakumon," 3.
86. In their research, Suzuki and Nagashima draw on primary sources from the eighteenth and nineteenth centuries, but it is clear that the ideas surrounding *gakumon* were already taking shape in the seventeenth century.

1. The Culture of the Written Word   313

87. Maryanne Wolf, *Proust and the Squid: The Story of Science and the Reading Brain* (New York: HarperCollins, 2007), 54, 60–65.
88. Wolf, *Proust and the Squid*, 60.
89. Wolf, *Proust and the Squid*, 61–62. These claims are supported by references to scientific papers; see unnumbered notes on 248–49.
90. Wolf, *Proust and the Squid*, 61.
91. Peter Francis Kornicki, *Languages, Scripts, and Chinese Texts in East Asia* (Oxford: Oxford University Press, 2018), 29.
92. Kornicki, *Languages*, 165, details how it was possible to read (silently or aloud) a Sinitic text in the vernacular. The words read in Sino-Japanese pronunciation needed to be reordered (Sinitic follows a subject-verb-object [SVO] order, while Japanese follows a subject-object-verb [SOV] order), particles had to be added, and inflections included.
93. Koizumi, "Learning to Read and Write," 98. On *sodoku*, see also Kornicki, *Languages*, 177–78.
94. *Jitsugokyō* (Edo: Tsuruya Kiemon, 1792), private collection, Suzuran Bunko, Cambridge, U.K. (no shelf mark). My analysis of *Jitsugokyō* does not follow any chronological arrangement. The primary sources are organized in a conceptual order, moving from texts whose treatment of the Sinitic text requires higher *kanbun* literacy to those that facilitate access to readers with *wabun* literacy.
95. Kornicki, *Languages*, 166.
96. *Jitsugokyō* (Edo: Hanabusa Bunzō, ca. 1843–1847), private collection, Suzuran Bunko, Cambridge, U.K. (no shelf mark).
97. *Jitsugokyō* (Edo: Moriya Jihee, 1863), private collection, Suzuran Bunko, Cambridge, U.K. (no shelf mark).
98. Wolf, *Proust and the Squid*, 123.
99. Kyokutei Bakin (author) and Okada Gyokuzan (illustrator), *Jitsugokyō eshō* (Osaka: Imazuya Tatsusaburō, Kawachiya Sōbee, Kawachiya Tasuke, 1812), private collection, Suzuran Bunko, Cambridge, U.K. (no shelf mark).
100. Kornicki, *Languages*, 190.
101. Kornicki, *Languages*, 191.
102. Yada Tsutomu, *Kokugo moji, hyōki shi no kenkyū* (Tokyo: Kyūko Shoin, 2012), 449–91, presents the first academic treatment of *sōrōbun*.
103. Kornicki, *Languages*, 47, briefly mentions *sōrōbun* as "a formal written style that bristles with Chinese characters but is undeniably Japanese" and is used "for regulations and correspondence in Japan."
104. *Shogaku bunshō narabi ni yorozu shitsukekata* (Kyoto: Nishimura Matazaemon, 1647), private collection, Suzuran Bunko, Cambridge, U.K. (no shelf mark), 6v.
105. Hackel, "Popular Literacy and Society," 88.
106. Wolf, *Proust and the Squid*, 114–62; Maria Nikolajeva, *Reading for Learning: Cognitive Approaches to Children's Literature* (Amsterdam: Benjamins, 2014), 15. Wolf introduces novice and expert readers in her account of how human beings develop the ability to read. Nikolajeva has adapted the idea to her work on children reading literature.
107. Asayama Irin'an, *Kiyomizu monogatari* (Kyoto: Tsurugaya Kyūbee, 1638), critical edition in *Kanazōshi shū*, ed. Watanabe Morikuni and Watanabe Kenji, Shin Nihon koten bungaku taikei 74 (Tokyo: Iwanami Shoten, 1991), 139–92. Hereafter cited as *Kiyomizu monogatari*.
108. *Kiyomizu monogatari*, 143.
109. *Kiyomizu monogatari*, 143.
110. *Kiyomizu monogatari*, 145.

111. *Kiyomizu monogatari*, 146.
112. *Kashōki atooi* ([Kyoto]: Yamamoto Shichirobee and Ogawa Ihee, 1672), diplomatic transcription in vol. 16 of *Kanazōshi shūsei*, ed. Asakura Haruhiko and Fukasawa Akio (Tokyo: Tōkyōdō Shuppan, 1995), 253–54.

2. The Publishing Business

1. Peter Kornicki, *The Book in Japan: A Cultural History from the Beginnings to the Nineteenth Century* (Honolulu: University of Hawai'i Press, 2001), 170–71.
2. Kornicki, *The Book in Japan*, 174, 176–77.
3. Kornicki, *The Book in Japan*, 200, 208–10.
4. Kornicki, *The Book in Japan*, 186, 226.
5. Jorge Carrión, *Bookshops*, trans. Peter Bush (London: MacLehose Press, 2016), 20.
6. Carrión, *Bookshops*, 27.
7. Konda Yōzō, *Edo no hon'ya san: Kinsei bunkashi no sokumen*, Heibonsha raiburarī 685 (Tokyo: Heibonsha, 2009); Nagatomo Chiyoji, *Edo jidai no tosho ryūtsū*, Bukkyō Daigaku ōryō bunka sōsho 7 (Kyoto: Bukkyō Daigaku Tsūshin Kyōikubu and Shibunkaku Shuppan, 2002); Suzuki Toshiyuki, *Ezōshiya: Edo no ukiyoe shoppu* (Tokyo: Heibonsha, 2010).
8. On *rakuchū rakugai zu byōbu*, see Matthew P. McKelway, *Capitalscapes: Folding Screens and Political Imagination in Late Medieval Kyoto* (Honolulu: University of Hawai'i Press, 2006). For details on the depiction of bookshops in *Funagi-bon* (Funagi manuscript; possibly ca. late Keichō era) and *Yūraku zu byōbu* (Folding screen with scenes of amusements; mid-seventeenth century), see Nagatomo, *Edo jidai no tosho ryūtsū*, 22.
9. Sumiyoshi Gukei, *Rakuchū rakugai zukan*, manuscript without colophon, ca. late seventeenth century, Tokyo National Museum, Tokyo (shelf mark: E0045242).
10. Sumiyoshi Gukei, *Tohi zukan* (also known as *Tohi emaki*), manuscript without colophon, ca. late seventeenth century, owned by Konbuin, Nara, housed in the Nara National Museum, Nara (no shelf mark).
11. For more information on Japanese early modern book formats, see Nakano Mitsutoshi, *Shoshigaku dangi: Edo no hanpon* (Tokyo: Iwanami Shoten, 1995), 60–69.
12. Hishikawa Moronobu, *Shokunin zukushi emaki*, manuscript without colophon, ca. 1682, British Museum, London (shelf mark: 1923, 1114, 0.2.1, 2). I am indebted to Tim Clark for introducing me to this scroll.
13. For details on *fukuro-toji*, see Suzuki Jun and Ellis Tinios, *Understanding Japanese Woodblock-Printed Illustrated Books: A Short Introduction to Their History, Bibliography and Format* (Leiden: Brill, 2013), 59–60.
14. It is worth mentioning that some of the tasks performed in the shop illustrated by Moronobu were at times delegated to specialists: block cutters (*hangiya*), makers of covers (*hyōshiya*), and craftsmen specializing in bindings (*kyōshiya*). For more about the production of early modern printed books, see Hashiguchi Kōnosuke, *Zoku wahon nyūmon: Edo no hon'ya to hon zukuri* (Tokyo: Heibonsha, 2007), 83–132. At the beginning of the nineteenth century books depicting the publication process increase in number. See, for example, *Atariyashita jihon-doiya* (It's a hit! The local book wholesaler [1802]; written and illustrated by Jippensha Ikku), available in English translation in Lawrence Marceau, "Behind the Scenes: Narrative and Self-Referentiality in Edo Illustrated Popular Fiction," in "Narrativity and Fictionality in Edo-Period Prose Literature," ed. Laura Moretti, special issue, *Japan Forum* 21, no. 3 (2010): 403–23.

15. Nagatomo Chiyoji, *Kinsei kashihon'ya no kenkyū* (Tokyo: Tōkyōdō Shuppan, 1982), 19–22; Nagatomo, *Edo jidai no tosho ryūtsū*, 85–89, 114–16.
16. Nagatomo, *Kinsei kashihon'ya*, 26–32; Nagatomo, *Edo jidai no tosho ryūtsū*, 117–22.
17. Kornicki, *The Book in Japan*, 175. See also Hashiguchi Kōnosuke, *Wahon nyūmon: Sennen ikiru shomotsu no sekai* (Tokyo: Heibonsha, 2005), 20–22, 63–65.
18. Yūsōan, *Inu Hyakunin isshu* (n.p. [Kyoto?]: publisher unknown, 1669), facsimile in *Inu Hyakunin isshu*, ed. Kisho Fukusei Kai (Tokyo: Yoneyamadō, 1919), 11v.
19. Hashiguchi, *Zoku wahon nyūmon*, 104–7.
20. For the poem in *Hyakunin isshu*, see Joshua S. Mostow, *Pictures of the Heart: The Hyakunin Isshu in Word and Image* (Honolulu: University of Hawai'i Press, 1996), 207: "As soon as it blows, / the autumn trees and grasses / droop, and this must be why, / quite rightly, the mountain wind / is called 'the ravager'" (*fuku kara ni / aki no kusaki no / shiworureba / mube yama-kaze wo / arashi to ifuramu*).
21. Kornicki, for example, explains the word *sōshiya* in the context of the seventeenth century as "a dealer in bound books, although later the word *sōshi* acquired connotations of lack of seriousness" (*The Book in Japan*, 175). Hashiguchi Kōnosuke associates *sōshiya* with cheap products that encompassed entertaining and practical texts and with the second half of the eighteenth century; *Zoku wahon nyūmon*, 51. For a detailed study of this type of publisher-bookseller, see Suzuki, *Ezōshiya*.
22. Hachimonjiya Jishō and Ejima Kiseki, *Yakusha kingeshō* ([Kyoto]: Hachimonjiya Hachizaemon and Ejimaya Ichirōzaemon, 1719), National Diet Library, Tokyo (shelf mark: い-80), 1r.
23. Miyako no Nishiki, *Genroku taiheiki* (Kyoto: Aoyama Ihee, 1702), critical edition in *Miyako no Nishiki shū*, ed. Nakajima Takashi, Sōsho Edo bunko 6 (Tokyo: Kokusho Kankōkai, 1989), 81–175. Hereafter cited as *Genroku taiheiki*.
24. *Genroku taiheiki*, 149.
25. *Genroku taiheiki*, 150. *Genroku taiheiki* assumes some familiarity on the part of the reader, as it offers a list of family names without specifying individual members.
26. Kojima Tokuemon, *Kyō habutae* (Kyoto: Tachibanaya Seian, 1705), Waseda University Library, Tokyo (shelf mark: ル04 03771), vol. 3, 16v (the pagination in this volume is problematic as there are two sets of f. 16). Hereafter cited as *Kyō habutae*.
27. On Izumoji Izumi no Jō, see Inoue Takaaki, *Kinsei shorin hanmoto sōran: Kaitei zōho*, Nihon shoshigaku taikei 76 (Musashimurayama: Seishōdō Shoten, 1998), 122. See also Nagatomo, *Edo jidai no tosho ryūtsū*, 15, and Konda, *Edo no hon'ya san*, 23–25. On Heirakuji, see Inoue, *Kinsei hanmoto shorin sōran*, 724. See also Nagatomo, *Edo jidai no tosho ryūtsū*, 15; Konda, *Edo no hon'ya san*, 25–27; and Kornicki, *The Book in Japan*, 208–9. The enduring popularity of the Heirakuji firm is such that it is still in operation in Kyoto as a publisher of Buddhist materials. It runs today under the name Heirakuji Shoten; https://www.heirakuji.co.jp/ (accessed November 14, 2019).
28. Konda, *Edo no hon'ya san*, 19. For facsimiles of book-trade catalogues (or *shojaku mokuroku*), see Keiō Gijuku Daigaku Fuzoku Kenkyūjo Shidō Bunko, ed., *Edo jidai shorin shuppan shojaku mokuroku shūsei*, 4 vols. (Tokyo: Inoue Shobō, 1962–1964). I refer to my previous work on *shojaku mokuroku* for details concerning them; see Laura Moretti, "The Japanese Early-Modern Publishing Market Unveiled: A Survey of Edo-Period Booksellers' Catalogues," *East Asian Publishing and Society* 2, no. 2 (2012): 199–308.
29. Oka Masahiko et al., eds., *Edo jidai shoki shuppan nenpyō* (Tokyo: Bensei Shuppan, 2011). Oka kindly granted me access to published and unpublished data in spreadsheets covering the period 1591–1704.

30. For example, I have counted only one name in the following instances (and all similar cases): Yamaguchi Ichirobee for 山口市良兵衛 and its graphic variant 山口市郎兵衛; Ichikawa Jihee for 市川次兵衛 and the version with a homophonic character, 市川治兵衛; Umemura Yaemon for 梅村弥衛門 and the version with an additional character, 梅村彌右衛門; Shorin Heibee 書林平兵衛 and the version followed by his personal name, 書林平兵衛愚常; Tokuda Jūbee for 徳田十兵衛 and the version with the indication that Tokuda is the family name, 徳田氏十兵衛. I have made a distinction in cases similar to the following: Yamamoto Shichibee 山本七兵衛 and Yamamoto Shichirobee 山本七郎兵衛; Kawasaki Shichirobee 川崎七郎兵衛 and Kawasaki Shichirōemon 川崎七郎衛門; Yamamoto Kuzaemon 山本九左衛門 and Yamamoto Kurōzaemon 山本九郎左衛門. I have also counted family names twice, like Heirakuji 平楽寺, and a specific person in that family, such as Herakuji Shōbee 平楽寺小兵衛.

31. I say a minimum of sixty-five publishers, because there are several books in the vernacular published in the same period with no publisher's name listed in their colophons.

32. *Kyō habutae*, vol. 3, 16v. Nakano was located on Teramachi Avenue, at the intersection with Gojō Avenue.

33. *Kōwakamai* texts deal with the warrior class and the Genpei War (1180–1185); they were intended for both performance and reading. For a discussion in English of *kōwakamai*, see R. Keller Kimbrough, "Late Medieval Popular Fiction and Narrated Genres: Otogizōshi, kōwakamai, sekkyō, and ko-jōruri," in *The Cambridge History of Japanese Literature*, ed. Haruo Shirane and Tomi Suzuki, with David Lurie (Cambridge: Cambridge University Press, 2015), 355–69, and James T. Araki, *The Ballad-Drama of Medieval Japan* (Berkeley: University of California Press, 1964). Kimbrough has confirmed fifty surviving *kōwakamai* texts, all of which were composed in the fifteenth century.

34. *Kagekiyo* ([Kyoto]: Nakano Dōya, 1632), National Institute of Japanese Literature (shelf mark: タ7-33).

35. The role of images in making texts more accessible is a matter of dispute. Julia K. Murray, for example, notes that in the late Ming (1368–1644) and early Qing (1644–1911) periods woodblock-printed illustrations "made the books appealing to a diverse constituency," and she discusses the role of pictures in a number of didactic stories, some related to Confucianism; "Didactic Illustrations in Printed Books," in *Printing and Book Culture in Late Imperial China*, ed. Cynthia J. Brokaw and Kai-wing Chow (Berkeley: University of California Press, 2005), 417. As Cynthia J. Brokaw notes, however, art historians of the Western tradition have called into question the belief that pictures could help the semiliterate to understand texts; "On the History of the Book in China," in Brokaw and Chow, *Printing and Book Culture*, 51n110. Nonetheless, cognitive research is exploring how images affect the brain and emotions. See Maria Nikolajeva, *Reading for Learning: Cognitive Approaches to Children's Literature* (Amsterdam: Benjamins, 2014), 95. On *tanrokubon*, printed books whose illustrations contain red, green, and yellow added by hand, see Kogorō Yoshida, *Tanrokubon: Rare Books of Seventeenth-Century Japan*, trans. Mark A. Harbison (Tokyo: Kodansha International, 1984).

36. See, for example, *Mongaku* ([Kyoto]: Nakano Dōya, 1632), Tōyō Bunko, Tokyo (shelf mark: 三 Fa に 15), and *Shinkyoku* ([Kyoto]: Nakano Dōya, 1632), Tōyō Bunko, Tokyo (shelf mark: 三 Ad 21). Both are available in photographic reproduction in *Kōwakamai, otogizōshi*, vol. Kinsei-hen 1 of *Iwazaki Bunko kichōbon sōkan*, ed. Tōyō Bunko and Nihon Koten Bungaku Kai (Tokyo: Kichōbon Kankōkai, 1974), 335–66, 397–433, respectively.

37. On *Fuji no hitoana sōshi*, see Koyama Kazunari, *Fuji no hitoana sōshi: Kenkyū to shiryō* (Tokyo: Bunka Shobō Hakubunsha, 1983), and on *Usuyuki monogatari*, see chapter 5 in the present volume.
38. Multiple copies of Nishimura Matazaemon's 1643 edition of *Jinkōki* can be found, for instance, in the Waseda University Library, Tokyo (shelf marks: イ16-00041, イ16-00042, and イ16-00043). Nakano Ichiemon, Nakano Dōya's elder brother, also issued three editions in 1632 and 1633. For a study of *Jinkōki*, see Yamazaki Yoemon, *Jinkōki no kenkyū* (Tokyo: Morikita Shuppan, 2012); Annick Horiuchi, *Japanese Mathematics in the Edo Period (1600–1868): A Study of the Works of Seki Takakazu (?–1708) and Takebe Katahiro (1664–1739)*, trans. Silke Wimmer-Zagier, Science Networks, Historical Studies 16 (Basel: Birkhäuser, 2010); Annick Horiuchi, "The *Jinkōki* Phenomenon: The Story of a Longstanding Calculation Manual in Tokugawa Japan," in *Listen, Copy, Read: Popular Learning in Early Modern Japan*, ed. Matthias Hayek and Annick Horiuchi, Brill's Japanese Studies Library 46 (Leiden: Brill, 2014), 253–87.
39. This analysis is based on four of the 1658 titles listed by Oka and housed in the National Diet Library, Tokyo: *Yokobue takiguchi no sōshi* (shelf mark: ∧42), *Mongaku* (shelf mark: 本別19-4), *Sannin hōshi* (shelf mark: 232-295), and *Atsumori* (shelf mark: 231-120).
40. On *Otogi bunko*, see Barbara Ruch, "Origins of *The Companion Library*: An Anthology of Medieval Japanese Stories," *Journal of Asian Studies* 30, no. 3 (May 1971): 593–610.
41. Sōshiya Tarōemon would later move to the intersection of Ryōgae-machi and Nijō Avenue. Similar publications were issued by booksellers called *hangiya* or *han'ya*. For example, Hangiya Mataemon はんぎや又右衛門 emerged around 1655 with the publication of *jōruri* booklets and Han'ya Seibee はんや清兵衛 with the guidebook to the Yoshiwara pleasure quarter titled *Azuma monogatari* in 1642. *Jōruriya* was another name for similar booksellers. Jōruriya Kiemon しやうるりや喜衛門, for instance, issued the Buddhist tale *Sekkyō karukaya* in 1631. An English translation is available in R. Keller Kimbrough, trans., *Wondrous Brutal Fictions: Eight Buddhist Tales from the Early Japanese Puppet Theater* (New York: Columbia University Press, 2015), 60–95.
42. *Nitan no Shirō* ([Kyoto]: Yamamoto Kyūbee, 1667), National Diet Library, Tokyo (shelf mark: わ-59).
43. Hashiguchi, *Zoku wahon nyūmon*, 102–7, identifies the cost of cutting the wooden blocks and that of paper made for the majority of the expenses involved in the production of commercially printed books.
44. For a discussion of other *sōshiya* who exhibit a similar page layout in their publications, see Mori Shirō, "Kinsei zenki Edo-ban no honbun hanshita," *Kyōto Furitsu Daigaku gakujutsu hōkoku jinbun* 64 (December 2012): 29–42.
45. For a discussion of the term *kusazōshi* in reference to picture books, see Kimura Yaeko, Uda Toshihiko, and Koike Masatane, eds., *Kusazōshi shū*, Shin Nihon koten bungaku taikei 83 (Tokyo: Iwanami Shoten, 1997), 593–640; Leon M. Zolbrod, "*Kusazōshi*: Chapbooks of Japan," *Transactions of the Asiatic Society of Japan*, 3rd ser., no. 10 (August 1968): 116–47; and Michael Emmerich, "Picture books: From Akahon to Kibyōshi and Gōkan," in *The Cambridge History of Japanese Literature*, ed. Haruo Shirane and Tomi Suzuki, with David Lurie (Cambridge: Cambridge University Press, 2016), 510–22.
46. Okamoto Masaru, *Shoki Kamigata kodomo ehon shū*, Kichō kotenseki sōkan 13 (Tokyo: Kadokawa Shoten, 1982); Okamoto Masaru, *Kodomo ehon no tanjō*, Shirīzu Nippon sōshi (Tokyo: Kōbundō, 1988). For an English introduction to these materials, see R.

Keller Kimbrough, "Bloody Hell! Reading Boys' Books in Seventeenth-Century Japan," *Asian Ethnology* 74, no. 1 (2015): 111–39.

47. *Utai no hisho* ([Edo]: Matsue Ichirobee, 1652), Kōzan Bunko, Nogami Memorial Noh Theatre Research Institute of Hōsei University, Tokyo; microfilm copy, National Institute of Japanese Literature, Tachikawa (microfilm number: 238-154-5). No copy of *Nyohitsu Ono Otsū tehon* seems to have survived.

48. Kashiwazaki Junko, "Matsue Sanshirō," *Gengo bunka* 32 (December 1995): 133–39; id., "Matsue Sanshirō sono ni," *Gengo bunka* 45 (December 2008): 3–16; Kashiwazaki Junko, ed., *Zōhō Shōkaiban shomoku*, Nihon shoshigaku taikei 96 (Tachikawa: Seishōdō Shoten, 2009); Kira Sueo and Kashiwazaki Junko, "Shōkaiban mokuroku ko (1)," *Nihon kosho tsūshin* 62, no. 7 (July 1997): 24–26; id., "Shōkaiban mokuroku ko (2)," *Nihon kosho tsūshin* 62, no. 8 (August 1997): 24–25; id., "Shōkaiban mokuroku ko (kan)," *Nihon kosho tsūshin* 62, no. 9 (September 1997): 24–25; and id., "Shōkaiban mokuroku ko (hoi)," *Nihon kosho tsūshin* 63, no. 3 (March 1998): 27. This publisher (and its succeeding generations) appears to have moved frequently; the first shop was in front of the Kaminari gate of Asakusa Temple (1650s), and by the 1680s it had been relocated to the commercial area of Nihonbashi (Nagatanigawa-machi, Yoko-chō). See also Inoue Takaaki, *Kinsei shorin hanmoto sōran*, 687–88.

49. *Shida* ([Edo]: Matsue, 1659), National Diet Library, Tokyo (shelf mark: 853-255). *Tengu no dairi* ([Edo]: Matsue, 1659), National Diet Library, Tokyo (shelf mark: り34).

50. On Urokogataya, see Kashiwazaki Junko, "Urokogataya," *Gengo bunka* 47 (December 2010): 61–74.

51. For an introduction to Urokogataya Magobee's activity in the second half of the eighteenth century, see Laura Moretti, *Recasting the Past: An Early Modern Tales of Ise for Children* (Leiden: Brill, 2016).

52. Fujita Rihee, *Edo kanoko* (Edo: Komori Tarobee, 1687), photographic reproduction in *Edo kanoko*, ed. Asakura Haruhiko (Tokyo: Sumiya Shobō, 1970), 265–66 (vol. 6, 16r–17r) for *shomotsuya*, and 276 (vol. 6, 27r) for *jōruri hon'ya*. Suzuki, *Ezōshiya*, 7–19, explains that *jihon'ya* and *ezōshiya* were the standard names used in Edo for booksellers of the same type as *sōshiya* in Kyoto.

53. For an account of the development of commercial publishing in Osaka, see Nagatomo, *Edo jidai no tosho ryūtsū*, 27–40, and Tajihi Ikuo, *Keihan bungei shiryō*, 5 vols., Nihon shoshigaku taikei 89 (1–5) (Tachikawa: Seishōdō Shoten, 2004–2007). See also Tajihi Ikuo, "Keihan hon'ya tentō zu (hoi)," *Ōsaka furitsu toshokan kiyō* 29 (March 1993): 1–16.

54. Tajihi, *Keihan bungei shiryō*, 5:4–5. The 1679 street directories *Naniwa suzume* (The Osaka sparrow) and *Naniwa zuru* (The Osaka crane), similar to *Kyō habutae* and *Edo kanoko*, provide further evidence that *shomotsuya*- and *sōshiya*-type booksellers were operating in the area of Osaka's Shinsai and Kōra bridges. See Nagatomo, *Edo jidai no toshi ryūtsū*, 28–30.

55. *Genroku taiheiki*, 97.
56. *Genroku taiheiki*, 97.
57. *Genroku taiheiki*, 97–98.
58. *Genroku taiheiki*, 160–63, gives a list of authors engaged in the production of *gakumon*.
59. Hōjō Hideo provides a detailed record of all the titles ascribed to Asai Ryōi in the various *shojaku mokuroku*; *Shinshū Asai Ryōi*, Kasama sensho 11 (Tokyo: Kasama Shoin, 1974), 9–31; *Kaitei zōho Asai Ryōi*, Kasama sōsho 26 (Tokyo: Kasama Shoin, 1972). Shirakura Kazuyoshi lists the various pen names of Asai Ryōi as they appear in the *shojaku mokuroku*; "Asai Ryōi: Nazo ni tsutsumareta jinbutsu," in "Kinsei shōsetsu

no sakusha-tachi," special issue, *Kokubungaku kaishaku to kanshō* 59, no. 8 (August 1994): 26.
60. For details of Asai Ryōi's life, see Hōjō, *Shinshu Asai Ryōi*, 43–79. For discussion of his affiliation with Shōganji, see Shirakura Kazuyoshi, "Asai Ryōi," 26–27.
61. On this point, see Ishikawa Tōru, "Asai Ryōi hitsu Nara ehon emaki no sonzai," *Chūsei bungaku* 47 (June 2002): 87–96, and Ishikawa Tōru, "Asai Ryōi jihitsu shiryō o megutte," *Kinsei bungei* 76 (July 2002): 1–13.
62. Hayashi Gitan, foreword to Asai Ryōi, *Inu hariko* (n.p.: publisher unknown, n.d.), Yūtoku Inari Jinja, Kashima; microfilm copy, National Institute of Japanese Literature, Tachikawa (microfilm number: ユ1-228-5), introduction 1r.
63. There is ongoing debate concerning what texts can be attributed to Asai Ryōi. See Emoto Hiroshi, "Asai Ryōi: Ryōi no kankai to songisaku josetsu," in "Kinsei bungaku (sanbun) ni miru ningenzō," special issue, *Kokubungaku kaishaku to kanshō* 66, no. 9 (September 2001): 49–55. See also Shirakura Kazuyoshi, "Asai Ryōi," 25, 28.
64. *Genroku taiheiki*, 148.
65. Santō Kyōden (author) and Utagawa Kunisada (illustrator), *Kabuki no hana botan dōrō* (Edo: Iwatoya Kisaburō, 1810), Waseda University Library, Tokyo (shelf mark: ヘ13 03204), vol. 1, 6v.
66. Kyokutei Bakin, *Kinsei mono no hon Edo sakusha burui*, critical edition in *Kinsei mono no hon Edo sakusha burui*, ed. Tokuda Takeshi (Tokyo: Iwanami Shoten, 2014), 148.
67. For more details, see Tsutsumi Kunihiko, "Suzuki Shōsan: Hatamoto bushi kara shūkyōsha e," in "Kinsei shōsetsu no sakusha-tachi," special issue, *Kokubungaku kaishaku to kanshō* 59, no. 8 (August 1994): 14–19, and Yasuda Bunkichi, "Suzuki Shōsan: Mikawa bushi no seishin to zen," in "Kinsei bungaku (sanbun) ni miru ningenzō," special issue, *Kokubungaku kaishaku to kanshō* 66, no. 9 (September 2001): 35–41. See also J. S. A. Elisonas, "Fables and Imitations. Kirishitan Literature in the Forest of Simple Letters," *Bulletin of Portuguese-Japanese Studies* 4 (2002): 9–36.
68. Royall Tyler, *Selected Writings of Suzuki Shōsan*, Cornell University East Asia Papers 13 (Ithaca, N.Y.: Cornell University Press, 1977), 1–2.
69. For further details, see Watanabe Kenji, "Tsujihara Genpo ryakufu," in *Kinsei daimyō bungeiken kenkyū* (Tokyo: Yagi Shoten, 1997), 22–27.
70. See details in Ichiko Teiji, "Nakagawa Kiun," in "Kinsei shōsetsu no sakusha-tachi," special issue, *Kokubungaku kaishaku to kanshō* 59, no. 8 (August 1994): 20–24; Ichiko Teiji, "Nakagawa Kiun," in "Kinsei bungaku (sanbun) ni miru ningenzō," special issue, *Kokubungaku kaishaku to kanshō* 66, no. 9 (September 2001): 42–48; and Matsuda Osamu, "Nakagawa Kiun: Hito to sono sakuhin," *Bungei to shisō* 22 (January 1962): 1–15.
71. Jerome J. McGann, *The Textual Condition*, Princeton Studies in Culture/Power/History (Princeton, N.J.: Princeton University Press, 1991), 60.
72. I am arguing here for a publishing model that is slightly different from the one proposed by Julie Nelson Davis for the eighteenth century. Davis recognizes the key role of publishers, stressing that the production of books was a collaborative process and the result of partnerships, but she also highlights the centrality of writers and designers; *Partners in Print: Artistic Collaboration and the Ukiyo-e Market* (Honolulu: University of Hawai`i Press, 2015).
73. L. Moretti, "Japanese Early Modern Publishing."
74. The idea of publishing genres is drawn from Victor Infantes's term *género editorial*; see Victor Infantes, "La prosa de ficción renacentista: Entre los géneros literarios y el género editorial," in *Actas del X Congreso de la Asociación Internacional de Hispanistas* (Barcelona: PPU, 1992), 471.

75. On the complex concept of genre, see, for example, Paolo Bagni, *Genere* (Florence: La Nuova Italia, 1997); Anis S. Bawarshi and Mary Jo Reiff, *Genre: An Introduction to History, Theory, Research, and Pedagogy* (West Lafayette, Ind.: Parlor Press and the WAC Clearinghouse, 2010); Thomas O. Beebee, *The Ideology of Genre: A Comparative Study of Generic Instability* (University Park: Pennsylvania State University Press, 1994); Arthur Asa Berger, *Popular Culture Genres: Theories and Texts*, Foundations of Popular Culture 2 (Newbury Park, Calif.: Sage Publications, 1992); Wai Chee Dimock, "Introduction: Genres as Fields of Knowledge," *PMLA* 122, no. 5 (October 2007): 1377–88; Garin Dowd, Lesley Stevenson, and Jeremy Strong, eds., *Genre Matters: Essays in Theory and Criticism* (Bristol: Intellect, 2006); Heather Dubrow, *Genre* (London: Methuen, 1982); David Duff, ed., *Modern Genre Theory*, Longman Critical Readers (London: Routledge, 2000); Alastair Fowler, *Kinds of Literature: An Introduction to the Theory of Genres and Modes* (Oxford: Clarendon Press, 1982); John Frow, *Genre*, The New Critical Idiom (London: Routledge, 2005); Gérard Genette et al., *Théorie des genres* (Paris: Seuil, 1986); Paul Hernadi, *Beyond Genre: New Directions in Literary Classification* (Ithaca, N.Y.: Cornell University Press, 1972); Marielle Macé, *Le genre littéraire* (Paris: Flammarion, 2013); Stephen Owen, "Genres in Motion," *PMLA* 122, no. 5 (October 2007): 1389–93; Sakamoto Kenzō, *"Wakeru" koto "wakaru" koto*, (Tokyo: Kōdansha, 1982); Margot Singer and Nicole Walker, eds., *Bending Genre: Essays on Creative Nonfiction* (London: Bloomsbury, 2013); and Yoshida Masayuki, *Bunruigaku kara no shuppatsu: Puraton kara konpyūta e* (Tokyo: Chūō Kōronsha, 1993).
76. Linda H. Chance, *Formless in Form: Kenkō,* Tsurezuregusa, *and the Rhetoric of Japanese Fragmentary Prose* (Stanford, Calif.: Stanford University Press, 1997), 8.
77. In the following chapters and for the books that I have chosen for my close-reading analysis I provide information on how these books were classified in book-trade catalogues. This showcases how the same title could and did migrate from one publishing genre to another over time.
78. As I mentioned in the introduction, modern literary histories organize seventeenth-century prose according to the modern genre of *kanazōshi*, which was conceived in the twentieth century. I have already challenged its validity and discussed its great limitation in my article "*Kanazōshi* Revisited: Reconsidering the Beginnings of Japanese Popular Literature in Print," *Monumenta Nipponica* 65, no. 2 (2010): 297–356.
79. Nakano Mitsutoshi, "Saikaku gesakusha setsu saikō: Edo no manako to gendai no manako o motsu imi," *Bungaku*, 15, no. 1 (January 2014): 148.
80. Moretti, "*Kanazōshi* Revisited," 311. Peter F. Kornicki comes to a similar conclusion in "Japan's Hand-Written Culture: Confessions of a Print Addict," *Japan Forum*, 31, no. 2 (2019): 280.
81. See, respectively, Manase Gensaku, *Nichiyō shokushō* (Kyoto: Fūgetsu Sōchi, 1642), National Diet Library, Tokyo (shelf mark: 特1-2816), and Manase Gensaku, *Nichiyō shokushō* ([Edo]: Matsue, 1673), Waseda University Library, Tokyo (shelf mark: 文庫31 E1787).
82. On the popularity enjoyed by *gunsho* in the Edo period, see Inoue Yasushi, *Kinsei kankō gunsho ron: Kyōkun, goraku, kōshō* (Tokyo: Kasama Shoin, 2014).
83. See, for example, Adam Kern, "Envisioning the Classics: The *Tale of the Heike* in Edo-Period Comic Books," in *Lovable Losers: The Heike in Action and Memory*, ed. Mikael S. Adolphson and Anne Commons (Honolulu: University of Hawai'i Press, 2015), 206–66.
84. See, for example, Yoshida Ippō, *Wakan gunsho yōran* (Osaka: Kichimonjiya Ichibee; Edo: Kichimonjiya Jirobee, 1770), National Diet Library, Tokyo (shelf mark: 856-62); Ōgō Shinsai and Makino Zenbee, *Wakan gundanki ryakkō tasei* (Kyoto: Izumoji

Bunjirō; Osaka: Akitaya Taemon; Edo: Suharaya Mohee, Kitajima Junshirō, Izumiya Zenbee, and Izumiya Kichibee, 1841), National Diet Library, Tokyo (shelf mark: 025.1-O783w).
85. Hayek and Horiuchi, *Listen, Copy, Read*, 1.
86. Koizumi Yoshinaga, "Learning to Read and Write—A Study of *Tenaraibon*," in Hayek and Horiuchi, *Listen, Copy, Read*, 91. See also Markus Rüttermann, "What Does 'Literature of Correspondence' Mean? An Examination of the Japanese Genre Term *ōraimono* and Its History," in Hayek and Horiuchi, *Listen, Copy, Read*, 139–60.
87. Moretti, "Japanese Early Modern Publishing," 235–41.
88. Research is needed to gauge to what extent other publishing genres like calendars (no. 13 in table 2.2) and pictures (no. 22 in table 2.2.) addressed novice readers.
89. On *kusazōshi* picture books, see note 45. *Kawaraban* were usually cheaply printed on a single sheet by anonymous publishers and focused on the reporting of contemporary news; in this sense they are akin to early modern European broadsheets and broadsides. For a discussion of the term *kawaraban*, see Ono Hideo, *Kawaraban monogatari: Edo jidai masu-komi no rekishi*, Fūzoku bunka sōsho 1 (Tokyo: Yūzankaku Shuppan, 1960), 10–12, and Sepp Linhart, "*Kawaraban*—Enjoying the News When News Was Forbidden," in *Written Texts–Visual Texts: Woodblock-Printed Media in Early Modern Japan*, ed. Susanne Formanek and Sepp Linhart, European Studies on Japan 3 (Amsterdam: Hotei, 2005), 231–33. The oldest examples of *kawaraban* date to 1615 and chronicle the siege of Osaka, with a gap until 1682 of the next known, documented *kawaraban* sheets. Many of the extant copies are facsimiles printed later in the Edo period. For details, see Ono Hideo, *Kawaraban monogatari*, 13–18.
90. They are the 1681, 1696, 1709, and 1715 catalogues. For details, see Moretti, "Japanese Early Modern Publishing," 293–95.
91. I thank Professor Hashiguchi Kōnosuke for clarifying that prices in book-trade catalogues must be viewed as retailers' prices.
92. Keiō Gijuku Daigaku, *Edo jidai shorin*, 2:163.
93. Keiō Gijuku Daigaku, *Edo jidai shorin*, 2:212.
94. Kornicki, *The Book in Japan*, 186.
95. Ono Takeo, *Edo bukka jiten*, (Tokyo: Tenbōsha, 2009), 207. During this period in Japan there were three types of silver monetary units: *kanme* 貫目, *monme* 匁, and *fun* 分. In addition there was the copper *mon* 文. One *monme* was equivalent to 10 *fun* and to approximately 67 copper *mon*. The exchange rate from silver to gold differed depending on the period, but 60 *monme* (4,000 *mon*) were equivalent to 1 gold *ryō* around 1700.
96. Ono Takeo, *Edo bukka*, 207.
97. Ono Takeo, *Edo bukka*, 215.
98. Ono Takeo, *Edo bukka*, 271.
99. Ono Takeo, *Edo bukka*, 346, 348.
100. Taniwaki Masachika, Sugimoto Yoshinobu, and Sugimoto Kazuhiro, eds., *Saikaku to ukiyozōshi kenkyū*, vol. 3 (Tokyo: Kasama Shoin, 2010); the spreadsheet in the book's CD-ROM contains prices recorded in Ihara Saikaku's works.
101. Ono Hideo, *Kawaraban monogatari*, 26–27. As mentioned, *kawaraban* were not included in book-trade catalogues.
102. The prices are retrieved from early modern book-trade catalogues. Careful handling of the four volumes containing the facsimiles of book-trade catalogues (Keiō Gijuku Daigaku, *Edo jidai shorin*) is needed as the index (vol. 4) contains omissions and mistakes. I do not provide records of prices for the primary sources that I mention only in passing as a complement to the main discussion.

3. Negotiating the Way

1. The system of affiliation to a Buddhist temple is known as *terauke seido* or *danka seido* and has been the object of extensive study in recent years. See, for example, Kenneth A. Marcure, "The Danka System," *Monumenta Nipponica* 40, no. 1 (Spring 1985): 39–67, and Nam-lin Hur, *Death and Social Order in Tokugawa Japan: Buddhism, Anti-Christianity, and the Danka System*, Harvard East Asian Monographs 282 (Cambridge, Mass.: Harvard University Asia Center, 2007), 1–30. Tamamuro Taijō has coined the term "funerary Buddhism" (*sōshiki bukkyō*) for a system whereby on the one hand parishioners had an obligation for ritual attendance, which in turn meant providing financial support to the temple, and, on the other, parish temples took care of the funerary and memorial services for members of a household generation after generation; see Tamamuro Taijō, *Sōshiki bukkyō* (Tokyo: Daihōrinkaku, 1963).
2. This data is based on research that I have previously conducted on *shojaku mokuroku*; see Laura Moretti, "The Japanese Early-Modern Publishing Market Unveiled: A Survey of Edo-Period Booksellers' Catalogues," *East Asian Publishing and Society* 2, no. 2 (2012): 199–308. It is worth noting that a similar preponderance of religious books is found in seventeenth-century England. "Probably about 40 per cent of all publications in the late Tudor and early Stuart periods were religious" (Thomas N. Corns, *A History of Seventeenth-Century English Literature* [Chichester: Wiley-Blackwell, 2014], 9). "Customers in early modern bookshops chose to spend far more of their money on religious books than they did on playbooks and other 'literary' publications" (Peter W. M. Blayney, "The Alleged Popularity of Playbooks," *Shakespeare Quarterly* 56, no. 1 [Spring 2005]: 47). See also H. S. Bennett, *English Books and Readers, 1558 to 1603: Being a Study in the History of the Book Trade in the Reign of Elizabeth I* (Cambridge: Cambridge University Press, 1965), 156.
3. On the idea of sectarianism, see Richard Bowring, *In Search of the Way: Thought and Religion in Early-Modern Japan, 1582–1860* (Oxford: Oxford University Press, 2017), 181.
4. On the "Confucian turn," see Bowring, *In Search of the Way*, 46–68. For a definition of "Chinese learning" and its use in lieu of neo-Confucianism, see Herman Ooms, "Introduction to 'The Nature of Early Tokugawa Confucianism' by Kurozumi Makoto," *Journal of Japanese Studies* 20, no. 2 (Summer 1994): 331–35, 337–75.
5. On vernacular Buddhism, see R. Keller Kimbrough and Hank Glassman, eds., "Vernacular Buddhism and Medieval Japanese Literature," special issue, *Japanese Journal of Religious Studies* 36, no. 2 (2009). On the Way of Man as promoted by Itō Jinsai 伊藤仁斎 (1627–1705), see, for example, Bowring, *In Search of the Way*, 121–36.
6. Tessa Watt writes about "popular piety" in seventeenth-century English cheap print and texts known as penny godlinesses; *Cheap Print and Popular Piety, 1550–1640*, Cambridge Studies in Early Modern British History (Cambridge: Cambridge University Press, 1991). On "small godly books," see Margaret Spufford, *Small Books and Pleasant Histories: Popular Fiction and Its Readership in Seventeenth-Century England* (Cambridge: Cambridge University Press, 1985), 194–218. Robert Mandrou has analyzed French examples of seventeenth- and eighteenth-century "faith and piety" (*foi et piété*) by looking at specific genres within the *bibliothèque bleue* (e.g., spiritual songs, instructions on Christian doctrine, books of devotion, and lives of saints); *De la culture populaire aux 17e et 18e siècles: La bibliothèque bleue de Troyes* (Paris: Imago, 1999), 87–110. The vast production of popular books published by societies aimed at the propagation of the Christian faith, like the Religious Tract Society (founded in 1799) and the Society for Promoting Christian Knowledge (founded in 1698), is also noteworthy.

7. Important work has been done by Victor H. Mair. See, for example, "Buddhism and the Rise of the Written Vernacular in East Asia: The Making of National Languages," *Journal of Asian Studies* 53, no. 3 (August 1994): 707–51. See also Peter Francis Kornicki, *Languages, Scripts, and Chinese Texts in East Asia* (Oxford: Oxford University Press, 2018), 217–71.
8. In their remarks on vernacular Buddhism in medieval Japan, R. Keller Kimbrough and Hank Glassman note that "medieval religious culture in Japan was fundamentally trans-sectarian, constituting a rich amalgam of diverse and occasionally incompatible elements, rather than an organized or internally consistent universe of practice and belief" ("Vernacular Buddhism," 202).
9. See the definition in Miyasaka Yūshō, ed., *Kana hōgo shū*, Nihon koten bungaku taikei 83 (Tokyo: Iwanami Shoten, 1964), 4. Janine Anderson Sawada, *Confucian Values and Popular Zen: Sekimon Shingaku in Eighteenth-Century Japan* (Honolulu: University of Hawai'i Press, 1993), 21, translates *kana hōgo* as "vernacular Dharma talks."
10. Katayama Naotsugu, *Makura no hibiki* (Kyoto: Hachio Ichibee and Matsumoto Kyūemon, 1688), Tenri University Library (shelf mark: 169-1~3). *Makura no hibiki* first appeared in the 1692 book-trade catalogue under the category of *kana washo*. The title was identified as "a tale about the Five Virtues" (*gojō no monogatari*). It reappears in the 1696, 1709, and 1715 catalogues. The price was fixed at 2 *monme* 5 *fun*.
11. Katayama, *Makura no hibiki*, vol. 3, 12v.
12. Mary Elizabeth Berry, *Japan in Print: Information and Nation in the Early Modern Period* (Berkeley: University of California Press, 2006), 209–13.
13. For a brief discussion, see Kornicki, *Languages*, 263. For a more in-depth study of Razan's vernacular translations, see Peter Kornicki, "Hayashi Razan's Vernacular Translations and Commentaries," in *Towards a History of Translating: In Commemoration of the 40th Anniversary of the Research Centre for Translation*, ed. Lawrence Wang-chi Wong (Hong Kong: Research Centre for Translation, 2013), 189–212.
14. See Takeda Yuki, "Hayashi Razan no *Daigaku* kaishaku o megutte," *Nihon kanbungaku kenkyū* 11 (March 2016): 27–54. This is not to deny that "scribal publication," as defined by Peter F. Kornicki, did exist; see P. F. Kornicki, "Manuscript, Not Print: Scribal Culture in the Edo Period," *Journal of Japanese Studies*, 32, no. 1 (Winter 2006): 23–52.
15. Ejima Tamenobu, *Mi no kagami* ([Kyoto]: Yoshinoya, 1659), photographic reproduction in vol. 25 of *Kinsei bungaku shiryō ruijū Kanazōshi hen*, ed. Kinsei Bungaku Shoshi Kenkyūkai (Tokyo: Benseisha, 1977), 3–118; critical edition in *Kanazōshi shū*, ed. Watanabe Morikuni and Watanabe Kenji, Shin Nihon koten bungaku taikei 74 (Tokyo: Iwanami Shoten, 1991), 271–319. Citations refer to the critical edition. Ejima Tamenobu, *Rihi kagami* ([Kyoto]: publisher unknown, 1664), National Institute of Japanese Literature, Tachikawa (shelf mark: ナ4-146-1~3); photographic reproduction of copy at the National Diet Library Tokyo, in vol. 25 of *Kinsei bungaku shiryō*, 121–274. The popularity of *Mi no kagami* was such that it circulated in at least five different editions. For details, see Watanabe Kenji, "Kaisetsu," in vol. 25 of *Kinsei bungaku shiryō*, 277–82. *Rihi kagami* has survived in only one edition, dated 1664, and is available in a handful of extant copies. In the 1666–1667 *shojaku mokuroku* only *Mi no kagami* appears, under the category of *washo narabi ni kanarui*. In the 1670 catalogue both titles are recorded under *kana washo* with Hyūga Ejima 日向江島 listed as their author. They continued to be recorded until 1715 under the same category. In the 1681 catalogue *Mi no kagami* (3 vols.) is listed with the price of 2 *monme*. It decreases in price to 1 *monme* 5 *fun* in the 1696 and 1709 catalogues; this increases

in the 1715 catalogue to 2 *monme* 5 *fun*. *Rihi kagami* (3 vols.) was slightly more expensive: 3 *monme* in 1681; 2 *monme* 3 *fun* in 1696, 1709, and 1715.

16. The first to connect this pen name to Ejima Tamenobu was Ryūtei Tanehiko 柳亭種彦 (1783–1842) in his notes to the manuscript copy of *Mi no kagami* kept at the University of Tokyo (Nanki Bunko). Matsuda Osamu was the first to write extensively on the subject; See Matsuda Osamu, "Nisshū hyōhaku yajin no shōgai," *Kokugo kokubun* 21, no. 6 (July 1952): 417–33. For more recent scholarship, see Shimosaka Noriko, "Ejima Tamenobu no shikan jijō to sono haikei," *Ehime kokubun to kyōiku* 36 (December 2003): 14–23, and Shimosaka Noriko, "Hyōhaku yajin Ejima Tamenobu no bungaku to shikan," in "Samurai no bungaku," special issue, *Edo bungaku* 31 (November 2004): 55–76.
17. See *Rihi kagami*, vol. 1, sec. 4, 7r–9r, 18r, and vol. 3, sec. 4, 8r.
18. *Rihi kagami*, vol. 2, sec. 1, 1r. In translating Confucian terms I use the terminology proposed by Bowring, *In Search of the Way*.
19. *Mi no kagami*, 274.
20. *Rihi kagami*, vol. 2, 9v–10r. To appreciate how Ejima's position is close to Zhu Xi's interpretation of human nature, see Bowring, *In Search of the Way*, 130–31.
21. For example, in *Rihi kagami* (vol. 1, sec. 6, 11r–14r) he describes a journey undertaken with friends to visit Nakayama no Kannon near Mount Arima. After debating about whether they should put their lives in danger by entering the cave where there is a statue of Kannon, Ejima sees a group of pilgrims. They are all young, and as he listens to their poems, he realizes that they have undertaken the journey to pray for the afterlife. At that point Ejima launches a bitter reproach of this kind of behavior, suggesting that it breaches the need for young people to be filial. The worries imposed on their parents by leaving them alone are condemned as nonfilial acts.
22. The metaphor of the mirror is by no means unique to Japan. Juanita Feros Ruys notes, for example, that the "mirror" was a specific didactic genre that remained prevalent from Carolingian times (750–887) until the eighteenth century; "Introduction: Approaches to Didactic Literature—Meaning, Intent, Audience, Social Effect," in *What Nature Does Not Teach: Didactic Literature in the Medieval and Early-Modern Periods* (Turnhout, Belg.: Brepols, 2008), 18. See also her contribution to the same volume "Didactic 'I's and the Voice of Experience in Advice from Medieval and Early-Modern Parents to Their Children," 136n27. It is tempting to connect the idea of texts conceived as mirrors to the notion of "mirroring" and the mirror neurons as studied by neuroscientists; see Bruce McConachie, *Engaging Audiences: A Cognitive Approach to Spectating in the Theatre* (New York: Palgrave Macmillan, 2008), 70–71.
23. I am indebted to Barry Pegg for the definition of "ancillary images," referring to illustrations "placed in the neighbourhood of the relevant text. . . . The exact relationship of the image to the text, however, is left for the reader to determine" ("Two-Dimensional Features in the History of Text Format: How Print Technology Has Preserved Linearity," in *Working with Words and Images: New Steps in an Old Dance*, ed. Nancy Allen [Westport, Conn.: Ablex Publishing, 2002], 170).
24. Maria Nikolajeva, *Reading for Learning: Cognitive Approaches to Children's Literature* (Amsterdam: Benjamins, 2014), 95.
25. Watt, *Cheap Print and Popular Piety*, 131–77, shows that images had a role even in a time when popular piety and cheap print were under the pressure of the iconoclastic turn promoted by the Reformation.
26. *Rihi kagami*, vol. 2, sec. 7, 9v–10r.
27. *Mi no kagami*, 319. For the reception history of *Tsurezuregusa* in the Edo period, see Linda H. Chance, "Constructing the Classic: *Tsurezuregusa* in Tokugawa Readings," *Journal of the American Oriental Society* 117, no. 1 (January–March 1997): 39–56.

28. *Rihi kagami*, vol. 3, 3r, 8r, 11v.
29. *Rihi kagami* vol. 2, 9r, and vol. 3, 17v.
30. There is lack of agreement on how to translate the Japanese word *mondō* (literally, "question and answer"). I opt for "dialogue," following the definition of the "dialogical sequence" (*séquence dialogale*) in Jean-Michel Adam, *Les textes: Types et prototypes*, 4th ed. (Paris: Colin, 2017), Kindle, chapter 5. Adam talks about a *séquence-échange*, made of an *intervention initiative* and an *intervention réactive*. These sequences of exchanges can be made up of two or more interventions. This is not to deny that in other contexts *mondō* can be more aptly translated as "debate."
31. *Rihi kagami*, vol. 2, sec. 10; vol. 3, sec. 5; and vol. 3, sec. 1, respectively.
32. *Rihi kagami*, vol. 1, sec. 3, 5v.
33. *Rihi kagami*, vol. 1, sec. 3, 7r.
34. *Mi no kagami*, 312.
35. On empathy and identification, see, for example, Nikolajeva, *Reading for Learning*, 84. See also McConachie, *Engaging Audiences*, 65–76.
36. *Mi no kagami*, 275–76.
37. *Rihi kagami*, vol. 3, sec. 11, 21r–22r. Ejima here quotes Confucius's *Analects* (J. *Rongo*) by giving the Chinese text (知之為知之不知為不知) and the interlinear translation in Japanese. See *Rongo*, critical edition in *Rongo*, ed. Kanaya Osamu (Tokyo: Iwanami Shoten, 1999), 43; English translation in Edward Slingerland, trans., *Confucius, Analects: With Selections from Traditional Commentaries* (Indianapolis: Hackett Publishing, 2003), 13. See also *Mi no kagami*, 275–76, 287. Cautioning against false pretenses is also a feature of other seventeenth-century didactic writings. The same saying appears in Yamaoka Genrin, *Tagami no ue* (Kyoto: Akitaya Heizaemon, 1657), diplomatic transcription in vol. 48 of *Kanazōshi shūsei*, ed. Hanada Fujio et al. (Tokyo: Tōkyōdō Shuppan, 2012), 5–6. Section 3 in the second volume reinforces this teaching. It should be noted that *Tagami no ue* generally includes a great deal of the intellectual ground that interests Ejima, but the style comes across as much more learned, with an abundance of quotations in *kanbun* from Chinese classics; these were made accessible through the use of reading glosses for each character. On *Tagami no ue*, see Miura Kunio, *Kanazōshi ni tsuite no kenkyū* (Tokyo: Ōfū, 1996), 124–69.
38. This teaching emerges in *Rihi kagami*, vol. 1, sec. 2, 3r–4r. The point is reiterated in other, coeval texts. For example, *Kashōki* includes a list of good and bad friends. People one should become acquainted with include those with compassion and with a strong sense of justice; those who like *gakumon*, are loyal, and understand filial piety; and those who are discreet and honest. Avoid contact with those who are lustful and drink, lie, lack filial piety and loyalty, and who are arrogant; Nyoraishi, *Kashōki* ([Kyoto]: publisher unknown, 1642), diplomatic transcription in vol. 14 of *Kanazōshi shūsei*, ed. Asakura Haruhiko and Fukasawa Akio (Tokyo: Tōkyōdō Shuppan, 1993), 137; see also vol. 1, sec. 30, 30v; *KS* 14:156.
39. *Mi no kagami*, 285. *Tagami no ue* (vol. 3, sec. 1; *KS* 48:33–36) also warns readers against the perils of losing one's mind over prostitutes (*keisei gurui*).
40. *Mi no kagami*, 301–2.
41. *Mi no kagami*, 309–11.
42. *Mi no kagami*, 290. Ejima here quotes Confucius's *Analects* by giving the Chinese text (朝聞道夕死可) and the interlinear translation in Japanese; see Kanaya, *Rongo*, 74; English translation in Slingerland, *Confucius*, 32.
43. *Mi no kagami*, 305.
44. *Mi no kagami*, 292–93; see also *Mi no kagami*, 301 (vol. 2, sec. 10), for the importance of distinguishing between private (*naigi*) and public (*kōgi*).

45. *Mi no kagami*, 298–99.
46. *Rihi kagami*, vol. 3, sec. 1, 1r–2v.
47. *Rihi kagami*, vol. 2, sec. 3, 2v–4r.
48. *Rihi kagami*, vol. 3, sec. 6, 11r–13r.
49. Tadao Sakai, "Confucianism and Popular Educational Works," in *Self and Society in Ming Thought*, ed. Wm. Theodore de Bary (New York: Columbia University Press, 1970), 347.
50. *Rihi kagami*, vol. 1, sec. 8, 16r–19r.
51. *Mi no kagami*, 318–19.
52. *Rihi kagami*, vol. 3, sec. 8, 15v–17r.
53. For example, in *Mi no kagami*, 287–88, Ejima cautions parents that they should never lie to their children.
54. *Rihi kagami*, vol. 2, sec. 6, 7r–8v.
55. *Mi no kagami*, 280–82; *Rihi kagami*, vol. 2, sec. 1, 1r–3v.
56. *Mi no kagami*, 314–15. *Inu makura*, also known as *Inu makura narabi ni kyōka*, is the work of Hata Sōha 秦宗巴 (1550–1607), a doctor employed by the shogun Tokugawa Ieyasu. It was published in 1600 using movable type. It is available in a critical edition in *Kanazōshi shū*, ed. Maeda Kingorō and Morita Takeshi, Nihon koten bungaku taikei 90 (Tokyo: Iwanami Shoten, 1965), 33–48, and in English translation in Edward Putzar, "*Inu Makura*: The Dog Pillow," *Harvard Journal of Asiatic Studies* 28 (1968): 98–113. *Mottomo no sōshi* was first published in 1632. It survives in printings dated to 1634, 1649, and 1673, as well in others without a colophon. See Saitō Tokugen, *Mottomo no sōshi* ([Kyoto]: Nakano Dōhan, 1634), critical edition in *Kanazōshi shū*, ed. Watanabe Morikuni and Watanabe Kenji, Shin Nihon koten bungaku taikei 74 (Tokyo: Iwanami Shoten, 1991), 53–138. A study of the reception history of *Makura no sōshi* in the Edo period can be found in Gergana Ivanova, *Unbinding* The Pillow Book: *The Many Lives of a Japanese Classic* (New York: Columbia University Press, 2018).
57. Asayama Irin'an, *Kiyomizu monogatari* (Kyoto: Tsurugaya Kyūbee, 1638), critical edition in *Kanazōshi shū*, ed. Watanabe Morikuni and Watanabe Kenji, Shin Nihon koten bungaku taikei 74 (Tokyo: Iwanami Shoten, 1991), 139–92. Citations refer to the critical edition. Tsurugaya Kyūbee probably inherited the 1638 printing blocks and inserted his own name in the colophon. It is unclear who produced the blocks in the first place. Other copies of *Kiyomizu monogatari* date to 1645 (Sugita Kanbee, Kyoto), 1682 (Urokogataya Sanzaemon, Edo), and 1689 (Nagata Chōbee, Kyoto); these exist alongside copies without colophons. *Kiyomizu monogatari* was listed in *shojaku mokuroku* as early as the 1666–1667 and remained a steady title until the 1715 catalogue. It was first listed under *washo narabi ni kanarui* and then moved to *kana washo* beginning in 1670. For this two-volume publication, the price was 1 *monme* 7 *fun* in the 1681 catalogue; it decreased to 1 *monme* 5 *fun* in the 1696 and 1709 catalogues, increasing to 2 *monme* 5 *fun* in the 1715 catalogue.
58. *Kiyomizu monogatari*, 142–56.
59. *Kiyomizu monogatari*, 156.
60. *Kiyomizu monogatari*, 157–66.
61. *Kiyomizu monogatari*, 177–92.
62. Emoto Hiroshi, *Kinsei zenki shōsetsu no kenkyū*, Kinsei bungaku kenkyū sōsho 12 (Tokyo: Wakakusa Shobō, 2000), 54.
63. *Kiyomizu monogatari*, 167–72.
64. *Kiyomizu monogatari*, 167.
65. *Kiyomizu monogatari*, 167.

66. *Kiyomizu monogatari*, 168.
67. *Kiyomizu monogatari*, 169.
68. *Kiyomizu monogatari*, 170.
69. *Kiyomizu monogatari*, 172.
70. *Minu kyō monogatari* ([Kyoto]: publisher unknown, 1659), photographic reproduction in *Kanazōshi shū*, Kinsei bungei sōkan 2 (Osaka: Han'an Noma Kōshin Sensei Kakō Kinen, 1970), 187–350. It was reissued by Itamiya Kichiemon (Kyoto) in 1679 under the new title of *Ikkyū shina monogatari* (Various tales of Ikkyū), National Diet Library, Tokyo (shelf mark: 212-33). *Minu kyō monogatari* appeared in *shojaku mokuroku* in 1670 under the label of *mai narabi ni sōshi*, moving to *monogatari-rui* after 1685. It remained a steady item in book-trade catalogues until 1715. Its three volumes were priced at 2 *monme* 5 *fun* (only in the 1681catalogue).
71. *Minu kyō monogatari*, vol. 1, 3v–14r.
72. *Minu kyō monogatari*, vol. 1, 5r.
73. *Minu kyō monogatari*, vol. 1, 10v.
74. *Gion monogatari* (n.p.: publisher unknown, n.d.), diplomatic transcription in vol. 22 of *Kanazōshi shūsei*, ed. Asakura Haruhiko, Fukasawa Akio, and Yanagisawa Masaki (Tokyo: Tōkyōdō Shuppan, 1998), 1–87. The author of *Gion monogatari* is unknown. A fair number of copies have survived, but none bears a colophon. *Gion monogatari* appears in *shojaku mokuroku* as early as the 1666–1667 catalogue and was continuously included until the 1715 book-trade catalogue. In the catalogues organized into categories, it follows soon after *Kiyomizu monogatari* under the label first of *washo narabi ni kanarui* and then of *kana washo* (beginning in 1670). In the 1675 book-trade catalogue it is described as a "response to *Kiyomizu monogatari*." In two volumes like *Kiyomizu monogatari*, it was more expensive than *Kiyomizu monogatari*, priced at 3 *monme* (1681 catalogue; later catalogues do not include a price).
75. *Gion monogatari*, vol. 1, 2v–3r; *KS* 22:4. *Gion monogatari* even mentions that *Kiyomizu monogatari* sold at two thousand to three thousand copies; *Gion monogatari*, vol. 1, 1r; *KS* 22:3.
76. Emoto, *Kinsei zenki shōsetsu*, 55.
77. *Gion monogatari*, vol. 1, 48r–48v; *KS* 22:46.
78. *Gion monogatari*, vol. 2, 4r–4v; *KS* 22:49–50.
79. *Gion monogatari*, vol. 2, 6r–6v; *KS* 22:51.
80. *Gion monogatari*, vol. 2, 5v; *KS* 22:51–52.
81. Sakai, "Confucianism," 338–39, notes a similar tendency toward syncretism (Daoism, Buddhism, and Confucianism) in popular educational works of the Ming period.
82. *Daibutsu monogatari* ([Kyoto]: publisher unknown, 1644), diplomatic transcription in vol. 47 of *Kanazōshi shūsei*, ed. Fukasawa Akio et al. (Tokyo: Tōkyōdō Shuppan, 2011), 59–89. It was issued twice, in 1642 and 1644, but there is no information on the publishers. Nichishin, *Tadasu monogatari* ([Kyoto]: publisher unknown, 1657) diplomatic transcription in vol. 47 of *Kanazōshi shūsei*, ed. Fukasawa Akio et al. (Tokyo: Tōkyōdō Shuppan, 2011), 119–66. Editions dating to 1660, 1678, 1706, 1777, 1816, and 1843 are known.
83. Royall Tyler, *Selected Writings of Suzuki Shōsan*, Cornell University East Asia Papers 13 (Ithaca, N.Y.: Cornell University Press, 1977), 4.
84. Suzuki Shōsan, *Mōanjō* (Kyoto: Hiroi Kyūzaemon, 1651), critical edition in *Kana hōgo shū*, ed. Miyasaka Yūshō, Nihon koten bungaku taikei 83 (Tokyo: Iwanami Shoten, 1964), 241–61. An English translation is available in Tyler, *Selected Writings*, 31–52. Its popularity is seen in the existence of multiple editions produced during the Edo period:

1651, 1653, 1655, 1664, 1727, 1778, 1824, and other undated editions. It was recorded in the 1666–1667 catalogue under *washo narabi ni kanarui* and then moved to *kana hōgo* beginning in 1670. In one volume, it was priced at 5 *fun* in 1681 and 1696. No price is given in 1709 and 1715.

85. Bowring, *In Search of the Way*, 27.
86. Charlotte Eubanks, "Illustrating the Mind: 'Faulty Memory' *Setsuwa* and the Decorative Sutras of Late Classical and Early Medieval Japan," in Kimbrough and Glassman, "Vernacular Buddhism," 217.
87. *Kannon-gyō hayayomi eshō* (Kyoto: Suharaya Heizaemon, n.d.), private collection, Suzuran Bunko, Cambridge, U.K. (no shelf mark); advertisement pasted on the back of the front cover.
88. *Kannon-gyō wadan shō* ([Kyoto]: Akitaya Seibee, 1661), private collection, Suzuran Bunko, Cambridge, U.K. (no shelf mark). Hereafter cited as *Kannon-gyō wadan shō*, 1661 edition. There is also a 1661 edition issued by Chōjiya Saburobee in Kyoto. It was reissued or reprinted in 1670, 1683, 1703, 1719; undated editions also exist. It is worth noting the involvement of two *sōshiya* in the publication of *Kannon-gyō wadan shō*—that is, the Kyoto-based Yamamoto Kyūbee and the Edo-based Urokogataya. Urokogataya even cut two sets of blocks: the first is dated 1683 and probably copied the page layout set out by Yamamoto Kyūbee; the second is a later edition published together with Edo-based publisher Nishimuraya Yohachi. This proves that publishers at the time considered *Kannon-gyō wadan shō* as a title that had market potential, appealing to both *mono no hon'ya* and *sōshiya*. It appeared in the 1670 catalogue under *kana hōgo* and was listed until 1715. An edition with illustrations (*eiri*) was also recorded in the 1675, 1692, and 1699 catalogues organized in publishing genres, and in the 1696, 1709, and 1715 catalogues organized in *i-ro-ha* order. In 1681 the price (for three volumes) was 2 *monme*. In 1696 the edition without illustrations (3 vols.) was priced at 1 *monme* 1 *fun*, while the illustrated edition (3 vols.) was 1 *monme* 2 *fun* (?). In the 1709 catalogue the price increased to 1 *monme* 5 *fun* for both. In 1715 the price went back to 2 *monme* for the edition without illustrations. No price was given for the illustrated edition. A further edition where the word *eshō* follows the title was recorded in 1692, 1696, 1709, and 1715. Further research needs to be conducted to understand what this *eshō* version refers to.
89. *Kannon-gyō wadan shō*, 1661 edition, vol. 1, 4r.
90. *Kannon-gyō wadan shō*, 1661 edition, vol. 1, 10r–10v.
91. It is hoped that future research will reveal whether specific Chinese texts were used as source texts for these exempla.
92. *Kannon-gyō wadan shō* (Edo: Urokogataya Magobee and Nishimuraya Yohachi, n.d.) Private collection, Suzuran Bunko, Cambridge, U.K. (no shelf mark), vol. 1, 9v–10r. The illustration on the 10r is based on the illustration included in *Kannon-gyō wadan shō* (Kyoto: Yamamoto Kyūbee, n.d.), vol. 1, 11r.
93. Hirata Shisui and Tsujimoto Motosada, *Kannon-gyō wadan shō zue* (Kyoto: Sakaiya Jinbee, 1833), private collection, Suzuran Bunko, Cambridge, U.K. (no shelf mark), vol. 1, 10v–11r.
94. On how basic emotions are innate as hardwired in the brain and evolutionarily conditioned see Nikolajeva, *Reading for Learning*, 81, 82, 133.
95. *Kannon-gyō wadan shō*, 1661 edition, vol. 2, 6v–7v.
96. The title *Kannon riyaku monogatari* appears in the introduction of the 1719 edition published by the Kyoto publisher Umemura Saburobee. See original in the National Institute of Japanese Literature, Tachikawa (shelf mark ヤ 5-371).

97. Blurb that appears at the back of Hirata Shisui, Tsujimoto Motosada, and Hishikawa Kiyoharu (illustrator), *Ikkyū shokoku monogatari zue* (Kyoto: Sakaiya Jinbee, 1836), private collection, Suzuran Bunko, Cambridge, U.K. (no shelf mark).
98. *Amida kyō wadan shō* (Kyoto: Nagata Chōbee, 1685), private collection, Suzuran Bunko, Cambridge, U.K. (no shelf mark, no folio number).
99. Kornicki, *Languages*, 191, 239. On the history of translation in the Edo period, see Rebekah Clements, *A Cultural History of Translation in Early Modern Japan* (Cambridge: Cambridge University Press, 2015).
100. Kornicki, *Languages*, 263.
101. Meghan Marie Hammond and Sue J. Kim, eds., *Rethinking Empathy through Literature*, Routledge Interdisciplinary Perspectives on Literature (New York: Routledge, 2014), 189. In her analysis of the medieval English text *Handlyng Synne*, Anne M. Scott examines the part played by narrative exempla in making complex ecclesiastical issues as palatable and memorable as possible in a vernacular text written for a wide readership; "'For lewed men y vndyr toke on englyssh tonge to make this boke': *Handlyng Synne* and English Didactic Writing for the Laity," in *What Nature Does Not Teach: Didactic Literature in the Medieval and Early-Modern Periods*, ed. Juanita Feros Ruys (Turnhout, Belg.: Brepols, 2008), 377–400.
102. Suzuki Shōsan, *Inga monogatari* (Kyoto: Zeniya, n.d.), hiragana version; diplomatic transcription in vol. 4 of *Kanazōshi shūsei*, ed. Asakura Haruhiko (Tokyo: Tōkyōdō Shuppan, 1983), 199–285. Suzuki Shōsan, Giun (editor), and Unpo (editor), *Inga monogatari* (n.p: publisher unknown, n.d.), katakana version; diplomatic transcription in vol. 4 of *Kanazōshi shūsei*, ed. Asakura Haruhiko (Tokyo: Tōkyōdō Shuppan, 1983), 287–368. Citations are from these transcriptions. "Zeniya" might refer to Zeniya Gihee on Horikawa Avenue. The hiragana version was issued in different editions, including one by Yamada Ichirobee (with eleven lines per half folio) and one anonymous (with twelve lines per half folio, later reissued by Chōjiya Kurōemon and in 1841 by Medokiya Shūhachi). Asakura Haruhiko opines that the Yamada Ichirobee edition precedes the Zeniya. Asakura also notes that Asai Ryōi has to be seen as the calligrapher of the preparatory text used to create the printing blocks. See *kaidai* in vol. 4 of *Kanazōshi shūsei*, 450–51. The katakana version was later reprinted by Yamamoto Heizaemon and by Chōjiya Kurōemon (dates known). The hiragana version of *Inga monogatari* appears in *shojaku mokuroku* for the first time in 1670 under the publishing genre of *kana hōgo*. The word *kana* (here indicating hiragana) follows the title and the number of volumes (six) matches with the hiragana version. The last appearance is in the 1715 catalogue. In the 1681 catalogue the price is 3 *monme* 5 *fun*, decreases to 2 *monme* 5 *fun* in 1696, goes back to 3 *monme* 5 *fun* in 1709 and 1715. The katakana version appears in the 1670 catalogue as a note in the entry for the hiragana version (the note mentioning *shin* 3, or 3 volumes in noncursive). It was indeed in three volumes, and in the 1675 catalogue organized in *i-ro-ha* order, the name of the author was recorded as Suzuki Shōsan. In the 1681 catalogue this version is slightly cheaper than the hiragana version (3 *monme*) but, considering that the latter had double the number of volumes, contained illustrations, and thus used more blocks and paper, the small difference in price is interesting. The price decreases to 2 *monme* 5 *fun* in 1696 but increases to 3 *monme* 5 *fun* in 1709, exactly like the six-volume hiragana version. It remains as such in the 1715 catalogue. For more details on the publication history of *Inga monogatari*, see Yoshida Kōichi, ed., *Inga monogatari*, Koten bunko 185 (Tokyo: Koten Bunko, 1962), 222–35.
103. *Inga monogatari*, katakana version, vol. 1, 2r–2v; *KS* 4:289.

104. Yoshida, *Inga monogatari*, 185:236, puts forward this date.
105. Carlo Ginzburg, *The Cheese and the Worms: The Cosmos of a Sixteenth-Century Miller*, trans. John and Anne Tedeschi (Baltimore: Johns Hopkins University Press, 2013), xxvi.
106. Ginzburg, *Cheese and Worms*, xxvi.
107. *Inga monogatari*, hiragana version, vol. 1, 3r–5v; *KS* 4:203–5.
108. I am using the Kyoto, n.p., n.d., hiragana version of *Inga monogatari*, private collection, Suzuran Bunko, Cambridge, U.K. (no shelf mark), vol. 1, 3r.
109. *Inga monogatari*, hiragana version, vol. 1, 1v; *KS* 4:201.
110. The introduction of Shimura Kunihiro and Suwa Haruo, eds., *Nihon setsuwa densetsu dai jiten* (Tokyo: Bensei Shuppan, 2000), underline the fact that the interest of *setsuwa* lies in its strange, miraculous nature regarding allegedly real events.
111. *Inga monogatari*, katakana version, vol. 1, 9r; *KS* 4:297. The image is from Suzuki Shōsan, Giun (editor), and Unpo (editor), *Inga monogatari* ([Kyoto]: [Chōjiya Kurōemon], n.d.), katakana version, private collection, Suzuran Bunko, Cambridge, U.K. (no shelf mark).
112. *Inga monogatari*, katakana version, vol. 1, 11v–12r; *KS* 4:298–99.
113. In her study of the Anglo-Latin version of the didactic text *Gesta Romanorum*, for example, Philippa Bright recognizes in the presence of dramatized scenes using direct speech a technique that enhances reader engagement; "Anglo-Latin Collections of the *Gesta Romanorum* and Their Role in the Cure of Souls," in Ruys, *What Nature Does Not Teach*, 410.
114. Nikolajeva, *Reading for Learning*, 95.
115. On ghost stories in the Edo period, see, for example, Tachikawa Kiyoshi, *Kinsei kaii shōsetsu kenkyū* (Tokyo: Kasama Shoin, 1979). See also Noriko T. Reider, "The Emergence of *Kaidan-shū*: The Collection of Tales of the Strange and Mysterious in the Edo Period," *Asian Folklore Studies* 60, no. 1 (2001): 79–99.
116. In *Shokoku inga monogatari* eighteen tales are selected from the five volumes of the hiragana version of *Inga monogatari* (there is no tale from the sixth volume) and crammed into twenty-eight folios in the pocket-size edition of a *chūbon*-size book; see *Shokoku inga monogatari* (n.p: publisher unknown, n.d.), photographic reproduction in *Inga monogatari*, ed. Yoshida Kōichi, Koten bunko 185 (Tokyo: Koten Bunko, 1962), 163–220. Hereafter *Shokoku inga monogatari*. For a comparison of the contents in the hiragana version and that in the abridged, see Yoshida, *Inga monogatari*, Koten bunko 185, 250–51. Aoki Rosui 青木鷺水 (also Hakubaien 白梅園 [1658–1733]), haikai poet and prolific prose writer, employed the same title for his six-volume version, *Shokoku inga monogatari* (Kyoto: Hishiya Jihee; Edo: Izumoji Shirobee, 1707), Tokyo University Library, Katei Bunko (shelf mark: 霞亭0230).
117. *Shokoku inga monogatari*, 1r–1v; *Shokoku inga monogatari*, 185:165–66.
118. The title *Ayame kagami* 善悪鑑 can be verified not only in the introduction but also in the *hashira dai* (the title inscribed in the center of the folio). This is not to deny the entertaining nature of *Inga monogatari* noted in Reider, "Emergence of *Kaidan-shū*," and examined in the passages quoted here.

4. Civility Matters

1. Eiko Ikegami, *Bonds of Civility: Aesthetic Networks and the Political Origins of Japanese Culture* (Cambridge: Cambridge University Press, 2005).

2. Ikegami, *Bonds of Civility*, 19.
3. Ikegami, *Bonds of Civility*, 324. Ikegami also writes, "They [Tokugawa people] were living in a society of hierarchical order in which specific forms of good manners were determined by recognizing one's relative social status in the context of a socially interactive occasion" (38).
4. Ikegami, *Bonds of Civility*, 327.
5. Ikegami, *Bonds of Civility*, 433n10, conflates *Ogasawara shorei taizen* with *Shorei daigaku*. Yet these are two different texts: *Ogasawara shorei taizen* was written by Okada Gyokuzan 岡田玉山 (also known as Hokkyō Gyokuzan 法橋玉山 [d. 1808]) and was first published in 1809. It remained in circulation into the Meiji period with an edition of 1881. The Union Catalogue of Early Japanese Books (http://base1.nijl.ac.jp/~tkoten/) lists two *Shorei daigaku*, one attributed to Tajma Yōgen 田島養元 (dates unknown) and the other to Takai Ranzan 高井蘭山 (1762–1838), issued possibly late in the Edo period by the Nagoya publisher Eirakuya Tōshirō.
6. Ikegami, *Bonds of Civility*, 347.
7. Ikegami, *Bonds of Civility*, 324.
8. Ikegami, *Bonds of Civility*, 367.
9. Ikegami, *Bonds of Civility*, 38.
10. Ikegami, *Bonds of Civility*, 329.
11. Ikegami, *Bonds of Civility*, 353, 371.
12. "For the most part, however, writers of Ekken's caliber were unusual in this genre, and most handbooks were clearly detached from any sort of moralizing" (Ikegami, *Bonds of Civility*, 329).
13. Anna Bryson, *From Courtesy to Civility: Changing Codes of Conduct in Early Modern England* (Oxford: Oxford University Press, 2004); Keith Thomas, *In Pursuit of Civility: Manners and Civilization in Early Modern England* (New Haven, Conn.: Yale University Press, 2018); and Peter Burke, Brian Harrison, and Paul Slack, eds., *Civil Histories: Essays Presented to Sir Keith Thomas* (Oxford: Oxford University Press, 2000). See also Norbert Elias, *The Civilizing Process*, ed. Eric Dunning, Johan Goudsblom, and Stephen Mennell, trans. Edmund Jephcott, rev. ed. (Oxford: Blackwell Publishing, 2000); first published in two volumes in German in 1939 as *Über den Prozeß der Zivilisation*.
14. Thomas, *In Pursuit of Civility*, 69.
15. Thomas, *In Pursuit of Civility*, 63–64, 69–74.
16. Thomas, *In Pursuit of Civility*, 343.
17. Elias, *The Civilizing Process*, 65. Elias's study must be used with caution; a strong Eurocentric bias permeates Elias's work, as is clear from the 1939 preface, in which he states, "Central to this study are the modes of behaviour considered typical of people who are civilized in a Western way" (ix). Ikegami Eiko remarks that "Elias was a man of his time and presumed a unitary model of civilization that other societies would eventually follow," while in the case of Tokugawa Japan "a different pattern of state formation could result in a different style of civility" (*Bonds of Civility*, 28). Bryson, *From Courtesy to Civility*, 11–16, 97–106, points to a number of weaknesses in Elias's work.
18. Elias, *The Civilizing Process*, 68–69.
19. Bryson, *From Courtesy to Civility*, 71.
20. Thomas, *In Pursuit of Civility*, 24.
21. Shimokōbe Shūsui, illus., *Ogasawara-ryū shitsukekata hyakka jō* (Osaka: Katsuoya Rokubee, 1770), Ajinomoto Foundation for Dietary Culture, Takanawa, Tokyo; digital version, National Institute of Japanese Literature, Tachikawa (shelf mark: DIG-AJNM-160); afterword appended to back cover.

332   4. Civility Matters

22. Mary Elizabeth Berry, *Japan in Print: Information and Nation in the Early Modern Period* (Berkeley: University of California Press, 2006).
23. On the Ogasawara school, see Futaki Ken'ichi, *Chūsei buke girei no kenkyū* (Tokyo: Yoshikawa Kōbunkan, 1985), and Higuchi Motomi, "Ogasawara ke oyobi Ogasawara ryū," in *Dai shoreishū: Ogasawara ryūrei hōdensho*, ed. Shimada Isao and Higuchi Motomi, Tōyō bunko 562 (Tokyo: Heibonsha 1993), 207–23. See also the short historical account in Ogasawara Keishōsai, *Utsukushii furumai: Ogasawara ryū reihō nyūmon* (Tokyo: Dankōsha, 2017), 10–12; Ogasawara Keishōsai, *Mite manabu Nihonjin no furumai: Ogasawara ryū reihō nyūmon* (Tokyo: Dankōsha, 2011), 3–4; and Ogasawara Kiyotada, *Ogasawara ryū no densho o yomu* (Tokyo: Nihon Budōkan, 2015), 1–52. Michael Kinski offers a very helpful synopsis in "Basic Japanese Etiquette Rules and Their Popularization: Four Edo-Period Texts, Transcribed, Translated, and Annotated," *Japonica Humboldtiana* 5 (2001): 66–67n11.
24. Kinski, "Basic Japanese Etiquette Rules," 67–68n12.
25. Kinski, "Basic Japanese Etiquette Rules," 67, 69, also suggests that the Ogasawara name became a sort of brand that bestowed legitimacy on any kind of etiquette text. Similarly, Ikegami, *Bonds of Civility*, 333, speaks of the "Ogasawara brand." It is worth stressing that although Kinski mentions the 1632 *Ogasawara hyakka jō*, he traces the tradition of the etiquette topics under study to the early eighteenth century because he is concerned mainly with rules of etiquette in household encyclopedias. This chapter demonstrates that the same tradition goes back to seventeenth-century popular prose.
26. *Ogasawara hyakka jō*, movable-type edition ([Kyoto]: publisher unknown, n.d.), National Diet Library, Tokyo (shelf mark: WA7-171). It is one volume that contains seventy-seven articles (not one hundred, as advertised in the title). It is not clear whether a second volume was also printed. This copy does not provide any information about the publisher or the date of publication. Hereafter cited as *Ogasawara*, movable-type edition.
27. *Ogasawara*, movable-type edition, 1r.
28. *Ogasawara*, movable-type edition, 1r–1v.
29. *Ogasawara*, movable-type edition, respectively 4r and 6v.
30. *Ogasawara*, movable-type edition, respectively 8r, 13v–14r, 9v, 10v–11r, and 14v.
31. On the popularity enjoyed by *gunsho* from the Genna to Kanbun eras, between 1615 and 1673, see Inoue Yasushi, *Kinsei kankō gunsho ron: Kyōkun, goraku, kōshō* (Tokyo: Kasama Shoin, 2014), 29–30, 48–53. As mentioned in chapter 2, *gunsho* formed a stand-alone category in book-trade catalogues.
32. *Ogasawara hyakka jō* ([Kyoto]: Nakano Ichiemon, 1632), National Diet Library, Tokyo (shelf mark: 855-35). Hereafter cited as *Ogasawara hyakka jō*, 1632 edition. On its numerous editions, see note 57. The title *Ogasawara hyakka jō* appeared regularly in book-trade catalogues from 1666–1667 until 1715. It moved from the category *washo narabi ni kanarui* to that of *shitsukekata-sho narabi ni ryōri-sho* in 1670. In one volume, it was priced cheaply: 5 *fun* in 1681, 3 *fun* in 1696, and 7 *fun* in 1709 and 1715.
33. *Ogasawara hyakka jō*, 1632 edition, afterword, 67r.
34. Berry, *Japan in Print*, 200, 207–8, 217–18, highlights the importance of the term *ban-min* in the context of the Genroku era (1688–1704). It is worth noting that commercial publishers made use of this concept as early as the 1630s. Sakai Tadao, "Confucianism and Popular Educational Works," in *Self and Society in Ming Thought*, ed. Wm. Theodore de Bary (New York: Columbia University Press, 1970), 346, reflects on a similar use of the Chinese word *fan-min* (which he translates as "ordinary people") in daily-life encyclopedias and morality books.

35. *Ogasawara hyakka jō*, 1632 edition, 1r–1v. Thomas, *In Pursuit of Civility*, 40, notes that in sixteenth-century Britain, "courtesy and civility became necessary qualifications for those seeking employment in a gentry household; and servants by imitation and out of deference often adopted genteel standards of appearance and behaviour, sometimes more genteel than those of their masters."
36. *Ogasawara hyakka jō*, 1632 edition, 1v–2r.
37. *Ogasawara hyakka jō*, 1632 edition, 2r.
38. *Ogasawara hyakka jō*, 1632 edition, 2v.
39. *Ogasawara hyakka jō*, 1632 edition, 2v.
40. *Ogasawara hyakka jō*, 1632 edition, 3r.
41. *Ogasawara hyakka jō*, 1632 edition, 3v–4r.
42. *Ogasawara hyakka jō*, 1632 edition, 3v.
43. *Ogasawara hyakka jō*, 1632 edition, 4r.
44. Included for the first time in the 1685 catalogue, the publishing genre of *kōshoku narabi ni rakuji* merged diverse typologies, including evaluations of actors and courtesans, Saikaku's *kōshokubon* (erotic tales), manuals related to sexual hygiene, and more generally books with sexually explicit pictures (referred to as *makura-e*). For a study of a few seventeenth-century texts belonging to this publishing genre, see Maria Bugno, "Shunpon: Intertextuality, Humour, and Sexual Education in Early-Modern Japan" (PhD diss., University of Cambridge, 2019).
45. *Ogasawara hyakka jō*, 1632 edition, 5v–6r.
46. *Ogasawara hyakka jō*, 1632 edition, 6v.
47. *Ogasawara hyakka jō*, 1632 edition, 7v.
48. *Ogasawara hyakka jō*, 1632 edition, 2v, 4r.
49. *Ogasawara hyakka jō*, 1632 edition, 4r, 7v.
50. *Ogasawara hyakka jō*, 1632 edition, 7v–10r, 10r–26r.
51. Bryson, *From Courtesy to Civility*, 67.
52. *Ogasawara hyakka jō*, 1632 edition, 26v–48v.
53. *Ogasawara hyakka jō*, 1632 edition, 35r.
54. *Ogasawara hyakka jō*, 1632 edition, 55r–56r.
55. *Ogasawara hyakka jō*, 1632 edition, 49r–54v.
56. "The tray is arranged as a *hikiwatashi*. You drink the first round of sake and then eat [hold in your mouth] a dried chestnut. You drink the second round of sake and eat [hold in your mouth] a piece of dried *konbu* seaweed. More sake is poured, and you drink again. This is called *sansan kudo*" (*Ogasawara hyakka jō*, 1632 edition, 54v). The verb *kuu* 喰ふ is used in describing what to do with the dried chestnuts and *konbu* seaweed. Eric C. Rath, *Food and Fantasy in Early Modern Japan* (Berkeley: University of California Press, 2010), 66–71, examines a similar example and explains that none of these foods were actually consumed; they were included on the tray for their symbolic value. So, we could take this verb in *Ogasawara hyakka jō* (1632 edition) to mean "to hold in one's mouth" rather than to actually consume. One wonders to what extent the Edo-period reader who had no access to the oral tradition could understand how *kuu* was used in this context.
57. The Union Catalogue of Early Japanese Books records the following editions: 1652, 1659, 1666, 1674, 1770, 1809, 1843, 1848, and 1853. There are also many examples that bear no publishing date.
58. For details, see Peter Burke, *The Fortunes of the Courtier: European Reception of Castiglione's Cortegiano* (Cambridge: Polity Press, 1995).
59. Elizabeth Wise, ed., *Debrett's Handbook: British Style, Correct Form, Modern Manners* (London: Debrett's, 2014), Kindle, cover and preface.

60. Umberto Eco, *On Literature*, trans. Martin McLaughlin (London: Vintage Books, 2006), 1.
61. In his *Shorei tōyō shū* (The collection for all immediate needs on etiquette; 1765), Tō Mitsunaka notes that "etiquette [*shorei*] and conduct [*shitsukekata*] are something that must be maintained by people of all sorts [*banmin*], high and low, at all moments of daily life, day and night, when standing or sitting. . . . Etiquette starts with knowing how to stand, how to sit, how to use one's hands and extends to handling all sorts of tools. If one does not know this, one will end up feeling insecure with others and be greatly scorned by people" (*Shorei tōyō shū* [Kyoto: Zeniya Shichirobee et al., 1765], private collection, Suzuran Bunko, Cambridge, U.K. [no shelf mark], front matter [*dai-i*], vol. 1, 2r–2v).
62. Ikegami, *Bonds of Civility*; Rebecca Corbett, *Cultivating Femininity: Women and Tea Culture in Edo and Meiji Japan* (Honolulu: University of Hawai`i Press, 2018).
63. Corbett, *Cultivating Femininity*, 33.
64. Cynthia J. Brokaw, *Commerce in Culture: The Sibao Book Trade in the Qing and Republican Periods*, Harvard East Asian Monographs 280 (Cambridge, Mass.: Harvard University Asia Center, 2007), 415.
65. Pierre Bourdieu, "The Forms of Capital," in *Handbook of Theory and Research for the Sociology of Education*, ed. John G. Richardson (Westport, Conn.: Greenwood Press, 1986), 241–58.
66. On sumptuary laws, see Donald H. Shively, "Sumptuary Regulation and Status in Early Tokugawa Japan," *Harvard Journal of Asiatic Studies* 25 (1964–1965): 123–64.
67. *Ogasawara-ryū shitsukekata hyakka jō* (Edo: Wan'ya Ihee, 1843), private collection, Suzuran Bunko, Cambridge, U.K. (no shelf mark). The colophon mentions a revised edition dated 1689, a new edition based on it and issued in 1805, and finally the 1843 new edition, probably based on both.
68. *Shogaku bunshō narabi ni yorozu shitsukekata* ([Kyoto]: Nishimura Matazaemon, 1634), Ehime University Library, Suzuka Bunko, Matsuyama; digital version, National Institute of Japanese Literature, Tachikawa (shelf mark: DIG-EMSK-482). Hereafter cited as *Shogaku bunshō*, 1634 edition. We know of the following editions/reprints: 1638, 1643, 1644, 1645, 1647, 1653, 1665, 1666, 1679, 1681, and 1682. There are also undated examples. Tachibana Yutaka, *Shokan sahō no kenkyū zokuhen* (Tokyo: Kazama Shobō, 1985), 1:123, mentions a 1630 copy in the collection of the linguist Iwabuchi Etsutarō. It is worth noting that *Ogasawara hyakka jō* was popular until the end of the Edo period, whereas *Shogaku bunshō* seems to have attracted little interest after the seventeenth century. It appeared regularly in book-trade catalogues, from 1666–1667 until 1715, under the title *Shogaku bunshō*. It moved from the category of *washo narabi ni kana-rui* to that of *shitsukekata-sho narabi ni ryōri-sho* in 1670. In one volume, it had a price similar to that of *Ogasawara hyakka jō*: 5 *fun* (1681) and 3 *fun* (1696 and 1709). No price is given in the 1715 catalogue. The catalogues also list *Shogaku bunshō zōho taizen* (Elementary letters: The great compilation with additions [in 3 or 5 volumes]), starting in 1670. It might refer to what is now known as *Shogaku bunshō shō* (Elementary letters: A commentary), but research is needed to confirm this.
69. *Shogaku bunshō*, 1634 edition, 42r–59r.
70. For example, another seventeenth-century title mentioned in book-trade catalogues is *Dai shorei shū* (Great collection of etiquette; also known as *Shorei shū* [Collection of etiquette]), attributed to Ogasawara Sadayoshi 小笠原貞慶 (1546–1595) and composed in 1576. In seventeen volumes, it was a rather bulky book, which made it quite a different product from the two titles discussed here.

71. See, for example, Takai Ranzan (editor), Nakamura Tsunetoshi (additions), and Kikukawa Eizan (illustrator), *Edo daisetsuyō kaidai-gura* (Nagoya: Eirakuya Tōshirō et al., 1863), private collection, Suzuran Bunko, Cambridge, U.K. (no shelf mark). The colophon mentions also an original edition dated 1704 and an enlarged and revised edition of 1833. At the end of the first volume is a section titled "Almost Everything You Need to Know About Contemporary Etiquette" (Tōryū shitsukekata taigai; 172v–75v). The compilers acknowledge that etiquette for the warrior class (*buke reishiki*) is of no use to those of the lower classes (*ika minkan*) but that table manners, including how to eat everyday food and serve dishes, are important regardless of social position. A lack of familiarity with these will result in someone's being labeled "rustic" (*nohi*). Social distinction between the warrior and lower classes is acknowledged, yet etiquette is described as a tool for self-affirmation, something that everyone needs to avoid being scoffed at as unsophisticated. More than a matter of class, it is one of sophistication. If one wants to avoid the label "rustic," it is important to master proper comportment, regardless of social status. For other materials, see Kinski, "Basic Japanese Etiquette Rules."
72. See the websites Ogasawara-ryū reihō, https://ogasawararyu-reihou.com/, and Ogasawara-ryū, http://www.ogasawara-ryu.gr.jp/ (both accessed December 16, 2019).
73. A list can be found at https://ogasawararyu-reihou.com/outline/books.html (accessed December 16, 2019).
74. Nancy Armstrong notes for Europe around the same period, "Until sometime around the end of the seventeenth century, the great majority of conduct books were devoted mainly to representing the male of the dominant class. . . . Ruth Kelso and Suzanne Hull have shown that during the sixteenth and seventeenth centuries there were relatively few books instructing women as compared to those available to men" ("The Rise of the Domestic Woman," in *The Ideology of Conduct: Essays in Literature and the History of Sexuality*, ed. Nancy Armstrong and Leonard Tennenhouse, Routledge Revivals [London: Routledge, 2014], 96–141). Armstrong also observes that things were different at the turn of the eighteenth century, with conduct books written for women outnumbering those for men; Nancy Armstrong and Leonard Tennenhouse, "The Literature of Conduct, the Conduct of Literature, and the Politics of Desire: An Introduction," in Armstrong and Tennenhouse, *The Ideology of Conduct*, 9.
75. See P. F. Kornicki, "Women, Education, and Literacy," in *The Female as Subject: Reading and Writing in Early Modern Japan*, ed. P. F. Kornicki, Mara Patessio, and G. G. Rowley (Ann Arbor: Center for Japanese Studies, University of Michigan, 2010), 7–38. Jamie Newhard is currently working on a book titled *A Market of Their Own: "Books for Women" in 17th and 18th Century Japan*. Ground-breaking work in Japanese has been done by Koizumi Yoshinaga, "Kinsei no nyohitsu tehon: Onna-bumi o meguru shomondai" (PhD diss., Kanazawa University, 1999). The category *nyosho* appeared for the first time in the 1670 *shojaku mokuroku*; see table 2.3.
76. *Onna kagami hidensho* (Kyoto: Noda Yahee, 1650), diplomatic transcription in vol. 10 of *Kanazōshi shūsei*, ed. Asakura Haruhiko and Fukasawa Akio (Tokyo: Tōkyōdō Shuppan, 1989), 3–77. Unless otherwise stated, I refer to this edition (cited as *Onna kagami*). In addition to the 1650 edition are the 1652 edition by Yamamoto Chōbee in three volumes without illustrations; a later reprint of the 1652 edition, in six volumes, with illustrations; the 1659 edition published in Edo by Matsue Ichirobee (illustrated); the edition by an Edo publisher known as Hon Toiya (illustrated; date unknown); the 1678 edition by Yorozuya Shōhee (illustrated); and the 1692 edition by Izumiya Mōhee (reprinted in 1699; illustrated). It is noteworthy that Matsue Ichirobee published two

different editions of his title, a version dated 1659 now housed in Tōyō Bunko (shelf mark: 三 Fa ろ 58) and an undated version at Tohoku University Library, Kano Bunko (shelf mark: 4547). *Onna kagami hidensho* appeared in book-trade catalogues from 1666–1667 until 1715, under the title *Onna kagami*. It moved from the category of *washo narabi ni kanarui* to that of *nyosho* in 1670. It was listed twice beginning with the 1675 catalogue: in three volumes and in six volumes with illustrations (*eiri*). The latter version is probably the revised edition of the 1652 edition by Yamamoto Chōbee. In the 1681 catalogue the three-volume *Onna kagami* was available in small and large formats, the former priced at 1 *monme* 2 *fun*, the latter at 1 *monme* 8 *fun*. The 1696, 1709, and 1715 catalogues dropped the two formats and priced the three-volume *Onna kagami* as follows: 1 *monme* 2 *fun* (1696) and 2 *monme* 2 *fun* (1709 and 1715). The six-volume edition with illustrations was more expensive, at 4 *monme* 5 *fun* in 1681. It decreased to 2 *monme* 8 *fun* (1696) and 3 *monme* 8 *fun* (1709 and 1715).

77. *Onna shikimoku* ([Kyoto]: publisher unknown, 1660), diplomatic transcription in vol. 11 of *Kanazōshi shūsei*, ed. Asakura Haruhiko and Fukasawa Akio (Tokyo: Tōkyōdō Shuppan, 1990), 141–73. Unless otherwise indicated, I refer to this edition (cited as *Onna shikimoku*). *Onna shikimoku* is also known in a 1751 edition by the Kyoto publisher Kagaya Uhee. The Union Catalogue of Early Japanese Books lists a 1754 edition, the details of which are unknown, and undated editions. *Onna shikimoku* appeared in book-trade catalogues from 1666–1667 to 1772. It moved from the category of *mai narabi ni sōshi* to that of *nyosho* in 1670. It was often recorded in combination with *Jubutsu monogatari* (The tale of Confucianism and Buddhism), and that is probably why it was recorded in three volumes. In the 1681 catalogue it was priced at 2 *monme* 5 *fun*. In the 1696 catalogue the price decreased to 1 *monme* 7 *fun*, only to increase again to 2 *monme* 7 *fun* in 1709. This price was confirmed in the 1715 catalogue. For a preliminary discussion of *Onna shikimoku* in English, see Marcia Yonemoto, "The Perils of the 'Unpolished Jewel': Defining Women's Roles in Household Management in Early Modern Japan," *U.S.-Japan Women's Journal*, no. 39 (2010): 38–62. *Onna shikimoku* is also mentioned in Risako Doi, "Beyond *The Greater Learning for Women*: Instructional Texts (*Joshiyō ōrai*) and Norms for Women in Early Modern Japan" (master's thesis, University of Colorado Boulder, 2011).
78. *Onna kagami*, vol. 1, 5r–6r; *KS* 10:8–9
79. The Five Hindrances stipulate that women cannot be reborn as a Brahman; Shakra; Lord of the Devas; a devil king; a wheel-turning king; or a Buddha.
80. *Onna kagami*, vol. 1, 5r–5v; *KS* 10:8.
81. *Onna kagami*, vol. 1, 5v–6r; *KS* 10:8–9.
82. *Onna shikimoku*, respectively vol. 1, 14r–19v and vol. 1, 20r–24v; *KS* 11:152–56, 157–60.
83. Ikegami, *Bonds of Civility*, 329.
84. *Onna kagami*, vol. 1, 6v; *KS* 10:9.
85. *Onna kagami*, vol. 1, 7r–7v, 13v; *KS* 10:9–10, 14.
86. *Onna kagami*, vol. 1, 7v–8r; *KS* 10:10. *Onna shikimoku* recommends that a woman be instructed in conduct (*gyōgi, sahō*) starting at age ten; vol. 1, 10r; *KS* 11:149.
87. *Onna kagami*, vol. 1, 7v; *KS* 10:9.
88. *Onna kagami*, vol. 1, 8v–13v; *KS* 10:10–14.
89. *Onna kagami*, vol. 1, 16r; *KS* 10:14.
90. *Onna kagami*, vol. 1, 17v–27v; *KS* 10:14–25.
91. *Onna kagami*, vol. 1, 28r–29r; *KS* 10:26.
92. *Onna kagami*, vol. 1, 29r–32r; *KS* 10:26–28.
93. *Onna kagami*, vol. 1, 31r–31v; *KS* 10:27–28.

94. *Onna kagami*, vol. 2, 3r–7v; *KS* 10:31–34 for written correspondence; vol. 2, 7v–21v; *KS* 10:34–43 for wedding ceremonies.
95. Marcia Yonemoto, *The Problem of Women in Early Modern Japan* (Oakland: University of California Press, 2016), 94, notes that "from the late seventeenth century on, numerous instructional manuals focusing on or containing information about marriage were published." *Onna kagami hidensho* can be viewed as the stepping-stone in this textual tradition.
96. "You first take a sip of sake, then eat a chestnut, then another sip, then eat a piece of seaweed, then another sip. This is called *san san kyūdo*" (My earlier remarks on the verb *kuu*, note 56, apply here as well.) *Onna kagami*, vol. 2, 16r; *KS* 10:40–41.
97. *Onna shikimoku*, vol. 1, 10v–13v; *KS* 11:149–52.
98. *Onna kagami*, vol. 2, 22v–23r; *KS* 10:46–47.
99. *Onna kagami*, vol. 2, 26r–29v; *KS* 10:49–52.
100. *Onna kagami*, vol. 3, 4r–20r; *KS* 10:55–67; from section 1 to 26.
101. *Onna kagami*, vol. 3, 20r–26r; *KS* 10:67–72.
102. *Onna kagami*, vol. 3, 23r; *KS* 10:69.
103. Bryson, *From Courtesy to Civility*, 39–40.
104. *Onna kagami*, vol. 3, 26r–52r; *KS* 10:72–77.
105. *Onna shikimoku*, vol. 1, 3r–7v; *KS* 11:144–47.
106. For example, *Onna yō chie kagami takara ori* (Precious collection that works as a mirror for women's wisdom) (Osaka: Kashiwaraya Seiemon, 1769), private collection, Suzuran Bunko, Cambridge, U.K. (no shelf mark). It contains a section called "Onna shorei shū" (Compendium of all etiquette for women). Inserted in the center section of the composite page, it lays out rules for conduct that include table manners and food service (15v–34v), together with advice on proper behavior in social settings (35r–41r). A brief section on marriage is seen in the lower section of the page (82v–86r). For a German translation and study of *Onna yō chie kagami takara ori*, see Stephan Köhn, *Traditionen idealisierter Weiblichkeit: Die "Kostbare Sammlung von Vorbildern weiblicher Weisheit" (Joyō chie kagami takaraori) als Paradebeispiel edozeitlicher Frauenbildung* (Wiesbaden: Harrassowitz, 2008). See also the review by Bettina Gramlich-Oka in *Monumenta Nipponica* 65, no. 1 (Spring 2010): 217–21.
107. *Onna kagami hidensho* (Kyoto: Yamamoto Chōbee, n.d.), 6 vols., reissue of the 1652 edition with added illustrations and content; private collection, Suzuran Bunko, Cambridge, U.K. (no shelf mark). Yamamoto's name is retained in the colophon of the reissue, though this is not proof he was still in charge of the project. Hereafter cited as *Onna kagami*, 1652 reprint.
108. *Onna kagami*, 1652 reprint, vol. 2, 16/2r–16/9v. The pagination is irregular, displaying 十六／二 and similar.
109. *Onna shorei shū* ([Kyoto]: Tanaka Bunnai, 1660), photographic reproduction in vol. 61 of *Edo jidai josei bunko* (Tokyo: Ōzorasha, 1997). Hereafter cited as *Onna shorei*. We know of two more editions published in Kyoto and dated 1660, by Yamada Ichirobee and Masuya Heibee. Other known dated editions/impressions are from 1675, 1678, 1683, 1685, 1688, and 1736. *Onna shorei shū* appeared in book-trade catalogues from 1666–1667 to 1715. In the 1666–1667 catalogue it was advertised in two versions: one in seven volumes and the other, in small size (*kohon*) in three volumes. This double format is retained in later catalogues, but there is confusion on the number of volumes, sometimes seven or six for both, other times in six and three volumes, respectively. It was first listed under the label of *washo narabi ni kanarui* and then under *nyosho* (beginning in 1670). In the 1681 catalogue the six-volume, probably large-size, format was priced at 5 *monme*,

338   4. Civility Matters

whereas the three-volume, small format was 3 *monme*. In the 1696 and 1709 catalogues only the six-volume edition was listed, for 3 *monme* 5 *fun*. The price increased to 4 *monme* 5 *fun* in the 1715 catalogue (only the six-volume version).

110. Rath, *Food and Fantasy*, 53.
111. *Ryōri monogatari* ([Kyoto]: publisher unknown, 1643), Tokyo Municipal Central Library, Kaga Bunko (shelf mark: 3800). Unless otherwise noted, I refer to this edition (cited as *Ryōri monogatari*). The oldest extant edition of *Ryōri monogatari* dates to 1643, even though an earlier version produced in the Keichō era was acknowledged in the first half of the twentieth century; see Harada Nobuo, *Edo no ryōri shi: ryōribon to ryōri bunka* (Tokyo: Chūō Kōronsha, 1989), 25–26. *Ryōri monogatari* was then recut in 1647 and 1649 (the latter extant in two impressions bearing slightly different colophons). There are also two 1664 editions: one produced in Kyoto by Takahashi Seibee and one in Edo by Matsue Ichirobee. There is also a 1670 *Ryōri hidenshō*: Ajinomoto Foundation for Dietary Culture, Takanawa, Tokyo; digital version, National Institute of Japanese Literature, Tachikawa (shelf mark: DIG-AJNM-20). It functions as an abridged version of *Ryōri monogatari*, starting with an explanation of the *hikiwatashi* tray for the wedding ceremony and then offering a selection of some of the sections of *Ryōri monogatari*. In 1684 a new edition of the same abridged text was issued in Osaka by Hon'ya Gohee. It is kept at the National Institute of Japanese Literature, Tachikawa (shelf mark: 49-97). The title *Ryōri monogatari* was not recorded as such in book-trade catalogues, and we probably need to look under the title *Ryōri sho* to gather information on how it was publicized. *Ryōri sho* appears in the 1670 to 1715 catalogues as part of *shitsukekata-sho narabi ni ryōri-sho*. It was available in both large and small formats, both in one volume. In 1681 the price for the large-format edition was 1 *monme* and that for the small-format one was 6 *fun*. The prices decreased in 1696 and 1709: the large-format edition was 7 *fun* and the small format was 4 *fun* in both. No price is recorded in 1715. A one-volume *Ryōri shō* (with the character 抄 instead of 書) features in the 1666–1667 catalogue under *washo narabi ni kanarui*. It might be the same as *Ryōri sho*.
112. *Ryōri monogatari*, 53v.
113. See Harada, *Edo no ryōri shi*, 14–17. Rath, *Food and Fantasy*, 85, notes that culinary books like *Ryōri monogatari* "were actually the first popular writings on cuisine and signaled the popularization of elite modes of dining and the broadening of authorship, readership, and subject matter of culinary texts."
114. Hannah Glasse, *The Art of Cookery Made Plain and Easy* (n.p: printed for the author, 1747), British Library, London (shelf mark: 1485 pp18); quotation from the introduction.
115. For the title slip of the 1643 edition in Ōei Bunko, see the exhibition catalogue Tōkyō Kasei Gakuin Seikatsu Bunka Hakubutsukan, ed., *Ōei Bunko ni miru Edo jidai no Ryōri monogatari: Dai nijūkai tokubetsuten mokuroku* (Tokyo: Hōbunsha, 2000), 6.
116. Harada, *Edo no ryōri shi*, 19–20. Harada also notes that the mention of red meat (*kedamono*)—namely, deer, badger, boar, rabbit, dog—in *Ryōri monogatari* is revealing. It accounts for a shift from medieval culinary writings that focused on vegetarian cuisine (*shōjin ryōri*) and accounts for popular eating habits that developed in households and outside regulated culinary practices.
117. *Ryōri monogatari*, 2r.
118. *Ryōri monogatari*, 17r–36v.
119. A table of contents does exist, as with the majority of the other books discussed in this chapter, but it merely gives the titles of the section, as I have done here. Rath, *Food and Fantasy*, 220n6, provides an English translation of the table of contents. He recognizes the presence of a table of contents in early modern culinary books as an innovation

4. Civility Matters   339

when compared with medieval culinary writings (57). He also infers that this table of contents made recipes easy to find (168). I would assert, however, that compared with other tables of contents in seventeenth-century books the one in *Ryōri monogatari* is too vague to be of much practical help in locating a specific recipe.

120. *Ryōri monogatari*, 17r–17v.
121. *Ryōri monogatari*, 15v–15r and 26v–47v.
122. *Ryōri monogatari*, 48r–53r.
123. For information on these two abridged editions, see note 111.
124. Rath, *Food and Fantasy*, 118–19.
125. *Ryōri monogatari* ([Edo]: Matsue, n.d.), National Institute of Japanese Literature, Tachikawa (shelf mark: 49-66). Hereafter cited as *Ryōri monogatari*, Matsue edition. Although no date is recorded in this specific copy, the blocks are those for the 1664 edition. See details in Kashiwazaki Junko, ed., *Zōho Shōkaiban shomoku*, Nihon shoshigaku taikei 96 (Tachikawa: Seishōdō Shoten, 2009), 24, 105, 133.
126. Francesca Bray, Vera Dorofeeva-Lichtmann, and Georges Métailié, eds., *Graphics and Text in the Production of Technical Knowledge in China: The Warp and the Weft*, Sinica Leidensia 79 (Leiden: Brill, 2007), 2–3.
127. *Ryōri kirigata hidenshō* ([Kyoto]: publisher unknown [private publication?], 1642), diplomatic transcription in vol. 1 of *Edo jidai ryōribon shūsei: Honkoku*, ed. Yoshii Motoko (Kyoto: Rinsen Shoten, 1978), 39–177.
128. Harada, *Edo no ryōri shi*, 29–32, notes that while *Ryōri monogatari* gives voice to the common people, *Ryōri kirigata hidenshō* borrows the authority of a well-established culinary school. Rath, *Food and Fantasy*, 57, exhibits a somewhat different view and identifies the value of this work as marking "the popularization of knowledge of the *hōchōnin*'s craft and signaled an end to their monopoly on culinary writings, as published culinary books began to dominate this field."
129. *Ryōri monogatari*, Matsue edition, 3r.
130. I use the term "intervisual," a combination of "intertextual" and "visual" as used in Maria Nikolajeva and Carole Scott, *How Picturebooks Work* (New York: Routledge, 2006), 228.
131. Here I make reference to *Onna jingi monogatari* (n.p: publisher unknown, n.d.), National Institute of Japanese Literature, Tachikawa (shelf mark: ﾁ4-397-1~2).
132. For a discussion of knife ceremonies in medieval Japan, see Rath, *Food and Fantasy*, 38–51.
133. *Yorozu kikigaki hiden* (Kyoto: Nishimura Matazaemon, 1652), Tokyo University Library, Tokyo; digital version, National Institute of Japanese Literature, Tachikawa. (shelf mark: DIG-TOKY-162). Unless otherwise stated, I refer to this edition (cited as *Kikigaki*). Other editions/impressions date from 1651, 1653, 1658 (two separate editions), and 1673. There are also copies without a colophon. For a study of the different editions see Iizuka Yōko, Kokubun Kyōko, and Yoshii Motoko, "*Yorozu kikigaki hiden* ni tsuite no kenkyū," *Tōkyō Kasei Gakuin Daigaku kiyō* 16 (October 1976): 23–106. Its presence in *shojaku mokuroku* is complex. It appears as *Kikigaki hidenshō* twice in the 1666–1667 catalogue (under *washo narabi ni kanarui*): one title is in two volumes, the other is in one and is accompanied by the description "small book" (*kohon*). A single-volume *Kikigaki hidenshō* was listed under *shitsukekata-sho narabi ni ryōri-sho* in the 1670 catalogue. It was accompanied by the description "methods of cooking" (*ryōri no shiyō*) and was available in small and big formats. It appeared regularly until 1699. The 1685 catalogue listed a two-volume *Kikigaki hiden* as part of *hinagata* (kimono-pattern) books and described it as an instruction book on how to dye cloth. It was retained in 1692, 1696, 1699, 1709, and 1715. In the 1681 catalogue only the one-volume

text appears. It was priced at 6 *fun* for the small size and at 1 *monme* for the big size. In the 1696, 1709, and 1715 catalogues only the two-volume text appears. It was priced at 8 *fun* (only in 1696 and 1709). Because the one-volume *Kikigaki hidenshō* contains sections that deal with dyeing cloth, further research needs to be done in order to understand the relationship between these two titles.

134. *Kikigaki*, 12v–13r.
135. *Yorozu kikigaki hiden* (n.p.: publisher unknown, 1651), Waseda University Library, Tokyo (shelf mark: 文庫 31 E0886).
136. *Yorozu kikigaki hiden*, 1651 edition, 32r–33r.
137. *Waka shokumotsu honzō* (n.p.: publisher unknown, 1630), National Diet Library, Tokyo (shelf mark: 特 1-788). Unless otherwise noted, I refer to this edition (cited as *Waka shokumotsu honzō*). There are editions/impressions dated to 1642, 1646, 1654, 1671, 1692, and 1694. There are also undated copies. It appeared as *Uta honzō* in book-trade catalogues from 1666–1667 to 1715, under the category of medical texts (*isho*). In 1692 it was listed as available in small and large sizes. It was accompanied by a note explaining that is was in hiragana. The 1681 catalogue lists it twice: at 8 *fun*, probably for the large size, and at 5 *fun* for the small one, both in one volume. In the 1696 catalogue we find a choice between the price of 6 *fun*, probably for the large-size format, and that of 4 *fun* for the small-size format. No price is recorded in the 1709 or 1715 catalogues. In the 1671 catalogue we also find an edition in seven volumes titled *Uta honzō zōho*, highlighting the presence of additions (*zōho*). It last appears in 1675. It probably refers to what is known today under the title *Shokumotsu waka honzō zōho* compiled by Yamaoka Genrin and published in 1667.
138. *Waka shokumotsu honzō* (Kyoto: Yasuda Jūbee, 1642), Waseda University Library, Tokyo (shelf mark: ニ1 2797), vol. 2, 18v.
139. Please note that not all syllables contain all the food types listed here. The choice to organize the text around natural products (raw or processed) and to indicate their medical properties is in line with the herbaria (*honzō*) that constituted an essential part of Chinese and Japanese medicine. See Kosoto Hiroshi, *Nihon kanpō tenseki jiten* (Tokyo: Taishūkan Shoten, 1999), 349–59.
140. *Waka shokumotsu honzō*, respectively vol. 1, 16r, 32v, 26v.
141. *Waka shokumotsu honzō*, respectively vol. 1, 29r, 15v, 9v.
142. The term "cultural literacy" was originally coined outside the context of Japan by Eric Donald Hirsch in *Cultural Literacy: What Every American Needs to Know* (New York: Vintage Books, 1988). Hirsch explains, "To be culturally literate is to possess the basic information needed to thrive in the modern world" (115).
143. Berry, *Japan in Print*, 211; see also 50, 195.
144. Berry, *Japan in Print*, 214, 217.
145. Berry, *Japan in Print*, 215, 217.
146. Berry, *Japan in Print*, 215.
147. Berry, *Japan in Print*, 216, notes that "even savants are unlikely to recognize every name [place-name]" and that "presumably versed in this coherent spatial order, readers make out odd references by analogy with what they know," but Berry fails to develop a line of inquiry as to how readers learn from Saikaku's fiction.
148. *Ikkyū shokoku monogatari* (Kyoto: Akai Chōbee, n.d.), Waseda University Library, Tokyo (shelf mark: ヘ13 03379), vol. 5, 8v–10v. It appeared in *shojaku mokuroku* as *Ikkyū shokoku banashi* from 1671 until 1715 in the category of *hanashi no hon* (or *hanashibon*). The price for this five-volume title is recorded as follows: 4 *monme* (1681), 2 *monme* 7 *fun* (1696, 1709, and 1715). On *Chikusai*, see chapter 7.

149. On how Abbott Ikkyū 一休 (1394–1481) was transformed into a fictional character in the seventeenth-century, see Oka Masahiko, *Ikkyū banashi: Tonchi kozō no raireki*, Seminā koten o yomu 7 (Tokyo: Heibonsha, 1995).

150. See, for example, *Shin Chikusai* (Kyoto: Nishimura Ichirōemon and Sakagami Shōbee, 1687), private collection, Suzuran Bunko, Cambridge, U.K. (no shelf mark), vol. 5, 1r–3v; diplomatic transcription of the copy at Tōyō Bunko in vol. 2 of *Nishimura bon shōsetsu zenshū*, ed. Nishimura Bon Shōsetsu Kenkyūkai (Tokyo: Benseisha, 1985), 261–63.

151. *Sanze aishō makura* (Edo: Iseya Ihee and Matsuzakaya Kihee, 1687), photographic reproduction and transcription in vol. 1 of *Edo enpon shūsei*, ed. Hayashi Yoshikazu (Tokyo: Kawade Shobō Shinsha, 2013), 197–245. Cited hereafter as *Sanze*. It did not appear in book-trade catalogues. A facsimile with German translation was published as a limited edition of three hundred copies in Berlin in 1982; see Nikolaus Ritter and Gabriele Hilpert Ritter, eds., *Sanze Aishō Makura: Ein horoskopisches "Kopfkissenbuch der dreifachen Seelenverwandtschaft" aus dem 17. Jahrhundert mit Holzschnitten von Moronobu Hishikawa*, trans. Terasaki Akiko and Gabriele Hilpert Ritter (Berlin: Edition BBW, 1982).

152. *Sanze*, 197; Shirakura Yoshihiko, *Eiri shunga ehon mokuroku* (Tokyo: Heibonsha, 2007), 148; Asano Shūgō, *Hishikawa Moronobu to ukiyo-e no reimei* (Tokyo: Tōkyō Daigaku Shuppankai, 2008), 137, 148.

153. *Onna kagami*, vol. 2, 7v–8r; *KS* 10:34.

154. *Sanze*, vol. 1, 3v–4r; 202.

155. *Sanze*, vol. 1, 4v–5r; 203.

156. *Sanze*, vol. 1, 5v–6r; 204. The illustration is very similar to that included in *Onna kagami hidensho* (Edo: Hon Toiya, n.d.), National Diet Library, Tokyo (shelf mark: わ159-123), vol. 2, 7r.

157. *Onna kagami*, vol. 2, 8v–10r; *KS* 10:34–36.

158. *Sanze*, vol. 1, 6v–7r; 206.

159. *Sanze*, vol. 1, 6v–7r; 206.

160. *Sanze*, vol. 1, 6v–7r; 206–7.

161. *Onna kagami*, vol. 2, 18r–19v; *KS* 10:43–44.

162. *Onna kagami*, vol. 2, 19v; *KS* 10:44.

163. *Sanze*, vol. 1, 9r; 209.

5. Say It in a Skillful Letter

1. Even the 1632 *Ogasawara hyakka jō*, the first conduct manual to reveal the secret and oral traditions surrounding etiquette (chapter 3), provides some basic instruction in the practice of letter writing. It cautions, for instance, against sending a letter written in a poor hand and criticizes a skilled calligrapher who resorts to the use of inferior-quality paper; *Ogasawara hyakka jō* ([Kyoto]: Nakano Ichiemon, 1632), National Diet Library, Tokyo (shelf mark 855-35), 6r–6v. As noted by Peter Burke, the connection between language, spoken or written, and civility was a feature of early modern Europe as well; "A Civil Tongue: Language and Politeness in Early Modern Europe," in *Civil Histories: Essays Presented to Sir Keith Thomas*, ed. Peter Burke, Brian Harrison, and Paul Slack (Oxford: Oxford University Press, 2000), 31–48. See also chapter 5 in Anna Bryson, *From Courtesy to Civility: Changing Codes of Conduct in Early Modern England* (Oxford: Oxford University Press, 2004).

2. Roger Chartier, "Introduction: An Ordinary Kind of Writing," in *Correspondence: Models of Letter Writing from the Middle Ages to the Nineteenth Century*, ed. Roger Chartier, Alain Boureau, and Cécile Dauphin, trans. Christopher Woodall (Cambridge: Polity Press, 1997), 6.
3. Eve Tavor Bannet, *Empire of Letters: Letter Manuals and Transatlantic Correspondence, 1680–1820* (Cambridge: Cambridge University Press, 2005), xvii.
4. Markus Rüttermann, "What Does 'Literature of Correspondence' Mean? An Examination of the Japanese Genre Term *ōraimono* and Its History," in *Listen, Copy, Read: Popular Learning in Early Modern Japan*, ed. Matthias Hayek and Annick Horiuchi, Brill's Japanese Studies Library 46 (Leiden: Brill, 2014), 139–60. For a recent and comprehensive study of *ōraimono*, see Ishikawa Matsutarō, *Ōraimono no seiritsu to tenkai* (Tokyo: Yūshōdō Shuppan, 1988). The connection between letter writing and *ōraimono* is discussed by Tachibana Yutaka in his foundational study of the history of letter writing in Japan, *Shokan sahō no kenkyū* (Tokyo: Kazama Shobō, 1977), 363–401; see also Tachibana Yutaka, *Shokan sahō no kenkyū zokuhen* (Tokyo: Kazama Shobō, 1985), 103–76.
5. Beginning in 1670 the number of albums must have been such that it resulted in the creation of an independent category in book-trade catalogues under the heading *ishizuri narabi ni hitsudō sho* 石摺并筆道書 (stone rubbings and calligraphy books).
6. David Pattinson, "The Market for Letter Collections in Seventeenth-Century China," *Chinese Literature: Essays, Articles, Reviews (CLEAR)* 28 (December 2006): 125–57, notes four types of letter collections in seventeenth-century China: anthologies of letters of a particular individual, letter-writing manuals, compilations of letters from earliest times to the Ming dynasty, and compendia of letters by writers from the late Ming through to the compilers' contemporaries. Work needs to be done on the publishing genres *ōraimono narabi ni tehon* and *ishizuri narabi ni hitsudō sho* in order to ascertain whether the same categories apply.
7. *Shoshin bunshō* (n.p.: publisher unknown, n.d.), Tokyo Gakugei University Library, Mochizuki Bunko, Tokyo (shelf mark: T1A0/74/68), vol. 1, 1r. The rhetoric of encouraging letter writing as a tool for promoting the Confucian Way has been noted also by Pattinson in his study of *chisu* (collections of letters) in seventeenth-century China; "Market for Letter Collections," 146, 147, and 150. Hwisang Cho has studied how in Korea the 1556 collection *Chujasŏ chŏryo* (The abbreviated essence of Master Zhu Xi's letters) was framed as a reading that facilitated the understanding of complex new Confucian theories; "The Epistolary Brush: Letter Writing and Power in Chosŏn Korea," *Journal of Asian Studies* 75, no. 4 (November 2016): 1055–81.
8. Markus Rüttermann has done important work on the history of epistolary etiquette in early modern Japan; see "'So That We Can Study Letter-Writing': The Concept of Epistolary Etiquette in Premodern Japan," *Japan Review* 18 (January 2006): 57–128. His analysis focuses on the development of descriptive letter-writing manuals and on the theoretical discourse around epistolary etiquette across centuries, from the Nara to the late Edo periods. While Rüttermann's work must be praised for being the first contribution in English on the subject and for its thoroughness, there is a great gap between the sixteenth century and the work of Kaibara Ekiken at the beginning of the eighteenth century, with the exception of a few lines on *Kiyomizu monogatari* and the significance of rites therein (80).
9. See chapter 4, note 68, for information on the publishing history of *Shogaku bunshō narabi ni yorozu shitsukekata*. Here I make reference primarily to *Shogaku bunshō narabi ni yorozu shitsukekata* (Kyoto: Nishimura Matazaemon, 1647), private

collection, Suzuran Bunko, Cambridge, U.K. (no shelf mark). Hereafter cited as *Shogaku bunshō*, 1647 edition.
10. Tachibana, *Shokan sahō no kenkyū*, 1:224–28, lists all the titles in the table of contents. Tachibana also offers a very brief linguistic analysis of this text (228–30).
11. The inclusion of a table of contents represents an important navigational tool that enhances the accessibility to knowledge. It must be noted, though, that the table of contents of the 1647 edition of *Shogaku bunshō* does not always match the text. The document to confirm receipt of money, for example, is listed as section 34 in the table of contents but is in fact section 35 in the text. For early modern Japanese books produced commercially we must keep in mind Bradin Cormack and Carla Mazzio's observation regarding early modern Western books, "technologies of navigation were not always useful" and "the *illusion* of navigability alone might make the book commercially attractive" (emphasis in original); *Book Use, Book Theory: 1500–1700* (Chicago: University of Chicago Library, 2005), 15. I am indebted to Ellis Tinios for alerting me to this secondary source.
12. "The text-constitutive category consists of both text-type formulae (such as address formulae, date formulae, salutation, and opening formulae, closing formulae and signatures) and text-structural formulae ... which mark the text structure and realize the transition of one part of the discourse to another" (Gijsbert Rutten and Marijke van der Wal, "Functions of Epistolary Formulae in Dutch Letters from the Seventeenth and Eighteenth Centuries," *Journal of Historical Pragmatics* 13 [January 2012]: 173–201).
13. *Shogaku bunshō*, 1647 edition, 1r (for the table of contents), 6v (for the corresponding section in the text). I have omitted the *kunten* marks in my transcription.
14. For a comprehensive study of the linguistic features characterizing *sōrōbun* as an artificial written language in documents from the Edo period onward, see Yada Tsutomu, *Kokugo moji, hyōki shi no kenkyū* (Tokyo: Kyūko Shoin, 2012), 449–91.
15. *Shogaku bunshō*, 1647 edition, 1v (for the table of contents), 9v (for the corresponding section in the text).
16. *Shogaku bunshō*, 1647 edition, section 35 (in the table of contents, section 34; "How to Write a Receipt"), 16v.
17. *Shogaku bunshō*, 1647 edition, respectively section 53, 26r–27r, and section 54, 27r–27v.
18. For these two types of letter-writing manuals (*artes dictandi*), see Carol Poster and Linda C. Mitchell, eds., *Letter-Writing Manuals and Instruction from Antiquity to the Present: Historical and Bibliographic Studies*, Studies in Rhetoric/Communication (Columbia: University of South Carolina Press, 2007), 4. For a definition of formularies, see Malcolm Richardson, "The *Ars dictaminis*, the Formulary, and Medieval Epistolary Practice," in Poster and Mitchell, *Letter-Writing Manuals*, 52.
19. When discussing Lawrence of Aquilegia's *Practica sive usus dictaminis* (ca. 1300?), for example, Richardson, "*Ars dictaminis*," 59–60, shows that it is possible to create a letter by simply assembling the formulas that can be found in this manual.
20. Namura Jōhaku, *Yorozu anshi tegata kagami* (Kyoto: Tanaka Shōbee, 1693), photographic reproduction in vol. 6 of *Kinsei bungaku shiryō ruijū Sankō bunken hen*, ed. Kinsei Bungaku Shoshi Kenkyūkai (Tokyo: Benseisha, 1976), 175–344.
21. Marcia Yonemoto, *The Problem of Women in Early Modern Japan* (Oakland: University of California Press, 2016), 54.
22. Yonemoto, *Problem of Women*, 63.
23. Yonemoto, *Problem of Women*, 65.
24. Kubota Yasu, *Onna shogaku bunshō* ([Kyoto]: publisher unknown, 1660), private collection, Koizumi Yoshinaga, Tokyo, (no shelf mark). I thank Koizumi Yoshinaga for

granting access to digital images of his original. Koizumi explains that it was probably published by the Kyoto bookseller Maruya Genpee; Koizumi Yoshinaga, "Kinsei no nyohitsu tehon: Onna-bumi o meguru shomondai" (PhD diss., Kanazawa University, 1999), 20; Koizumi Yoshinaga, *Nyohitsu tehon kaidai*, Nihon shoshigaku taikei 80 (Musashimurayama: Seishōdō Shoten, 1998), 21–22. See also Koizumi Yoshinaga, "Ōraimono kaidai" (accessed December 17, 2019), http://www.bekkoame.ne.jp/ha/a_r/B40.htm. *Onna shogaku bunshō* first appeared in the 1670 book-trade catalogue and was retained until 1715. It was usually listed under the category of *nyosho*, with the exception of the 1692 catalogue, where it appears under *ōraimono narabi ni tehon*. In 1681 the price for this three-volume publication was 2 *monme* 5 *fun*. It increased slightly in 1696, 1709, and 1715 to 2 *monme* 7 *fun*. A *Zōho Onna shogaku bunshō* (3 vols.) was recorded in 1685, 1692, and 1699, in the first two catalogues under *ōraimono narabi ni tehon* and in the last one as a *nyosho*. There is no trace of this in the Union Catalogue of Early Japanese Books.

25. Koizumi, "Kinsei no nyohitsu tehon," 20, observes that Yasu should be viewed as one of the most prominent female intellectuals of the seventeenth-century. Also noted is that her daughter Kubota Tsuna signed the 1687 textbook *Onna imagawa*, which was probably published in Kyoto by Fukumori Saburōbee (20). Ishikawa Tōru, "Isome Tsuna no ōraimono," *Geibun kenkyū* 95 (2008): 170–76, argues that Kubota Tsuna is the same person as Isome Tsuna, a well-known calligrapher who worked on illustrated manuscripts as well as on *ōraimono* textbooks. On Isome Tsuna, see also Koizumi Yoshinaga, "Isome Tsuna no joyō bunshō," *Edo-ki onna kō* 8 (1997): 48–74.

26. The only exceptions can be found toward the end, after letter 25 in *Shogaku bunshō* and letter 3, vol. 3, in *Onna shogaku bunshō*. Male-oriented contents, including *renga* poetry (letter 26), medicine (letter 27), and military arts (letter 28) are substituted with contents more suitable to women—namely, the game of shells (vol. 3, letter 4), etiquette for women (vol. 3, letter 5), and music (vol. 3, letter 6). The lists continue to match until the letter that would accompany a person going to another province. Thereafter, *Shogaku bunshō* continues with business-like correspondence and then formal texts, while *Onna shogaku bunshō* ends with instructions on how to write on the paper accompanying gifts. Tachibana, *Shokan sahō no kenkyū*, 231–33, reproduces the table of contents of *Onna shogaku bunshō*, Koizumi, *Nyohitsu tehon kaidai*, 22, identifies the 1629 *Shogaku bunshō shō* as the direct source of *Onna shogaku bunshō*. More research needs to be done to ascertain the relationship between *Onna shogaku bunshō*, *Shogaku bunshō narabi ni yorozu shitsukekata*, and *Shogaku bunshō shō*, but it is beyond the scope of my analysis here.

27. *Onna shogaku bunshō*, vol. 1, 20r–20v.

28. This calligraphic style became widespread among the court aristocracy in the mid-Heian period. Beginning in the Kamakura period it represented a writing style appropriate for both court and military aristocratic women but was by no means confined to women. It was normally used in poetry and letters. For a discussion of this style, see Koizumi, "Kinsei no nyohitsu tehon," 41–61. Creative uses of the spatial layout of texts is not limited to Japan. Chosŏn Korea, for example, saw the emergence of "spiral letters." For details, see Cho, "The Epistolary Brush."

29. On *chirashi-gaki* in the Heian period, see Thomas LaMarre, *Uncovering Heian Japan: An Archaeology of Sensation and Inscription* (Durham, N.C.: Duke University Press, 2000), 114. On the aesthetics at play in *chirashi-gaki*, see Noriko Kaya, "The Aesthetic Characteristics of *Kana* Seen in *Chirashi-gaki*," in *Buchstaben der Welt—Welt der Buchstaben*, ed. Martin Roussel and Ryōsuke Ōhashi, Morphomata 12 (Munich: Fink,

2014), 139–59. Helen Magowan, doctoral candidate at the University of Cambridge, is exploring whether the shift to typography in the Meiji period corresponded to the decline of this type of text.
30. Paul Zukofsky reflects on the musical composition by Yuji Takahashi titled *Chirashi-gaki* (Dispersed calligraphy); "Chirashi Gaki," Musical Observations, Inc. (accessed September 14, 2019), http://www.musicalobservations.com/pour_un_Haydn/chirashi-gaki.html.
31. Koizumi, "Kinsei no nyohitsu tehon," 136–45.
32. Helen Magowan is working on a sophisticated reading of *nyohitsu*, moving away from the notion of gender and advancing the idea of a register indexed by several variables and appropriate for certain social contexts.
33. The distinction between Latin and vernacular seems very important in the discussion of Western *ars dictaminis*, for example, in the context of sixteenth-century England. See W. Webster Newbold, "Letter Writing and Vernacular Literacy in Sixteenth-Century England," in Poster and Mitchell, *Letter-Writing Manuals*, 127–40.
34. "Above all, literature keeps language alive as our collective heritage. . . . By helping to create language, literature creates a sense of identity and community" (Umberto Eco, *On Literature*, trans. Martin McLaughlin [London: Vintage Books, 2006], 2–3).
35. Bannet, *Empire of Letters*, 64.
36. On the publication histories of *Onna kagami hidensho* and *Onna shikimoku*, see notes 76 and 77 in chapter 4. *Onna shikimoku* ([Kyoto]: publisher unknown, 1660), diplomatic transcription in vol. 11 of *Kanazōshi shūsei*, ed. Asakura Haruhiko and Fukasawa Akio (Tokyo: Tōkyōdō Shuppan, 1990), vol. 2, 9r–13v; *KS* 11:166–70. Hereafter cited as *Onna shikimoku*. *Onna kagami hidensho* (Kyoto: Noda Yahei, 1650), diplomatic transcription in vol. 10 of *Kanazōshi shūsei*, ed. Asakura Haruhiko and Fukasawa Akio (Tokyo: Tōkyōdō Shuppan, 1989), vol. 2, 3r–7v; *KS* 10:30–34. Hereafter cited as *Onna kagami*.
37. Marcia Yonemoto, "The Perils of the 'Unpolished Jewel': Defining Women's Roles in Household Management in Early Modern Japan," *U.S.-Japan Women's Journal*, no. 39 (2010): 53.
38. *Onna shikimoku*, vol. 2, 9r; *KS* 11:166. Rüttermann, "'So That We Can Study,'" 67 clarifies that as far back as the early thirteenth century Prince Shukaku Hōshinnō arranged formulas in his *Shōsoku jitei hishō* (Secret treatise of letters kept in one's ears) according to the relationship between the sender and the addressee. The classification of letters according to the hierarchical relation between the addresser and the addressee can also be seen in Western *ars dictaminis*, the reason for which lies in the connection between rhetoric and its application in letter writing. See, for example, Richardson, "Ars dictaminis," 61, and Newbold, "Letter Writing," 130.
39. "Fumi no kakiyō jō-chū-ge no koto," *Onna kagami*, vol. 2, 3r; *KS* 10:30.
40. *Onna shikimoku*, vol. 2, 10r–10v; *KS* 11:167.
41. *Onna shikimoku*, vol. 2, 11r; *KS* 11:168; *Onna kagami hidensho*, vol. 2, 5r; *KS* 10:32.
42. *Onna shikimoku*, vol. 2, 14v; *KS* 11:171.
43. Ogawa Takeo, "Chūsei ensho bunreishū no seiritsu: *Horikawa-in enjo awase* kara *Shika kenro shū* e," *Bulletin of the National Institute of Japanese Literature* 30 (2004): 53–94, indicates that the oldest surviving manuscript dates to 1442. The core of the original text is believed to be a collection of courtly poetic love exchanges, but Ogawa notes that all extant manuscripts include an additional section with samples of love letters unrelated to the original poetic gathering. Markus Rüttermann has also examined the structure and language used in *Horikawa-in enjo awase*; "Nihon chūsei no kesōbun

sahō ni tsuite: *Ensho bunrei* o jiku ni," in *Nihon bunka no kaishaku: Roshia to Nihon kara no shiten*, ed. James C. Baxter (Kyoto: Kokusai Nihon Bunka Kenkyū Sentā, 2009), 165–83. Teruoka Yasutaka, *Nihon no shokan tai shōsetsu* (Tokyo: Echigoya Shoten, 1943), 38–40, even recognizes in *Horikawa-in enjo awase* the very origin of Japanese epistolary novels (*shoken tai shōsetsu*). Joshua S. Mostow, offers a different view: "The first true epistolary narrative also dates from this century [the tenth], the *Takamitsu Diary* (*Takamitsu nikki*, also known as the *Tōnomine Shōshō monogatari*), which records letters exchanged between Fujiwara no Takamitsu (fl. 939–977/985), his wife and his sister, after his precipitous decision to renounce the world and enter cloistered religious life" ("*The Tale of Light Snow*: Pastiche, Epistolary Fiction and Narrativity Verbal and Visual," in "Narrativity and Fictionality in Edo-Period Prose Literature," ed. Laura Moretti, special issue, *Japan Forum* 21, no. 3 [2010]: 366). Kathryn Lowry discusses love letters (*qingshu*) as a distinct literary genre in miscellanies, encyclopedias for daily use, and epistolary guides published in China during the late sixteenth and early seventeenth centuries; "Duplicating the Strength of Feeling: The Circulation of *Qingshu* in the Late Ming," in *Writing and Materiality in China: Essays in Honor of Patrick Hanan*, ed. Judith T. Zeitlin, Lydia H. Liu, and Ellen Widmer (Cambridge, Mass.: Harvard University Asia Center, 2003), 239–72.

44. Yuasa Yoshiko has conducted a systematic survey of the Edo-period printed editions of *Shika kenro shū* and has organized them according to three main lineages: one based on the 1660 edition, one on its undated facsimile, and one on the 1698 edition; *Kinsei shōsetsu no kenkyū: Keimōteki bungei no tenkai* (Tokyo: Kyūko Shoin, 2017), 22–52.

45. See Teruoka, *Nihon no shokan tai shōsetsu*, 40–49.

46. *Usuyuki monogatari* ([Kyoto]: Nakano Dōya, 1632), critical edition in *Urami no suke, Usuyuki monogatari*, ed. Kikuchi Shin'ichi (Osaka: Izumi Shoin, 1994), 37–75. Hereafter cited as *Usuyuki monogatari*, 1632 edition. For a comprehensive and detailed survey of all the editions of *Usuyuki monogatari*, see Matsubara Hidee, "*Usuyuki monogatari* hanpon kō," in *Usuyuki monogatari to otogizōshi, kanazōshi* (Osaka: Izumi Shoin, 1997), 48–73. In this chapter I refer to several editions. In book-trade catalogues *Usuyuki monogatari* appeared as a steady item from 1666–1667 to 1715, included in the category of *mai narabi ni sōshi*. For the two-volume edition, the price was 8 *fun* in 1681 and 1696. There are no prices in the 1709 and 1715 catalogues.

47. I use the term "master plot" here as defined by H. Porter Abbott as "stories that we tell over and over in myriad forms" (*The Cambridge Introduction to Narrative*, 2nd ed. [Cambridge: Cambridge University Press, 2008], 46). I am not, however, operating on the idea that master plots "connect vitally with our deepest values, wishes, and fears" and are endowed with "moral force" (46, 48). Similarly, I do not wish to discuss the potential of master plots as deeply embedded in "national cultures" (47). Here I would equate the notion of a "master plot" with that of the "story skeleton" as defined by Roger C. Schank in the field of artificial intelligence. Schank has done foundational work on how story skeletons affect memory, how storytelling and understanding are functionally identical, and on the mechanism whereby stories are produced from "the gist of a story" and out of a database of story skeletons; *Tell Me a Story: Narrative and Intelligence* (Evanston, Ill.: Northwestern University Press, 2000), 147–88.

48. *Usuyuki monogatari* ([Kyoto]: publisher unknown, 1636), National Diet Library, Tokyo (shelf mark: WB2-3); hereafter cited as *Usuyuki monogatari*, 1636 edition. *Usuyuki monogatari* ([Kyoto]: Yamamoto Kyūzaemon, 1664), National Diet Library, Tokyo (shelf mark: 857-95); hereafter cited as *Usuyuki monogatari*, 1664 edition.

49. Mostow, "*Tale of Light Snow*," 364. The intertextual relationship between *Usuyuki monogatari* and Muromachi-period tales is also analyzed in Watanabe Morikuni,

"*Usuyuki monogatari* to otogi-zōshi," *Kinsei bungei* 22 (1973): 1–12. Lowry, "Duplicating the Strength of Feeling," notes a similar intertextual stance in love letters published in late-Ming China, where poetry, quatrains, lyrics, and excerpts from dramas interweave in a sophisticated pastiche.
50. Mostow, "*Tale of Light Snow*," 384.
51. *Usuyuki monogatari*, 1664 edition, vol. 1, 3v–4r, 9v–10r; vol. 2, 3v–4r, 9v–10r.
52. I borrow this term from Schank, *Tell Me a Story*, 37–40.
53. *Usuyuki monogatari* (Tokyo: Izumoji Manjirō, 1895), private collection, Suzuran Bunko, Cambridge, U.K. (no shelf mark), vol. 1, 1v.
54. Noda Hisao, *Nihon kinsei shōsetsu shi: Kanazōshi hen* (Tokyo: Benseisha, 1986), 86.
55. Nishimura Mitatsu, *Shokoku shinjū onna* (Edo: Nishimura Hanbee; Kyoto: Nishimura Ichirōemon and Sakagami Shōbee, 1686), Katei Bunko, Tokyo (shelf mark: 霞亭0167), vol. 2, 8v.
56. Ejima Kiseki, *Sakiwake gonin musume* (Kyoto: Hishiya Jihee, 1735), National Diet Library, Tokyo (shelf mark: 京-212), vol. 2, 5v.
57. Maeda Sawa, *Onna sewa yōbunshō taisei* (Osaka: Yorozuya Hikotarō; Edo: Suhara Mohee, 1700), Hirosaki City Public Library, Hirosaki; microfilm copy, National Institute of Japanese Literature, Tachikawa (microfilm number: 272-399-3). The presence of *Usuyuki monogatari* in this book was first identified in Matsubara, "*Usuyuki monogatari* hanpon kō," 58.
58. There are subtle changes in the text, such as the fact that Sonobe no Emon does not die at the age of twenty-six but continues to practice Buddhist ascetics until he is eighty-five; see *Onna sewa yōbunshō taisei*, vol. 3, 19v.
59. Rankeishi (calligrapher) and Ōmori Yoshikiyo (illustrator), *Shin Usuyuki monogatari* (Kyoto: Kawakatsu Gorōemon; Edo: Masuya, 1716), private collection, Suzuran Bunko, Cambridge, U.K. (no shelf mark).
60. It is noteworthy that the popularity of this love story was such that it inspired early modern theater. The play *Shin Usuyuki monogatari*, originally conceived for the puppet theater, was first staged in the fifth month of 1741 at the Osaka theater Takemoto-za. Act 1, scene 1 adapts three of the four key moments already identified in this chapter: Sonobe Saemon falls in love with Usuyuki after viewing a poem written by her that is affixed to a cherry tree; promised in marriage, they exchange letters with the help of Magaki, Usuyuki's maidservant, and Tsumahee, Saemon's footman. The plot is developed in new directions.
61. *Usugumo monogatari* (Kyoto: Mizuta Jinzaemon, 1659), photographic reproduction in vol. 14 of *Kinsei bungaku shiryō ruijū Kanazōshi hen*, ed. Kinsei Bungaku Shoshi Kenkyūkai (Tokyo: Benseisha, 1974), 295–358. All citations (as *Usugumo monogatari*) are to the 1659 edition. Also known as *Usugumo koi monogatari*, it was reprinted in 1667 in Edo by Matsue Ichirobee. In book-trade catalogues it appeared as a regular item from 1666–1667 to 1715. It was originally listed in the category of *mai narabi ni sōshi* but migrated to *monogatari-rui* in 1685. It was recorded as *Usugumo koi monogatari* in catalogues organized around publishing genres and as *Usugumo monogatari* in those following the *i-ro-ha* order. The price for this two-volume publication remained steady at 8 *fun* in 1681, 1696, 1709, and 1715. A hand scroll with illustrations attributed to Miyagawa Chōshun 宮川長春 (1683–1753) is preserved in the Mary Griggs Burke Collection, New York. For more information on this manuscript, see Yasuhara Makoto, "Bāku korekushon shozō den Miyagawa Chōshun *Usugumo monogatari* shōkai: Shoshi to honkoku," *Rikkyō Daigaku Nihon bungaku*, no. 105 (December 2010): 46–52.
62. Noda, *Nihon kinsei shōsetsu shi*, 355.

348   5. Say It in a Skillful Letter

63. This literary device is generally referred to as *kōkō tan*. See, for example, Sano Daisuke, *Kō no kenkyū: Kōkyō chūshaku to kōkō tan to no bunseki* (Tokyo: Kenbun Shuppan, 2016). For a study of filial piety in Edo-period culture and literature, see Katsumata Motoi, *Oya kōkō no Edo bunka* (Tokyo: Kasama Shoin, 2017).
64. *Usugumo monogatari*, vol. 1, 1v. *Nijūshikō* was circulating in manuscript form during the medieval period and was printed as early as the seventeenth century, first in movable-type, and then in 1632 and in 1656, among other editions. For an English translation of a version published in Osaka sometime between circa 1716 and 1729, see R. Keller Kimbrough, trans., "Translation: The Twenty-Four Filial Exemplars," *Japan Review*, no. 34 (2019): 69–94.
65. *Usugumo monogatari*, vol. 1, 4r.
66. This trope is known as *mōshigo tan* in Japanese literature. See, for example, Fujishima Hidetaka, "Mōshigo tan kōseijō no mondai ten: Otogizōshi o chūshin to shite," *Chūsei bungaku* 16 (May 1971): 18–22; Fujishima Hidetaka, "Mōshigo tan no keisei," *Kanazawa Kōgyō Daigaku kenkyū kiyō* 2 (April 1972): 59–71; and Minobe Shigekatsu, "Mōshiko tan no kōzō," *Kokubungaku kaishaku to kanshō* 56, no. 10 (October 1991): 135–40.
67. *Usugumo monogatari*, vol. 1, 6v–7r.
68. *Usuyuki monogatari*, 1632 edition, 40; *Usugumo monogatari*, vol. 1, 6v; illustration on 6r.
69. *Usuyuki monogatari*, 1632 edition, 40.
70. *Usugumo monogatari*, vol. 1, 7r.
71. Schank, *Tell Me a Story*, 186, speaks of skeleton stories used "as a contrast rather than as a framework" and of stories that "rely upon failed expectations about what is likely to happen next by implicitly invoking a story skeleton and then abandoning it when least expected." Schank explains that the effect of this contrast is humor; *Usugumo monogatari* shows that other outcomes are possible.
72. *Usugumo monogatari*, vol. 1, 7v.
73. Izayoi hears from Usugumo about her lovesickness and replies, "Don't be silly, my lady! Do you really suffer for something so easily solved? It is normal in this world to love and to be loved. From now on, leave this to me. I will solve it for the best" (*Usugumo monogatari*, vol. 1, 8v).
74. Yuasa, *Kinsei shōsetsu no kenkyū*, 89–90.
75. *Usugumo monogatari*, vol. 1, 16r.
76. *Usugumo monogatari*, vol. 2, 19r–19v.
77. The celebration of the wedding is suggested by the penultimate illustration, which offers a visual trope of the nuptial rituals similar to what was seen in chapter 4; *Usugumo monogatari*, vol. 2, 35r. Here, though, the parents are not portrayed; in their place are Aoyagi and Izayoi. This change stresses their crucial roles in supporting both protagonists.
78. *Usugumo monogatari*, vol. 2, 20v–24r.
79. *Usugumo monogatari*, vol. 2, 21r. Princess Mano later appeared in the 1680 *Meijo nasake kurabe*, in which she was an example of ideal compassion and love. In this version, the girl's parents are not mentioned. The emperor still leaves the court and hides his real identity in order to remain near the young girl. But here it is Princess Mano who catches sight of him in the fields, falling in love with him despite his allegedly lower status. The ending is unchanged, with the girl becoming the emperor's wife. An English translation of the passage in question is found in Maria Bugno, "Shunpon: Intertextuality, Humour, and Sexual Education in Early-Modern Japan" (PhD diss., University of Cambridge, 2019), 43–44.

80. In the version included in *Meijo nasake kurabe* Princess Mano has a place in the love story in her taking notice of the emperor, although we are far removed from the proactiveness demonstrated in *Usugumo monogatari*.
81. *Usugumo monogatari*, vol. 2, 21v–22v.
82. *Usugumo monogatari*, vol. 2, 24r.
83. *Nishikigi* (n.p.: publisher unknown, n.d.), National Diet Library, Tokyo (shelf mark: 京-145). Hereafter cited as *Nishikigi*. The only dated edition is the 1661, and the Union Catalogue of Early Japanese Books (http://base1.nijl.ac.jp/~tkoten/) records two copies (one at the Hiroshima University Library and one in Ryūmon Bunko, Nara). *Nishikigi* first appeared in the 1670 book-trade catalogue under the category of *nyosho*. It was advertised as "a list of love letters" (*koi no fumi zukushi nari*). In the 1675 catalogue, Asai Ryōi was listed as the author, although to date there is no evidence to support this attribution. In the 1681 catalogue, the price for the five volumes was 4 *monme* 5 *fun*. It decreased to 2 *monme* 7 *fun* in the 1696 and 1709 catalogues. It went up to 3 *monme* 7 *fun* in the 1715 catalogue.
84. Cormack and Mazzio, *Book Use, Book Theory*, 24.
85. Yuasa, *Kinsei shōsetsu no kenkyū*, 99.
86. *Nishikigi*, vol. 5, 15v–17v. Yuasa, *Kinsei shōsetsu no kenkyū*, 100, points out that *hatsu no koi* (first love) and its explanation quotes almost verbatim the same explanation given in the *ruidai shū* titled *Waka dairin gushō* (A humble treatise on the forest of the topics for poetry), composed in the Muromachi period and first published in 1637. The passage on first love uses the description in *Waka dairin gushō* and selects two poems from the thirty-seven included in this poetry anthology; Yamashina Tokio (compiler), *Waka dairin gushō* (n.p.: publisher unknown, n.d.), Hirosaki City Public Library, Hirosaki; microfilm copy, National Institute of Japanese Literature, Tachikawa (microfilm number: 272-129-7), vol. 4, 3r. I could not identify similar descriptions for the remaining five entries, although the *waka* appear in *Waka dairin gushō*.
87. *Nishikigi*, vol. 5, 15r–22r. Yuasa, *Kinsei shōsetsu no kenkyū*, 100–101, identifies *Karin ryōzai shū* (Collection of good materials for the forest of poetry), attributed to Ichijō Kaneyoshi 一条兼良 (1402–1481) and first printed in 1643, as the source for this section.
88. *Nishikigi*, vol. 1, 14r–24r. Yuasa, *Kinsei shōsetsu no kenkyū*, 101–12, examines two other sections: "The Very First Love: Approaching a Young Girl" and "Concealed Love."
89. *Nishikigi*, vol. 1, 14v. Yuasa, *Kinsei shōsetsu no kenkyū*, 119, notes that this poem also appears in *Waka dairin gushō*, although the last verse differs slightly: *omoi aru to mo* becomes *omoi aru to wa*.
90. *Nishikigi*, vol. 1, 14v.
91. The reference to *Shin Senzai waka shū* is justified by the fact that the author of *Nishikigi* mentions the title of this anthology as a source used for the expression *shinobu koi*; *Nishikigi*, vol. 5, 15v.
92. Joshua S. Mostow and Royall Tyler, trans., *The Ise Stories: Ise monogatari* (Honolulu: University of Hawai'i Press, 2010), 14–16.
93. *Nishikigi*, vol. 5, 20r. The note first gives a synonym for *ho ni araware* as *ho ni izuru* and explains the meaning as *kokoro no omoi o arawasu* (literally, "to reveal the feelings of one's heart").
94. *Nishikigi*, vol. 1, 14v.
95. *Nishikigi*, vol. 1, 15v.
96. *Nishikigi*, vol. 1, 22r.
97. *Nishikigi*, vol. 2, 2v.

350   5. Say It in a Skillful Letter

98. *Nishikigi*, vol. 2, 4v.
99. *Nishikigi*, vol. 1, 12v.
100. Noda, *Nihon kinsei shōsetsu shi*, 516.
101. Noda, *Nihon kinsei shōsetsu shi*, 516–17. Noda's view accords with Teruoka, *Nihon no shokan tai shōsetsu*, 60. Yuasa Yoshiko problematizes this assessment by treating *Nishikigi* also as a form of *yomimono* (story to be read): "While [*Nishikigi*] retains the nature of an educational text about poetic knowledge, it also departs from this by describing love stories between men and women of the seventeenth century" (Yuasa, *Kinsei shōsetsu no kenkyū*, 112).
102. Chartier, "Introduction," "*Secrétaires* for the People? Model Letters of the *Ancien Régime*," in *Correspondence*, 5, 7, 98–100.
103. For example, Richardson, "*Ars dictaminis*," 56, notes that "medieval letters were intended to be read aloud to the recipient rather than silently and in private." Bannet, *Empire of Letters*, 47–49, also explores this reading mode.
104. *Kōshoku Nishikigi* (Edo: Nishimura Hanbee; Kyoto: Nishimura Ichirōemon, [1692]), diplomatic transcription in *Kōshoku fumi denju, Kōshoku Nishikigi*, ed. Yoshida Kōichi, Koten bunko 604 (Tokyo: Koten Bunko, 1997), 331–448. *Shin Nishikigi monogatari* (Edo: Yamazaki Kinbee, 1758), Art Research Center, Ritsumeikan University, Kyoto (shelf mark: hayBK02-0026).
105. There are only two documented copies of *Nasake no uwamori*. The first is a photographic reproduction and transcription of an original, whose whereabouts are unknown, in vol. 1 of *Edo enpon shūsei*, ed. Hayashi Yoshikazu (Tokyo: Kawade Shobō Shinsha, 2013), 247–94. This copy has three distinct internal titles: *Nasake* (abbreviation for *Nasake no uwamori* in the *hashira-dai*), *Danjo ōnure e makura* (The great illustrated pillow of love between men and women) at the beginning of the first volume, and *Yamato chiwa no ōyose* (The great collection of lovers' talk) at the beginning of the third volume. Hayashi Yoshikazu (104) opines that these two titles might have been added at a later stage, thereby canceling out the earlier title. The other copy is in the private collection Suzuran Bunko, Cambridge, U.K., and is not complete (only vol. 1 survives; two folios are missing). In this copy there is no title preceding the introduction. Judging from the condition of the printed surface, it appears to be an earlier printing using the same blocks. *Nasake no uwamori* is not included in book-trade catalogues. It was probably published in the 1680s.
106. *Nasake no uwamori*, vol. 1, 1r; 249.
107. For other examples, see Bugno, "Shunpon," chapter 3; Joshua S. Mostow, *Courtly Visions: The Ise Stories and the Politics of Cultural Appropriation* (Leiden: Brill, 2014), 243–73.
108. *Nasake no uwamori*, vol. 1, 5v; 255. The text uses the expression *inamono goto no naki*. While the main meaning of *inamono* is "strange things" or "miraculous things," I would interpret it here as a metonym of *en* (love bond) from the saying *en wa inamono ajina mono* (love bonds are a strange and wondrous thing). That is why I suggest that the meaning is "no love bond materializes."
109. *Nasake no uwamori*, vol. 2, 3v–4r; 266–67.
110. See Mostow and Tyler, *The Ise Stories*, 43–44.
111. These two characters appear as part of a longer text that reads 圖育風獨一 on a folding screen used by Moronobu in the 1683 *Koi no tanoshimi* (The pleasure of love; 3v–4r). The image is reproduced in the exhibition catalogue Tanabe Masako, ed., *Shoki ukiyoe ten: Han no chikara, fude no chikara* (Chiba: Chiba City Museum of Art, 2016), no. 33. The same compound, but inversed, also appears in the hanging scroll

attributed to Moronobu and known under the title *Shitsunai yūraku zu* (Image of indoor entertainments; n.d.); see Tanabe, *Shoki ukiyoe ten*, no. 44. The connection with Hikkaidō is suggested by Tanabe, *Shoki ukiyoe ten*, no. 42, when discussing the character 獨 as it appears in Moronobu's *Yoshiwara no tei* (Images from Yoshiwara; 1681–1684) as well as in *Nasake no uwamori* (vol. 1, 5v–6r; 254). The calligrapher Hikkaidō was celebrated for his *Sangoku hikkai zensho* (Compilation of the sea of brush across three countries, 20 vols.; originally published in 1650).

112. *Nasake no uwamori*, vol. 1, 1v–2r; 250.
113. Hishikawa Moronobu, illus., *Genji Yamato e kagami*. Edo: Urokogataya, 1685, private collection, Ebi Bunko, U.K. (shelf mark: EbiM001), vol. 2, 18r.
114. *Nishikigi*, vol. 5, 1r–1v.
115. *Nishikigi*, vol. 5, 3v.
116. *Nasake no uwamori*, vol. 1, 2r; 250.
117. *Nasake no uwamori*, vol. 1, 2v–3r; 251.
118. *Nasake no uwamori*, vol. 1, 2v; 251.
119. *Nishikigi*, vol. 5, 7r. *Nasake no uwamori* uses the phrasing almost verbatim, adding the following description to "the next world": "where there is no need to worry about hiding from people's eyes" (*hitome tomo shinoburu tomo naki nochi no yo*); see *Nasake no uwamori*, vol. 1, 3r; 251.
120. *Nishikigi*, vol. 5, 7v.
121. *Nasake no uwamori*, vol. 2, 5v–6r; 269–70.
122. *Nishikigi*, vol. 5, 15v–16v.
123. *Nasake no uwamori*, vol. 2, 16r; 269–70.
124. *Nishikigi*, vol. 5, 18v–22v.
125. Saikaku's disciple Hōjō Dansui 北条団水 (1663–1711) edited the work and oversaw the posthumous publication of *Yorozu no fumi hōgu* in 1696; Ihara Saikaku and Hōjō Dansui, *Yorozu no fumi hōgu* (Edo: Yorozuya Seibee; Osaka: Kariganeya Shōhee; Kyoto: Uemura Heizaemon, 1696), critical edition with translation in modern Japanese in vol. 15 of *Ketteiban Taiyaku Saikaku zenshū*, ed. Asō Isoji and Fuji Akio (Tokyo: Meiji Shoin, 1993), 139–273. For English-language studies, see Virginia Marcus, "A Miscellany of Old Letters: Saikaku's *Yorozu no Fumihōgu*," *Monumenta Nipponica* 40, no. 3 (Autumn 1985): 257–64, and Susanna Fessler, "Scraps of Wisdom: Ihara Saikaku's *Yorozu no fumihōgu*," *Journal of the Association of Teachers of Japanese* 31, no. 2 (October 1997): 52–72.
126. Marcus, "Miscellany of Old Letters," 260.

6. A Commitment to the Present

1. Bradin Cormack and Carla Mazzio, *Book Use, Book Theory: 1500–1700* (Chicago: University of Chicago Library, 2005), 79.
2. Todd W. Reeser and Steven D. Spalding, "Reading Literature/Culture: A Translation of 'Reading as a Cultural Practice,'" in "Resources in Stylistics and Literary Analysis," special issue, *Style* 36, no. 4 (Winter 2002): 670.
3. See, for example, Constantine Nomikos Vaporis, *Breaking Barriers: Travel and the State in Early Modern Japan*, Harvard East Asian Monographs 163 (Cambridge, Mass.: Harvard University Press, 1995), and Laura Nenzi, *Excursions in Identity: Travel and the Intersection of Place, Gender, and Status in Edo Japan* (Honolulu: University of Hawai'i Press, 2008).

4. See Mary Elizabeth Berry, *Japan in Print: Information and Nation in the Early Modern Period* (Berkeley: University of California Press, 2006), 54–103, 139–84; Marcia Yonemoto, *Mapping Early Modern Japan: Space, Place, and Culture in the Tokugawa Period, 1603–1868* (Berkeley: University of California Press, 2003); and Nicolas Fiévé, "Kyoto's Famous Places: Collective Memory and 'Monuments' in the Tokugawa Period," in *Japanese Capitals in Historical Perspective: Place, Power and Memory in Kyoto, Edo and Tokyo*, ed. Nicolas Fiévé and Paul Waley (London: RoutledgeCurzon, 2003), 153–71.
5. Daniel Woolf, "News, History, and the Construction of the Present in Early Modern England," in *The Politics of Information in Early Modern Europe*, ed. Brendan Dooley and Sabrina A. Baron, Routledge Studies in Cultural History 1 (London: Routledge, 2011), 80.
6. Akira Hayami notes that "the structure of society in Tokugawa Japan was also systematically premised on the development of a certain level of money economy. That is precisely why the shogunate, from its inception, established and simultaneously began the minting of gold, silver, and copper coins. A portion of yearly taxes was paid in cash, and over half the tax paid in rice was converted into cash. Once converted into cash it was used to purchase necessary goods. With that in mind, we may see that the common description of Tokugawa Japan as 'a rice economy' cannot be taken literally" ("Introduction: The Emergence of 'Economic Society,'" in *Emergence of Economic Society in Japan, 1600–1859: Early Modern*, ed. Akira Hayami, Osamu Saitō, and Ronald P. Toby, vol. 1 of *The Economic History of Japan: 1600–1990* [Oxford: Oxford University Press, 2004], 22).
7. For a discussion of these factors and others, see, for example, Suzuki Kōzō, *Edo no keizai seisaku to gendai—Edo ga wakareba ima ga mieru* (Tokyo: Bijinesu Kyōiku Shuppansha, 1993), 5–23.
8. Hayami, "Introduction," 11.
9. Penelope Francks, *The Japanese Consumer: An Alternative Economic History of Modern Japan* (Cambridge: Cambridge University Press, 2009), 11–73.
10. Ethan Segal, "Money and the State: Medieval Precursors of the Early Modern Economy," in *Economic Thought in Early Modern Japan*, ed. Bettina Gramlich-Oka and Gregory Smits, Monies, Markets, and Finance in East Asia, 1600–1900, vol. 1 (Leiden: Brill, 2010), 22, 25. Segal observes that copper cash (*zeni*) had been in circulation in medieval Japan, and that for the first century of Tokugawa rule "people continued to use imported Chinese cash, especially Ming *Eiraku* (C: *Yongle*) coins and privately minted medieval counterfeit coins (*bita sen*), in their daily business dealings" (41).
11. The supply of money "increased tremendously during the first half of the seventeenth century" (Matao Miyamoto, "Quantitative Aspects of Tokugawa Economy," in Hayami, Saitō, and Toby, *Emergence of Economic Society*, 59).
12. Donald H. Shively, "Sumptuary Regulation and Status in Early Tokugawa Japan," *Harvard Journal of Asiatic Studies* 25 (1964–1965): 135.
13. Shively, "Sumptuary Regulation," 150, describes *hatamoto* as those who were "direct vassals of the Bakufu, its first military arm as well as civil administrators."
14. Shively, "Sumptuary Regulation," 135.
15. Shively, "Sumptuary Regulation," 126.
16. *Jinkyōron* (Kyoto: Ōmiya Jirokichi, n.d.), photographic reproduction in vol. 21 of *Chōhōki shiryō shūsei*, ed. Nagatomo Chiyoji (Kyoto: Rinsen Shoten, 2006), 5–99. Hereafter cited as *Jinkyōron*. The oldest extant edition is titled *Kingin mannōgan* and dates to 1687 (Settsu: Morita Shōtarō). We know of 1690, 1694, 1753, 1833, and 1843 editions/

reprints. There are also specimens with no colophon. It appeared sporadically in book-trade catalogues under the title *Jinkyōron* first in 1692 and then in 1696, 1709, and 1715. In the 1692 catalogue it was categorized under *kana washo*. In the 1696, 1709, and 1715 catalogues the price for this three-volume publication was 2 *monme* 3 *fun*.

17. Nagatomo Chiyoji is, to my knowledge, the only scholar to devote at least a few pages to this primary source; see Nagatomo Chiyoji, *Edo jidai no shomotsu to dokusho* (Tokyo: Tōkyōdō Shuppan, 2001), 127–45, and his *Chōhōki no chōhōki: Seikatsu shi hyakka jiten hakkutsu* (Kyoto: Rinsen Shoten, 2005), 30–31. Nagatomo's research reconstructs the publication history of *Jinkyōron*. The Osaka publisher Morita Shōtarō 森田庄太郎, already known as the principal publisher of Ihara Saikaku's prose, issued the text in 1687 under the new title *Kingin mannōgan* 金銀万能丸 and then again in 1694 with the new title *Kanemochi chōhōki* 金持重宝記. By the time the Kyoto publisher Ōmiya Jirōkichi 近江屋次郎吉 bought the blocks from Morita and reprinted the work in Kyoto (n.d.), the title had become *Jinkyōron ichimei Kanemochi chōhōki* (*Jinkyōron*, also known as *Kanemochi chōhōki*). The choice of these titles tells readers the text is about money and its power.
18. *Jinkyōron*, 2v.
19. *Jinkyōron*, 15r.
20. *Jinkyōron*, 18r–19v.
21. *Jinkyōron*, 24v–25v.
22. *Jinkyōron*, 38r.
23. *Jinkyōron*, 26v.
24. There are at least three medieval tales that have wealth as the main theme: *Umezu no chōja monogatari* (The millionaire of Umezu), *Hōman chōja* (The millionaire full of treasures), and *Fukutomi sōshi* (The king of farts). For transcriptions, see Yokoyama Shigeru and Matsumoto Ryūshin, eds., *Muromachi jidai monogatari taisei* (Tokyo: Kadokawa Shoten, 1974–1989), vols. 2, 12, and 11, respectively. For a discussion of *Umezu no chōja monogatari* and two other texts not mentioned here, see Fabio Rambelli, "The Mystery of Wealth and the Role of Divinities: The Economy in Pre-Modern Japanese Fiction and Practice," in "Buddhism and Business: South and East Asian Perspectives," special issue, *Hualin International Journal of Buddhist Studies* 2, no. 2 (2019): 163–201.
25. Rambelli, "Mystery of Wealth," explains that "wealth is described in medieval Japan as the result of the interaction with the Invisible World of gods and spirits—as retribution from some deity for good actions and moral behaviour" (174).
26. *Umezu no chōja monogatari* starts with the wife of Sakon no Jō resolving to commit suicide to escape poverty. Her husband convinces her not to do so by recounting three stories of similar instances that are in keeping with *setsuwa* literature and set in India, China, and Japan, respectively. The alternative to suicide is to place faith in Ebisu, one of the Seven Gods of Good Fortune. The importance of faith is further stressed in *Hōman chōja*; the core of the story involves the unveiling of Hōman's true treasures. As Hōman opens the boxes we discover that his real treasures are a copy of the Lotus Sutra and the words *namu Amida butsu*. True wealth is ultimately the Buddhist faith.
27. Rambelli, "Mystery of Wealth," notes the motif of wealth bestowed as a reward for filial piety in the medieval tale *Daikoku mai* (179).
28. For example, Sakon no Jō and his wife in *Umezu no chōja monogatari* combine their faith in Ebisu with an altruistic nature. He ceases working in the fields to help a young nun who asks the way; the reward for accompanying her is ten copper coins (*zeni*). His wife buys rice cakes with this money and shares the food with an old street beggar. The remainder of the story reveals that the old beggar was none other than

Ebisu, and together with the other Gods of Good Fortune, Ebisu decides to live with Sakon no Jō for the rest of his life.

29. *Ichimori chōja* (n.p.: publisher unknown, [Enpō era (1673–1681)]), Tokyo University Library, Katei Bunko, Tokyo. Shelf mark: 霞亭0113. It was part of the *Yamato Nijūshikō* or the Japanese equivalent of the *Twenty-Four Paradigms of Filial Piety*.

30. Asai Ryōi, *Kanninki* ([Kyoto]: Araki Rihee, 1659), diplomatic transcription in vol. 20 of *Kanazōshi shūsei*, ed. Asakura Haruhiko and Fukasawa Akio (Tokyo: Tōkyōdō Shuppan, 1997), 93–294. The oldest edition dates to 1655, and subsequent editions/impressions date to 1664, 1671, 1684–1688, 1700, 1701, 1704, 1818, and 1824, together with several undated versions. *Kanninki* appeared in book-trade catalogues from 1667–1669 to 1715, first under the category of *washo narabi ni kanarui* and then under that of *kana washo*. The cost varies over time: 8 *monme* (1681), 4 *monme* 5 *fun* (1696), 5 *monme* 5 *fun* (1709), and 6 *monme* 5 *fun* (1715) for eight volumes. It also inspired a number of other publications, including *Shin kanninki* (The new *Chronicle of Patience*; 1708), *Kōshoku kanninki* (The erotic *Chronicle of Patience*; 1698), and *Ehon kanninki* (The illustrated *Chronicle of Patience*; 1823).

31. *Kanninki*, vol. 3, 16v–18v; *KS* 20:168–71.

32. Soga Kyūji, *Iguchi monogatari* (Kyoto: Yoshinoya Gonbee, 1662), diplomatic transcription in vol. 2 of *Kanazōshi shūsei*, ed. Asakura Haruhiko (Tokyo: Tōkyōdō Shuppan, 1981), 105–323. *Iguchi monogatari* was listed in book-trade catalogues from 1670 to 1715, categorized under *kana washo*. Its price was somewhat high because it appeared in eight volumes: 12 *monme* (1681), 6 *monme* (1696), 7 *monme* (1709), and 10 *monme* (1715).

33. *Iguchi monogatari*, vol. 6, 18r–45v, *KS* 2:251–64. This section is incorrectly numbered as 16 in the original, instead of 12.

34. *Iguchi monogatari*, vol. 6, 20r; *KS* 2:252–53.

35. *Iguchi monogatari*, vol. 6, 21r–21v; *KS* 2:253.

36. *Chōjakyō* (n.p.: publisher unknown, 1627), movable-type edition, Waseda University Library, Tokyo (shelf mark: へ13 04176. If not otherwise indicated, I refer to the 1627 edition (cited as *Chōjakyō*). *Chōjakyō* appeared for the first time in movable type in 1627; woodblock-printed versions were issued in 1627 and 1628. Apart from modifications in the use of kana and kanji, the text remained unaltered, even in its horizontal-book format, which was rather unusual for the early seventeenth century. *Chōjakyō* survived well beyond the seventeenth century. It was, for example, released in 1762. The same blocks were then sold to the Osaka publisher Sakaiya Shinbee (with Yamashiroya Sahee in Edo probably working as a distributor) and were reprinted in 1846. Despite the fact that the Union Catalogue of Early Japanese Books (http://base1.nijl.ac.jp/~tkoten/) lists this late *Chōjakyō* as a different work from the seventeenth-century *Chōjakyō*, I argue that it is essentially the same text, albeit in a new, revised edition. It is also worth noting that *Chōjakyō* was incorporated into other texts in the seventeenth century. *Iguchi monogatari* (see note 32) used it as part of vol. 6, section 16. *Ima Chōja monogatari*, ascribed to Nishizawa Ippū 西沢一風 (1665–1731) and probably published in the early eighteenth century, is a pastiche of *Chōjakyō* and *Iguchi monogatari*. A diplomatic transcription of *Ima Chōja monogatari* (Kyoto: Nishizawashi Ippū; n.d.) is available in vol. 5 of *Kanazōshi shūsei*, ed. Asakura Haruhiko (Tokyo: Tōkyōdō Shuppan, 1984), 323–47. For more details about the publication history of *Chōjakyō*, see Asakura Haruhiko, ed., *Chōjakyō*, Koten bunko 82 (Tokyo: Koten Bunko, 1954). *Chōjakyō* appeared in book-trade catalogues from 1666–1667 to 1772. It was first listed under the publishing genre *washo narabi ni kanarui*, beginning in 1670 it was relocated under *mai narabi ni sōshi*, and in 1685 it moved to *monogatari-rui*. In 1772, when entirely new categories were applied, it was included in the category *kyōkun*

6. A Commitment to the Present   355

(educational books). In one volume, it was a cheap publication: 3 *fun* (1681, 1696, and 1709, although not entirely legible) and 6 *fun* (1715). An English translation of the 1627 text can be found in G. W. Sargent, *The Japanese Family Storehouse; or, The Millionaires Gospel Modernized* (Cambridge: Cambridge University Press, 1969), 239–44. Translations in this chapter are mine.

37. *Chōjakyō* (Kyoto: Tsujii Kichiemon; Osaka: Araki Sahee, 1762), Osaka University Library, Ninchōji Bunko; microfilm copy, National Institute of Japanese Literature, Tachikawa (microfilm number: 228-66-10). Hereafter cited as *Chōjakyō*, 1762 edition.
38. *Chōjakyō*, 1762 edition, 2r.
39. *Nioi bukuro* (Kyoto: Nagaharaya Magobee, 1681), diplomatic transcription in vol. 55 of *Kanazōshi shūsei*, ed. Hanada Fujio et al. (Tokyo: Tōkyōdō Shuppan, 2016), 113–36; quotation from *Nioi bukuro*, vol. 1, 15r; *KS* 55:122. See also chapter 1, note 25.
40. In the celebrated *The Complete English Tradesman* (1726), Daniel Defoe characterizes pleasures and diversions, even those lawful and apparently innocent, as "a thief to business." Only pleasure "in the shop" is allowed as prudent; anything foreign to a tradesman's shop, referred to exotic diversions, can damage one's business. Chapter 10 alerts the reader to another cause for economic disaster: an expensive way of living; *The Complete English Tradesman* (London, 1726; Edinburgh, 1839); Project Gutenberg 2004, http://www.gutenberg.org/files/14444/14444-h/14444-h.htm.
41. *Chōjakyō*, 16r. A similar distinction is made in *Iguchi monogatari*, vol. 2, sec. 20, 35r–36v; *KS* 2:154–55.
42. *Chōjakyō*, 9v.
43. David Atherton, "Making Money Talk: Economic and Literary Form in the Fiction of Ihara Saikaku" (paper presented at the Association for Asian Studies Conference, Chicago, Ill., March 28, 2015). I thank David for sharing his unpublished paper with me.
44. Normally scholars refer to section 16 in volume 6 of *Iguchi monogatari* as the only part of the text devoted to wealth because this section uses *Chōjakyō* by rearranging the order of the contents and by adding a few passages. In reality there are many more sections in *Iguchi monogatari* that deal with money and wealth: vol. 1, secs. 9, 10, 11, 13, 14; vol. 2, secs. 1, 5, 17, 18, 20; vol. 4, sec. 14; vol. 5, secs, 9, 17; vol. 6, sec. 16; vol. 7, sec. 3, and vol. 8 sec. 3.
45. *Iguchi monogatari*, vol. 4, 26r–27v; *KS* 2:200–202.
46. *Iguchi monogatari*, vol. 4, 26r–26v; *KS* 2:200–01.
47. *Iguchi monogatari*, vol. 4, 26v; *KS* 2:201.
48. *Iguchi monogatari*, vol. 7, 7v–8r; *KS* 2:271–72.
49. *Iguchi monogatari*, vol. 2, 29v–34v; *KS* 2:150–54
50. *Iguchi monogatari*, vol. 2, 30v; *KS* 2:151.
51. Samukawa Masachika, *Shison kagami* ([Kyoto]: Fukumori Heizaemon, 1673), National Diet Library, Tokyo (shelf mark: り-36). Although I refer to the 1673 original, a critical edition can be found in *Kinsei chōnin shisō*, ed. Nakayama Yukihiko, Nihon shisō taikei 59 (Tokyo: Iwanami Shoten, 1975), 17–84. It was reissued in 1710 and 1733. *Shison kagami* first appeared in the 1675 catalogue and remained a listed item until 1715. It was first categorized under *kana washo* and then moved to *monogatari-rui* in 1685. The price for this three-volume publication was 3 *monme* in 1681 and then decreased to 2 *monme* 2 *fun*.
52. Noda Hisao, *Nihon kinsei shōsetsu shi: Kanazōshi hen* (Tokyo: Benseisha, 1986), 514. Tetsuo Najita notes that *Shison kagami* underscores the importance of moral dignity as *the* teaching that ought to be transmitted across generations and stresses the moral equality among human beings; *Visions of Virtue in Tokugawa Japan: The Kaitokudō Merchant Academy of Osaka* (Honolulu: University of Hawai'i Press, 1997), 23–25.

53. *Shison kagami*, vol. 2, 4r–4v.
54. *Shison kagami*, vol. 2, 4v.
55. *Shison kagami*, vol. 2, 4v.
56. *Zeraku monogatari* (Kyoto: Yamamori Rokubee, n.d.), critical edition in *Kanazōshi shū*, ed. Watanabe Morikuni and Watanabe Kenji, Shin Nihon koten bungaku taikei 74 (Tokyo: Iwanami Shoten, 1991), 193–270. Hereafter cited as *Zeraku*. Partial translation in *A Kamigata Anthology: Literature from Japan's Metropolitan Centers, 1600–1750*, ed. Sumie Jones and Adam L. Kern, with Kenji Watanabe (Honolulu: University of Hawai'i Press, 2020), 329–54. It is noteworthy that the second volume, of interest here, is not included in the translation. *Zeraku monogatari* appeared in book-trade catalogues from 1666–1667 to 1715. It was categorized under *mai narabi ni sōshi*. In three volumes, it was priced at 2 *monme* 5 *fun* in 1681 and then decreased to 2 *monme* in 1696, 1709, and 1715.
57. *Zeraku*, 244.
58. *Iguchi monogatari*, vol. 1, 22v; *KS* 2:122.
59. *Kanninki*, vol. 2, 9r; *KS* 20:128.
60. *Kanninki*, vol. 2, 3r; *KS* 20:124.
61. *Iguchi monogatari*, vol. 1, 24r; *KS* 2:123; see also *Iguchi monogatari*, vol. 1, 26v; *KS* 2:125.
62. *Iguchi monogatari*, vol. 1, 27r; *KS* 2:125.
63. *Shison kagami*, vol. 1, 15r.
64. Atherton, "Making Money Talk."
65. For a discussion of the Way of the merchant, see Richard Bowring, *In Search of the Way: Thought and Religion in Early-Modern Japan, 1582–1860* (Oxford: Oxford University Press, 2017), 156–62. More specifically on the work of Ishida Baigan 石田梅岩 (1685–1744) and its significance, see Kawaguchi Hiroshi, "Economic Thought Concerning Freedom and Control," in Gramlich-Oka and Smits, *Economic Thought*, 47–66. See also Najita, *Visions of Virtue*, and Ichiro Horide, *The Mercantile Ethical Tradition in Edo Period Japan: A Comparative Analysis with Bushido* (Singapore: Springer, 2019). Horide mentions the seventeenth century, with a focus on how Shinto, Confucianism, and Buddhism influenced the mercantile ethic (63–76). Rambelli, "Mystery of Wealth," mentions that "competing economic discourses proliferate" in the Edo period, with the emergence of anti-Buddhist formulations (196), but does not delve into an analysis of early modern Japan.
66. For a history of famines in early modern Japan, see Kikuchi Isao, *Kinsei no kikin* (Tokyo: Yoshikawa Kōbunkan, 1997).
67. On *kawaraban*, see chapter 2, note 89. It is only in the eighteenth century that there are examples of *kawaraban* dealing with a fire; see Sepp Linhart, "Kawaraban—Enjoying the News When News Was Forbidden," in *Written Texts–Visual Texts: Woodblock-Printed Media in Early Modern Japan*, ed. Susanne Formanek and Sepp Linhart, European Studies on Japan 3 (Amsterdam: Hotei, 2005), 237.
68. *Yakushi tsūya monogatari* ([Kyoto]: publisher unknown, [1643]), Waseda University Library, Tokyo (shelf mark: ヘ 13 01699). Hereafter cited as *Yakushi tsūya monogatari*. It was reissued under two different titles: *Fukusai monogatari* (The tale of Fukusai) and *Nezumi monogatari* (The tale of rats); dates are unknown. In one volume, it was recorded in book-trade catalogues from 1666–1667 to 1715. It was originally categorized under *mai narabi ni sōshi*, moved to the category of *monogatari-rui* in 1685, and then back to *mai narabi ni sōshi* in 1699. The price in 1681 was 8 *fun*. No prices are recorded in later catalogues. Asai Ryōi, *Musashi abumi* (Kyoto: Nakamura Gohee, 1661), National Diet Library, Tokyo (shelf mark: 841-35). Hereafter cited as *Musashi abumi*. It was

reissued in 1676 and 1772, and there are a few undated editions. It was a regular title in book-trade catalogues from 1670 to 1715. It was originally included under *hanashi no hon* (or *hanashibon*), moved to the category of *monogatari-rui* in 1685, and then to *mai narabi ni sōshi* in 1699. The price for this two-volume title was 1 *monme* 7 *fun* in 1681; it decreased slightly to 1 *monme* 5 *fun* in 1696 and 1709; no price is given in 1715. Asai Ryōi, *Kanameishi* (n.p.: publisher unknown, [ca. 1662–1663]), critical edition in *Kanazōshi shū*, ed. Taniwaki Masachika, Oka Masahiko, and Inoue Kazuhito, Shinpen Nihon koten bungaku zenshū 64 (Tokyo: Shōgakukan, 1999), 11–83. Hereafter cited as *Kanameishi*. No other edition/reprint is known. It appeared in book-trade catalogues from 1670 to 1715. It was originally listed under *hanashi no hon* (or *hanashibon*), moved to the category of *monogatari-rui* in 1685, and then to *mai narabi ni sōshi* in 1699. The price for its three volumes was 2 *monme* 8 *fun* in 1681. No price is recorded in later catalogues. *Inu Hōjōki* (Kyoto: Yamamoto Shichirobee, 1682), diplomatic transcription in vol. 4 of *Kanazōshi shūsei*, vol. 4, ed. Asakura Haruhiko (Tokyo: Tōkyōdō Shuppan, 1983), 153–75. Hereafter cited as *Inu Hōjōki*. No other edition/reprint is known. It appeared in the 1675 (only in the catalogue in *i-ro-ha* order), 1685, and 1692 book-trade catalogues. In the latter two it was listed as a *monogatari-rui*. No price is available as it does not appear in catalogues that record prices. Only *Musashi abumi* has been partially translated, by Henry D. Smith II and Steven Wills, in Jones and Kern, *A Kamigata Anthology*, 410–39. All translations in this chapter are mine.

69. *Hinin taiheiki* (n.p.: publisher unknown, [1688]), National Diet Library, Tokyo (shelf mark: 212-38). There are few extant copies but none present a colophon. It is worth noting that it was listed in book-trade catalogues as a war tale (*gunsho*). The two groups of outcasts presented in *Hinin taiheiki* are *kojiki* (or *hinin* 非人) and *hinin* 貧人. Drawing on the historical work by Okamoto Ryōichi, Ohara Tōru explains that *kojiki* were poor beggars but were part of the urban social structure and had specific duties within the community, whereas *hinin* were ad hoc mendicants who fled to Osaka to avoid starvation; they saw *kojiki* as a threat in the competition for the little available food. Whether *Hinin taiheiki* chronicled a real event has yet to be substantiated. See Ohara Tōru, "*Hinin taiheiki* no sōsaku ishiki," *Ronkyū Nihon bungaku* 58 (May 1993): 25–34, and his "Jiken no bungeika—kanazōshi no hōhō, *Hinin taiheiki* no baai," *Buraku mondai kenkyū kiyō* 148 (September 1999): 2–16. Ohara also offers an interesting rationale for the choice of the medieval war tale *Taiheiki* as a text to be emulated when recounting a story concerning *hinin*; see his "*Hinin taiheiki* no haikei to tokushitsu," *Ronkyū Nihon bungaku* 67 (December 1997): 25–34. *Hinin taiheiki* is viewed as a text that criticizes the power of the four chiefs (*chōri*) in charge of *kojiki*; see Maeshiba Ken'ichi, *Kanazōshi: Konton no shikaku*, Izumi sensho 89 (Osaka: Izumi Shoin, 1995), 218–43. In English a short introduction to this text, with a focus on the historical background, can be found in Kyoko Selden, "Introduction to the *Hinin Taiheiki: The Paupers' Chronicle of Peace*," *Asia-Pacific Journal: Japan Focus* 14, no. 4 (July 2016): 1–8.

70. *Kanameishi*, 67. On borrowings from *Hōjōki* in Asai Ryōi's work, see Akahane Manabu and Matsuura Kōhei, eds., *Ihon Musashi abumi to kenkyū*, Mikan kokubun shiryō 4-ki 7-satsu (Toyohashi: Mikan Kokubun Shiryō Kankōkai, 1977), 99. Maeshiba, *Kanazōshi*, 215, following the work of Ogawa Takehiko, also mentions a connection between *Hōjōki* and *Yakushi tsūya monogatari*.

71. Peter Kornicki, "Narrative of a Catastrophe: *Musashi abumi* and the Meireki Fire," in "Narrativity and Fictionality in Edo-Period Prose Literature," ed. Laura Moretti, special issue, *Japan Forum* 21 (2010): 354–55. Selden, "Introduction," talks of a "parody on

the *Hōjōki* . . . using mongrels as characters," but no mongrels appear at any point in the text.
72. For a comparison of the two texts, see Maeshiba, *Kanazōshi*, 197–200.
73. Maeshiba, *Kanazōshi*, 191–94, suggests that in this case *inu* should be considered simply as a synonym for "updated" (*tōdai*).
74. Nicholas Daly, "The Volcanic Disaster Narratives: From Pleasure Garden to Canvas, Page, and Stage," *Victorian Studies* 53, no. 2 (Winter 2011): 255–85. Gennifer Weisenfeld effectively discusses the disaster pictures produced in the wake of the 1923 Kantō earthquake and explores how they "engaged the public gaze to produce emotions such as marvel, horror, sorrow, and pity" (*Imaging Disaster: Tokyo and the Visual Culture of Japan's Great Earthquake of 1923* [Berkeley: University of California Press, 2012], 83).
75. *Yakushi tsūya monogatari*, vol. 1, 3r.
76. *Musashi abumi*, vol. 1, 3r.
77. *Musashi abumi*, vol. 1, 3r, 3v; vol. 2, 1r, 4r, 16r, respectively.
78. *Kanameishi*, 15, 42.
79. *Musashi abumi*, vol. 1, 3r–3v.
80. *Musashi abumi*, vol. 2, 1v–3r. In the recently published English translation, Smith and Wills have chosen to cut all these passages for the sake of readability (unfortunately without indicating where the cuts were made). While the decision is understandable, it seems to me that it forgoes an important aspect of the nature of this text.
81. *Musashi abumi*, vol. 2, 6v–9r.
82. *Musashi abumi*, vol. 2, 15r (the folio number is "10 *mata* 15").
83. *Musashi abumi*, vol. 2, 15v.
84. *Musashi abumi*, vol. 1, 5r, 7r, 19r.
85. *Musashi abumi*, vol. 2, 16v.
86. *Kawaraban* on 1852 Osaka fire, pasted in the album titled *Shūkojō*, private collection, Suzuran Bunko, Cambridge, U.K. (no shelf mark). Hereafter cited as *Kawaraban* 1852.
87. *Musashi abumi*, vol. 1, 1v–2r.
88. *Kawaraban* 1852.
89. This is by no means peculiar to early modern Japan. For example, Christian Rohr speaks of "educated and literary exaggerations of relatively ordinary natural events as catastrophic" when examining European sources from the late Middle Ages; "Writing a Catastrophe: Describing and Constructing Disaster Perception in Narrative Sources from the Late Middle Ages," *Historical Social Research/Historische Sozialforschung* 32, no. 3 (121) (2007): 88–102.
90. *Musashi abumi*, vol. 2, 30r.
91. *Kanameishi*, 17.
92. *Kanameishi*, 33.
93. *Yakushi tsūya monogatari*, 5r–5v.
94. *Inu Hōjōki*, vol. 1, 1v–4r; *KS* 4:155–57.
95. *Musashi abumi*, vol. 2, 27v–30r.
96. *Kanameishi*, 66–70.
97. *Kanameishi*, 70.
98. Nakagawa Kiun, *Kyō warabe* (Kyoto: Hachimonjiya Gohee, 1658), National Institute of Japanese Literature, Tachikawa (shelf mark: 99-172-1~6), vol. 2, 8r. A partial English translation by Marcia Yonemoto can be found in Jones and Kern, *A Kamigata Anthology*, 138–46. It does not include the passage on Mimizuka. Michael A. Levine comments extensively on the fact that the first volume of *Kanameishi* applies a descriptive style that was typical of *meishoki* and examines the passage on Mimizuka from

this point of view; "Chronicling Catastrophe and Constructing Urban Deconstruction: Asai Ryōi's *Musashi Abumi* and *Kanameishi*" (master's thesis, University of Colorado Boulder, 2016), 66–73.
99. Asai Ryōi, *Kanameishi* (N.p: publisher unknown, [ca. 1662–1663]), National Diet Library, Tokyo (shelf mark: 京-160), vol. 1, 11v and 13r, respectively.
100. *Kanameishi*, 26. For the poem in *Ise monogatari*, see Joshua S. Mostow and Royall Tyler, trans., *The Ise Stories: Ise monogatari* (Honolulu: University of Hawai'i Press, 2010), 36. Levine, "Chronicling Catastrophe," 62–65, looks at the presence of the punning poems that punctuate the first volume of *Kanameishi* and argues that they serve "as a counterpoint to the portrayed chaos and trauma."
101. *Kanameishi*, 15, 38, respectively.
102. *Kanameishi*, 54.
103. *Musashi abumi*, vol. 2, 19r.
104. *Musashi abumi*, vol. 2, 24v–27r. An English translation of this passage can be found in Kornicki, "Narrative of a Catastrophe," 347–61. See also the translation by Smith and Wills in Jones and Kern, *A Kamigata Anthology*, 437–38.
105. *Kanameishi* does something similar when noting that the daily laborers working on the restoration of Daibutsu Hall failed to realize that the building was shaking because of an earthquake and imagined that this was a punishment inflicted on them by the Buddha for the dismantling of sacred statues: "They thought they had fallen into the eighth and most painful of the Buddhist hells [*mugen jigoku*]" (*Kanameishi*, 23).
106. Kornicki, "Narrative of a Catastrophe," 357. David Atherton stresses the use of medieval narrative motifs in "Sōzōteki hakai: Chūsei to kinsei no kakehashi toshite no *Musashi abumi*," in vol. 4 of *Nihon bungaku no tenbō o hiraku*, ed. Komine Kazuaki (Tokyo: Kasama Shoin, 2017), 38–43.
107. Kornicki, "Narrative of a Catastrophe," 357.
108. Levine, "Chronicling Catastrophe," 38–39.
109. Smith and Wills in their introduction to the translation of *Musashi abumi*, in Jones and Kern, *A Kamigata Anthology*, 411.
110. *Musashi abumi*, vol. 2, 26r.
111. *Musashi abumi*, vol. 2, 27r.
112. Regina Bendix, "Reflections on Earthquake Narratives," *Western Folklore* 49, no. 4 (October 1990): 331–47.
113. Bendix, "Reflections," 341–42.
114. Bendix, "Reflections," 342.
115. *Musashi abumi*, vol. 1, 5r.
116. *Musashi abumi*, vol. 1, 7v, 20v–21r, respectively.
117. *Musashi abumi*, vol. 2, 5v.
118. *Musashi abumi*, vol. 1, 21r.
119. *Musashi abumi*, vol. 1, 22v–23r.
120. Levine, "Chronicling Catastrophe," 51. For much later materials that combine reports of the disaster with other materials, including narratives, Stephan Köhn uses the term "disaster collages"; "Between Fiction and Non-fiction—Documentary Literature in the Late Edo Period," in Formanek and Linhart, *Written Texts–Visual Texts*, 283–310. Köhn has published other work on later Edo-period disaster narratives, including *"Berichte über Gesehenes und Gehörtes aus der Ansei-Zeit" (Ansei kemmonshi): Kanagaki Robuns (1829–1894) Bericht über das große Ansei-Erdbeben 1855 als Repräsentant des Genres der "Katastrophendarstellungen,"* 2 vols. (Wiesbaden: Harrassowitz 2002); "Die genretheoretische Einordnung von Katastrophendarstellungen: Der Weg zum Konzept eines

neuen Genrebegriffes," *NOAG* 167-170 (2000-2001): 105-36; "Ansei kenmonshi — Kanagaki Robuns Bericht über das große Ansei-Erdbeben 1855," in *Referate des 10. deutschsprachigen Japanologentags vom 9. bis 12. Oktober 1996 in München*, ed. Ulrich Apel, Jossi Holzapfel, and Peter Pörtner (Munich: Iudicium 1997), 291-300.

121. *Kanameishi*, 53.
122. *Kanameishi*, 19-20.
123. *Kanameishi*, 21-22.
124. *Inu Hōjōki*, vol. 1, 13r-13v; *KS* 4:162-63.
125. *Inu Hōjōki*, vol. 1, 13v-14r; *KS* 4:163.
126. *Inu Hōjōki*, vol. 1, 13v-14r; *KS* 4:163.
127. *Inu Hōjōki*, vol. 1, 3v; *KS* 4:156.
128. *Inu Hōjōki*, vol. 1, 14r; *KS* 4:163.
129. *Inu Hōjōki*, vol. 1, 13r; *KS* 4:162.
130. In the Western context, Bendix, "Reflections," 333, stresses the power of narrative and sees in self-oriented tales "the primary means at an individual's disposal to regain order out of chaos." The humorous treatment of a traumatic experience is interpreted as "a celebration of the liminal and hence disorderly state brought on by an earthquake" (344). Elliott Oring, in his analysis of riddles/jokes related to the explosion of the space shuttle *Challenger* in 1989, quotes a variety of studies that discuss humor as a coping mechanism that assists people in distancing themselves from the horror of an event; "Jokes and the Discourse on Disaster," *Journal of American Folklore* 100, no. 397 (July-September 1987): 281. Erik Bond has studied the writings produced in seventeenth-century England concerning London's Great Fire of 1666, with a focus on Samuel Pepys's *Diary* entries. He introduces the notion of "rebuilding from trauma," with the message of hope being delivered via the image of citizens rebuilding their city alongside a monarch who is committed to "redress"; "Historicising the 'New Normal': London's Great Fire and Genres of Urban Destruction," *Restoration* 31, no. 2 (Fall 2007): 43-64.
131. Bendix, "Reflections," 334.
132. Atherton, "Sōzōteki hakai," examines Rakusaibō's "voice" as a reenactment of the medieval trope of confession (*sange-mono*). He views it as a "subjective" voice that punctuates the more objective one describing the catastrophe as a whole. Atherton, however, does not explore the importance of storytelling as a coping mechanism in dealing with trauma, which is foregrounded here.
133. *Kanameishi*, 78.
134. *Kanameishi*, 81.
135. Maeshiba, *Kanazōshi*, 202, notes that at this point in Japanese history Hiden-in was a hamlet of outcasts.
136. *Inu Hōjōki*, vol. 2, 19v-21v; *KS* 4:166-68.
137. *Inu Hōjōki*, vol. 2, 31v-32r; *KS* 4:174.
138. Ohara Tōru explains that the trope of a night spent in prayer at a Buddhist temple is borrowed from the thirty-fifth book of *Taiheiki*; "Hinin taiheiki no sōsaku ishiki," 25. See the same remark in Maeshiba, *Kanazōshi*, 171.
139. *Kanameishi*, 30-32.
140. *Inu Hōjōki*, vol. 1, 8v-10r; *KS* 4:159-60.
141. *Kanameishi*, 37.
142. *Kanameishi*, 56-60.
143. *Kanameishi*, 77.
144. *Yakushi tsūya monogatari*, 11v.

145. *Yakushi tsūya monogatari*, 11v.
146. See *Yakushi tsūya monogatari*, 12v–13v, 13v–14v, 14v–17r, respectively.
147. *Yakushi tsūya monogatari*, 19r, 21v–22r.
148. Maeshiba Ken'ichi pushes this interpretation even further, suggesting that Yakushi and the Twelve Heavenly Generals mirror the structure of the local government (*machigumi*). In his view Yakushi personifies the town elders (*machidoshiyori*) and the Guardians are the Group of Five Persons (*gonin-gumi*). Maeshiba explains that part of the job of this form of local government was to pass legislation over to the citizens. In this regard, he argues that the emphasis on curtailing excessive expenditure echoes the sumptuary laws, with the nine articles issued in the eighth month of 1642 more specifically in mind. He also maintains that the author must have been someone very close to the local government; *Kanazōshi*, 185–87.
149. *Yakushi tsūya monogatari*, 22r–23r.
150. *Musashi abumi*, vol. 2, 20v.
151. *Musashi abumi*, vol. 2, 23r.
152. *Musashi abumi*, vol. 2, 23v, 31r.
153. Atherton, "Sōzōteki hakai," 42–43.
154. *Inu Hōjōki*, vol. 2, 23v–30v; *KS* 4:169–74.
155. *Inu Hōjōki*, vol. 2, 31r–31v; *KS* 4:174.
156. Cathy Caruth, *Unclaimed Experience: Trauma, Narrative, and History* (Baltimore: Johns Hopkins University Press, 2016), 7–8, 59–69.
157. Trauma is described as a wound of the mind that "is experienced too soon, too unexpectedly, to be fully known and is therefore not available to consciousness until it imposes itself again, repeatedly, in the nightmares and repetitive actions of the survivors" (Caruth, *Unclaimed Experience*, 4; see also 11–12, 18–19, 65, and 66).
158. "I believe that one of the principal functions of literature lies in these lessons about fate and death. Perhaps there are others, but for the moment none springs to mind" (Umberto Eco, *On Literature*, trans. Martin McLaughlin [London: Vintage Books, 2006], 15).

7. The Triumph of Plurality

1. Roland Barthes, *The Pleasure of the Text*, trans. Richard Miller (New York: Hill and Wang, 1975), 14; emphasis in original.
2. In introducing their edited volume on didactic literature in England, Natasha Glaiyser and Sara Pennell remark that the study of didactic texts lacks "thorough and critically sophisticated treatment," as noted in the introduction, and that "at stake are academic judgments of what constitutes a valid text for study. In cultural histories of the early modern period the 'literary' text has tended to assume an ascendancy over those texts that had practical application" (*Didactic Literature in England, 1500–1800: Expertise Constructed* [Aldershot, Hants., U.K.: Ashgate Publishing, 2003], 1–2).
3. Franco Moretti, *Distant Reading* (London: Verso, 2013), 180.
4. Roger Chartier, *The Order of Books: Readers, Authors, and Libraries in Europe Between the Fourteenth and the Eighteenth Centuries*, trans. Lydia G. Cochrane (Stanford, Calif.: Stanford University Press, 1994); Roger Chartier, "Libraries Without Walls," in "Future Libraries," special issue, *Representations* 42 (Spring 1993): 38–52; D. F. McKenzie, *Bibliography and the Sociology of Texts* (London: British Library, 1986), 9. Elizabeth Salter, for example, has written her history of popular reading in medieval

362 7. The Triumph of Plurality

England based on a similar assumption; *Popular Reading in English c. 1400–1600* (Manchester: Manchester University Press, 2012).

5. Barthes, *Pleasure of the Text*, 18, 31.
6. Peter Stallybrass was the first to propose the concept of "discontinuous reading"; "Books and Scrolls: Navigating the Bible," in *Books and Readers in Early Modern England*, ed. Jennifer Andersen and Elizabeth Sauer (Philadelphia: University of Pennsylvania Press, 2002), 42–79. See also Eve Tavor Bannet, *Eighteenth-Century Manners of Reading: Print Culture and Popular Instruction in the Anglophone Atlantic World* (Cambridge: Cambridge University Press, 2017).
7. Bannet, *Eighteenth-Century Manners*, 4.
8. The exception is a mention of the text in Richard Lane, "The Beginnings of the Modern Japanese Novel: Kana-zōshi, 1600–1682," *Harvard Journal of Asiatic Studies* 20, no. 3/4 (December 1957): 670n46. I have also briefly commented upon it in Laura Moretti, "*Kanazōshi* Revisited: Reconsidering the Beginnings of Japanese Popular Literature in Print," *Monumenta Nipponica* 65, no. 2 (2010): 328–29.
9. *Jigabachi monogatari* ([Kyoto]: Nakano Gorōzaemon, 1661), diplomatic transcription in vol. 33 of *Kanazōshi shūsei*, ed. Asakura Haruhiko (Tokyo: Tōkyōdō Shuppan, 2003), 105–231. Hereafter cited as *Jigabachi*. It was reprinted in 1665 and 1702, and there are several examples without a colophon. It was also issued under the new title *Zoku chomonjū* (*A Collection of Notable Things Heard*: A sequel) by the Kyoto publisher Tanakaya Jisuke, but the date is unknown; National Diet Library, Tokyo (shelf mark: 237-34). In book-trade catalogues *Jigabachi monogatari* was categorized as a *hanashi no hon* (or *hanashibon*) from 1670 to 1675, and from 1685 it was listed under *monogatari-rui*. It moved to *mai narabi ni sōshi* in the 1699 catalogue. The price was 5 *monme* for six volumes (1696, 1709, and 1715). There is no record in the 1681 catalogue.
10. *Jigabachi*, vol. 1, 1v; *KS* 33:108.
11. *Jigabachi*, vol. 1, 1r; *KS* 33:108. Bannet, *Eighteenth-Century Manners*, 92, identifies a similar strategy in the new print genres designed for a broad readership that were issued in eighteenth-century England. She also underscores that "to read was to hear someone speaking to you through the medium of a letter, essay, or book"; see also 92–95.
12. *Jigabachi*, vol. 5, 18v; *KS* 33:205. The text uses *mōshi mairase sōrō* for what I translate as "do recount." I interpret is as *mōshi mairase sōrae*.
13. *Jigabachi*, vol. 1, 20r–21v; *KS* 33:124–25.
14. Bannet, *Eighteenth-Century Manners*, 15.
15. For example, section 60 in volume 4 of *Jigabachi monogatari* comments on section 11 of *Tsurezuregusa*; *Jigabachi monogatari*, vol. 4, 46v–47r; *KS* 33:187. Sections 13 and 26 in volume 3 recount episodes related to Sei Shōnagon; *Jigabachi*, vol. 3, 12r–13r, 24v–25r; *KS* 33:155–56, 166.
16. Linda H. Chance, *Formless in Form: Kenkō,* Tsurezuregusa, *and the Rhetoric of Japanese Fragmentary Prose* (Stanford, Calif.: Stanford University Press, 1997), 244.
17. Noda Hisao, *Nihon kinsei shōsetsu shi: Kanazōshi hen* (Tokyo: Benseisha, 1986), 479–83.
18. Lane, "Beginnings," 670n46.
19. Moretti, "*Kanazōshi* Revisited," 329.
20. Bannet, *Eighteenth-Century Manners*, 104, notes something similar for British pronouncing anthologies.
21. Vol. 1, secs., 4 and 9; vol. 2, sec. 23; vol. 3, secs. 10, 16, and 24; vol. 4, sec. 55; and vol. 5, sec. 13; *Jigabachi*, vol. 1, 6r, 12v–13r; vol. 2, 27r–31r; vol. 3, 11r–11v, 15r–17r, 21v–24v; vol. 4, 43r–44v; vol. 5, 13v–14r; *KS* 33:110, 116, 132–35, 154–55, 158–61, 163–66, 184–85, 200–201.

22. *Jigabachi*, vol. 4, 43v–44r; *KS* 33:184–85.
23. See Laura Moretti, "Adaptation as a Strategy for Participation: The *Chikusai* Storyworld in Early Modern Japanese Literature," *Japanese Language and Literature* 54, no. 1 (March 2020): 81.
24. *Jigabachi*, vol. 5, 13v–14r; *KS* 33:200–201.
25. Suzuki Tōzō, *Nazo no kenkyū* (Tokyo: Tōkyōdō, 1963).
26. Vol. 2, secs. 29 and 35; vol. 3, secs. 6 and 14; vol. 4, sec. 36; vol. 5, sec. 5; vol. 6, the opening section (with no identification number); *Jigabachi*, vol. 2, 33v–36r, 37v–38r; vol. 3, 5v–10v, 13r–15r; vol. 4, 29r–34v; vol. 5, 4v–11r; vol. 6, 25r–30r; *KS* 33:137–38, 141, 150–54, 156–57, 171–76, 192–98, 211–15.
27. *Jigabachi*, vol. 3, 5v–10v; *KS* 33:150–54.
28. *Jigabachi*, vol. 3, 10r; *KS* 33:153.
29. *Jigabachi*, vol. 4, 38v; *KS* 33:179.
30. *Jigabachi*, vol. 4, 45v; *KS* 33:186.
31. *Jigabachi*, vol. 4, 46r; *KS* 33:186–87.
32. Although the cultural context is different, this approach is not so far removed from the goals of eighteenth-century English "miscellarian" texts: "Toleration of all sorts of Readers to indulge themselves uncensored and uncontrolled, in the Perusal of all such Writings as their various Humours and Tastes shall respectively dispose them to"; quoted in Bannet, *Eighteenth-Century Manners*, 172.
33. Also quoted in the introduction; Donald Keene, *World Within Walls: Japanese Literature of the Pre-modern Era, 1600–1867* (New York: Columbia University Press, 1999), 159.
34. E. Taylor Atkins, *A History of Popular Culture in Japan: From the Seventeenth Century to the Present* (London: Bloomsbury, 2017), 66.
35. Peter Kornicki, *The Book in Japan: A Cultural History from the Beginnings to the Nineteenth Century* (Honolulu: University of Hawai'i Press, 2001), 334–35. See also Sumie Jones and Adam L. Kern, with Kenji Watanabe, eds., *A Kamigata Anthology: Literature from Japan's Metropolitan Centers, 1600–1750* (Honolulu: University of Hawai'i Press, 2020), 56–57. For an in-depth study of censorship edicts in the Edo period, see Yamamoto Hideki, *Edo jidai santo shuppanhō taigai: Bungakushi shuppanshi no tame ni* (Okayama: Okayama Daigaku Bungakubu, 2010).
36. Vol. 1, secs. 5, 7, 8, 12, 14, 16, and 17; vol. 2, secs. 27 and 39; vol. 3, secs. 12, 28, and 31; vol. 4, secs. 35 and 43; vol. 5, secs. 1, 18, and 19; vol. 6, sec. 27; *Jigabachi*, vol. 1, 6r–6v, 8v–12v, 12v, 17v, 17v–18r, 18r–19v, 19v–20r; vol. 2, 33r, 39r–39v; vol. 3, 11v–12r, 25r–25v, 26v; vol. 4, 29r, 37r–37v; vol. 5, 3r–3v, 20r–23r, 23v–24r; vol. 6, 35r–47r; *KS* 33, 110, 112–15, 115, 120, 120–21, 121–23, 123–24, 137, 142, 155, 166–67, 168, 171, 178, 191, 206–9, 209–10, 219–31.
37. *Jigabachi*, vol. 5, 20r–23r; *KS* 33:206–9.
38. Vol. 5, secs. 13 and 14, mentioned in passing in discussing humorous stories; *Jigabachi*, vol. 5, 13v–14r, 14r–18v; *KS* 33:200, 201–5.
39. *Jigabachi*, vol. 2, 37r; *KS* 33:140.
40. *Jigabachi*, respectively vol. 2, secs. 36, 40, 44; and vol. 3, secs. 11, 20; *Jigabachi*, vol. 2, 38v, 39v–40r, 41r; vol. 3, 11v, 18r; *KS* 33:141, 142–43, 144, 155, 160–161.
41. *Jigabachi*, vol. 3, 27r; *KS* 33:168.
42. Asai Ryōi, *Ukiyo monogatari* ([Kyoto]: Hiranoya Sahee, ca. 1665), critical edition in *Kanazōshi shū*, ed. Taniwaki Masachika, Oka Masahiko, and Inoue Kazuhito, Shinpen Nihon koten bungaku zenshū 64 (Tokyo: Shōgakukan, 1999), 85–224. Hereafter cited as *Ukiyo monogatari*. The date of publication is suggested in Maeda Kingorō, "*Ukiyo monogatari* zakkō," in *Kinsei bungaku zakkō* (Tokyo: Bensei Shuppan, 2005), 64–94. *Ukiyo monogatari* was available in two editions. The first has eleven lines per

364   7. The Triumph of Plurality

half folio, and the earliest extant example has no colophon; it was later reprinted by the Kyoto publisher Hiranoya Sahee. The second has fourteen lines per half folio and was first seen in the 1670 edition published by Matsue Ichirobee. At this stage the text was renamed *Ukiyo banashi* (Stories of the floating world). Evidence suggests that the same set of blocks continued to be used in 1737 by Taharaya Heibee and then probably in 1757 under the new title *Zoku Kashōki*. *Ukiyo monogatari* appeared in book-trade catalogues in 1666–1667, starting under the publishing genre of *washo narabi ni kanarui* and moving to *kana washo*. It last appeared in the 1729 catalogue under *kana mono sōshi rui*. The price for the five volumes was 4 *monme* 5 *fun* (1681, 1696, 1709, and 1715). The title *Zoku kashōki* appears only in the 1772 catalogue under the category of *kidan* (strange tales). A partial translation can be found in Haruo Shirane, *Early Modern Japanese Literature: An Anthology, 1600–1900* (New York: Columbia University Press, 2002), 29–32, and a complete English translation is available in Daniel Lewis Barber, "Tales of the Floating World: The *Ukiyo monogatari* of Asai Ryōi" (master's thesis, Ohio State University, 1984). All translations here are mine.

43. Lane, "Beginnings," 675.
44. Barber, "Tales," 34.
45. Donald H. Shively, "Popular Culture," in vol. 4 of *The Cambridge History of Japan*, ed. John Whitney Hall and James L. McClain (Cambridge: Cambridge University Press, 1991), 730.
46. *Ukiyo monogatari*, 89.
47. Matsue Ichirobee reduced the number of illustrations and made substantial changes to the visual details, although the general feeling of the illustrations remained the same. He also added captions. Whenever Ukiyobō features in the illustrations, which account for the vast majority of them, his name appears at the beginning of the caption. The image is from the later reprint of *Ukiyo monogatari* titled *Zoku Kashōki*. *Zoku Kashōki* recycled the blocks by the Osaka publisher Taharaya Heibee, who probably used Matsue Ichirobee's blocks. Here I use the later reprint of *Zoku Kashōki* (Osaka: Kichimonjiya Ichibee and Kichimonjiya Genjūrō; Edo: Kichimonjiya Jirobee, n.d.), private collection, Suzuran Bunko, Cambridge, U.K. (no shelf mark), vol. 3, 9r.
48. Noda Hisao, "*Ukiyo monogatari* no igi," reprinted in vol. 2 of *Kanazōshi kenkyū sōsho*, ed. Fukasawa Akio and Kikuchi Shin'ichi (Tokyo: Kuresu Shuppan, 2006), 202, 206–7, 213.
49. Taniwaki Masachika, notes at the top of the page of the critical edition, *Ukiyo monogatari*, 137, 139 (comments in red; no note numbers).
50. Taniwaki, notes at the top of the page of the critical edition, *Ukiyo monogatari*, 143, 148, 157, 161, 171, and 179 (comments in red; no note numbers).
51. Taniwaki, notes at the top of the page of the critical edition, *Ukiyo monogatari*, 195 (comments in red; no note number).
52. Keene, *World Within Walls*, 158, 160.
53. Barber, "Tales," 8.
54. Lane, "Beginnings," 672.
55. Lane, "Beginnings," 671, 675.
56. Shirane, *Early Modern Japanese Literature*, 29.
57. Shively, "Popular Culture," 730.
58. *Ukiyo monogatari*, 121.
59. Respectively, vol. 2, sec. 8; vol. 3, sec. 1; vol. 4, sec. 4; *Ukiyo monogatari*, 139–41, 150–51, 192–93. Other comic sections include Ukiyobō's mistake in quoting from a Noh drama

he has been asked to perform that leads to the recollection of another embarrassing story about a professional performer who appeared onstage at the wrong moment (vol. 3, sec. 11; *Ukiyo monogatari*, 176–78); a story about a painter who is accused of drawing egrets badly and who defends his work (vol. 3, sec. 12; *Ukiyo monogatari*, 178–79); and a tale about a person who bought a cow of poor quality and challenges the seller only to be silenced with a series of puns (vol. 4, sec. 2; *Ukiyo monogatari*, 188–89).

60. The narrator remarks that "because Ukiyobō was naturally absentminded, on many occasions he was laughed at" (*Ukiyo monogatari*, 176).
61. On Ikkyū, see chapter 4, note 149.
62. In vol. 1, sec. 10 Ukiyobō visits Kyoto (*Ukiyo monogatari*, 111–17); in vol. 2, sec. 3 he goes from Kyoto to Osaka (*Ukiyo monogatari*, 123–27); in vol. 2, sec. 5 he visits Tennōji in Osaka (*Ukiyo monogatari*, 131–34); in vol. 2, sec. 6 he visits Sumiyoshi Shrine (*Ukiyo monogatari*, 134–37); and vol. 2, sec. 7 he goes to Shinoda Forest (*Ukiyo monogatari*, 137–39). See also Laurence Bresler, "The Origins of Popular Travel and Travel Literature in Japan" (PhD diss., Columbia University, 1975), 359–423.
63. Mary Elizabeth Berry, *Japan in Print: Information and Nation in the Early Modern Period* (Berkeley: University of California Press, 2006), 153, uses the term in her discussion of the early street directories produced, notably, after *Ukiyo monogatari*.
64. On *michiyukibun*, see, for example, Tsunoda Ichirō, "Michiyukibun kenkyū joron 1," *Hiroshima Joshi Daigaku kiyō* 1 (March 1966): 1–10; Tsunoda Ichirō, "Michiyukibun kenkyū joron 2," *Hiroshima Joshi Daigaku kiyō* 5 (March 1970): 1–13; Jacqueline Pigeot, "Otogizōshi ni okeru michiyukibun," *Bungaku* 43, no. 6 (June 1975): 718–27; and Jacqueline Pigeot, *Michiyuki-bun: Poétique de l'itinéraire dans la littérature du Japon ancien* (Paris: Collège de France, Institut des Hautes Études Japonaises, 2009).
65. *Ukiyo monogatari*, 112.
66. Nakagawa Kiun, *Kyō warabe* (Kyoto: Hachimonjiya Gohee, 1658), National Institute of Japanese Literature, Tachikawa (shelf mark: 99-172-1~6), vol. 2, 15v.
67. Asai Ryōi, *Tōkaidō meishoki* (n.p.: publisher unknown, n.d.), critical edition in *Tōkaidō meishoki*, ed. Asakura Haruhiko, 2 vols., Tōyō bunko 346, 361 (Tokyo: Heibonsha, 1979); Tōyō bunko 361, p. 231, for a brief reference to Gojō no Tenjin.
68. Lane, "Beginnings," 672.
69. *Ukiyo monogatari*, 187.
70. *Ukiyo monogatari*, 187.
71. *Ukiyo monogatari*, 106; vol. 1, sec. 7.
72. *Ukiyo monogatari*, 106–9; vol. 1, sec. 8.
73. Taniwaki, *Ukiyo monogatari*, 106n30.
74. *Ukiyo monogatari*, 144–45; vol. 2, sec. 10.
75. *Ukiyo monogatari*, 108.
76. Taniwaki, 108n17, discusses this as an attempt to circumvent the 1657 ordinance on war tales. He quotes the ordinance in the afterword to the critical edition of *Ukiyo monogatari*, 634: "If you publish a war tale [*gunsho*], you must write your address, let the magistrates know, and ask for instructions." On the same ordinance, see also Konda Yōzō, *Edo no kinsho*, Edo sensho 6 (Tokyo: Yoshikawa Kōbunkan, 1981), 56; Kumakura Isao, *Kan'ei bunka no kenkyū* (Tokyo: Yoshikawa Kōbunkan, 1988), 83.
77. *Ukiyo monogatari*, 127–29.
78. Keene, *World Within Walls*, 159.
79. Shirane, *Early Modern Japanese Literature*, 29.
80. *Ukiyo monogatari*, 187.

81. *Ukiyo monogatari*, 188.
82. *Ukiyo monogatari*, 151–55.
83. *Ukiyo monogatari*, 151–55.
84. *Ukiyo monogatari*, 157–59.
85. *Ukiyo monogatari*, 160–61.
86. On the publication history of *Zoku Kashōki*, see note 47. On *Kashōki* see ch. 1, note 83.
87. *Ukiyo monogatari*, 190–92; vol. 4, sec. 3.
88. *Ukiyo monogatari*, 206–9; vol. 5, sec. 1.
89. *Ukiyo monogatari*, 141–43; vol. 2, sec. 9.
90. *Ukiyo monogatari*, 141–42.
91. Keene, *World Within Walls*, 157, 159.
92. Isoda Dōya, *Chikusai* (n.p.: publisher unknown, n.d.), critical edition (Kan'ei era, 1624–1644) in *Kanazōshi shū*, ed. Maeda Kingorō and Morita Takeshi, Nihon koten bungaku taikei 90 (Tokyo: Iwanami Shoten, 1965), 89–159. Hereafter cited as *Chikusai*. More information about the publishing history is given in the main body of this section. *Chikusai* was a steady item in book-trade catalogues from 1666–1667 to 1715. It was recorded as *Chikusai monogatari* under the category of *mai narabi ni sōshi* but in 1685 it migrated to *monogatari-rui*. The price for two volumes was 1 *monme* 8 *fun* in 1681, decreasing to 1 *monme* 5 *fun* in 1696 and 1709, and increasing to 2 *monme* 5 *fun* in 1715. An almost complete translation of the movable-type edition appears in Bresler, "Origins." A partial translation of the Kan'ei era woodblock edition is available in Edward Putzar, trans., "*Chikusai Monogatari*: A Partial Translation," *Monumenta Nipponica* 16, no. 1/2 (April–July 1960): 161–95. All translations here are mine.
93. L. Moretti, "Adaptation as a Strategy for Participation," 67–113.
94. Bannet, *Eighteenth-Century Manners*, 210–11; emphasis added.
95. For details, see Sasano Ken, *Kinsei kayō shū*, Koten zensho (Tokyo: Asahi Shinbunsha, 1956), 176. For information in English on Dōya's life, see Bresler, "Origins," 199.
96. There is the argument that publishers based in Edo might not have had access to earlier movable type editions; however, it is also true that no attempt was made to make *Chikusai* into something less fragmentary. This decision is telling, thus prompting my line of inquiry.
97. Photographic reproductions of different editions and details of the publishing history can be found in *Chikusai monogatari shū*, ed. Maeda Kingorō, Kinsei bungei shiryō 11 (Tokyo: Koten Bunko, 1970), and in *Kinsei bungaku shiryō ruijū Kanazōshi hen*, ed. Kinsei Bungaku Shoshi Kenkyūkai (Tokyo: Benseisha, 1978), vols. 30 and 31.
98. David McCraw, "Criss-Cross: Introducing Chiasmus in Old Chinese Literature," *Chinese Literature: Essays, Articles, Reviews (CLEAR)* 28 (December 2006): 67–124.
99. *Chikusai*, 159.
100. Lane, "Beginnings," 676–77; Jones and Kern, *A Kamigata Anthology*, 55; Bresler, "Origins," 192.
101. *Chikusai*, 92.
102. *Kyō warabe*, vol. 2, 1r–4r. A description similar to that of *Kyō warabe* is encountered with little variation in *Tōkaidō meishoki*, 166. See also other, coeval *meishoki*, including Yamamoto Taijun, *Rakuyō meisho shū* (Collection of famous places in the capital) ([Kyoto]: Hanji Nihee, 1658), National Institute of Japanese Literature, Tachikawa (shelf mark: 99-55-1-12), vol. 4, 3r–5r; Asai Ryōi (author), Yoshida Hanbee (illustrator), *Dekisai kyō miyage* (Dekisai's souvenir from the capital) (Kyoto: Yamaguchi Ichirobee,

1678), National Institute of Japanese Literature, Tachikawa (shelf mark: ヤ6-277-1~7), vol. 3. 7v–10r.
103. *Chikusai*, 94. The passage in *Kyō warabe* is in vol. 1, 13r–14v. It displays unrelated content.
104. For a discussion of *Nise monogatari*, see Jack Rucinski, trans., "A Japanese Burlesque: Nise Monogatari," *Monumenta Nipponica* 30, no. 1 (Spring 1975): 1–18. See also Laura Moretti, "Nise monogatari: Parodi to kokkei," in *Warai to sōzō*, ed. Howard Hibbett (Tokyo: Benseisha, 2000), 43–59; Laura Moretti, "Kinsei shoki, zenki no sanbun bungaku ni okeru *Ise monogatari* no kakinaoshi, parodi oyobi shin tenkai," in *Ise monogatari sōzō to hen'yō*, ed. Yamamoto Tokurō and Joshua Mostow, 269–301 (Osaka: Izumi Shoin, 2010).
105. "When he arrived at Kitano Shrine and looked around" (*Kitano no yashiro ni mairite mireba*; beginning episode 1); "When he looked in yet again another direction" (*mata aru kata o mite areba*; beginning of episodes 2, 3, 4, 5, and 8; or *sate aru kata o mite areba* beginning of episodes 6, 9 and 11; or *sate katagata o mite areba*, beginning of episode 7). *Chikusai*, 94–130.
106. Bresler, "Origins," 190.
107. *Chikusai*, 94–96.
108. *Chikusai*, 100.
109. I use "omnipresent," not "omniscient," because the use of honorifics demonstrates that this narrator is not able to extract himself from the narrative world and yet he is able to travel freely in space and time as an omniscient narrator should do.
110. *Chikusai*, 100–101.
111. *Chikusai*, 105.
112. This poem is constructed around multiple puns. The word *hidarai* is plays on "tub" and "vagina"; *toku nori* can mean either "the law explained" (説く法) or "paste" (解く糊), used to lubricate the vagina. *Namagusaki* means "stinky," a reference to mucus, but it is also a term referring to depraved monks (*namagusa bōzu*).
113. *Chikusai*, 111–30.
114. Noda Hisao identifies a connection with *Uraminosuke* for this section of *Chikusai*, but fails to engage with the potential unleashed by this intertextual borrowing and downplays the passage as spurious; see Noda Hisao, *Kinsei shoki shōsetsu ron* (Tokyo: Kasama shoin, 1978), 105.
115. Iwata Jun'ichi, *Honchō nanshoku kō—Nanshoku bunken shoshi* (Tokyo: Hara Shobō, 2002).
116. "With the early modern period, when the figure of the monk is distanced from literature and when the power held by temples is weakened, *chigo monogatari* disappear . . . the male love previously seen among monks is now depicted as belonging to the world of the warrior. This point clearly derives from the different social realities of the medieval period and of the early modern period" (Ichiko Teiji, *Chūsei shōsetsu no kenkyū* [Tokyo: Tōkyō Daigaku Shuppankai, 1955], 140). On medieval *chigo monogatari*, see Margaret H. Childs, "Chigo Monogatari: Love Stories or Buddhist Sermons?" *Monumenta Nipponica* 35, no. 2 (Summer 1980): 127–51.
117. Shibayama Hajime, *Edo nanshoku kō: Wakashu hen* (Tokyo: Hihyōsha, 2001), 199–211; Hanada Fujio, "Chikusai azuma kudari kō," *Ōtsuma Joshi Daigaku kiyō* 23 (March 1991): 52–54.
118. *Chikusai*, 132.
119. *Chikusai*, 147–48, 150, and 158.

368　7. The Triumph of Plurality

120. *Chikusai*, 150. For the passage in *Ise monogatari*, see Joshua S. Mostow and Royall Tyler, *The Ise Stories:* Ise monogatari (Honolulu: University of Hawai'i Press, 2010), 33–34.
121. *Chikusai*, 158. For the passage in *Ise monogatari*, see Mostow and Tyler, *The Ise Stories*, 36.
122. Kakei (compiler), *Fuyu no hi* (n.p.: publisher unknown, [1684]) critical edition in *Bashō shichibu shū*, ed. Shiraishi Teizō and Ueno Yōzō, Shin Nihon koten bungaku taikei 70 (Tokyo: Iwanami Shoten, 1990), 1–28. The English translation is from Haruo Shirane, *Traces of Dreams: Landscape, Cultural Memory, and the Poetry of Basho* (Stanford, Calif.: Stanford University Press, 1998), 123.
123. *Chikusai ryōji no hyōban* (Osaka: Shorin Shōtarō, 1685), diplomatic transcription in vol. 48 of *Kanazōshi shūsei*, ed. Hanada Fujio et al. (Tokyo: Tōkyōdō Shuppan, 2012), 176. For a study of *Chikusai ryōji no hyōban*, see Laura Moretti, "Chikusai ryōji no hyōban ron: Hyōban no keitai to sono imi," *Kinsei shoki bungei* 18 (December 2001): 47–68. Shorin Shōtarō is probably another name for Morita Shōtarō.
124. *Chikusai*, 136–46. This section displays another significant difference between movable-type and woodblock-printed editions—namely, the latter adds a new episode about a pregnant woman suffering from bleeding.
125. *Chikusai*, 137.
126. Anrakuan Sakuden, *Seisuishō*, critical edition of multiple early modern editions in *Seisuishō*, ed. Suzuki Tōzō, 2 vols. (Tokyo: Iwanami Shoten, 1986), 1:195–96. Hereafter cited as *Seisuishō*.
127. This comic technique is used in later *hanashibon*. For example, Sakauchi Naoyori, *Karukuchi ōwarai* ([Kyoto]: Kobayashi Kuzaemon and Ōsumi Hachirobee, 1680), reads, "In Kyoto there was a doctor called Dōun Sōdearō [Dōun 'So It Should Be']. This nickname derived from the fact that looking first at the physiognomy of his patient he was wont to say, 'Your pulse says that you should have a headache. Don't you have a headache?' If the answer was, 'Yes, I have a headache,' his comment was, 'As it should be,' but even if the answer was, 'No, I don't have a headache,' his response was the same, 'As it should be'" (*Karukuchi ōwarai*, vol. 4, 2v–4r, in *Hanashibon taikei*, ed. Mutō Sadao and Oka Masahiko, 20 vols. [Tokyo: Tōkyōdō Shuppan, 1975–1979], CD-ROM).
128. *Chikusai*, 137–38 and 141. The humorous use of eggplants to cool down something appears in *Seisuishō*: "A man entered a bath filled with hot water and said, 'How hot this water is! I cannot stand it. Bring some pickles.' 'What do you use them for?,' somebody asked. 'When a soup is too hot, you put pickles in it to cool it down,' answered the man" (vol. 1, 146).
129. *Chikusai*, 138.
130. *Chikusai*, 143.
131. *Chikusai*, 145–46.
132. Barthes, *Pleasure of the Text*, 9.
133. Moretti, "*Kanazōshi* Revisited," 340.
134. Margot Singer and Nicole Walker, eds., *Bending Genre: Essays on Creative Nonfiction* (London: Bloomsbury, 2013), 4.
135. I am indebted to Mary Elizabeth Berry for suggesting the idea of "way finding."

Bibliography

Primary Sources

Note: Works whose author is unknown are listed by title.

Amida kyō wadan shō 阿弥陀経和談抄. Kyoto: Nagata Chōbee 永田長兵衛, 1685. Private collection, Suzuran Bunko, Cambridge, U.K. No shelf mark.

Anrakuan Sakuden 安楽庵策伝. *Seisuishō* 醒睡笑. Critical edition of multiple early modern editions in *Seisuishō*, edited by Suzuki Tōzō. 2 vols. Tokyo: Iwanami Shoten, 1986.

Aoki Rosui 青木鷺水. *Shokoku inga monogatari* 諸国因果物語. Kyoto: Hishiya Jihee 菱屋治兵衛; Edo: Izumoji Shirobee 出雲寺四良兵衛, 1707. Tokyo University Library, Katei Bunko. Shelf mark: 霞亭0230.

Asai Ryōi 浅井了意 (author), Yoshida Hanbee 吉田半兵衛 (illustrator). *Dekisai kyō miyage* 出来斎京土産. Kyoto: Yamaguchi Ichirobee 山口市郎兵衛, 1678. National Institute of Japanese Literature, Tachikawa. Shelf mark: ヤ6-277-1~7.

Asai Ryōi 浅井了意(author). *Inu hariko* 狗張子. N.p.: publisher unknown, n.d. Yūtoku Inari Jinja, Kashima. Microfilm copy, National Institute of Japanese Literature, Tachikawa. Microfilm number: ユ1-228-5.

——. *Kanameishi* かなめ石 / 艱難目異志. N.p.: publisher unknown, [ca. 1662–1663]. Critical edition in *Kanazōshi shū*, edited by Taniwaki Masachika, Oka Masahiko, and Inoue Kazuhito, 11–83. Shinpen Nihon koten bungaku zenshū 64. Tokyo: Shōgakukan, 1999.

——. *Kanameishi* 艱難目異志. N.p.: publisher unknown, [ca. 1662–1663]. National Diet Library, Tokyo. Shelf mark: 京-160.

——. *Kanninki* 堪忍記. [Kyoto]: Araki Rihee 荒木利兵衛, 1659. Diplomatic transcription in vol. 20 of *Kanazōshi shūsei*, edited by Asakura Haruhiko and Fukasawa Akio, 93–294. Tokyo: Tōkyōdō Shuppan, 1997.

——. *Kyō suzume* 京雀. [Kyoto]: Yamada Ichirobee 山田市郎兵衛, 1665. National Diet Library, Tokyo. Shelf mark: 京乙:252.

——. *Musashi abumi* むさしあぶみ. Kyoto: Nakamura Gohee 中村五兵衛, 1661. National Diet Library, Tokyo. Shelf mark: 841-35.

——. *Tōkaidō meishoki* 東海道名所記. N.p.: publisher unknown, n.d. Critical edition in *Tōkaidō meishoki*, edited by Asakura Haruhiko, 2 vols. Tōyō bunko 346, 361. Tokyo: Heibonsha, 1979.

——. *Ukiyo monogatari* 浮世物語. [Kyoto]: Hiranoya Sahee 平野屋佐兵衛, ca. 1665. Critical edition in *Kanazōshi shū*, edited by Taniwaki Masachika, Oka Masahiko, and Inoue Kazuhito, 85–224. Shinpen Nihon koten bungaku zenshū 64. Tokyo: Shōgakukan, 1999.

Asayama Irin'an 朝山意林庵. *Kiyomizu monogatari* 清水物語. Kyoto: Tsurugaya Kyūbee 敦賀屋九兵衛, 1638. Critical edition in *Kanazōshi shū*, edited by Watanabe Morikuni and Watanabe Kenji, 139–92. Shin Nihon koten bungaku taikei 74. Tokyo: Iwanami Shoten, 1991.

Atsumori あつもり / 敦盛. Kyoto: Yamada Ichirobee 山田市郎兵衛, 1658. National Diet Library, Tokyo. Shelf mark: 231-120.

Chikusai ryōji no hyōban 竹斎療治之評判. Osaka: Shorin Shōtarō 書林庄太郎, 1685. Diplomatic transcription in vol. 48 of *Kanazōshi shūsei*, edited by Hanada Fujio, Iriguchi Atsushi, Nakajima Jirō, Yasuhara Makoto, and Laura Moretti, 175–201. Tokyo: Tōkyōdō Shuppan, 2012.

Chōjakyō 長者教. Kyoto: Tsujii Kichiemon 辻井吉右エ門; Osaka: Araki Sahee 荒木佐兵衛, 1762. Osaka University Library, Ninchōji Bunko. Microfilm copy, National Institute of Japanese Literature, Tachikawa. Microfilm number: 228-66-10.

Chōjakyō 長者教. N.p.: publisher unknown, 1627. Movable-type edition. Waseda University Library, Tokyo. Shelf mark: ヘ13 04176.

Daibutsu monogatari 大仏物語. [Kyoto]: publisher unknown, 1644. Diplomatic transcription in vol. 47 of *Kanazōshi shūsei*, edited by Fukasawa Akio, Itō Shingo, Iriguchi Atsushi, Hanada Fujio, Yasuhara Makoto, and Wada Yasuyuki, 59–89. Tokyo: Tōkyōdō Shuppan, 2011.

Ejima Kiseki 江島其磧. *Sakiwake gonin musume* 咲分五人娘. Kyoto: Hishiya Jihee 菱屋治兵衛, 1735. National Diet Library, Tokyo. Shelf mark: 京-212.

Ejima Tamenobu 江島為信. *Mi no kagami* 身の鏡. [Kyoto]: publisher unknown, n.d. Private collection, Suzuran Bunko, Cambridge, U.K. No shelf mark.

——. *Mi no kagami* 身の鏡. [Kyoto]: Yoshinoya 芳野屋, 1659. Photographic reproduction in vol. 25 of *Kinsei bungaku shiryō ruijū Kanazōshi hen*, edited by Kinsei Bungaku Shoshi Kenkyūkai, 3–118. Tokyo: Benseisha, 1977. Critical edition in *Kanazōshi shū*, edited by Watanabe Morikuni and Watanabe Kenji, 271–319. Shin Nihon koten bungaku taikei 74. Tokyo: Iwanami Shoten, 1991.

——. *Rihi kagami* 理非鏡. [Kyoto]: publisher unknown, 1664. National Institute of Japanese Literature, Tachikawa. Shelf mark: ナ4-146-1~3. Photographic reproduction of copy at the National Diet Library, Tokyo, in vol. 25 of *Kinsei bungaku shiryō ruijū Kanazōshi hen*, edited by Kinsei Bungaku Shoshi Kenkyūkai, 121–274. Tokyo: Benseisha, 1977.

Enomoto Yazaemon 榎本弥左衛門. *Mitsugo yori no oboe* 三子より之覚. Diplomatic transcription in *Enomoto Yazaemon oboegaki: Kinsei shoki shōnin no kiroku*, edited by Ōno Mizuo, 15–120. Tōyō bunko 695. Tokyo: Heibonsha, 2001.

——. *Yorozu no oboe* 万之覚. Diplomatic transcription in *Enomoto Yazaemon oboegaki: Kinsei shoki shōnin no kiroku*, edited by Ōno Mizuo, 121–352. Tōyō bunko 695. Tokyo: Heibonsha, 2001.

Fudanzakura 不断桜. Manuscript at Tenri Central Library (Wataya Bunko), transcribed in vol. 11 of *Mikan zappai shiryō*, edited by Suzuki Katsutada, 不1–不9. Okazaki: Suzuki Katsutada, 1961.

Fujita Rihee 藤田理兵衛. *Edo kanoko* 江戸鹿子. Edo: Komori Tarobee 小森太郎兵衛, 1687. Photographic reproduction in *Edo kanoko*, edited by Asakura Haruhiko. Tokyo: Sumiya Shobō, 1970.

Fukutomi sōshi 福富草紙. Medieval period. Diplomatic transcriptions of two different manuscripts in vol. 11 of *Muromachi jidai monogatari taisei*, edited by Yokoyama Shigeru and Matsumoto Ryūshin, 335–52. Tokyo: Kadokawa Shoten, 1983.

Gion monogatari 祇園物語. N.p.: publisher unknown, n.d. Diplomatic transcription in vol. 22 of *Kanazōshi shūsei*, edited by Asakura Haruhiko, Fukasawa Akio, and Yanagisawa Masaki, 1–87. Tokyo: Tōkyōdō Shuppan, 1998.

Hachimonjiya Jishō 八文字屋自笑 and Ejima Kiseki 江島其磧. *Yakusha kingeshō* 役者金化粧. [Kyoto]: Hachimonjiya Hachizaemon 八文字屋八左衛門 and Ejimaya Ichirōzaemon 江嶋屋市良左衛門, 1719. National Diet Library, Tokyo. Shelf mark: い-80.

Hata Sōha 秦宗巴. *Inu makura narabi ni kyōka* 犬枕并狂哥. N.p.: publisher unknown, n.d. Critical edition in *Kanazōshi shū*, edited by Maeda Kingorō and Morita Takeshi, 33–48. Nihon koten bungaku taikei 90. Tokyo: Iwanami Shoten, 1965.

Hinin taiheiki 貧人太平記. N.p.: publisher unknown, [1688]. National Diet Library, Tokyo. Shelf mark: 212-38.

Hirata Shisui 平田止水 and Tsujimoto Motosada 辻本基定. *Kannon-gyō wadan shō zue* 観音経和談鈔図会. Kyoto: Sakaiya Jinbee 堺屋仁兵衛, 1833. Private collection, Suzuran Bunko, Cambridge, U.K. No shelf mark.

Hirata Shisui 平田止水, Tsujimoto Motosada 辻本基定, and Hishikawa Kiyoharu 菱川清春 (illustrator). *Ikkyū shokoku monogatari zue* 一休諸国物語図会. Kyoto: Sakaiya Jinbee 堺屋仁兵衛, 1836. Private collection, Suzuran Bunko, Cambridge, U.K. No shelf mark.

Hishikawa Moronobu 菱川師宣, illus. *Genji Yamato e kagami* 源氏大和絵鑑. Edo: Urokogataya 鱗形屋, 1685. Private collection, Ebi Bunko, U.K. Shelf mark: EbiM001.

——. *Nasake no uwamori* 情のうわもり. N.p.: publisher unknown, ca. 1680s. Photographic reproduction and transcription in vol. 1 of *Edo enpon shūsei*, edited by Hayashi Yoshikazu, 247–94. Tokyo: Kawade Shobō Shinsha, 2013.

——. *Nasake no uwamori* 情のうわもり. Edo: Urokogataya 鱗形屋, n.d. Vol. 1 only. Private collection, Suzuran Bunko, Cambridge, U.K. No shelf mark.

——. *Shokunin zukushi emaki* 職人尽絵巻. Manuscript without colophon, ca. 1682. British Museum, London. Shelf mark: 1923, 1114, 0.2.1, 2.

Hōjō Dansui 北条団水. *Chūya yōjinki* 昼夜用心記. Kyoto: Izutsuya Shōbee 井筒屋庄兵衛 and Yurugi Jihee 万木治兵衛; Edo: Suharaya Mohee 須原屋茂兵衛, 1707. Nakanoshima Toshokan, Osaka. Microfilm copy, National Institute of Japanese Literature, Tachikawa. Microfilm number: 66-1-4.

Hōman chōja ほうまん長者. Medieval period. Diplomatic transcriptions of different originals in vol. 12 of *Muromachi jidai monogatari taisei*, edited by Yokoyama Shigeru and Matsumoto Ryūshin, 342–52. Tokyo: Kadokawa Shoten, 1984.

Ichimori chōja 市守長者. N.p.: publisher unknown, [Enpō era (1673–1681)]. Tokyo University Library, Katei Bunko, Tokyo. Shelf mark: 霞亭0113.

Ihara Saikaku 井原西鶴 and Hōjō Dansui 北条団水. *Yorozu no fumi hōgu* 万の文反古. Edo: Yorozuya Seibee 万屋清兵衛; Osaka: Kariganeya Shōhee 雁金屋庄兵衛; Kyoto: Uemura Heizaemon 上村平左衛門, 1696. Critical edition with translation in modern Japanese in vol. 15 of *Ketteiban Taiyaku Saikaku zenshū*, edited by Asō Isoji and Fuji Akio, 139–273. Tokyo: Meiji Shoin, 1993.

Ikkyū shina monogatari 一休品物語. Kyoto: Itamiya Kichiemon 伊丹屋吉右衛門, 1679. National Diet Library, Tokyo. Shelf mark: 212-33.

Ikkyū shokoku monogatari 一休諸国物語. Kyoto: Akai Chōbee 赤井長兵衛, n.d. Waseda University Library, Tokyo. Shelf mark: へ13 03379.

Inu Hōjōki 犬方丈記. Kyoto: Yamamoto Shichirobee 山本七郎兵衛, 1682. Diplomatic transcription in vol. 4 of *Kanazōshi shūsei*, edited by Asakura Haruhiko, 153–75. Tokyo: Tōkyōdō Shuppan, 1983.

Isoda Dōya 磯田道冶. *Chikusai* 竹斎. N.p.: publisher unknown, n.d. Critical edition (Kan'ei era, 1624–1644) in *Kanazōshi shū*, edited by Maeda Kingorō and Morita Takeshi, 89–159. Nihon koten bungaku taikei 90. Tokyo: Iwanami Shoten, 1965.

Jigabachi monogatari 似我蜂物語. [Kyoto]: Nakano Gorōzaemon 中野五郎左衛門, 1661. Diplomatic transcription in vol. 33 of *Kanazōshi shūsei*, edited by Asakura Haruhiko, 105–231. Tokyo: Tōkyōdō Shuppan, 2003. See also *Zoku chōmonjū*.

Jinkyōron 人鏡論. Kyoto: Ōmiya Jirokichi 近江屋治郎吉, n.d. Photographic reproduction in vol. 21 of *Chōhōki shiryō shūsei*, edited by Nagatomo Chiyoji, 5–99. Kyoto: Rinsen Shoten, 2006.

Jitsugokyō 実語教. Edo: Hanabusa Bunzō 英文蔵, ca. 1843–1847. Private collection, Suzuran Bunko, Cambridge, U.K. No shelf mark.

Jitsugokyō 実語教. Edo: Moriya Jihee 森屋治兵衛, 1863. Private collection, Suzuran Bunko, Cambridge, U.K. No shelf mark.

Jitsugokyō 実語教. Edo: Tsuruya Kiemon 鶴屋喜右衛門, 1792. Private collection, Suzuran Bunko, Cambridge, U.K. No shelf mark.

Kagekiyo 景清. [Kyoto]: Nakano Dōya 中野道也, 1632. National Institute of Japanese Literature, Tachikawa. Shelf mark: タ7-33.

Kaibara Ekiken 貝原益軒. *Wazoku dōjikun* 和俗童子訓. Osaka: Shibukawa Seiemon 渋川清右衛門, 1710. Critical edition in *Yōjōkun, Wazoku dōjikun*, edited by Ishikawa Ken, 193–280. Tokyo: Iwanami Shoten, 1961.

Kakei 荷兮, comp. *Fuyu no hi* 冬の日. N.p.: publisher unknown, [1684]. Critical edition in *Bashō shichibu shū*, edited by Shiraishi Teizō and Ueno Yōzō, 1–28. Shin Nihon koten bungaku taikei 70. Tokyo: Iwanami Shoten, 1990.

Kannon-gyō hayayomi eshō 観音経早読絵抄. Kyoto: Suharaya Heizaemon すはらや平左衛門, n.d. Private collection, Suzuran Bunko, Cambridge, U.K. No shelf mark.

Kannon-gyō wadan shō 観音経和談抄. Edo: Urokogataya Magobee 鱗形屋孫兵衛 and Nishimuraya Yohachi 西村屋与八, n.d. Private collection, Suzuran Bunko, Cambridge, U.K. No shelf mark.

Kannon-gyō wadan shō 観音経和談抄. [Kyoto]: Akitaya Seibee 秋田屋清兵衛, 1661. Private collection, Suzuran Bunko, Cambridge, U.K. No shelf mark.

Kannon-gyō wadan shō 観音経和談抄. Kyoto: Umemura Saburobee 梅村三郎兵衛, 1719. National Institute of Japanese Literature, Tachikawa. Shelf mark: ヤ5-371.

Kannon-gyō wadan shō 観音経和談抄. Kyoto: Yamamoto Kyūbee 山本九兵衛, n.d. Private collection, Suzuran Bunko, Cambridge, U.K. No shelf mark.

Kashōki atooi 可笑記跡追. [Kyoto]: Yamamoto Shichirobee 山本七郎兵衛 and Ogawa Ihee 小川井兵衛, 1672. Diplomatic transcription in vol. 16 of *Kanazōshi shūsei*, edited by Asakura Haruhiko and Fukasawa Akio, 211–84. Tokyo: Tōkyōdō Shuppan, 1995.

Katayama Naotsugu 方山直次. *Makura no hibiki* 枕のひゞき. Kyoto: Hachio Ichibee 八尾市兵衛 and Matsumoto Kyūemon 松本九右衛門, 1688. Tenri University Library, Tenri. Shelf mark: 169-1~3.

Kawachiya Yoshimasa 河内屋可正. *Kashō zakki* 可正雑記. Diplomatic transcription of the manuscript in the private collection of the Tsuboi family, in *Kashō zakki*, vol. 41 of *Ōtani Joshi Daigaku Shiryōkan hōkokusho*, edited by Ōtani Joshi Daigaku Shiryōkan, 1–87. Tondabayashi: Ōtani Joshi Daigaku Shiryōkan, 1999.

———. *Kawachiya Yoshimasa kyūki* 河内屋可正旧記. Diplomatic transcription in *Kawachiya Yoshimasa kyūki*, edited by Nomura Yutaka and Yui Kitarō, Seibundō shiryō sōsho 1. Tokyo: Seibundō Shuppan, 1970.

[*Kawaraban* on Osaka fire, 1852]. In album entitled *Shūkojō* 集古帖. Private collection, Suzuran Bunko, Cambridge, U.K. No shelf mark.

Kojima Tokuemon 小嶋徳右衛門. *Kyō habutae* 京羽二重. Kyoto: Tachibanaya Seian 橘屋清安, 1705. Waseda University Library, Tokyo. Shelf mark: ル04 03771.

Kōshoku Nishikigi 好色にしき木. Edo: Nishimura Hanbee 西村半兵衛; Kyoto: Nishimura Ichirōemon 西村市郎右衛門, [1692]. Diplomatic transcription in *Kōshoku fumi denju*, *Kōshoku Nishikigi*, edited by Yoshida Kōichi, 331–448. Koten bunko 604. Tokyo: Koten Bunko, 1997.

Kubota Yasu 窪田やす. *Onna shogaku bunshō* 女初学文章. [Kyoto]: publisher unknown, 1660. Private collection, Koizumi Yoshinaga. Tokyo. No shelf mark.

Kyokutei Bakin 曲亭馬琴. *Kinsei mono no hon Edo sakusha burui* 近世物之本江戸作者部類. Critical edition in *Kinsei mono no hon Edo sakusha burui*, edited by Tokuda Takeshi. Tokyo: Iwanami Shoten, 2014.

Kyokutei Bakin 曲亭馬琴 (author) and Okada Gyokuzan 岡田玉山 (illustrator). *Jitsugokyō eshō* 実語教絵抄. Osaka: Imazuya Tatsusaburō 今津屋辰三郎, Kawachiya Sōbee 河内屋惣兵衛, Kawachiya Tasuke 河内屋太助, 1812. Private collection, Suzuran Bunko, Cambridge, U.K. No shelf mark.

Maeda Sawa 前田さわ. *Onna sewa yōbunshō taisei* 女世話用文章大成. Osaka: Yorozuya Hikotarō 萬屋彦太郎; Edo: Suhara Mohee 須原茂兵衛, 1700. Hirosaki City Public Library, Hirosaki. Microfilm copy, National Institute of Japanese Literature, Tachikawa. Microfilm number: 272-399-3.

Makieshi Genzaburō 蒔絵師源三郎, illus. *Jinrin kinmōzui* 人倫訓蒙図彙. [Kyoto]: Heirakuji 平楽寺; Osaka: Murakami Seizaburō 村上清三郎; Edo: Murakami Gorobee 村上五郎兵衛, 1690. Critical edition in *Jinrin kinmōzui*, edited by Asakura Haruhiko. Tōyō bunko 519. Tokyo: Heibonsha 1990.

Manase Gensaku 曲直瀬玄朔. *Nichiyō shokushō* 日用食性. [Edo]: Matsue 松会, 1673. Waseda University Library, Tokyo. Shelf mark: 文庫31 E1787.

———. *Nichiyō shokushō* 日用食性. Kyoto: Fūgetsu Sōchi 風月宗知, 1642. National Diet Library, Tokyo. Shelf mark: 特1-2816.

Minu kyō monogatari 見ぬ京物語. [Kyoto]: publisher unknown, 1659. Photographic reproduction in *Kanazōshi shū*, Kinsei bungei sōkan 2, 187–350. Osaka: Han'an Noma Kōshin Sensei Kakō Kinen, 1970.

Miyako no Nishiki 都の錦. *Genroku taiheiki* 元禄大平記. Kyoto: Aoyama Ihee 青山為兵衛, 1702. Critical edition in *Miyako no Nishiki shū*, edited by Nakajima Takashi, 81–175. Sōsho Edo bunko 6. Tokyo: Kokusho Kankōkai, 1989.

Mongaku 文覚. [Kyoto]: Nakano Dōya 中野道也, 1632. Tōyō Bunko, Tokyo. Shelf mark: 三 Fa に 15. Photographic reproduction in *Kōwakamai, otogizōshi*, vol. Kinsei-hen 1 of *Iwazaki Bunko kichōbon sōkan*, edited by Tōyō Bunko and Nihon Koten Bungaku Kai, 335–66. Tokyo: Kichōbon Kankōkai, 1974.

Mongaku 文覚. [Kyoto]: Yamada Ichirobee 山田市郎兵衛, 1658. National Diet Library, Tokyo. Shelf mark: 本別19-4.

Nakagawa Kiun 中川喜雲. *Kyō warabe* 京童. Kyoto: Hachimonjiya Gohee 八文字屋五兵衛, 1658. National Institute of Japanese Literature, Tachikawa. Shelf mark: 99-172-1~6.

Namura Jōhaku 苗村常伯. *Nan chōhōki* 男重宝記. Kyoto: Nakagawa Hikosaburō 中川彦三郎 and Yamatoya Kanshichirō 大和屋勘七良, 1693. Critical edition in *Onna chōhōki Nan chōhōki: Genroku wakamono kokoroe shū*, edited by Nagatomo Chiyoji, 197–381. Tokyo: Shakai Shisōsha, 1993.

———. *Onna chōhōki* 女重宝記. Edo: Yorozuya Seibee 万屋清兵衛; Osaka: Itan'ya Tarōemon 伊丹屋太郎右衛門; Kyoto: Yoshinoya Jirobee 吉野屋次郎兵衛, 1692. Critical edition in *Onna chōhōki Nan chōhōki: Genroku wakamono kokoroe shū*, edited by Nagatomo Chiyoji, 9–196. Tokyo: Shakai Shisōsha, 1993.

———. *Yorozu anshi tegata kagami* 万案紙手形鑑. Kyoto: Tanaka Shōbee 田中庄兵衛, 1693. Photographic reproduction in vol. 6 of *Kinsei bungaku shiryō ruijū Sankō bunken hen*, edited by Kinsei Bungaku Shoshi Kenkyūkai, 175–344. Tokyo: Benseisha, 1976.

Nichishin 日心. *Tadasu monogatari* 糺物語. [Kyoto]: publisher unknown, 1657. Diplomatic transcription in vol. 47 of *Kanazōshi shūsei*, edited by Fukasawa Akio, Itō Shingo, Iriguchi Atsushi, Hanada Fujio, Yasuhara Makoto, and Wada Yasuyuki, 119–66. Tokyo: Tōkyōdō Shuppan, 2011.

Nioi bukuro 匂ひ袋. Kyoto: Nagaharaya Magobee 永原屋孫兵衛, 1681. Diplomatic transcription in vol. 55 of *Kanazōshi shūsei*, edited by Hanada Fujio, Ōkubo Junko, Nakajima Jirō, and Yuasa Yoshiko, 113–36. Tokyo: Tōkyōdō Shuppan, 2016. See also *Shorei kyōkun kagami*.

Nishikigi 錦木. N.p.: publisher unknown, n.d. National Diet Library, Tokyo. Shelf mark: 京-145.

Nishikigi 錦木. N.p.: publisher unknown, n.d. Private collection, Suzuran Bunko, Cambridge, U.K. No shelf mark.

Nishimura Mitatsu 西村未達. *Shokoku shinjū onna* 諸国心中女. Edo: Nishimura Hanbee 西村半兵衛; Kyoto: Nishimura Ichirōemon 西村市郎右衛門 and Sakagami Shōbee 坂上勝兵衛, 1686. Katei Bunko, Tokyo. Shelf mark: 霞亭0167.

Nishizawa Ippū 西沢一風. *Ima Chōja monogatari* 今長者物語. Kyoto: Nishizawashi Ippū 西沢氏一夫, n.d. Diplomatic transcription in vol. 5 of *Kanazōshi shūsei*, edited by Asakura Haruhiko, 323–47. Tokyo: Tōkyōdō Shuppan, 1984.

Nitan no Shirō 二たん乃四郎. [Kyoto]: Yamamoto Kyūbee 山本九兵衛, 1667. National Diet Library, Tokyo. Shelf mark: わ-59.

Nyoraishi 如儡子. *Kashōki* 可笑記. [Kyoto]: publisher unknown, 1642. Diplomatic transcription in vol. 14 of *Kanazōshi shūsei*, edited by Asakura Haruhiko and Fukasawa Akio, 131–376. Tokyo: Tōkyōdō Shuppan, 1993.

Ogasawara hyakka jō 小笠原百箇条. [Kyoto]: Nakano Ichiemon 中野市右衛門, 1632. National Diet Library, Tokyo. Shelf mark: 855-35.

Ogasawara hyakka jō 小笠原百箇条. Movable-type edition. [Kyoto]: publisher unknown, n.d. National Diet Library, Tokyo. Shelf mark: WA 7-171

Ogasawara-ryū shitsukekata hyakka jō 小笠原流躾方百箇條. Edo: Wan'ya Ihee 椀屋伊兵衛, 1843. Private collection, Suzuran Bunko, Cambridge, U.K. No shelf mark.

Ōgō Shinsai 大郷信斎 and Makino Zenbee 牧野善兵衛. *Wakan gundanki ryakkō taisei* 和漢軍談紀略考大成. Kyoto: Izumoji Bunjirō 出雲寺文治郎; Osaka: Akitaya Taemon 秋田屋太右衛門; Edo: Suharaya Mohee 須原屋茂兵衛, Kitajima Junshirō 北島順四郎, Izumiya Zenbee 和泉屋善兵衛, and Izumiya Kichibee 和泉屋吉兵衛, 1841. National Diet Library, Tokyo. Shelf mark: 025.1-O783w.

Onna jingi monogatari 女仁義物語. N.p.: publisher unknown, n.d. National Institute of Japanese Literature, Tachikawa. Shelf mark: ナ4-397-1~2.

Onna kagami hidensho 女鏡秘伝書. Edo: Hon Toiya 本問屋, n.d. National Diet Library, Tokyo. Shelf mark: わ159-123.

Onna kagami hidensho 女鏡秘伝書. Kyoto: Noda Yahee 野田弥兵衛, 1650. Diplomatic transcription in vol. 10 of *Kanazōshi shūsei*, edited by Asakura Haruhiko and Fukasawa Akio, 3–77. Tokyo: Tōkyōdō Shuppan, 1989.

Onna kagami hidensho 女鏡秘伝書. Kyoto: Yamamoto Chōbee 山本長兵衛, n.d. 6 vols. Reissue of 1652 edition with added content. Private collection, Suzuran Bunko, Cambridge, U.K. No shelf mark.

Onna kagami hidensho 女鏡秘伝書. Kyoto: Yamamoto Chōbee 山本長兵衛, 1652. 3 vols. Private collection, Suzuran Bunko, Cambridge, U.K. No shelf mark.

Onna shikimoku 女式目. N.p.: publisher unknown, n.d. Private collection, Suzuran Bunko, Cambridge, U.K. No shelf mark.

Onna shikimoku 女式目. [Kyoto]: publisher unknown, 1660. Diplomatic transcription in vol. 11 of *Kanazōshi shūsei*, edited by Asakura Haruhiko and Fukasawa Akio, 141–73. Tokyo: Tōkyōdō Shuppan, 1990.

Onna shorei shū 女諸礼集. [Kyoto]: Tanaka Bunnai 田中文内, 1660. Photographic reproduction in vol. 61 of *Edo jidai josei bunko* (unpaginated). Tokyo: Ōzorasha, 1997.

Onna yō chie kagami takara ori 女用智恵鑑宝織. Osaka: Kashiwaraya Seiemon 柏原屋清右衛門, 1769. Private collection, Suzuran Bunko, Cambridge, U.K. No shelf mark.

Rankeishi 蘭嵠子 (calligrapher) and Ōmori Yoshikiyo 大森善清 (illustrator). *Shin Usuyuki monogatari* 新薄雪物語. Kyoto: Kawakatsu Gorōemon 川勝五郎右衛門; Edo: Masuya 桝屋, 1716. Private collection, Suzuran Bunko, Cambridge, U.K. No shelf mark.

Rongo 論語. Critical edition in *Rongo*, edited by Kanaya Osamu. Tokyo: Iwanami Shoten, 1999.

Ryōri hidenshō 料理秘伝抄. N.p.: publisher unknown, 1670. Ajinomoto Foundation for Dietary Culture, Takanawa, Tokyo. Digital version, National Institute of Japanese Literature, Tachikawa. Shelf mark: DIG-AJNM-20.

Ryōri hidenshō 料理秘伝抄. [Osaka]: Hon'ya Gohee 本や五兵衛, 1684. National Institute of Japanese Literature, Tachikawa. Shelf mark: 49-97.

Ryōri kirigata hidenshō 料理切形秘伝抄. [Kyoto]: publisher unknown [private publication?], 1642. Diplomatic transcription in vol. 1 of *Edo jidai ryōribon shūsei: Honkoku*, edited by Yoshii Motoko, 39–177. Kyoto: Rinsen Shoten, 1978.

Ryōri monogatari 料理物語. [Edo]: Matsue 松会, n.d. National Institute of Japanese Literature, Tachikawa. Shelf mark: 49-66.

Ryōri monogatari 料理物語. [Kyoto]: publisher unknown, 1643. Tokyo Municipal Central Library, Kaga Bunko, Tokyo. Shelf mark: 3800.

Saitō Tokugen 斎藤徳元. *Mottomo no sōshi* 尤之双紙. [Kyoto]: Nakano Dōhan 中野道伴, 1634. Critical edition in *Kanazōshi shū*, edited by Watanabe Morikuni and Watanabe Kenji, 53–138. Shin Nihon koten bungaku taikei 74. Tokyo: Iwanami Shoten, 1991.

Sakauchi Naoyori 坂内直頼. *Karukuchi ōwarai* 軽口大わらひ. [Kyoto]: Kobayashi Kuzaemon 小林久左衛門 and Ōsumi Hachirobee 大角八郎兵衛, 1680. Diplomatic transcription in *Hanashibon taikei*, edited by Mutō Sadao and Oka Masahiko. 20 vols. Tokyo: Tōkyōdō Shuppan, 1975–1979. CD-ROM.

Samukawa Masachika 寒河正親. *Shison kagami* 子孫鑑. [Kyoto]: Fukumori Heizaemon 福森兵左衛門, 1673. National Diet Library, Tokyo. Shelf mark: り-36. Critical edition in *Kinsei chōnin shisō*, edited by Nakamura Yukihiko, 17–84. Nihon shisō taikei 59. Tokyo: Iwanami Shoten, 1975.

Sannin hōshi 三人法師. [Kyoto]: Yamada Ichirobee 山田市郎兵衛, 1658. National Diet Library, Tokyo. Shelf mark: 232-295.

Santō Kyōden 山東京伝 (author) and Utagawa Kunisada 歌川国貞 (illustrator). *Kabuki no hana botan dōrō* 戯場花牡丹燈籠. Edo: Iwatoya Kisaburō 岩戸屋喜三郎, 1810. Waseda University Library, Tokyo. Shelf mark: ヘ13 03204.

Sanze aishō makura 三世相性枕. Edo: Iseya Ihee 伊勢屋伊兵衛 and Matsuzakaya Kihee 松坂屋喜兵衛, 1687. Photographic reproduction and transcription in vol. 1 of *Edo enpon shūsei*, edited by Hayashi Yoshikazu, 197–245. Tokyo: Kawade Shobō Shinsha, 2013.

Sasayama Baian 笹山梅庵. *Tenarai shiyō shū* 手習仕用集. Osaka: Kichimonjiya Ichizaemon 吉文字屋市左衛門, n.d. Sakata Shiritsu Toshokan, Sakata. Microfilm copy, National Institute of Japanese Literature, Tachikawa. Microfilm number: 26-153-16.

———. *Terako seikai no shikimoku* 寺子制誨之式目. Osaka: Kawachiya Shinjirō 河内屋新次郎 and Kawachiya Tasuke 河内屋太助, 1835. Posthumous printed edition. Tottori Kenritsu Toshokan, Tottori. Digital version, National Institute of Japanese Literature, Tachikawa. Shelf mark: DIG-TOKT-11.

Shida 信田. [Edo]: Matsue 松会, 1659. National Diet Library, Tokyo. Shelf mark: 853-255.

Shimokōbe Shūsui 下河邊拾水, illus. *Ogasawara-ryū shitsukekata hyakka jō* 小笠原流躾方百箇條. Osaka: Katsuoya Rokubee 勝尾屋六兵衛, 1770. Ajinomoto Foundation for Dietary Culture, Takanawa, Tokyo. Digital version, National Institute of Japanese Literature, Tachikawa. Shelf mark: DIG-AJNM-160.

Shin Chikusai 新竹斎. Kyoto: Nishimura Ichirōemon 西村市郎右衛門 and Sakagami Shōbee 坂上庄兵衛, 1687. Private collection, Suzuran Bunko, Cambridge, U.K. No shelf mark. Diplomatic transcription of copy at Tōyō Bunko in vol. 2 of *Nishimura bon shōsetsu zenshū*, edited by Nishimura Bon Shōsetsu Kenkyūkai, 201–71. Tokyo: Benseisha, 1985.

Shinkyoku 新曲. [Kyoto]: Nakano Dōya 中野道也, 1632. Tōyō Bunko, Tokyo. Shelf mark: 三 Ad 21. Photographic reproduction in *Kōwakamai, otogizōshi*, vol. Kinsei-hen 1 of *Iwazaki Bunko kichōbon sōkan*, edited by Tōyō Bunko and Nihon Koten Bungaku Kai, 397–433. Tokyo: Kichōbon Kankōkai, 1974.

Shin Nishikigi monogatari 新にしき木物語. Edo: Yamazaki Kinbee 山崎金兵衛, 1758. Art Research Center, Ritsumeikan University, Kyoto. Shelf mark: hayBK02-0026.

Shinpan Heianjō narabi ni rakugai no zu 新板平安城并洛外之図. [Kyoto]: Itsutsuya Kichibee いつゝや吉兵衛, 1680. National Diet Library, Tokyo. Shelf mark: WB39-5.

Shogaku bunshō narabi ni yorozu shitsukekata 初学文章并万躾方. Kyoto: Nishimura Matazaemon 西村又左衛門, 1647. Private collection, Suzuran Bunko, Cambridge, U.K. No shelf mark.

Shogaku bunshō narabi ni yorozu shitsukekata 初学文章并万躾方. [Kyoto]: Nishimura Matazaemon 西村又左衛門, 1634. Ehime University Library, Suzuka Bunko, Matsuyama. Digital version, National Institute of Japanese Literature, Tachikawa. Shelf mark: DIG-EMSK-482.

Shokoku inga monogatari 諸国ゐんくわ物かたり. Abridged edition of *Inga monogatari*. N.p.: publisher unknown, n.d. Photographic reproduction in *Inga monogatari*, edited by Yoshida Kōichi, 163–220. Koten bunko 185. Tokyo: Koten Bunko, 1962.

Shorei kyōkun kagami 諸礼教訓鏡. Later edition of *Nioi bukuro*. Kyoto: Kikuya Shichirobee 菊屋七郎兵衛, after 1738. British Museum, London. Shelf mark: 1979,0305,0.31.

Shoshin bunshō 初心文章. N.p.: publisher unknown, n.d. Tokyo Gakugei University Library, Mochizuki Bunko, Tokyo. Shelf mark: T1A0/74/68.

Soga Kyūji 曽我休自. *Iguchi monogatari* 為愚痴物語. Kyoto: Yoshinoya Gonbee 吉野屋権兵衛, 1662. Diplomatic transcription in vol. 2 of *Kanazōshi shūsei*, edited by Asakura Haruhiko, 105–323. Tokyo: Tōkyōdō Shuppan, 1981.

Sumiyoshi Gukei 住吉具慶. *Rakuchū rakugai zukan* 洛中洛外図巻. Manuscript without colophon, ca. late seventeenth century. Tokyo National Museum, Tokyo. Shelf mark: E0045242.

———. *Tohi zukan* 都鄙図巻. Also known as *Tohi emaki* 都鄙絵巻. Manuscript without colophon, ca. late seventeenth century. Owned by Konbuin, Nara. Nara National Museum, Nara. No shelf mark.

———. *Tohi zukan* 都鄙図巻. Manuscript without colophon, ca. late seventeenth century. Chester Beatty Library, Dublin. Shelf mark: CBL J 1120.

Suzuki Shōsan 鈴木正三. *Inga monogatari* 因果物語. [Kyoto]: publisher unknown, n.d. Hiragana version. Private collection, Suzuran Bunko, Cambridge, U.K. No shelf mark.

——. *Inga monogatari* 因果物語. Kyoto: Zeniya 錢屋, n.d. Hiragana version. Diplomatic transcription in vol. 4 of *Kanazōshi shūsei*, edited by Asakura Haruhiko, 199–285. Tokyo: Tōkyōdō Shuppan, 1983.

——. *Mōanjō* 盲安杖. Kyoto: Hiroi Kyūzaemon, 廣井久左衛門, 1651. Critical edition in *Kana hōgo shū*, edited by Miyasaka Yūshō, 241–61. Nihon koten bungaku taikei 83. Tokyo: Iwanami Shoten, 1964.

Suzuki Shōsan 鈴木正三, Giun 義雲 (editor), and Unpo 雲歩 (editor). *Inga monogatari* 因果物語. [Kyoto]: [Chōjiya Kurōemon 丁子屋九郎右衛門], n.d. Katakana version. Private collection, Suzuran Bunko, Cambridge, U.K. No shelf mark.

——. *Inga monogatari* 因果物語. N.p.: publisher unknown, n.d. Katakana version. Diplomatic transcription in vol. 4 of *Kanazōshi shūsei*, edited by Asakura Haruhiko, 287–368. Tokyo: Tōkyōdō Shuppan, 1983.

Takai Ranzan 高井蘭山 (editor), Nakamura Tsunetoshi 中村経年 (additions), and Kikukawa Eizan 菊川英山 (illustrator). *Edo daisetsuyō kaidai-gura* 江戸大節用海内蔵. Nagoya: Eirakuya Tōshirō 永楽屋東四郎 et al., 1863. Private collection, Suzuran Bunko, Cambridge, U.K. No shelf mark.

Tengu no dairi てんぐのだいり. [Edo]: Matsue 松会, 1659. National Diet Library, Tokyo. Shelf mark: り34.

Tō Mitsunaka 藤允中. *Shorei tōyō shū* 諸礼当用集. Kyoto: Zeniya Shichirobee 錢屋七郎兵衛 et al., 1765. Private collection, Suzuran Bunko, Cambridge, U.K. No shelf mark.

Umezu no chōja monogatari 梅津長者物語. Medieval period. Diplomatic transcriptions of three manuscripts in vol. 2 of *Muromachi jidai monogatari taisei*, edited by Yokoyama Shigeru and Matsumoto Ryūshin, 558–84. Tokyo: Kadokawa Shoten, 1974.

Usugumo monogatari 薄雲物語. Also known as *Usugumo koi monogatari* 薄雲恋物語. Kyoto: Mizuta Jinzaemon 水田甚左衛門, 1659. Photographic reproduction in vol. 14 of *Kinsei bungaku shiryō ruijū Kanazōshi hen*, edited by Kinsei Bungaku Shoshi Kenkyūkai, 295–358. Tokyo: Benseisha, 1974.

Usuyuki monogatari 薄雪物語. [Kyoto]: Nakano Dōya 中野道也, 1632. Critical edition in *Urami no suke, Usuyuki monogatari*, edited by Kikuchi Shin'ichi, 37–75. Osaka: Izumi Shoin, 1994.

Usuyuki monogatari 薄雪物語. [Kyoto]: publisher unknown, 1636. National Diet Library, Tokyo. Shelf mark: WB2-3.

Usuyuki monogatari 薄雪物語. [Kyoto]: Yamamoto Kyūzaemon 山本九左衛門, 1664. National Diet Library, Tokyo. Shelf mark: 857-95.

Usuyuki monogatari 薄雪物語. Tokyo: Izumoji Manjirō 出雲寺万次郎, 1895. Private collection, Suzuran Bunko, Cambridge, U.K. No shelf mark.

Utai no hisho 謡之秘書. [Edo]: Matsue Ichirobee 松会市郎兵衛, 1652. Kōzan Bunko, Nogami Memorial Noh Theatre Research Institute of Hōsei University, Tokyo. Microfilm copy, National Institute of Japanese Literature, Tachikawa. Microfilm number: 238-154-5.

Waka shokumotsu honzō 和歌食物本草. Also known as *Uta honzō* 歌本草. Kyoto: Yasuda Jūbee 安田十兵衛, 1642. Waseda University Library, Tokyo. Shelf mark: ニ01 02797.

Waka shokumotsu honzō 和歌食物本草. Also known as *Uta honzō* 歌本草. N.p.: publisher unknown, 1630. National Diet Library, Tokyo. Shelf mark: 特1-788.

Yakushi tsūya monogatari 薬師通夜物語. [Kyoto]: publisher unknown, [1643]. Waseda University Library, Tokyo. Shelf mark: へ 13 01699.

Yamamoto Taijun 山本泰順. *Rakuyō meisho shū* 洛陽名所集. [Kyoto]: Hanji Nihee no Jō 板司仁兵衛尉, 1658. National Institute of Japanese Literature, Tachikawa. Shelf mark: 99-55-1~12.

Yamaoka Genrin 山岡元隣. *Tagami no ue* 他我身の上. Kyoto: Akitaya Heizaemon 秋田屋平左衛門, 1657. Diplomatic transcription in vol. 48 of *Kanazōshi shūsei*, edited by Hanada Fujio, Iriguchi Atsushi, Nakajima Jirō, Yasuhara Makoto, and Laura Moretti, 1–94. Tokyo: Tōkyōdō Shuppan, 2012.

Yamashina Tokio 山科言緒, comp. *Waka dairin gushō* 和歌題林愚抄. N.p.: publisher unknown, n.d. Hirosaki City Public Library, Hirosaki. Microfilm copy, National Institute of Japanese Literature, Tachikawa. Microfilm number: 272-129-7.

Yokobue takiguchi no sōshi よこぶえたきぐちのさうし. [Kyoto]: Yamada Ichirobee 山田市郎兵衛, 1658. National Diet Library, Tokyo. Shelf mark: ヘ42.

Yorozu kikigaki hiden 万聞書秘伝. Kyoto: Nishimura Matazaemon 西村又左衛門, 1652. Tokyo University Library, Tokyo. Digital version, National Institute of Japanese Literature, Tachikawa. Shelf mark: DIG-TOKY-162.

Yorozu kikigaki hiden 万聞書秘伝. N.p.: publisher unknown, 1651. Waseda University Library, Tokyo. Shelf mark: 文庫31 E0886.

Yoshida Ippō 吉田一保. *Wakan gunsho yōran* 和漢軍書要覧. Osaka: Kichimonjiya Ichibee 吉文字屋市兵衛; Edo: Kichimonjiya Jirobee 吉文字屋次郎兵衛, 1770. National Diet Library, Tokyo. Shelf mark: 856-62.

Yūsōan 幽双庵. *Inu Hyakunin isshu* 犬百人一首. N.p. [Kyoto?]: publisher unknown, 1669. Facsimile in *Inu Hyakunin isshu*, edited by Kisho Fukusei Kai. Tokyo: Yoneyamadō, 1919.

Zeraku monogatari 是楽物語. Kyoto: Yamamori Rokubee 山森六兵衛, n.d. Critical edition in *Kanazōshi shū*, edited by Watanabe Morikuni and Watanabe Kenji, 193–270. Shin Nihon koten bungaku taikei 74. Tokyo: Iwanami Shoten, 1991.

Zoku chomonjū 続著聞集. Later edition of *Jigabachi monogatari*. Kyoto: Tanakaya Jisuke 田中屋治助, n.d. National Diet Library, Tokyo. Shelf mark: 237-34.

Zoku Kashōki 続可笑記. Later edition of *Ukiyo monogatari*. Osaka: Kichimonjiya Ichibee 吉文字屋市兵衛 and Kichimonjiya Genjūrō 吉文字屋源十郎; Edo: Kichimonjiya Jirobee 吉文字屋治郎兵衛, n.d. Private collection, Suzuran Bunko, Cambridge, U.K. No shelf mark.

Secondary Sources

Abbott, H. Porter. *The Cambridge Introduction to Narrative*. 2nd ed. Cambridge: Cambridge University Press, 2008.

Adam, Jean-Michel. *Les textes: Types et prototypes*. 4th ed. Paris: Colin, 2017. Kindle.

Adams, Thomas R., and Nicolas Barker. "A New Model for the Study of the Book." In *A Potencie of Life: Books in Society*, edited by Nicolas Barker, 5–43. London: British Library, 2001.

Akahane Manabu and Matsuura Kōhei, eds. *Ihon Musashi abumi to kenkyū*. Mikan kokubun shiryō 4-ki 7-satsu. Toyohashi: Mikan Kokubun Shiryō Kankōkai, 1977.

Andries, Lise, and Geneviève Bollème. *La bibliothèque bleue: Littérature de colportage*. Paris: Laffont, 2003.

Andries, L., G. Bollème, B. Bricout, P. Burke, P. Carile, M. Di Nardi, G. Dotoli, D. Gallingani, R. Muchembled, J.-P. Oddos, and V. Pompejano. *La "Bibliothèque bleue" nel Seicento; o, Della letteratura per il popolo*. Bari: Adriatica; Paris: Nizet, 1981.

Araki, James T. *The Ballad-Drama of Medieval Japan*. Berkeley: University of California Press, 1964.

Armstrong, Nancy. "The Rise of the Domestic Woman." In *The Ideology of Conduct: Essays in Literature and the History of Sexuality*, edited by Nancy Armstrong and Leonard Tennenhouse, 96–141. Routledge Revivals. London: Routledge, 2014.

Armstrong, Nancy, and Leonard Tennenhouse. "The Literature of Conduct, the Conduct of Literature, and the Politics of Desire: An Introduction." In *The Ideology of Conduct: Essays in Literature and the History of Sexuality*, edited by Nancy Armstrong and Leonard Tennenhouse, 1–24. Routledge Revivals. London: Routledge, 2014.
Asakura Haruhiko, ed. *Chōjakyō*. Koten bunko 82. Tokyo: Koten Bunko, 1954.
Asano Shūgō. *Hishikawa Moronobu to ukiyo-e no reimei*. Tokyo: Tōkyō Daigaku Shuppankai, 2008.
Ashton, John. *Chapbooks of the Eighteenth Century*. London: Skoob Books, 1992. First published by Chatto and Windus in 1882.
Atherton, David. "Making Money Talk: Economic and Literary Form in the Fiction of Ihara Saikaku." Paper presented at the Association for Asian Studies Conference, Chicago, Ill., March 28, 2015.
———. "Sōzōteki hakai: Chūsei to kinsei no kakehashi toshite no *Musashi abumi*." In vol. 4 of *Nihon bungaku no tenbō o hiraku*, edited by Komine Kazuaki, 38–43. Tokyo: Kasama Shoin, 2017.
Atkins, E. Taylor. *A History of Popular Culture in Japan: From the Seventeenth Century to the Present*. London: Bloomsbury, 2017.
———. "Popular Culture." In *A Companion to Japanese History*, edited by William Tsutsui, 460–76. Malden, Mass.: Blackwell Publishing, 2007.
Baetens, Jan, and Hugo Frey. *The Graphic Novel: An Introduction*. Cambridge: Cambridge University Press, 2015.
Bagni, Paolo. *Genere*. Florence: La nuova Italia, 1997.
Bannet, Eve Tavor. *Eighteenth-Century Manners of Reading: Print Culture and Popular Instruction in the Anglophone Atlantic World*. Cambridge: Cambridge University Press, 2017.
———. *Empire of Letters: Letter Manuals and Transatlantic Correspondence, 1680–1820*. Cambridge: Cambridge University Press, 2005.
Barber, Daniel Lewis. "Tales of the Floating World: The *Ukiyo monogatari* of Asai Ryōi." Master's thesis, Ohio State University, 1984.
Barthes, Roland. *The Pleasure of the Text*. Translated by Richard Miller. New York: Hill and Wang, 1975.
Bawarshi, Anis S., and Mary Jo Reiff. *Genre: An Introduction to History, Theory, Research, and Pedagogy*. West Lafayette, Ind.: Parlor Press and the WAC Clearinghouse, 2010.
Beebee, Thomas O. *The Ideology of Genre: A Comparative Study of Generic Instability*. University Park: Pennsylvania State University Press, 1994.
Bendix, Regina. "Reflections on Earthquake Narratives." *Western Folklore* 49, no. 4 (October 1990): 331–47.
Benedict, Barbara M. *Curiosity: A Cultural History of Early Modern Inquiry*. Chicago: University of Chicago Press, 2001.
Bennett, H. S. *English Books and Readers, 1558 to 1603: Being a Study in the History of the Book Trade in the Reign of Elizabeth I*. Cambridge: Cambridge University Press, 1965.
Berger, Arthur Asa. *Popular Culture Genres: Theories and Texts*. Foundations of Popular Culture 2. Newbury Park, Calif.: Sage Publications, 1992.
Berlyne, Daniel E. "Curiosity and Exploration." *Science* 153 (July 1966): 25–33.
Berry, Mary Elizabeth. *Japan in Print: Information and Nation in the Early Modern Period*. Berkeley: University of California Press, 2006.
Blayney, Peter W. M. "The Alleged Popularity of Playbooks." *Shakespeare Quarterly* 56, no. 1 (Spring 2005): 33–50.
Bond, Erik. "Historicising the 'New Normal': London's Great Fire and Genres of Urban Destruction." *Restoration* 31, no. 2 (Fall 2007): 43–64.

Bourdieu, Pierre. "The Forms of Capital." In *Handbook of Theory and Research for the Sociology of Education*, edited by John G. Richardson, 241–58. Westport, Conn.: Greenwood Press, 1986.
———. *The Rules of Art: Genesis and Structure of the Literary Field.* Translated by Susan Emanuel. Cambridge: Polity Press, 1996.
Bowring, Richard. *In Search of the Way: Thought and Religion in Early-Modern Japan, 1582–1860.* Oxford: Oxford University Press, 2017.
Bray, Francesca, Vera Dorofeeva-Lichtmann, and Georges Métailié, eds. *Graphics and Text in the Production of Technical Knowledge in China: The Warp and the Weft.* Sinica Leidensia 79. Leiden: Brill, 2007.
Bresler, Laurence. "The Origins of Popular Travel and Travel Literature in Japan." PhD diss., Columbia University, 1975.
Bright, Philippa. "Anglo-Latin Collections of the *Gesta Romanorum* and Their Role in the Cure of Souls." In *What Nature Does Not Teach: Didactic Literature in the Medieval and Early-Modern Periods*, edited by Juanita Feros Ruys, 401–24. Turnhout, Belg.: Brepols, 2008.
Brokaw, Cynthia J. *Commerce in Culture: The Sibao Book Trade in the Qing and Republican Periods.* Harvard East Asian Monographs 280. Cambridge, Mass.: Harvard University Asia Center, 2007.
Brokaw, Cynthia J., and Kai-wing Chow, eds. *Printing and Book Culture in Late Imperial China.* Berkeley: University of California Press, 2005.
Brooks, Jeffrey. *When Russia Learned to Read: Literacy and Popular Literature, 1861–1917.* Studies in Russian Literature and Theory. Evanston, Ill.: Northwestern University Press, 2003.
Bryson, Anna. *From Courtesy to Civility: Changing Codes of Conduct in Early Modern England.* Oxford: Oxford University Press, 2004.
Bugno, Maria. "Shunpon: Intertextuality, Humour, and Sexual Education in Early-Modern Japan." PhD diss., University of Cambridge, 2019.
Burke, Peter. "A Civil Tongue: Language and Politeness in Early Modern Europe." In *Civil Histories: Essays Presented to Sir Keith Thomas*, edited by Peter Burke, Brian Harrison, and Paul Slack, 31–48. Oxford: Oxford University Press, 2000.
———. *The Fortunes of the* Courtier: *European Reception of Castiglione's* Cortegiano. Cambridge: Polity Press, 1995.
———. *Languages and Communities in Early Modern Europe.* Cambridge: Cambridge University Press, 2004.
———. *Popular Culture in Early Modern Europe.* 3rd ed. London: Routledge, 2017. First published in 1978.
———. *Social History of Knowledge: From the* Encyclopédie *to Wikipedia.* Cambridge: Polity Press, 2012.
———. *Social History of Knowledge: From Gutenberg to Diderot.* Cambridge: Polity Press, 2000.
Burke, Peter, Brian Harrison, and Paul Slack, eds. *Civil Histories: Essays Presented to Sir Keith Thomas.* Oxford: Oxford University Press, 2000.
Carrión, Jorge. *Bookshops.* Translated by Peter Bush. London: MacLehose Press, 2016.
Caruth, Cathy. *Unclaimed Experience: Trauma, Narrative, and History.* Baltimore: Johns Hopkins University Press. 2016.
Chance, Linda H. "Constructing the Classic: *Tsurezuregusa* in Tokugawa Readings." *Journal of the American Oriental Society* 117, no. 1 (January–March 1997): 39–56.
———. *Formless in Form: Kenkō,* Tsurezuregusa, *and the Rhetoric of Japanese Fragmentary Prose.* Stanford, Calif.: Stanford University Press, 1997.

Chartier, Roger. "Introduction: An Ordinary Kind of Writing." In *Correspondence: Models of Letter Writing from the Middle Ages to the Nineteenth Century*, edited by Roger Chartier, Alain Boureau, and Cécile Dauphin, translated by Christopher Woodall, 1–23. Cambridge: Polity Press, 1997.

———. "Libraries Without Walls." In "Future Libraries." Special issue, *Representations* 42 (Spring 1993): 38–52.

———. *The Order of Books: Readers, Authors, and Libraries in Europe Between the Fourteenth and the Eighteenth Centuries*. Translated by Lydia G. Cochrane. Stanford, Calif.: Stanford University Press, 1994.

———. "*Secrétaires* for the People? Model Letters of the *Ancien Régime*." In *Correspondence: Models of Letter Writing from the Middle Ages to the Nineteenth Century*, edited by Roger Chartier, Alain Boureau, and Cécile Dauphin, translated by Christopher Woodall, 59–112. Cambridge: Polity Press, 1997.

Chartier, Roger, and Hans-Jürgen Lüsebrink, eds. *Colportage et lecture populaire: Imprimés de large circulation en Europe, XVIe–XIXe siècles*. Actes du colloque des 21–24 avril 1991, Wolfenbüttel. Paris: IMEC, 1996.

Chia, Lucille. *Printing for Profit: The Commercial Publishers of Jianyang, Fujian (11th–17th Centuries)*. Harvard-Yenching Institute Monograph Series 56. Cambridge, Mass.: Harvard University Asia Center for the Harvard-Yenching Institute, 2002.

Chia, Lucille, and Hilde De Weerdt, eds. *Knowledge and Text Production in an Age of Print: China, 900–1400*. Sinica Leidensia 100. Leiden: Brill, 2011.

Childs, Margaret H. "*Chigo Monogatari*: Love Stories or Buddhist Sermons?" *Monumenta Nipponica* 35, no. 2 (Summer 1980): 127–51.

Cho, Hwisang. "The Epistolary Brush: Letter Writing and Power in Chosŏn Korea." *Journal of Asian Studies* 75, no. 4 (November 2016): 1055–81.

Clements, Rebekah. *A Cultural History of Translation in Early Modern Japan*. Cambridge: Cambridge University Press, 2015.

Cohen, Margaret. *The Sentimental Education of the Novel*. Princeton, N.J.: Princeton University Press, 1999.

Corbett, Rebecca. *Cultivating Femininity: Women and Tea Culture in Edo and Meiji Japan*. Honolulu: University of Hawai'i Press, 2018.

Cormack, Bradin, and Carla Mazzio. *Book Use, Book Theory: 1500–1700*. Chicago: University of Chicago Library, 2005.

Corns, Thomas N. *A History of Seventeenth-Century English Literature*. Chichester: Wiley-Blackwell, 2014.

Cowan, Edward J., and Mike Paterson. *Folk in Print: Scotland's Chapbook Heritage, 1750–1850*. Edinburgh: John Donald / Birlinn, 2007.

Daly, Nicholas. "The Volcanic Disaster Narrative: From Pleasure Garden to Canvas, Page, and Stage." *Victorian Studies* 53, no. 2 (Winter 2011): 255–85.

Darnton, Robert. *The Case for Books: Past, Present, and Future*. New York: Public Affairs, 2009.

Davis, Julie Nelson. *Partners in Print: Artistic Collaboration and the Ukiyo-e Market*. Honolulu: University of Hawai'i Press, 2015.

Dawkins, Richard. *The Selfish Gene*. 30th anniversary ed. Oxford: Oxford University Press, 2006. First published in 1976.

Defoe, Daniel. *The Complete English Tradesman*. London 1726, Edinburgh 1839. Project Gutenberg, 2004. http://www.gutenberg.org/files/14444/14444-h/14444-h.htm.

Denecke, Wiebke, and Kano Kimiko, eds. *Nihon bungaku shi*, vol. 2. Tokyo: Bensei Shuppan, 2017.

Dimmock, Matthew, and Andrew Hadfield, eds. *Literature and Popular Culture in Early Modern England*. London: Ashgate Publishing, 2009.
Dimock, Wai Chee. "Introduction: Genres as Fields of Knowledge." *PMLA* 122, no. 5 (October 2007): 1377–88.
Doi, Risako. "Beyond *The Greater Learning for Women*: Instructional Texts (*Joshiyō ōrai*) and Norms for Women in Early Modern Japan." Master's thesis, University of Colorado Boulder, 2011.
Dore, Ronald P. *Education in Tokugawa Japan*. London: Routledge and Kegan Paul, 1965.
Dotoli, Giovanni. *Letteratura per il popolo in Francia (1600–1750): Proposte di letture della "Bibliothèque bleue."* Biblioteca della ricera 4. Fasano: Schena, 1991.
Dowd, Garin, Lesley Stevenson, and Jeremy Strong, eds. *Genre Matters: Essays in Theory and Criticism*. Bristol: Intellect, 2006.
Dubrow, Heather. *Genre*. London: Methuen, 1982.
Duff, David, ed. *Modern Genre Theory*. Longman Critical Readers. London: Routledge, 2000.
Eco, Umberto. *On Literature*. Translated by Martin McLaughlin. London: Vintage Books, 2006.
Elias, Norbert. *The Civilizing Process*. Edited by Eric Dunning, Johan Goudsblom, and Stephen Mennell. Translated by Edmund Jephcott. Rev. ed. Oxford: Blackwell Publishing, 2000. First published in German as *Über den Prozeß der Zivilisation*, 1939.
Elisonas, J. S. A. "Fables and Imitations: Kirishitan Literature in the Forest of Simple Letters." *Bulletin of Portuguese-Japanese Studies* 4 (2002): 9–36.
Emmerich, Michael. "Picture Books: From Akahon to Kibyōshi and Gōkan." In *The Cambridge History of Japanese Literature*, edited by Haruo Shirane and Tomi Suzuki, with David Lurie, 510–22. Cambridge: Cambridge University Press, 2016.
——. *The Tale of Genji: Translation, Canonization, and World Literature*. New York: Columbia University Press, 2013.
Emoto Hiroshi. "Asai Ryōi: Ryōi no kankai to songisaku josetsu." In "Kinsei bungaku (sanbun) ni miru ningenzō." Special issue, *Kokubungaku kaishaku to kanshō* 66, no. 9 (September 2001): 49–55.
——. *Kinsei zenki shōsetsu no kenkyū*. Kinsei bungaku kenkyū sōsho 12. Tokyo: Wakakusa Shobō, 2000.
Eubanks. Charlotte. "Illustrating the Mind: 'Faulty Memory' *Setsuwa* and the Decorative Sutras of Late Classical and Early Medieval Japan." In "Vernacular Buddhism and Medieval Japanese Literature," edited by R. Keller Kimbrough and Hank Glassman. Special issue, *Japanese Journal of Religious Studies* 36, no. 2 (2009): 209–30.
Farris, William Wayne. *Daily Life and Demographics in Ancient Japan*. Michigan Monograph Series in Japanese Studies 63. Ann Arbor: Center for Japanese Studies, University of Michigan, 2009.
Fessler, Susanna. "Scraps of Wisdom: Ihara Saikaku's *Yorozu no fumihōgu*." *Journal of the Association of Teachers of Japanese* 31, no. 2 (October 1997): 52–72.
Fiévé, Nicolas. "Kyoto's Famous Places: Collective Memory and 'Monuments' in the Tokugawa Period." In *Japanese Capitals in Historical Perspective: Place, Power and Memory in Kyoto, Edo and Tokyo*, edited by Nicolas Fiévé and Paul Waley, 153–71. London: RoutledgeCurzon, 2003.
Ford, Wyn. "The Problem of Literacy in Early Modern England." *History* 78, no. 252 (February 1993): 22–37.
Fowler, Alastair. *Kinds of Literature: An Introduction to the Theory of Genres and Modes*. Oxford: Clarendon Press, 1982.

Francks, Penelope. *The Japanese Consumer: An Alternative Economic History of Modern Japan*. Cambridge: Cambridge University Press, 2009.
Fróis, Luís. *Tratado das contradições e diferenças de costumes entre a Europa e o Japão*. Macau: Instituto Português do Oriente, 2001.
Frow, John. *Genre*. The New Critical Idiom. London: Routledge, 2005.
Fujishima Hidetaka. "Mōshigo tan kōseijō no mondai ten: Otogizōshi o chūshin to shite." *Chūsei bungaku* 16 (May 1971): 18–22.
———. "Mōshigo tan no keisei." *Kanazawa Kōgyō Daigaku kenkyū kiyō* 2 (April 1972): 59–71.
Fukasawa Akio. *Saitō Chikamori (Nyoraishi) denki shiryō*. Tokorozawa: Kinsei Shoki Bungei Kenkyūkai, 2010.
Fukasawa Akio and Kikuchi Shin'ichi, eds. *Kanazōshi kenkyū bunken mokuroku*. Osaka: Izumi Shoin, 2004.
———. *Kanazōshi kenkyū sōsho*. 8 vols. Tokyo: Kuresu Shuppan, 2006.
Futaki Ken'ichi. *Chūsei buke girei no kenkyū*. Tokyo: Yoshikawa Kōbunkan, 1985.
Gallagher, Catherine. "Historical Scholarship." In *Introduction to Scholarship in Modern Languages and Literatures*, edited by David G. Nicholls, 171–93. 3rd ed. New York: Modern Language Association of America, 2007.
Gallagher, Catherine, and Stephen Greenblatt. *Practicing New Historicism*. Chicago: University of Chicago Press, 2000.
Genette, Gérard, et al. *Théorie des genres*. Paris: Editions du Seuil, 1986.
Ginzburg, Carlo. *The Cheese and the Worms: The Cosmos of a Sixteenth-Century Miller*. Translated by John and Anne Tedeschi. Baltimore: Johns Hopkins University Press, 2013. First published in Italian as *Il formaggio e i vermi: Il cosmo di un mugnaio del '500*, 1976.
Glaisyer, Natasha, and Sara Pennell, eds. *Didactic Literature in England, 1500–1800: Expertise Constructed*. Aldershot, Hants., U.K.: Ashgate Publishing, 2003.
Glasse, Hannah. *The Art of Cookery Made Plain and Easy*. N.p.: printed for the author, 1747. British Library, London. Shelf mark: 1485 pp18.
Goodwin, Jonathan, and John Holbo, eds. *Reading Graphs, Maps, Trees: Responses to Franco Moretti*. Anderson, S.C.: Parlor Press, 2011.
Gramlich-Oka, Bettina. Review of *Traditionen idealisierter Weiblichkeit: Die "Kostbare Sammlung von Vorbildern weiblicher Weisheit" (Joyō chie kagami takaraori) als Paradebeispiel edozeitlicher Frauenbildung*, by Stephan Köhn. *Monumenta Nipponica* 65, no. 1 (Spring 2010): 217–21.
Greenblatt, Stephen. *Shakespearean Negotiations: The Circulation of Social Energy in Renaissance England*. Oxford: Clarendon Press, 2001.
———. "What Is the History of Literature?" *Critical Inquiry* 23, no. 3 (Spring 1997): 460–81.
Gundry, David J. *Parody, Irony and Ideology in the Fiction of Ihara Saikaku*. Brill's Japanese Studies Library 58. Leiden: Brill, 2017.
Hackel, Heidi Brayman. "Popular Literacy and Society." In *Cheap Print in Britain and Ireland to 1660*, edited by Joad Raymond, 88–100. The Oxford History of Popular Print Culture, vol. 1. Oxford: Oxford University Press, 2011.
Hammond, Meghan Marie, and Sue J. Kim, eds. *Rethinking Empathy through Literature*. Routledge Interdisciplinary Perspectives on Literature. New York: Routledge, 2014.
Hanada Fujio. "Chikusai azuma kudari kō." *Ōtsuma Joshi Daigaku kiyō* 23 (March 1991): 43–55.
Harada Nobuo. *Edo no ryōri shi: ryōribon to ryōri bunka*. Tokyo: Chūō Kōronsha, 1989.
Harvey, William. *Scottish Chapbook Literature*. Paisley, U.K.: Alexander Gardner, 1903.
Hashiguchi Kōnosuke. *Wahon nyūmon: Sennen ikiru shomotsu no sekai*. Tokyo: Heibonsha, 2005.

———. *Zoku wahon nyūmon: Edo no hon'ya to hon zukuri*. Tokyo: Heibonsha, 2007.
Hayami, Akira. "Introduction: The Emergence of 'Economic Society.'" In *Emergence of Economic Society in Japan, 1600–1859: Early Modern*, edited by Akira Hayami, Osamu Saitō, and Ronald P. Toby, 1–35. Vol. 1 of *The Economic History of Japan: 1600–1990*. Oxford: Oxford University Press, 2004.
Hayek, Matthias, and Annick Horiuchi, eds. *Listen, Copy, Read: Popular Learning in Early Modern Japan*. Brill's Japanese Studies Library 46. Leiden: Brill, 2014.
He, Yuming. *Home and the World: Editing the "Glorious Ming" in Woodblock-Printed Books of the Sixteenth and Seventeenth Centuries*. Harvard-Yenching Institute Monograph Series 82. Cambridge, Mass.: Harvard University Asia Center, 2013.
Hernadi, Paul. *Beyond Genre: New Directions in Literary Classification*. Ithaca, N.Y.: Cornell University Press, 1972.
Higuchi Motomi. "Ogasawara ke oyobi Ogasawara ryū." In *Dai shorei shū: Ogasawara ryūrei hōdensho*, edited by Shimada Isao and Higuchi Motomi, 207–23. Tōyō bunko 562. Tokyo: Heibonsha 1993.
Hirsch, Eric Donald. *Cultural Literacy: What Every American Needs to Know*. New York: Vintage Books, 1988.
Hōjō Hideo. *Kaitei zōho Asai Ryōi*. Kasama sōsho 26. Tokyo: Kasama Shoin, 1972.
———. *Shinshū Asai Ryōi*. Kasama sensho 11. Tokyo: Kasama Shoin, 1974.
Horide, Ichiro. *The Mercantile Ethical Tradition in Edo Period Japan: A Comparative Analysis with Bushido*. Singapore: Springer, 2019.
Horiuchi, Annick. *Japanese Mathematics in the Edo Period (1600–1868): A Study of the Works of Seki Takakazu (?–1708) and Takebe Katahiro (1664–1739)*. Translated by Silke Wimmer-Zagier. Science Networks. Historical Studies 16. Basel: Birkhäuser, 2010.
———. "The *Jinkōki* Phenomenon: The Story of a Longstanding Calculation Manual in Tokugawa Japan." In *Listen, Copy, Read: Popular Learning in Early Modern Japan*, edited by Matthias Hayek and Annick Horiuchi, 253–87. Brill's Japanese Studies Library 46. Leiden: Brill, 2014.
Horton, H. Mack, trans. *Laughs to Banish Sleep*. Hollywood, Calif.: Highmoonoon, 2001.
Howell, David L. *Geographies of Identity in Nineteenth-Century Japan*. Berkeley: University of California Press, 2005.
Hunter, J. Paul. *Before Novels: The Cultural Contexts of Eighteenth-Century English Fiction*. New York: Norton, 1990.
Hur, Nam-lin. *Death and Social Order in Tokugawa Japan: Buddhism, Anti-Christianity, and the Danka System*. Harvard East Asian Monographs 282. Cambridge, Mass.: Harvard University Asia Center, 2007.
Ichiko Teiji. *Chūsei shōsetsu no kenkyū*. Tokyo: Tōkyō Daigaku Shuppankai, 1955.
———. "Nakagawa Kiun." In "Kinsei bungaku (sanbun) ni miru ningenzō." Special issue, *Kokubungaku kaishaku to kanshō* 66, no. 9 (September 2001): 42–48.
———. "Nakagawa Kiun." In "Kinsei shōsetsu no sakusha-tachi." Special issue, *Kokubungaku kaishaku to kanshō* 59, no. 8 (August 1994): 20–24.
Iizuka Yōko, Kokubun Kyōko, and Yoshii Motoko. "*Yorozu kikigaki hiden* ni tsuite no kenkyū." *Tōkyō Kasei Gakuin Daigaku kiyō* 16 (October 1976): 23–106.
Ikegami, Eiko. *Bonds of Civility: Aesthetic Networks and the Political Origins of Japanese Culture*. Cambridge: Cambridge University Press, 2005.
Infantes, Victor. "La prosa de ficción renacentista: Entre los géneros literarios y el género editorial." In *Actas del X Congreso de la Asociación Internacional de Hispanistas*, 467–74. Barcelona: PPU, 1992.
Inoue Tadashi. *Kaibara Ekiken*. Jinbutsu sōsho. Tokyo: Yoshikawa Kōbunkan, 1989.

Inoue Takaaki. *Kinsei shorin hanmoto sōran: Kaitei zōho*. Nihon shoshigaku taikei 76. Musashimurayama: Seishōdō Shoten, 1998.
Inoue Yasushi. *Kinsei kankō gunsho ron: Kyōkun, goraku, kōshō*. Tokyo: Kasama Shoin, 2014.
Ishikawa Ken. *Terakoya: Shomin kyōiku kikan*. Nihon rekishi shinsho. Tokyo: Shibundō, 1960.
Ishikawa Matsutarō. *Ōraimono no seiritsu to tenkai*. Tokyo: Yūshōdō Shuppan, 1988.
Ishikawa Tōru. "Asai Ryōi hitsu Nara ehon emaki no sonzai." *Chūsei bungaku* 47 (June 2002): 87–96.
———. "Asai Ryōi jihitsu shiryō o megutte." *Kinsei bungei* 76 (July 2002): 1–13.
———. "Isome Tsuna no ōraimono." *Geibun kenkyū* 95 (2008): 170–76.
Ivanova, Gergana. *Unbinding The Pillow Book: The Many Lives of a Japanese Classic*. New York: Columbia University Press, 2018.
Iwata Jun'ichi. *Honchō nanshoku kō—Nanshoku bunken shoshi*. Tokyo: Hara Shobō, 2002.
Johnson, Jeffrey. "The Carnivalesque in Saikaku's Oeuvre." In *Bakhtinian Theory in Japanese Studies*, edited by Jeffrey Johnson, 19–51. Lewiston, N.Y.: Mellen Press, 2001.
———. "Novelness in Comical Edo Fiction: A Carnivalesque Reading of Ihara Saikaku's *Kōshoku ichidai otoko*." PhD diss., University of Washington, 1994.
Johnson, Samuel. *The Rambler*, vol. 2. London, 1794.
Jones, Sumie, and Adam L. Kern, with Kenji Watanabe, eds. *A Kamigata Anthology: Literature from Japan's Metropolitan Centers, 1600–1750*. Honolulu: University of Hawai'i Press, 2020.
Kashiwazaki Junko. "Matsue Sanshirō." *Gengo bunka* 32 (December 1995): 133–39.
———. "Matsue Sanshirō sono ni." *Gengo bunka* 45 (December 2008): 3–16.
———. "Urokogataya." *Gengo bunka* 47 (December 2010): 61–74.
———, ed. *Zōho Shōkaiban shomoku*. Nihon shoshigaku taikei 96. Tachikawa: Seishōdō Shoten, 2009.
Katsumata Motoi. *Oya kōkō no Edo bunka*. Tokyo: Kasama Shoin, 2017.
Kawaguchi Hiroshi. "Economic Thought Concerning Freedom and Control." In *Economic Thought in Early Modern Japan*, edited by Bettina Gramlich-Oka and Gregory Smits, 47–66. Monies, Markets, and Finance in East Asia, 1600–1900, vol. 1. Leiden: Brill, 2010.
Kaya, Noriko. "The Aesthetic Characteristics of *Kana* Seen in *Chirashi-gaki*." In *Buchstaben der Welt—Welt der Buchstaben*, edited by Martin Roussel and Ryōsuke Ōhashi, 139–59. Morphomata 12. Munich: Fink, 2014.
Keene, Donald. *World Within Walls: Japanese Literature of the Pre-modern Era, 1600–1867*. New York: Columbia University Press, 1999.
Keiō Gijuku Daigaku Fuzoku Kenkyūjo Shidō Bunko, ed. *Edo jidai shorin shuppan shojaku mokuroku shūsei*. 4 vols. Tokyo: Inoue Shobō, 1962–1964.
Kelly, Gary. "General Editor's Introduction." In *Cheap Print in Britain and Ireland to 1660*, edited by Joad Raymond. The Oxford History of Popular Print Culture, vol. 1. Oxford: Oxford University Press, 2011.
Kern, Adam. "Envisioning the Classics: The *Tale of the Heike* in Edo-Period Comic Books." In *Lovable Losers: The Heike in Action and Memory*, edited by Mikael S. Adolphson and Anne Commons, 206–66. Honolulu: University of Hawai'i Press, 2015.
Kidd, Celeste, and Benjamin Y. Hayden. "The Psychology and Neuroscience of Curiosity." *Neuron* 88, no. 3 (November 2015): 449–60.
Kikuchi Isao. *Kinsei no kikin*. Tokyo: Yoshikawa Kōbunkan, 1997.
Kim Hŭnggyu. *Understanding Korean Literature*. Translated by Robert J. Fouser. New York: Routledge, 2016.

Kim Hŭnggyu and Peter H. Lee. "Chosŏn Fiction in Korean." In *A History of Korean Literature*, edited by Peter H. Lee, 273–87. Cambridge: Cambridge University Press, 2003.

Kimbrough, R. Keller. "Bloody Hell! Reading Boys' Books in Seventeenth-Century Japan." *Asian Ethnology* 74, no. 1 (2015): 111–39.

———. "Late Medieval Popular Fiction and Narrated Genres: Otogizōshi, kōwakamai, sekkyō, and ko-jōruri." In *The Cambridge History of Japanese Literature*, edited by Haruo Shirane and Tomi Suzuki, with David Lurie, 355–69. Cambridge: Cambridge University Press, 2015.

———, trans. "Translation: The Twenty-Four Filial Exemplars." *Japan Review*, no. 34 (2019): 69–94.

———, trans. *Wondrous Brutal Fictions: Eight Buddhist Tales from the Early Japanese Puppet Theater*. New York: Columbia University Press, 2015.

Kimbrough, R. Keller, and Hank Glassman, eds. "Vernacular Buddhism and Medieval Japanese Literature." Special issue, *Japanese Journal of Religious Studies* 36, no. 2 (2009).

Kimura Yaeko, Uda Toshihiko, and Koike Masatane, eds. *Kusazōshi shū*. Shin Nihon koten bungaku taikei 83. Tokyo: Iwanami Shoten, 1997.

Kinsei Bungaku Shoshi Kenkyūkai, ed. *Kinsei bungaku shiryō ruijū Kanazōshi hen*, vols. 30 and 31. Tokyo: Benseisha, 1978.

Kinski, Michael. "Basic Japanese Etiquette Rules and Their Popularization: Four Edo-Period Texts, Transcribed, Translated, and Annotated." *Japonica Humboldtiana* 5 (2001): 63–123.

Kira Sueo and Kashiwazaki Junko. "Shōkaiban mokuroku ko (1)." *Nihon kosho tsūshin* 62, no. 7 (July 1997): 24–26.

———. "Shōkaiban mokuroku ko (2)." *Nihon kosho tsūshin* 62, no. 8 (August 1997): 24–25.

———. "Shōkaiban mokuroku ko (kan)." *Nihon kosho tsūshin* 62, no. 9 (September 1997): 24–25.

———. "Shōkaiban mokuroku ko (hoi)." *Nihon kosho tsūshin* 63, no. 3 (March 1998): 27.

Kitō Hiroshi. *Jinkō kara yomu Nihon no rekishi*. Tokyo: Kōdansha, 2000.

Kobayashi Akio. *Chappu bukku no sekai: Kindai Igirisu shomin to renkabon*. Tokyo: Kōdansha, 2007.

Köhn, Stephan. "Ansei kenmonshi—Kanagaki Robuns Bericht über das große Ansei-Erdbeben 1855." In *Referate des 10. deutschsprachigen Japanologentags vom 9. bis 12. Oktober 1996 in München*, edited by Ulrich Apel, Jossi Holzapfel, and Peter Pörtner, 291–300. Munich: Iudicium 1997.

———. "Berichte über Gesehenes und Gehörtes aus der Ansei-Zeit" (Ansei kemmonshi): *Kanagaki Robuns (1829–1894) Bericht über das große Ansei-Erdbeben 1855 als Repräsentant des Genres der "Katastrophendarstellungen."* Wiesbaden: Harrassowitz, 2002.

———. "Between Fiction and Non-fiction—Documentary Literature in the Late Edo Period." In *Written Texts–Visual Texts: Woodblock-Printed Media in Early Modern Japan*, edited by Susanne Formanek and Sepp Linhart, 283–310. European Studies on Japan 3. Amsterdam: Hotei, 2005.

———. "Die genretheoretische Einordnung von Katastrophendarstellungen: Der Weg zum Konzept eines neuen Genrebegriffes." *NOAG* 167–70 (2000–2001): 105–36.

———. *Traditionen idealisierter Weiblichkeit: Die "Kostbare Sammlung von Vorbildern weiblicher Weisheit" (Joyō chie kagami takaraori) als Paradebeispiel edozeitlicher Frauenbildung*. Wiesbaden: Harrassowitz, 2008.

Koizumi Yoshinaga. *Edo no ko sodate yomihon*. Tokyo: Shōgakukan, 2007.

———. "Isome Tsuna no joyō bunshō." *Edo-ki onna kō* 8 (1997): 48–74.

———. "Kinsei no nyohitsu tehon: Onna-bumi o meguru shomondai." PhD diss., Kanazawa University, 1999.

———. "Learning to Read and Write—A Study of *Tenaraibon*." In *Listen, Copy, Read: Popular Learning in Early Modern Japan*, edited by Matthias Hayek and Annick Horiuchi, 91–138. Brill's Japanese Studies Library 46. Leiden: Brill, 2014.
———. *Nyohitsu tehon kaidai*. Nihon shoshigaku taikei 80. Musashimurayama: Seishōdō Shoten, 1998.
———. "Ōraimono kaidai." Accessed December 17, 2019. http://www.bekkoame.ne.jp/ha/a_r/B40.htm.
Konda Yōzō. *Edo no hon'ya san: Kinsei bunkashi no sokumen*. Heibonsha raiburarī 685. Tokyo: Heibonsha, 2009.
———. *Edo no kinsho*. Edo sensho 6. Tokyo: Yoshikawa Kōbunkan, 1981.
Kornicki, Peter F. *The Book in Japan: A Cultural History from the Beginnings to the Nineteenth Century*. Honolulu: University of Hawai'i Press, 2001.
———. "Hayashi Razan's Vernacular Translations and Commentaries." In *Towards a History of Translating: In Commemoration of the 40th Anniversary of the Research Centre for Translation*, edited by Lawrence Wang-chi Wong, 189–212. Hong Kong: Research Centre for Translation, 2013.
———. "Japan's Hand-Written Culture: Confessions of a Print Addict." *Japan Forum*, 31, no. 2 (2019): 272–84.
———. *Languages, Scripts, and Chinese Texts in East Asia*. Oxford: Oxford University Press, 2018.
———. "Manuscript, Not Print: Scribal Culture in the Edo Period." *Journal of Japanese Studies* 32, no. 1 (Winter 2006): 23–52.
———. "Narrative of a Catastrophe: *Musashi abumi* and the Meireki Fire." In "Narrativity and Fictionality in Edo-Period Prose Literature," edited by Laura Moretti. Special issue, *Japan Forum* 21 (2010): 347–61.
———. Review of *Novel Japan: Spaces of Nationhood in Early Meiji Narrative, 1870–88*, by John Pierre Mertz. *Journal of Japanese Studies* 31, no. 2 (Summer 2005): 502–5.
———. "Women, Education, and Literacy." In *The Female as Subject: Reading and Writing in Early Modern Japan*, edited by P. F. Kornicki, Mara Patessio, and G. G. Rowley, 7–38. Ann Arbor: Center for Japanese Studies, University of Michigan, 2010.
Kosoto Hiroshi. *Nihon kanpō tenseki jiten*. Tokyo: Taishūkan Shoten, 1999.
Koyama Kazunari. *Fuji no hitoana sōshi: Kenkyū to shiryō*. Tokyo: Bunka Shobō Hakubunsha, 1983.
Kumakura Isao. *Kan'ei bunka no kenkyū*. Tokyo: Yoshikawa Kōbunkan, 1988.
LaMarre, Thomas. *Uncovering Heian Japan: An Archaeology of Sensation and Inscription*. Durham, N.C.: Duke University Press, 2000.
Lane, Richard. "The Beginnings of the Modern Japanese Novel: *Kana-zōshi*, 1600–1682." *Harvard Journal of Asiatic Studies* 20, no. 3/4 (December 1957): 644–701.
Levine, Michael A. "Chronicling Catastrophe and Constructing Urban Deconstruction: Asai Ryōi's *Musashi Abumi* and *Kanameishi*." Master's thesis, University of Colorado Boulder, 2016.
Linhart, Sepp. "*Kawaraban*—Enjoying the News When News Was Forbidden." In *Written Texts–Visual Texts: Woodblock-Printed Media in Early Modern Japan*, edited by Susanne Formanek and Sepp Linhart, 231–50. European Studies on Japan 3. Amsterdam: Hotei, 2005.
Lipking, Lawrence. "A Trout in the Milk." In *The Uses of Literary History*, edited by Marshall Brown, 1–12. Durham, N.C.: Duke University Press, 1995.
Litman, Jordan A. "Curiosity and the Pleasures of Learning: Wanting and Liking New Information." *Cognition and Emotion* 19, no. 6 (2005): 793–814.

———. "Measuring Epistemic Curiosity and Its Diversive and Specific Components." *Journal of Personality Assessment* 80, no. 1 (February 2003): 75–86.
Lowry, Kathryn. "Duplicating the Strength of Feeling: The Circulation of *Qingshu* in the Late Ming." In *Writing and Materiality in China: Essays in Honor of Patrick Hanan*, edited by Judith T. Zeitlin, Lydia H. Liu, and Ellen Widmer, 239–72. Cambridge, Mass.: Harvard University Asia Center, 2003.
Macé, Marielle. *Le genre littéraire*. Paris: Flammarion, 2013.
Macfarlane, Robert. *The Gifts of Reading*. London: Penguin Books, 2017.
Maeda Kingorō, ed. *Chikusai monogatari shū*. Kinsei bungei shiryō 11. Tokyo: Koten Bunko, 1970.
———. "*Ukiyo monogatari* zakkō." In *Kinsei bungaku zakkō*, 64–94. Tokyo: Bensei Shuppan, 2005.
Maeshiba Ken'ichi. *Kanazōshi: Konton no shikaku*. Izumi sensho 89. Osaka: Izumi Shoin, 1995.
Mair, Victor H. "Buddhism and the Rise of the Written Vernacular in East Asia: The Making of National Languages." *Journal of Asian Studies* 53, no. 3 (August 1994): 707–51.
Mandrou, Robert. *De la culture populaire aux 17e et 18e siècles: La bibliothèque bleue de Troyes*. Paris: Imago, 1999. First published in 1964.
Manguel, Alberto. *Curiosity*. New Haven, Conn.: Yale University Press, 2015.
Marceau, Lawrence. "Behind the Scenes: Narrative and Self-Referentiality in Edo Illustrated Popular Fiction." In "Narrativity and Fictionality in Edo-Period Prose Literature," edited by Laura Moretti. Special issue, *Japan Forum* 21 (2010): 403–23.
Marcon, Federico. *The Knowledge of Nature and the Nature of Knowledge in Early Modern Japan*. Chicago: University of Chicago Press, 2015.
Marcure, Kenneth A. "The Danka System." *Monumenta Nipponica* 40, no. 1 (Spring 1985): 39–67.
Marcus, Virginia. "A Miscellany of Old Letters: Saikaku's *Yorozu no Fumihōgu*." *Monumenta Nipponica* 40, no. 3 (Autumn 1985): 257–64.
Matsubara Hidee. "*Usuyuki monogatari* hanpon kō." In *Usuyuki monogatari to otogizōshi, kanazōshi*, 48–73. Osaka: Izumi Shoin, 1997.
Matsuda Osamu. "Nakagawa Kiun: Hito to sono sakuhin." *Bungei to shisō* 22 (January 1962): 1–15.
———. "Nisshū hyōhaku yajin no shōgai." *Kokugo kokubun* 21, no. 6 (July 1952): 417–33.
McClain, James L. *A Modern History of Japan*. New York: Norton, 2002.
McConachie, Bruce. *Engaging Audiences: A Cognitive Approach to Spectating in the Theatre*. New York: Palgrave Macmillan, 2008.
McCraw, David. "Criss-Cross: Introducing Chiasmus in Old Chinese Literature." *Chinese Literature: Essays, Articles, Reviews (CLEAR)* 28 (December 2006): 67–124.
McDermott, Joseph P. *A Social History of the Chinese Book: Books and Literati Culture in Late Imperial China*. Hong Kong: Hong Kong University Press, 2006.
McFadden, George. "'Literature': A Many-Sided Process." In *What Is Literature?*, edited by Paul Hernadi, 49–61. Bloomington: Indiana University Press, 1978.
McGann, Jerome J. *The Textual Condition*. Princeton Studies in Culture/Power/History. Princeton, N.J.: Princeton University Press, 1991.
McKay, Barry. *An Introduction to Chapbooks*. Oldham, U.K.: Incline Press, 2003.
McKelway, Matthew P. *Capitalscapes: Folding Screens and Political Imagination in Late Medieval Kyoto*. Honolulu: University of Hawai`i Press, 2006.
McKenzie, D. F. *Bibliography and the Sociology of Texts*. London: British Library, 1986.

Meriton, John, and Carlo Dumontet. *Small Books for the Common Man: A Descriptive Bibliography.* London: British Library, 2010.
Minobe Shigekatsu. "Mōshiko tan no kōzō." *Kokubungaku kaishaku to kanshō* 56, no. 10 (October 1991): 135–40.
Miura Kunio. *Kanazōshi ni tsuite no kenkyū.* Tokyo: Ōfū, 1996.
Miyamoto Mataji. *Kōnoike Zen'emon.* Jinbutsu sōsho. Tokyo: Yoshikawa Kōbunkan, 1986.
——. "Kōnoike Zen'emon ke no kakun ni tsuite." *Kokumin keizai zasshi* 110, no. 3 (September 1964): 36–58.
Miyamoto, Matao. "Quantitative Aspects of Tokugawa Economy." In *Emergence of Economic Society in Japan, 1600–1859: Early Modern*, edited by Akira Hayami, Saitō Osamu, and Ronald P. Toby, 36–84. Vol. 1 of *The Economic History of Japan: 1600–1990.* Oxford: Oxford University Press, 2004.
Miyasaka Yūshō, ed. *Kana hōgo shū.* Nihon koten bungaku taikei 83. Tokyo: Iwanami Shoten, 1964.
Mizutani Futō. *Kinsei retsudentai shōsetsu shi.* 2 vols. Tokyo: Shun'yōdō, 1897.
Moretti, Franco. *Atlas of the European Novel: 1800–1900.* London: Verso, 1999.
——. *Distant Reading.* London: Verso, 2013.
——. *Graphs, Maps, Trees: Abstract Models for a Literary History.* London: Verso, 2005.
——. "The Slaughterhouse of Literature." *Modern Language Quarterly* 61, no. 1 (2000): 207–27.
Moretti, Laura. "Adaptation as a Strategy for Participation: The *Chikusai* Storyworld in Early Modern Japanese Literature." *Japanese Language and Literature* 54, no. 1 (March 2020): 67–113.
——. "Chikusai ryōji no hyōban ron: Hyōban no keitai to sono imi." *Kinsei shoki bungei* 18 (December 2001): 47–68.
——. "A Forest of Books: Seventeenth-Century Kamigata Commercial Prose." In *The Cambridge History of Japanese Literature*, edited by Haruo Shirane and Tomi Suzuki, with David Lurie, 396–402. Cambridge: Cambridge University Press, 2016.
——. "The Japanese Early-Modern Publishing Market Unveiled: A Survey of Edo-Period Booksellers' Catalogues." *East Asian Publishing and Society* 2, no. 2 (2012): 199–308.
——. "*Kanazōshi* Revisited: Reconsidering the Beginnings of Japanese Popular Literature in Print." *Monumenta Nipponica* 65, no. 2 (2010): 297–356.
——. "Kinsei shoki, zenki no sanbun bungaku ni okeru *Ise monogatari* no kakinaoshi, parodi oyobi shin tenkai." In *Ise monogatari sōzō to hen'yō*, edited by Yamamoto Tokurō and Joshua Mostow, 269–301. Osaka: Izumi Shoin, 2010.
——. "Nise monogatari: Parodi to kokkei." In *Warai to sōzō*, edited by Howard Hibbett, 43–59. Tokyo: Benseisha, 2000.
——. *Recasting the Past: An Early Modern* Tales of Ise *for Children.* Leiden: Brill, 2016.
Mori, Maryellen Toman, trans. *The Peony Lantern.* Hollywood, Calif.: Highmoonoon, 2000.
Mori Shirō. "Kinsei zenki Edo-ban no honbun hanshita." *Kyōto Furitsu Daigaku gakujutsu hōkoku jinbun* 64 (December 2012): 29–42.
Mostow, Joshua S. *Courtly Visions: The* Ise Stories *and the Politics of Cultural Appropriation.* Leiden: Brill, 2014.
——. *Pictures of the Heart: The* Hyakunin Isshu *in Word and Image.* Honolulu: University of Hawai'i Press, 1996.
——. "*The Tale of Light Snow*: Pastiche, Epistolary Fiction and Narrativity Verbal and Visual." In "Narrativity and Fictionality in Edo-Period Prose Literature," edited by Laura Moretti. Special issue, *Japan Forum* 21, no. 3 (2010): 363–87.

Mostow, Joshua S., and Royall Tyler, trans. *The Ise Stories: Ise monogatari*. Honolulu: University of Hawai'i Press, 2010.
Murray, Julia K. "Changing the Frame: Preface and Colophons in the Chinese Illustrated Book *Dijian tushuo* (The Emperor's Mirror, Illustrated and Discussed)." *East Asian Library Journal* 12, no. 1 (Spring 2006): 20–67.
———. "Didactic Illustrations in Printed Books." In *Printing and Book Culture in Late Imperial China*, edited by Cynthia J. Brokaw and Kai-wing Chow, 417–50. Berkeley: University of California Press, 2005.
Nagatomo Chiyoji. *Chōhōki no chōhōki: Seikatsu shi hyakka jiten hakkutsu*. Kyoto: Rinsen Shoten, 2005.
———. *Edo jidai no shomotsu to dokusho*. Tokyo: Tōkyōdō Shuppan, 2001.
———. *Edo jidai no tosho ryūtsū*. Bukkyō Daigaku ōryō bunka sōsho 7. Kyoto: Bukkyō Daigaku Tsūshin Kyōikubu and Shibunkaku Shuppan, 2002.
———. *Edo shomin no dokusho to manabi*. Tokyo: Benseisha, 2017.
———. *Kinsei kashihon'ya no kenkyū*. Tokyo: Tōkyōdō Shuppan, 1982.
———. *Kinsei no dokusho*. Nihon shoshigaku taikei 52. Musashimurayama: Seishōdō Shoten, 1987.
Najita, Tetsuo. *Visions of Virtue in Tokugawa Japan: The Kaitokudō Merchant Academy of Osaka*. Honolulu: University of Hawai'i Press, 1997.
Nakabe Yoshiko. *Kinsei toshi no seiritsu to kōzō*. Tokyo: Shinseisha, 1967.
Nakano Mitsutoshi. *Gesaku kenkyū*. Tokyo: Chūō Kōronsha, 1981.
———. "Gesaku no han'i: *Ichidai otoko* shushō o rei ni shite." In *Kinsei bungaku fukan*, edited by Hasegawa Tsuyoshi, 77–92. Tokyo: Kyūko Shoin, 1997. Later reprinted as "Gesaku no kakuritsu: *Ichidai otoko* shushō o rei ni shite." In *Jūhasseiki no Edo bungei: Ga to zoku no seijuku*, 123–42. Tokyo: Iwanami Shoten, 1999.
———. "Jūnanaseiki no shōsetsu shi: Watakushi no gesakuron josetsu." In "Saikaku chōhatsu suru tekisuto," edited by Kigoshi Osamu. Special issue, *Kokubungaku kaishaku to kanshō* (March 2005): 19–27.
———. "Saikaku gesakusha setsu saikō: Edo no manako to gendai no manako o motsu imi." *Bungaku*, 15, no. 1 (January 2014): 140–57.
———. *Shoshigaku dangi: Edo no hanpon*. Tokyo: Iwanami Shoten, 1995.
———. "Tōsho sakki setcho *Jūhasseiki no Edo bungei* shoka hyō ni." *Ga zoku* 8 (2000): 70–93.
Nenzi, Laura. *Excursions in Identity: Travel and the Intersection of Place, Gender, and Status in Edo Japan*. Honolulu: University of Hawai'i Press, 2008.
Neuburg, Victor E. *The Batsford Companion to Popular Literature*. London: Batsford Academic and Educational, 1982.
———. *Popular Literature: A History and Guide, from the Beginning of Printing to the Year 1897*. London: Woburn Press, 1977.
Newbold, W. Webster. "Letter Writing and Vernacular Literacy in Sixteenth-Century England." In *Letter-Writing Manuals and Instruction from Antiquity to the Present: Historical and Bibliographic Studies*, edited by Carol Poster and Linda C. Mitchell, 127–40. Studies in Rhetoric/Communication. Columbia: University of South Carolina Press, 2007.
Nikolajeva, Maria. *Reading for Learning: Cognitive Approaches to Children's Literature*. Amsterdam: Benjamins, 2014.
Nikolajeva, Maria, and Carole Scott. *How Picturebooks Work*. New York: Routledge, 2006.
Nisard, Charles. *Histoire des livres populaires; ou, De la littérature du colportage*. Paris: Dentu, 1864.
Noda Hisao. *Kinsei shoki shōsetsu ron*. Tokyo: Kasama shoin, 1978.

———. *Nihon kinsei shōsetsu shi: Kanazōshi hen*. Tokyo: Benseisha, 1986.
———. "*Ukiyo monogatari* no igi." Reprinted in vol. 2 of *Kanazōshi kenkyū sōsho*, edited by Fukasawa Akio and Kikuchi Shin'ichi, 202–13. Tokyo: Kuresu Shuppan, 2006.
Obiechina, Emmanuel. *An African Popular Literature: A Study of Onitsha Market Pamphlets*. Cambridge: Cambridge University Press, 1973.
Ogasawara Keishōsai. *Mite manabu Nihonjin no furumai: Ogasawara ryū reihō nyūmon*. Tokyo: Dankōsha, 2011.
———. *Utsukushii furumai: Ogasawara ryū reihō nyūmon*. Tokyo: Dankōsha, 2017.
Ogasawara Kiyotada. *Ogasawara ryū no densho o yomu*. Tokyo: Nihon Budōkan, 2015.
Ogasawara-ryū. Accessed December 16, 2019. http://www.ogasawara-ryu.gr.jp/.
Ogasawara-ryū reihō. Accessed December 16, 2019. https://ogasawararyu-reihou.com/.
Ogawa Takeo. "Chūsei ensho bunreishū no seiritsu: *Horikawa-in enjo awase* kara *Shika kenro shū* e." *Bulletin of the National Institute of Japanese Literature* 30 (2004): 53–94.
Ohara Tōru. "*Hinin taiheiki* no haikei to tokushitsu." *Ronkyū Nihon bungaku* 67 (December 1997): 25–34.
———. "*Hinin taiheiki* no sōsaku ishiki." *Ronkyū Nihon bungaku* 58 (May 1993): 25–34.
———. "Jiken no bungeika—kanazōshi no hōhō, *Hinin taiheiki* no baai." *Buraku mondai kenkyū kiyō* 148 (September 1999): 2–16.
Oka Masahiko. *Ikkyū banashi: Tonchi kozō no raireki*. Seminā koten o yomu 7. Tokyo: Heibonsha, 1995.
Oka Masahiko, Ichiko Natsuo, Ōhashi Tadayoshi, Okamoto Masaru, Ochiai Hiroshi, Kira Sueo, Suzuki Toshiyuki, Horikawa Takashi, Yanagisawa Masaki, and Wada Yasuyuki, eds. *Edo jidai shoki shuppan nenpyō*. Tokyo: Bensei Shuppan, 2011.
Okamoto Masaru. *Kodomo ehon no tanjō*. Shirīzu Nippon sōshi. Tokyo: Kōbundō, 1988.
———. *Shoki Kamigata kodomo ehon shū*. Kichō kotenseki sōkan 13. Tokyo: Kadokawa Shoten, 1982.
Ono Hideo. *Kawaraban monogatari: Edo jidai masu-komi no rekishi*. Fūzoku bunka sōsho 1. Tokyo: Yūzankaku Shuppan, 1960.
Ono Takeo. *Edo bukka jiten*. Tokyo: Tenbōsha, 2009.
Ooms, Herman. "Introduction to 'The Nature of Early Tokugawa Confucianism' by Kurozumi Makoto." *Journal of Japanese Studies* 20, no. 2 (Summer 1994): 331–35, 337–75.
Oring, Elliott. "Jokes and the Discourse on Disaster." *Journal of American Folklore* 100, no. 397 (July–September 1987): 276–86.
Orsini, Francesca. *Print and Pleasure: Popular Literature and Entertaining Fictions in Colonial North India*. New Delhi: Permanent Black, 2009.
Owen, Stephen. "Genres in Motion." *PMLA* 122, no. 5 (October 2007): 1389–93.
Parker, Holt N. "Toward a Definition of Popular Culture." *History and Theory* 50 (May 2011): 147–70.
Patterson, Annabelle. "Historical Scholarship." In *Introduction to Scholarship in Modern Languages and Literatures*, edited by Joseph Gibaldi, 183–200. 2nd ed. New York: Modern Language Association of America, 1992.
Pattinson, David. "The Market for Letter Collections in Seventeenth-Century China." *Chinese Literature: Essays, Articles, Reviews (CLEAR)* 28 (December 2006): 125–57.
Payne, Michael, ed. *The Greenblatt Reader*. Oxford: Blackwell Publishing, 2005.
Pegg, Barry. "Two-Dimensional Features in the History of Text Format: How Print Technology Has Preserved Linearity." In *Working with Words and Images: New Steps in an Old Dance*, edited by Nancy Allen, 164–79. Westport, Conn.: Ablex Publishing, 2002.

Petit, Nicolas. *L'éphémère, l'occasionnel et le non livre à la bibliothèque Sainte-Geneviève (XVe–XVIIIe siècles)*. Paris: Klincksieck, 1997.
Pigeot, Jacqueline. *Michiyuki-bun: Poétique de l'itinéraire dans la littérature du Japon ancien*. Paris: Collège de France, Institut des Hautes Études Japonaises, 2009.
———. "Otogizōshi ni okeru michiyukibun." *Bungaku* 43, no. 6 (June 1975): 718–27.
"Pītā Bāku [Peter Burke] no shigoto: Bunkashi kenkyū no genzai." Special issue, *Shisō* 1074 (October 2013).
Poster, Carol, and Linda C. Mitchell, eds. *Letter-Writing Manuals and Instruction from Antiquity to the Present: Historical and Bibliographic Studies*. Studies in Rhetoric/Communication. Columbia: University of South Carolina Press, 2007.
Preston, Cathy L., and Michael J. Preston, eds. *The Other Print Tradition: Essays on Chapbooks, Broadsides, and Related Ephemera*. New Perspectives in Folklore. New York: Garland Publishing, 1995.
Putzar, Edward, trans. "*Chikusai Monogatari*: A Partial Translation." *Monumenta Nipponica* 16, no. 1/2 (April–July 1960): 161–95.
———. "*Inu Makura*: The Dog Pillow." *Harvard Journal of Asiatic Studies* 28 (1968): 98–113.
Rambelli, Fabio. "The Mystery of Wealth and the Role of Divinities: The Economy in Pre-Modern Japanese Fiction and Practice." In "Buddhism and Business: South and East Asian Perspectives." Special issue, *Hualin International Journal of Buddhist Studies* 2, no. 2 (2019): 163–201.
Rath, Eric C. *Food and Fantasy in Early Modern Japan*. Berkeley: University of California Press, 2010.
Raymond, Joad, ed. *Cheap Print in Britain and Ireland to 1660*. The Oxford History of Popular Print Culture, vol. 1. Oxford: Oxford University Press, 2011.
———. "Introduction: The Origins of Popular Print Culture." In *Cheap Print in Britain and Ireland to 1660*, edited by Joad Raymond, 1–14. The Oxford History of Popular Print Culture, vol. 1. Oxford: Oxford University Press, 2011.
Reider, Noriko T. "The Emergence of *Kaidan-shū*: The Collection of Tales of the Strange and Mysterious in the Edo Period." *Asian Folklore Studies* 60, no. 1 (2001): 79–99.
Reeser, Todd W., and Steven D. Spalding. "Reading Literature/Culture: A Translation of 'Reading as a Cultural Practice.'" In "Resources in Stylistics and Literary Analysis." Special issue, *Style* 36, no. 4 (Winter 2002): 659–75.
Richardson, Malcolm. "The *Ars dictaminis*, the Formulary, and Medieval Epistolary Practice." In *Letter-Writing Manuals and Instruction from Antiquity to the Present: Historical and Bibliographic Studies*, edited by Carol Poster and Linda C. Mitchell, 52–66. Studies in Rhetoric/Communication. Columbia: University of South Carolina Press, 2007.
Ritter, Nikolaus, and Gabriele Hilpert Ritter, eds. *Sanze Aishō Makura: Ein horoskopisches "Kopfkissenbuch der dreifachen Seelenverwandtschaft" aus dem 17. Jahrhundert mit Holzschnitten von Moronobu Hishikawa*. Translated by Terasaki Akiko and Gabriele Hilpert Ritter. Berlin: Edition BBW, 1982.
Robson, Mark. *Stephen Greenblatt*. London: Routledge, 2008.
Rohr, Christian. "Writing a Catastrophe: Describing and Constructing Disaster Perception in Narrative Sources from the Late Middle Ages." *Historical Social Research/Historische Sozialforschung* 32, no. 3 (121) (2007): 88–102.
Rosenblatt, Louise M. *The Reader, the Text, the Poem: The Transactional Theory of the Literary Work*. Carbondale: Southern Illinois University Press, 1978.
Rubinger, Richard. *Popular Literacy in Early Modern Japan*. Honolulu: University of Hawai'i Press, 2007.
Ruch, Barbara. "Origins of *The Companion Library*: An Anthology of Medieval Japanese Stories." *Journal of Asian Studies* 30, no. 3 (May 1971): 593–610.

Rucinski, Jack, trans. "A Japanese Burlesque: *Nise Monogatari*." *Monumenta Nipponica* 30, no. 1 (Spring 1975): 1–18.
Rutten, Gijsbert, and Marijke van der Wal. "Functions of Epistolary Formulae in Dutch Letters from the Seventeenth and Eighteenth Centuries." *Journal of Historical Pragmatics* 13 (January 2012): 173–201.
Rüttermann, Markus [Ryuttāman Marukusu]. "Nihon chūsei no kesōbun sahō ni tsuite: Ensho bunrei o jiku ni." In *Nihon bunka no kaishaku: Roshia to Nihon kara no shiten*, edited by James C. Baxter, 165–83. Kyoto: Kokusai Nihon Bunka Kenkyū Sentā, 2009.
———. "'So That We Can Study Letter-Writing': The Concept of Epistolary Etiquette in Premodern Japan." *Japan Review* 18 (January 2006): 57–128.
———. "What Does 'Literature of Correspondence' Mean? An Examination of the Japanese Genre Term *ōraimono* and Its History." In *Listen, Copy, Read: Popular Learning in Early Modern Japan*, edited by Matthias Hayek and Annick Horiuchi, 139–60. Brill's Japanese Studies Library 46. Leiden: Brill, 2014.
Ruys, Juanita Feros, ed. *What Nature Does Not Teach: Didactic Literature in the Medieval and Early-Modern Periods*. Turnhout, Belg.: Brepols, 2008.
Ryan, Marie-Laure. "The Modes of Narrativity and Their Visual Metaphors." *Style* 26, no. 3 (Fall 1992): 368–87.
———. "Narrativity and Its Modes as Culture-Transcending Analytical Categories." In "Narrativity and Fictionality in Edo-Period Prose Literature," edited by Laura Moretti. Special issue, *Japan Forum* 21, no. 3 (2010): 307–23.
———. "Toward a Definition of Narrative." In *The Cambridge Companion to Narrative*, edited by David Herman, 22–35. Cambridge: Cambridge University Press, 2007.
Sado Emi. "Nōson shakai ni okeru Genroku bunka no juyō keitai." *Tachibana shigaku* 14 (1999): 26–50.
Saitō Seiji. "Edo jidai no toshi jinkō." *Chiiki kaihatsu* 9 (September 1984): 48–63.
Sakai, Tadao. "Confucianism and Popular Educational Works." In *Self and Society in Ming Thought*, edited by Wm. Theodore de Bary, 331–66. New York: Columbia University Press, 1970.
Sakakibara Satoru. "Sumiyoshi Gukei hitsu *Tohi zu* kaidai." *Kobijutsu* 88 (October 1988): 48–75.
Sakamoto Kenzō. *"Wakeru" koto "wakaru" koto*. Tokyo: Kōdansha, 1982.
Salter, Elizabeth. *Popular Reading in English, c. 1400–1600*. Manchester: Manchester University Press, 2012.
Sanders, Eve Rachele, and Margaret W. Ferguson, eds. "Literacies in Early Modern England." Special issue, *Critical Survey* 14, no. 1 (2002).
Sano Daisuke. *Kō no kenkyū: Kōkyō chūshaku to kōkō tan to no bunseki*. Tokyo: Kenbun Shuppan, 2016.
Sargent, G. W. *The Japanese Family Storehouse; or, The Millionaires Gospel Modernized*. Cambridge: Cambridge University Press, 1969.
Sasano Ken. *Kinsei kayō shū*. Koten zensho. Tokyo: Asahi Shinbunsha, 1956.
Sawada, Janine Anderson. *Confucian Values and Popular Zen: Sekimon Shingaku in Eighteenth-Century Japan*. Honolulu: University of Hawai'i Press, 1993.
Schank, Roger C. *Tell Me a Story: Narrative and Intelligence*. Evanston, Ill.: Northwestern University Press, 2000.
Scott, Anne M. "'For lewed men y vndyr toke on englyssh tonge to make this boke': *Handlyng Synne* and English Didactic Writing for the Laity." In *What Nature Does Not Teach: Didactic Literature in the Medieval and Early-Modern Periods*, edited by Juanita Feros Ruys, 377–400. Turnhout, Belg.: Brepols, 2008.

Segal, Ethan. "Money and the State: Medieval Precursors of the Early Modern Economy." In *Economic Thought in Early Modern Japan*, edited by Bettina Gramlich-Oka and Gregory Smits, 21–45. Monies, Markets, and Finance in East Asia, 1600–1900, vol. 1. Leiden: Brill, 2010.
Selden, Kyoko. "Introduction to the *Hinin Taiheiki: The Paupers' Chronicle of Peace*." *Asia-Pacific Journal: Japan Focus* 14, no. 4 (July 2016): 1–8.
Shibata Jun. "Kinsei zenki ni okeru gakumon no rekishiteki ichi." *Nihonshi kenkyū* 247 (March 1983): 112–36.
Shibayama Hajime. *Edo nanshoku kō: Wakashu hen*. Tokyo: Hihyōsha, 1993.
Shimazaki, Satoko. *Edo Kabuki in Transition: From the Worlds of the Samurai to the Vengeful Female Ghost*. New York: Columbia University Press, 2016.
Shimosaka Noriko. "Ejima Tamenobu no shikan jijō to sono haikei." *Ehime kokubun to kyōiku* 36 (December 2003): 14–23.
———. "Hyōhaku yajin Ejima Tamenobu no bungaku to shikan." In "Samurai no bungaku." Special issue, *Edo bungaku* 31 (November 2004): 55–76.
Shimura Kunihiro and Suwa Haruo, eds. *Nihon setsuwa densetsu dai jiten*. Tokyo: Bensei Shuppan, 2000.
Shirakura Kazuyoshi. "Asai Ryōi: Nazo ni tsutsumareta jinbutsu." In "Kinsei shōsetsu no sakusha-tachi." Special issue, *Kokubungaku kaishaku to kanshō* 59, no. 8 (August 1994): 25–29.
Shirakura Yoshihiko. *Eiri shunga ehon mokuroku*. Tokyo: Heibonsha, 2007.
Shirane, Haruo, ed. *Early Modern Japanese Literature: An Anthology, 1600–1900*. New York: Columbia University Press, 2002.
———. *Traces of Dreams: Landscape, Cultural Memory, and the Poetry of Basho*. Stanford, Calif.: Stanford University Press, 1998.
Shively, Donald H. "Popular Culture." In vol. 4 of *The Cambridge History of Japan*, edited by John Whitney Hall and James L. McClain, 706–70. Cambridge: Cambridge University Press, 1991.
———. "Sumptuary Regulation and Status in Early Tokugawa Japan." *Harvard Journal of Asiatic Studies* 25 (1964–1965): 123–64.
Singer, Margot, and Nicole Walker, eds. *Bending Genre: Essays on Creative Nonfiction*. London: Bloomsbury, 2013.
Slater, Candace. *Stories on a String: The Brazilian Literatura de Cordel*. Berkeley: University of California Press, 1982.
Slingerland, Edward, trans. *Confucius, Analects: With Selections from Traditional Commentaries*. Indianapolis: Hackett Publishing, 2003.
Spufford, Margaret. *Small Books and Pleasant Histories: Popular Fiction and Its Readership in Seventeenth-Century England*. Cambridge: Cambridge University Press, 1985.
Stallybrass, Peter. "Books and Scrolls: Navigating the Bible." In *Books and Readers in Early Modern England*, edited by Jennifer Andersen and Elizabeth Sauer, 42–79. Philadelphia: University of Pennsylvania Press, 2002.
Suzuki Jun and Ellis Tinios. *Understanding Japanese Woodblock-Printed Illustrated Books: A Short Introduction to Their History, Bibliography and Format*. Leiden: Brill, 2013.
Suzuki Ken'ichi. *Jūnanaseiki no bungaku*. Vol. 1 of *Kinsei bungaku shi kenkyū*. Tokyo: Perikansha, 2017.
———. "Jūnanaseiki no bungaku: Sono tayōsei." In "Jūnanaseiki no bungaku." Special issue, *Bungaku* 11, no. 3 (May–June 2010): 32–43.
Suzuki Kōzō. *Edo no keizai seisaku to gendai—Edo ga wakareba ima ga mieru*. Tokyo: Bijinesu Kyōiku Shuppansha, 1993.

Suzuki Sadami. *The Concept of "Literature" in Japan*. Translated by Royall Tyler. Kyoto: International Research Center for Japanese Studies, 2006.
Suzuki Toshiyuki. *Ezōshiya: Edo no ukiyoe shoppu*. Tokyo: Heibonsha, 2010.
——. "Gakumon to bungei to seikatsu to: Kinsei kōki minshū no gakugei sekai." In "Bungaku to gakumon no aida: Kinsei bungaku." Special issue, *Bungaku* 8, no. 3 (May–June 2007): 39–50.
Suzuki Tōzō. *Nazo no kenkyū*. Tokyo: Tōkyōdō, 1963.
Tachibana Yutaka. *Shokan sahō no kenkyū*. Tokyo: Kazama Shobō, 1977.
——. *Shokan sahō no kenkyū zokuhen*. Tokyo: Kazama Shobō, 1985.
Tachikawa Kiyoshi. *Kinsei kaii shōsetsu kenkyū*. Tokyo: Kasama Shoin, 1979.
Tajihi Ikuo. *Keihan bungei shiryō*. 5 vols. Nihon shoshigaku taikei 89 (1–5). Tachikawa: Seishōdō Shoten, 2004–2007.
——. "Keihan hon'ya tentō zu (hoi)." *Ōsaka furitsu toshokan kiyō* 29 (March 1993): 1–16.
Takahashi Satoshi. *Edo no kyōiku ryoku*. Tokyo: Chikuma Shobō, 2007.
Takeda Yuki. "Hayashi Razan no *Daigaku* kaishaku o megutte." *Nihon kanbungaku kenkyū* 11 (March 2016): 27–54.
Tamamuro Taijō. *Sōshiki bukkyō*. Tokyo: Daihōrinkaku, 1963.
Tanabe Masako, ed. *Shoki ukiyoe ten: Han no chikara, fude no chikara*. Chiba: Chiba City Museum of Art, 2016.
Taniwaki Masachika, Sugimoto Yoshinobu, and Sugimoto Kazuhiro, eds. *Saikaku to ukiyozōshi kenkyū*, vol. 3. Tokyo: Kasama Shoin, 2010.
Teruoka Yasutaka. *Nihon no shokan tai shōsetsu*. Tokyo: Echigoya Shoten, 1943.
Thomas, Keith. *In Pursuit of Civility: Manners and Civilization in Early Modern England*. New Haven, Conn.: Yale University Press, 2018.
——. "The Meaning of Literacy in Early Modern England." In *The Written Word: Literacy in Transition*, edited by Gerd Baumann, 97–131. Wolfson College Lectures 1985. Oxford: Clarendon Press, 1986.
Thompson, Roger. *Samuel Pepys' Penny Merriments*. London: Constable, 1976.
Tōkyō Kasei Gakuin Seikatsu Bunka Hakubutsukan, ed. *Ōei Bunko ni miru Edo jidai no Ryōri monogatari: Dai nijūkai tokubetsuten mokuroku*. Tokyo: Hōbunsha, 2000.
Tsunoda Ichirō. "Michiyukibun kenkyū joron 1." *Hiroshima Joshi Daigaku kiyō* 1 (March 1966): 1–10.
——. "Michiyukibun kenkyū joron 2." *Hiroshima Joshi Daigaku kiyō* 5 (March 1970): 1–13.
Tsutsumi Kunihiko. "Suzuki Shōsan: Hatamoto bushi kara shūkyōsha e." In "Kinsei shōsetsu no sakusha-tachi." Special issue, *Kokubungaku kaishaku to kanshō* 59, no. 8 (August 1994): 14–19.
Tucker, Mary Evelyn. *Moral and Spiritual Cultivation in Japanese Neo-Confucianism: The Life and Thought of Kaibara Ekken, 1630–1740*. SUNY Series in Philosophy. Albany: State University of New York Press, 1989.
Tyler, Royall. *Selected Writings of Suzuki Shōsan*. Cornell University East Asia Papers 13. Ithaca, N.Y.: Cornell University Press, 1977.
Umihara Tetsu. *Kinsei no gakkō to kyōiku*. Kyoto: Shibunkaku Shuppan, 1988.
Vaporis, Constantine Nomikos. *Breaking Barriers: Travel and the State in Early Modern Japan*. Harvard East Asian Monographs 163. Cambridge, Mass.: Harvard University Press, 1995.
Vivero, Roderigo de. *An Account of Japan, 1609*. Translated by Caroline Stone. Edinburgh: Hardinge Simpole, 2015.
Watanabe Kenji. "Tsujihara Genpo ryakufu." In *Kinsei daimyō bungeiken kenkyū*, 22–27. Tokyo: Yagi Shoten, 1997.

Watanabe Morikuni. "*Usuyuki monogatari* to otogi-zōshi." *Kinsei bungei* 22 (1973): 1–12.
Watt, Tessa. *Cheap Print and Popular Piety, 1550–1640*. Cambridge Studies in Early Modern British History. Cambridge: Cambridge University Press, 1991.
Weisenfeld, Gennifer. *Imaging Disaster: Tokyo and the Visual Culture of Japan's Great Earthquake of 1923*. Berkeley: University of California Press, 2012.
Wise, Elizabeth, ed. *Debrett's Handbook: British Style, Correct Form, Modern Manners*. London: Debrett's, 2014. Kindle.
Wolf, Maryanne. *Proust and the Squid: The Story of Science and the Reading Brain*. New York: HarperCollins, 2007.
Woolf, Daniel. "News, History, and the Construction of the Present in Early Modern England." In *The Politics of Information in Early Modern Europe*, edited by Brendan Dooley and Sabrina A. Baron, 80–117. Routledge Studies in Cultural History 1. London: Routledge, 2011.
Yada Tsutomu. *Kokugo moji, hyōki shi no kenkyū*. Tokyo: Kyūko Shoin, 2012.
Yamamoto Hideki. *Edo jidai santo shuppanhō taigai: Bungakushi shuppanshi no tame ni*. Okayama: Okayama Daigaku Bungakubu, 2010.
Yamazaki Yoemon. *Jinkōki no kenkyū*. Tokyo: Morikita Shuppan, 2012.
Yasuda Bunkichi. "Suzuki Shōsan: Mikawa bushi no seishin to zen." In "Kinsei bungaku (sanbun) ni miru ningenzō." Special issue, *Kokubungaku kaishaku to kanshō* 66, no. 9 (September 2001): 35–41.
Yasuhara Makoto. "Bāku korekushon shozō den Miyagawa Chōshun *Usugumo monogatari* shōkai: Shoshi to honkoku." *Rikkyō Daigaku Nihon bungaku*, no. 105 (December 2010): 46–52.
Yokota Fuyuhiko. *Nihon kinsei shomotsu bunka shi no kenkyū*. Tokyo: Iwanami Shoten, 2018.
Yonemoto, Marcia. *Mapping Early Modern Japan: Space, Place, and Culture in the Tokugawa Period, 1603–1868*. Berkeley: University of California Press, 2003.
——. "The Perils of the 'Unpolished Jewel': Defining Women's Roles in Household Management in Early Modern Japan." *U.S.-Japan Women's Journal*, no. 39 (2010): 38–62.
——. *The Problem of Women in Early Modern Japan*. Oakland: University of California Press, 2016.
Yoshida, Kogorō. *Tanrokubon: Rare Books of Seventeenth-Century Japan*. Translated by Mark A. Harbison. Tokyo: Kodansha International, 1984.
Yoshida Kōichi, ed. *Inga monogatari*. Koten bunko 182, 185. Tokyo: Koten Bunko, 1962.
Yoshida Masayuki. *Bunruigaku kara no shuppatsu: Puraton kara konpyūta e*. Tokyo: Chūō Kōronsha, 1993.
Yoshie Hisaya. *Saikaku: Hitogokoro no bungaku*. Osaka: Izumi Shoin, 1988.
——. *Saikaku: Shisō to sakuhin*. Tokyo: Musashino Shoin, 2004.
Yuasa Yoshiko. *Kinsei shōsetsu no kenkyū: Keimōteki bungei no tenkai*. Tokyo: Kyūko Shoin, 2017.
Zaid, Gabriel. *So Many Books*. Translated by Natasha Wimmer. London: Sort of Books, 2004.
Zolbrod, Leon M. "*Kusazōshi*: Chapbooks of Japan." *Transactions of the Asiatic Society of Japan*, 3rd ser., no. 10 (August 1968): 116–47.
Zorzi, Marino. *La vita nei libri: Edizioni illustrate a stampa del quattro e cinquecento dalla Fondazione Giorgio Cini*. Gorizia: Edizioni della Laguna, 2003.
Zukofsky, Paul. "Chirashi Gaki." Musical Observations, Inc. Accessed September 14, 2019. http://www.musicalobservations.com/pour_un_Haydn/chirashi-gaki.html.

Index

Abbott, H. Porter, 346n47
Abe no Seimei monogatari (The story of Abe no Seimei), 3
adaptations, 16, 23, 100, 169, 194, 199, 279, 289, 297, 366n93
Akira Hayami, 223, 352n6
Akitaya Heizaemon, 2–3, 20, 325n37
Akitaya Seibee, 118, 328n88
allusions, intertextual: and *Chikusai*, 279, 281, 287, 298; in disaster narratives, 234; in *Jigabachi monogatari*, 261; in love letters, 195, 202, 203–4, 206, 207, 212, 215, 219; visual (intervisuality), 154, 156–57, 162–63
alternate attendance (*sankin kōtai*), 274
Amida kyō wadan shō (The Amida Sutra explained and commented upon), 122
Analects (Confucius), 104, 111, 325n37, 325n42
animals: attachment to, 107; and karma, 258, 260–61, 264; as pets, 102, 106
Annaisha (The guide), 3
Anrakuan Sakuden, 3
Aoki Rosui, 330n116
Ariwara no Narihira, 210–11, 287
artisans, 28, 31, 66, 67, 108, 228, 307n4

Art of Cookery Made Plain and Easy, The (Glasse), 159, 160
Asai Ryōi, 3, 78, 83–84, 272, 318n59, 319n63, 329n102, 349n83. See also *Kanameishi*; *Kanninki*; *Kyō suzume*; *Musashi abumi*; *Ukiyo monogatari*
Asano Shūgō, 170
Asayama Irin'an, 65
Atherton, David, 229, 233, 251–52, 355n43, 359n106, 360n132
Atkins, E. Taylor, 263
aurality. *See* orality
authors, 113, 292–93; celebrity, 82, 85, 96; collective, 22, 68, 82–86, 280, 281, 319n72; and publishing genres, 84, 87, 292, 296. *See also* narrators

Bakhtin, Mikhail, 124
banmin (all people), 174, 252, 332n34, 334n61; and etiquette books, 139–40, 144, 145, 148, 149, 153
Bannet, Eve Tavor, 24, 178, 191, 257, 259, 279
Barber, Daniel Lewis, 266, 270
Barthes, Roland, 24, 255–57, 265, 286, 292, 296
Bendix, Regina, 243, 247
Berlyne, Daniel, 18

Berry, Mary Elizabeth, 18–19, 99, 137, 167–68, 175, 271
bibliothèque bleue (blue-covered paperbacks), 10, 11, 322n6
Bonds of Civility (Eiko Ikegami), 23
Book in Japan, The (Kornicki), 67
books, printed: bindings of, 71; circulation of, 43–48, 66; costs of publishing, 72, 79, 82, 94, 154, 306n88; formats of, 70, 72; learning literacy from, 50–51; publishers' modifications to, 85–86, 96, 145, 154–58, 161–64, 276–77, 280. *See also* genres, publishing; illustrations; prices; textual instability
bookshops: high-end (*mono no hon'ya, shomotsuya, shomotsu doiya*), 72–74, 74, 76, 77–78, 81, 81–82, 96, 118; in Kyoto, 2–3, 67–68; low-end (*sōshiya*), 72, 74, 77–79, 80, 81–82, 93, 96, 118, 315n21, 317n41, 318n52; overlapping between high- and low-end, 72–74, 76, 77, 78, 96; signs on, 37, 69, 71, 72; visual depictions of, 50, 69–71, 73, 81. *See also* publisher-booksellers
Bourdieu, Pierre, 14, 145
Bowring, Richard, 97, 113
Bray, Francesca, 161
Bresler, Laurence, 282, 284
Brokaw, Cynthia J., 11, 145, 316n35
Brooks, Jeffrey, 10, 11
Bryson, Anna, 135, 136, 142, 153
Buddhism: in *Chikusai*, 284; and commercial publishing, 3, 22–23, 76, 83, 97–132, 133; commodification of, 99, 113–23; vs. Confucianism, 100, 101, 106, 107–13; criticism of, 100, 111, 276, 284–85; debates on, 224–26; and disaster narratives, 248–49, 252; and etiquette for women, 150; and humor, 271; in *Jigabachi monogatari*, 259, 261, 263–64; and money, 226, 230, 353n26, 356n65; and moral instruction, 32, 123–31, 179, 294; Nichiren, 110; publishing genres for, 88, 89, 98–99; Pure Land, 110, 264; sectarianism in, 97–98, 322n3; Shingon, 76; syncretism in, 107, 108, 113, 150, 323n8, 327n81; and temple affiliation, 97, 322n1; in *Ukiyo monogatari*, 270, 273; women in, 120–21, 285; Zen, 84, 258, 264. *See also kana hōgo; kana washo*
Burke, Peter, 16, 18, 341n1

calendars, 19, 88, 89, 321n88
calligraphy: copybooks for, 80, 90, 179, 191–92, 199; in letter-writing manuals, 185–87, 189, 190, 191–92, 198–99, 202, 219; in love stories, 202, 214; manuals on, 50, 90, 179, 190, 342nn5–6; models for, 185–86; and publishing genres, 89, 90; scattered style (*chirashi-gaki*) of, 186–87, 190, 198, 199, 344nn28–29; and social status, 191–93, 219; styles of, 29, 51, 53, 78, 189; visual depictions of, 34–38, 40, 41, 42; by women, 80, 186–89, 192, 198, 344n25. *See also tenarai; terakoya*
Carrión, Jorge, 68
Caruth, Cathy, 24, 253
Castiglione, Baldassare, 144
catalogues, book-trade (*shojaku mokuroku*), 3, 17, 22, 43–48, 310n53, 315n28; on authors, 83, 84; continuity in, 297; cookbooks in, 161, 166; etiquette books in, 134, 140; *kanbun* vs. *wabun* texts in, 45–48, 89–90; organization of, 43, 86; prices in, 93–96, 321n102; publishing genres in, 68, 86–93, 179, 296, 320n77, 342n5; religious books in, 97–98, 114, 122, 124; on *Ukiyo monogatari*, 266, 278; and women, 149, 150, 186
censorship, 17, 263, 274–75, 297, 305n72, 363n35
Chance, Linda H., 86–87, 259
Chartier, Roger, 178, 208, 222, 257
Cheng, King of Chu, 227
chigo monogatari, 367n116
Chikusai, 95, 168, 169, 257, 278–91, 291, 292; and Buddhism, 284–85; and chiastic structure, 281; and collective memory, 287, 288; and didacticism, 284, 285; and humor, 283, 285, 287, 288–90; illustrations in, 280; and intertextuality, 279, 281, 287, 298; as jestbook, 288–90; and Matsuo Bashō, 288; and medicine, 288; price of, 95, 366n92; publication history of, 280–81, 366n92, 366n97; and publishing genres, 366n92; and travel,

280, 281–83, 286–87, 288, 290; and *Usuyuki* master plot, 286
Chikusai kyōka banashi (The story of Chikusai's mad poems), 280
Chikusai ryōji no hyōban (*Chikusai*: An evaluation of its medicine), 288
China: chiastic structure in, 281; in disaster narratives, 238, 250, 254; etiquette in, 137, 152; letter anthologies in, 342n6; love letters in, 346n43, 347n49; poetry of, 52, 84, 109; popular literature in, 10, 11, 298; publishing industry in, 10; religious syncretism in, 327n81
Chinese, literary. See *kanbun*
Chinese learning, 98, 137, 264, 322n4; *wabun* texts on, 100–107
chirashi-gaki (scattered writing style), 186–87, 190, 198, 199, 344nn28–29
Chōjakyō (The millionaire's doctrine), 227–29, 230, 232, 354n36
Chōjiya Kurōemon (publisher), 128, 329, 330n111
Chousi jinnang (Precious guide to social exchange), 145
Christianity, 84, 98, 322n6
civility. See etiquette
clothing, 165, 170; in etiquette manuals, 150, 153, 156–57; *hinagata* (kimono patterns) books, 156, 157, 339n133
Cohen, Margaret, 13, 305n75
colophons, 86, 93, 124, 165, 166; publishers recorded in, 4, 22, 75–76, 78, 316n30
commoners, 96, 135, 145, 147; literacy of, 25–26, 27, 31, 32, 33, 52, 66
Confucianism: and authors, 83, 84; vs. Buddhism, 100, 101, 106, 107–13; and commercial publishing, 3, 23, 97–132, 133; commodification of, 99, 100–107; and education, 48, 52; and etiquette, 137, 150, 342n7; and *gakumon*, 52, 103–4, 106, 108, 179; and illustrations, 101, 102, 316n35; and money, 224–26, 356n65; popularization of, 100, 131; in publishing genres, 88, 89, 98–99; and social status, 101–2, 102–3; syncretism in, 107, 108, 113, 150, 327n81; in *Ukiyo monogatari*, 270, 273; in vernacular texts, 32, 100–107, 226, 294

cookbooks, 90, 158–64, 298; and cultural capital, 161, 167, 176; and etiquette manuals, 160, 176; and household management, 164–67; illustrations in, 161–64; prices for, 338n111; tables of contents in, 338n119. See also *shitsukekata-sho narabi ni ryōri-sho*
copybooks (*tehon*), 49, 89, 90, 179, 311n66; for calligraphy, 80, 191–92; for love letters, 194, 195, 198, 210, 211
Corbett, Rebecca, 145
Cormack, Bradin, 205, 222
Cortegiano (Castiglione), 144
courtesan critiques, 7, 80, 91
cultural capital, 295; and cookbooks, 161, 167, 176; and etiquette manuals, 145, 148, 158, 167, 176; and narrative capital, 169
cultural literacy, 45, 117, 340n142; and etiquette manuals, 137, 144; and letter-writing manuals, 182, 207; and narrative vs. nonnarrative texts, 167–69; and national identity, 19, 168; playing with, 168–69; of women, 203
culture: and literature, 8–9, 15–17; popular, 10, 15–17, 23, 124, 132, 305n69; as text, 9
curiosity, 1, 4, 207, 259, 296, 297; and disaster narratives, 235, 245; epistemic, 18, 20, 24, 222, 306nn78–79; pleasure of, 279; purposive vs. digressive, 24, 279, 285, 291, 306n87
currency, 224, 321n95, 352n6, 352n10. See also money
cursive script (*sōsho*): in book-trade catalogues, 89; kana in, 48, 49, 60, 89, 117, 140; kanji in, 52, 53, 60, 62, 89, 192; and *tenarai*, 62, 64. See also *kaisho*

Daibutsu monogatari (Tales of the Great Buddha), 113, 327n82
Daigaku (The Great Learning), 95
Daikoku (god of wealth), 248–49, 250–51
Dai shorei shū (Great collection of etiquette; Ogasawara Sadayoshi), 334n70
Daly, Nicholas, 235
Daoism, 327n81

400 Index

Davis, Julie Nelson, 319n72
Debrett's Handbook, 144–45, 148
De civilitate morum puerilium (Erasmus), 135–36, 153
Defoe, Daniel, 355n40
dialogical format (*mondō*), 163, 325n30; in Buddhist and Confucian popular texts, 102, 107–13, 123, 132, 224, 231; in disaster narratives, 248–49; and empowerment, 102–3, 248–49; in *Jigabachi monogatari*, 262; with knowledgeable interlocutor, 65, 108; on money, 224; in *Ukiyo monogatari*, 266, 267, 271, 275
dictionaries, 88, 89, 205, 206, 217, 218
didacticism, 4, 7, 8, 9, 12, 20–21, 304n59, 316n35; in *Chikusai*, 291; in disaster narratives, 246, 250–51, 253; in English literature, 12, 329n101, 361n2; and etiquette, 135, 136, 150, 176; and *gakumon*, 51–52, 179; and humor, 14–15, 108, 111, 297; in *Jigabachi monogatari*, 259, 261, 263, 265; as *kyōkunsei*, 14; in literary histories, 7, 14, 276; mirror as genre of, 324n22; and money, 226–27, 228, 229, 353n25; in texts for women, 3, 150; and trauma, 246; in *Ukiyo monogatari*, 270, 278. *See also* knowledge: ethical; literature: didactic
Didactic Literature in England, 1500–1800, 12
Dimmock, Matthew, 16
direct speech, 130, 330n113
disaster narratives, 24, 223, 233–53, 254, 295; on behavior, 242–43, 246, 247, 249, 250, 253, 254; on catastrophic nature of events, 234, 238–44, 241, 246, 252, 254, 358n89; coping with trauma in, 235, 246–53, 254; and didacticism, 246, 250–51, 253; and *Hōjoki*, 234, 357n70; horror in, 234, 235, 244–46; humor in, 241, 242, 246, 247, 249, 253, 360n130; illustrations of, 238–40, 358n74; as news, 234, 235–37, 246, 254; redress in, 251–53; social criticism in, 250–51; sounds in, 244, 246; and storytelling, 247–49; Western, 235, 243, 244, 358n89, 360n130
documents, official, 31, 39, 62

Early Modern Japanese Literature (ed. Haruo Shirane), 270
earthquakes, 223, 233–35, 238–39, 241, 243, 243–44, 245–47, 249–50, 358n74
Eboshi ori (The fold of the *eboshi*), 203
Eco, Umberto, 2, 9, 19, 144, 190, 254
Edo: book publishers in, 45, 68, 80–81, 96; book-trade catalogues from, 44, 46; fire in, 234–36, 237, 244, 251–52; population of, 43
Edo daisetsuyō kaidai-gura (Takai Ranzan, ed., Kikukawa Eizan, illus.), 335n71
Edo kanoko (The Edo fawn), 81
education. *See gakumon*; *tenarai*
Ejima Tamenobu (Ejima Sansui), 100–107, 109, 138, 306n87, 324nn16–21; on Buddhism, 100, 106; on etiquette, 105–6, 133; on filial piety, 106; and first-person narration, 102; on funerals, 106; on *gakumon*, 103; mirror metaphor of, 101–2, 107, 113; on moderation, 104–5, 232; and neo-Confucianism, 100–101; and quotations from Chinese, 104; and readers, 102, 103–4, 107, 258; on secret traditions, 101–2. *See also Mi no kagami*; *Rihi kagami*
Elias, Norbert, 135–36, 331n17
Emoto Hiroshi, 109, 112
English literature. *See* European literature
Enomoto Otake, 33
Enomoto Yazaemon, 32–33, 49, 311n70
Erasmus, 135–36
etiquette (*sahō, shitsukekata, rei*), 133–77; and breaking secrecy, 137–49; and Confucianism, 137, 150, 342n7; and cultural capital, 145, 148, 158, 167, 176; and cultural literacy, 137, 144; Ejima Tamenobu on, 105–6, 133; in European literature, 135, 136, 142, 153, 333n35, 335n74; and food culture, 158–61; of funerals, 106; and money making, 229; and national identity, 135, 149, 152; and orality, 134, 137–39, 139, 143–44, 173; and social harmony, 135–36; and social status, 23, 134–37, 139–49, 152–54, 157–58, 176, 191, 295, 331n3, 335n71; of table manners, 134, 142–43, 152–53, 158, 335n71, 337n106; of weddings, 143,

151–52, 157, 170–73; for women, 142, 149–58, 176, 337n109, 344n26
etiquette manuals, 133–77, 297–98; in book-trade catalogues, 92, 134, 140; clothing in, 150, 153, 156–57; didacticism of, 135, 136, 137, 150, 176; how to read, 144–48; illustrations in, 145, 149, 154–58, 164, 177; and narrative capital, 170; prices of, 140, 158, 332n32, 334n68, 336nn76–77, 337n109; and publisher-booksellers, 137–49, 176, 177; readers of, 135, 139–40, 144, 153–54, 176–77; on sexuality, 142, 173–74. See also *shitsukekata-sho narabi ni ryōri-sho*
Eubanks, Charlotte, 114
European literature: didacticism in, 12, 329n101, 361n2; disaster narratives in, 235, 358n89, 360n130; etiquette in, 135–36, 142, 153, 333n35, 335n74; and Latin, 16, 98, 311n61, 330n13, 345n33; and letteracy, 178; miscellanies in, 259, 279, 363n32; and orality, 309n46, 362n11; popular, 8, 10–11, 302nn35–36, 322n2, 322n6, 355n40; and popular literacy, 308n16

famine, 223, 233–35, 238, 245–46, 248–51, 250, 251. See also disaster narratives
fiction, 1, 10; and didacticism, 7, 20, 123, 138; epistolary, 219–20, 346n43; and letter writing, 180, 193, 193–204, 207–8, 219; and literary history, 4, 5, 7, 9, 12, 19, 168, 169, 175, 270; narrative, 5, 11, 15, 168, 295–96; vs. nonfiction, 5–7, 12, 91, 126, 255, 256, 259; and publishing genres, 91. See also narrative; *setsuwa* stories; storytelling
filial piety (*kōkō*), 32, 52, 91, 95, 276, 348nn63–64; in Buddhist and Confucian texts, 98, 103–4, 106, 113, 131, 295, 324n21, 325n38; in disaster narratives, 237, 251; and etiquette, 137, 151, 152; in love stories, 200; and money, 226–27, 353n27
Five Relations, 48, 52, 66, 108, 112, 150, 163
food culture, 137, 143, 158–61, 166–69, 176; professional chefs in, 158, 161, 164, 171, 339n128
Francks, Penelope, 223

French literature, 10, 11, 13, 305n75, 322n6
Fróis, Luís, 307n14
frugality (*shimatsu, ken'yaku*), 24, 153, 221, 224, 228–33; in Buddhist and Confucian texts, 131, 295; in disaster narratives, 250–51; and *gakumon*, 51; vs. parsimony/avarice, 224, 228; and social status, 224, 228, 232–33. See also sumptuary laws
Fudanzakura (Never-ending blossoms), 4, 299n7
Fūgetsu Sōchi, 90
Fuji no hitoana sōshi (The tale of the Fuji cave), 76, 95
Fujiwara no Takamitsu, 346n43
Fukasawa Akio, 301n22, 312n83
Fukutomi sōshi (The king of farts), 353n24
Fun'ya no Yasuhide, 72
furigana (reading glosses), 57, 58, 60, 61

gakumon (advanced learning), 51–53, 312n83; big learning (*daigaku*), 52; and Confucianism, 52, 103–4, 106, 108, 179; and *kanbun*, 51–52, 53, 64; and novice readers, 64–66, 132; outside book learning, 65–66, 103, 325n38; small learning (*shōgaku*), 52, 90; and *tenarai*, 28–29, 48, 51–53, 64; and *wabun*, 51, 57, 65, 82. See also *tenarai*
Gallagher, Catherine, 8, 9
Gekō (On the way home; *Kiyomizu monogatari*), 108–9
gender: and etiquette, 142, 151, 152–53, 176; gendered translations, 186–87, 190, 207; inversion of, 180, 200–204, 219; and kanji, 49; and letter-writing manuals, 23, 180, 186–90, 219. See also women
Genji monogatari (The Tale of Genji; Murasaki Shikibu), 3, 72, 204, 215, 261, 283
Genji Yamato e kagami (The mirror of Japanese pictures of The Tale of Genji; Hishikawa Moronobu), 215
genkai (vernacular explanations), 100, 323n13
Genpei War (1180–1185), 316n33
genre hybridism, 292

genres, publishing, 17–18, 21, 68, 96, 142, 149, 253, 256; and authors, 84, 87, 292, 296; in book-trade catalogues, 86–93; for Buddhism and Confucianism, 88, 89, 98–99; for etiquette, 92, 134, 151; formulation of, 319n74; and *Jigabachi monogatari*, 259, 265; lists of, 88–89, 92; vs. modern literary genres, 22, 86–87, 292, 296, 298; porosity of, 23, 87, 113, 137, 177, 220, 222, 297; reorganization of, 91–93; and *Ukiyo monogatari*, 270, 278
Genroku taiheiki (Record of the great peace of the Genroku era; Miyako no Nishiki), 74, 76, 77, 81, 82–83, 84
Genshin, 99
gesaku (playful writings), 12–14, 15, 20, 260
Gesta Romanorum, 330n113
ghost stories, 3, 84, 130
Ginzburg, Carlo, 124
Gion monogatari (The tale of Gion), 111–12; price of, 327n74; and publishing genres, 327n74; on syncretism, 112
Giun, 128
Glaisyer, Natasha, 12, 361n2
Glasse, Hannah, 159
Godaigō, Emperor, 262
Goshūi waka shū (Collection of gleanings continued), 206
government, Tokugawa: criticism of, 262–63, 272–75, 276, 291, 361n148; currency of, 224; in disaster narratives, 251–52, 254. *See also* censorship; social criticism
Gramsci, Antonio, 17
Great Meireki Fire (Edo; 1657), 94
Greenblatt, Stephen, 1, 9
guilds, booksellers' (*hon'ya nakama*), 74, 78, 177
gunsho (publishing genre; military books and war tales), 47, 357n69; in book-trade catalogues, 46, 88, 89; and Ejima Tamenobu, 100; as historical narratives, 90, 297, 320n84; numbers of, 46, 88; ordinance on, 365n76; popularity of, 90, 139, 320n82, 332n31

Hackel, Heidi Brayman, 64
Hadfield, Andrew, 16

Ha kirishitan (Christian countered; Suzuki Shōsan), 84
Hanada Fujio, 286
hanashibon (publishing genre; jestbooks; *hanashi no hon*), 92, 340n148, 357n68, 362n9, 368n127; and *Chikusai*, 288–90, 290; and *Jigabachi monogatari*, 259–60, 265; and *Ukiyo monogatari*, 270–71, 278, 291
Hanaway, William L., 11
Hanaya (*jōruri* text), 78
Hangiya Mataemon, 317n41
Hannya kyō wadan shō (The Perfection of Wisdom Sutra explained and commented upon), 122
Hannya shingyō (Heart Sutra), 271
Han'ya Seibee, 317n41
Hanyū no monogatari (The tale of Hanyū), 202
Harada Nobuo, 159
Haruo Shirane, 270
Hashiguchi Kōnosuke, 44, 45, 72, 306n88, 314n14, 315n21, 317n43, 321n91
Hata Sōha, 106, 326n56
Hayashi Gitan, 84
Hayashi Hakusui (Izumoji Izumi no Jō), 74, 315n27
Hayashi Razan, 95, 100
Hayashi Yoshikazu, 170, 350n105
He, Yuming, 11
Heian tales, 45, 72, 74, 193–94, 195
heihō (art of war), 100. *See also gunsho*
Heike monogatari (*The Tales of Heike*), 90
Hikkaidō (Masaki Seishin), 214, 351n111
hinagata (books of kimono patterns), 156–57, 339n133
Hinin taiheiki (The paupers' chronicle of peace), 234, 357n69
hiragana, 261, 283; in Buddhist and Confucian texts, 100, 113, 114, 117; in etiquette manuals, 140; and *gakumon*, 65; *Inga monogatari* in, 123, 124–26, 127, 129, 130; in interlinear translations, 57, 60; and kanji, 49, 61, 76, 78, 79, 82, 90, 113, 123, 124–25; and literacy, 27, 29, 32, 48, 53, 60, 61, 64, 140, 294; variants of, 48, 60, 311n65. *See also wabun* (vernacular) literacy
Hirata Shisui, 120

Hishikawa Moronobu, 71, 80, 85, 170, 219, 280; and Hikkadō, 351n111. See also *Nasake no uwamori*

Hōjō Dansui, 67, 351n125

Hōjōki (*An Account of My Hut*; Kamo no Chōmei), 235, 248; and disaster narratives, 234, 357n70

Hokekyō (Lotus Sutra), 115

Hokekyō wadan shō (The Lotus Sutra explained and commented upon), 122

Hōman chōja (The millionaire full of treasures), 353nn24–26

honji mono (type of narrative structure), 91

Horikawa-in enjo awase (The collection of love letters of Horikawa-in), 193–94, 345n43

household manuals, 77, 95, 164–67, 264–65. See also *Shogaku bunshō narabi ni yorozu shitsukekata*; *Yorozu kikigaki hiden*

Howell, David L., 26, 309n47

how-to manuals, 21, 24, 222–23, 264, 305n74; and disaster narratives, 250; pleasure in, 137, 148, 164, 295; problematizing, 229, 232–33, 253. See also cookbooks; etiquette manuals; letter-writing manuals

humor, 11, 82, 85, 169, 297, 348n71; in *Chikusai*, 283, 285, 287, 288–90; and didacticism, 14–15, 108, 111, 297; in disaster narratives, 241, 242, 246, 247, 249, 253, 360n130; in *Jigabachi monogatari*, 259–61, 262, 265; and riddles, 260–61; in *Ukiyo monogatari*, 257, 270, 271, 277, 364n59. See also *hanashibon*

Hunter, Paul, 8–9

hyōbanki (critiques), 7, 80, 91

Ichimori chōja, 226, 354n29

Ichiro Horide, 356n65

Igaku nyūmon (Introduction to medicine; Li Chan), 89–90

Iguchi monogatari (Foolish tales), 227, 229–33; and *Chōjakyō*, 354n36, 355n44; and frugality, 229–30; on moderation, 232–33; price of, 354n32; and publishing genres, 354n32

Ihara Saikaku, 25, 175, 333n44, 351n125, 353n17; and cultural literacy, 19, 137, 168, 169; on economic issues, 233; epistolary fiction by, 219–20; fame of, 82–83; and literary history, 6, 7, 13–15, 19, 21. See also *Kōshoku ichidai otoko*

Ikegami, Eiko, 23, 134–35, 144, 145, 149, 150, 331n3, 331n17

Ikkadō (Setsurin), 186

Ikkyū, 271, 298

Ikkyū banashi (Stories about Ikkyū), 95

Ikkyū shina monogatari (Various tales of Ikkyū), 327n70

Ikkyū shokoku monogatari (Tales of Ikkyū from all the provinces), 168–69, 175, 340n148

Ikusa mai (Dance of the armies), 80

illustrations, 71, 79, 80, 82, 268, 269, 280, 324n23, 364n47; borrowing of, 162–64; in Buddhist and Confucian texts, 101, 102, 118–20, 122, 126, 127, 131, 316n35, 324n25, 328n88, 329n102; in cookbooks, 161–64; in disaster narratives, 238–40, 358n74; in etiquette manuals, 145–47, 149, 154, 154–58, 164, 177; in love stories, 195–98, 208–10, 213–16, 219; and popular literature, 76, 316n35

illustrators, 85, 210, 222, 280, 296

Ima Chōja monogatari (Nishizawa Ippū), 354n36

Inga monogatari (Tales of karmic causality; Suzuki Shōsan), 123–31, 132, 226; abridged version of, 330n116; attachment in, 125–30; in hiragana, 123, 124–26, 127, 129, 130; in katakana, 124–30, 226; price of, 329n102; publication history of, 123–24, 329n102; and publishing genres, 329n102

Inoue Shinkai, 100

intellectual property, 85, 177

Inu hariko (The paper-mâché dog; Asai Ryōi), 83–84

Inu Hōjōki (The bastard *Hōjōki*), 238, 245–49, 249; and *Hōjōki*, 234, 247–48; and horror, 245–46; narrator in, 248; and news, 235; price of, 357n68; and publishing genres, 357n68; relief for victims in, 251–52. See also disaster narratives

Inu Hyakunin isshu (One hundred poets, one hundred poems: A bastard version; Yūsōan), 72–74, 79, 94, 283

Inu makura (*The Dog Pillow*; *Inu makura narabi ni kyōka*; Hata Sōha), 107, 326n56
Iriguchi Atsushi, 367n114
Ise monogatari (*The Tales of Ise*), 3, 5; and *Chikusai*, 281, 283, 285–87, 286; intertextual allusions to, 195, 206, 212, 213, 241, 281, 283, 285, 287; and love letters, 204; and *Nasake no uwamori*, 212–13; and *Nishikigi*, 204, 206; translations of, 310n59; and *Usuyuki monogatari*, 195
Ishida Baigan, 356n65
Ishikawa Ken, 31
ishizuri narabi ni hitsudō sho (publishing genre; stone rubbings and calligraphy books), 46, 86, 342nn5–6
Isoda Dōya, 280

Japanese language. *See* hiragana; vernacular Japanese
jestbooks. *See* hanashibon
Jigabachi monogatari (The tale of a sand wasp), 257–65, 266, 270, 274–77; and aurality, 258, 265; and Buddhism, 259, 261, 263–64; and cognitive engagement, 264; conflicting views in, 262–63; humor in, 259–61, 262, 265; as jestbook, 259–60; and *kana hōgo*, 264; as miscellarian prose, 257, 259, 262, 263, 291; as practical manual, 264; price of, 362n9; and publishing genres, 362n9; and *Usuyuki* master plot, 261
Jing shang bao dian (Golden rules of business success), 231
Jinkōki (Inexhaustible treatise), 77, 317n38
Jinkyōron (On the mirror of human beings), 224–26, 352n16
Jitsugokyō (Teachings of the words of truth; Kūkai), 54–57, 58, 62, 64, 313n94
Jitsugokyō eshō (Kyokutei Bakin), 59
Johnson, Samuel, 306n87
Jones, Sumie, 282
jōruri texts, 72, 78, 79, 81, 96, 105, 317n41
Jubutsu monogatari (The tale of Confucianism and Buddhism), 336n77
jubutsuron (debates between Confucianism and Buddhism), 99

Kabuki, 5, 17, 91, 105, 260, 305n72
Kabuki no hana botan dōrō (Flower of Kabuki, the peony lantern ghost story; Santō Kyōden), 84
Kagekiyo (ballad-drama), 76, 77, 95
Kaibara Ekiken, 27, 28, 48–49, 51, 53, 54, 150, 311n70, 342n8
kaisho (noncursive script), 48, 52, 89, 90, 115, 138, 140, 329n102
kakekotoba (pivot words), 206, 287
Kamo no Chōmei, 234, 248
kana (syllabaries), 29, 48–49, 53, 60. *See also* hiragana; katakana
kana bussho (*kana hōgo*; publishing genre Buddhist texts in vernacular), 22, 98, 99, 111, 113, 131, 132, 133, 264, 285, 328n84, 328n88, 329n102
kana hōgo. *See kana bussho*
Kanameishi (The keystone; Asai Ryōi), 234, 235, 238–42, 245–47; and catastrophe, 238; horror in, 245; humor in, 249; illustrations of, 238–41; narrator in, 247; practical advice in, 250; price of, 357n68; and publishing genres, 357n68; and superstition, 249–50
kana mono sōshi rui (publishing genre), 364n42
kana washo (Japanese books in kana), 22, 91, 92, 98, 99, 113, 131, 132, 133, 229, 264, 278, 323n10, 323n15, 326n57, 327n74, 353n16, 354n30, 354n32, 355n51, 364n42
kanazōshi (modern genre for seventeenth-century prose literature), 5, 6, 17, 84, 268, 297, 300n12, 305n74, 320n78
kanbun (literary Chinese, Sinitic), 53, 294–95; and *gakumon*, 51–52, 64; hybrid (*sōrōbun*), 23, 60, 61–62, 64, 181, 185, 189, 190, 219, 295, 313n102; interlinear translations of, 57, 59, 60, 64, 103, 104, 115, 121, 131, 264, 275, 325n37, 326n42; prices of texts in, 94–95; reading aids for, 54–61, 62, 64, 95, 100, 103, 115, 121, 122, 325n37; *sodoku*, 54, 64, 313n92; texts in, 27, 45–48, 83, 87–90, 94–95, 114, 115, 131; vernacular reading of (*kanbun kundoku*), 54–60, 61
kanbun literacy, 48, 61; and authors, 83, 85; education in, 51–53, 54; and multiple literacies, 60; and publishers, 66, 86–90,

Index 405

96; and *wabun* literacy, 57, 60, 64, 90, 180, 190, 313n94. See also *gakumon*
Kanemochi chōhōki (The treasury of wealthy people), 224–26, 253n17. See also *Jinkyōron*; *Kingin mannōgan*
kanji (Chinese characters): cursive, 52, 53, 60, 62, 89, 192; and *gakumon*, 29, 48, 49, 52, 53, 54; and gender, 49; with hiragana, 49, 61, 76, 78, 79, 82, 90, 113, 123, 124–25; with katakana, 100, 123, 138; and literacy, 27, 32; and *tenarai*, 51, 52, 53, 64, 311n63; vernacular readings of, 54–60, 61, 64, 78
Kanninki (The chronicle of patience; Asai Ryōi), 226; filial piety in, 227; on moderation, 232; price of, 354n30; and publishing genres, 354n30
Kannon-gyō (Kannon Sutra), 115, 117, 283
Kannon-gyō hayayomi eshō (The Kannon Sutra for easy reading and with illustrations), 114–15
Kannon-gyō wadan shō (The Kannon Sutra explained and commented upon), 115–22, 123; illustrations in, 119–20, 283; and interlinear translation, 115; narrative anecdotes in, 118; price of, 328n88; and publishing genres, 328n88; and translation of sutras, 121, 122
Kannon-gyō wadan shō zue (The Kannon Sutra explained, commented upon, and illustrated; Hirata Shisui and Tsujimoto Motosada), 119, 120, 121
Kannon riyaku monogatari (Tales of the miraculous power of Kannon), 121
Kantō earthquake (1923), 358n74
Kanzeon bosatsu fumon bon (*Kannon-gyō*), 115, 117
karma, 131, 259, 264; and animals, 258, 260–61; and marriage, 175; and money, 226–27, 229, 231; and social status, 264. See also *Inga monogatari*; *Shokoku inga monogatari*
Karukuchi ōwari (Sakauchi Naoyori), 368n127
Kashiwazaki Junko, 80
Kashōki (Record that makes laughter possible; Nyoraishi), 276, 277, 278, 312n83, 325n38
Kashōki atooi (Record that makes laughter possible, a follow-up), 65–66

Kashōki hyōban (Record that makes laughter possible: An evaluation; Asai Ryōi), 276
kasho narabi ni monogatari (publishing genre; books of poetry and monogatari), 194
katakana: *Inga monogatari* in, 60, 123–30, 140, 226, 329n102; and kanbun, 61, 95, 100; with kanji, 57, 90, 100, 123, 138; and literacy, 29, 32, 49, 60, 61; *okurigana* suffixes in, 54, 56, 57; and prices, 95
Katayama Naotsugu, 97, 221
Katsuoya Rokubee, 136
Kawachiya Rihee, 75, 93
Kawachiya Yoshimasa, 25, 31–32, 33, 49, 51, 52, 65
Kawachiya Yoshimasa kyūki (Old records of Kawachiya Yoshimasa), 31–32
kawaraban (news sheets), 93, 95, 96, 321n89, 321n101; and disaster narratives, 24, 234, 236–37
Kayoi Komachi (Noh play), 204
Keene, Donald, 263, 268, 278
Keian ofuregaki (The Keian proclamation), 28
Kelly, Gary, 10
Kern, Adam L., 282
Kichimonjiya (publisher), 277
kidan (strange tales), 364n42
Kikigaki hidenshō (The commentary on the secret tradition of things heard and recorded; alternative title for *Yorozu kikigaki hiden*), 165, 339n133
Kikukawa Eizan, 335n71
Kikuya Shichirobee, 308n25
Kingin mannōgan (The almighty medication for money), 224–26, 353n17. See also *Jinkyōron*; *Kanemochi chōhōki*
Kinsei mono no hon Edo sakusha burui (Early modern books and a taxonomy of Edo authors; Kyokutei Bakin), 84
Kinsei shōsetsu shi (Noda Hisao), 6
Kinski, Michael, 138, 332n25
Kiyomizu monogatari (The tale of Kiyomizu; Asayama Irin'an), 107–13, 121, 225; Buddhism vs. Confucianism in, 108–9; as *gakumon*, 65; price of, 95, 326n57; and publishing genres, 326n57

knowledge: democratizing, 140, 143, 158, 176, 219; ethical, 14, 15, 23, 51, 66, 107, 113, 131, 133, 176, 179, 221, 296; and etiquette, 134, 138, 139, 150, 153, 170, 173, 176; vs. information, 18–19, 306n82; interpersonal, 12, 14, 23, 107, 111, 113, 134, 138, 139, 140, 143, 167, 175, 176, 177, 178, 181, 193, 218, 256, 296; and letter writing, 178, 193, 220; of limits, 104–5, 232; and money making, 228–29, 232, 233; national, 19, 99, 135, 168; and novice readers, 66, 99, 107, 124, 175, 177, 297; pleasure from, 1–2, 17, 19–20, 24, 107, 134, 167, 254, 256, 272, 295, 298, 306n87; practical, 24, 165, 221–23, 229, 250, 259, 264–65, 270, 277–78; profit from, 1–2, 4, 17, 19–21, 85–86, 107, 132, 167, 218, 254, 256, 258, 259, 295; and reading, 9, 12, 15, 107, 221–22; secret, 101, 123–24, 132, 137–49, 150, 159, 161, 164, 167, 176, 177; societal, 14, 15, 18, 23, 134, 176, 178, 218. *See also* didacticism; *gakumon*; narrative capital; reading: efferent vs. aesthetic
Kobayashi Sōemon, 165
Koizumi Yoshinaga, 54, 185–86, 190, 311n66
Kojima Tokuemon, 74
Kokon gunri mondō (Dialogues on the principles of warfare past and present: Ejima Tamenobu), 100
Kōkyō (*The Classic of Filial Piety*), 52, 95
Konda Yōzō, 25–26, 47, 75
Kōnoike Naofumi (Shinroku; Shin'emon), 33, 51
Kōnoike Shinzaemon, 33
Kōnoike Zen'emon, 33, 309n38
Korean literature, 10, 122, 298, 342n7, 344n28
Kornicki, Peter F., 53, 54, 61, 67–68, 72, 94, 122, 242, 308n24, 311n65, 315n21
kōshokubon (erotica), 81, 82, 86, 333n44. See also *kōshoku narabi ni rakuji*
Kōshoku ichidai otoko (*The Life of an Amorous Man*; Ihara Saikaku), 5, 50, 81, 95, 266
kōshoku narabi ni rakuji (publishing genre; erotica and diversions), 92, 142, 211, 333n44
Kōshoku Nishikigi (The amorous *Nishikigi*), 210

kōwakamai (texts of ballad dramas), 76, 78, 80, 89, 91, 95, 203, 316n33
Kubota Muneyasu, 186
Kubota Tsuna, 344n25
Kudari Chikusai banashi (The story of Chikusai moving east), 280. See also *Chikusai*
Kūkai, 54
Kumarajū (Kumārajīva), 111
kunten (reading marks), 54–57, 60, 62, 64, 95, 100, 103, 115. See also *kanbun*; translations, vernacular
kusazōshi (cheap picture books), 72, 74, 79, 81, 93, 96, 317n45
Kyō habutae (Kyoto silk; street directory), 74, 76, 77, 81
kyōka (mad verse), 279–85, 288–89
kyōkun-sho (*kyōkun*; educational books), 91, 98, 354n36
Kyokutei Bakin, 59, 84
Kyō suzume (The Kyoto sparrow; Asai Ryōi), 37, 39, 40–42, 78, 95
Kyoto: books printed in, 45, 47; book-trade catalogues from, 44, 46; earthquake in, 234, 238; and Edo fire, 237; population of, 43; publisher-booksellers in, 2–3, 67–68, 74–80, 82, 96; Teramachi Street in, 2, 298
Kyō warabe (Denizens of Kyoto; Nakagawa Kiun), 238, 241, 272, 283, 358n98

Lane, Richard, 4–7, 259, 265, 266, 270, 282
Latin, 16, 98, 311n61, 330n13, 345n33
letteracy, 23, 178–79, 180–90, 218, 219, 220; definition of, 178; and social status, 190–93. See also letter-writing manuals
letters: in etiquette manuals, 142; and fiction, 23, 180, 193–210, 219; and narrativity, 180, 219–20; reading aloud of, 185, 210, 350n103; and social status, 181, 190–93, 219, 345n38; of women (*nyohitsu*), 80, 190, 345n32; writing styles in, 23, 61–62, 64, 180, 181, 185, 187, 189, 190, 219, 295
letter-writing manuals, 23, 178–220, 297–98; calligraphy in, 179, 185–87, 189, 190, 191–92, 198–99, 202, 219; commentaries in, 181, 182, 185, 189–90, 192, 218; and cultural literacy, 182, 207; and erotica, 210–11;

formulas in, 63, 180–85; and gender, 180, 186–90, 219; multiple literacies in, 180, 190; and narrative capital, 180, 199, 210, 218, 219; and publisher-booksellers, 179, 218; templates in, 3, 149, 180–85, 188–90, 192, 195, 198, 198–200, 208; for women, 186–93, 207, 219

Levine, Michael A., 242, 245, 358n98

libraries, lending (*kashihon'ya*), 71, 310n58

Lipking, Lawrence, 8

literacies, multiple, 4, 16, 22, 27, 53–64, 283, 310n61; education in, 48–53; in letter-writing manuals, 180, 190; and popular reader, 66; and publishing industry, 54, 66, 67, 68. See also *kanbun* literacy; readers: expert; readers: novice; *wabun* (vernacular) literacy

literacy: benefits of, 29–30, 32; of commoners, 25–26, 27, 31–33, 66; education in, 48–53; and etiquette manuals, 153; evidence for, 31–39; and letteracy, 179, 218; of merchants, 25–26, 26, 28–29, 31–33, 66, 311n70; of peasants, 26, 28, 28–29, 31, 66; and political power, 308n27; popular, 16, 22, 27, 64, 66, 311n61, 362n11; promotion of, 28–30, 39, 66, 67; rates of, 39–48, 66; and social order, 28, 308n16; and social status, 26–29, 39, 52, 53, 66, 294; subscriptional, 26, 307n10; in visual arts, 34–38; of women, 26, 29–30, 35, 49, 66, 191, 294, 308n24. See also *kanbun* literacy; literacies, multiple; *wabun* (vernacular) literacy

literary history, 4, 8, 9, 10, 12, 14, 16, 21, 78, 79, 91, 210, 220, 255, 257, 265, 267, 291, 295, 301n24, 320n78. See also literature: democratic view of

literature: democratic view of, 8, 10, 301n30; didactic, 8, 12, 99, 123, 256, 361n2; elitist (*bungaku*), 1–7, 13, 16, 304n66, 305n77; epistemic function of, 9, 12, 14, 20, 168, 175, 180, 198, 207, 211, 220, 256, 295, 297; and literary canon, 1, 2, 4, 6, 8–10, 14, 16, 24, 180, 270; transformative, 2, 4, 9, 20, 23, 24, 101, 131, 134, 145, 148, 150, 157, 222, 223, 229, 258, 261, 295

literature, popular: emotional bonds in, 102, 103–4, 107, 117, 119, 258; illustrations and, 76, 316n35; international, 8, 10–11, 11, 298, 302nn35–37, 303nn38–39, 322n2, 322n6, 329n101, 355n40; and popular culture, 15–17; popular piety in, 98, 322n6; publisher-booksellers of, 15–16, 292–93, 297; scholarship on, 10–12; textual strategies for, 64, 82, 102, 113, 114, 115, 122, 131, 153, 205, 246, 265. See also literature: didactic

Literature and Popular Culture in Early Modern England, 16

love letters, 23, 180, 193–218, 345n43; allusions in, 195, 202–4, 206, 207, 212, 215, 219; in China, 346n43, 347n49; and fiction, 23, 193–204, 207–8, 219; in love stories, 193–200, 200–204; manuals for, 194, 195, 198–99, 219; prices of, 346n46, 347n61, 349n83; and sexuality, 210–18; and types of love, 204–10

love stories, 175, 194, 211, 258, 261, 265, 286, 291, 295, 347n60, 349n80; allusions to, 203–4; calligraphy in, 202, 213–14; empowerment of women in, 200–204; illustrations in, 195–98, 208–10, 213–16, 219; and poetry, 350n101; social status in, 203–4. See also *Usuyuki monogatari*: master plot of

Macfarlane, Robert, 2

Maeshiba Ken'ichi, 361n148

magazines, modern, 259, 265

Magowan, Helen, 345n29, 345n32

mai narabi ni sōshi (publishing genre; *kōwakamai* and booklets), 89, 90, 91, 327n70, 336n77, 346n46, 347n61, 354n36, 356n56, 356n68, 357n68, 362n9, 366n92

mairase sōrōbun, 23, 60, 62, 64, 187, 189, 190, 219, 295; in love stories, 195, 199, 203, 207

makura-e (sexually explicit pictures), 333n44

Makura no hibiki (Pillow's echoes; Katayama Naotsugu), 97, 99, 221; price of, 323n10; and publishing genres, 323n10

Makura no sōshi (*The Pillow Book*, Sei Shōnagon), 106, 326n59

Manase Gensaku, 90

Mandrou, Robert, 10
Manguel, Alberto, vii, 18
Marcon, Federico, 303n49
Marcus, Virginia, 220
Masuya Heibee, 337n109
Matsue (Shōkai; publisher), 81, 90, 166, 171, 318n49, 320n81, 339n125
Matsue Ichirobee, 80, 81, 90, 161, 162, 318n47, 335n76, 338n111, 347n71, 364n42, 364n47
Matsue Sanshirō, 80, 318n48
Matsunaga Teitoku, 84
Matsuo Bashō, 288
Mazzio, Carla, 205, 222
medical texts (publishing genre; *isho*), 88, 89–90, 166–67, 254, 340n137
meishoki. *See* travel writing
meisho zukushi (publishing genre; books on famous places), 92, 270
Mencius, 105
merchants, 49, 51, 247, 267, 307n4; and book publishing, 67; and bookshops, 69, 72, 74, 83; criticism of, 108, 275–76; in disaster narratives, 251; and etiquette manuals, 140, 145, 153, 185; literacy of, 25–26, 28–29, 31–33, 66, 311n70; as readers, 80, 81, 191; Way of, 233, 356n65; wives of, 29, 153, 191; and writing, 39, 41
michiyukibun style, 271–72, 286–87
millionaires (*chōja*), 226–27, 229, 231–32, 248, 253–54
Mi no kagami (A mirror for yourself; Ejima Tamenobu), 100–107, 278; price of, 323n15; and publishing genres, 323n15. *See also* Ejima Tamenobu
Minu kyō monogatari (Tales of the unseen capital), 111; price of, 327n70; and publishing genres, 327n70
mirror, metaphor of, 101–2, 107, 113, 131, 150, 185, 258, 272, 324n22
miscellanies, 142, 160, 180, 205, 219, 220, 257, 262, 263, 266, 270, 277, 291; in European literature, 259, 279, 363n32; and *zuihitsu*, 102, 259. *See also* Chikusai; *Jigabachi monogatari*; reading: discontinuous; *Ukiyo monogatari*; writing, discontinuous
Mitsugo yori no oboe (Recollections from the age of three; Enomoto Yazaemon), 32–33

Miyagawa Chōshun, 347n61
Miyako no Nishiki, 74, 83. *See also* authors: celebrity of
Mizushima Bokuya, 138
Mizuta Jinzaemon, 200
Mizutani Futō, 5
Mōanjō (A staff to guide the blind; Suzuki Shōsan), 113, 327n84
money, 223–33; and Buddhism, 226, 230, 353n26, 356n65; in *Chōja nidai nashi*, 231; in disaster narratives, 250; and economy, 223–24; and frugality, 24, 51, 131, 153, 221, 224, 228, 229–32, 233, 295; investment of, 228; and karma, 226–27, 229, 231; making of, 24, 223, 227–29, 253; as medicine, 229–30; and moral behavior, 226–27, 229, 353n25; praise of, 224–26; and publishers, 44–45; and social status, 232–33, 253, 352n6. *See also* currency; prices; sumptuary laws
monks, 26, 32, 54, 69, 81, 98, 237, 247, 252, 266, 267, 271, 309n47; as authors, 83, 84, 99; criticism of, 110–11, 249, 276, 284–85; dialogue with, 111–13, 224, 262, 263, 284; and learning (*gakumon*), 47; and writing, 36, 37, 70, 179
monogatari-rui (publishing genre; *monogatari*-type books), 92, 327n70, 347n61, 354n36, 355n51, 356n68, 357n68, 362n9, 366n92
mono no hon'ya. *See* bookshops
Moretti, Franco, 4, 9, 256
Morita Shōtarō, 352n16, 353n17, 368n123
Moro Chōbee, 33
mōshigo tan (literary motif), 200, 348n66
Mostow, Joshua S., 195
Mottomo no sōshi (rewriting of *Makura no sōshi*), 107, 326n56
Mudan dengji (*Botan tōki*; The peony lantern), 84
Murakami Kanbee, 68, 74, 89
Muromachi tales, 76, 78, 80, 91, 95, 195, 346n49
Murray, Julia K., 316n35
Musashi abumi (Stirrups of Musashi; Asai Ryōi), 234–38, 242–47; and catatastrophe, 238, 242; horror in, 244–45; humor in, 242–43, 249; narrator in, 247; as news, 235–37; price of,

356n68; and publishing genres, 356n68; redress in, 251–52. *See also* disaster narratives

Nagashima Hiroaki, 52
Nagatomo Chiyoji, 25–26, 44, 47, 71, 353n17
Nakabe Yoshiko, 43
Nakagawa Kiun, 84, 241
Nakano Dōya, 76, 77, 96, 317n38, 346n46
Nakano Gorōzaemon, 257
Nakano Ichiemon, 139, 148, 317n38, 332n32
Nakano Jinbee, 81
Nakano Kozaemon, 76
Nakano Mitsutoshi, 8, 12–16, 19, 20, 21, 44, 87
Namura Jōhaku, 28–29, 49, 185
Nan chōhōki (A treasury for men; Namura Jōhaku), 28–29, 185
nanshoku (male-male love), 286, 367n116
narrative: and narrative anecdotes (exempla), 117–20, 123–31, 226, 258, 264; and narrative personas, 102–3, 258, 263–64; vs. nonnarrative, 5–6, 12, 91, 167–76, 177, 207–8, 220, 255, 256, 259, 262, 268, 272–73, 278, 284–85, 291, 293, 295–96
narrative capital, 23, 169, 170, 222, 296; and letter-writing manuals, 180, 199, 210, 218, 219; and readers, 175, 177
narrativity, 5, 6, 7, 15, 18, 262, 295; modes of, 23, 300n16. *See also* fiction; narrative; storytelling
narrators, 175, 200, 202, 265, 275; of disaster narratives, 237, 247–48, 249, 253; dispensing teachings, 123, 227, 229; and emotions, 130; first-person, 65, 102, 108–9, 111, 258; multiple, 248; and narrativity, 5; in nonnarrative texts, 5, 207–8, 217; omnipresent, 284–85, 286, 367n109; personas of, 102–3, 258, 263–64; third-person, 247, 274, 284
Nasake no uwamori (Heightened feelings; illus. Hishikawa Moronobu), 180, 210–18, 350n105; ABC of love in, 217–18; and *Nishikigi*, 211, 213, 214, 215, 217, 218
national identity, Japanese, 23, 135, 149, 152, 168
natural disasters. *See* disaster narratives
Nendaiki (Chronicles), 238
neo-Confucianism, 100, 322n4

Newhard, Jamie, 335n75
New Historicism, 9–10, 301n30
Nijūshikō (Twenty-Four Paradigms of Filial Piety), 200, 348n64
Nikolajeva, Maria, 12, 64, 130
Nioi bukuro (The scented pouch), 30, 228, 355n39
Nisard, Charles, 10
Nise monogatari (The fake *Tales of Ise*), 283
Nishikigi (The winged spindle tree), 204–10, 220; glossary in, 205, 206, 217, 218; love letters in, 180, 208; and *Nasake no uwamori*, 211, 213, 214, 215, 217, 218; price of, 349n83; and publishing genres, 349n83; and *Usuyuki monogatari*, 204, 206, 208
Nishimura Ichirōemon, 83, 347n55, 350n104
Nishimura Mataemon, 81, 86
Nishimura Matazaemon, 3, 20, 77–78, 78, 83, 86, 96, 148, 298, 317n38
Nishimuraya Yohachi, 118, 119, 328n88, 328n92
Nishizawa Ippū, 83, 354n36
Nitan no Shirō (The warrior Nitan no Shirō), 79
nobility, court, 26, 35, 192, 202, 224, 225, 264, 309n47
Noda Hisao, 6, 198, 200, 208, 231, 259, 265, 268, 367n114
Noda Yahee, 149
Noh theater, 3, 31, 32, 49, 92, 204, 284
novel, the (*shōsetsu*), 5, 6, 8, 10, 13, 279
novice readers, 22, 27, 93, 96, 116, 117, 122, 140, 143, 294, 295; authors for, 83; definition of, 64; and etiquette manuals, 139, 148, 149; and *gakumon*, 64–66, 132; and knowledge, 99, 124, 175, 177, 297; and moral teachings, 99, 131–32; and multiple literacies, 64, 66; and narrative capital, 175; and publisher-booksellers, 72, 76, 81, 86, 294, 296–97; and *wabun* literacy, 64
nyohitsu ("the woman's brush"), 80, 190, 345n32
Nyohitsu Ono Otsū tehon (Woman's brush: A copybook from Ono Otsū), 80
Nyoraishi, 312n83
nyosho (publishing genre; books for women), 23, 92, 137, 149, 176, 335n75, 336nn76–77, 337n109, 344n24, 349n83

Obiya Chōkurō, 80
Obiya Jirōkichi, 80
Ogasawara hyakka jō (The hundred articles of the Ogasawara school), 137, 138–49, 151, 152, 158, 159, 332n26, 341n1; movable-type edition of, 138–39; price of, 332n32; and publishing genres, 332n32; and secret traditions, 139, 140; and table manners, 142–43; and wedding ceremonies, 143; woodblock printed edition of, 139–40
Ogasawara Keishōsai, 148
Ogasawara-ryū shitsukekata hyakka jō (One hundred articles on the Ogasawara-style etiquette), 136, 145, 146, 147, 331n21, 334n67
Ogasawara Sadayoshi, 334n70
Ogasawara school, 137, 144, 145, 148–49, 154, 159, 173, 176, 177, 332n23, 332n25
Ogasawara shorei taizen (The complete book of Ogasawara school manners; Okada Gyokuzan), 134
Ogawa Takeo, 194, 345n43
Ohara Tōru, 357n69, 360n138
Okada Gyokuzan, 59, 331n5
Oka Masahiko, 22, 75–77, 80, 81, 315n29
Okamoto Masaru, 80
okurigana (suffixes in katakana), 54, 56, 60
Ōmiya Jirōkichi, 353n17
Ōmori Yoshikiyo, 199
Onna chōhōki (A treasury for women; Namura Jōhaku), 29, 49, 151, 185
Onna imagawa (textbook), 344n25
Onna jingi monogatari (Tales of female virtue), 162–64, 339n131. See also Ryōri monogatari
Onna kagami hidensho (Book on the secret tradition of the mirror for women), 29–30, 137, 149–58, 176, 341n156; illustrated edition of, 154–58; on letter writing, 191–93; on morality, 150; price of, 336n76; and publishing genres, 336n76; readership of, 153; and table manners, 152–53; and wedding ceremonies, 151–52. See also Sanze aishō makura
Onna sewa yōbunshō taisei (Collection of letters useful for women's daily business), 198

Onna shikimoku (Rules for women), 29, 137, 150–54, 176, 217; on letter writing, 178, 189, 191–93; on morality, 150; price of, 336n77; and publishing genres, 336n77; readership of, 153; and wedding ceremonies, 152
Onna shogaku bunshō (Elementary letter writing for women), 186–90, 198; price of, 344n24; and publishing genres, 344n24. See also nyohitsu; Shogaku bunshō
Onna shorei shū (Compendium of the complete etiquette for women), 154, 157, 337n109
Onna yō chie kagami takara ori (Precious collection that works as a mirror for women's wisdom), 337n106
Ono Otsū, 80
ōraimono ("things coming and going"; educational materials), 90, 178–79, 311n66
ōraimono narabi ni tehon (publishing genre; ōraimono and copybooks), 89, 90, 179, 342n6, 344n24
orality: and disaster narratives, 242, 243; of English texts, 309n46; and etiquette manuals, 134, 137–49, 143–44, 173, 333n56; and food culture, 158, 176; and learning, 65–66, 132, 191, 294; and letter writing, 191; of moral teachings, 23, 65, 130, 132; and print culture, 21, 176, 177, 258, 265, 294, 297; vs. reading, 23, 39, 65, 107, 132, 143, 174, 258, 265, 297; and storytelling, 242, 243; of sutras, 113–14; and voices in books, 132
Orsini, Francesca, 10
Osaka, 43, 45, 49, 82, 83, 100, 248, 267, 271, 275; fire in, 236–37, 237; publisher-booksellers in, 78, 81, 96, 136, 318n54
Otogi bōko (Hand puppets; Asai Ryōi), 3, 84
Otogi bunko (The companion library), 78
otogizōshi (Muromachi monogatari), 78, 91
outcasts, 26, 234, 250, 309n47, 357n69

peasants (hyakushō), 31, 108, 307n4; vs. government, 262, 263, 267, 272, 273, 274, 276, 277; and learning, 51; and literacy, 26, 28–29, 31, 66; and money, 228; as readers, 26, 28, 66

Pennell, Sara, 12, 361n2
Pepys, Samuel, 11, 360n130
pillow words, 212, 217
pleasure: aesthetic, 169, 175, 186, 214, 222, 259; vs. bliss, 256–57, 296; and bookshops, 1–4; and curiosity, 279; and disaster narratives, 235; from financial profit, 20; from how-to manuals, 144, 148, 166, 193, 220, 222; from knowledge, 1–2, 17, 19–20, 24, 107, 134, 167, 222, 254, 256, 272, 295, 298, 306n87; and plurality, 107, 144, 167, 272, 282, 286, 290, 291, 292; of reading, 2, 9, 24, 107, 144, 148, 156, 158, 167, 214, 220, 257, 272, 282, 286, 290, 291; sensual, 205, 213. *See also* profit
Pleasure of the Text, The (Barthes), 255
pleasure quarters, 5, 29, 71, 164, 205, 254, 267; guides to (*yūjo hyōbanki*), 80, 91
poetry: anthologies of, 3, 81, 205; authors of, 31, 84, 104; in book-trade catalogues, 45, 46, 47, 88; Chinese, 52, 84, 88, 109, 264, 275; gatherings for, 145; haikai, 31, 49, 84, 89, 90, 100, 204, 212; *hokku*, 174, 288; and *kanbun* vs. *wabun* literacy, 90; *kyōka* (mad verse), 279–85, 288; in letters, 194, 195, 219, 350n101; in love stories, 204, 205, 206, 212, 215, 217; in miscellanies, 258, 264; publishing genres for, 88, 89, 90, 92, 194, 205; *renga*, 88, 90, 258, 284; *waka*, 45, 72, 90, 166–67, 194, 204, 205, 206, 212, 217, 241
Popular Literacy in Early Modern Japan (Rubinger), 22
population, urban, 43, 45, 47, 309n47
Practicing New Historicism (Gallagher and Greenblatt), 9
present-mindedness, 221–54, 286; and disaster narratives, 233–53; and moneymaking, 223–33
Preston, Cathy and Michael, 10
prices, 15, 44, 50, 68, 72, 93–96, 96, 294, 321n91, 321n102, 340n148, 354n30, 354n32, 355n51, 356n56, 356n68, 357n68, 362n9, 366n92; of Buddhist and Confucian texts, 101, 124, 323n10, 323n15, 326n57, 327n70, 327n74, 328n84, 328n88, 329n102; of cookbooks, 338n111, 340n133, 340n137; of etiquette manuals, 140, 144, 158, 332n32, 334n68, 336nn76–77, 337n109; and greed, 250, 252, 274–75; of *kyōkun* (educational books), 354n36; of letter-writing manuals, 344n24; of love letters, 346n46, 347n61, 349n83; of moneymaking books, 353n16, 354n36; and reading marks, 95
printing: movable-type, 44, 138, 194, 195, 234, 280, 299n7, 326n56, 354n36; woodblock, 3, 20, 44, 45, 71, 114, 139–40, 234, 280, 299n7
profit: financial, 17, 20, 44, 47, 86, 124, 132, 154, 177, 222, 225, 259, 261, 275, 276; from how-to books, 148, 158, 167, 254, 295; from knowledge, 1–2, 4, 17, 19–21, 85–86, 107, 132, 167, 218, 254, 256, 258, 259, 295; from letter-writing manuals, 220; and morality, 14; and pleasure, 4, 15, 19–20, 256, 259, 295, 298; and publisher-booksellers, 17, 20, 44, 47, 86, 124, 132, 154, 177, 222, 259. *See also* money; reading: efferent vs. aesthetic
prostitutes, 104, 325n39. *See also* pleasure quarters
publisher-booksellers, 2–4, 15–16, 67–96, 292–93, 297, 314n14; and Buddhism, 3, 22–23, 76, 83, 97–132, 133; and censorship, 17, 263, 274–75, 297, 305n72; in China, 10; in colophons, 4, 22, 75–76, 78, 316n30; and Confucianism, 3, 23, 97–132, 133; costs to, 72, 79, 82, 94, 154, 306n88, 317n43; and curiosity, 18; in Edo, 45, 68, 80–81, 82, 96; and financial profit, 17, 20, 44, 47, 86, 124, 132, 154, 177, 222, 259; itinerant (*gyōshō hon'ya*), 71; in Kyoto, 2–3, 67–68, 74–80, 82, 96; modifications to books by, 85–86, 96, 145, 154–58, 161–64, 276–77, 280; and multiple literacies, 54, 66, 67, 68; and novice readers, 72, 76, 81, 86, 294, 296–97; numbers of, 74–82; numbers of books printed by, 43–48; and numbers of readers, 22, 48, 66; in Osaka, 81, 96, 318n54; textual strategies of, 64, 82, 102, 114, 122, 131, 205, 238–39; types of, 72–74, 81. *See also* authors: collective; bookshops; genres, publishing

412 Index

Rakuchū rakugai zukan (Scroll illustrated with scenes in and around the capital; Sumiyoshi Gukei), 69
rakugo (comic storytelling), 3
Rakusaibō, 237, 242–43, 247
Rankeishi (calligrapher), 199
Rath, Eric C., 158, 161
readers, 22, 25–66, 27, 292–93, 300n10; aesthetic engagement of, 4, 18, 23, 107, 137, 148, 157, 167, 169, 175, 176, 177, 178, 186, 187, 193, 207, 211, 214, 219, 222, 251, 259, 265, 295; cognitive engagement of, 4, 17, 18, 23, 114, 121, 131, 137, 168, 170, 175, 193, 207, 208, 212, 218, 222, 254, 256, 258, 264, 286, 295; diversity of, 95, 96; emotional bonds with, 103–4, 107, 117, 126, 130; emotional engagement of, 4, 18, 23, 102, 118, 119, 121, 131, 137, 175, 193, 198, 207, 211, 219, 245, 251, 254, 258, 258; of etiquette manuals, 135, 139–40, 144, 153–54, 176–77; expert, 64, 66, 86, 96, 175, 177, 294; of household manuals, 165–66; of letter-writing manuals, 185–86; marginalia by, 164, 165–66; and narrative capital, 175, 177; numbers of, 25, 48, 66; and numbers of printed books, 43–48; and publishing genres, 86, 89, 90, 92; of sutras, 114, 115, 121. *See also* literacies, multiple; literacy; novice readers
reading: and aurality, 23, 65, 107, 132, 258, 265, 297; discontinuous, 24, 257, 259, 263, 266, 270, 271, 272, 277, 286, 290, 296, 362n6; discontinuous vs. continuous, 265, 278, 279–80, 291–92; efferent, 145, 153, 154, 161, 177, 222, 229; efferent vs. aesthetic, 12, 20, 23, 107, 148, 157, 167, 176, 220, 222, 251, 256, 272, 295; modes of, 24; and plurality, 222, 255–93; retrospective, 301n23. *See also* orality; pleasure: of reading
Rihi kagami (A mirror of right and wrong behavior; Ejima Tamenobu), 100–107, 278; price of, 324n21; and publishing genres, 324n21. *See also* Ejima Tamenobu
Rosenblatt, Louise M., 12
Rubinger, Richard, 22, 26, 30, 43, 61, 191
ruidai waka shū (type of *waka* poetry anthologies), 205

Rüttermann, Markus, 178, 179, 342n8, 345n43
Ryan, Marie-Laure, 5, 300n16
Ryōri hidenshō (A commentary on the secret tradition of cookery), 159, 160, 338n111
Ryōri kirigata hidenshō (Secret writings on culinary slicing), 161, 339n128
Ryōri monogatari (Food tales), 158–61, 165, 169, 171; illustrated edition of, 161–64; and *Onna jingi monogatari*, 162; price of, 338n111; and publishing genres, 338n111
Ryūtei Tanehiko, 324n16

Saionji Kinfuji, 224
Saitō Seiji, 43
Sakai Tadao, 106
Sakaiya Jinbee, 119, 121
Sakakibara Satoru, 34
Sakiwake gonin musume (The multicolored five young girls; Ejima Kiseki), 198
samurai, 29, 33, 224, 288, 307n4, 309n47; and Buddhism vs. Confucianism, 111–12; and censorship, 263; criticism of, 108, 109, 250, 262, 267, 276; in disaster narratives, 250; etiquette for, 134, 137, 138–39, 142, 145, 146, 148; literacy of, 26, 27, 28, 98; masterless (ronin), 109; and money, 225, 231; and *nanshoku*, 284, 286, 290, 367n116; as readers, 25, 27, 35, 38, 47, 81, 98, 310n58
Santō Kyōden, 84
Sanze aishō makura (The pillow of affinities across three generations), 23, 169–75, 177, 341n151; and *Onna kagami hidensho*, 170, 171, 173, 174, 175
Sasayama Baian, 30, 50–51
Sawa (calligrapher), 198
Schank, Roger C., 346n46, 348n71
secret traditions, 123, 124, 176, 177; of cookery, 159, 161, 164, 167, 338n111; disclosing of, 23, 101, 132, 134, 137–49, 176; of etiquette, 137–49; in titles, 29, 78, 79, 137, 150, 159, 164, 165, 345n38
Segal, Ethan, 224
Sei Shōnagon, 259
Seisuishō (Laughter to banish sleep), 289, 368n126

Sentō shinwa (*Jiandeng xinhua*; New stories under the lamplight), 84
setsuwa stories, 123–31, 126, 226, 259, 330n110, 353n26
sexuality, 152, 297; and etiquette manuals, 142, 173–74; and love letters, 210–18. See also *kōshokubon*
Shibata Jun, 26, 28, 49
Shibayama Hajime, 286
Shibukawa Seiemon, 78, 307n13
Shida (About Shida), 80, 95
Shika kenro shū (Anthology of beautifully crafted words), 194, 204, 346n44
Shimazaki, Satoko, 17
Shin Senzai waka shū (New Collection of a Thousand Years), 206, 349n91
Shinto, 88, 89, 113, 224–26, 356n65
Shin Usuyuki monogatari (New Tale of Usuyuki), 199, 210; as play, 347n60
Shirakura Yoshihiko, 170
Shisho (The Four Books), 52
Shisho taizen (annotated Four Books), 72, 94
Shison kagami (The mirror for posterity), 231, 233, 355n52; price of, 355n51; and publishing genres, 355n51
Shison seishi jōmoku (Articles with admonitions for the progeny; Kōnoike Shinzaemon), 33
Shitsukekata chikuba shō (A treatise on etiquette and wooden horses), 139
shitsukekata-sho narabi ni ryōri-sho (publishing genre; books on manners and cookery), 23, 92, 134, 137–49, 158, 164, 176; examples of, 332n32, 334n68, 338n111, 339n133
Shively, Donald H., 224, 266, 270
Shōgaku (The Small Learning), 52
Shogaku bunshō narabi ni yorozu shitsukekata (Elementary letters and all forms of etiquette), 78, 148–49, 152, 190, 343n11, 344n26; on letter writing, 3, 62, 63, 180–86; price of, 95, 334n68; and publishing genres, 334n68
Shokoku inga monogatari (Tales of karma across the provinces), 130–31, 330n116

Shokoku shinjū onna (Women's double suicides around the provinces), 198
Shokunin zukushi emaki (Craftsmen of various trades; Hishikawa Moronobu), 71
Shokushō nōdoku (*Nichiyō shokushō nōdoku*; Bad and good properties of food; Manase Gensaku), 90
shomotsuya. See bookshops
Shorei daigaku (Tajima Yōgen or Takai Ranzan), 331n5
Shorei kyōkun kagami (The mirror of etiquette and morals; alternative title for *Nioi bukuro*), 308n25
Shorei tōyō shū (The collection for all immediate needs on etiquette; Tō Mitsunaka), 133, 334n61
Shoshin bunshō, 179, 181, 342n7
shoshū hōgo (vernacular Dharma talks for all schools), 99
Shōsoku jitei hishō (Secret treatise of letters kept in one's ears; Shukaku Hōshinnō), 345n38
Shūkojō (album), 236
shunga, shunpon (erotic art), 170, 210
Sima Guang, 277–78
Sinitic. See *kanbun*
Slater, Candace, 10
Small Books and Pleasant Histories (Spufford), 10
Smith, Henry D., 242
social criticism, 108–9, 111, 249, 250, 262–63, 267, 272–78, 276, 291, 361n148. See also censorship; government, Tokugawa
social status: and calligraphy, 193; in census, 309n47; and Confucianism, 101–2, 102–3; in disaster narratives, 249, 250; and etiquette, 23, 134–49, 152–54, 157–58, 176, 191, 295, 331n3, 335n71; four estates in, 26, 28, 29, 108, 307n4; and frugality, 228, 232–33; in *Jigabachi monogatari*, 262, 264; and karma, 264; and letters, 181, 190–93, 219, 345n38; and literacy, 26–28, 39, 52, 53, 66, 294; in love stories, 203–4; and money, 232–33, 253, 352n6; in *Ukiyo monogatari*, 276

sōrōbun (hybrid literary Chinese), 23, 60, 61–62, 64, 181, 185, 189, 190, 219, 295, 313nn102–3. See also *mairase sōrōbun*
sōshi (booklets), 91–92, 93
sōshiya. See bookshops
Sōshiya Tarōemon, 78
sōsho. See cursive script
Spufford, Margaret, 10, 11
Stallybrass, Peter, 24, 257, 362n6
storytelling: and cookbooks, 161–64; in disaster narratives, 242, 246, 247, 253; in etiquette manuals, 166, 167, 177; and narrative, 5, 167, 208; and story skeletons, 194, 199, 200, 204, 207, 219, 261, 346n47; and trauma, 246–47, 253, 360n132
Sugawara no Michizane, 285
Sugimura Jihee, 170
Sumiyoshi Gukei, 34–38, 49, 50, 69, 70
sumptuary laws, 145, 224, 228, 233, 277, 361n148
sutras, 113–22
Suzuki Sadami, 304n66
Suzuki Shōsan, 84, 113, 123–31, 327n84, 329n102
Suzuki Toshiyuki, 52
Suzuki Tōzō, 261
syncretism, 107, 108, 113, 131, 132, 150, 264, 323n8, 327n81

tables of contents, 102, 113, 153, 170, 265, 270, 338n119; in letter-writing manuals, 180, 182, 205, 343n11
Tadasu monogatari (Tales of Tadasu), 113
Tagami no ue (The life of others; Yamaoka Genrin), 3, 221, 325n37, 325n39
Taharaya Heibee, 364n42
Taiheiki, 357n69
Tajihi Ikuo, 81, 318n53
Takahashi Gozaemon, 161
Takamitsu nikki (Takamitsu Diary), 346n43
Taniwaki Masachika, 268, 273, 276
Tao Zhu Gong (Fan Li), 231
tehon. See copybooks
tenarai (writing and reading), 32, 61, 90, 179, 267; age for, 33, 48, 311n70; and *gakumon*, 28–29, 48–53, 64; instruction in, 28–30, 48–52, 307n14; and letter-writing manuals, 191; and *wabun*, 53, 61, 64; for women, 29–30, 154, 155, 217
Tenarai shiyō shū (A collection to be used for learning to write; Sasayama Baian), 50
Tengu no dairi (The palace of Tengu), 80, 95
Terako seikai no shikimoku (Rules on the prohibitions for pupils of *terakoya* schools; Sasayama Baian), 30
terakoya (*tenaraisho*; writing schools), 49–50, 54, 261, 294, 312n70; visual depictions of, 50, 70
Tetsuo Najita, 355n52
textbooks, 179, 311n66, 344n25. See also *ōraimono*
textual compression, 79, 80, 82
textual instability, 85, 297
Thomas, Keith, 135, 136, 307n10, 308n16, 309n46, 310n61
Tohi zukan (or *Tohi emaki*; Scroll illustrating town and country; Sumiyoshi Gukei; Konbuin), 49–50, 70
Tohi zukan (Scroll illustrating town and country; Sumiyoshi Gukei; Chester Beatty), 34–38, 70
Tōkaidō meishoki (Record of famous places along the Tōkaidō; Asai Ryōi), 272
Tō Mitsunaka, 133, 334n61
Tomiyama Dōya, 280
townspeople (*chōnin*), 25–26, 29, 111, 153, 224, 270, 275, 276
Toyotomi Hideyoshi, 238
translations: vernacular, 310n59, 323n13; of Buddhist and Confucian texts, 98, 104, 114, 115–17, 121, 122, 131, 294–95; gendered, 186–87, 190, 207; interlinear, 57, 59, 60, 64, 103, 104, 115–17, 121, 131, 264, 275, 325n37, 325n42; in Korea, 122. See also *wadan shō*
travel writing (*meisho zukushi*, *meisho michi no ki*, *meishoki*), 2, 19, 85, 92, 222–23, 254, 278, 291, 358n98, 366n102; in *Chikusai*, 280, 281–83, 286–87, 288, 290; prices of, 95; street directories, 39, 40, 41, 42, 74, 81, 271, 318n54, 365n63; in *Ukiyo monogatari*, 270, 271–72, 275
Tsujihara Genpo, 84
Tsujimoto Motosada, 120

Tsurezuregusa (*Essays in Idleness*), 5, 102, 259
tsurimono narabi ni ezu (publishing genre; hanging scrolls and pictures), 89, 90
Tsurugaya Kyūbee, 313n107, 326n57
Tyler, Royall, 84, 113

ukiyo (floating world), 252, 266–67, 268
Ukiyo monogatari (*Tales of the Floating World*; Asai Ryōi), 104–5, 257, 266–78, 280, 281, 287, 291; conflicting views in, 277; as guidebook, 271–72; illustrations in, 268, 269, 364n47; as jestbook, 270–71, 278, 291; and *Kashōki*, 276–77; as mirror for politicians, 272–76; as miscellarian prose, 266, 270, 273, 277, 278; price of, 363n42; and publishing genres, 363n42; social criticism in, 276
Umezu no chōja monogatari (The millionaire of Umezu), 353n24, 353n26, 353n28
United States, earthquake in, 243–44
Unpo, 123, 128
Uraminosuke, 367n114
Urokogataya (publisher), 80, 91, 210, 280, 318n50, 328n88, 351n113
Urokogataya Kahee, 80
Urokogataya Magobee, 81, 118, 119
Urokogataya Sanzaemon, 81, 326n57
Ushiwaka sennin kiri hashi Benkei (Little Yoshitsune slays a thousand, and Benkei on the bridge), 79
Usugumo monogatari (The tale of Usugumo), 180, 206, 208, 212; allusions in, 203–4; gender inversion in, 200–204, 219; price of, 347n61; and publishing genres, 347n61. See also *Nishikigi*; *Usuyuki monogatari*
Usuyuki monogatari (The tale of Usuyuki), 76, 180, 194–200, 204, 206, 208, 212, 219, 220, 298; and *Chikusai*, 286; illustrations in, 195–98; and *Ise monogatari*, 195; and *Jigabachi monogatari*, 261; as letter-writing manual, 198–200; as love story, 195–98; master plot of, 23, 194, 195, 199, 200–204, 205, 211, 219, 261, 286; and Muromachi tales, 346n49; price of, 346n46; and publishing genres, 346n46.

See also *Nishikigi*; *Usugumo monogatari*
Uta honzō zōho (*Waka shokumotsu honzō*), 340n137
Utai no hisho (The secret book on Noh texts), 80

vernacular European languages, 16, 98, 311n61, 345n33
vernacular Japanese. See *wabun*
Vivero y Velasco, Rodrigo de, 43

wabun (vernacular) literacy (kana-mainly literacy), 3, 4, 16, 22, 49, 76, 81, 82, 98, 99, 131; and authors, 83; and cognitive efficiency, 53; and high-end bookshops, 72; and hiragana, 27, 29, 31, 32, 48, 53, 60, 61, 64, 294; and *kanbun* literacy, 57, 60, 64, 90, 180, 190, 313n94; and multiple literacies, 60; and publishing genres, 89, 92, 93; and reading glosses, 54–62, 64, 100, 103, 104, 117, 121, 122, 325n37; and *tenarai*, 53, 61, 64. See also literacies, multiple; novice readers; translations: vernacular; vernacular European languages
wabun texts: authors of, 31–32, 82–86; in book catalogues, 45–48, 86–93; and *gakumon*, 51, 57, 65, 82; numbers of, 45–47, 76; publishers of, 1–4, 22, 76–82, 96; readers of, 27, 31–32, 64–66. See also *wabun* (vernacular) literacy
wadan shō (friendly commentaries) on sutras, 115–22
Waka dairin gushō (A humble treatise on the forest of the topics for poetry), 349n86
Waka shokumotsu honzō (Food and medical herbs in poem form), 166–67, 169, 340n137
Wan'ya Ihee, 145
washo narabi ni kanarui (publishing genre; Japanese books and books in kana), 88, 90, 91–92; Buddhist and Confucian texts as, 232n15, 326n57, 327n74, 328n84; cookbooks as, 338n115; etiquette manuals as, 332n32, 334n68, 336n76, 337n109; household manuals as, 339n133; miscellanies as, 354n30, 364n42; moneymaking manuals as, 354n36

Wazoku dōjikun (Japanese traditional teachings for children; Kaibara Ekiken), 28, 48
wedding ceremonies: cookbooks on, 160–61, 338n111; etiquette of, 143, 151–52, 157, 170–73; and sex, 175; visual tropes of, 160, 171–74, 348n77
Wills, Steven, 242
Wolf, Maryanne, 53, 57, 64
women, 71, 104, 106; books for (*nyosho*), 23, 92, 137, 149, 176, 186, 335n75, 336nn76–77, 337n109, 344n24; and book-trade catalogues, 149, 150, 186; brush of (*nyohitsu*), 62, 80, 190, 345n32; in Buddhism, 120–21, 285; calligraphy by, 80, 186–89, 198, 344n25; categories of, 29; didactic texts for, 3, 150; empowerment of, 200–204, 297; etiquette for, 11, 134, 137, 149–54, 156, 176, 335n74; humble forms of language for, 152; letter-writing manuals for, 186–93, 207, 219; literacy of, 26, 29–30, 35, 49, 66, 294, 308n24; and love letters, 195, 198, 216; and *mairase-sōrōbun*, 62, 187, 189, 190, 207, 219; and marriage, 150–52, 154, 175, 176, 337n95, 337n106; *tenarai* for, 154, 155, 217
Woolf, Daniel, 223
writing, discontinuous, 257, 259, 263, 265, 270, 277, 278, 280, 286, 291, 292

Yakusha kingeshō (Actors' golden makeup), 74
Yakushi (Buddha of healing), 248–49
Yakushi tsūya monogatari (The tale of the wake of the Buddha Yakushi), 234, 235, 238, 262, 275; criticism of samurai in, 250; frugality in, 250–51; multiple narrators in, 248; price of, 356n68; and publishing genres, 356n68. *See also* disaster narratives
Yamada Ichirobee, 78, 91, 123, 124, 309n42, 329n102, 337n109
Yamada Kihee, 93

Yamamoto Chōbee, 154, 336n76
Yamamoto Kyūbee, 78–79, 96, 162, 317n42, 328n88, 328n92
Yamaoka Genrin, 221, 340n137
Yasu (calligrapher), 186, 192, 344n25
Yasuda Jūbee, 166
Yoda Nagayasu, 310n58
Yokawa hōgo (Dharma talks at Yokawa; Genshin), 99
Yokota Fuyuhiko, 27, 45, 310n58
yomihon (genre), 84
yomimono (story to be read), 350n101
Yonemoto, Marcia, 185–86, 191
Yorozu anshi tegata kagami (A mirror for ten thousand letter templates; Namura Jōhaku), 185
Yorozu kikigaki hiden (The secret tradition of things heard and recorded), 78, 164–67, 264; price of, 339n133; and publishing genres, 339n133
Yorozu no fumi hōgu (A miscellany of old letters; Ihara Saikaku), 219–20
Yorozu no oboe (A myriad of memories; Enomoto Yazaemon), 32
Yoshida Kōichi, 125
Yoshie Hisaya, 21
Yuasa Yoshiko, 202, 205, 208, 350n101
yūmin (idlers), 108
Yūsōan, 72, 74

Zaid, Gabriel, 2, 294
Zen'aku monogatari (Tales of good and evil; alternative title for *Kashōki atooi*), 65–66
Zeniya (publisher), 123, 124, 329n102
Zeraku monogatari (The story of Zeraku), 231–32; price of, 356n56; and publishing genres, 356n56
zokkai, 95
Zoku Kashōki (later ed. of *Ukiyo monogatari*), 269, 276–77, 364n42, 364n47
Zoku Nishikigi (*Nishikigi* continued), 210
Zukofsky, Paul, 187

GPSR Authorized Representative: Easy Access System Europe, Mustamäe tee
50, 10621 Tallinn, Estonia, gpsr.requests@easproject.com

www.ingramcontent.com/pod-product-compliance
Lightning Source LLC
Chambersburg PA
CBHW021928290426
44108CB00012B/759